DATE DUE

IN
SPITE OF
INNOCENCE

IN

SPITE OF

✳ INNOCENCE

Erroneous Convictions
in Capital Cases

MICHAEL L. RADELET

HUGO ADAM BEDAU

CONSTANCE E. PUTNAM

Boston Northeastern University Press

Northeastern University Press

Copyright 1992 by Michael L. Radelet, Hugo Adam Bedau, and Constance E. Putnam

Library of Congress Cataloging-in-Publication Data

Radelet, Michael L.
   In spite of innocence : erroneous convictions in capital cases /
Michael L. Radelet, Hugo Adam Bedau, Constance E. Putnam
       p.   cm.
   Includes bibliographical references and index.
   ISBN 1-55553-142-3 (cloth)
       1. Judicial error—United States   2. Homicide—United States.
3. Capital punishment—United States.   I. Bedau, Hugo Adam.
II. Putnam, Constance E.   III. Title.
KF9756.R33   1992
347.73'12—dc 20
[347.30712]   92-17899

Designed by Virginia Evans

Composed in Sabon by Coghill Composition Co., Richmond, Virginia. Printed and bound by The Maple Press, York, Pennsylvania. The paper is Sebago Antique, an acid-free sheet.

MANUFACTURED IN THE UNITED STATES OF AMERICA
97 96 95 94 93   5 4 3 2

POLONIUS: My lord, I will use them
according to their desert.

HAMLET: God's bodkin, man, much better:
Use every man after his own
desert, and who shall scape
whipping? Use them after your
own honor and dignity—the
less they deserve, the more
merit is in your bounty.

Hamlet, Act II, Scene ii

✴ CONTENTS

THIS BOOK is the product of thirty years of intermittent research. A few words about its history will help the reader understand and appreciate its contents. In 1964 one of us (H. A. Bedau) published a nineteen-page essay on miscarriages of justice in capital cases in the United States. That essay was accompanied by an inventory, spanning the years 1893 through 1962, of seventy-four such cases. It was the first attempt anyone had made to collect in one place information on all errors of this sort. Another essay (also by Bedau), published in 1982, discussed the problem of verifying miscarriages of justice but did not attempt to expand the inventory of cases.

In 1983 collaborative efforts were initiated by another of us (M. L. Radelet), aiming at a truly comprehensive and detailed study of the problem. Four years later the results of that work were published (by Bedau and Radelet) in the November 1987 issue of the *Stanford Law Review*. In that article we identified and described the cases of 350 defendants we believed had been wrongfully convicted in capital (or potentially capital) cases in the period from 1900 to 1985. We also described with some care how we had interpreted the concepts "miscarriage of justice" and "(potentially) capital" case, and what criteria and evidence we had used to evaluate cases for inclusion in our inventory. Finally, we tried to show how the risk of executing the innocent was relevant to the ongoing debate over whether to retain, expand, or abolish the death penalty. At the request of then-Attorney General Edwin Meese, III, two attorneys in the Department of Justice—Stephen J. Markman and Paul G. Cassell—roundly criticized some aspects of that research and argument in the November 1988 issue of the *Stanford Law Review*, to which we (Bedau and Radelet) replied in the same issue.

Since 1985, when a preliminary version of our research was released to the press, our work has received widespread and continuing publicity in law journals, in newspapers and magazines (from the *New York Times* to *Playboy*), and on television talk shows. One of our findings even showed up in a line spoken by Cher in her 1987 movie, *Suspect*. We are naturally gratified by the interest the public has shown in what we have written; we hope it attests to a recognition of the importance of the problems we have been exploring as well as to the fact that the individual stories behind these cases are often hair-raising. (Everyone knows that a good story is more gripping than the best sociological research or philosophical analysis. We must not, however, lose sight of the fact that the miscarriages we recount have ruined or irreversibly damaged the lives of hundreds of innocent persons.)

With that in mind, in 1987 the two academics (Bedau and Radelet) invited a writer (C. E. Putnam) to join in the three-way collaboration that has produced this book. Our aim has been to present in a less-academic style the cases and some of the issues discussed in the law review article by Bedau and Radelet. Accordingly, in this book the reader will find none of the tabular data and little of the conceptual analysis and argument of that article. We have also taken the opportunity to correct errors that have come to our attention during the past four years.

Neither grave miscarriages of justice in capital cases nor our discovery of them ended in 1987. The Inventory of Cases in this book catalogues the results of our research through the summer of 1991; sixty-six more cases have been added to the list. Thus, the book covers all but the final decade of the twentieth century and provides once again what we claimed for the 1987 article—a base line for future research into the general problem of wrongful convictions in capital or potentially capital cases in this century in the United States.

Since 1983 our research has benefited from the assistance and initiative of countless secretaries, librarians, academics, attorneys, activists, and others throughout the country as they learned of the research project. Without their help we could never have produced this book.

For her special encouragement and support, Lisa Radelet has our thanks. For information on particular cases we are indebted to David Bruck, Robert Bryan, Watt Espy, Jonathan Gradess, Paul Keve, James McCloskey, Gene Miller, Marty Rosenbaum, and Margaret Vandiver. For help in documenting their own cases, we are grateful to Joseph Green Brown, Willie Brown, Robert K. Domer, and Buzz Fay; for help unraveling his father's case, we thank Sam Reese Sheppard. It is a pleasure to thank Virginia Mulle for her research assistance. We also owe a debt of gratitude to those who took the time to read and suggest improvements in earlier drafts of various chapters: Sylvan Barnet, Christine Bastianelli, Judith Bastianelli, Katie Crane, Dana Grossman, Margaret Henderson, William Leffler, Barry Pelzner, Susan Pollack, Craig Putnam, Fran Putnam, Michael Putnam, Ross Putnam, Sarah Putnam, Spencer Putnam, Lisa Radelet, Donald Robb, Stephen Spaulding, and Karen Taylor. For financial support during the year in which the bulk of the book was written, Michael Radelet wishes to acknowledge NIMH Grant No. 5 T32 MH 1516-14, administered through the Family Research Laboratory,

University of New Hampshire, and the special assistance of David Finkel-
hor, Murray Straus, and other colleagues in New Hampshire.

Summer 1992   MICHAEL L. RADELET
                                                         HUGO ADAM BEDAU
                                                    CONSTANCE E. PUTNAM

* IN
SPITE OF
INNOCENCE

 INTRODUCTION

A T A B O U T half past eight on the evening of Monday, October 23, 1989, the telephone rang at Officer Gary McLaughlin's desk. He picked it up immediately, answering, "State Police, Boston." From the other end of the line he heard a man's voice: "My wife's been shot. I've been shot." Thus began a thirteen-minute, life-or-death conversation between Officer McLaughlin and the caller.

McLaughlin quickly learned that the man on the line, using a car phone as he sat behind the steering wheel, was Charles Stuart. Half an hour earlier Stuart and his wife, Carole, had been at Brigham and Women's Hospital attending a birthing clinic. Carole DiMaiti Stuart was pregnant with their first child. Now, slumped down on the seat next to her husband, she bled profusely; a bullet had been fired point-blank into her face. Stuart himself had been shot in the stomach. Minutes later a patrol car arrived, and the young couple was on its way to the hospital emergency room.

When the police arrived at the crime scene, so did the media. Starting with the eleven o'clock news on television that night, the media flooded the country with stories and pictures of the crime and its victims. For several days the nation's attention was fixed on their fate. Carole Stuart died, as did the couple's premature child delivered by Caesarean section. For countless Americans, the brutal attack on a young couple about to become parents—attractive, white, professional, still in their twenties—was a nightmare suddenly made real.

Right behind the police and the news media came the politicians. In 1989 Massachusetts was one of fourteen states in the nation that did not punish any kind of murder with the death penalty. The day after Carole Stuart's death, the chairman of the Massachusetts State GOP, Raymond Shamie, flanked by his party's gubernatorial candidates, held a news conference at the State House urging speedy enactment of death penalty legislation. Representative John H. Flood, a Democrat seeking his party's nomination for governor, filed a death penalty bill in the legislature. Attorney General Francis X. Bellotti, also a Democrat and a rival for the gubernatorial nomination, said he would himself willingly pull the switch of the electric chair on the killer. At Carole Stuart's funeral, a thousand people—led by Governor Michael Dukakis—paid their last respects.

Under considerable public pressure to solve the crime, the police promptly began their search for the murderer. Charles Stuart, out of danger and recovering from his stomach wound, was able to provide some help. He described the gunman as 6' tall, black, and about 30 years old. Not much, but still something for the police to go on. The next day Stuart elaborated on his description of the killer, and the police circulated the information. So did the Boston papers. By Wednesday evening, two days after the crime, Police Commissioner Francis Roache could report to the media that Stuart's description, along with fingerprint evidence from his automobile, was yielding good leads. "We have reduced our list of suspects to a chosen few," he said.

The police concentrated their attention on the Mission Hill district near the hospital. Mission Hill is on the border between the Fenway—part of Boston's middle-class, still-fashionable Back Bay—and Roxbury, where some of the city's poorest neighborhoods are found. Not normally a setting for street violence of the sort found in Boston's less well integrated areas, Mission Hill was soon overrun with law-enforcement officers. Residents felt besieged as platoons of police swept through the area, looking for the black killer. Search efforts were concentrated on the public-housing projects in the district, home mainly to blacks and other minorities.

On November 10, two weeks after the Stuart murder, police in the Boston suburb of Burlington arrested a Willie Bennett on a traffic offense. Less than three days later, he was arraigned by the authorities in Brookline—a mile or so from the Mission Hill district where the Stuart murder had occurred—for armed robbery of a video store. Bennett, who had a previous criminal record, was 39 years old and black. Just after Christmas, the Boston police showed a photograph of Bennett to Charles Stuart; they also arranged a line-up with Bennett in it for Stuart to review. He promptly fingered Bennett as the man who looked "most like" the killer of his wife. Thus, within six weeks of the crime, it appeared the police had their man. The newspapers applauded and turned to other stories.

Shortly thereafter, the case was suddenly turned inside out. On the morning of January 5, 1990, readers of the *Boston Globe* were stunned when they saw the bold headline: "STUART DIES IN JUMP OFF TOBIN BRIDGE AFTER POLICE ARE TOLD HE KILLED HIS WIFE." Incredible though it seemed, it was true. Apparently from well before the murder, Stuart had carefully woven a fabric of lies as he plotted the death of his pregnant wife. For reasons still not altogether clear, he too was dead, an apparent suicide.

The news that Stuart himself might have been the killer led Willie Bennett to say that his life had "been ruined and no one is willing to take responsibility." His anger and bitterness were understandable. Through an improbable pattern of bad luck, he had come very close to being indicted for a crime he had nothing to do with.

Why? Because he had an arrest record in other cases, including armed robbery. Because the police were under intense pressure to solve the crime. Because Bennett more or less fit the description provided by a seemingly unimpeachable eyewitness to the crime. And, above all, because the public—clamoring for some way to express its indignation—found him a plausible target.

There seems to be no doubt about Willie Bennett's complete innocence. Fortunately, the truth—or enough of it—emerged in time to spare him not only a trial for murder but all of the possible undeserved consequences of such a trial. Bad as Bennett's ordeal was, the system did not come close to convicting him. And it is, of course, erroneous *conviction*, not merely wrongful *arrest*, that is the crucial threshold to undeserved punishment—whether years in prison or death in the execution chamber. Crossing that threshold from accusation and indictment to a guilty verdict is one of the gravest steps the system can take. Only two steps are more serious: actually sentencing the defendant to death, and carrying out the execution.

The Willie Bennett case marks one end of the spectrum on which miscarriages of justice in capital cases occur. The case of James Adams marks the other. On May 10, 1984, Adams was executed in Florida for murder. (As Adams was being executed in the electric chair in Florida State Prison and as death penalty opponents stood in silent vigil across the street, an unidentified man drove by in a pickup truck, and with a thumbs-up gesture shouted, "Fry the nigger!") No national publicity surrounded this case, which had stretched out over a decade. It had begun on the morning of November 12, 1973, with the murder of Edgar Brown in Ft. Pierce, Florida. Brown was found badly beaten, allegedly during the course of a robbery in his home. A 61-year-old rancher and former deputy sheriff, Brown died the next day. Adams was promptly arrested, tried, and convicted.

During the penalty phase of his trial, the State called only one witness, a Tennessee sheriff, who testified that Adams had escaped from prison there after conviction for rape. Adams's public defender called no witnesses, and the jury spent a mere five minutes deliberating over the sentence. Four months and three days after the crime, St. Lucie County Circuit Judge Wallace Sample, concurring with the jury's recommendation, sentenced James Adams to death.

Barely more than a week before the execution, Adams's appellate attorneys, led by West Palm Beach public defenders Richard Burr and Craig Barnard, filed with Governor Bob Graham their second request for executive clemency. In their application, the lawyers presented for the first time facts relating to Adams's background and the circumstances surrounding his conviction, asserting:

> We believe, as strongly as human beings can believe, that the life of James Adams is in your hands today solely because he is a poor black Southerner. . . . The outcome of Mr. Adams's every involvement in the criminal justice system since 1955 has been influenced by his race or by the race of the victims of his alleged crimes.

Adams's first encounter with the law had come in 1955 when he was convicted of assault and battery. In 1957 he and his brother were convicted of petit larceny (they had stolen a pig for their family's dinner table), and Adams was sentenced to one year in jail. He was not provided with counsel in connection with either of these two convictions. During his incarceration for stealing the pig, he was once beaten unconscious with a bat by a jailer and severely beaten on other occasions as well. He suffered dizzy spells, blackouts, and blurred vision as a result of these beatings, and he bore their marks until his death.

In October 1962, Adams was convicted of rape. The records of this conviction did not become available to the attorneys fighting for Adams's life until December 1983. No blacks had been included among the five hundred persons on the list from which the jurors at his trial were selected. In addition, the white victim had repeatedly referred to her assailant as a "nigger." Despite the lack of any physical evidence of rape—it was simply her word against his—Adams was convicted. He was sentenced to ninety-nine years in prison.

Under decisions of the United States Supreme Court, Adams's first two convictions ought to have been ruled unconstitutional because he had been denied the assistance of counsel. Racial discrimination in the selection of the jury made the rape conviction also constitutionally defective.

Nonetheless, all three convictions were cited by the prosecution as aggravating factors in the sentencing phase of Adams's Florida trial, and they no doubt played a role in the jury's decision to recommend a death sentence.

After Adams had served nine years of his prison sentence for rape, the Tennessee Board of Probation and Paroles found his behavior "exemplary" and recommended to the governor that his sentence be commuted to time served. The governor refused, on the ground that the district attorney who had prosecuted Adams objected. A year later, the Board of Probation and Paroles decided not to recommend release, because the district attorney still opposed such a move.

At the time, Adams was not being housed as one might think a convicted rapist would be; he was a "trusty" at a correctional facility for teenaged girls. As part of his job he had access to state-owned vehicles. When he was told that he would not be released until the prosecutor dropped his objections, Adams—heartbroken (he had done all he could to earn release)—drove off in one of the prison trucks. Ten months later he was arrested for the murder in Florida.

The killer had entered Edgar Brown's unoccupied home on the morning of November 12, 1973. Sometime later Brown returned home, where he was attacked and beaten with a fireplace poker. Adams's car had been parked in the driveway, and it was seen traveling to and from the victim's home. One witness, Willie Orange, positively identified Adams as the driver of the car; a second witness, John Thompkins, "thought" Adams was the driver. The car was located later that day at a shop where it had been left for the repainting job Adams had been planning for months. Adams claimed his car had been driven that morning, at 10:00 or 10:15 A.M. (one half hour before the assault) by a friend, Vivian Nickerson, and another man, Kenneth Crowell. According to Adams, while they were off in his car—precisely at the time of the homicide—he was at the Nickerson home playing cards.

The victim, it was known, always carried between $700 and $1500 in cash; no cash was found in his wallet after the assault. When Adams was arrested, he had only $185 with him. He also had a credible explanation for the source of this money: His employer had recently lent him $200. The State offered no explanation of what it thought had happened to the other $500 to $1300 that Brown would have been carrying and that had in all likelihood been taken by his killer. One bill in Adams's possession had a dried patch of O-positive blood on it, consistent with the blood of the victim—and that of 45 percent of the rest of the population.

The one person who had a chance to identify the killer at Brown's home was Foy Hortman. He testified that he drove up to the house shortly after Brown had returned home and heard a woman shout from inside,

"In the name of God, don't do it!" He then saw and briefly spoke with someone leaving the house, but failed to identify Adams as that person. More than that, he testified that the person he spoke with was blacker than Adams and, unlike Adams, had no mustache. On the day of the homicide, Hortman viewed a police line-up that included Adams and said he was positive that none of the men was the person he had seen leaving the Brown house. Nonetheless, at trial Hortman testified that Adams "may or may not have been" the person at the scene. (A logician would call that remark a tautology, but the jury appears to have been influenced by it.)

John Thompkins testified that he thought it was James Adams he had seen driving a car to the victim's home shortly before the homicide. "It had to be [Adams]," Thompkins said, "because he throwed up his hand at me, because everybody that passed there don't hardly wave at you unless you know him." Not a very precise or damning statement, yet the State relied heavily on it.

Willie Orange, on the other hand, did positively identify Adams as driving the car away from the Brown home. His was the sole testimony that placed Adams near the crime scene. Perhaps not so incidentally, it later turned out that Orange believed Adams was having an affair with his wife. During the clemency hearing, three witnesses were located who had heard Orange stating before the trial that he was going to testify against Adams because of this affair. One witness quoted Orange as saying before the trial, "I'm going to send him [Adams] because he's been going with my wife." A polygraph administered to Orange to support Adams's appeal for clemency in 1984, while hardly conclusive, indicated that Orange was being deceptive when he testified at the trial.

Vivian Nickerson, the person Adams said had access to his car at the time of the homicide, was 15 years old. She was very large for her age and had a strikingly masculine appearance. In fact, she resembled James Adams, and her height, size, and complexion fit Hortman's eyewitness description better than Adams's did. It is possible that she was the person Hortman saw leaving the victim's house. If she was, that would explain another loose end not tied up by the State's theory of the crime: Hers could have been the woman's voice Hortman testified he had heard coming from inside the house. Yet no photos of Vivian Nickerson were shown to Hortman, and he never saw her in a police line-up.

Interestingly enough, Nickerson was called by Adams to corroborate his alibi at trial. She was a reluctant witness, however, and ended up hurting his case. By claiming that he had not arrived at her house until 11:00 A.M., she undermined his testimony. In a pretrial deposition, given under oath, she had stated that Adams reached her house prior to 10:30 and that she had then borrowed his car. In other words, contrary to what she claimed during the trial, Nickerson when deposed had said that Adams was at her house and that she was driving his car at the time of the crime. This inconsistency was by no means a minor one; unfortunately, Adams's defense counsel never confronted Nickerson with the contradiction.

The most significant blow to the State's case against Adams arose from evidence not presented at trial. En route to the hospital in an ambulance with her husband, Mrs. Brown found strands of hair clasped in his hand—hair presumably pulled from the head of his assailant. The State's crime laboratory compared these hairs with samples of Adams's hair and determined that although the hair was "very dark brown, Negroid, [and] curly," Adams was definitely not its source. This report, however, was not released until three days after Adams had been sentenced. Even then, when it could have been used to support a request for a new trial, it was not given to the defense attorneys.

In their 1984 clemency papers, Adams's attorneys succinctly stated their case as follows:

> In sum, had all of the evidence raising doubt about Mr. Adams's guilt been submitted to the jury, there would have been at least a reasonable doubt about Mr. Adams's guilt. The evidence would have shown that the only person who had an opportunity to observe the perpetrator was "positive" that Mr. Adams was not that person. The evidence would have shown that Willie Orange's identification of Mr. Adams as the person driving away from Brown's house was wholly unbelievable because of his stated motive to "get" James Adams. The evidence would have shown that a specimen of hair asserted by the investigating deputy to have been recovered from the hand of Mr. Brown in the ambulance after the assault against him could not have come from James Adams. . . . Had the jury been told about Vivian Nickerson's sworn testimony less than two months before James Adams's trial which unequivocally corroborated Mr. Adams's testimony that he was continuously at Ms. Nickerson's house from before the homicide until well after the homicide, the jury would have been more likely to suspect Vivian Nickerson as the perpetrator than James Adams.

No doubt due process of law failed rather badly in the Adams case, and these deficiencies played a critical role in his conviction and death sentence. But was Adams truly innocent? Did he deserve to be acquitted on the ground that he had no involvement in the murder of Edgar Brown, even though members of the trial jury—given the evidence before them—believed otherwise? Adams's postconviction attorneys, Burr and Barnard, thought so. We think so. But from the moment Adams was executed, it became virtually impossible to resolve the issue one way or the other. There is no legal forum in which the innocence of the dead can be officially confirmed, or even satisfactorily investigated. The court of public opinion—such as it is—is the only recourse, and James Adams was too obscure, too bereft of friends and supporters with time and money, to have his claim of innocence tested and vindicated posthumously in that forum.

Once Adams was dead, his attorneys had to turn their full attention to the plight of other death row clients. Time spent re-investigating the circumstances of the Edgar Brown murder in the hope of vindicating the late James Adams was time denied to clients still alive but facing the electric chair. No newspaper editor or team of reporters, no investigative journalist, has seen fit (so far as we know) to re-open the Adams case. Instead, a giant question mark continues to haunt his execution, a question mark that will probably never be removed. A rare case? Perhaps, but not unique. We know of nearly two dozen cases in this century where the evidence similarly suggests that the wrong person was convicted of murder or rape, sentenced to death, and executed.

Between the case of Willie Bennett—arrested and accused of a capital crime but then released as innocent even before trial—and that of James Adams—executed despite unresolved questions strongly suggesting his innocence—there are hundreds of other cases in which innocent persons were convicted of a capital (or potentially capital) crime but were then fortunate enough to have their innocence established, thus saving them from a lifetime behind bars or, worse, an execution. This book is principally about these grave errors—wrongful convictions in capital cases, spread across the United States during this century. In each of the cases we discuss, the wrong person was charged with and convicted of criminal homicide (or of the then-capital offense of rape). One such case is that of Melvin Reynolds.

The crime was a ghastly and frightening one, which angered the whole community. During the afternoon of May 26, 1978, 4-year-old Eric Christgen disappeared while in the care of his father's secretary, running errands in downtown St. Joseph, Missouri. She promptly searched for Eric in the immediate vicinity but could not find him. Some hours later the police organized a full-scale search and, joined by dozens of concerned citizens, swept the entire area of the city along the banks of the Missouri. Finally, following up some vague leads, searchers found the child's mutilated body in dense underbrush along the river bank just a few minutes' walk from the shopping mall. An autopsy revealed that the boy had been sexually abused before he died of suffocation. As the distraught father said to newspaper reporters, "Things like this do not happen in St. Joseph, but rather in faraway places like New York or Chicago. But indeed, it did happen here."

The local police systematically rounded up well over a hundred possible suspects, including "every known pervert in town," as one of the officers crassly put it. More than two hundred leads were investigated. One suspect, a 64-year-old man in poor health, was terrified by the police interrogation; shortly afterwards, he went into convulsions and died. "Heart attack," the death certificate said. His friends were convinced that he had been literally scared to death.

Suspicion then fell on Melvin Reynolds, 25, one of the many who had joined in the search for the boy's killer. An anonymous tip had informed the police that Reynolds had been seen at the mall on the day of the murder, in Eric's company. When the police asked Reynolds to confirm this tip, he at first denied it, but later conceded that he had been at the mall on the fateful day. That was all the police needed to take him in for a polygraph test. Terribly agitated, Reynolds spent four hours on the lie detector; even so, the results strongly indicated that he was not the man the police were looking for. Reynolds was released.

The authorities were not through. Investigation into Reynolds's youth revealed that he had suffered sexual abuse himself at the hands of older boys; his sexual identity had wavered during adolescence, with various homosexual episodes marking his path to maturity. Rumors circulated (which later proved to be unfounded) that Reynolds had once sexually abused his 3-year-old nephew.

During the summer of 1978 Reynolds became engaged to Rita Anderson; they planned to get married in October. But when October rolled around, Reynolds was taken in for another polygraph examination, and the wedding was postponed. A few weeks later detectives had Reynolds hypnotized, hoping to gather evidence against him. In December they arranged to give him a sodium amytal—"truth serum"—injection.

Through all this investigation, not to say harassment, Reynolds obliged the police at every turn. He never had the assistance he desperately needed of a lawyer to help him protect his rights. Then, under the truth serum, he let slip the words, "Before I killed . . . before I went to the unemployment office . . . ." This convinced the police they should keep him under surveillance, and two months later, on Valentine's Day 1979, they brought him in for yet another round of questioning. Still cooperative, he spent fourteen hours in the basement of the police headquarters as he was grilled anew. The police accused him of various thefts and told him that if he went to jail he would never be married. But they were willing to suspend further charges for the petty larcenies, they said, provided he would help them solve the Christgen murder.

The scene in the police basement, as Terry Ganey describes it in his book, *St. Joseph's Children*, was pathetic. After denying once again that he had killed the boy, Reynolds finally looked up at his interrogator "appeasingly, like a dog with his ears pressed back against his head," and said, "I'll say so if you want me to." To be sure, this was not a very convincing confession, but it was better than nothing. Once they had made this breakthrough in Reynolds's resistance, the police were able to persuade the hapless young man to embellish his confession with enough details to warrant their arresting him. The police chief, James Hayes, eagerly called a press conference to announce that the Christgen murder had been solved.

The prosecutor, Michael Insco, was more cautious; prior to making any announcements to the press, he wanted Reynolds to bolster his confession by showing the police exactly where he had disposed of the boy's body. Reynolds dutifully did as he was asked, more or less, and his rather vague indication of the general area along the river bank, which was the best he could do, was precise enough for Chief Hayes. The chief's enthusiasm swept away the remaining doubts shared by the prosecutor, Detective Robert Eaton (who had led the search for Eric's body), and Terry Boyer (who had conducted the polygraph tests on Reynolds).

Joe Holtslag, the local FBI agent, was less easily convinced. From the start he had thought that an altogether different kind of person was the killer. His belief was based mainly on a description given to police by a Jeff Davey, who had telephoned authorities shortly after the murder to report that he had seen an older man with a young boy not far from where Eric was eventually found. Davey had supplied further details under hypnosis, which Holtslag had not forgotten. They pointed away from Reynolds. So did alibi testimony from a neighbor of Reynolds's, who claimed she had seen him within minutes of the abduction more than a mile from the mall.

The trial began in October 1979. Reynolds's counsel, Lee Nation, attempted to convince the jury that the confession had been given under duress. His effort was to no avail. Reynolds himself took the stand to retract his confession, explaining that he had falsely admitted to the crime because he was scared of what the police would do if he refused. The entire case for the defense took just forty minutes. The jury needed seven hours and only one ballot to reach its verdict: Guilty of murder in the second degree, with punishment of life imprisonment.

One might well wonder why Reynolds was convicted only of second-degree murder, rather than of first-degree or capital murder. As occurs in many cases, the jury in the Reynolds case evidently was convinced that the defendant had killed the victim—but not with premeditation. Perhaps the second-degree murder conviction was intended as a way of showing some mercy; perhaps it was the easy way to reach a unanimous verdict quickly. For whatever reason, although members of the jury wanted Reynolds severely punished, they did not want him sent to the electric chair.

Melvin Reynolds had for years shown symptoms of mild mental retardation. Despite that, he was aware that his conviction left a problem hardly anyone else seemed to notice. "What really bothers me," Ganey quotes him as saying, "is that whoever did it, they're still out on the streets, laughing about it." Not bad for an I.Q. of 75.

No sooner was Reynolds behind bars in Missouri State Penitentiary than the sexual abuse that had plagued his youth began again, this time in terrifying earnest. He had been in prison only a few months when he was jumped, gagged, and gang-raped in the prison kitchen by six inmates. The next day, six others replayed the scenario in a trash bin. Later, yet another group had their way with him in the prison gym. No relief was in sight. Then came word that the Missouri Supreme Court had turned down his appeal. All signs pointed to a lifetime of physical and emotional abuse in prison for Melvin Reynolds.

Three years after Reynolds entered prison, residents of St. Joseph were again shocked by news of a child abductor in their midst. Half a block from where Eric Christgen had disappeared, a 10-year-old boy was grabbed by a man who said he was a security guard. The boy escaped, unharmed, but a day later 11-year-old Michelle Steele failed to arrive home after a dental appointment downtown; the next morning her naked body was found on the bank of the Missouri River, a mile from where Eric's body had been left. She had been raped and murdered.

The day Michelle Steele was killed, a man identifying himself as Richard M. Clark of Davenport, Iowa, walked into the State Mental Hospital in St. Joseph, sobbing and begging for help. It turned out that he had been seen near the spot where Michelle's body was found, and that he had identified himself to the police at that time as Richard Harris. Routine checking quickly revealed that Clark and Harris were one and the same person. Furthermore, nylon cords in his possession, footprints at the crime scene matching his shoes, bite marks on the girl's body matching his dental pattern—all pointed to Clark-Harris as the wanted killer. He was promptly arrested.

The police soon discovered that the man they had in custody was actually Charles Hatcher, 54—a man with a history of arrest and incarceration for sordid crimes involving murder, rape, sodomy, and assault going back to the early 1950s. By 1980 there was no doubt that Hatcher was psychotic and extremely dangerous. His most recent return to society had come only two months prior to the murder of Michelle Steele.

A few weeks before he was set to be tried for her murder, Hatcher wrote a note from his cell and handed it to a sheriff's deputy. "Please call the FBI," it said, "and tell them I would like to see them today. Very important case." Responding to the note was Joe Holtslag, the FBI agent who had had his doubts about Melvin Reynolds's guilt in the Christgen murder. Intensive discussion between Holtslag and Hatcher soon convinced the FBI agent that Hatcher was involved in numerous unsolved murders. No one except the killer could give details that fit together so well with what the police knew about those various crimes. Then, as discussion between them continued, Holtslag suddenly realized he was looking at someone who matched the description given under hypnosis four years earlier by Jeff Davey of the man he had seen with a young boy on the day Eric Christgen disappeared.

At that point, Hatcher proved not to be such a cooperative prisoner after all. Although he made it known that the conviction of the innocent Reynolds had preyed on his mind, and that to correct this injustice he had decided to confess, Hatcher clearly was going to do it his way. He chose to feed Holtslag the details indicating his involvement in the Christgen crime piecemeal, and weeks went by as Hatcher slowly spelled out his story.

The St. Joseph authorities—Chief Hayes and prosecutor Insco in particular—were at first inclined to scoff at Hatcher's revelations, arguing that most of them were common knowledge and the rest dubious or inaccurate. Then, abruptly, Hatcher dropped his mincing manner and talked freely with an assistant prosecutor from Insco's office. Insco himself began to swing around to believing Hatcher, though it wasn't an easy conversion. As he explained to Terry Ganey, "You can imagine the difficulty I had convincing myself that Melvin Reynolds didn't commit the crime. I was the one that prosecuted Reynolds. . . . I was pretty reluctant to admit it."

Yet bit by bit, re-investigation of the crime and Hatcher's report of his movements on May 26, 1978, convinced even the skeptical prosecutor. Charged with the murder of Eric Christgen, Hatcher simplified matters (contrary to his attorney's advice) by pleading guilty in court before the judge who had presided over the Reynolds trial. He also announced that he wanted to be sentenced to death. The court met him halfway: He was immediately found guilty of first-degree murder and sentenced to fifty years in prison. With that verdict, the Missouri courts repeated a lesson taught by hundreds of other murder trials across the land: One and the same crime can be judged to be murder, in either the first degree or the second degree—with enormously different consequences for the guilty defendant—depending on unpredictable and adventitious circumstances.

Even so, it was several months before Melvin Reynolds was released from prison. If the psychotic serial murderer Hatcher had not happened to read about Reynolds's conviction in a detective magazine and decided to implicate himself, Reynolds would still be behind bars for a crime he did not commit. Prosecutor Insco later told a *Los Angeles Times* reporter, "I feel fortunate that I've had an opportunity to straighten out my own mistake." A lawyer in the office of the federal attorney in Kansas City added, "The disturbing part is not so much that a mistake was made, but that so many mistakes were made." Perhaps an editorial on the case in the *St. Louis Post-Dispatch* put it best: "The Reynolds case says something about confessions and police methods used to extract them, even when these methods fall short of outright physical brutality. Under the stress of constant harassment, individuals can reach breaking points. . . . Suppose Mr. Reynolds had been executed for the murder?"

Hatcher's confession closed the Eric Christgen murder case and freed Reynolds. Hatcher was then quickly tried and convicted of the murder of Michelle Steele. Three months later he was dead; prison guards found him hanged in his cell, an apparent suicide. He never revealed all the details of his other crimes. Who knows whether Melvin Reynolds, now free, was the only innocent person convicted for any of them?

One naturally wonders how frequently such terrible miscarriages of justice actually occur. Most Americans do not seriously distrust our criminal justice system or the efficiency and dedication of law enforcement officers. At the same time, we know that public servants are not infallible, and that honest errors and occasionally outright corruption do occur. How frequently in the past has the criminal justice system failed in a capital case to convict only the guilty? What explains these failures? How likely are they to happen in the future? How, if at all, can they be remedied or prevented?

The framework for answering questions such as these is provided by two basic concepts that govern the inclusion of the cases discussed in this book. One of these concepts concerns the kind of *crime* involved. The other concerns the kind of *error*.

The crime. All but a few of the cases collected and described in the following pages are those in which a person was wrongfully convicted of criminal homicide, usually first-degree murder. Most of the cases we have chosen for detailed discussion involve defendants who were sentenced to death. In the majority of the four hundred cases in our files, the sentence was not death, but imprisonment—as in the Reynolds case. From our perspective, the error is equally grave whether the sentence is life in prison or death, though the stakes are obviously higher when an innocent person faces death.

Cases of wrongful conviction of criminal homicide appear in our Inventory of Cases even when the crime occurred in a jurisdiction with no death penalty. Murder has been a capital crime in most American jurisdictions during most of this century. Furthermore, the public tends to think of every murder case as a "capital" offense, no matter what the current statutory punishment may be. We can learn about the fallibility of the criminal justice system in capital cases even when the death penalty is not actually involved.

Finally, we have also included a few cases of wrongful conviction of rape in jurisdictions where, at the time, rape was a capital offense and the defendant was sentenced to death. The death penalty for rape was abolished nationwide in 1977, as a result of the Supreme Court's ruling in *Coker v. Georgia*. But because about 10 percent of all executions in the nation in this century have been for rape, we think it important to include such cases when they have involved miscarriages of justice. Further research would almost certainly uncover many more cases of wrongful conviction for this crime.

As explained above, we do not count cases like that of the falsely accused Willie Bennett, because he was never convicted. Wrongful accusation, arrest, indictment, and trial—even on a capital charge—do not suffice to bring the accused defendant within our purview.

The error. Taken broadly, there are many kinds of error that can result in a miscarriage of justice, whether in a capital case or not. Suppose, for example, a defendant is convicted of murder, and then later evidence shows that the killing was in self-defense. Surely, a *murder* conviction in such a case—perhaps conviction of any crime whatever—would be a miscarriage of justice. Nevertheless, we ignore such cases, as long as there is no reason to doubt that the accused actually did cause the death of the deceased. Similarly, a conviction of murder is surely a miscarriage of justice when the accused is insane, even if the jury (for whatever reason) fails to learn of the defendant's mental illness or to accept the insanity plea. Insane defendants are not legally or morally responsible for their criminal acts; they should be found not guilty by reason of insanity (or, under some recent laws, found guilty but insane). We exclude all cases of this sort, too, again provided that the accused really did cause the death of the victim.

We also exclude miscarriages of justice, even in capital cases, where only the procedure leading to the conviction violated the guilty defendant's right to due process of law. Although we grant that such errors are of the utmost gravity and should be corrected, we have left aside all cases of that sort as long as there is reason to believe that the defendant really did cause the victim's death. A defendant in a capital case whose conviction rests in part on due-process error, no matter how serious or flagrant the error, is not for that reason innocent as charged. Thus, throughout this book, when we refer to miscarriages of justice, we mean cases where there was more than due-process error—as we believe is true, for instance, in the James Adams case.

What kinds of cases are left? Only what we call *wrong-person convictions,* and they fall into two categories. The rarest is where there is no murder (or rape) victim at all; the "deceased" turns out to be alive (or the rape victim to have consented). Far more common is the kind of case where the crime did, indeed, occur, but where the authorities convicted the wrong person. Using the criteria of crime and error explained here, we have identified 416 cases in which the wrong person was convicted of murder (or of capital rape and then sentenced to death) in the United States so far in this century. All together, roughly a third of the defendants whose cases we discuss were not merely convicted, but also sentenced to death.

Knowing the kind of crime and the kind of error we are interested in does not, by itself, tell us whether a given case really involves a miscarriage of justice. To make that decision, we have relied on *evidence* that falls into two categories. The more important kind of evidence is *official judgments of error.* (About 90 percent of the cases in this book belong to this category.) Such judgments can take several different forms, and they can be delivered by any of the three branches of government. They may be found in a commutation or a pardon, or in the award of an indemnity to the convicted defendant after release (by special act of the legislature, or after litigation in the courts). They may take the form of a reversal of the criminal conviction by an appellate court, followed by a further judgment: a prosecutor's decision not to seek another trial for the defendant, a jury's decision to acquit at retrial, a judge's directed verdict of acquittal. Obviously, the more of these official actions there are in a given case, the more complete is the evidence of official belief in the defendant's innocence—and, to that extent, the more compelling the inference that the defendant really is innocent.

The second category of evidence consists of *unofficial judgments.* There is no limit to the variety of this kind of evidence. The following examples are typical but by no means exhaustive: The supposed crime turns out never to have taken place at all, even though the jury thought otherwise; the real culprit confesses or is identified but never arrested, indicted, or convicted; a state official (such as a prison warden) investigates the case and concludes that the courts were wrong and that the convicted defendant really is innocent—but no extrajudicial official action comes to the defendant's aid; the defendant's attorney or family uncovers crucial evidence showing that the defendant is innocent, but cannot convince any court or official body (as happened in the James Adams case). Or perhaps other students of the case, journalists or scholars, re-examine all the available evidence and conclude that the defendant cannot be guilty.

These are the sorts of evidence that led to our judgment that miscarriages of justice resulting in the execution of the innocent have occurred. To the best of our knowledge, no state or federal officials have ever acknowledged that a wrongful execution has taken place in this century.

As for the causes of the errors, our research has shown that the two most frequent are perjury by prosecution witnesses and mistaken eyewitness testimony. Accordingly, in Part I of this book, "Bearing False Witness," we have devoted three chapters to cases where one or both of these causes are prominent factors. In Chapter 1, we look closely at the story of James Foster (Georgia, convicted and sentenced in 1956); the good-faith testimony of a woman who believed she saw him murder her husband sent him to death row. The case of Isidore Zimmerman (New York, 1937), told in Chapter 2, illustrates how false testimony deliberately fabricated by "witnesses" coached by the prosecution can convict an innocent man. Chapter 3 is the story of Randall Dale Adams (Texas, 1976); perjured testimony provided by none other than the real culprit led to Adams's wrongful conviction.

Perhaps the most dramatic, even if not the most frequent, cases of miscarriage of justice occur when community passion is aroused against vulnerable defendants. Part II, "Pride and Prejudice," contains three chapters on cases that illustrate different forms of such passion. In Chapter 4, we review one of the most famous capital cases of the century, the wrongful convictions of Tom Mooney and Warren Billings (California, 1916), in which political prejudice fueled by patriotic fervor led to judicial error. In the next two chapters we examine the ugly fruits of white racism. Chapter 5 tells the story of three young blacks—Charles Greenlee, Samuel Shepherd, and Walter Irvin (Florida, 1949)—erroneously convicted of the then-capital crime of rape in an atmosphere of violence and near-lynching. Chapter 6 examines the more recent ordeal of Clarence Brandley (Texas, 1980).

Among the most troubling causes of miscarriage of justice are failures in police work—whether from negligent and incompetent investigation of the crime or more sinister motives—and overzealous prosecution. In Part III, "Corrupt Practices," we focus on a small sampling of the many cases in our files that illustrate these themes. Chapter 7 relates the story of Lloyd Miller (Illinois, 1956), victim of a coerced confession and the suppression by the prosecution of exculpatory evidence. In Chapter 8, we examine the case of Mary Katherin Hampton (Louisiana, 1961), pressured to plead guilty despite no evidence whatever of her involvement in the crime—except the vengeful testimony by her alleged accomplice (a pathological liar himself under death sentence). Chapter 9 relates one of the most flagrant cases of injustice in our files, that of Jerry Banks (Georgia, 1975), sentenced to death as a result of police tampering with the evidence and withholding potentially exculpatory evidence from the defense.

In Part IV, "Rush to Judgment," we examine four quite different cases, each of which presents the spectacle of someone making the defendant fit the crime. In Chapter 10, we tell the story of James Richardson (Florida, 1968), a handy suspect and easy target without effective defense against official belief in his guilt. Chapter 11 examines the plight of Floyd Fay (Ohio, 1978), convicted on the basis of an ambiguous tip—from the dying victim—linked by the police to misinterpreted polygraph evidence. The next chapter focuses on the case of Earl Charles (Georgia, 1975), whose prior criminal record made him vulnerable to indictment and whose truthful alibi the jury refused to believe. The final chapter presents the case of Robert Domer (Ohio, 1963), a victim of misleading circumstantial evidence par excellence.

During this century in the United States, more than seven thousand men and women have been legally executed for capital crimes. Many thousands more have been sentenced to death. Probably a quarter of a million persons have been convicted of criminal homicide. The errors, blunders, and tragedies recounted in the pages of this book barely scratch the surface of this vast output of the nation's criminal justice system. Some of these stories we have rescued from near oblivion, but although our research has often broken new ground, we know that it is far from complete. Hundreds of cases, many of them involving miscarriages of justice every bit as serious as any we describe, almost certainly remain to be investigated. Unknown hundreds of other cases have completely disappeared from sight; we will never know whether justice was done to the defendant. This is especially true of the cases from earlier in the century, or those where the defendant was a member of a repressed minority—a Native American or Hispanic, a recent immigrant, a black. We believe, however, that we have provided a solid base line for future investigations.

PART ONE

BEARING

FALSE

WITNESS

1 ✸ | THE

EX-CONVICT

AND THE

EX-POLICEMAN

ATTORNEY HENRY DAVIS, handling the prosecution for the State of Georgia, was confident as he led his middle-aged witness through her testimony for the benefit of the jury. Camie Drake was perfect. As Davis posed the questions, her answers spelled out the tragic events of the summer evening at home that had brought her to the witness box.

While her husband Charlie was watching television in the living room, an intruder burst into the house. In the bathroom getting ready for bed, Camie hadn't heard anything, but when she emerged she saw Charlie making a dash for the bedroom, where he kept a gun by the bedside. That's when she saw the intruder, hard on Charlie's heels. Charlie reached his gun all right; he even managed to shoot it once. He missed. The burglar fired back, pumping four bullets into Charlie Drake, and the terrified Camie ran for the telephone. The gunman sprang at her, shoved his gun in her face, and ripped the phone from her hand—using it to knock her to the floor. Dazed but still conscious, she got a good look at him. Charlie, bleeding profusely, did not survive long.

Once Camie Drake had related these incidents, the stage was set for Davis to ask her the crucial questions. "Mrs. Drake, have you seen the intruder, or the man who was in your house that night—who was in your bedroom shooting your husband—since that night?"

"I have."

"Could you tell us when you saw him?"

"I saw him the week after my husband's funeral—that's the week following the time he was killed."

"Where did you see him?"

"In my home."

"Have you seen the man since?"

"I have seen him since."

"Is he in the court room?"

"He is. He is sitting over there."

"The one at the corner?"

"The one at the corner."

"Is that the man that was in your house?"

"That's the man."

"Is he the man that shot your husband?"

"He is the man that shot my husband."

The words "He is the man that shot my husband," uttered from the witness stand by Charles Drake's widow, Camie, sealed the fate of James Fulton Foster, on trial for murder. The jury deliberated barely more than four hours that hot summer day in 1956 before returning with a verdict of guilty. As soon as the polling of the jury was finished, Judge J. Julian Bennett, serving on his first case as a trial judge, ordered Foster to rise. Without further ado, Judge Bennett was about to pass sentence on the guilty man. Defense attorney James Horace Wood shouted out an angry protest, shocked that there would not even be the usual respite of a couple of days between the verdict and the pronouncement of the sentence. Judge Bennett ignored him. Looking solemnly at Foster, he intoned: "You will be put to death between the hours of 10 A.M. and 3 P.M. on September seventeenth at the State Penitentiary at Reidsville, in a manner prescribed by the sovereign State of Georgia. May God have mercy on your soul."

It was already August 18; Foster had only thirty days to live. Georgia was about to execute an innocent man.

Jefferson, the county seat of Jackson County, is in the Georgia Piedmont, some forty miles northeast of Atlanta and just a few minutes' drive from the university town of Athens. Pine and oak and choking vines cover the bright red earth. Summers are hot and humid. Jefferson is known beyond the county borders, if at all, as the place where ether was first used as an anaesthetic in a surgical operation. The Crawford W. Long Medical Museum honors the physician who performed the historic operation in 1842. Jefferson was, in 1956, a very quiet and very southern country town. A Confederate statue dominated the town square; the somewhat run-down county court house was perched on the hill overlooking the square. Jefferson's two thousand residents were mostly farmers or mill workers and those who served them.

Among those in service jobs was Charles Drake, 57, owner of a general store on the main road leading out of town toward Gainesville, Georgia. On the morning of June 20, 1956, the people of Jefferson were shocked to learn that Charlie—a big, strapping fellow, well known and well liked—had been brutally murdered. The crime was, according to one newspaper account, "the most vicious in the history of Jackson County." No one could remember the last time a victim of attempted robbery had been murdered in Jefferson.

Drake, "a good, honest, Christian man" in the words of one neighbor, was in the habit of carrying $5,000 in a wad of bills stuffed in his shirt pocket—and most people in the area knew it. This was the money willed to him by his father, Drake had told just about everyone, to be used for the care of his aging mother. Flashing it from time to time was his way of making the point that he wasn't using it—that he didn't need financial assistance from anyone, not even his own father. In the aftermath of the murder, it was easy to assume the burglar had intended to rob Charlie. But if so, whoever broke into the Drake house was a better gunman than thief; when the police arrived, the money was still in the dead man's shirt pocket.

Seven weeks after the crime, the police charged James Foster, 38, with the murder of Charles Drake. An itinerant housepainter, Foster had been arrested because of an unrelated matter shortly after Drake was killed. The indirect way he came to be viewed as a suspect in the Drake murder is revealing.

On the Friday night after the Tuesday of the murder, Foster and a woman acquaintance and two other couples had been cruising around looking for beer. Since Jackson County was dry, that meant finding the local bootleggers, which they did. Then, a few hours after they had set out, the six of them—a bit inebriated—checked into overnight cabins in Cleveland, Georgia. They were by that time about twenty miles from Gainesville, where Foster lived in a boarding house. The next morning they drove off without paying. As if this weren't enough to make the manager angry, someone in the group had let a burning cigarette get out of control. A mattress fire, which Foster's companions thought they had put out, flared up after they left, ruining the mattress and causing considerable damage to the interior of the cabin.

On Monday, Foster returned to his housepainting job in Gainesville, which lies between Cleveland and Jefferson. That day—three days after the motel fire—the local police chief and Fred Culberson of the Georgia Bureau of Investigation (GBI) paid a visit to Foster and told him they wanted to talk to him about the motel episode. He didn't argue. In no time, Foster and his five companions were in police custody.

The others were soon freed, after each agreed to pay a share of the bill at the motel (including enough to cover the fire damage), but Foster was detained. In his pocket the police had found a release card from the Florida prison where he had just spent more than a year after being convicted as an accessory to armed robbery. As soon as the GBI officials learned they were holding a drifter with an out-of-state prison record for robbery who had been arrested only an hour's drive from where Drake was murdered, they wanted to question him further.

The GBI agent, Culberson, knew that Mrs. Drake had gotten a good look at the murderer, and he wanted to see whether she could identify Foster. Without explaining what he was doing, he drove Foster to the Drake house. Foster had no idea why the GBI was interested in him or why Culberson and Hightower, a second GBI agent, wanted some woman in Jefferson to give him the once-over. (This was hardly a case of Foster's "voluntarily" submitting himself "for the purpose of others identifying him," as the Georgia Supreme Court later described it.) Foster was given no warning at all that he was being put into a potentially incriminating situation, nor did he realize that there was no lawful warrant (and therefore no legal authority) for anyone to take him to the Drake home without asking for his consent.

They arrived at the house and walked in. Culberson told Foster to wait in the living room. He did as he was told, and was standing alone, framed in the doorway, as Mrs. Drake entered. When she saw Foster, she lunged for him and had to be restrained by Hightower. "Why did you kill my husband?" she screamed at Foster. "How could you do it?" She burst hysterically into tears, and the GBI men attempted to calm her down.

Foster, horrified, suddenly realized what was happening. He later told his attorney that he "almost started to shake," he was so scared. "Lady, for God's sake," he begged her, "please don't make a mistake. I'm in enough trouble already." But Mrs. Drake, ignoring his plea, told him first to stand in one spot, then to move to another, and so on, thus putting him in various places where she had seen the murderer the night her husband died. Seeing him in these positions confirmed her first impression. Although Mrs. Drake's identification of Foster as her husband's killer was hardly the product of a properly conducted police line-up, the two GBI agents were convinced by her reactions that they had their man.

Under indictment for the murder of Drake, Foster needed an attorney. Because he had no funds of his own to hire one, on August 7—six weeks after his arrest—the court appointed James Horace Wood and Floyd Hoard to defend him. Both attorneys were local, though Wood had only recently moved back to the area. Hoard, 29, was a serious man, thoroughly devoted to the law. He had passed the bar examination without attending law school, having instead learned law the old-fashioned way, by apprenticeship. His mentor had been his father-in-law, a distinguished Jackson County lawyer. Wood, on the other hand, had spent sufficient time in formal education to earn two law degrees. Before returning to Jackson County at age 44 to hang out his shingle, he had traveled widely. He had served with the United States Army in Germany and then established a good practice in Atlanta. But he was, he had concluded, basically a country boy who wanted nothing more than to prove himself to the people among whom he had grown up.

A court-appointed case, one involving a vicious murder at that, was not exactly what Wood had had in mind as a way to start his local career. The trial was scheduled to open in only six days, however, so he and Hoard set immediately to work. From the first interview, Wood doubted his client's guilt. There was an uncontrived simplicity and directness to the story Foster told his attorneys; he never faltered or hesitated, as someone making it up might, when he recounted where he had been on the night of the murder.

The accused man had no difficulty supplying Wood and Hoard with the details of his whereabouts. Early on the evening of June 19, he said, he was sitting on the porch of the rooming house in Gainesville where he had been living for about a month. A young woman acquaintance had phoned him and proposed that the two of them go out for the evening. Foster liked the idea, but he had no car, and she lived in New Holland—too far to walk from Gainesville. Two of his fellow boarders at the house obliged him, though, and the three drove out to the girl's house. Accompanied by Foster's date and her sister-in-law and the women's three children, they then went in search of some after-hours bootleg beer. Off to the Three Gables, the nearest bar, back to Gainesville, over to Pendergrass by way of Talmo for more beer (they got a bit lost on the back roads), to Gainesville again, and then to New Holland. They pretty much cruised away the night.

Though Wood had had experience as the defense attorney in more than a dozen previous murder cases, he had never had an alibi from a client that matched Foster's for sheer detail. If his account was true, there was no chance that Foster had murdered anyone in Jefferson. Gradually Wood came to believe that, since Foster had been held for more than six weeks before he was charged with the Drake murder and assigned legal counsel, even the authorities didn't think they had much of a case against him.

All Wood needed was corroboration. In the course of the next few days, he and Floyd Hoard proceeded to track down Foster's several companions and to interview these potential witnesses one by one. Each confirmed detail after detail of Foster's story; three declared themselves ready to testify that Foster had been with them at the time of the murder and that they had never been nearer than eight or nine miles to the Drake house in Jefferson. By that time, Wood and Hoard were thoroughly convinced: Their client was innocent and was going to be tried for a murder he had not committed.

Wood's pretrial investigations turned up other evidence to support his conclusion as well. Mrs. Drake had told the police that the burglar was wearing army fatigues; Foster owned no such clothes. The intruder obviously had brought a gun with him; Foster claimed to have had no gun since he had arrived in Georgia, and no gun had been found. Foster was slight and wiry and about medium height, no more than 5'7"; Mrs. Drake had initially described the murderer as a big strong man. (He had to be, she said, in order to "handle" her two-hundred-pound husband.) No fingerprint evidence from the crime scene implicated Foster. Nor was there any evident motive, since so far as anyone knew Foster had never been to Jefferson and therefore presumably did not know about the roll of bills Charlie Drake liked to carry. Even a lie detector test that the GBI ran prior to charging Foster turned up nothing.

Best of all, Wood had found a witness, Betty Williams, who would testify that she had given directions to Foster and his friends, temporarily lost, from the porch of her house in Talmo—within minutes of the time Drake was murdered several miles away in Jefferson. She would also testify that Foster was wearing light-colored pants at the time, not the army fatigues that Mrs. Drake said the intruder-murderer was wearing. Her testimony on Foster's appearance was especially important, because of the one enormous obstacle that stood in the way of his acquittal: Mrs. Drake's eyewitness identification. Wood's belief in his client's innocence was not shaken by Mrs. Drake's identification, any more than it was by Foster's previous record and the fact that he was a drifter, or by the absence of another suspect. These factors did, however, leave him uneasy about what the trial's outcome might be.

Wood and Hoard were exhausted by the time the trial began. When they took the case, they had realized that even working ten hours a day would give them only about sixty hours to get ready—unlikely to be anywhere nearly enough time. In fact they had worked far more than that and were still a long way from feeling adequately prepared when they appeared in court the day the trial opened. Because of the extensive publicity the case had received, the lawyers' first move was to request a change of venue. A series of articles in the Jackson County *Herald* had spelled out sufficient details of Foster's past to make it clear to even casual readers that, whatever else was true, the man charged with murder was an ex-con. The County Board of Commissioners had also offered a much-publicized reward in the Drake killing.

Wood called two witnesses, the chairman of the Board of Commissioners and the editor of the *Herald*, in an attempt to demonstrate that Foster could not receive a fair trial in Jackson County. Judge Bennett wasted no time in setting the speedy pace that he was to insist on throughout the trial. When the editor proved unwilling to commit himself as to whether he thought a fair trial was possible after what had appeared in the paper, saying he would "need time to think about it," the judge cut him off and denied the change-of-venue motion.

The defense lawyers next moved for a continuance, on the ground that they had not had enough preparation time. That motion, too, was denied, even more quickly than the first one. The trial would go forward immediately, whether Wood was ready or not.

On the witness stand, Mrs. Drake told her story slowly and precisely. Her presentation had a plain, unvarnished quality to it, and her story—full of details—was convincing; Mrs. Drake came across as an unimpeachable eyewitness. She alone had seen everything from shortly after the moment the intruder entered her house. Referring to the burglar, she said to the jury: "He stood by me for an instant and he threw his gun on me. I saw him well. I saw his whole features, his eyes and his mouth, while standing there." It was a few minutes later in her testimony, under the careful prompting of the prosecutor, that Camie Drake pointed across the court room at James Foster and uttered the damning words: "He is the man that shot my husband."

Foster's attorneys felt helpless, according to Wood's own later account of this crucial phase of the trial. "She has the hearts of the jury in the palm of her hand," he despaired. "How can I come along at this point and attempt to destroy her identification of Foster without running the risk of gaining only scorn from the jury?" His concern was not without basis. Mrs. Drake was more than a witness. She was also a grieving widow, and a well-known one at that. Any challenge to her account of events could easily be interpreted as a callous lack of sympathy for her grief.

When it was Wood's turn to cross-examine Mrs. Drake, he warmed to the task slowly. He was tired and uncertain how best to proceed, as any attorney might be after working around the clock for days in the pell-mell rush to judgment imposed by the trial court. Despite his worries about alienating the jury, Wood tried mightily to shake Mrs. Drake's testimony and her recollection of the murder. First he grilled her about the exact height of the intruder—she insisted she knew—and then he got her to admit that she was not certain about her own husband's weight or height. He then turned to other details: Which part of the telephone had the intruder used to club her to the floor? (Oddly, no one had checked the phone for fingerprints.) What was the exact time of the break-in? Which of the intruder's facial features allegedly matched Foster's? Again and again, Mrs. Drake answered his questions vaguely and hesitantly, but she nonetheless left the witness stand with no noticeable cracks in her composure or her testimony.

With the cross-examination of Mrs. Drake finished, the State put another witness on the stand, J. C. Dameron. Brought into court directly from his jail cell, where he had met Foster a few weeks earlier, Dameron testified that Foster had boasted to him about the Drake murder. Dameron's testimony rapidly deteriorated into incoherence and implausibility, however; he contradicted himself and could not supply the details he claimed to have heard. The prosecution was visibly embarrassed, and for a moment the defense experienced a flicker of hope. If the prosecutors were so desperate they would resort to a witness of this sort, Wood reasoned, they must know their case was weak. Although Wood in his cross-examination effectively destroyed Dameron's credibility as a witness, he knew it would take more than that to neutralize the powerful effect of Mrs. Drake's testimony.

Foster's own appearance on the witness stand didn't help much. He admitted, even prior to cross-examination, that he had "just got out of the penitentiary in Florida" before the Drake murder. He allowed that he had been "a very bad man" for part of his life. (Indeed he had, as his wife and seven children, abandoned in South Carolina, could attest.) Bible in hand, Foster gave his alibi and prayed aloud to the jury that "you fellows will believe me." But his evident sincerity and piety could not blot out the admitted prison record or the information published in the Jackson County *Herald* about his prior conviction, sentence, and release.

Wood had a dozen other witnesses prepared to support Foster's alibi or discredit details in Mrs. Drake's testimony. As a group, they accomplished little of either goal. Bobby Smith, for example, who lived in the same boarding house as Foster, actually ended up being something of a liability. The defense had wanted him simply to corroborate that Foster lived at the boarding house, that Foster had bought pink pants from him, and that Foster had been wearing them the night of June 19. Smith did testify to all of that, but the prosecution managed to get him thoroughly confused on cross-examination, which raised questions about his reliability. The prosecution also got from him the information that he had recently found a pair of army fatigue pants lying around at the boarding house. As Smith stepped down, the possibility that those pants belonged to Foster hung ominously in the air.

The defense's prime alibi witness was Betty Williams. Having no direct involvement with Foster and his companions, she had nothing to gain by providing an alibi for him, which helped make her testimony convincing. Wood described Williams as "our clean-up hitter," and indeed she did much better than the others. She gave precise and definite testimony, stating clearly that she had seen Foster at her house in Talmo about the time of the murder in Jefferson nearly ten miles distant. Cross-examination failed to damage her credibility. This was, as Wood put it, the "time-and-distance alibi, all wrapped up pretty." Yet even so, when Betty Williams was done, the jury was still free to speculate: If the stated time of either the murder in Jefferson or the encounter in Talmo were off by just a few minutes, and if Foster had driven at breakneck speed from Talmo to Jefferson, he could have killed Drake, time-and-distance alibi notwithstanding.

The jurors must have believed something of this sort, because their verdict agreed with Mrs. Drake's version of the murder.

No sooner had Foster been sentenced to death than his attorneys, Wood and Hoard, asked to be relieved of their duties as court-appointed counsel. They wanted to continue the fight working independently, even though it would mean doing so on their own time and money. (That was essentially what they'd been doing anyway, given the low fees for court-appointed work.)

To their surprise and relief, Wood and Hoard began to hear sympathetic voices in the community. Several individuals came forward to indicate they thought that Foster had not had a fair trial, that he might have been a victim of mistaken identity. Wood, having lost the case, had felt very much alone at first. As it became clear that the jury had not spoken for the entire community, however, and as support for Foster mounted, Wood's faith in the basic goodness of the people among whom he had grown up was slowly restored. Within a few days of the end of the trial, the James Foster Defense Fund had been organized, and a rally was being planned. The banquet hall at the Andrew Jackson Hotel in Commerce, where Wood had his law office, was reserved.

On the day of the rally, the hall was already full an hour before the public meeting was scheduled to begin. When he learned this, Wood arranged for the event to be moved to the city park in Jefferson. Then, minutes before the rally was to start, Foster's wife and six of the seven Foster children serendipitously arrived in Wood's office from their home in South Carolina. Wood took them with him to the park, where both he and Mrs. Foster spoke briefly to the crowd of a thousand, many no doubt drawn by curiosity but some obviously also eager to help Foster and his lawyer. Whatever the motivation for attendance, the results were impressive; it was like having half the population of Jefferson gathered in one place.

Wood later commented on how the meeting buoyed his spirits. The sight of "good honest faces" and the thought of people "rising up, by peaceful means, to correct an injustice" were reassuring. "We were," he said, "on the road back." By the end of the public meeting the Defense Fund had more than $1200, and a special purse of $88.20 had been raised directly for Mrs. Foster and the children. As September came to a close, thanks to additional contributions (often in dollar or half-dollar amounts), the Defense Fund held more than $2000.

In the first post-trial weeks, as Wood worked on the appeal he had filed for Foster (which had resulted in an automatic stay of execution), other encouraging developments were taking place. Most importantly, Judge Julian Bennett—so apparently unsympathetic to Wood's and Hoard's efforts on behalf of their client—had to face election (he had been appointed to the bench, to fill out another judge's unexpired term). He was soundly beaten, winning only eighteen votes out of hundreds cast. With such a dramatic and public demonstration of the people's lack of confidence in him, the lame-duck judge promptly resigned without waiting for his term to expire. Wood could dare to hope he might have better luck the next time around, with a more cooperative judge.

The solicitor general for Jackson County, Hope Stark—who had directed the prosecution in the Foster trial—was also no friend of Wood or of Wood's client. In the same election in which Bennett was so spectacularly rejected, Stark did not even seek re-election; he was succeeded by one of Wood's friends, a former law school classmate. That, too, made a little optimism seem warranted.

Not everything was going smoothly, however. Funds were always short. With little hard cash to offer, Wood had difficulty finding a private investigator to follow up the leads he had uncovered. And not everyone was ready to celebrate the formation and growth of the Defense Fund. The Gainesville *Daily Times*, for instance, remained unimpressed by the suggestion that Foster might be innocent. An editorial in the paper argued: "If the convicted man needs public contributions in order to continue his legal fight for life, no doubt he can find them. We would hate to execute an innocent man. By the same reasoning, we dislike building phony sympathy for a guilty one and dislike further heartache being brought to those who have suffered because of the death of Charles Drake."

Then, on a routine visit with his client at the jail, Wood was appalled to learn that his co-counsel, Hoard, had advised Foster to plead guilty if he won a new trial. A guilty plea, Hoard knew, would reduce the likelihood of Foster being sentenced to death a second time. But Foster told Wood he had refused. "I'd rather die like a dog," he said, "than admit to a lie like that." Wood was furious with Hoard for what he saw as a betrayal. When he confronted Hoard with what Foster had reported, Hoard confirmed it; Wood simmered in anger. Although Hoard continued to work on the case, relations between the two men soured.

September became October before the transcription of the trial record, which ran to more than four hundred pages, was finished. Another month passed before the transcript could be suitably copied for filing with the appeal. More months went by as Wood researched the law, looking for the strongest grounds on which to base his argument for a new trial.

Finally, in April 1957, the hearing on the motion was held. The outcome was a crushing defeat for Wood; every point he had raised was denied. On appeal to the Georgia Supreme Court later that year, the result was the same: Motion denied. In unanimously rejecting attorney Wood's argument for a new trial, the court particularly noted the eyewitness testimony of Mrs. Drake and Foster's alleged jail-house confession to J. C. Dameron. As the court saw it, Foster's guilt was proved beyond a reasonable doubt: "The evidence fully supported the verdict." Wood filed a motion for a rehearing, which was likewise denied. Foster was discouraged; Wood could do little but promise to take the case on further appeal into the federal courts.

Without any warning, a break came in the form of a phone call to Wood from an Atlanta attorney. Jimmy Venable, a friend of Wood's, had been following the Foster case in the papers, never dreaming he might have a role to play in it. Then the girl friend of a client of his, Lonnie Neal, informed Venable that Neal had information he wanted to share about the Foster case. Getting to Neal would be easy, Venable assured Wood, since Neal was in the Fulton County jail in Atlanta. Eager to learn more, Wood went to Atlanta to interview him.

A career criminal, Neal was angry at a former partner in crime, Charles Paul ("Rocky") Rothschild, over a division of the spoils. When he learned of Foster's conviction and death sentence, he decided to tip off Foster's attorney that it was Rothschild, not Foster, who had killed Charlie Drake. As Wood later reported their conversation, Neal insisted, "I figured that it wasn't right for an innocent fellow to die for a crime that a bum like that Rothschild committed." Neal then proceeded to relate to Wood details of conversations between himself and Rothschild that left little doubt about Foster's innocence and Rothschild's guilt—if Neal could be believed.

When a reporter for the *Atlanta Constitution* heard about Neal's story, headlines in the paper announced: "NEW EVIDENCE GIVES HOPE TO DOOMED MAN." The story told how the GBI investigators were following Neal's leads, and how they had never been fully convinced of Foster's guilt. But the next day the *Constitution* reported skepticism on the part of John Brooks, the local sheriff in Jackson County; Neal, he pointed out, was a jailbird with a long criminal record. (Sheriff Brooks seemed unaware of the irony in his remarks: At Foster's trial, the prosecution had not hesitated to use testimony from a convicted criminal, J. C. Dameron. Wood also learned that, soon after the trial, the police had quietly released Dameron from jail—suggesting that a deal had been made in exchange for his testimony.)

The *Constitution* article gave undeserved credit to the GBI for following up on Neal's leads. It was initially Wood alone who set to work tracking down Rothschild. A resident of Cairo, Illinois, Rocky Rothschild had been a police officer until 1953, when he was accused of using unnecessary violence during an arrest. Unfortunately for Rothschild, the suspect he roughed up turned out to be the son of a powerful local politician. As a result of that incident, Rothschild was peremptorily dismissed from the force. He promptly turned to robbery, safecracking, and burglary—mostly at what looked like a comfortable distance, far to the east, in Georgia and South Carolina. He was frequently back in Cairo, however, where his former colleagues on the police force kept tabs on his comings and goings. They knew how bitter and angry he was over his dismissal, and some of them suspected his new line of work was not entirely aboveboard.

Wood persuaded Floyd Hoard to drive him to Cairo, where he hoped to learn more about Rothschild's activities around the time of the murder. Among other things, he had always wondered whether it might be possible to locate the murder weapon. When he mentioned this to Deputy Sheriff Buck Self, one of the people he interviewed in Cairo, Self suddenly pulled his own gun from its holster and offered it to Wood. "I think this is the gun you want," he said of the .357 Magnum. It turned out Buck had bought the weapon from a Cairo tavern owner, who in turn had obtained it from Rocky. Self was confident in his identification of this particular weapon, because of an unusual and unmistakable mark on the cylinder. He had recognized the gun when he acquired it, having noticed it when Rothschild had proudly shown it to him some months earlier.

Subsequent test firings of the Rothschild-Self revolver, performed by the crime laboratory in Atlanta, confirmed that bullets from that gun bore identical markings to the bullets that had killed Charlie Drake. Back in Cairo on a second trip, Wood learned that Self had acquired the weapon from the tavern owner about two weeks after the Drake murder. Furthermore, Wood discovered that no one had seen Rothschild in Cairo for approximately a week before and a week after the day of the murder.

Cheered by this news, the next day Wood was in the hallway of the Cairo court house, preparing to interview the tavern keeper to check out the dates of his acquisition and sale of the gun. Suddenly he was hailed by a stranger—none other than his prime suspect. Rothschild had evidently learned about Wood's arrival in town and that he was asking questions. He recognized Wood from photos in the news coverage of the Foster case. The conversation that then unfolded between lawyer-detective Wood and criminal-suspect Rothschild was marked by caution on both sides.

Rothschild inquired whether Wood was in town to try to pin the Drake killing on him, and Wood—by his own later account trying in vain to sound candid—lied that he wasn't. The two men chatted warily a bit more and then went their separate ways. Wood was struck with Rothschild's poise and intelligence and noted that he was "an excellent conversationalist." Rothschild, he said, came across as an "all-American boy."

Wood was nevertheless convinced that Rothschild was a murderer. But when Wood eventually tracked down the tavern owner, the man flatly refused to provide any information—let alone sign any papers—concerning the gun then in Wood's possession. Wood surmised that Rothschild had gotten to the tavern owner first and had used whatever means were necessary to convince him to remain silent.

During the two years that had elapsed since Wood's original assignment to the Foster case in the summer of 1956, his law practice had not grown the way he had hoped it would. Although some prospective clients could unquestionably be numbered among the supporters of the James Foster Defense Fund, many others could not. They took their business elsewhere, because they disapproved of Wood's refusal to abandon Foster to what they believed was a well-deserved fate in the electric chair. But Wood himself was also partially to blame for the poor business. The main explanation for the fitful and disappointing beginning of his new practice was his preoccupation, even obsession, with trying to save his death row client. He had little time or energy to attend to the needs of other clients.

The lack of anything remotely like steady income from fees was a constant problem. The Defense Fund never raised much money after the first flurry of contributions. What there was quickly disappeared in expenses incurred by Wood's endless telephone calls, trips to and from Atlanta and Cairo, and preparation of legal papers. At one point, the utility company turned off the electricity in Wood's office; his secretary moved the typewriter under a skylight so she could see to work, and more than once Wood himself had to resort to using a flashlight. His rent was months overdue, he was behind on car payments, and two local banks were hounding him to make good on various overdrafts.

As for Rothschild, his fortunes at last also took a turn for the worse. In May 1958, he was successfully extradited by out-of-state authorities after a grand jury indictment for robbery. Unfortunately for Wood, it was South Carolina that first laid claim to the elusive ex-policeman; he was wanted there for a burglary at a cotton gin. Georgia, where Rothschild had come under suspicion for a grocery store robbery, would have to wait. Some of the fallout from the extradition did help Wood's case, however, when a picture of Rothschild's arrest appeared in a South Carolina paper. A delivery man saw that photo and identified the policeman-turned-burglar as the hitchhiker he had picked up in the early morning hours, the day after the murder, about fifty miles from the Drake home.

Meanwhile, in early June, Wood's latest motions in the Georgia courts to re-open the case were turned down, and a new date was set for James Foster's execution: June 21, 1958. Understandably, Foster again became depressed, even though Wood professed greater confidence than ever that he could save his client.

Hoping to extract a confession from Rothschild, Wood arranged to visit him in the jail in Spartanburg, South Carolina. Superficially as affable as ever, Rothschild listened with increasing agitation and dismay to Wood's account of the evidence accumulating against him. Nonetheless, he continued to maintain that he knew nothing about the Drake murder.

Despite lacking the confession and affidavit he had hoped to get from Rothschild, Wood filed a special motion on June 10, only eleven days before the scheduled execution, on the ground that he had newly discovered evidence. This time he was successful. The execution date was cancelled, and the motion was set for argument on July 2. In the interval, Rothschild was convicted of the South Carolina cotton gin robbery and was sentenced to five years in prison. Mrs. Drake, on the second anniversary of her husband's murder, was taken to visit Rothschild, but she did not recognize him and was unwilling to revise or revoke her trial testimony against Foster.

Wood's best hope of a case against Rothschild at that point lay in persuading another of Rothschild's former partners in crime, William Patterson, to give incriminating testimony. Patterson, like Rothschild, was then in the South Carolina state prison in Columbia, having been convicted of robbery in Spartanburg. But despite being assured that it might help him win an earlier release, Patterson at first refused to budge, insisting he had nothing to say. Then suddenly, on July 2—eleven days after Foster had been scheduled to die and at the very time Wood's motion on new evidence was being heard—Patterson finally agreed to give a statement to the chief of the South Carolina Law Enforcement Division. As anticipated, his statement implicated Rothschild in the Drake killing.

Still better news greeted Wood as he was beginning a short Fourth of

July holiday. Floyd Hoard called to tell him that Rocky Rothschild, worn down by the combination of evidence against him and his own guilty conscience, had chosen Independence Day to sign a full confession. His statement, which ran to twenty-five hundred words, was duly sworn to and notarized in the presence of several witnesses. In it, Rothschild spelled out in full detail the story of the crime; he also explained what had finally moved him to confess.

"I make this statement," he said at the end, "because since I have been or was first locked up . . . I have been worried and my conscience has been hurting me and I have read the Bible and prayed and when I would wake up at night, I would always see Mrs. Drake, and knowing that a man, named James F. Foster, had been sentenced to death twice for the 1956 robbery slaying, which I committed, has been constantly on my conscience and my mind." Like Foster at trial, Rothschild had in the end turned to his Bible. "What made me think so much of Foster," he continued, "was a chapter I read in the Bible, St. Matthew, Chapter 5, Verse 10: 'Blessed are they which are persecuted for righteousness' sake; for theirs is the kingdom of heaven.' Foster was definitely being persecuted. May God return him to his wife and family and may he have a long and happy life."

A week later, Rothschild was taken under guard to Jefferson to re-enact the crime. At one point, he indicated some underbrush and told the police, "There's where I hid the fatigues"—the clothes he had worn on the night of the crime. And sure enough, when the police looked, they found a rotting pair of army fatigue trousers hidden in the grass and weeds.

The most extraordinary moment of the whole case occurred in front of the court house in Jefferson, just prior to Rothschild's re-enactment of the crime. Foster, still in custody, was brought out to meet Rothschild. A large crowd had gathered, including the former housepainter's wife and children. With newspaper and television crews all around, Foster and Rothschild approached each other. "Rocky," Foster said, "I've waited quite a while for this moment. I owe you a lot. It must have taken guts to do what you did."

Rothschild, struggling for control, replied, "I owe you quite a bit, too. I'm glad to see you, and I wish you all the luck in the world now that you're back with your family. I hope that you and your wife and your children will have a long, happy life." The two men embraced, sobbing; the photographers' bulbs flashed. Foster's wife fainted, and he seemed dazed. "I don't know what to say. There are so many things I could say. I just don't know, I'm dumbfounded." Ten days later, on the strength of Rothschild's stunning confession, Foster was granted a new trial and released on $500 bond.

In early August, Rothschild was indicted for the murder of Charles Drake. Rocky turned State's witness against an accomplice, A. D. Allen, who was then also indicted. Despite vigorous efforts by Allen's defense attorney to discredit everything Rothschild said, Allen was found guilty with recommendation for mercy and was sentenced to life in prison. Rothschild pleaded guilty and was also sentenced to life; his belated cooperation with the State saved him from the death sentence that had originally been meted out unjustly to Foster.

In September, Foster appeared in court for his second trial. The prosecutors suggested to Wood that they would be willing simply to drop the charges. Wood rejected the idea; he wanted a jury to hear the evidence and acquit his client, once and for all. After a brief statement from Sheriff Brooks identifying the Rothschild confession, a profusion of thanks by Foster himself—once again on the witness stand, Bible in hand—and further statements from Hoard and Wood, the jury announced its verdict without even leaving the court room: Not guilty.

With his family in tow, Foster was soon on his way home to South Carolina. Four months later, Wood tried to get some compensation for his client for the two years he had spent on death row, wrongfully convicted. The lower house of the Georgia Legislature voted an indemnity of $2,500, but the state senate failed to approve it. The bill died, and Foster never received a cent.

A few loose ends remained. Rothschild claimed in his confession that he had thrown the murder weapon, "a .38 Police Positive," into the water off a bridge in Jefferson. This cast some doubt on the story told by Deputy Sheriff Self about the .357 Magnum—and on the ballistics tests—but no such weapon was found. More significantly, after his sentencing for the Drake murder, Rothschild repudiated his confession. (He thereby made himself unavailable as a State's witness and in the process enabled Allen to appeal his conviction successfully.)

Rothschild's retraction of his confession did little to change people's minds, however. No one any longer seriously doubted that he was guilty of the Drake murder and that Foster was innocent—except, perhaps, the shaken Mrs. Drake. After Foster's acquittal, she told an interviewer: "I thought I was right. Now I just don't know. I certainly don't want to see anyone suffer for anything he didn't do, but I was completely honest. It's a terrible thing to see your husband killed before your eyes and almost be killed yourself." Foster himself said of Mrs. Drake, "She only made an honest mistake."

Years later, after being released on parole from prison in Georgia, Rothschild reverted to his criminal ways. Arrested in North Carolina, he was serving a life sentence for burglary when he died of a heart attack in 1976.

James Foster settled down again in Greer, South Carolina. There he resumed his responsibilities as a husband and father and took up once more the trade of housepainter.

✳

SINCERE YET MISTAKEN eyewitness testimony clinched the case against Foster, as it has against many other defendants in capital cases. The fact that eyewitness testimony cannot always be trusted was drawn to public attention earlier in this century by Harvard's professor of experimental psychology Hugo Münsterberg, who staged a "shooting" in his classroom to prove to skeptical students that witnesses to the same event do not tell the same story. Since then, countless investigations have confirmed that such testimony is often unreliable. Among many cases we cite illustrating the point, two from California a half century apart provide especially good examples.

During the late 1940s, lawyer-turned-detective-writer Erle Stanley Gardner created the Court of Last Resort—a small, private organization devoted to rectifying miscarriages of justice in serious felony cases where innocent defendants had been put behind bars. None was more of a cliff-hanger than the case that inspired Gardner to create his Court in the first place. It occurred virtually on his doorstep, in central California, among the human tide washed up by migrations from the Dust Bowl during the Great Depression.

In August 1943, a badly injured 13-year-old girl was found along the banks of the Feather River in Yuba City, half an hour's drive north of Sacramento. She and her family, like thousands of others, eked out a living picking peaches in nearby orchards. Near death when she was found by friends and family, she gasped out, "Don't let that old red-headed man get me, Daddy." Although promptly hospitalized, the child died.

A few hundred yards from where she had been found was a boathouse regularly used by three men, including William Marvin Lindley, known to one and all as "Red" because of his red hair. Lindley, 49—uneducated, illiterate, and not in the best mental health—was another itinerant farm worker. He had arrived in that part of California some years earlier from Texas, where he had served a prison term for burglary. Police soon located a teenaged sheepherder who claimed to have seen the girl fighting off Lindley on the riverbank. Another prosecution witness testified that while he and Lindley were in jail prior to trial, Lindley confessed, saying, "I might as well tell you I followed this little girl to the river and grabbed her and choked her and throwed her in the bushes and went back to the bunk house for an alibi." The case appeared to be open and shut.

Lindley's testimony during the trial (which was delayed a year on the ground that he was incompetent to be tried) amounted mostly to denial of any such confession, denial of harming the girl, and offer of a rather vague alibi. His court-appointed attorney could do little in the face of testimony to the contrary, and Red Lindley was convicted of first-degree murder and sentenced to death.

Los Angeles attorney Al Matthews, Jr., became interested in the case, and his volunteer efforts secured a hearing for Lindley. There it was established that the young sheepherder was color blind and of such marginal intelligence as to be barely capable of giving reliable testimony. Matthews also established that another red-headed farm worker had been in the vicinity of the crime; some witnesses had noticed scratch marks on his face, and others said that during a drunken brawl the night of the murder he had even confessed to assaulting the girl. Despite these facts, the California Supreme Court affirmed Lindley's conviction and sentence.

Unwilling to surrender his client to the gas chamber, Matthews wrote to Erle Stanley Gardner—wealthy, famous, with easy access to publicity and the ear of officials—urging him to get involved. He did, and he later prefaced his own account by observing, "I know of no case which gives a better example of the dangers inherent in capital punishment."

By tracing out in precise detail the movements of Lindley, the girl, and witnesses in the vicinity, Gardner broke the case wide open. He showed that at the very time the sheepherder claimed to have seen Lindley taking the girl into the willows by the river, Lindley was in fact riding in an automobile with her father! With this rock-solid alibi for Lindley in his pocket, Gardner personally wrote to each member of the state supreme court, the governor, and the attorney general, laying out his analysis. A stay of execution was duly issued.

But Lindley's travail was not over. In January 1946 he came within a few hours of the gas chamber; another reprieve came in July, only two days before his rescheduled execution. Again in October he won a reprieve, this time with a week to spare. The pendulum stopped swinging only in April 1947, when Gardner was able to persuade Governor Earl Warren to commute the death sentence to life imprisonment.

Lindley, however, had all but collapsed under the strain of the previous three years. He was declared insane and disappeared from sight into the recesses of California's prison for the criminally insane.

Erle Stanley Gardner's final reflections on the case deserve to be remembered: "Because of the identification made by the dying girl . . . [and] the so-called eyewitness identification by the young sheepherder, the police became convinced that Lindley was the murderer. They diligently searched for any evidence that would enable the prosecutor to build a good case against Lindley in court, and they brushed aside any evidence which might have pointed to developments that would have been in Lindley's favor."

A MORE RECENT California case presents another variation on the theme of sincere but untrustworthy eyewitness testimony. Late on a February evening in 1978, several shots were fired from a passing car at some youths in the Mexican-American community of Duarte, on the northeastern fringe of Los Angeles. As the gunmen drove off, one of the boys died. Police quickly arrived, took descriptions of the assailants and their vehicles, and only a few blocks away saw what they thought was the getaway car. They soon surrounded the area, where teenagers were partying, and arrested Gordon Castillo Hall, 16, whom they found hiding in some nearby bushes. Later that night in a police line-up, Hall was identified by two of the victim's brothers, who had also been targets of the gunman.

Hall claimed he was completely innocent. He insisted he had been at the yard party all evening, and one of his friends confirmed his statement. Although Hall admitted he had run and hidden from the police, he said it was not because he had shot and killed anyone. The reason was rather that attending the party violated the terms of his probation for involvement in a grafitti-painting incident. Nevertheless, the eyewitness testimony by the victim's brothers and the lack of convincing alibi testimony sufficed to convince the jury. Hall was convicted of first-degree murder, but—perhaps because of his youth—he was spared a death sentence.

State Senator H. L. Richardson represented the district in which Duarte is located. Prompted by pressure from Hall's family and friends in the Latino community there, he urged the Los Angeles County Sheriff's Department to re-investigate the crime. A major break came when the two brothers recanted their trial testimony. They then testified in writing and under oath that they had erroneously identified Hall; he was not the gunman, and they had not seen him at the scene of the crime. Instead, they claimed, a man named Oscar Sanchez was the guilty one. One of the brothers explained that after closer examination of both Hall and Sanchez, he became convinced that his original identification had been in error. The other brother allowed that he, too, had wrongly identified Hall because (as one newspaper reported) he was "distraught about his brother's death" and careless in noticing what the gunman really looked like.

The prosecution disputed the legitimacy of the new testimony but stopped short of denying that there was no ulterior motive for the change in the brothers' stories. Meanwhile, the defense had discovered another eyewitness; she identified Sanchez and a third man, Alfred Reyes, as the two who had fired the fatal shots. She also knew Hall and denied he had been involved. Although Reyes admitted he had been at the party, he denied any role in the crime and accused Sanchez of driving the getaway car. He did not mention Hall at all. Other witnesses added to the weight of evidence mounting against Reyes and Sanchez.

Why had none of this come out in the original trial? Because, said the supreme court of California when it reviewed the case in 1981, Hall's defense was wholly inadequate. His attorney had no investigator to dig up leads (much less follow them), paid no serious attention to the possibility that Sanchez rather than Hall was guilty, and never contested the improprieties in the police line-up that led to the identification of Hall as the killer. What the attorney did do was convince Hall's family to mortgage their home to pay his $10,000 fee.

But, as is so often the case, the inferior defense Hall received was something of a side issue. Mistaken eyewitness identification, however inadvertently or "honestly" tendered, was the critical factor in Hall's conviction. Fittingly, perhaps, it was *accurate* eyewitness testimony that set the record straight. Speaking for a majority of the California Supreme Court, Judge Stanley Mosk observed that the new evidence from witnesses was "amply sufficient to undermine the entire case of the prosecution, because it eviscerates the key trial testimony against petitioner [Hall] and clearly implicates a different culprit." In December 1981, after serving nearly three years in prison, Hall was released. Two months later the prosecution recommended that all charges against Hall be dropped, and the judge so ordered.

2 ✸ | "ME, THEY WERE BURYING ALIVE"

IN THE 1930s, when the nation was in the throes of the Great Depression, New York's Lower East Side was jammed with people struggling just to get by. Money was scarce, food was scarce, work was scarce. Young men roamed the streets, looking for whatever odd jobs they could find.

Samuel Cooperstein was more or less making a go of it, with his Boulevard Restaurant. Though he was not Dutch, people called him the "Dutchman" and referred to his place as the "Dutchman's." His was a popular gathering spot. More than just a restaurant, the Dutchman's was a tearoom, a coffeehouse, an everyday hangout—and sometimes a gambling joint.

Actually, the Boulevard Restaurant was nothing but a long room with makeshift partitions, on the second floor of an unprepossessing building at 144 Second Avenue (just a block down the street from the corner where the Second Avenue Deli does business today). Not a very fancy place, but then the Lower East Side has never been a very fancy place. Most of the Dutchman's clientele dropped by only when they had a little money. A few others showed up more regularly, even without money, drawn by card games and looking for companionship. The policemen on the beat put in periodic appearances, especially in the spring of 1937. There had been a holdup at the Boulevard in March, which had netted the robbers $1500. Knowing that where there is gambling there is money (and thus a tempting target for robbery), and knowing that the March crime had not yet been solved, the police kept a close eye on the place.

On April 9, 1937, it was business as usual at the Boulevard. As Friday night turned to the Saturday morning of April 10, Detectives John R. Gallagher and Michael J. Foley made a routine visit to the Dutchman's. They climbed the double flight of stairs to the narrow, low-ceilinged room. When they entered, they heard laughter and conversation; smoke filled the air. They saw nothing to report and turned to leave.

Cooperstein recognized the policemen despite their plainclothes dress and invited them to stay for a cup of coffee, no charge. The two police officers sat flanking the Dutchman, at a table some two dozen feet from the entrance. The door opened and shut repeatedly, as people came and went. Cooperstein put in an order for a couple of milks and a coffee for his guests. The door to the landing opened again. Gallagher and Foley, with an unobstructed view of the doorway, were in the best position to see the man who entered. He had a .32 pistol in his hand.

Right behind him was another man, unarmed. "This is a stickup. Everybody up!" he rasped. Two more young men joined the invading party. While the first two headed toward the kitchen, the third stood guard at the door. He also had a pistol. The fourth young man, armed with a .38, moved directly toward the Dutchman and the pair of officers and ordered them to the rear of the restaurant. It apparently had not dawned on him or the others that their captive clientele might include policemen.

Suddenly there was a burst of shots; it wasn't clear who fired first, or where the shots were coming from. People dropped to the floor or ducked under tables. Amazingly, only two men were hit. One was Detective Foley, the other was the third intruder. He abandoned his post as guard, but he was shot again as he staggered out the door. Foley emptied his gun and then fell back into his chair, bleeding profusely. Meanwhile, in the kitchen, the cook was sitting alone over a cup of coffee when a couple of the stickup men burst in. Detective Gallagher corralled them there and managed to phone for re-inforcements. "Signal 30"—felony in progress—went out over the police radios. In a matter of seconds, other officers patrolling in the area began to arrive.

The scene at the Boulevard was chaotic. Patrons of the restaurant testified later to the frantic activity. Gallagher looked for the gun the robbers had apparently disposed of in the kitchen; it later turned out to have been dropped in a flour barrel. Foley, though badly wounded, held his gun on the two men brought back from the kitchen. Only he knew that his weapon was already empty. Fights broke out as enraged customers tried to jump the holdup men, once it appeared safe to do so. Newly arrived police officers had their hands full trying to contain the action.

The two men Gallagher had rounded up in the kitchen were easily identified: Arthur "Hutch" Friedman and Dominick Guariglia. Their companion who had been standing watch at the door had disappeared, but was apprehended a few hours later. With one police bullet in his chest and another in his arm, Joseph Harvey O'Loughlin delivered himself to the emergency room of the nearest hospital. There he became the third member of the holdup gang to be taken into custody.

The next evening, April 10, Detective Foley died of his wounds. He was no longer merely an officer wounded in the line of duty, but a martyr to the cause of public safety. The desire to catch everyone in any way connected with the raid on the Boulevard Restaurant rose to a fever pitch. Michael Foley's death, his fellow officers were determined, would not go unavenged.

Before long, Guariglia talked. His rambling remarks alerted police to the possibility that several other men were involved. Philip "Sonny" Chaleff came under particular suspicion, and the police started looking for him. Five days later, hearing he was wanted, Chaleff saved the police further trouble by turning himself in. For three hours he protested his innocence, but he finally confessed to having been an unarmed participant in planning the raid. Insisting he had never been in the restaurant itself, he said he had been only the look-out man.

The police became convinced that at least six men had had something to do with the holdup, though they still had only four under arrest and did not know who the others were. They proceeded to file murder charges, as a result of which the four known culprits—Friedman, Guariglia, O'Loughlin, and Chaleff—were indicted on April 23, a scant two weeks after the bungled robbery. The police continued working on the case, determined to find the rest of the gang so they could be arrested and indicted as well.

Within less than eight weeks, they had almost succeeded. They had the names of two more men who were clearly involved. Benjamin "Little Benny" Ertel was the fourth of those who had burst into the Boulevard Restaurant in the wee hours of April 10, and Isidore "Little Chemey" Perlmutter (though he was not one of the actual armed gang) had been on hand for some of the planning sessions. With that, the police had worked out very nearly everything: who had helped to plan and orchestrate the attack on the Boulevard, who had actually been there, who had been armed—and who had shot Detective Foley.

The only thing they didn't know for sure was where the guns had come from. To make the case tight, they needed an "armorer." Then the name of Isidore "Beansy" Zimmerman came up. The police were told that he, too, had been in on the planning sessions and that he knew about the guns. That was all the authorities needed to conclude that Zimmerman was their man. For one thing, the police already knew him; they had picked Zimmerman up fourteen months earlier as a suspect in another murder case. Though they had released him in the end, they remembered Zimmerman; the decision to arrest him was an easy one. A second, modified indictment followed on June 21, which listed seven persons: the four named in the first indictment, the two not yet apprehended (Ertel and Perlmutter), and Isidore Zimmerman.

Actually, any of a number of feckless young men in the area near the Dutchman's might have been plausible candidates for arrest. To be sure, Friedman and Guariglia had been caught in the act, as had been—to all intents and purposes—O'Loughlin. But the net that brought in Chaleff and Zimmerman, and the names of Perlmutter and Ertel, could easily have included others. It just happened not to. Crisscrossing paths created a tangled web around that group of unemployed and bored young men. They and their friends appeared almost like interchangeable parts as they moved from one hangout to another: Muskin's Restaurant, Tobias Hanover's candy store, the Madison Bar and Grill, Artie's Poolroom, the Scammel Street Boys' Club, Louis Golden's Bar and Grill, Loew's movie house, an empty building here or there. Sometimes an off-duty cab would serve as a meeting place for "friends" to whom some money or favor was likely owed. None of the young men stayed in any one place very long. All of them were generally looking for a little action.

The shifting cast of characters would make it difficult to determine later which of these friends had spent the afternoon or evening of April 9, or the early hours or April 10, in each other's company. Abe Kirschner was a friend of Hutch Friedman's; so were Joseph Reibach and Isidore Meichenbaum. They had spent time together on April 9. Guariglia met O'Loughlin and Ertel at one point, though everyone knew he didn't like either of them, and then they had gone their separate ways. They met again later and ran into Perlmutter and Friedman. But in between? And prior to their first meeting? By the time it mattered, no one was able to recall with any certainty.

Danny Rose. "Popeye" Cooperman. Salvatore Scalogna, Buddy Boyles, and Philip "Footke" Savoy. Each of them seemed to have had some connection with the guns used at the Dutchman's, but it was all rather vague. Furthermore, "Chester," "Smitty," and "Fat"—three other youths from the neighborhood—had all spent time with one or another of the accused robbers at critical points just prior to the invasion of the Boulevard. But the police never showed an interest in these three, especially once Guariglia, Friedman, and O'Loughlin—the clearly guilty parties—had all implicated Zimmerman, and Danny Rose had testified that Zimmerman knew someone in the group had guns. When Rose said he remembered telling Beansy Zimmerman about the guns, that linked Zimmerman directly with the murder. It also fit neatly with the testimony of Popeye Cooperman, who said he had heard Zimmerman volunteering to ask Rose for guns. Cooperman and Rose admitted their own involvement in the crime, but the prosecution found it more convenient to believe their testimony about the others (especially Zimmerman) than to indict them, because that testimony gave the prosecutors what they needed: In Beansy Zimmerman, they had the armorer, the crucial supplier of the guns—one of which had been used to kill Detective Foley. Actual evidence that Zimmerman had played a role in obtaining the guns, apart from the testimony given under pressure by Rose and Cooperman, was nonexistent. But the police and prosecutors, sliding over the lack of confirmation from any other sources, chose to be content with what they had. They then further concluded (on what basis is not clear) that Zimmerman had planned the robbery.

Everyone agreed that Zimmerman was not involved in the actual holdup in any direct way, and no one ever disputed his claim that he had not set foot in the Dutchman's that Friday night or Saturday morning. His own account was that he had spent the evening with his girl friend, a lass with a "pretty little Irish face" and a "cute little turned-up nose." But of course an alibi of that sort is not enough to make a person innocent of behind-the-scenes complicity. If Zimmerman knowingly provided weapons for the felony, he was an "accessory before the fact" and under the law just as guilty as the person who fired the bullet that killed Detective Michael Foley. And from the standpoint of the prosecutor, convicting the gun supplier was essential. Eager to have justice done on Foley's behalf and in his memory, the prosecution wanted no obvious gaps in the case. The failure to take Little Benny and Little Chemey into custody made it all the more important to have someone to label as the first link in the chain of events that led to Foley's murder.

When the trial started, the defense table consisted of twelve attorneys who together summoned twenty-four witnesses. The prosecution called sixty. Not surprisingly, given the number of witnesses, testimony was confusing and sometimes contradictory; the trial lasted twenty days. The five defendants were tried together despite the fact that each had a different lawyer or team of lawyers. Zimmerman's lawyer, James Murray, made a motion for a separate trial for his client—so obviously in a different category from the others, as both Murray and Zimmerman saw it—but Judge Charles C. Nott, Jr., denied the motion. In so doing, he denied Zimmerman a chance to establish a separate identity for himself. Instead, Zimmerman was repeatedly linked with the known culprits by virtue of his name always showing up on the list of defendants. Oddly, even so, only rarely during the trial did anyone mention Zimmerman explicitly. Most of the time it was as if everyone had forgotten that he, too, was on trial—let alone trial for his life. (Years later, Zimmerman's lawyer rightly called his client "the forgotten man.") It was almost as if Zimmerman's name had been added to the list inadvertently, and no one had bothered to delete it; none of the damning evidence presented against the four known culprits—Friedman, Guariglia, O'Loughlin, and Chaleff—implicated Zimmerman. The truth was that he had essentially nothing to do with the defendants or the case. When the prosecution mentioned him along with the other defendants, however, the testimony against them was nonetheless applied to him bit by bit as well.

Three witnesses for the prosecution turned out to be particularly devastating for Zimmerman. He later described them as "millstones" around his neck. The prosecution handled these witnesses very effectively, however, and no one on the jury seemed to notice or care how unsavory these three characters were.

One of the millstones was Tobias Hanover, who owned and ran the candy shop that served as one of the meeting places for the young men in the neighborhood. Simply by being in his store, he had been a witness (though not a very attentive one) to the comings and goings of several of the defendants on the evening of April 9. For business reasons, however, Hanover wanted nothing to do with the case, and during the trial his chief concern was getting out of the witness box and back to his shop as quickly as possible. Anxious lest he damage his own reputation or that of his business any further, he gave information under oath that he thought would get him off the hook. In the process he conveyed greater certainty than he actually had, "definitely" placing Beansy with the conspirators at some point during the evening of the crime. If Zimmerman had been meeting with the known gunmen, as Hanover's testimony implied, he must have been plotting with them. Vague and unreliable though Hanover's recollections were, they became part of the record.

Danny Rose and Popeye Cooperman were the other two millstones. Given that they could easily have been defendants themselves, there was some reason to be skeptical about their motivation in testifying. When they appeared as witnesses for the prosecution, one might have wondered whether they had been granted immunity in exchange for their cooperation. In fact, Judge Nott acknowledged that Cooperman was an accomplice, though he stopped just short of saying the same about Rose. The lead attorney for the prosecution—Jacob J. Rosenblum—skillfully reminded the jury, however, that the question of Rose's or Cooperman's guilt was not the issue before it. The jury's views on that subject, he pointed out, were irrelevant. What mattered was Rose's testimony that Zimmerman knew about the guns, and Cooperman's claim that both

Rose and Zimmerman were with him when he walked to the place where the guns were hidden.

The upshot of the testimony from these two witnesses was that Zimmerman knew about the guns used in the holdup and that he was involved in supplying them to the actual robbers. The likelihood that Rose and Cooperman would say anything to keep themselves as far removed from suspicion as possible never came up at the trial. They had good reason to connect Zimmerman (or, for that matter, anyone they could) with the guns. Zimmerman's lawyer tried to show how patently self-serving Cooperman's testimony was. He argued that the jury ought to give no credence to testimony from an acknowledged accomplice in the crime. The argument was to no avail.

On April 14, 1938, ten months after the filing of the second indictment, a jury convicted Isidore Zimmerman and his co-defendants of first-degree murder. Even before the sentencing eight days later, Zimmerman knew that all five of them were headed for the electric chair.

Now, more than half a century later, no one can go back and sort out exactly what influenced the jury. Zimmerman's testimony should have raised serious questions about the two contradictory statements the police had taken from him. After he had made the first statement, he was released. He was then brought in for questioning again, and made a second statement in which he admitted knowing where some guns were hidden (though he consistently denied handling the guns or knowing about a plan to use them in a felony). While his second statement was being taken, however, there were numerous interruptions, and some of what he said was modified before it was written down for his signature. When he testified in court later, Zimmerman said he had been told more than once to "answer that question in a different way." And it was only after he had made the second statement the way the authorities wanted it that he was held in jail.

The jury failed to grasp the significance of these irregularities or to see that the dubious testimony of an unwilling bystander like Hanover and two sleazy characters like Rose and Cooperman hardly constituted proof of Zimmerman's guilt "beyond a reasonable doubt." The stories these three told, however, were the stories the prosecutor wanted the jury to hear—and the jury apparently believed them. Furthermore, the prosecution succeeded in convincing the jury that most of the points the defense team brought up were mere "side shows." They would be better described as violations of due process, for they included police brutality, perjured testimony, forced confessions, statements taken without benefit of witnesses and with no records kept, altered documents, and suppressed evidence.

Any one of these flaws by itself, had the trial judge so ruled, might have destroyed the prosecution's case. All were swept aside. Jacob Rosenblum, in summation for the prosecution, earnestly told the jury that he thought the case was "pretty nearly perfect." The defendants, he said, had developed the side shows because "they are so guilty." He stressed his years of experience both as a defense lawyer and as a prosecutor, strongly implying that no reasonable person could possibly doubt his judgment.

What he did not tell the jury was that three different pretrial statements had been supplied by Danny Rose. Nor did Rosenblum ever explain why those pretrial statements were not used at the trial. He did not tell how the statements conflicted with each other on the critical issue of when or whether Zimmerman had any knowledge of what the guns were going to be used for. Neither did Rosenblum spell out the details of the off-the-record discussions between the police and Rose before and after Rose's recorded statements, which resulted in various remarkable modifications of his second and third statements. The problem—from the prosecution's point of view—was the wild inconsistency of Rose's three statements, which suggested that Rose had been coached along the way. Furthermore, although the third statement fit the prosecution's version of the story virtually to a tee, it included clear evidence of Rose's complicity in other felonious activities. Allowing into evidence against Zimmerman even this most useful of Rose's pretrial statements would have demonstrated unequivocally how unreliable a witness Rose was.

Rosenblum also did not tell the jury how clearly Rose had recalled, under questioning at the time the third statement was taken, his own earlier assertion that Zimmerman had nothing to do with the crime. Instead, at the trial, Rose testified under oath that he had no recollection of ever having exonerated Zimmerman. Thus, introducing the third pretrial statement would have devastated the prosecution's case, because it would have impeached Rose's credibility as a witness. It would also have provided the jury with irrefutable evidence of Zimmerman's complete innocence.

None of this emerged at the trial in 1938.

Many years later, together with Francis Bond, Zimmerman wrote a book about his case—*Punishment Without Crime.* How utterly incomprehensible he found his situation constitutes a major theme of his story. Knowing he was innocent made the idea of being sentenced to die in the electric chair totally unbelievable, literally incredible. In the book, he makes clear how unprepared a person is for being arrested, indicted, and found guilty of a crime committed by someone else. No one is taught how to react to being sentenced to death. For Zimmerman, the primary sensation was an indescribable numbness. The past became a confusing blur that had lost its meaning. There was no future. Only the present was real, and that verged on the surreal.

Nothing can make a person ready for life on death row: the grinding monotony of the routine, the uncertainty, the dull pointlessness of existence. Zimmerman turned bitter. More than once during his long ordeal he stopped bothering to tell people he was innocent; no one who believed in him seemed able to do anything about his plight anyway. And most people simply did not, could not, would not accept the possibility that he was innocent.

Family visits to the prison were infrequent, and unpleasant, for Zimmerman. They did afford a break in the routine. But they also forced him to witness his mother's tears and his father's efforts to cheer her up. Worst of all was the responsibility that fell to Zimmerman, as he saw it, of buoying up his parents' spirits and insisting he was hopeful when he was not. He hated himself for lying to his family; he hated feeling he had to lie. There was little or nothing to be hopeful about, as far as he could see. His first appeal, for example, had led only to an affirmation of the original verdict. (The court did officially acknowledge that he had not been present at the scene of the crime, but that concession did him no good.)

The community at large did not, however, completely abandon the five condemned men. On January 11, 1939, the five mothers joined seventy-five other concerned citizens in a meeting with Governor Herbert H. Lehman to beg for executive clemency. They presented a petition with thirty-five thousand signatures to buttress their plea.

The governor stalled, and execution day—January 26, 1939—arrived. Zimmerman had already lived nine months on death row. The day had finally come when he and his four co-defendants were to die. (Philip Chaleff, the second member of the group besides Zimmerman who everyone agreed had never entered the restaurant, had meanwhile suffered diabetic comas. He had been given insulin shots to keep him alive so he could be put to death.) As dawn broke over Sing Sing Prison, Beansy Zimmerman had every reason to think it would be his last day.

Zimmerman numbly went through the pre-execution rituals. The last meal (choose whatever you want), and music (you get to choose that, too) played on the wind-up phonograph. The barber shaves your scalp so the electrodes can fit snugly against your bare skin. The tailor slits one of your trouser legs for another electrode. Officials treat you with unaccustomed politeness. A final family visit—how do you say good-bye when you know it is forever? What should your last words be? Beansy's mother stayed away, unable to face such finality.

And then, two hours before he was to be executed, Zimmerman was told that Governor Lehman had commuted his death sentence (and Philip

Chaleff's) to life in prison. The governor had expressed doubts about Zimmerman's guilt, pointing out that the conviction rested on the word of Cooperman and Rose—who were, Lehman was convinced, themselves accomplices in the crime despite their never having been indicted.

At first, Zimmerman was more angry than relieved at the governor's action. Clemency, too, was incomprehensible; by that time Zimmerman knew enough about prison to be certain he had no desire to spend the rest of his life there. He had watched others go to their deaths: While he sat on death row, nine Sing Sing inmates had been executed. He had no wish to join them, yet it did seem it might be better to be done with it all. And when Guariglia, O'Loughlin, and Friedman were in fact executed as scheduled that January day, Zimmerman began to comprehend that the real agony was only beginning for him and for Chaleff. Death may be forever. But living out a life sentence in prison stretches the future into its own peculiar kind of eternity.

The death sentence and the approach of execution day had both been nightmarish. Execution would have brought an end to all that. Instead, at the time of the commutation (Zimmerman later said) he felt he had been condemned all over again, to go on living the nightmare. "I wasn't dead, no. But every day from now on they'd bury me a little more. . . . Me, they were burying alive. And I could live to be a hundred."

In the end, though, Isidore Zimmerman decided he would not let the nightmare take over his life. He would also not let the world forget "the forgotten man." The way he and his loyal supporters kept up the fight for his freedom is a remarkable story of perseverance and determination. Zimmerman knew he was innocent, of course, but by the time his sentence had been commuted, he had learned enough to know that innocence was no guarantee the truth would ever come out.

Attorney Maurice Edelbaum proved to be the key. Zimmerman had had half a dozen lawyers before Edelbaum came on the scene, and they had worked hard for him. Bernard Burkaloff, for instance, had done a fine piece of work during a coram nobis hearing in 1956 taking apart Jacob Rosenblum, the prosecutor who had initially handled the case against Zimmerman. Despite his efforts, however, the petition for a new trial had been denied, and Burkaloff had withdrawn from the case—as he had warned Zimmerman he felt he would have to do, win or lose. A few months after that, a friend and fellow inmate at the prison in Dannemora arranged for the disappointed and discouraged Zimmerman to talk with *his* lawyer. Zimmerman was skeptical; the friend pressed, saying the lawyer was worth talking to. "He's a good man," he insisted.

Zimmerman's first impressions of Maurice Edelbaum were not altogether favorable. Edelbaum was a good listener, it was immediately apparent, and clearly intelligent. But he seemed cold and unsympathetic—until after Zimmerman had poured out his story in rapid-fire fashion. Before Edelbaum left the prison that day, he had agreed to take Zimmerman's case without fee. Zimmerman later recalled that Edelbaum ended their initial interview by saying, "Mr. Zimmerman, you're a man on his way out of prison." And though no one could have known it then, the day Zimmerman met Edelbaum turned out to be a dramatic turning point.

Years afterward, Zimmerman was quoted as saying, "I wrote a million letters and tried a million actions, but nothing happened till Mr. Edelbaum came into the picture." It took six years, but thanks to Edelbaum's efforts, on January 11, 1962, a writ of coram nobis was granted by the New York Court of Appeals. The writ vacated Zimmerman's conviction and remanded him for a new trial. Almost twenty-five years had passed since Detective Foley's death and Isidore Zimmerman's indictment.

The Court of Appeals based its order for a new trial on the testimony of Danny Rose, whose statements at the 1938 trial had sealed Zimmerman's fate. Rose had denied making any pretrial statements to the prosecutors. But Edelbaum—a short, chunky, intense man who wore big glasses with black frames and used vigorous gestures to make his points—was both energetic and persistent. He eventually learned about the statements Rose had made on three separate occasions, and he was able to show the court that, in addition to being inconsistent with what Rose said at the trial, the statements actually supported Zimmerman's claim of innocence.

Edelbaum also demonstrated that the prosecution had made no effort at trial to correct what it knew was a blatant lie when Rose denied having made any pretrial statements. In sum, Edelbaum persuaded the court that Zimmerman's conviction was based on perjured testimony, prosecutorial inaction in revealing the perjury to the defense or to the jury, and suppression of the statements that might well have convinced the jury of Zimmerman's innocence. On hearing the judge's order for Beansy's release, Zimmerman's 76-year-old father leaped to his feet, charged across the room to hug his son, and impulsively planted a big kiss on Edelbaum's cheek. The exonerated and exhilarated defendant announced, "I feel like I'm back from the grave."

Three weeks after the granting of the writ, on the recommendation of the district attorney, the indictment was dismissed.

And so truth did triumph, but the ring of victory had a distressingly hollow sound. In addition to losing twenty-four years of his life, Zimmerman was saddled with a "record" he neither earned nor deserved. Neither could he ignore or discard it. Back on the street and part of the real world again, he was unable for long stretches at a time to find any work. When he did find jobs, they didn't pay enough for him to support himself or allow him—a man who as a teenager had thought about becoming a lawyer—to use his intelligence. And though at long last Isidore Zimmerman was able to share life with his father, his mother had died before he was released from prison. The initial injustice generated a long catalogue of injustices.

Zimmerman continued to fight to clear his name. Within ninety days of his release from prison, he had filed a damage suit for $2 million against New York City for his erroneous conviction. In 1963 he lost the suit; the court ruled he had not shown that the district attorney's conduct was the *cause* of his conviction. In 1966 he tried again; the second suit was dismissed on the ground of prosecutorial immunity. "Plaintiff's remedy, if any, lies with the Legislature," wrote the court.

Zimmerman would not give up the struggle. To succeed, however, he had to follow a convoluted route. In order to file a suit against the State, he first had to persuade the New York Legislature to pass a special bill giving him permission to sue. Then, even if the bill passed, it would merely open the court's doors for him. No verdict in his favor was assured, no remedy was guaranteed. Most observers gave him little chance; former prisoners are not popular constituents, especially when they are asking legislators to acknowledge that the criminal justice system has badly blundered.

Nonetheless, Zimmerman took the first hurdle in stride: The legislature passed his bill. The second hurdle turned out to be higher, however. Governor Nelson Rockefeller vetoed the bill, so Zimmerman had to start over. Once again the legislature passed a bill granting him permission to sue, and once again the bill was vetoed. Then a third round: Zimmerman fought for the bill, the legislature passed it, the governor vetoed it. Finally, however, when the enabling legislation was passed for a fourth time—in 1981—the new governor, Hugh Carey, signed it. Zimmerman at last had the State's permission to sue the State.

His day in the Court of Claims came in May of 1982. Once Danny Rose's pretrial statements were a matter of public record, the State of New York could no longer seriously argue that Zimmerman might have been guilty. So when Isidore Zimmerman appeared in court for the last time, the State simply conceded that he was completely innocent. The only remaining question was how much this innocent man should be compensated for his close encounter with the electric chair and his twenty-four years behind bars. What dollar value should be attached to such an experience? Zimmerman had, by the skin of his teeth, escaped execution. He asked for $10 million.

On May 31, 1983, Judge Joseph Modugno decided on a compensation of $1 million. He never revealed what formula he had used to arrive at this figure, only a tenth of what Zimmerman had requested. Zimmerman was unhappy, but at 66 he was also an old man, tired and badly in need of cash. Though a substantial chunk of the award would go for his legal and other expenses, any award at all accomplished his most important goal: Complete vindication. On June 30, 1983, Zimmerman picked up his check. After expenses were paid, he pocketed about $660,000.

July, August, and September of 1983 were good months for Isidore Zimmerman. He bought a new car, spent a few days in the Catskills with the woman he had married soon after his release from prison, and began making plans for the rest of his life. They were never carried out. On October 13, 1983—fourteen weeks after receiving his hard-won check—Isidore Zimmerman suffered a fatal heart attack. He had spent twenty-four of his sixty-six years in prison for a crime the State finally admitted he had no part in. Though Isidore Zimmerman committed no crime, the State of New York nearly sent him to his grave.

✳

MISTAKES in identification based on sincere belief are, as shown in Chapter 1, one thing; false eyewitness identification teased out by the police or in other ways fraudulently produced are another matter entirely. What happened to Zimmerman in New York during the Great Depression has happened to many others. Two fairly recent cases further illustrate some of the forms such errors can take.

In February 1974, in a motel room in Albuquerque, New Mexico, evidence of a brutal murder was reported to the police. Days later the mutilated body of a young homosexual male was found in an arroyo just east of town. Speculation among local pathologists suggested that the killers might have been a band of roving homosexuals, perhaps motorcyclists. A couple of weeks later word reached the Albuquerque police that a vanload of five bikers from the Vagos Motorcycle Club in suburban Los Angeles had been arrested in Oklahoma City on a robbery charge. With photos in hand of the deceased and of the five men—Thomas Gladish, Ronald Keine, Clarence Smith, Arthur Smith, and Richard Greer—two sheriff's detectives made inquiries at gay bars in Albuquerque. Only when they also went to a cheap motel frequented by gays did they hit paydirt. Judy Weyer, a part-time maid, said she recognized the bikers. The police thus had her testimony that the bikers had been in Albuquerque. Then, in a further series of statements to the police, Weyer progressively amplified her initial story into an eyewitness account of a murder that included sodomy, shooting, and the dumping of the victim's body in Albuquerque. Thinking the bikers might be the fugitive murderers, the New Mexico police went to Oklahoma to investigate. The five motorcyclists were promptly arrested and booked for murder, and Judy Weyer became the "woman forced to witness mutilation."

In May, the trial opened in an atmosphere of chaos. Albuquerque residents were shocked to learn that these violent California motorcyclists had come to their town. In the court room, the five defendants—in clean suits, but long-haired and bearded—looked as though they had been sent straight from Central Casting for their roles as Biker Terrorists. Weyer's testimony, despite some backing and filling on her part under cross-examination, was convincing enough for the jury to ignore its inconsistencies. The case was clinched when two other witnesses, a father and son, testified that they had seen the biker gang in Albuquerque on the day of the murder.

The bikers produced an alibi: They had been in Los Angeles at the time of the crime, and they had a trail of fuel purchases on stolen credit cards that tracked their way east to Oklahoma to prove it. The prosecution dismissed this as an elaborate ruse to throw the police off their trail. After fifteen hours of deliberation, the jury filed its verdict and sentence: Guilty of first-degree murder, death in New Mexico's gas chamber. (Charges were dismissed against Arthur Smith; Judy Weyer simply forgot to implicate him in the murder orgy.)

In September 1975, sixteen months after the trial, a young drifter and former mental patient, Kerry R. Lee, walked into a South Carolina police station and confessed to the Albuquerque murder. A quarrel over drugs—not homosexual savagery—had provoked the murder, he said. Checking out Lee's confession proved conclusively that he was, indeed, guilty. A gun, discovered two months previously near the site where the victim's body had been found, was determined to be the murder weapon. This gun was also identified as stolen from the father of a young woman Lee had dated. The girl friend testified that Lee had told her he had killed a man, and that she had seen him the morning after the murder, splattered with blood. A tow-truck operator identified Lee as the man whose car he had helped pull out of the arroyo only hours after the crime. Three months later, in November 1975, all charges against the four defendants who had been erroneously convicted were dismissed, and they walked out of prison free men.

Between the time when the bikers were arrested and Lee's startling confession, the *Detroit News* had become interested in the case when it turned out that three of the five defendants (and the victim) originally hailed from the Detroit area. The paper's inquiries were jump-started when a letter was received from the girl friend of one of the defendants, in which she wrote, "I can't sit by and watch four guys who are innocent go to their death for something they didn't do." Such letters are common enough to be routinely ignored—but this one, thanks to a twist of fate, reached receptive eyes.

Veteran reporters assigned to the story soon discovered that the prosecution's star witness, Judy Weyer, had been carefully coached in her pretrial statements and threatened with perjury if she failed to back them up in open court. Her initial remarks to the police may have been given in good faith, but her trial testimony was not. The lurid tale she told, of torture by the homosexual biker terrorists, she herself later admitted was a complete fabrication—developed with the complicity of the police. She claimed that the chief of detectives had promised to pay her way through secretarial school if she testified against the defendants, and that he threatened her with five years in prison for perjury if she did not. Other changes and errors in her testimony emerged under probing by *News* reporters, all duly published in a series of articles the paper correctly described as based on "one of the most extensive criminal investigations in American journalistic history."

J U S T   A   F E W   D A Y S before the Albuquerque murder that imperiled the lives of four Los Angeles bikers, two white hitchhikers were thumbing a ride south of Fort Myers, on the Gulf Coast of Florida not far from the Everglades. Terry Milroy, 27, was headed for a job in the Florida Keys. His hitchhiking companion, 16-year-old Cynthia Nadeau, was a runaway from Rhode Island living by her wits. Soon the two of them were picked up by a black man driving a truck. Half an hour later Milroy was dead from a pistol shot and Nadeau, raped and bleeding, had been abandoned on the roadside. Although there is no evidence that law enforcement officers encouraged perjury in this case, there is strong evidence that they jumped at the opportunity to build a case even when they knew all they had was totally unreliable testimony.

Days later Fort Myers police showed Cynthia a Polaroid photograph of a black man picked up near Leesburg, 220 miles to the north. She examined it for a couple of minutes and, visibly shaken, identified the man as the murderer-rapist. The man in the photo was Delbert Lee Tibbs. Later, Nadeau picked him out of a police line-up, positively identifying him despite the fact that his physical features were at variance with the description she had originally given the police.

Tibbs had been hitchhiking his way back to Chicago when a Florida Highway Patrol trooper stopped him, claiming he looked like a man wanted in Fort Myers. After being photographed, Tibbs was released; no reason to arrest him had emerged. When Cynthia Nadeau identified him, however, the Highway Patrol organized a regional search. A few days later Tibbs was found, hitchhiking again, this time in Mississippi. All this attention from the police was new to him. Prior to this trip, Tibbs's only brushes with the law had been receiving a couple of traffic tickets. Suddenly, however, he was in custody and on his way to Fort Myers, awaiting charges for murder and rape. In 1974 rape was a capital offense in Florida, but only if the victim was a child. The death penalty for first-degree murder had no such limitations—quite the contrary, if the victim was white and the defendant black.

In December Tibbs went on trial before an all-white jury. Cynthia Nadeau's testimony constituted the whole of prosecutor James R. Long's case. Despite extensive efforts by the police, no other witnesses had been found who could place Tibbs anywhere near Fort Myers at the time of the crime. Defense counsel tried to show how unreliable a witness Nadeau, a heavy user of drugs, was (she had admitted being high just before the crime). No murder weapon, no other physical evidence, no theory of how Tibbs was supposed to have had access to a truck or to have disposed of it played a role in the prosecution's case. The only corroboration for any of Nadeau's testimony came from Tibbs's cell mate (himself a convicted rapist), who testified that while awaiting trial Tibbs had confessed the crime to him. (This testimony was later discredited, when the cell mate admitted it had been given in the hope of leniency in his own case.)

Tibbs took the stand in his own defense and argued alibi: He had been in Daytona Beach for several days before and after the crime. Written records supported his statement. Tibbs, it emerged, did not fit the negative stereotype of the young, urban, single black male. He was college educated and a determined poet, had been active in the civil rights struggles of the 1960s, and at the time of his arrest was in the midst of a coast-to-coast journey "to experience firsthand the woes and wonders of the world" (as one newspaper reporter deftly phrased it) before returning to his studies at Chicago Theological Seminary. His many northern friends were quick to come to his aid as he faced Florida's capital charges.

Less than three days were needed to complete the trial and less than ninety minutes for members of the jury to reach their verdict. They found Tibbs guilty of rape and murder, and they recommended a death sentence. Judge Thomas Shands, although he had authority under Florida's recently enacted death penalty statute to override the jury's sentencing recommendation, instead readily concurred.

Two years later, Florida's supreme court announced its decision on Tibbs's appeal. By a vote of four to three, the judges overturned the conviction on the unusual ground that the weight of the evidence simply did not support the jury's verdict. The jail-bird testimony was worthless, and Nadeau's testimony was at best highly dubious. Declaring its "considerable doubt that Delbert Tibbs is the man who committed the crimes," the court ordered him retried. Fort Myers officials were furious;

Long, the prosecutor, complained, "I have never heard an appellate court reverse a conviction because of questioning the credibility of a witness. . . ."

For five years following his release, Tibbs's fate hung in the balance as his attorneys and the State of Florida argued over whether the evidence from the first trial, having been judged insufficient to convict, could be used again in a new trial without subjecting Tibbs to double jeopardy (prohibited by the fifth amendment). In June 1982 the State's argument prevailed, opening the door for a second trial.

Two months later, however, State Attorney Joseph D'Allesandro announced he would not retry Tibbs. His principal witness, Cynthia Nadeau, had by then become a confirmed drug addict, thereby completely destroying any credibility she might ever have had as a witness. And another transformation had taken place in the interval. James Long, who had successfully prosecuted Tibbs, told Tibbs's attorneys that the original investigation of the crime had been "tainted from the beginning and the [police] investigators knew it." Long vowed that if Tibbs were retried, he would testify for the defense.

In the years since his release, Delbert Tibbs has often lectured publicly and testified at legislative hearings against the death penalty. As he has said—and no one knows better than he—"It's quite easy to build a criminal case against an innocent person."

3 | CHANCE

 | ENCOUNTERS

DURING THE boom times of the 1970s, Dallas was a prime destination for anyone looking for work. Among those who saw Dallas as a land of opportunity was 27-year-old Randall Dale Adams, a 1967 high school graduate from Grove City, Ohio. Adams was the youngest of five children; his father, a miner, had died of black-lung disease in 1960. When Randall reached Dallas in early November 1976, he quickly found a job repairing wooden pallets—the movable platforms used in factories and warehouses to store heavy materials. In his first two weeks, he showed up regularly and on time. He worked hard, and the boss liked him.

David Ray Harris, a 16-year-old from East Texas, also viewed Dallas as full of inviting opportunities, but of a rather different sort. For Harris, Dallas was above all a place to go (even if it meant stealing a car) when he was bored, to find alcohol and drugs. He was, by most measures, a troubled kid. In 1975 he had committed several burglaries and stolen a car in his home town of Vidor, Texas. Following another burglary in April 1976, he was formally declared a juvenile delinquent and placed on probation.

On Friday, November 26, 1976, in search of a more exciting Thanksgiving holiday than Vidor could provide, David Harris decided to leave town. He stole a 1972 Mercury Comet, some tools, and money from a neighbor; he also took a shotgun and a .22-caliber pistol of his father's. He then drove toward Dallas, three hundred miles to the northwest. After spending the night in a Houston parking lot, he reached Dallas the next morning and picked up a hitchhiker. It was Randall Adams. From that moment, Harris, Adams, and the city of Dallas became knotted together in a way that took a dozen years to untangle.

That morning, Adams had arrived at the shop as usual. He found no one there, and the place was tightly locked; it was, after all, the long Thanksgiving weekend. Adams decided there was no point in hanging around. When he left, however, his car promptly ran out of gas. Carrying an empty plastic milk jug, he walked to the nearest gas station, only to learn from the attendant that it was illegal in Texas to put gasoline into such containers. Unsure what to do, he started back along Fort Worth Avenue toward the spot where he had left his car. He was still on foot when a kid driving a blue Comet pulled over and offered him a lift. Adams accepted. In addition to being out of gas, he was shivering and cold. Before coming to Texas, he had most recently been in Florida, and he was unprepared for the sudden onset of cold weather. It would turn out to be the coldest November 27 in Dallas history.

David Harris and Randall Adams spent that Saturday afternoon driving around Dallas in Harris's stolen car, smoking marijuana, drinking beer, and visiting pawnshops to get cash in exchange for the tools Harris had stolen. In the evening, they went to a drive-in theater where two soft-core porn movies were showing: *The Student Body* and *The Swinging Cheerleaders*.

The stories later told by Harris and by Adams begin to diverge at this point. Harris said they didn't leave the movie until after midnight, and that he knew how late it was because he had seen a clock when he went to buy popcorn at the concession stand. Adams, on the other hand, while conceding that he had spent the day with Harris and that they had gone to the movies together, insisted that he had tired of both Harris and the movie, and that they had left about 9:30. Shortly afterward, Adams contended, he was dropped by Harris at a convenience store near the Comfort Motel, where he was staying. Harris then drove away, while Adams (as he told it) bought something to drink at the store and returned to his motel room in time for the end of the Carol Burnett Show. He watched the beginning of the ten o'clock news and fell asleep.

A little after midnight—in the early morning of Sunday, November 28—the stolen blue Mercury Comet, being driven with no headlights, was stopped by Dallas Police Officers Robert Wood and Teresa Turko. As Wood approached the driver's side, the driver reached under the front seat and grabbed a pistol. Five shots rang out. Officer Wood fell dead. The driver stomped on the accelerator, and the Comet sped off into the night. Officer Turko, throwing her half-finished milkshake aside, jumped into action. She fired five shots of her own at the speeding car, though she wasn't sure whether she had hit it. Later she also realized she hadn't gotten the license number or noticed the make of the car, though she did remember that it was blue.

Later that day, Harris returned to Vidor. He spent the next few days with friends, to whom he bragged that he had "offed a pig" in Dallas. He burglarized a house and, using a rifle, robbed a convenience store. He later tried to blame these two crimes on friends. On December 5, with nine days of freedom in the little blue car behind him, Harris was arrested for auto theft. He was released to the custody of his parents; the authorities had no inkling that he might be involved in something much more serious than car theft.

Two weeks passed. The killing of Robert Wood was the first murder of a police officer in the history of Dallas to remain unsolved for more than forty-eight hours. Pressure to find the killer was intense. Then the Vidor police learned about the self-incriminating statements Harris had made concerning the Dallas murder, and they re-arrested him. Harris told them he had only been boasting, to "impress" his friends. But the gun he had stolen, which was found in a nearby swamp, turned out to be the murder weapon, and Harris finally admitted having been present when Officer Wood was killed. He was, he said, a passenger in the car while it was being driven by the hitchhiker, Randall Adams. He all but said that Adams had committed the murder.

Adams had continued to go to work regularly after the murder, so the police had no difficulty tracking him down. The day after Harris implicated him, Dallas police officers surrounded the pallet factory, checked to make sure there were no escape routes, and moved in. Flashing their badges, they made an easy arrest; totally unsuspecting, Adams did not resist. He did, however—immediately and consistently—insist on his innocence to anyone who would listen.

Once in custody, Adams was given a polygraph exam and asked about the murder of Officer Wood. He failed the test. (Harris had also been tested; he passed.) Because so-called lie detector tests are so unreliable, Texas does not allow the results to be presented to juries. Even so, Adams's failed exam helped re-inforce for the prosecutors what they wanted to believe: Adams was their man.

Apart from the dubious evidence of the polygraph, the case against Adams was weak. The person who should have been the prosecution's key witness—Officer Turko, partner to Officer Wood—couldn't remember any helpful details, though she seemed certain there had been only one person in the car. Furthermore, Adams hardly had the criminal record of a ruthless cop-killer. His only prior offenses were a drunk-driving conviction and a minor A.W.O.L. violation, the sole blemish on his record during three years of service as an army paratrooper.

There was, in fact, nothing to incriminate Adams except David Harris's word. No one seemed to notice that it was not Adams, but Harris, who—driving a stolen car, carrying stolen guns, and already on probation for other crimes—had motives for wanting to avoid even a casual encounter with the police. He had been on something of a crime spree in his home town of Vidor in the days following Officer Wood's murder, where despite his youth he was already well known to the police. If Adams was not the culprit, the only other plausible suspect was Harris himself.

From the prosecution's point of view, however, there was one major argument in favor of focusing attention on Adams rather than Harris: This was a cop killing. An unwritten law in Dallas (and a lot of other places) is that those who kill cops deserve the severest penalty, and in Texas that means death. But Texas law does not permit a death sentence for offenders under the age of 17. Thus Harris, even if convicted, could not be sentenced to death. Adams could be.

Directing the prosecution was Dallas District Attorney Henry Wade (who had earlier gained a footnote in history as the defendant in the 1970 abortion case, *Roe v. Wade*). Wade, according to a Dallas writer, was "a mighty figure who brooked no dissent and made no apologies. He judged his prosecutors . . . on their won-lost records: They were given raises and promotions according to their success in obtaining criminal convictions." The prosecutors in this case, needless to say, wanted a conviction, and they wanted a death sentence. They indicted Randall Dale Adams for capital murder, and on March 28, 1977, jury selection began. The trial opened a month later.

The chief prosecution witness was none other than David Harris. He stuck to his version of the story: He and Adams had not left the drive-in until after midnight; when they left, Adams was driving. As the passenger, Harris was able to slump down on the floor of the car when they were pulled over so he could not be seen. When Officer Wood walked up to the window on the driver's side, Adams pulled a gun from under the front seat and shot him five times.

The jurors were told about Harris's various brushes with the law prior to the Wood murder, but the judge would not permit them to hear about the series of offenses Harris committed after returning to Vidor from Dallas. Neither were they told about a propensity he had shown over the years to blame his crimes on friends or casual companions. Harris stated (though not in the presence of the jury) that he and the prosecutors had not worked out any deals on the December crimes in Vidor in exchange for his testimony against Adams. Curiously enough, however, after Harris incriminated Adams, all the charges against Harris for those crimes were dropped.

Throughout the trial, Adams was confident of acquittal. But on the last day of testimony, a Friday, the prosecution sprang a surprise. Three eyewitnesses came forward, all of whom said they had driven by the scene of the crime as the shooting was taking place. This was the first indication that anyone besides the killer and the two police officers had been anywhere in the vicinity. One of those who said he had driven by, Michael Randell, testified that he had seen two people in the stopped car, and that it was Adams behind the wheel. The other two eyewitnesses, Robert and Emily Miller, had driven by together but testified separately. Each said only one person was in the car; each said it was Adams. Mrs. Miller further claimed that she had picked Adams out of a police line-up.

Adams and his attorneys were stunned. They had had no idea that these witnesses would be testifying, or that they even existed. Texas law is clear on the point: The prosecution must inform the defense about witnesses it intends to call—unless they are rebuttal witnesses. Because these three had been called only to contradict Adams's testimony that he had been asleep at the time of the murder, the prosecution was not required to say anything about them ahead of time.

The defense team was further alarmed when, over the weekend, they heard rumors that Robert and Emily Miller had lied on the stand. On Monday the defense tried to recall all three of the surprise witnesses, but the prosecutor, Douglas D. Mulder, said the Millers had left for Illinois and could not be located. By odd coincidence, neither was Michael Randell anywhere to be found. (Only much later did it turn out that the Millers had simply moved from a Dallas hotel to a West Dallas motel— and that Mulder knew it.)

The defense attorneys next demanded that Mulder allow them to see all the written statements made by these three witnesses prior to the trial. (Although prosecutors are required to give the defense any sworn statements by witnesses, Mulder had failed to do so.) From Emily Miller's statement, the defense learned that she had originally told police the person she saw in the car was a "Mexican or very light-skinned black man." If this statement could have been used by the defense, it would have seriously undermined Mrs. Miller's trial testimony, because Adams is white. Meanwhile, her husband, it turned out, hadn't signed an affidavit at all until after the trial started—more than five months after the murder. And Michael Randell hadn't signed an affidavit until Adams's picture had been published in the Dallas newspapers.

When the defense team tried to get the affidavits shown to the jury, the judge would not allow it. To present this confusing and conflicting information would be unfair, he ruled, because the witnesses were no longer in the court room and therefore could not be cross-examined.

There were additional important documents that neither the defense attorneys nor the jury saw at the time of the trial. One was the original police report of the murder. In it, Officer Teresa Turko had said the windows of the car were so dirty that she couldn't see the culprit clearly—except for two things. Wood's killer, she had stated, was wearing a coat with a turned-up fur collar; David Harris had testified that he, not Randall Adams, had been wearing such a coat. But Turko had also stated that the killer had hair the color and style of Adams's rather than Harris's. If her report had been available to the defense and the jury, these contradictory observations would have further undermined the prosecution's case.

An investigator from Mulder's office had also written a memorandum that indicated there had been no midnight showing of *The Swinging Cheerleaders*. This was fully consistent with Adams's account of the evening he and Harris had spent together—and inconsistent with Harris's. Both Harris and Adams said they had left in the middle of the film, but Harris said their departure was at midnight. Unfortunately for Adams, the investigator's memo—like the original police department report—surfaced only much later. When it did, it was supported by an observation from the managers of the theater. They knew the theater had closed early that particular evening, they said, because it was such an unusually cold night. The drive-in didn't have heaters for even the few cars that had shown up.

The prosecution had ambushed the defense with its three unannounced witnesses. On Monday afternoon, stymied in their every effort to counter the unexpected testimony, the defense attorneys made their final arguments to the jury. Douglas Mulder closed for the prosecution with a flourish, reminding the jury with dramatic imagery of the "thin blue line of men and women who daily risk their lives by walking into the jaws of death" to protect the rest of us.

The jury began its deliberations on May 2, 1977. Early the next morning, they found Randall Dale Adams guilty of capital murder. All that remained to be decided was his sentence.

In Texas, capital trials are divided into two stages. In the first, the jury determines only guilt or innocence. If the defendant is found not guilty, there is no second stage. But if the defendant is found guilty, the jury reconvenes to decide the sentence. In the process, the jury is required to consider three issues, the most controversial of which is whether the defendant is likely to be a continuing threat to society. More precisely, in the language of the statute, the jury must decide whether there is, "beyond a reasonable doubt," a "probability" that the defendant "would commit criminal acts of violence" in the future. This question is difficult, if not impossible, to answer. There is of course always a possibility that any person might, under some circumstances, commit a "criminal act of violence." But such a possibility hardly constitutes a probability.

Even the American Psychiatric Association (APA) has taken the position that neither psychiatrists nor any other experts can accurately predict future violent behavior. The association has repeatedly affirmed that efforts to make such predictions must be viewed with great caution. In the APA's words, "The unreliability of psychiatric predictions of long-term future dangerousness is by now an established fact within the profession." Two of three predictions of future dangerousness are wrong, the APA insists, and psychiatrists are no better at predicting dangerousness than any amateur who has access to the relevant statistics.

These pronouncements by the professional organization notwithstanding, several Texas psychiatrists have gone on the stand to make the very kinds of predictions their colleagues have insisted are unreliable. They have testified in capital trials that the convicted defendant will, unless executed, constitute a continuing threat to society. Two of those psychiatrists testified for the prosecution during the sentencing phase of Adams's trial. The first was Dr. John Holbrook, former chief of psychiatric services for the Texas Department of Corrections. The second, another Dallas psychiatrist, was Dr. James Grigson, a man who has made something of a specialty of providing this service to the State. By 1990 he had examined 12,000 criminals, including more than 1,400 murderers and nearly 400 capital-murder defendants; he had testified in 124 Texas capital trials. In 115 of them, the jury had returned a death sentence.

Grigson is a mild-mannered man with the demeanor of television's Dr. Marcus Welby. Unlike the fictional doctor, however, Dr. Grigson uses his medical training not to save lives, but to legitimate taking them. For years, critics of capital punishment in Texas and elsewhere have called him "Dr. Death."

Even if dangerousness cannot be predicted, the testimony of "Dr. Death" and others like him can be. Drs. Holbrook and Grigson, claiming to rely on medical science, duly testified that Randall Adams would indeed be dangerous in the future if he were not executed. It did not matter that Adams had no prior criminal record. Grigson even managed to turn Adams's claim of innocence against him. Insisting he was innocent and continuing at his job in the days immediately after the murder showed that Adams had none of the normal human feelings of pity, regret, or remorse. Or so Dr. Grigson told the jury.

After hearing the psychiatrists' testimony, the jury was persuaded that Adams would be "a continuing threat to society." On May 3, 1977, Judge Don Metcalfe did what the law required of him and sentenced Randall Dale Adams to death. Adams was moved to the Ellis I Unit of the Texas Department of Corrections, in Huntsville, Texas—better known to the outside world as death row.

A couple of days after the guilty verdict, a woman who had worked with the Millers (the couple who claimed to have driven by the murder scene) sent a note to Dennis White, one of the defense attorneys. Her information was devastating to the prosecution's case against Adams. Among other things, she said the Millers had bragged that they really weren't able to identify who was driving the car, but that they were going to get their hands on the $21,000 reward anyway.

White, suspecting that prosecutor Mulder had withheld information, sought an investigation of Mulder's conduct and a new trial for Adams. The FBI refused his request, however, and White's motion for a new trial was dismissed. A civil suit he filed against the Dallas district attorney's office was likewise dismissed. And with that, Dennis White—depressed, bitter, and embarrassed about his failure to save Adams—gave up not just on the Adams case, but on the practice of law altogether.

Adams was in need of a lawyer nonetheless. All criminal cases in Texas are reviewed by the state's highest criminal court, the Texas Court of Criminal Appeals, and death penalty cases are subject to automatic review. An appellate attorney is assigned to handle the appeal in cases where the defendant cannot afford private counsel, and Dallas attorney Melvyn Carson Bruder was appointed to argue Adams's appeal.

On January 31, 1979, Adams's first appeal was unanimously denied. Two months later, on April 5, 1979, Judge Don Metcalfe scheduled Adams's execution for May 8, 1979. One week before the death date, Associate Justice Lewis F. Powell, Jr., of the United States Supreme Court ordered a stay, and the Court agreed to hear the case.

At issue before the Supreme Court was not whether Adams was innocent, but a technicality having to do with the exclusion of potential jurors at trial. During jury selection, people in the jury pool had been asked whether the possibility of a death sentence "would affect [their] deliberations on any issue of fact," including their deliberations on the three questions to be raised during the penalty phase of the trial if they convicted the defendant. Those who answered "Yes" were excluded from the jury. The Supreme Court ruled, however, that this procedure had kept off the jury those "whose only fault was to take their responsibilities with special seriousness or to acknowledge honestly that they might or might not be affected." Accordingly, on June 25, 1980, the Court reversed Adams's death sentence and ordered a new trial for the sentencing phase of the case. The guilty verdict was left intact.

District Attorney Wade was outraged and publicly predicted that a new jury would resentence Adams to death. Then, almost as quickly, he changed his mind, saying that although Adams deserved to die it was a waste of money to go through a resentencing trial. He asked Governor Bill Clements to commute Adams's sentence to life imprisonment. On July 11, 1980—two weeks and two days after the Supreme Court's decision—the governor complied. Adams was no longer under sentence of death, but neither was he free. The commutation meant he faced a life in prison.

Adams wanted another day in court so he could establish his innocence. Defense attorney Bruder again went to the Texas Court of Criminal Appeals; another year passed. Finally, in September 1981, the court ruled that the commutation had effectively removed Adams's right to a new hearing; the judgment imposing a life sentence was affirmed. Bruder refused to have anything more to do with the case. Having saved his client's life, he concluded he had done his job. Adams had no apparent place to turn; he quietly began to serve his sentence.

Then Hollywood came to town and transformed the case. In March 1985 a young film producer and former private detective, Errol Morris, interviewed Adams in connection with a documentary film he planned to make about the notorious Dr. James Grigson. Grigson's testimony had, after all, put nails in the coffins of dozens of death row prisoners, and Morris realized the career of "Dr. Death" contained the ingredients of an unusual story.

Initially, Morris assumed that Adams and all the others whom Grigson had helped send to death row were guilty. But something about Adams struck him. He couldn't get out of his mind the way, during the interview, Adams "kept talking about 'the kid, the kid.' " He decided to read the transcript of Adams's trial. The more he read, the more convinced he became that Adams might be innocent after all. Morris couldn't let it go. In fact, he got so interested in Adams's story that he set aside his plans for a "Dr. Death" film and instead made a film about the Randall Dale Adams case. While work on the film proceeded, Morris teamed up with Houston attorney Randy Schaffer (who had entered the case in 1982). The two worked tirelessly, seeking a new trial.

Morris's film *The Thin Blue Line* was released in August 1988. Actors were used only to re-enact the murder scene. Otherwise, the film consists almost exclusively of monologues by most of the principals in the case—including Adams, Harris, and the three surprise witnesses. As the film develops, the audience sees and hears for itself the inconsistencies and outright lies that sent Adams to death row. Viewers also see, perhaps to their amazement, that when David Harris was interviewed for the film in 1988, he was himself then on death row.

One of the problems in murder cases where innocent defendants are convicted is that the true killer remains at large, as dangerous as ever. The criminal record amassed by David Harris during the years Randall Adams was in prison is sobering. Within months of Adams's conviction in 1977, Harris enlisted in the United States Army. In January 1978, home in Vidor for Christmas leave, he was charged with assault (later dismissed when the victim decided not to press charges). Still in the army and stationed in Germany, he committed several burglaries in June and stole some money in September. Convicted of these offenses, he was sentenced to eight months in Leavenworth.

Five months after his release from prison and the army, Harris was arrested in California for kidnapping, armed robbery, burglary, attempted burglary, and attempted robbery. In February 1980 he was sentenced to six and a half years for these crimes. He was paroled in December 1984, having just celebrated his twenty-fourth birthday. Then in 1985, back in Texas, he broke into an apartment in Beaumont and abducted a woman from her bed. He shot and murdered her boyfriend, who was attempting to protect her. That was the crime that finally put Harris on death row in Huntsville, seven years after he had helped send Adams there.

In December 1986, six years after his commutation, Adams (with the help of Schaffer and Morris) at last succeeded in getting a court to hear his motion for a new trial. Federal magistrate John Tolle was appointed to hear the case and to recommend whether Adams should be retried. Everyone knew that Tolle had worked in the office of the Dallas County district attorney at the time of Adams's original trial, but Tolle insisted he had had nothing to do with the Adams case. In May 1988, after reviewing the evidence, he recommended against a new trial.

What Tolle had not revealed was that it was he who had handled prosecutor Douglas Mulder's defense when Adams's trial attorney, Dennis White, filed the $5 million suit against the prosecutor. When that fact surfaced in August, the recommendation against retrial was withdrawn. In late November 1988 the request for a new trial was reassigned to Judge Larry Baraka of the State District Court in Dallas. Baraka had succeeded the original trial judge; he, too, had earlier served as an assistant district attorney in Henry Wade's office. Unlike the others, however, he was prepared to listen.

Morris and Schaffer had uncovered important information to present to the judge, including the fact that Officer Turko had been hypnotized before she was able to state anything about the killer's hair style. The defense team had never been told either about her hypnosis or about her initial statement that she could neither see nor identify the killer.

Judge Baraka was told about Mrs. Miller's original statement that the killer was black or Mexican. He heard—contrary to her trial testimony— that she had *not* picked Adams out of a line-up; indeed, she had first picked another man, and the police officer in charge of the line-up had had to identify Adams for her. This made her testimony nothing short of perjury. The judge heard how robbery charges against her daughter, pending at the time of the Adams trial, were dropped after Mrs. Miller's testimony. He heard Robert Miller admit he had lied, that he really hadn't seen anything on the night of Officer Wood's murder.

The judge also heard that witness Michael Randell had lied when he told the jury he was returning from a basketball game at the time he drove past the murder scene. Morris's film shows Randell admitting that he had been out cheating on his wife that night, and drinking; by his own account, he was drunk.

Baraka further heard about the memo found in Mulder's files showing that the prosecution knew the times of the film showings at the drive-in on the night of November 27, and that these times confirmed Adams's testimony rather than Harris's. The judge heard, too, how Morris had learned from the theater managers that the concession stand was never open past 10:30 P.M. This was inconsistent with the portion of Harris's story where he claimed to have noticed the time ("around midnight") on the concession-stand clock when he went to buy popcorn.

Among others who testified at Judge Baraka's three-day hearing was Adams's former attorney, Dennis White. He recounted exactly why he had left the practice of law after the Adams trial and entered the real estate business: His work had been primarily in real estate law, not criminal defense, and yet he had been appointed to defend Adams. He knew he had failed at Adams's trial to make some timely objections and to seek information that would have helped his client. He went on to express how outraged and upset he had been at what seemed to him to be a blatant miscarriage of justice. "The system of justice totally miscarried in this case. . . . They took the real killer, David Harris, and made him a witness against Randall Dale Adams."

Most importantly, Judge Baraka heard Harris recant his testimony against Adams, essentially admitting sole responsibility for the killing. The *Dallas Morning News* reported Morris's contention that Harris, except for his original trial testimony against Adams, had been "confessing to Wood's death for years—to friends in Vidor immediately after the shooting, to a cell mate while in prison in California, to reporters since the release of the film and this week to a judge. 'He's been saying this for a long time,' Morris said. 'The question is, when are people going to start listening to these confessions?' "

On the last day of the hearing, Gus Rose, the chief homicide detective assigned to the Wood murder, testified that Adams had never denied committing the crime. At that point defense attorney Randy Schaffer pulled out a transcript of Morris's filmed interview of Rose. There one could plainly see that Rose had told Morris, for the film, just the opposite, namely that Adams "almost over-reacted his innocence—he protested he hadn't done anything, couldn't imagine why we were bringing him in."

The defense argued not only that Adams was innocent, but that the prosecutors at the time of the trial knew he was.

The hearing ended on December 1. The next day, Judge Baraka recommended to the Texas Court of Criminal Appeals that Adams be given a new trial. Although he rejected more than half of the complaints made by Adams's attorney, Judge Baraka found support for the claims that the prosecution had withheld exculpatory evidence and that the defense counsel had been inadequate.

Although Judge Baraka "stopped short of finding Adams innocent," the *Austin American Statesman* reported that he said "if he were to make a decision based on the evidence, he would find Adams not guilty." And the judge had further stated, according to the *Dallas Morning News*, that Harris's admission "that Adams was not even in the car when Wood was shot amounted essentially to a confession."

On January 30, 1989, Dallas County District Attorney John Vance, Henry Wade's successor, announced that his office had no objection to Judge Baraka's decision. Stating that he still believed Adams was guilty, he conceded that there were enough questions to warrant a new trial. On that day, Judge Baraka wrote a letter to the Texas Board of Pardons and Paroles giving his support to the defense's request that Adams be paroled as soon as possible.

A month later, parole was nonetheless denied. One member of the board, Reuben Torres, was reported to have said, "I was not reviewing the case for whether the man was innocent or guilty, I was reviewing it for parole consideration. I had to presume that the man is guilty."

Randy Schaffer, Adams's attorney, was infuriated by Torres's reasoning. The board's decision "defied all logic," he said. "It's illogical to say they gave him a special review because there was new evidence of his innocence, and then deny him parole because you can't consider new evidence of his innocence." It was, he fumed, a case of "the collision of intellectual dishonesty and total stupidity."

Within a week, however, Adams's luck finally changed. On March 1, the Texas Court of Criminal Appeals unanimously reversed Adams's murder conviction and, pending a new trial, ordered his immediate release from the state prison and his return to the custody of the Dallas sheriff.

Emily Miller's testimony had especially provoked the court's ire, despite her claim during the hearing that Errol Morris, when interviewing her, had said, "It's just a movie. Anything you don't remember, I'll remember for you." She had lost all credibility. Judge M. P. Duncan, agreeing with Judge Baraka, concluded that "the State was guilty of suppressing evidence favorable to the accused, deceiving the trial court during the applicant's trial, and knowingly using perjured testimony." The court's ruling endorsed Judge Baraka's findings in their entirety.

Two weeks later, Judge Baraka held a hearing on Adams's appeal to be released on bond pending retrial. Prosecutor Winfield Scott protested vigorously. When Baraka ruled that Adams could go free on a $50,000 personal recognizance bond, the prosecution took its case to another judge, who promptly raised the bond to $100,000 cash. Not to be outbid, film maker Morris announced he would put up the money himself. It never came to that, however. After talking to Baraka, the second judge revoked the higher amount; bond was set at $50,000 after all, and Adams was free to go on his own recognizance.

Finally, on March 21, 1989—exactly twelve years and three months after being taken into custody—Randall Dale Adams was released. Two days later, District Attorney Vance announced that no retrial would be held. Within a fortnight of Adams's release, the two prosecutors who had represented the State at the November hearings before Judge Baraka announced their resignations from the Dallas County district attorney's office. Both declined to give reasons. Winfield Scott, the prosecutor who had fought Adams's release on bail, was fired.

Grigson did not find Adams's release by the courts a cause for any professional embarrassment. He still believes that Adams is guilty of murdering Officer Wood, and that history will vindicate him when Adams kills again. (Serving as an expert witness for the prosecution in the 1990 Texas murder trial of Gayland Bradford, Grigson managed once again to work in a remark about his certainty that Randall Adams is a murderer and will kill again.)

In retrospect, it is not hard to see why Adams was convicted. To be sure, it was David Harris who was found in a stolen car, who disposed of the murder weapon, and who had a criminal record. But Harris was also, by his account, an extremely well placed eyewitness to the crime he said was committed by Randall Adams. Harris's accusation was critical. Coupled with Adams's unconvincing alibi, his status as a newcomer to Texas, and the fact that the murder victim was a police officer, it was devastating. That the setting was Dallas County, where, as one reporter wrote, " 'law and order' means law and order and where prosecutors don't lose," no doubt made matters worse. There were no rogue cops in this story, just law enforcement officers rightfully outraged at the murder of a comrade. They wanted to see the killer brought to justice. The prosecutors may not have cooperated with the defense to the full extent required by law, but presumably they honestly believed they had solved the crime and convicted the true killer.

Under Texas law, Randall Adams cannot receive any restitution from the State. Despite that, and despite his loss of more than twelve years of freedom, he showed no bitterness when interviewed shortly after his release at his mother's Ohio home. He was even willing to express his faith in the courts. "I believe the system of American justice is basically good," he said, "because if it weren't, I wouldn't be sitting here today."

Adams's mother had other concerns. "After all this is over," she said in an interview two days after her son had come home, "I'd like to write a letter to David Harris and tell him that God loves him, whether he thinks anyone else does or not. I don't like what he did, and I don't like what he did to Randy, but he . . . was just a scared 16-year-old. . . . It's these professional men I don't understand. To go to law schools and then just turn around and decide you're going to put an innocent man on death row."

The innocent man was already looking ahead. "I'm not bitter at all," Randall Adams said; "I will not let the past ruin what lies ahead for me."

TROUBLING AS IT IS when an eyewitness in good faith implicates an innocent defendant, it is far worse when the police or prosecution connive with a witness to give false testimony. Worst of all is when an eyewitness implicates someone knowing that person is innocent—and knowing it because the witness is the real culprit. Perjury of this sort belongs in fiction, not in real court rooms. Yet that is precisely what David Harris did to Randall Adams in a Dallas court room, and it has happened many times elsewhere. Among the cases in recent years that present the same deplorable spectacle as the Adams case did are two involving black defendants—one in Massachusetts and one in New York.

In November 1973, three black youths from a local housing project entered a jewelry shop in Roxbury, a couple of miles from downtown Boston. Their purpose was robbery. As they were emptying the jewelry trays, an off-duty police officer, John Schroeder, entered the store. Attempting to thwart the robbery in progress, he was shot and killed. Within a day, however, thanks to efficient police work, the three robbers were rounded up.

One of the three youths mentioned a "lighter-skinned black girl," 18 or so, and identified her as the driver of their getaway car. As an accomplice under the felony-murder rule, she was as guilty as the one who fired the fatal bullet. In the course of plea-bargaining conversations among the defendants, their attorneys, and the prosecution, two of the defendants—Nathanial Williams and Anthony Irving—agreed to testify against the triggerman, Terrell Walker, and against "Sue," the woman driver. In exchange, the prosecution agreed to accept their pleas of guilty to second-degree murder. A few months later, "Sue" was located and arrested in Rochester, New York.

"Sue" turned out to be Ella Mae Ellison. She was not exactly a girl of 18—she was 27. Nor was she "lighter-skinned"; her skin was quite dark. At the time of the robbery, she was on her way home from a shopping expedition. Three months later she moved back to Rochester to be near her parents. Ellison had no criminal record, and unlike the three youths, she was not a drug addict. But she did know Williams, Irving, and Walker; in fact, she had driven them in her car more than once. Perhaps their familiarity with her 1969 Ford LTD helped give them the idea of describing it to the police as their getaway car. Charged with first-degree murder and armed robbery, Ellison pleaded not guilty. The jury thought otherwise and sentenced her to two concurrent life sentences in prison.

In May 1976, Williams and Irving recanted their trial testimony, admitting there had been no fourth participant in the crime and that Ellison had no connection with their getaway car or the robbery. They had, they said, invented "Sue" in order to shift blame from Irving, at 17 the youngest of the three robbers. They also declared (in the words of the appellate court) that "they had felt compelled to plea bargain and testify against the defendant [Ellison] out of fear of the death penalty." This, despite the fact that in 1973 the death sentence for felony-murder armed robbery had been declared unconstitutional in Massachusetts. (One of the many curiosities of the death penalty is that although there seems considerable doubt whether it deters would-be criminals, there is little doubt that fear of the harsher penalty often deters even the innocent from pleading not guilty.)

In July 1978, the Supreme Judicial Court of Massachusetts unanimously reversed Ellison's conviction. As is often the case, technicalities (as the lay observer tends to view violations of due process of law) played a conspicuous role in the court's judgment. But the root of the matter was that the three guilty defendants had falsely implicated in their crime someone they knew was innocent. There was no evidence, not even circumstantial, pointing in Ellison's direction. And, as the court observed, it was implausible that a mother of four in her middle twenties, working part-time, receiving money from her father, and having no criminal record whatever, would join a band of youthful heroin users in a poorly planned crime, in exchange for a meager share of the proceeds—none of which was ever found in her possession.

PRIOR TO the Adams case in Texas, probably no case of perjury by the real killer has received more publicity in recent years than that of Nathaniel Carter in New York City. The story began in 1981, on another September afternoon, when Clarice Herndon, a 60-year-old resident of the Cambria Heights district in the borough of Queens, was found murdered. The pathologist recorded twenty-seven stab wounds in her body from a penknife.

Her foster daughter, Delissa Carter, told authorities that a strange man had broken into the house, attacked both women, and murdered Mrs. Herndon. Three days later, under questioning from skeptical police officers, she changed her story. She had been attacked, she then said, as cuts on her arms proved, but the murderer was not a stranger. It was her ex-husband, Nathaniel Carter, who had remarried and moved to Ossining (known far and wide in earlier years as the site of New York's death row prison, Sing Sing). The police promptly located and arrested Carter.

In the rush to get him indicted before the three-day holding limit expired, the district attorney's office never asked Delissa Carter to sign a waiver of immunity. As a result, once she testified before the grand jury, she was immune from prosecution connected with the murder. Lucky for her.

Nathaniel Carter, 30 years old and recently laid off from his job, was not a plausible suspect. Friends described him as "guileless and deeply religious"; he had no prior record and no known motive for the murder. Nevertheless, his ex-wife testified at trial that he had simply burst into the Herndon home and, for no apparent reason, started attacking the two women. When his turn came to testify, Carter told the court he had been in Westchester, miles away. Two witnesses backed him up, but the jurors believed Delissa. They convicted Nathaniel of second-degree murder and sentenced him to twenty-five years to life in prison. (It could easily have been worse. Fortunately for Carter, New York's death penalty statute in 1982 did not apply to murders like Mrs. Herndon's.)

Marie Parker, the mother of Carter's second wife, refused to believe her son-in-law was guilty. She obtained the help of a Peekskill detective, James Nelson, and later the town's police commissioner, Walter Kirkland. Together they investigated the case further and agreed with her: Nathanial Carter was innocent.

Early in 1983 they secured a lawyer from New York Legal Aid to file an appeal for Carter. Their investigations turned up evidence that the first Mrs. Carter had a violent temper. They also found a witness who told them she had passed the Herndon residence shortly prior to the murder, heard screams from two women indoors, and saw Delissa Carter run from the house with blood on her hands. (The police, as it later turned out, had had this testimony within days of the murder, but for some reason had failed to follow it up.) Further investigation of Carter's alibi confirmed it almost to the minute: Carter was, as he had testified, thirty miles away when Mrs. Herndon was murdered.

By then the district attorney's office for Queens had agreed to re-open the case. Assistance from an informant enabled prosecutors to get onto a hidden tape recorder Delissa's flat statement that "Carter hadn't done it." A few days later, in the police station, she told detectives, "I killed my [foster] mother."

The district attorney went back to court, having agreed to give Delissa Carter complete immunity from a charge of perjury. Nathaniel Carter listened while she spelled out how she and Mrs. Herndon had started fighting when she blamed the older woman for negligence resulting in the death of her baby daughter in a household fire a few months earlier. As tempers between the women mounted, Delissa grabbed a knife and stabbed, and stabbed again. Judge John J. Leahy ordered that Nathaniel Carter's conviction be overturned and that he be immediately freed.

After Carter's release, Philip Shenon, a *New York Times* reporter who had covered the case in detail, observed that "the police, the prosecutors and a defense lawyer may all have made serious errors—of negligence or incompetence—that could have kept Mr. Carter in prison for life and that [could have] allowed the real killer to go free." Carter's Legal Aid attorney, William E. Hellerstein, commented, "If New York State had the death penalty, God only knows what would have happened to this poor man."

PART TWO

PRIDE

AND

PREJUDICE

4 POLITICAL CRIMES AND PUNISHMENTS

J ULY 22, 1916—Preparedness Day in San Francisco. For months, enthusiastic planners had been working to create a great patriotic spectacle to show support for American entry into the war and to flex their muscles for all slackers, pacifists, and socialists to see. The centerpiece of the day's celebrations was to be an impressive parade up Market Street, San Francisco's main thoroughfare. Flags at curbside waved bravely along the parade route, and thousands of eager spectators filled the sidewalks. Shortly after noon, a block away from the Ferry Building on the Embarcadero, the first marching units stepped off.

Suddenly, at the corner of Steuert and Market, a huge blast occurred, sending bits of metal flying in every direction and hurling bodies like jackstraws across the pavement. A dense cloud of smoke boiled up, obscuring the scene. As it cleared, horrified spectators saw that the paving stones were wet with blood. Pieces of human flesh were scattered about; the injured were groping for safety and calling for help. Nearby delivery trucks were pressed into service to haul the dead, the dying, and the wounded to Harbor Emergency Hospital; its staff was soon overwhelmed. In the days that followed, the nation learned that the bomb blast at the Preparedness Parade had been a ghastly terrorist attack that left ten dead and forty wounded.

Within a few months, two men would become more famous than any of the bomb's immediate victims. Warren K. Billings and Thomas J. Mooney, labor agitators and anarcho-socialists, would be convicted of setting off the explosion and murdering innocent bystanders. Billings would be sentenced to prison for life; Mooney would be sentenced to die on the gallows at San Quentin Prison.

When they met in San Francisco in 1913, Tom Mooney was in his early thirties and Billings just 20. The local militant labor movement brought them together; along with other radicals and reformers, they were active in Bay Area strikes, including a major one in the summer of 1913 against the Pacific Gas & Electric Company (PG&E), a private utility monopoly. Violence on both sides of the picket lines was common. Striking workers used dynamite to destroy the property of capitalists; the capitalists for their part employed private detectives (especially from the Pinkerton Agency) to arrest and convict agitators—always a "frame-up," if one could believe the labor spokesmen.

Mooney and Billings joined the picket lines against PG&E. Billings, along with some other strikers, stole dynamite from local construction projects, presumably for later use against the company's installations. In September of 1913, three years before the Preparedness Day bombing, Billings was in fact caught red-handed by Pinkerton agents who had infiltrated the strikers; he was carrying a suitcase crammed with sixty sticks of dynamite. The police, PG&E attorneys, and Pinkertons believed that Billings was linked with Mooney in a conspiracy to blow up a PG&E generating plant. They had no evidence, however, and Mooney was never arrested or charged. Billings denied involvement in any such conspiracy, but he was easily convicted of illegally transporting explosives and sentenced to two years in Folsom Prison. This was the first time Billings and Mooney were implicated in what some considered a terrorist plot against the established order. Billings's conviction was integral to the conspiracy theory that later engulfed them both.

Three months after Billings's conviction, a police tip-off led to Mooney's arrest. Sailing a skiff east across San Francisco Bay, Mooney and two friends had run aground in shallow water off Richmond; they walked ashore to wait for higher tide the next day. When they returned to their boat, the police were already there. The skiff, it turned out, was loaded with guns and materials used in dynamiting. Martin Swanson, the head Pinkerton detective employed by PG&E, let it be known that he believed the explosives were to be used by the strikers against PG&E installations. The newspapers broadcast this allegation across California, and a second major element in the Mooney-Billings conspiracy theory was in place.

At trial, Mooney and the others were charged with illegal possession of high explosives, though Mooney claimed he knew nothing of the contraband. The defense alleged that the guns and other things found in the skiff had in fact been planted by company detectives or others in their employ. Furthermore, since no dynamite, nitroglycerin, or guncotton was found, expert witnesses ended up debating before the jury such questions as whether percussion caps were "explosives." Convicting the three defendants proved impossible; juries split twice on the verdict, and at a third trial all the defendants were acquitted. Mooney's friends in the labor movement, who believed from the start that he had been framed by Swanson, were overjoyed. What the jury believed was never clear, but it certainly had not been stacked with laborites, radicals, or friends of the accused. In any event, by the end of 1913, both Billings and Mooney had been arrested (and Billings convicted) for crimes involving bombs. They were on their way to fame among Bay Area radical groups, and infamy among the authorities.

A year after his acquittal, Mooney—by then secretary of San Francisco's International Workers Defense League—marked himself publicly as a dangerous agitator when he sent a threatening telegram (with copies to the local newspapers) to Governor Hiram Johnson of California. Mooney was angered by Johnson's refusal to use his clemency powers on behalf of two labor agitators serving a prison sentence for murder. They had been arrested and tried under circumstances that violated what today would be regarded as elementary rights of due process.

Mooney's wire read in part: "There are some workers at least, Governor Johnson, who will not accept as final your decision . . . and from now on they will attempt to use the only kind of reasoning that will eventually reach you. . . . And so if violence is committed, Governor Johnson is responsible for it. . . ." A letter from Mooney to Governor William Spry of Utah on behalf of Joe Hill, a labor radical under death sentence there, contained similar threats of violence. These two public missives, first the telegram and then the letter, helped confirm the image of Mooney as an irresponsible agitator who would stop at nothing. How much bluster and how much genuine threat Mooney's demands for clemency actually contained was never determined. But before long, he would have reason to regret these two literary outbursts.

Several months before the Preparedness Parade, Mooney hammered yet another nail into what later nearly became his coffin when he joined with Alexander Berkman to found a new radical paper, with the prophetic title *Blast*. Berkman was well known to authorities across the nation as the anarchist who had attempted to assassinate Pennsylvania millionaire capitalist Henry Clay Frick in 1892. The *Blast* was soon publishing revolutionary propaganda. Mooney's contributions were confined to a diatribe attacking the Pacific Coast Defense League, one of the major sponsors of the Preparedness Parade scheduled for mid-1916. But *Blast* editorials led the way in denunciations of the Preparedness Day celebration for its nativism, militarism, and enthusiastic embrace of Manifest Destiny.

Concurrently, anarchist threats (real or imagined) of assassination and revolutionary labor violence were being made with disturbing frequency from one end of the nation to the other. The resulting public anxiety was considerable. In San Francisco, William Randolph Hearst's *Examiner* warned its readers of possible local anarchist uprisings. Not to be outdone by its rival, the *Chronicle* proposed that all anarchists should be permanently deported to an offshore island, where they could harm only each other.

A month prior to the Preparedness Parade, a utility power line was dynamited in San Bruno, just south of San Francisco. Detective Swanson, by then in the direct employ of PG&E, believed Mooney was responsible. As later testimony revealed, he attempted to get evidence against Mooney by bribing Israel Weinberg, a San Francisco taxi driver whose son was taking music lessons from Mooney's wife, Rena; with the same purpose in mind, Swanson befriended Billings, who had been released from prison some months earlier. Neither effort produced anything for Detective Swanson. Furthermore, Mooney was promptly informed by both Weinberg and Billings of Swanson's attempts to pry information out of them, helping to confirm suspicions in radical circles that Swanson was out to get Mooney.

In the days immediately after the Preparedness Day bombing, the San Francisco press, led by Hearst's *Examiner*, pointed the finger of guilt at the local anarchists. Who else was capable of such indiscriminate terror launched in the heart of the city? Anyone could see the similarity between the infamous anarchist bombing in Chicago's Haymarket Square (1886) and the bombing in San Francisco. No one could ignore that Alex Berkman, would-be anarchist assassin, was then working in San Francisco as editor of the *Blast* and that Mooney was closely associated with that project. In addition, Berkman's erstwhile lover, the notorious radical agitator "Red Emma" Goldman, was at that very moment on a lecture tour in the Bay Area; sizable crowds in San Francisco heard her speak on such topics as "Anarchism and Human Nature." She had been scheduled to deliver an antipreparedness speech two days before the parade, only to have it canceled because it conflicted with a previously scheduled talk by another anticapitalist.

Responsible citizens demanded that those guilty of the bombing be arrested, and rewards totaling several thousand dollars (generous for those days) were offered for information leading to convictions. Six thousand people crowded into San Francisco's Civic Auditorium to hear members of the city's Law and Order Committee (a direct descendant of the old vigilante groups from half a century earlier) denounce lawlessness and social disorder, including especially labor unrest. Provocateurs and agitators were put on notice that they were unwelcome and could expect no mercy if caught. A bomb scare preceding the meeting underscored the need for vigilance.

During the first day or two after the parade bombing, Mooney's name was conspicuous by its absence from public discussion. Privately, however, several leading citizens informed the police that they believed Mooney to be responsible. Chief among these informants was Detective Martin Swanson. District Attorney Charles Fickert inquired of him whether he knew of any possible suspects; Mooney and Billings were among those he named. Within a few days, the district attorney's office and the police had lost interest in other suspects and were concentrating their efforts on the doomed pair. Fickert had also quietly hired Swanson as a special investigator.

Was this an effort by the prosecution and the police to frame Mooney and Billings from the start, to accuse them without any evidence? Possibly, but there is no solid basis for such a claim. More likely (given events and testimony that emerged years later), Detective Swanson— confident that Mooney and Billings were guilty of many crimes and unstinting in his efforts to get the authorities to see facts his way— succeeded in convincing Fickert and others that the two labor radicals were behind the Preparedness Day bombing.

Believing that Mooney and Billings were their prime suspects, the police promptly arrested two of their associates, Edward Nolan and Israel Weinberg, with the scant respect for procedural niceties typical of the day: no arrest warrants, no notice of the charges, no opportunity to seek legal counsel. Illegal searches and seizures at Mooney's house and the offices of the *Blast* followed. Billings was found in a San Francisco medical clinic being treated for a skin rash. Mooney, on vacation with his wife some miles to the north, read in the newspaper that he was the object of a "nationwide search." He promptly wired the authorities (with a copy to a San Francisco newspaper), "My movements are and have been an open book. Will return by next train to San Francisco." The police didn't wait; they intercepted the Mooneys on their way back into the city and took them both into custody. Thus, within four days of the bombing, the police believed they had arrested all the conspirators and solved the crime.

Under police interrogation, Mooney denied having anything to do with the bombing, refused to answer questions about Billings, and insisted on his alibi: At the time of the explosion, he and his wife were on the roof of their house, along the parade route, more than a mile up Market Street from the scene of the crime.

Meanwhile, trial by newspaper, aided and abetted by the police and prosecution, proceeded apace. District Attorney Fickert, who had larger political ambitions, fancied from the outset that a successful prosecution of the bombers could win him the keys to the governor's mansion in Sacramento. In remarkably similar columns, the city's newspapers spread story after story against the two defendants: Billings when arrested was said to have been seeking medical aid in the aftermath of the explosion; Mooney was reported to have fled the city only to be caught by alert police.

All of these stories were based on information planted by the authorities. None of it was true. Fickert told the press: "I believe Mooney had determined to bring about a reign of terror in San Francisco, and that he and Nolan had wild ideas about getting control of labor by what they call 'direct action,' which is another way of saying murder." Other unsolved bombings and attempted bombings in the region were laid at their door as well, all without any evidence implicating Mooney and Billings, and without any criminal charges being filed against them.

Prior to their arrest, Mooney and the others had not been identified by anyone as having been in the vicinity of Steuert and Market. Nor had any witness come forward to give testimony that would have led the police to suspect them. Neither did the police offer to the grand jury any physical evidence that could be said to connect the accused to the crime. What the district attorney did offer the grand jury was flimsy indeed: the materials (with which it was said bombs might be manufactured) taken from Nolan's basement, Mooney's motorcycle (which had been parked in Nolan's basement), and a key (which had been in Mooney's possession) to Nolan's basement. The defendants were truculent before the grand jury and repeatedly protested the refusal of the authorities to let them obtain legal counsel; Mooney, Billings, and Nolan in fact refused to testify.

The prosecution's idea of how to build the case against each defendant was straightforward enough. Mooney and Billings were known to the Bay Area police as anticapitalist agitators and worse. They were also thought to be experienced in handling explosives. Mooney was friends with the notorious anarchist Alex Berkman, himself implicated in prior bombings. Further, Mooney and Billings were in the vanguard of the opposition to the Preparedness Day celebrations. In an attempt to disrupt the parade, so the prosecution theory went, the two conspirators had fashioned a time bomb in a pipe and packed it with scrap metal in a suitcase. Billings had then carried it onto the roof of a Market Street building that overlooked the parade, with the intention of throwing it into the street below. Deciding that was unworkable, he had joined Mooney and walked a few blocks to Steuert Street; there they had left the suitcase on the sidewalk and made their escape. Rena Mooney, Ed Nolan, and Israel Weinberg were co-conspirators, and their conduct had been interwoven with that of the two principals.

In support of this theory, the prosecution argued four main points. First, the defendants were the kind of men who would commit just this sort of crime. Second, the behavior of the defendants after their arrest showed their consciousness of guilt. Third, various articles were found in the rooms of the defendants that linked them in a conspiracy and marked them as the makers of a bomb. Finally—this was new, a linchpin in the case—eyewitness testimony placed the defendants at the scene of the crime with a heavy and suspicious-looking suitcase in hand.

Each of the accused had been indicted on eight counts of murder, one for each of the bombing victims who had died by the time the indictments were filed. The prosecution decided to try the five defendants on one count at a time, and separately. Billings was to be tried first, and thus it was at his trial that the prosecution had its first opportunity to lay out its case and the supporting evidence. The eyewitness testimony presented to the jury was without doubt the most convincing feature of the case against Billings. No fewer than nine witnesses claimed to have seen him in the vicinity of the bombing. Seven said they had seen him at 721 Market Street, ten blocks from the scene of the crime, about a half hour before the explosion. Two of these witnesses said they had seen him carrying a suitcase (one of them added that he had helped Billings carry it onto the roof of the building), and two others—Mellie Edeau and her daughter Sadie—claimed they had seen him leaning over the roof holding a suitcase and that they had then seen him on the street below a few minutes later. Still another witness said he had seen Billings a block away from the corner of Steuert Street just minutes before the explosion.

Probably the most persuasive testimony came from Estelle Smith (who had earlier testified before the grand jury) and John McDonald. Smith said Billings had walked into the office where she worked as a dental assistant at 721 Market; he had claimed to be a photographer with camera equipment in his suitcase and to be looking for a way onto the roof. She had been struck, she said, by his evident nervousness and the sheer panic he exhibited when she reached over to help him move his suitcase. Nonetheless, she had let him onto the roof, and she supposed he had come down some minutes later. If he had, then he would have had just enough time to walk down Market to Steuert.

McDonald was the only witness who claimed to have seen both Billings and Mooney at the site of the bombing a few minutes before the explosion. He said he not only had seen Billings leave a suitcase on the sidewalk but had also observed how both Billings and Mooney checked their watches, looked up at the large clock on the Ferry Building tower a block away, and then disappeared into the crowd.

How reliable were these various bits of testimony? How were the witnesses (none of whom knew Billings) able to identify him as the man they had seen carrying the suitcase, in the office, on the rooftop, in the street? None of these eyewitnesses had gone to the police on his or her own initiative prior to the arrests of Billings and Mooney. None had picked Billings out of a police line-up. Years later, the defense learned that each of the witnesses first saw the two defendants behind bars in jail, after being shown their photographs from police files.

The initial descriptions McDonald gave ("medium height") of the two men he claimed to have seen at the scene of the bombing bore no resemblance to the actual characteristics of the two defendants (Billings was short, Mooney tall)—a fact not revealed until fifteen years after the trial. Smith's precise characterization of a scar on Billings's hand turned out to place it on the wrong hand; curiously, the same error had been made a few days before her testimony in two of the local newspapers. And what she had to say about the clothing worn by Rena Mooney (whom she placed with Billings at 721 Market a half hour before the bombing) subsequently proved completely inconsistent with a photograph taken of Mooney at her home minutes after the bombing.

It also turned out that Estelle Smith's uncle had been convicted of a murder for which she, too, had been indicted though not prosecuted, and that her father was serving a term in Folsom Prison. Her mother had earlier testified before the grand jury that she had seen Mooney and Billings at 721 Market; in a letter to her husband, she explicitly linked the authorities' eagerness to have her testify with their willingness to seek his early parole. None of this evidence, which should have provoked questions about the crucial testimony of Estelle Smith, was put before the jury in either the Billings or the Mooney trial.

Despite all the damning eyewitness testimony against him, Billings insisted that on the afternoon of the Preparedness Day parade he was never on Market Street or at the corner of Steuert. In fact he was, as he claimed to be, several blocks away from Market Street: At the time of the bombing, he was near Union Square defacing parked cars by spraying paint remover on them—his way of retaliating for the use of scab labor in the auto factories. Unfortunately for Billings, the evidence supporting his alibi emerged only much later, not at his trial. When he was arrested, he said nothing about his actual whereabouts, because he thought the police wanted him for defacing the cars. He thereby unwittingly suppressed the best possible evidence against his direct involvement in the bombing.

Although Mooney was tried separately from Billings, the defense entered evidence of his alibi at Billings's trial. Testimony of eyewitnesses placed him at his and Rena's studio apartment at 975 Market. Photographs that the defense did not know about until years later showed the Mooneys watching the parade from their rooftop, with friends, at the very time of the explosion. These photographs would later pose a problem for the prosecution's theory of the crime. If the bomb was set off by a timer or by remote control, then the photographs were of little value. But no evidence of any significance was ever produced by the prosecution to show that the bomb had been triggered by such a device. The earlier testimony that had placed Billings on a rooftop at 721 Market with the intention of throwing a *time bomb* is baffling; it would make sense, however, if the bomb had a percussion charge. But a percussion bomb could not have been set off by a suitcase left on the curb—or by the defendants, if their alibis were true.

The link between Billings and the bomb fragments gathered at the site of the explosion was weak. Some ball bearings had been found in Billings's room, but those picked up in the street were not of the same size. The pistol cartridges evidently used in the bomb were not unusual, and nothing much could be inferred from the presence of similar ammunition at Billings's residence.

If the eyewitness testimony was so weak and the physical evidence implicating the defendant so meagre, why did the jury convict Billings? Several factors probably explain the prosecution's success. All accounts indicate that Estelle Smith was a very sympathetic witness, and none of the evidence that might have impeached her testimony was ever put before the trial jury. Although Billings, testifying in his own defense, gave a clear and accurate account of his itinerary during the crucial period (he even acknowledged that he had been defacing scab-made cars), the prosecution was able to capitalize on the way his testimony did not correspond with what he had told the police when he was first arrested. Furthermore, Billings already had a criminal record that tied him to possession and (presumably) intended use of explosives.

Above all, there was the organizing structure of the case as presented by the prosecution: namely, that Billings and Mooney, two well-known radical agitators, were the principal figures in an anarchist conspiracy. District Attorney Fickert developed that theme at length in his summation to the jury, as he spread before his audience allegation after allegation for which no supporting evidence had appeared at the trial. He denounced Billings at length, claiming that he "probably delighted in hearing the cries of the [injured] women and children . . . ," and then added, "I can find no comparison between this defendant and any other animal that breathes, except the hyena. . . ." The defense agreed that the root of the case was a conspiracy, but they insisted it was a conspiracy "spawned in the brain of a private detective named Martin Swanson, and hatched in the super-heated perfervid imaginations of the Smiths . . . and the McDonalds, and fostered and brought into being and reared by the Fickerts. . . ."

The jury believed otherwise and found Billings guilty. The assistant district attorney, James Brennan, had tried the case, but he had found himself increasingly distressed over Fickert's management of the prosecution. During the final statement to the jury, Brennan argued that although Billings was guilty, he was "a mere puppet" who might "clear up this story" if spared a death sentence. Brennan's nagging doubts were apparently shared by members of the jury: They sentenced Billings to life in Folsom Prison.

With the trial of Billings successfully concluded, the prosecution turned its attention to Mooney, believed to be the mastermind behind the bombing. In Mooney's corner was attorney Bourke Cockran. No Clarence Darrow, Cockran was nevertheless a successful New York politician, intelligent and skillful as a trial lawyer. Though Cockran had little experience in criminal defense, competence of counsel never really became an issue in the Mooney-Billings case.

A few days before the trial opened, Fickert staged a raid on the offices of the *Blast*—this time with a search warrant and maximum newspaper publicity—claiming that it was there that "the bomb plot was hatched." He impounded various letters, on the ground that they contained "damning information." When later published in the newspapers, they proved to be of singular inconsequence. The prosecution nevertheless maintained that in materials to which the press had no access (and that were never introduced before any court) there was evidence of a plan to assassinate Governor Johnson. Even the *New York Times* carried that story.

Not surprisingly, the prosecution once again stressed the theme of an anarchist conspiracy in its opening statement to the jury. What Fickert chose to enter as evidence differed, however, in important ways from what was seen by the jury that convicted Billings. For one thing, Fickert was about to unveil a new star witness, Frank G. Oxman. An Oregon rancher who enjoyed being in the limelight, Oxman took the defense completely by surprise. He was convincing on the witness stand, and his testimony was critical to Mooney's conviction. He claimed he had been on the corner of Steuert and Market, had seen Mooney and Billings leaving a suspicious suitcase on the sidewalk, and had watched them and others come and go. Furthermore, he insisted he was confident of his identifications, even though he could not describe how the defendants had been dressed. There were, to be sure, discrepancies between his testimony and that provided against Billings by other witnesses. But then, eyewitnesses rarely agree on everything, and the worst conflicts were avoided by the prosecution's decision not to have all its witnesses against Billings also testify against Mooney.

Oxman's reliability became the major focus of defense efforts on appeal in the years after the trial. As evidence eventually showed, Oxman had entered the case on his own initiative when he learned of the reward money offered for information leading to the arrest of the Preparedness Day bombers. He had arranged for a friend in Oregon to draft an anonymous letter to Fickert, informing him that an unnamed "reputable Oregon businessman" had vital testimony to give in the case.

When Fickert's office finally tracked Oxman down, he was on a business trip in Kansas. There he decided to make a notarized statement of his testimony. The statement was not located by the defense until 1924, and apparently it had never been sent to Fickert's office prior to or during the trial. Internally, the statement was full of troubling inconsistencies; more important, it differed markedly from the testimony Oxman later gave under oath at the trial. Whether Fickert would have put Oxman on the stand to testify against Mooney if he had known of this statement is anybody's guess. In the hands of the defense, Oxman's notarized statement would have destroyed him as a witness (as eventually it did). Furthermore, instead of implicating Billings and Mooney, it virtually exonerated them. For example, Oxman claimed that the two men carrying the deadly suitcase at the bombing scene were "talking in a foreign language . . . I could not understand." Had that remark come to the defense's attention, it would have gone a long way toward clearing Mooney and Billings, since neither of them spoke any language other than English.

Indeed, in later years it emerged that Oxman almost certainly was not even in San Francisco at the time of the bombing. It also turned out that just before the Mooney trial, Oxman had written a school friend of his son's, Ed Rigall, asking him to come to the trial and vouch for having met Oxman at the scene of the bombing. This was Oxman's idea of how to provide support for his testimony. In the letter, Rigall was offered a share in the reward. There was only one snag. Rigall, who lived in Grayville, Illinois, had never been to San Francisco (as he later admitted) in his life—much less at the corner of Steuert and Market moments before the Preparedness Day bomb exploded. But with the inducement of a share in the reward, Rigall journeyed to the city in time for the trial. Naturally, the prosecution was overjoyed to have this corroborating witness for Oxman's testimony. Before the time came to put Rigall on the stand, however, he got cold feet and told the prosecution the truth. As a result, his testimony was not used after all.

What is striking is that Fickert's staff completely failed to check out either Rigall's story or, for that matter, Oxman's. If they had, they would have discovered that neither witness was telling the truth. Fickert was never able to give a satisfactory explanation for these failures, and they fueled defense charges that his office knowingly used perjured testimony to secure Mooney's conviction. But no court, state or federal, ever agreed on this point, and Fickert remained adamant in his denials all the way to his grave. The damning letter from Oxman soliciting Rigall's perjury, like Oxman's Kansas City affidavit, was not located by the defense until years after the trial.

At Mooney's trial, the principal arrow in the quiver of the defense was the result of a more careful examination of the photo evidence used at Billings's trial. Those pictures, as everyone knew, showed Tom and Rena on their apartment rooftop, watching the parade; barely visible in the background was a clock outside a jeweler's shop. The photographer had supplied the crucial photographs not to the defense but to the prosecution, however. Thus the defense had not seen the negatives at Billings's trial—and without a court order to obtain them for scrutiny prior to Mooney's trial would never have been able to have enlargements of the clock face made. Once enlargements were produced from the negatives, the photos clearly showed the hands reading 1:58, 2:01, and 2:04—the very moments before and after the explosion.

How the testimony that convicted Billings was to be made consistent with these photos of the Mooneys was never explained. Supposing that the explosion was caused by a time bomb raised all the absurdities of the testimony against Billings, which alleged that he was on a rooftop intending to drop or throw a suitcase bomb onto the parade, something no one familiar with high explosives would do with a time bomb.

The fine hand of Martin Swanson appeared behind the scenes. One person who had served as a witness for the defense at the Billings trial reported that she had been cautiously threatened not to testify again in Mooney's defense—and that the man who had threatened her was Detective Swanson. But the prosecution of course refused to put Swanson on the stand, and so the defense was unable to cross-examine him for his hidden role in the case. The story of the threat, like so much of the evidence relevant to the case, did not become public until years later.

As for physical evidence connecting the bombing to Mooney, the prosecution had none. In the closing argument, not to be outdone by his chief, the assistant district attorney, Edwin Cunha (who had done the day-to-day trial work), spoke in florid terms to the jury; he tugged at their heartstrings with imagined pleas from the children of one of the bombing victims and ended with a dramatic call to patriotism and citizenship: "I hope I can say . . . that you did your duty, gentlemen, that you walked out of this court room like American citizens. I want you to return your verdict promptly . . . kicking the props from under anarchy in San Francisco, kicking the props out of indecency and lawlessness in San Francisco. . . ." The *Chronicle* reported that jurors and spectators alike wept.

Some six hours later, at 9:30 in the evening of February 9, 1917, the jurors returned their verdict: Guilty of first-degree murder. They added no recommendation on the sentence. Under California law, that meant only one thing. The sentence would be death by hanging at San Quentin Prison.

When the jury's verdict was announced without recommendation for mercy, Mooney's mother and sister burst into tears and shrieks, and they had to be helped from the court room. Rena Mooney was told in her jail cell of her husband's fate. Formal sentencing was scheduled for a fortnight later, at which time the death date on the gallows was set for May 17.

In the period immediately after the trial, the prosecution's entire case against Mooney nearly fell apart. Through an incredible stroke of luck, the reliability of Oxman's testimony was abruptly put in doubt, leading the defense to move for a new trial, and to demand that Oxman be tried for perjury and that Fickert himself be recalled by the voters for subornation to perjury. These developments were unwittingly fueled by Ed Rigall, back in Illinois, when he learned of Mooney's conviction. Approached by investigators whom he believed to be on Fickert's staff, he showed them photocopies of Oxman's letters soliciting his corroborating testimony. But the investigators were actually working for the defense! Rigall didn't really care. He refused to turn over the letters to the defense, however, because in the meantime he and his lawyer, Claude Ellis, had concluded that the letters were documents of considerable value. They did their best to sell the letters to the defense for $10,000. After weeks of haggling over the money, including a marathon all-night bargaining session, the defense managed to persuade Rigall and Ellis to give up the damning letters without receiving any money for them. They then wasted no time in having the story told in the San Francisco newspapers. In those days, perjury in a capital case was itself subject to the death penalty under California law.

These revelations sent shocks through Fickert's office. When Judge Franklin Griffin (Mooney's trial judge) read the Oxman letters, he called for a conference in his chambers with the attorneys on both sides. As Cunha, for the prosecution, started to say something about technicalities, Griffin interrupted sharply. "This is no time for technicalities," he said. "A man's liberty is at stake." Griffin wanted Mooney to have a new trial, but the matter was no longer under his jurisdiction.

Oxman, however, was arrested and arraigned in late April. Fickert's office fought hard to prevent Oxman's trial; they lost that battle but won the next one, when Oxman was acquitted. One of the city's newspapers announced the outcome in blunt words: "OXMAN WHITEWASHED. VERDICT NO SURPRISE. TRIAL PROVES FARCE." During these proceedings, only a month before Mooney's scheduled execution, Fickert published a long statement in the newspaper, denouncing the side show over the Oxman letters as the direct result of "a formulated policy of those bloodthirsty anarchists to escape punishment for their crime." The defense efforts to secure Mooney a new trial on the strength of the Oxman letters had come to nought.

With the two main defendants now convicted, the prosecution moved against the other three. At the trial of Rena Mooney, the theme of conspiracy again dominated the prosecution's argument. The testimony of its witnesses differed only in details from that offered earlier against Billings and Mooney. Conspicuously absent was Oxman; he had returned to his Oregon ranch. One new witness, Samuel Samuels, testified that he had given Rena "niter" (nitroglycerin) that she said she wanted to use in her garden. The prosecution claimed the conspirators wanted it to manufacture explosives.

This time, however, the defense was able to mount effective criticism of the prosecution's case. Rena took the stand in her own defense and proved a credible witness. After three days of deliberation, the jury returned a verdict of not guilty. But since she, like the other defendants, was also under seven other murder indictments, Fickert had her immediately re-arrested. Months passed before the prosecution stopped threatening to retry her on the remaining charges; in the end Fickert was forced to drop those other indictments, one by one. By that time, Rena Mooney had spent nearly half a year behind bars.

Three months after Rena Mooney's acquittal, the prosecution turned to Weinberg and Nolan. Their fate was quickly settled. Weinberg's trial was brief; virtually no evidence was presented linking him to the bombing (Oxman again failed to appear), and he was promptly acquitted. Two days later, the trial against Nolan was scheduled to commence; it was abruptly abandoned without explanation. No further charges were brought against either defendant, but Fickert nevertheless opposed bail, and it was months before Weinberg and Nolan were released.

Meanwhile, the real trial for Billings, and especially Mooney, had truly begun. Staring Mooney in the face was a death sentence, scheduled to be carried out on May 17, 1917. By then, thanks to the worldwide radical press, Tom Mooney had an international reputation as a working-class hero; as the execution day neared, riots erupted outside the American Embassy in Russia. Deeply concerned over the international impact of the trial and troubled by the many loose ends in the prosecution's case, President Woodrow Wilson telegraphed Governor William D. Stephens, advising him not to wait for the outcome of Mooney's appeal to the state supreme court, but to commute the death sentence to life in prison. The plea was ignored, but the execution was stayed by the court pending completion of the appeal.

Six months later, the Federal Mediation Commission was created to investigate and recommend resolution of labor-management conflicts in the western states that were hampering the war effort. Armed with this authority, the commission (principally in the person of Felix Frankfurter, later a justice of the United States Supreme Court) also looked into the Mooney-Billings case. The commission's secret report recommended postponing the execution, and a new trial for Mooney. Again the president communicated privately with the governor. When Fickert learned of these extraordinary interventions, he was furious. He presumably felt vindicated when the state appellate court unanimously turned down Mooney's appeal, affirming his conviction and sentence.

Mooney's lawyers promptly filed a plea for clemency with Governor Stephens. In what may have been an act of bravado, Mooney personally flung down a gauntlet to the governor. He demanded either to be given a new trial—his principal, perhaps only, chance for vindication through the legal process—or to be hanged.

When the California Supreme Court denied Mooney's appeal on March 1, 1918, his conviction and sentence were reaffirmed. To Judge Griffin, increasingly convinced that Tom Mooney had been convicted unfairly, fell the responsibility of setting a new death date: August 23, 1918. Mooney was transferred from the San Francisco jail north across the Bay to San Quentin Prison, to await execution. In an attempt to put the issue to one side during the period prior to the November elections (Governor Stephens found himself pitted against Fickert, who was running for governor on an "Americanism or Anarchism" campaign), Stephens granted a reprieve until December 13.

Other forces were also on the move in support of Mooney. No less a figure than publishing magnate William Randolph Hearst had changed his mind about Mooney's guilt, and he publicly explained why in his New York paper, the *American*. In San Francisco, Hearst hired Fremont Older as the new editor of his afternoon paper, the *Call*. Older was one of Mooney's earliest and strongest supporters; for years he had been the editor of the *Call*'s rival afternoon paper, the *Bulletin*.

Just a month prior to the scheduled December execution, "Mooney Day" was celebrated by his supporters in most of the major cities of the nation. But time was running out. The appellate courts had proved of no help, Fickert's office vigorously opposed every postconviction stratagem of the defense, and the governor's position was an impenetrable mystery. Yet the agitation for pardon, release, a new trial—*anything* to redress the wrong Mooney had suffered—continued unabated. Abruptly, in the last days of November and just two weeks before the scheduled execution, Governor Stephens announced his decision: He would not pardon Mooney, and he would not order a new trial. But he would, and did, commute Mooney's death sentence to life imprisonment.

Mooney, far from being grateful, was—according to the prison warden who took him the news—"belligerent, and he berated the governor for not granting him a complete pardon." Mooney spoke grandiloquently for himself in a letter he immediately wrote to Governor Stephens: "It is my life you are dealing with. I demand that you revoke your commutation of my death sentence to a living death. I prefer a glorious death at the hands of my traducers, you included, to a living grave. I am innocent. I demand a new and a fair trial or my unconditional liberty through a pardon."

With the crisis of the scheduled execution over (Mooney apparently never believed that he would hang), the defense faced new challenges in trying to get him released. The story of that struggle and its eventual success is too complex and lengthy to retell here in the detail it deserves. In brief, however, those years are marked by several significant developments in the case.

The courts offered no relief, but not for want of effort either from Mooney or from his attorneys. The disappointing climax of their efforts came in 1937, when the state court in San Francisco delivered its verdict on Mooney's petition for habeas corpus (originally filed in 1932). In nearly a hundred pages of text, the court rejected every contention of the appellant. (In fact, the only victory Mooney ever won in the courts was in 1935, when the United States Supreme Court ordered the California courts to grant him a hearing on his habeas petition.) In particular, the court declared that none of the prosecution witnesses was a perjurer, in effect clearing Fickert of having knowingly relied on perjured testimony.

Still, the defense had marshaled an impressive case; its briefs and their appendices filled twenty large volumes, a massive compilation of thousands of pages and hundreds of exhibits. It did not persuade the courts, but it did persuade most others who were willing to study it.

Sympathy for the defendants also came from various administrative bodies, beginning with the Federal Mediation Commission in 1917. In 1932 the Wickersham Commission, appointed by President Herbert Hoover to inquire into corruption of the administration of criminal justice across the country, decided to investigate the Mooney-Billings case. Without speaking directly to the issue of the defendants' innocence, the commission's secret report left no doubt of its opinion that the trials were a travesty of justice. Once made public, the report was yet another pronouncement that persuaded informed students of the case, even if it had no effect on the courts.

As the years went by, the prosecution (or what was left of it) watched its case deteriorate, bit by bit. Fickert, who never won the governorship he craved, was a pathetic figure in the end. He retired to obscurity and virtual poverty on his ranch in central California; he was unable to keep up alimony payments to his wife, who had divorced him because of his gambling and drinking habits. In the court of informed public opinion, if not the law courts of California or the United States, the prosecution witnesses whose testimony was largely responsible for the convictions were discredited out of their own mouths. John McDonald and Estelle Smith, eventually located years later by the defense team, completely reversed their testimony. Of course, even their recantations may have been suspect; who knows when an avowed perjurer has finally decided to tell the truth? But others less easily impeached also came forward, having changed their minds.

Police Detective Draper Hand explained how, under orders from Swanson, he had made sure that Oxman would be able to testify in court as to the license number of Weinberg's jitney by taking him to see it. Earl Hatcher, whose corroborating testimony had been crucial to Oxman's account of when he arrived in San Francisco on Preparedness Day, decided his loyalty had lasted long enough. Annoyed at Oxman's refusal to give him a loan he desperately needed, he told a version of the events completely different from the one he had given at Mooney's trial. James Brennan, who had successfully prosecuted the case against Billings, decided that the entire effort to convict Mooney and Billings had been trumped up out of antisocialist paranoia in Fickert's office, something to which he refused any longer to be a party. Fickert's successor as district attorney, Matthew Brady, agreed to support the Mooney pardon petition. So did Mooney's trial judge, Franklin Griffin, and nine of the ten surviving jurors. So, too, did Captain Duncan Matheson, head of the Bomb Bureau in the San Francisco Police Department and thus in charge of the original investigation into the Preparedness Day bombing. On the other side of the ledger, over the years not a cubit had been added to the prosecution's case: no newly discovered evidence of any kind, no hitherto silent eyewitness, nothing.

There was also a growing feeling among San Franciscans and other Californians that the case simply had to be put to rest, and that the only way to do this was to give both Mooney and Billings what they wanted: Freedom. Yet governor after governor—first Stephens, then Richardson, followed by Young, Rolph, and Merriam—refused to intervene. Not so

Governor Culbert L. Olson. He recognized, as some of the others surely must have, the need to close the case for good. The difference was that he also firmly believed in Mooney's and Billings's innocence.

Olson, a liberal and an avowed New Dealer, was elected in 1938 on the Democratic ticket; he was the first of his party to go to Sacramento since 1899. He had previously been one of the leaders in the California Legislature in the endeavor to get that body to intervene on behalf of Mooney and Billings. His efforts and those of others in the legislature had gained some support in the climate of a depression-torn economy when the populace was angry with do-nothing gubernatorial leadership.

The day after his inauguration, Olson announced he would consider a pardon for Mooney, and less than a week later the hearing was held in the state Capitol in Sacramento, with Mooney present. To the cheers of the hundreds assembled, the governor handed Mooney an official document, handsomely printed in black and green ink on heavy folio paper, declaring that his conviction and death sentence were wholly dependent on perjured testimony and granting him a complete, unconditional pardon.

The next day, January 8, 1939, the Mooney case ended as it had begun, with a giant parade up San Francisco's Market Street. A graying and paunchy Tom Mooney led the way as thousands marched from the Ferry Building to the Civic Center, some two miles to the west.

Mooney's intermittent poor health betrayed him outside the prison walls as it had periodically interfered with his activities inside; he spent most of his long-awaited freedom in the hospital. In 1942, three years after finally being released, he died at the age of 58.

Securing release for Warren Billings, because of his prior prison record, was more difficult. Not until ten months after Mooney's triumphant march up Market Street was Governor Olson able to secure the approval of the requisite state authorities. And at that, the best he could get for Billings was a commutation to time served. He apologized for not being able to grant a full pardon, saying, "I believe you have served a prison sentence for a crime you did not commit."

Billings was able to savor freedom much longer than Mooney. He spent nineteen years plying the trade of watchmaker, which he had learned in Folsom; he remained active in the California labor movement even after his retirement in 1959, and he did prisoner rehabilitation work (both before and after being badly beaten and robbed of $11.00 by a just-released convict). He also headed the California Committee for the Release of Morton Sobell, who had been convicted in 1951 along with "atom spies" Julius and Ethel Rosenberg on what Billings and many others believed to be perjured testimony.

Even Billings's repeated attempts to obtain a pardon rarely got him ir .o the news. Not until twenty-two years after his release did his stubborn insistence on staying in California to fight for his rights finally pay off. In 1961, Governor Edmund "Pat" Brown, with the concurrence of the California Supreme Court, finally granted Billings a full pardon.

✳

THE MOONEY-BILLINGS CASE is not unique in having political dimensions. There have been numerous other cases in which the prominence of the victim or the partisan political sentiments of the prosecutor, when coupled with the marginal social status of the defendant, have aroused the public and captured the nation's attention. Arguably the two most famous such cases in this century are those of Sacco and Vanzetti in Massachusetts in the 1920s and the Lindbergh baby kidnapping in New Jersey for which Hauptmann was convicted in 1936.

At about 3:00 P.M. on April 15, 1920, two men were murdered during a payroll robbery in South Braintree, a dozen miles or so from downtown Boston. The crime was punishable by a mandatory death penalty. Arrested were two Italian immigrants, Bartolomeo Vanzetti, 32, and Nicola Sacco, 29, the "poor fish-peddlar and good shoemaker" of later novels, plays, and poems. Self-professed anarchists, Sacco (a draft dodger who had fled briefly to Mexico in 1917) and Vanzetti (recently convicted of armed robbery in nearby Bridgewater and awaiting sentencing) were arrested, tried, convicted, and sentenced to death in the atmosphere of xenophobic patriotism that marked the great "Red Scare" of the early 1920s. They were eventually executed in April 1927. During the seven years their case dragged on, the struggle of the two defendants captured national and international attention.

Looking back at the case today, few would dispute the egregious violations in due process of law that marked the conduct of Norfolk County's prosecutor, Frederick Katzmann, and the rulings from the trial bench of Judge Webster Thayer. Motion after motion for postconviction relief was denied, and appeals filed in state and federal courts were routinely turned down. In 1977, on the fiftieth anniversary of the executions, a special proclamation by Governor Michael Dukakis, based on an exhaustive study of the entire record by his chief legal counsel, Daniel Taylor, pronounced the trial riddled with error: Prosecutor Katzmann had been guilty of "knowingly" using "unfair and misleading evidence," of refusing to investigate "new exculpatory evidence," and of flagrant appeals to the jury's "prejudice and bias" against foreigners and anarchists. Judge Thayer had ruled, again and again, in a "prejudicial" manner—not to mention his off-the-bench behavior ("Did you see what I did with those anarchist bastards the other day? I guess that will hold them for a while" was his most flagrant remark, made to a friend after denying defense motions for a new trial).

But due-process violations alone do not establish the innocence of a defendant. Were Sacco and Vanzetti not only the victims of an unfair trial and its aftermath, but really innocent as well? William Young and David Kaiser, in their 1985 review of the case, are the most recent to go on record in the affirmative: "Taken together [all the evidence currently available] leads to the conclusion that Sacco and Vanzetti, two innocent men, most probably were framed for a murder they did not commit."

Others are not so sure, notably the historian Francis Russell, whose two books on the case argue strongly for the defendants' guilt. In 1986 he presented what he regarded as clinching new evidence: hearsay from several aging anarchists who were part of the Sacco-Vanzetti defense committee from the start. They finally admitted, according to Russell, that they knew their comrade Sacco was guilty (and Vanzetti, too, but only as an accessory after the fact), and that the defendants' unwavering protestations of their innocence were lies.

What convicted the two anarchists was principally the physical evidence that linked them directly to the murder of the two payroll guards: the .32 Colt pistol taken from Sacco at his arrest, and the bullets later extracted from one of the victims. The prosecution's own ballistics expert, however—Captain William Proctor—advised prosecutor Katzmann that he would refuse to testify the bullets came from Sacco's pistol (an extremely widely sold type of gun, of which there thousands were in circulation). Katzmann instead got Proctor to say in court that the markings on the fatal bullets were "consistent" with having been fired from Sacco's weapon. Critics of the way the case ended have from that moment forward contended that the integrity of the bullets—and the gun—was in doubt. At a minimum, three things would need to be established to remove that doubt: that the gun used in the test firings by the prosecution was the gun taken from Sacco, that the bullets extracted from the victim matched the test-fired slugs, and that the bullets and the gun introduced into evidence were what they were purported to be.

Regardless of what the jury believed, the evidence submitted at trial failed to establish these propositions. In subsequent years efforts to reinvestigate the matter, beginning with comparison microscope tests made in 1927, simply have proved inconclusive. Today, it is impossible to verify whether any—much less all—of the three crucial propositions are true.

In 1987, Charles Whipple, then a retired senior editor of the *Boston Globe*, wrote that fifty years earlier, when he was a cub reporter, a Boston police ballistics expert who had been involved behind the scenes in the Sacco-Vanzetti case divulged a blockbusting secret. "We switched the murder weapon," he said, adding that if Whipple printed this shocking news, "I'll call you a liar." If the officer told Whipple the truth, this confirms the worst fears of those who do not believe Sacco was guilty—namely that the integrity of the crucial physical evidence was completely ruined.

Based on our reading of the shelf-full of books on the case, we agree with Justice Felix Frankfurter and Herbert Ehrmann (of counsel to the defendants in 1926–27), and with such recent scholars as Young and Kaiser, whose close study of the record persuades them the two defendants were innocent. Some readers, of course, may prefer to join Louis Joughlin and Edmund Morgan, who prefaced their 1948 book on the case thus: "Were Sacco and Vanzetti guilty of murder? . . . We do not know—and we do not believe that human judgment will ever be in a position to arrive at absolute certainty in this case."

TWO YEARS before Sacco and Vanzetti were executed, the world was thrilled by the courageous and pioneering nonstop solo flight across the Atlantic by the young American aviator Charles Lindbergh. From the moment he landed safely in Paris, "Lindy" was a household name, and his fame knew no limits. He was unquestionably the most admired American of his generation.

Several years later, after marriage to the debutante daughter of Governor Dwight Morrow of New Jersey and the birth of a son, Lindbergh was back in the news. The nation learned to its horror that Charles, Jr., not quite two years old, had been kidnapped and was being held for ransom. Kidnapping for ransom was the crime of the hour in the 1920s and early 1930s; one estimate has it that between the Great Crash in 1929 and the inauguration of Franklin Delano Roosevelt in 1933, there were at least twenty-five hundred kidnappings. The Lindberghs were merely the latest among the wealthy and prominent to have a child stolen and held in exchange for a large sum of money.

The ransom was paid, but the baby was not returned. Instead, in May 1932, five weeks after the kidnapping, a tiny body identified as that of Charles Augustus Lindbergh, Jr., was found in a shallow roadside ditch a few miles from the family home in Hopewell, New Jersey. State and federal investigators, followed by a swarm of journalists, fanned out across the Middle Atlantic states, following every lead, rumor, and possibility. Each tidbit of information reported in the papers or over the radio was eagerly snapped up by the public.

Two years of frantic activity passed. Then, in August 1932, a major break came when one of the marked ransom notes was passed at a gas station in upper Manhattan. It came from the hand of a German immigrant and war veteran, an expert carpenter by trade, Richard Hauptmann, 35. Despite his attempts to explain how the bills had come into his possession, he was promptly arrested. From that day until his death in New Jersey's electric chair in April 1936, Hauptmann protested his innocence.

One rarely remembered curiosity of this case that reflects its extraordinary salience arises from the fact that under New Jersey law in 1932, neither kidnapping, kidnapping for ransom, nor murder in the course of kidnapping was a capital crime. How, then, could Hauptmann have been lawfully executed for the Lindbergh kidnap-murder? He was successfully prosecuted for homicide in the course of *burglary*, entering a dwelling with the intent to commit a felony. What felony? Theft of the baby and its clothing. By this stratagem prosecutor David Wilentz, the youthful and politically ambitious attorney general of New Jersey, catered to public clamor and impressed his many admirers with his resourcefulness. Amazingly, the jury accepted his theory of the crime despite no evidence of any sort linking Hauptmann to the baby or the stolen clothes.

Jim Fisher, a criminal justice professor, lawyer, and former FBI agent who wrote a 1987 book about the case, believes that Hauptmann was, indeed, the kidnapper and murderer and that he received due process of law throughout his trial and appeals. Others who have carefully studied the case in recent years, notably journalist Anthony Scaduto and BBC commentator Ludovic Kennedy, disagree.

The crucial test of Hauptmann's guilt was the one piece of physical evidence introduced at the trial that connected him with the kidnapping. This was the oddly constructed ladder (twenty feet long, in three sections) found leaning against the outside wall of the Lindbergh home, reaching to the nursery window. The prosecution claimed it was used by the kidnapper; the defense said it was a prop planted to conceal an inside job.

Trial testimony asserted that a piece of the wood—designated as Rail 16—used to build the ladder was made from a strip of attic flooring in Hauptmann's house in the Bronx. The evidence connecting the two pieces was the alleged matching of the grain and the knots; the claim that Rail 16 came from Hauptmann's attic rested entirely on prosecution testimony and the way the nail holes in the wood strip matched those in the joists underneath. Attorney General Wilentz viewed this as his most important bit of evidence against Hauptmann. Post-trial interviews with the jurors revealed that they regarded it the same way.

The connection was weak at best, however, and probably fraudulent. Several wood experts with different professional backgrounds examined Rail 16 and the supposedly matching strip of attic flooring, and they virtually laughed at the prosecution's evidence. Wilentz (knowingly?) used a photograph of the flooring, of unauthenticated date, to undercut a defense expert whose testimony had cast doubt on the integrity of the wood exhibits. The prosecution had never allowed the defense to examine the attic, but evidence gathered at the behest of the then-governor of New Jersey, Harold Hoffman, just before Hauptmann's execution (and not published until later) indicated that Rail 16 had never been part of the attic flooring at all. Although the nail holes in the joists fit precisely with those in the board, laboratory tests showed that the joist holes were too new and shallow to have been genuine. Explanation? Someone had taken a piece of wood, cut it to fit with the attic flooring, briefly nailed it down, and then removed the board and extracted the nails.

Kennedy, alone among recent writers on the Hauptmann case, quotes the crucial portions of that technical report. Scaduto, who seems unaware of it, nonetheless elaborates in detail a plausible account of how the police (perhaps with the prosecution) contrived and used this piece of fake evidence. Kennedy quotes Scaduto's hypothesis and endorses it. But Fisher neither cites the laboratory report nor mentions, much less tries to refute, the Scaduto hypothesis, although he was clearly aware of it (he frequently mentions Scaduto's views in his own footnotes). The careful reader of these three recent studies must come away with shaken confidence in Fisher's thoroughness and thus in his judgments. Moreover, although Fisher gives Kennedy an occasional footnote, he makes no effort at all to deal with the mass of evidence that Kennedy offers in support of Hauptmann's innocence.

What will probably prove to be the definitive study of the case is now being researched and written by Robert Bryan, long-time attorney to the aged Anna Hauptmann (Richard Hauptmann's widow); together they have worked unstintingly to vindicate her husband. Bryan's forthcoming book, based in part on a vast quantity of new material obtained from state and federal government files, we believe will prove once and for all that Hauptmann was innocent.

No future or other official tribunal is likely to review the verdict against Hauptmann any more than it will the verdicts against Sacco and Vanzetti (or the notorious "atom spies," Ethel and Julius Rosenberg, executed in 1953 for espionage). The criminal justice system is not equipped to deal with such issues once a defendant has been executed. These remain matters of judgment that must be based on the best extralegal and nonjudicial investigations scholarship can provide.

5 ✳ WHITE MOBS, BLACK VICTIMS

MORE THAN ONCE, central Florida's air has been filled with the acrid smell of racist conflagrations. More than once, angry whites have burned down entire black communities. The so-called Rosewood Massacre, for example, began during New Year's week in 1923. A settlement with no white residents seventy years ago, Rosewood is located in the swamps just nine miles inland from scenic Cedar Key on the Gulf. A young white woman who lived three miles out of town claimed that a black man had entered her home in the predawn darkness, beaten her, and stolen her money. The culprit fled to the black community, where he was hidden by a sympathetic resident. A tracking dog soon led a white mob to the hiding place, but by the time the dog arrived, the man had vanished.

Armed white men, believing the woman's assailant was black, began to pour into Rosewood from neighboring communities. Seven days later, Rosewood had been burned to the ground. Dozens of buildings, homes to nearly two hundred people, had gone up in flames and smoke. The number who died in the Rosewood Massacre is uncertain; some say it was as many as 150. Almost all were blacks. Many were children. Among the dead was the man in whose home the assailant had temporarily hidden. No whites were ever arrested for participation in the riot.

A generation later, in the early morning hours of Saturday, July 16, 1949, word spread through the communities of central Florida's Lake County, north and west of Orlando, that another violent racial clash was on the horizon. A 17-year-old white woman reported she had been attacked and raped by four black men, near the hamlet of Groveland. "LAKE COUNTY BRIDE KIDNAPED," blared the headlines of Orlando's *Sunday Sentinel-Star* the next day. The article reported that "many outraged citizens" had vowed, "We'll wait and see what the law does, and if the law doesn't do it right, we'll do it."

On that Saturday night, even before those newspapers had been distributed and read, several hundred angry whites descended on the county jail in Tavares, twenty miles from Groveland. They demanded release of the three black suspects who had been arrested for the crime. But Willis V. McCall, the 40-year-old Lake County sheriff who would eventually gain international notoriety in this and other cases, persuaded the mob that the three men had been removed and turned over to state custody. He even let the victim's husband and her father search the jail. The frustrated mob departed and drove to Groveland.

The mob concentrated its rage on a black neighborhood with twenty-five residents, known locally as "Stuckey's Still." Luckily, Groveland's four hundred black residents had anticipated their imminent danger. With the assistance of sympathetic whites, they had abandoned their homes and fled the area. Still, numerous dwellings of black residents in Stuckey's Still were damaged. At least three were destroyed, including the house of one of the suspects, as the mob drove wildly around town setting fires and shooting randomly into blacks' homes.

The next morning, in response to a request from Sheriff McCall, Governor Fuller Warren activated the National Guard. Even so, on Monday night the fires continued, and cars were stopped by whites "looking for Negroes." Some of the cars cruising through the area sported out-of-state licenses; what had begun as a purely local matter had quickly escalated into a classic white-against-black confrontation of much broader proportions. Feelings ran high. Throughout Lake County, crosses were burned. Miraculously, no one was injured by the mob—or at least no injuries were formally reported. It took three hundred troops five days to restore a semblance of order. None of the white rioters was ever arrested.

Within hours of the initial report to the police by the alleged victim, three black men had been arrested: Walter Lee Irvin, Samuel Shepherd, and Charles Greenlee stood accused of kidnapping and raping a white woman, Norma Padgett, and of assaulting her husband, Willie. A fourth suspect, Ernest Thomas, initially managed to elude the posse that was sent to hunt him down. Ten days after the reported crime, the lynch mob finally caught up with him. They discovered him sleeping in the woods near Greenville, 150 miles northwest of Groveland, and without further ado he was shot and killed. The local paper ran an article stating that "two or three hundred men were said to have participated in the chase, and some reports put the number at a thousand." A coroner's jury later accepted the posse's version of the shooting: Thomas, although he had a pistol, was killed resisting arrest. No one ever made an effort to explain how Thomas could possibly have thought a solo stand against the hundreds of armed pursuers could succeed.

On the Tuesday following the alleged gang rape, even before order had been restored but with three of the four suspects in custody, Orlando's *Morning Sentinel* featured another bold headline about the mob violence in Lake County. Prominent in the upper center of the front page was a large drawing of four electric chairs. Signs reading "The Lake County Tragedy" and "Supreme Penalty" were pinned to the chairs in the drawing. The caption for the picture gave a clear message: "No Compromise!" Public opinion was being simultaneously expressed and inflamed.

Shortly after the three young men had been arrested, the president of the Orlando branch of the NAACP alerted staff in the organization's national headquarters to the case and requested assistance. Within twenty-four hours Franklin Williams, an attorney with the NAACP Legal Defense and Educational Fund in New York, was on his way to Florida. The stage was set for another tragedy of the American South. The basic plot was familiar, and the principal roles had been assigned. Like many other cases below the Mason-Dixon line, this one involved the alleged rape of a white woman by several black youths. As was typical in such cases, the judge and all members of the jury would be white. Once again the fairness of the southern judicial system itself would be on trial every bit as much as the defendants.

In 1949, Charlie Greenlee was 16 years old. Gainesville, in north-central Florida's Alachua County, was not a bad place to live. But Charlie was the only male in a houseful of females, and two of his sisters had recently been killed in a hideous accident—run over by a train. Charlie's mother took the deaths of her children badly. She went on and on about her "babies"; she spent her days at home, crying all the time. Charlie couldn't stand it. Every now and then he just left, going to meet friends, trying to get away from it all.

In Gainesville Charlie had befriended Ernest Thomas, and on Friday, July 15, he and Ernest hitchhiked to Thomas's home town of Groveland, two counties away, looking for work. People said Thomas was in some kind of trouble having to do with gambling. Because Charlie was a friend of Ernest's, the same people figured he was probably involved in gambling, too. But whether that was true and whether that was the reason they went to Groveland on a hot July night was never clear. Within a short time it didn't matter any more, because the two young men were caught up in something far more serious.

In the early morning hours of Saturday, July 16, Charlie was hanging around a gas station on the outskirts of town (where Ernest had left him a short while before), when a police car pulled up. The officers searched Charlie and found he was carrying a gun; they promptly arrested him for vagrancy. Only much later did the police tell Charlie he was one of four black men wanted for assaulting a white man named Willie Padgett and then kidnapping and raping his wife. Charlie could make no sense of this. He had not seen a white couple meeting the Padgetts' description, on a side road in a stalled car (where the attack was said to have taken place) or anywhere else. Indeed, when the Padgetts first saw Charlie Greenlee in police custody, they did not implicate him. That was hardly surprising, given that the rape had supposedly occurred at the very time Charlie was being arrested nineteen miles away. Besides, he later insisted, he wasn't stupid. If he had known a white woman had been raped somewhere in the vicinity, he would have left town. He knew enough to know something like that meant bad news for any black man in the area.

Another thing that didn't make sense was that the crime was supposed to have been carried out by a gang of four men. But Charlie had spent the evening either alone or with only one other person—not three others— and that was his friend Ernest Thomas. Ernest was also charged with the crime, but neither Charlie nor anyone else ever got to talk to him about it. As Charlie later learned, an armed posse found Ernest asleep in a wooded area near the Georgia border where they shot and killed him on the spot.

Well, at least Charlie wasn't dead. But he was in jail, and he found himself thrown in with the other two men, slightly older than he (in their early twenties), charged with the same crime. He had never met Walter Irvin and Sammy Shepherd before. They would eventually get to know each other quite well.

Sammy Shepherd and Walter Irvin were ex-army buddies; each had done two hitches. During their second tour of duty they had served a prison sentence for "misappropriation of government property," resulting in dishonorable discharges. Once the two young men were back home in Lake County, they continued to spend time in each other's company, partly out of habit and partly because Sammy planned to marry Walter's sister.

Lake County in 1949 was not a very comfortable place for blacks, though Sammy's father, Henry Shepherd, had actually done quite well. He had worked diligently to build up his little farm by reclaiming some swamp land. Ironically, his efforts brought him difficulties as well as satisfaction. Shepherd's white neighbors, some of them none too well off themselves, were able to get along with blacks as long as the blacks could be ignored. But Henry Shepherd did not fit their stereotype of the lazy black; they were irritated by the way his steady hard work tended to show them up. Shepherd managed both to survive the harassment and to improve his family's standard of living.

One might have thought this would be a tolerable atmosphere for Sammy to return to, but his army experience and the sense of independence he had gained from it made him unwilling to be squeezed into the traditional Lake County mold for young black males. That would have had him looking for work with one of the local citrus growers, a powerful group of white farmers disdainful of the poor blacks in the area. Sammy refused even to try to land such a job. He knew the growers desperately needed laborers, but he also knew they did not treat their hired help with any dignity. He would have none of it. Sammy's attitude, coupled with his father's relative success, made the Shepherds appear "uppity" to some whites.

Against this backdrop, on Friday, July 15, 1949, Sammy and Walter Irvin drove into Orlando, looking for something to do. The long, steamy evening of a hot Florida night added to their restlessness. They wandered from bar to bar, drinking idly and whiling away the time. Hours later, too bored to continue their barhopping any longer, they drove back to Groveland. Sammy returned the car he had borrowed from his older brother.

A few hours later, early in the morning of July 16, Sammy and Walter were arrested, accused of kidnapping and raping a young white woman named Norma Padgett and of assaulting her husband, Willie. The police had driven Willie through the black neighborhood, where he identified the car Sammy had been using and then identified Sammy and Walter as his assailants. The two men were baffled, since neither of them had ever seen Willie or Norma Padgett before. Even more baffling was finding that they were co-defendants with two other young men; according to the Padgetts, the crime had been committed by four blacks. One of the other two suspects, Ernest Thomas, they did know. But Ernest, they later found out, ran from the police and ten days later was shot and killed by a posse. The fourth defendant was a 16-year-old kid from a small place just north of Gainesville, a friend of Ernest's whom Sammy and Walter had never met. His name, they soon discovered, was Charlie Greenlee.

In the jail cells, the police tied Irvin, Shepherd, and Greenlee by their arms to overhead pipes. Cut glass was scattered on the floor. The young men's shoes were taken away from them; every time they moved, their feet got cut. They were also beaten, leaving them with bruises all over their bodies. Greenlee and Shepherd, desperate to end the torture, finally confessed to the crime. Irvin, despite the mistreatment, stubbornly refused to say he was guilty.

Norma Padgett was pretty, or at least that's what Willie Padgett apparently thought. But Willie was a bit on the tough side, and sometimes when he got mad, he hit Norma. She didn't like it, and neither did her parents. Norma kept running home to them, complaining about Willie, and they finally said he couldn't see her any more even though he was her husband. It was a year after their wedding; she was still only 17, and he was just 21.

On Friday night, July 15, 1949, Willie went by his in-laws' house, hoping they would let him see his wife. He persuaded them everything would be all right if she went with him to a dance, and Norma agreed to go. But later that evening, as Willie subsequently told the story, while they were driving along a back road the weak battery in his car caused it to stall and then stop. Another car pulled up, and someone inside asked what the trouble was; Willie gladly accepted the offer of help from the four black men in the car. Then, the next thing he knew, the four guys had jumped him and beaten him up rather badly. They also attacked Norma, but instead of beating her up they drove off—taking her with them. Willie finally got his car started again and set out after Norma's abductors. In Leesburg, about twenty miles north of Groveland, he told a gas station attendant that he had been attacked and that his wife had been kidnapped.

Around dawn, with the help of a deputy sheriff, Willie finally found Norma. She had been picked up near a restaurant on the edge of Groveland, by the owner's son. She hadn't mentioned to him that anything was wrong, and she appeared calm. But after she and Willie talked for a few minutes, Norma told the deputy sheriff that she had been kidnapped and raped by four black men. They had offered her a ride into town, she reported, but she had said she'd rather walk, and they left her in a field. She claimed to have hidden in the woods until daybreak.

The grand jury that indicted Greenlee, Shepherd, and Irvin was assembled in great haste a mere four days after the crime. The indictments followed just as quickly, while the National Guard was still patrolling the streets. The trial was to be held at the end of August, just a month away.

Barely a week before the trial was scheduled to open, Franklin Williams, the Legal Defense Fund lawyer from New York, finally found an attorney with a Florida license willing to take the case. Alex Akerman, Jr., a Georgia native and graduate of the (then) all-white University of Florida Law School, had just completed a term as the only Republican in the Florida House of Representatives. For this case he chose two assistants—one a black attorney from Daytona Beach.

The first thing Akerman did was to ask for a one-month extension so that he and his assistants could meet with the three defendants, familiarize themselves with the circumstances of the crime, and look for possible witnesses. Judge Truman Futch granted him three days. Akerman then petitioned for a change of venue on the ground that negative pretrial publicity made it impossible for his clients to receive a fair trial. Judge Futch denied the petition. Akerman also argued that seating one black on the grand jury did not offset the unfairness of twenty-five years of systematic exclusion of blacks from juries. But Judge Futch had testimony to the contrary from two locally prominent citizens. E. I. Burleigh, the mayor of nearby Tavares, claimed that race relations in Lake County were good. And F. L. Hampton, a black insurance agent, insisted that interracial relations in Lake County were "the best in Florida." The judge concluded that having one black on the grand jury *was* enough to show there was no "systematic exclusion" of blacks going on, whatever might have been true in the past. A trial jury of twelve white men was selected.

Almost four hundred spectators, including seventy-five blacks, watched the trial. Both Willie and Norma Padgett took the witness stand. Each told the same story, including that Norma had been raped by four blacks. Oddly enough, however, the prosecution—led by attorney J. W. Hunter—offered no medical evidence of rape, simply stating that such evidence wasn't necessary. And although the Padgetts had initially disagreed about whether Charlie Greenlee was one of the men involved in the crime, during the trial they both testified that he was. Their eyewitness identifications were critical to the case against all three defendants. Norma identified the "nigger Irvin" as the one who sat next to her during the abduction, at least until the point where "the Thomas nigger" got into the back seat.

That wasn't all of the damaging testimony. Deputy Sheriff James L. Yates presented in evidence several plaster casts, made at the scene of the abduction, of tire tracks and footprints. Since the tire-track casts were later matched to the car that all parties agreed Shepherd had borrowed from his brother, and the footprint casts matched Irvin's shoes, the evidence appeared conclusive. Only much later would questions be raised about the authenticity of the casts.

Sheriff McCall testified that he had confessions from the three accused, but for some reason he never entered them as evidence. Perhaps it was because he in fact had only two confessions; perhaps it was because the confessions were not exactly voluntarily given, or complete. It didn't matter. The members of the jury knew about the confessions anyway, because the newspapers had done a good job of spreading the word after

Sheriff McCall's early announcement that the defendants had admitted their guilt. The newspaper accounts didn't bother to qualify McCall's sweeping statement by referring to Irvin's refusal to confess, nor did they mention (even if they knew or guessed) anything about the brutal police tactics used to extract the two confessions McCall did have. These inconsistencies and omissions had little or no effect on the jury.

The three defendants took the witness stand, each testifying on his own behalf. There were no other defense witnesses. The jury deliberated a mere hour and a half before announcing the verdict. All three defendants were found guilty. The sentence for Shepherd and for Irvin was death. Greenlee, because he was so young, was sentenced to life imprisonment.

Beginning in 1944, the office of sheriff in Lake County was held by Willis V. McCall. A local boy, born in 1910, McCall had started a dairy venture and then worked as a citrus fruit inspector for nine years before he decided he'd like to be sheriff. He had no training or prior experience in law enforcement, but he had the support of the big citrus growers, who practically ran the county. McCall said he was a "lawan'order" sort of man—he liked to run the phrase together in one word. His swaggering style and the Stetson he always wore made him seem larger than life, and he was easily elected. He did things his own way and quickly earned a reputation for heavy-handed techniques, but few people complained; McCall was just another local officer of the law doing his job. In 1950 he was elected to a second term.

Late in 1951, two years after the Groveland trial, McCall ceased to be just one more county sheriff. On November 6 of that year, he drove 120 miles north to the prison in Raiford to pick up two of his death row prisoners, Shepherd and Irvin, and return them to the county jail in Tavares. Thanks to the vigorous efforts of the defense team, the United States Supreme Court had overturned Irvin's and Shepherd's convictions and ordered a new trial. Sheriff McCall took upon himself the task of delivering the two men to their pretrial hearing.

They never got there. Off on a back road as he drove into Lake County, McCall slowed to a stop and got out to check a tire he thought was going flat. He decided the tire should be changed and ordered his two passengers, handcuffed together in the back seat, to get out and do the job for him. McCall testified later that Shepherd and Irvin rushed him and tried to take his weapon, in a desperate attempt to escape. To protect himself and prevent them from fleeing, he said, he shot them both. Shepherd died almost instantly. Irvin—despite bullet wounds in his chest, neck, and head—survived.

Sheriff McCall's actions raised questions in the minds of some, but he was cleared of any wrongdoing after a coroner's inquest into Shepherd's death and praised for his actions "in the line of duty and in defense of his own life." Not everyone thought so highly of the sheriff's conduct, though. At the urging of the NAACP, Governor Warren appointed a special investigator. Once again, no proof was found of criminal wrongdoing, but this time Sheriff McCall was criticized for not using "maximum precaution" in transporting his two prisoners. He never did explain why he had both prisoners in his car without having a deputy ride with him. (Instead of accompanying McCall, James L. Yates—the deputy sheriff who had introduced the plaster tire casts at the trial—followed in a second squad car. Yates confirmed McCall's story: The prisoners had tried to disarm McCall, and he shot them in self-defense. Never mind that Irvin and Shepherd were unarmed and handcuffed together.)

Throughout the 1950s and 1960s, Sheriff McCall was returned to office at every election. He kept doing things his way, despite numerous charges of corruption and abuse of office. Not until 1971, and then only after a federal court order, did he remove the "White Waiting Room" and "Colored Waiting Room" signs outside his office. And only after Governor Reubin Askew had suspended him for kicking a black prisoner to death (McCall was acquitted of second-degree murder in that case) did he finally lose an election, late in 1972. But that was all much later.

Bleeding from several bullet wounds, Walter Lee Irvin lay beside the road and pretended to be dead. Next to him in the sand, handcuffed to his wrist, his friend Sammy Shepherd lay absolutely motionless.

The news that they would get a new trial had raised Irvin's and Shepherd's spirits considerably, and being picked up for the pretrial hearing had been a hopeful sign. But, according to Irvin's story, McCall and Yates had threatened them as soon as they got outside the prison gate, and the two young men began to think perhaps nothing had changed after all. Irvin and Shepherd had grown accustomed to that kind of treatment, since Sheriff McCall had made it clear from the start that he wanted them dead. Thus, once they were on their way, when he started driving erratically and said he thought he was getting a flat tire, Walter and Sammy were nervous. Then the sheriff pulled over and abruptly ordered the two of them out of the car. Just as suddenly, McCall shot first Shepherd and then Irvin. For no reason Irvin could figure, other than pure hate, Sheriff McCall had killed Sammy and tried to kill him.

Under oath, later, Irvin swore that he had heard McCall mutter, "I got rid of them, killed the sons of bitches." According to Irvin, McCall then radioed to Deputy Yates, following in another car, and reported that the two prisoners had tried to jump him. "I did a good job," he said. When Yates arrived, he shined his flashlight into Irvin's eyes. Irvin blinked.

"That son of a bitch is not dead, let's kill him," Yates said, and he proceeded to shoot. His revolver misfired, however, and it was only after he and McCall had coolly examined the gun and switched weapons that Yates was able to shoot again. This time, a bullet lodged in Irvin's neck. Still he lived.

Lying in the hospital, weak from his wounds, Irvin was repeatedly questioned. He told the same story each time, even with McCall watching and listening from the doorway. Once he gave his account of what had happened in the presence of the prosecuting attorney, J. W. Hunter. Knowing he was quite possibly dying from his wounds, Irvin also persisted in telling the earlier part of the story the way he had told it from the time he was indicted and charged in the Norma Padgett incident. He was, he declared, completely innocent. And he continued to insist on his innocence even when Hunter offered him a reduced sentence if he would admit complicity in the rape.

At the pretrial hearing, Irvin still refused to plea bargain, and his case went back to trial as ordered by the Supreme Court. The defense had raised the issue of whether blacks had been unfairly excluded from the jury, but the Court had had far more sweeping concerns about the case. The unanimous reversal of the judgment of Florida's supreme court came not primarily because "the method of jury selection discriminated against the Negro race." That, in the words of Justice Robert H. Jackson, would be to "stress the trivial and ignore the important." More significant was the prejudicial pretrial publicity. The first trial, he insisted, "took place under conditions and was accompanied by events which would deny defendants a fair trial before any kind of jury. . . . The case presents one of the best examples of one of the worst menaces to American justice."

This time a change of venue was permitted, though only to the next county; the new trial site was a mere forty miles away, in Ocala, and Judge Truman Futch would preside again. Instead of Franklin Williams, the New York office of the NAACP Legal Defense Fund sent the LDF's black director (a future Supreme Court justice), Thurgood Marshall, and a young white attorney (later to become executive director of the LDF), Jack Greenberg. They arrived in Orlando on a Saturday night, where the Ku Klux Klan met them with a torch-light parade. In deference to local customs, Marshall stayed with a black family in the area, and Greenberg registered at a hotel. Throughout the night, Klan members circled his hotel in their trucks, waving torches. Greenberg would recall, years later, that he got very little sleep that night.

The second trial proceeded essentially the way the first one had. The chief difference had to do with the plaster casts. Expert testimony for the defense established that the casts of Irvin's shoes had been formed from footprints made with empty boots. In other words, the plaster molds used as evidence against the accused had been deliberately faked, just as Irvin had argued from the outset. The casts had been made by Deputy Sheriff James L. Yates, who had accompanied McCall the day he picked Irvin and Shepherd up at Raiford prison.

(Interestingly enough, a decade later Deputy Yates apparently used the same technique to help convict two other blacks. Jerry Chatman and Robert Shuler were sentenced to death in 1960 for raping a Lake County white woman. Twelve years after their sentencing, a United States District Court judge vacated those convictions, finding that the plaster casts of the footprints incriminating Chatman and Shuler had not been made at the scene of the crime at all, but at the sheriff's office.)

Despite Irvin's continued insistence on his innocence, the new evidence about the plaster casts, and the spirited defense presented by Greenberg and Marshall, Irvin was again found guilty and again sentenced to death. According to one writer, Marshall was "stunned by the verdict" and "came out of court fighting back tears." He promised Irvin's mother, "We're going to stick by you. . . . We are going to keep on fighting." The conviction was upheld by the state supreme court, however, and two years after Irvin's second conviction, the United States Supreme Court dashed all hopes of judicial intervention by refusing to hear the case. Soon after, Governor Charley Johns announced that he would not grant clemency.

Ernest Thomas had been killed by a posse. Sammy Shepherd had been shot dead by Sheriff Willis McCall. Charlie Greenlee was serving a life sentence. And for Walter Irvin, once again on death row, time was running out.

A new governor, LeRoy Collins, took office in 1955. Collins was deluged with letters on behalf of Irvin. Inspired in part by editorials in the *St. Petersburg Times*—based on investigative work done by reporter Norman Bunin—Governor Collins decided to look into the case again. The more he looked, the more concerned he became. He was unhappy about the way the arrests and the trial had been carried out. He was appalled by Sheriff McCall. Collins asked Bill Harris, one of his assistants, to take charge of carefully re-investigating the already much-reviewed case. Harris uncovered numerous blunders in the way the case had been handled, and he raised several questions that had either never been asked or never been answered. He thus demonstrated how incomplete the investigation of the crime had been, while also drawing attention to loopholes in the testimony on which the prosecution had largely rested its case.

The only physical evidence the prosecutor had ever produced against Irvin and his co-defendants were the plaster casts of footprints and tire tracks, supposedly made at the scene of the crime. But Harris pointed out that despite Yates's claim that he had been making plaster casts for years, he had testified he did not understand what "integrity of footprints" meant. There was also another, more troubling, issue. One of McCall's deputies had seized the car and driven it to the sheriff's office when McCall made the arrest. Realizing that the deputy could have driven to the crime scene and made the tracks before returning to the office, Governor Collins concluded that Irvin's guilt had not been established "in an absolute and conclusive manner," beyond a reasonable doubt. He recommended clemency.

On December 15, 1955, the Florida Cabinet, acting as the State Pardon Board, reported its unanimous decision. Walter Lee Irvin's death sentence was commuted to life imprisonment. That was as close to a formal recognition of his innocence as Irvin would ever get.

Even though reporter Norman Bunin had found evidence that showed it was physically impossible for Charlie Greenlee to have been at the scene of the crime at the time it was supposed to have taken place, Greenlee's conviction had never been appealed. The risk of his being found guilty again and of then being sentenced to death was considered too great. There was no reason to think that if he did win a new trial his jury would be any less white or any more sympathetic to a young black than the first one. And so there the matter rested until July 26, 1960, when Charlie Greenlee was paroled. Another eleven and a half years went by before his civil rights were officially restored, when—more than twenty years after the night Norma Padgett was allegedly attacked—his sentence was commuted to time served. Today Charles Greenlee lives in Tennessee, no doubt still trying to put the whole thing behind him.

Walter Irvin had also applied for release in 1960, but his application was denied because he had served less than ten years of his life sentence. After eight more years, on June 16, 1968, Irvin was finally granted parole. Officials prescribed that he live in Miami, a safe distance from Groveland and Lake County, and there he began to forge a new life. He got on as well as could be expected; he had a perfect parole record.

Nine months after Irvin was released from prison, one of his uncles died back home in Lake County. Walter decided to go to the funeral. Shortly after arriving in Lake County, Walter Lee Irvin—at the age of forty-one—dropped dead of a heart attack.

❋

THE LYNCH-MOB atmosphere in which Greenlee, Irvin, and Shepherd faced trial for their lives has occurred again and again in this century. Two earlier cases, one from Arkansas in 1919 and another from Alabama in 1931, are among the many that dramatically display the ugly way white racism has corrupted criminal justice for blacks.

Elaine, Arkansas, is a small farming town southwest of Memphis, near the Mississippi River. During 1919, rumors circulated of impending violence organized by blacks and aimed at whites. Suddenly, on October 1, full-scale warfare broke out. The headline in Little Rock's daily paper shrieked: "DESPERATE FIGHTING BETWEEN WHITES AND NEGROES." Reports of more than a thousand blacks with high-powered rifles quickly brought armed whites to the Elaine area, by the carload, from towns on both sides of the river. The ensuing shoot-out left casualties among whites and blacks alike.

A special investigation ordered by Governor Charles Brough confirmed white beliefs: "The present trouble with the negroes of Phillips County is not a race riot. It is a deliberately planned insurrection of the negroes against the whites, directed by an organization known as the 'Progressive Farmers' and 'Household Union of America,' established for the purpose of banding negroes together for the killing of white people. . . ."

By early November, an all-white grand jury had indicted 122 blacks for a variety of crimes connected with the disturbance. (No whites were charged with any crime.) By the time the local courts were finished, 67 of those indicted had been sentenced to prison for terms of varying length, 28 for crimes such as "nightriding" and 39 for second-degree murder. In a series of earlier separate trials, a dozen others—Frank Moore, Ed and Frank Hicks, J. E. Knox, Paul Hall, Ed Coleman, Albert Giles, Joe Fox, John Martin, Alf Banks, Jr., Will Wordlow, and Ed Ware—were convicted of first-degree murder and condemned to death.

Judicial proceedings against the twelve sentenced to death took barely more than a fortnight. The all-white juries deliberated only briefly—in one case for nine minutes, in another for four. In one instance, where five men were tried together, the jury took a mere seven minutes to bring in its verdicts and death sentences. The American Legion Post in nearby Helena forwarded a strongly worded petition to Governor Brough demanding that he not commute any of the sentences. Threats of lynching smoldered in the air. (In the year after the Elaine trials, fifty-seven black Americans were lynched; between 1882 and 1927, Arkansas alone averaged six lynchings a year.)

Not everyone believed the official story of the riot. In fact, as that version of events was subjected to more and more scrutiny over the years, it was thoroughly discredited. One of the first outsiders to look into the disturbance and the trials was Walter F. White of the NAACP (created a decade earlier as an antilynching group). His research documented an entirely different account of the so-called riots, one that stands virtually unchallenged today. At considerable risk to his own safety, White made inquiries in Phillips County and found that there was a widespread peonage system that kept black farm laborers in wretched poverty and permanent debt. On September 30, a group of black laborers met at their village church in Hoop Spur, near Elaine, not to instigate a race war but simply to discuss ways of peacefully remedying their situation. There *was* no incipient black insurrection. Rumors of an uprising caused nervous white racists to fire into the church, however, and some of the blacks then fired back in self-defense. The story that blacks had set about starting a race war was nothing more than a cover-up for ruthless white suppression of black protest at their plight and of their lawful efforts to create organizations that would improve their condition. There was no reason to believe that any of the blacks convicted of murder had actually killed anyone.

The NAACP undertook to defend the prisoners, especially the dozen under death sentence. The defense team assembled was led by an unusual trio: George W. Murphy, an aging but distinguished Confederate War veteran practicing in Little Rock; Moorefield Storey, a Boston Brahmin and president of the NAACP; and Scipio Africanus Jones, a black ex-slave who was also an attorney in Little Rock. Arguing for a new trial, they raised a series of objections: Adverse pretrial publicity had prejudiced the community against the defendants, blacks had been systematically excluded from the grand and petit juries, and the confessions from Banks and Wordlow had been obtained by brutal torture.

As the true story of the Elaine shootings became known, Arkansas courts and government officials gradually began to look for face-saving ways to free the wrongly convicted prisoners. Bringing that to pass would eventually require the intervention of federal courts as well. The Arkansas Supreme Court reversed the convictions of Ware, Wordlow, Giles, Fox, Banks, and Martin, but only on the technical ground that their juries had failed to indicate in their verdicts the precise degree of murder (first or second) of which the defendants were guilty. The court let stand the convictions and death sentences of the other six defendants. When Ware and his five co-defendants were retried in 1920, they were again convicted—this time of first-degree murder—and they were again sentenced to death. The convictions and sentences for Moore, Knox, Hall, Coleman, and the Hicks brothers remained intact.

In June 1921, two days before the scheduled executions of Moore and his five co-defendants, their desperate attorneys sought state habeas corpus relief. It was denied. Thus was born the landmark Supreme Court case of *Moore v. Dempsey*. In February 1923, with the Court's opinion written by Justice Oliver Wendell Holmes, Jr., a rehearing was ordered on the dismissal of the habeas petition. The Court established that if state criminal procedures meet a high enough standard, the federal courts will turn a blind eye to the results—but that in this case Arkansas's procedures clearly failed to meet the standard. (This important ruling has since been reaffirmed many times.)

Meanwhile, in April 1923, all charges against Ware and his co-defendants had been dropped because the several delays by the prosecution in initiating their retrial violated Arkansas law. By June they were free men.

The legal proceedings set in motion by the Court's ruling in *Moore* were suddenly interrupted in November 1924, when Governor Thomas McRae commuted each of the remaining six death sentences to twelve years' imprisonment. In January 1925, as he was about to exit office, the governor granted each defendant an "indefinite furlough." They had been, he said, "model prisoners." They, too, were free men again. Thus, after six years, the last of the twelve men sentenced to death in the Elaine "riot" was finally freed; the other sixty-seven wrongly convicted defendants, those who had been sentenced to prison terms of varying lengths, were also released.

IN MARCH 1931, the Great Depression set thousands of Americans to "riding the rails" in freight cars across the countryside. Most of them were sneaking free rides, hoping to find work in another town; some were just traveling in search of adventure. In the northeast corner of Alabama, as a freight train slowly made its way southwest, a posse of white men had assembled in the rail yard in Paint Rock. Up the line some white hobos had complained to the stationmaster that several blacks had thrown them off the train. A telephone call to the local deputy sheriff was all it had taken to organize the score of armed men gathered by the tracks. Jackson County Sheriff M. L. Wann had ordered his deputy to arrest the blacks and take them to Scottsboro, the county seat. During the next few years, Scottsboro, Alabama, would become famous as another small town where white racism corrupted the local criminal justice system, another small town where innocent blacks, accused of capital crimes against whites, were persecuted.

When the train stopped, the posse searched it from end to end and quickly rounded up nine black teenagers, one white youth, and two young white women. Within minutes, Ruby Bates, one of the two females, told the deputy sheriff that she and her friend, Victoria Price, had been raped by the blacks. (A few days later, Price would elaborate at great length on her ordeal in the freight car. The stories both women told would be confirmed by the white youth.)

News of the alleged rapes spread rapidly, and rumors magnified the brutality of the crime. By evening a mob of hundreds had surrounded the local jail. Cries of "Give 'em to us" and "Let those niggers out" punctuated the night air. Sheriff Wann, fearful he was about to have a lynching on his hands, arranged for a National Guard caravan to take the prisoners to safer custody. In this atmosphere Scottsboro's "nigger rape case" began.

Standing accused of the capital crime of rape (punishable by an optional death penalty that was effectively mandatory when the victim was white and the offender black) were Charles Weems, 20, and Ozie Powell, Clarence Norris, Olen Montgomery, William Roberson, Haywood Patterson, Eugene Williams, and Andrew and Leroy ("Roy") Wright—all in their late teens, except Williams and Roy Wright, who were 13. Solicitor H. G. Bailey announced he would seek the death penalty for all the defendants. Six of the seven members of the local bar refused to accept assignment to the defense. The seventh, 70-year-old Milo Moody, found the lure of the fee (though not, apparently, the injustice of the arrests) irresistible. A Chattanooga attorney, Stephen Roddy, reluctantly agreed to serve as co-counsel. Trial was set for early April. Defendants Norris and Weems were to go before the judge first.

Hours before court was in session, thousands of whites crowded the court-house square. Machine guns manned by National Guard troops pointed ominously at the restless throng. In the court room, Roddy's first motion—a change of venue, on grounds of adverse pretrial publicity—was denied. In short order the all-white, male jury was selected. Victoria Price, decked out in new clothes, took the stand and told in colorful detail how six of the nine defendants had raped her. The following day, Ruby Bates took the stand; in a more subdued manner she told much the same story, though many details in her account differed from those Price had related. Medical testimony confirmed that each of the women had recently had sexual intercourse but failed to confirm any claims of accompanying violence.

The defense had nothing to offer except the unsupported testimony of the defendants. Roddy was shocked to hear one of them, Clarence Norris, shout out under cross-examination—with no warning and no explanation—"They all raped her, every one of them." With that accusation in open court, the prosecution was confident of the outcome. About an hour later, the jury foreman intoned: "We find the defendants guilty of rape and fix their sentence at death." The throng of spectators, inside and outside the court room, roared approval. The rest of the defendants (except for Roy Wright, the youngest, who was spared by a hung jury) were dealt with in much the same manner. All eight were headed for the electric chair. (Roy Wright was convicted soon enough, but he was sentenced only to prison.)

Within days the case became a national cause célèbre. In the years ahead the struggle to save the "Scottsboro Boys," as they became known, pitted the American Communist Party's International Labor Defense Committee against the NAACP. Each championed the defendants, and each sought to control the appellate litigation, which focused on the violations of due process and of equal protection of the law. When *Powell v. Alabama* was finally decided by the U.S. Supreme Court in 1932, it established the important precedent that—at least in capital cases—a defendant is entitled to legal counsel well before walking into court to face trial. No such counsel had been provided for the Scottsboro Boys.

The underlying facts of the case as they eventually emerged showed that the two women had completely fabricated the story of rape. Exactly what did happen to them on the freight train was never established to everyone's satisfaction, but unbiased observers—from the local black community in 1931 all the way to Governor George Wallace in 1976— eventually concluded that it did not include rape by any of the young blacks.

The complex and lengthy legal process that began in 1931 stretched out for nearly thirty years. The convictions of Patterson and Norris were overturned on appeal, but at their retrials they were reconvicted and sentenced to death. The courageous trial judge, James Horton, set aside both the verdict and the sentence, and ordered a third trial. The two defendants were again tried, convicted, and sentenced to death. In 1935 the Supreme Court, in another landmark ruling, *Norris v. Alabama,* reversed the verdict on the ground of improper exclusion of blacks from the trial jury. A year later Patterson was again convicted, but this time sentenced to seventy-five years instead of death. In 1937 Norris was also reconvicted and—for the third time—sentenced to death.

The convictions of the other six defendants were also overturned on appeal. Andrew Wright was reconvicted and sentenced to ninety-nine years, Weems reconvicted and sentenced to seventy-five years. Charges were eventually dropped against Roy Wright, Williams, Montgomery, and Roberson. In 1938 Norris's sentence was commuted to life. Weems was paroled in 1943, Norris and Andrew Wright a year later. Powell was released on parole in 1946. Patterson's career was more colorful: He escaped in 1948, fled to Michigan, and successfully fought extradition to Alabama. Two years later, however, after telling his story in the book *Scottsboro Boy,* he was back in prison on a manslaughter charge. He died there in 1952. In 1976 Alabama granted Norris, by then the sole surviving defendant, an unconditional pardon based on evidence of his and his co-defendants' innocence. The nine defendants had spent a total of 104 years in prison for a crime that never occurred.

6

※

"SINCE YOU'RE THE NIGGER, YOU'RE ELECTED"

T HE BUS carrying the Bellville, Texas, girls' volleyball team pulled into the parking lot at Conroe High School—a sprawling split-level school on a hill just west of I-45, about forty miles north of Houston. It was 9:10 in the morning on Saturday, August 23, 1980; the volleyball tournament the Bellville team had entered would soon begin. The girls—stiff and restless after a sixty-mile bus ride— jumped out, eager to warm up for their first game of the day.

On the bus with the coach and the players was the team's student manager, Cheryl Dee Fergeson. With a bag of volleyballs slung over her shoulder, she was the last to get off. Coach Susan Norris, discovering there was a half hour before the team was scheduled to play, herded Cheryl and the players away from the main complex of the high school and over to a smaller practice gym for a quick scrimmage. "Fergy," as the manager was called, put down the bag of balls, her purse, and the scorebook on the gym floor; she then turned and walked back into the empty hall through which they had all just come.

About to begin her junior year at Bellville High, 16-year-old Cheryl Fergeson had numerous extracurricular interests. Besides playing volley- ball she was a photographer for the *Hoof-Beat,* the school paper; she was active in Girl Scouts; she loved to ride her horse, Bandit. In her spare time, she had a job at the Bellville skating rink. She planned to become a dental hygienist.

Fergy was 5'7", with longish blond hair, hazel eyes, and a nice smile.

According to her aunt, she was "quiet, but popular"; her neighbor and close friend Wendy Honeycutt described her as "an angel." Wendy's and Fergy's fathers were close friends, as their mothers had been. But Cheryl's mother had died of cancer, and Wendy's parents had divorced. That gave the girls something in common—each lived with her father. Even though Wendy was two years younger than Cheryl, the girls spent a lot of time together.

On that Saturday morning at Conroe High School, one of the Bellville players, Cheryl Bradford, went to the girls' rest room before joining the others in the warm-up. As she came back into the gym, she passed Fergy in the hall, apparently also on her way to the rest room. When the warm-up got under way, someone noticed that Fergeson had failed to return; the coach sent a couple of the girls to find her. They looked in vain. Soon the whole team had been organized into search parties. They combed the school, looked in the bus, and even checked a nearby service station. Nobody could find Cheryl Fergeson. The opposing team was by then ready and waiting to play, however, so Mrs. Norris decided the Bellville team would start without its manager.

When the game was over, Cheryl still hadn't appeared. The hunt began anew and quickly intensified. After nearly two hours of extensive but fruitless searching by numerous individuals, two school janitors finally discovered Cheryl, dead, in a loft where theater props were kept above the stage in the school's auditorium. Her body was hidden under a sheet of plywood, nude except for a pair of sweat socks. The rest of her clothes were nowhere in sight. An autopsy later made it clear that Cheryl had been strangled; the marks on her neck were consistent with bruises from a belt. Contusions on her arms suggested that she had been forcibly held. Further evidence that considerable force had been used came from a mark on her back. She had been wearing a chain with a crucifix, which had slid around between her shoulder blades. There it left its distinctive imprint. Cheryl had also been raped, quite possibly after she lost consciousness or even after she had died.

Suspicion fell first on the two janitors who had found the girl's body— Henry "Icky" Peace and his supervisor, Clarence Brandley. Within hours of the murder they had been questioned, fingerprinted, and asked for hair and blood samples. Two days later they were taken to Houston and subjected to polygraph tests. Both men passed, and both were released. The town of Conroe, however, was in an uproar. Summer was coming to an end, and the school year was about to start. Parents threatened to keep their children (especially the girls) at home unless the murderer had been arrested by the time school registration was completed. Town and school officials alike recognized that they had to act fast if the growing panic and outrage were not to overwhelm the community.

Texas Ranger Wesley Styles was asked to cut short his vacation and go to Conroe so that he could head up the probe. He complied promptly. After meeting with Montgomery County District Attorney James Keeshan and the Conroe police, he went straight to the high school. By then it was Friday afternoon, the last day of registration; school would begin the following Monday. Six days had passed since the murder. Time was running out for the authorities, and they needed to do something. Well aware of this, Ranger Styles—only a few hours after he had come onto the case and with the entire investigative squad from the police department at his side—arrested Clarence Brandley on a charge of capital murder. With a suspect in custody, school could safely start.

There were, in all, five janitors who had been working at the high school on the Saturday morning Cheryl Fergeson was murdered. Knowing that Icky Peace and Clarence Brandley had earlier passed lie detector tests and been released, Ranger Styles brought in the other three—Gary Acreman, John Sessum, and Sam Martinez—for questioning. He then took them, together, on a "walk through" of the crime. When that was completed, Acreman, Sessum, and Martinez gave their statements—which agreed in all important particulars. Each of the three gave an alibi for the other two. The defense would later allege that once Styles had arrested Brandley, he coached the other janitors, shaping a plausible and consistent story that could be used first to implicate and then to convict Brandley.

The first hint that Brandley might be charged with the crime had come on the day of the murder, when he and Peace were initially interviewed by the police. According to Peace, the officer conducting the interview had said, "One of you two is going to hang for this." And then, turning to Brandley, he added, "Since you're the nigger, you're elected."

Founded in the 1880s, Conroe began as a railroad headquarters for Montgomery County farming and logging concerns; the town lies in the Piney Woods section of East Texas. Fifty years later, it enjoyed a renewed surge of growth as an oil boomtown. By 1980 the town had a population of about eighteen thousand. Housing was largely segregated, with the majority of the small black population hunkered down in modest homes literally on the other side of the tracks. Hispanics and poor whites lived either on the edge of the black ghetto or outside town in trailers and shacks half hidden among the pine trees. Such prosperity as there was among the town's residents belonged primarily to the white upper class. And though close to Houston, Conroe was—and is—nowhere nearly so cosmopolitan as its much larger neighbor. The Ku Klux Klan was still active in Montgomery County, and political power was the preserve of the whites. For Brandley, a black, to be the supervisor of an otherwise all-white janitorial staff was unusual. He was unlikely to find a better job.

During the 1970s, the population of the county had swelled, but the influx was predominantly of whites. As a result, the black population had dwindled to less than 5 percent of the total, and the number of blacks who showed up on jury panels was consequently very small. Even those few blacks were routinely struck from trial juries. Local lawyers could recall only one time, in 1978, when a black (a police officer) had sat on a criminal jury.

Montgomery County was thus not a particularly comfortable place for blacks in trouble with the law, and memories of what had happened on previous occasions in Conroe to blacks suspected of sex crimes involving whites did nothing to lessen the tension that built up around Clarence Brandley. In 1922 a black man accused of raping a white woman was burned alive while chained to a stake on the lawn of the county court house. In 1937 a black man had the audacity to appeal his conviction in a similar case. The United States Supreme Court had ruled that he should have a new trial, but on the first day of the court proceedings the rape victim's husband shot the defendant in the head while he sat in the court room. Later, at the public prosecutor's urging, the husband was acquitted of murder. Then, in the 1970s, a black teenager was shot and killed while in police custody. The white officer who shot him was rumored to be angry because the victim had been dating his niece. The officer was not found guilty of any crime.

From the start, Brandley steadfastly insisted that he was innocent. Though he and Peace had found the body, he said he knew nothing of what had happened to the girl. There were some difficulties with his story, however, and some gaps in it. For one thing, Brandley was alone at the time of the murder (he claimed he had been in the custodian's office), which meant he had no one to vouch for him. He was supposedly the only one of the custodians who had a set of keys to the various buildings and locked rooms around the school, including the auditorium where Cheryl Ferge-son's body was found.

Furthermore, some of the evidence, even if it did not directly implicate him, was nevertheless consistent with Brandley's having committed the crime. The dead girl's clothes were discovered two days after her murder in a plastic bag, of the sort used by the custodians at the high school, in a dumpster behind the school buildings. Strings like those on the janitors' mops were found on her jeans. Three hairs were found on her body that were "the same in all observable characteristics" as Brandley's (or so the prosecution claimed—the hairs were never officially tested). Inconclusive circumstantial evidence of this sort was all the police had to go on.

In their statements to the police, janitors Gary Acreman, John Sessum, and Sam Martinez each told a story that helped fit the pieces together—though Sessum indicated he was not happy about the investigative tactics being used. The three men did not claim to have seen the crime being committed, but they did say they had seen the victim enter a rest room near the auditorium and that Brandley had arrived shortly afterwards, carrying rolls of toilet paper. They each added that, when told there was a girl inside, Brandley replied he was headed for the boys' bathroom, not the girls'. He then sent all three of the janitors to do a chore in another building, while he remained behind. As they walked away, the saw Brandley entering a nearby janitor's closet. Once the trio got to the entrance of the second building, they had to wait nearly forty-five minutes before Brandley arrived with the keys to let them in. At 11:00 A.M., the work done, Brandley told the men that they could go home.

The fourth white janitor, Icky Peace, was the one who—in Clarence Brandley's company—had actually found the girl's body. His account of events leading up to that discovery, while consistent with what his three colleagues had related, added details that cast suspicion on Brandley's behavior. Peace was planning to give Brandley a ride home, so he did not leave with the others when they were dismissed. Thus he was with Brandley when, a few minutes later, the two of them met members of the Bellville volleyball team, looking for their missing student manager. The two janitors joined the search. Brandley, Peace claimed, right away suggested that Peace check the loft over the auditorium. When Peace found nothing, Brandley sent him to look again. Still nothing. This was not good enough for Brandley, who went with Peace for a third look. Urged by Brandley to "look real good," Peace lifted a sheet of plywood and found the body under it. Brandley coolly took the girl's pulse, according to Peace, and then rushed off to notify the authorities.

Five days after his arrest, Brandley agreed to appear before an all-white grand jury. There he tried to spell out his own account of what had happened. He admitted he had sat around smoking a cigarette and listening to the radio when he should have been working. That, he said, was why the other janitors had to wait for him nearly half an hour. This discrepancy on the elapsed time—the others had said they waited forty-five minutes—was only one of the ways that Brandley's account did not jibe with the consistent story given by the white janitors. Furthermore, Brandley's admission of his apparently casual attitude toward his work made him look untrustworthy.

The judge initially assigned to try the case, Lee Alworth, stepped aside (voluntarily), but only after Brandley's lawyers, Don Brown and George Morris, accused him of bias. Hence it was before Judge Sam Robertson, Jr., that Brandley was tried in Montgomery County Court in December

1980. Like the grand jury, the trial jury was all white. Brandley testified on his own behalf, telling essentially the same story as he had from the beginning. The other janitors stuck to their stories, as well. Afterwards, the defense speculated that Brandley had perhaps done himself more harm than good. The way he had openly disagreed with several whites—indeed, he had directly contradicted them—could well have alienated the jury.

Nonetheless, a hung jury saved Brandley from conviction when one juror, William Srack, refused to vote for guilt. Srack later recounted that his fellow jurors had accused him of being a "plant" (though planted by whom, they did not say). He also said he had been called a "nigger lover" during jury deliberations. And when his vote was publicly revealed, he received a barrage of harassing phone calls. For months after the trial ended, his phone would immediately ring again every time he replaced the receiver. Srack reported the harassment to the police, and an officer came to his house to investigate. After answering the phone, the officer confirmed Srack's claim: The anonymous callers were conveying messages such as "We're going to get you, nigger lover."

The second trial took place early in February 1981, again in Conroe, before another judge, John Martin. This time, on his attorney's advice, Brandley did not testify. Neither, curiously enough, did John Sessum. The prosecution apparently decided it did not need him and could not afford to risk having him raise doubts about the story the other white janitors were telling. (Later, the defense learned Sessum had been threatened with jail for perjury if he did not stick to the agreed-upon written statement.) The other white janitors once more testified that only Brandley had keys to the auditorium where the girl's body was found. They also again supported each other's alibis, while Clarence Brandley was still not able to produce any witness who could verify precisely where he was at the time of the murder.

Additional evidence introduced at the second trial included the testimony of Danny Taylor, a junior at Conroe High who had worked with the janitorial staff for a few days earlier in the summer (until he was fired). He said that one day he and Brandley had been standing together when a group of female students walked by. Taylor recalled that Brandley had said, "If I got one of them alone, ain't no tellin' what I might do." It was also brought out that, at the time he was arrested for Cheryl Fergeson's murder, Brandley was on probation for possessing a sawed-off shotgun, a weapon he had allegedly used to try to force a woman to have sex with him. He denied the allegation, but the clear suggestion to the jury was that Brandley had an uncontrolled sexual appetite.

Medical experts testified that Brandley's belt, 1.25 inches wide, was consistent with whatever was used to strangle the victim. Morbidly titillating was the information given to the jury about Brandley's second job: He worked part-time at a funeral home. The prosecution reminded the jury that the autopsy had shown the victim had been raped after she had lost consciousness, or perhaps even after she had died. Only someone who was not repulsed by dead bodies, someone like a funeral home employee, could have committed such a crime. Perhaps, District Attorney Keeshan suggested ghoulishly in his closing arguments, Brandley was a necrophiliac, a depraved sex maniac. The prosecution further pointed out to the jury that funeral home employees put dead people's clothes in a bag, just as the killer had put Cheryl's clothes in a bag after murdering her. The defense immediately objected to these suggestions, calling them "inflammatory," but the objection was overruled.

On February 13, 1981, Clarence Lee Brandley was convicted of murder. The next day—Valentine's Day—as recommended by the jury, Judge Martin sentenced him to death.

The foreman of the jury at the second trial was later quoted as saying racism was not a factor in the case. "If there was racism involved," he said, "it was behind the scenes and it was something the jury didn't know anything about. There very definitely wasn't any racial overtone to the jury." There was no denying, however, that once again a black man charged with raping and murdering a white teenaged girl had faced an all-white jury; the prosecution had used its peremptory challenges to exclude all of the qualified blacks from the trial jury.

Eleven months after the conviction, while Brandley's attorneys were preparing an appeal, they uncovered some disturbing news. Some of the evidence used to convict Brandley, evidence that could have been used to implicate others, had mysteriously disappeared while in the hands of the prosecution during the trial. For example, photographs of Brandley taken on the day of the murder, which the defense contended would have shown that he was not wearing a belt, were gone. This was extremely important, since although Cheryl Fergeson (her team mates agreed) had been wearing a belt with her jeans, the prosecution maintained that Brandley's belt was the murder weapon. Also missing were the hair samples the Conroe police had found near the victim's vagina and on her socks, which might have been useful in identifying the true culprit. Three of the hairs, of Caucasian origin, were reddish blond; they were not Fergeson's, and they could not possibly have been Brandley's.

In all, 166 of the 309 exhibits used at trial had vanished. Even before the first trial, spermatozoa taken from the girl's body had been discarded by the county medical examiner. Thus there was no possibility of running the sophisticated tests on these samples that might have eliminated Brandley as a suspect.

The missing items later became one of the many issues in dispute;

Brandley's supporters thought the prosecution had purposely destroyed them so that Brandley could not be exonerated, and that the judge and district attorney had deliberately hidden from the defense the fact that the evidence had been lost. The district attorney called such claims "preposterous." If evidence had been lost, he insisted, it was simply a matter of sloppy police work.

Brandley's conviction and death sentence were reviewed by the Texas Court of Criminal Appeals in May 1985, four and a half years after his conviction. Despite numerous challenges raised by the defense, including that the evidence was insufficient to support the conviction, the appeal was denied with only two justices dissenting. "No reasonable hypothesis is presented by the evidence to even *suggest*," the court emphasized, "that someone other than [Brandley] committed the offense." That November, Brandley was given his first execution date: January 16, 1986. The reason for choosing that date emerged only later.

Brandley's attorneys promptly filed a writ of habeas corpus on the ground that the lost evidence had deprived Brandley of his right to a fair trial. Once before, in early 1982, they had tried to force the question of whether the evidence had been deliberately misplaced or destroyed. They had confronted Judge Martin with the fact that they knew about the missing evidence, only to have Martin and District Attorney Keeshan persist with their claims that there had been no misconduct, and no collusion between them. The defense's repeated requests for a hearing on the matter had been denied, and Judge Martin was later unwilling to discuss these requests or to acknowledge any confrontation in which the defense had threatened to have him removed from the case. Even so, a few days after the issue was again raised, Judge Martin decided to recuse himself, and the case was turned over to its fourth judge, Lynn Coker.

This time the defense team was awarded the habeas hearing for Brandley that it so desperately needed. Scheduled for the summer of 1986, the hearing meant that Brandley's January death date was canceled.

About this time, the first real break in the Brandley case came, almost six years after the crime. Brenda Medina, a young woman from neighboring Cut 'n' Shoot, Texas, came forward with dramatic new information. She claimed that her former common-law husband, James Dexter Robinson, had confessed to the murder. Medina had not bothered to report this to anyone, because she had thought he was just bragging. Not one to read newspapers or watch the news on television, she had been completely oblivious of the ugly murder of Cheryl Fergeson in August 1980, even though the victim was a girl her own age and the crime had been committed in a nearby community. Medina did not learn about the case until a neighbor happened to mention it to her in early 1986. That was the first time she had heard about a man having been convicted of murdering a girl at the very time Robinson had told her he had done just that. She also learned then that the convicted man was waiting to be executed for the crime.

At her neighbor's suggestion, Medina talked to a lawyer; he in turn urged her to go to the district attorney, Peter Speers III. (By that time, Keeshan had been appointed a state district judge by Governor Mark White; Speers, one of his young assistants, had succeeded him both as district attorney and as chief prosecutor in the Brandley case.) Speers did not believe Medina's story. Because she was facing charges herself for stealing money from her employer, he thought her entirely unreliable. He later claimed that meant he was not obligated to share with the defense the information she had provided him. The lawyer with whom Medina had first conferred thought otherwise, however, and saw to it himself that the defense learned about Medina. Richard Reyna, the private investigator working for the defense, tracked down Medina and—after she had passed a polygraph test—obtained her sworn statement.

Judge Coker presided over the 1986 habeas hearing in Conroe. John Sessum, the janitor who had testified at the first trial but not at the second, used the occasion to recant his trial testimony. This time he said he had seen one of his fellow janitors, Gary Acreman, talking with the victim for several minutes shortly before the murder, and that Acreman had later threatened him with "trouble" if he mentioned anything about it. He repeated the testimony he had given at the first trial (the testimony that led to his not being used by the prosecution in the second trial) to the effect that he had been threatened with jail if he did not stick to his written statement.

Acreman's father-in-law, Edward Payne, also testified. He acknowledged to the court that on the night of the murder Acreman had told him where the victim's clothes were hidden—two days before the police actually located them. Payne further informed the court that when he tried to report this to the district attorney he was told the office was not interested. "I've already made my case," Payne said the district attorney had told him. Later, according to what Payne told one interviewer, two unidentified men had beaten him, warning him to "keep your goddam mouth shut."

Brenda Medina was the next witness for the defense. She stated bluntly and directly that James Dexter Robinson had confessed to the murder. Robinson, also white, was a former janitor at Conroe High; he had been fired about a month prior to the murder. He came home one night late in August, Medina testified, and told her he was going to South Carolina for a while and would send for her later (she was pregnant with his child), because he had "killed a girl" and hidden the body. By the next morning he had in fact gone, leaving a pair of blood-stained sneakers behind. That had been the end of it, for Medina, at the time. Only after she learned about Cheryl Fergeson's murder years later did it occur to Medina that Robinson might have been telling the truth, and that the blood spattered on his sneakers might very well have been Cheryl's.

Robinson himself also appeared at the evidentiary hearing. He testified that indeed he had told Medina he was leaving town because he had killed a girl, but he claimed he had manufactured the story simply to scare her. She was hassling him because of her pregnancy, he insisted, and he thought he could get her off his back if she were scared enough about what he might do to her.

Acreman, now suspected by the defense of being the co-perpetrator of the murder, had not said anything about Robinson in his trial testimony. Neither had anyone else. No mention whatever had been made of Robinson's presence at the school on August 23, 1980. At the 1986 hearing, however, Acreman testified that he remembered having seen Robinson at the school, though only briefly, on the day of the murder.

Despite all this new testimony—Sessum saying Acreman talked with the victim, Payne saying Acreman knew where the victim's clothes were before the police found them, Acreman saying Robinson was at the school on the day in question, Robinson admitting he told Medina he had killed a girl, Medina saying Robinson had confessed to the murder—Judge Coker remained unimpressed. In October he recommended that Brandley's request for a new trial be denied, and on December 22 the Texas Court of Criminal Appeals followed his advice.

As 1986 ended, Brandley's situation looked bleak. By that time, however, the case had attracted tremendous attention not just in the black communities of Conroe and Houston, but among human rights advocates nationwide as well. In late February 1987, responding to a new execution date having been set, a thousand protestors marched through the streets of Conroe. Waving signs with slogans like "Stop the Racist Death Penalty," the crowd cheered as speakers denounced capital punishment and demanded Brandley's freedom. Hundreds turned out at Conroe College (a small black Bible school) for a barbecued chicken dinner, arranged as a fund-raiser for Brandley's appeals. A "Free Clarence Brandley" coalition was formed, and $80,000 was raised to help pay legal fees. Ministers, civil rights leaders, and even some politicians—including United States Representative Mickey Leland—joined the call for a stay of execution and a re-opening of the case.

A thousand citizens protesting a black man's impending execution in East Texas in the 1980s? An extraordinary phenomenon, to say the least. The last time there had been a public protest of an American execution on this scale was when Caryl Chessman (who was white) was executed in

California in May 1960. Certainly, massive protests on behalf of death row inmates are not common.

With execution day—March 26, 1987—just around the corner, the number of public protest meetings grew. On one occasion, two hundred protestors gathered in Austin, the state capital. Their voices strengthened by the presence of three members of the state legislature and representatives from the human rights group Amnesty International, they protested the conviction and demanded an appointment with the governor. The governor's office and the state pardons board were flooded with letters and phone calls. Eventually even Attorney General Jim Mattox joined the cry for a stay of execution, not because he was convinced of Brandley's innocence, but because he agreed that Brandley's attorneys deserved more time to gather evidence.

Meanwhile, a strong and talented ally had joined the defense team. In November 1986 the phone had rung in the office of Centurion Ministries in Princeton, New Jersey. Clarence Brandley's brother, the Reverend Ozell Brandley, was calling James McCloskey. A former seminary student, McCloskey had abandoned studies leading to a traditional ministerial position in favor of working full-time to secure freedom for innocent prisoners. McCloskey had received many similar calls; since 1983 he had helped to free a half dozen prisoners erroneously convicted of rape, murder, and other serious felonies. Centurion Ministries—unlike Gardner's Court of Last Resort in the 1940s—was a low-budget organization, however, so McCloskey could help very few of the hundreds who requested his assistance. Ozell Brandley pleaded with McCloskey to come to Houston and investigate his brother's case. McCloskey had to be in New Orleans in mid-February on other business, and while there he decided to fly on to Houston to see what he could learn about the Brandley case. Once in Houston, he met with Mike DeGeurin and Paul Nugent (Brandley's appeal attorneys), with trial attorney Don Brown (George Morris had succumbed to cancer without knowing whether his efforts on Brandley's behalf would be successful), and with investigator Richard Reyna.

On March 2, Texas Independence Day, McCloskey visited Brandley on Texas's death row, twelve miles north of Huntsville. Brandley "didn't try to sell me on his innocence," McCloskey told a reporter. "He simply answered all the questions that I asked in a very simple, basic, forthright way. I walked away from that three-and-a-half hours thinking, 'This guy's innocent as a baby—and nobody believed him at the trial.' " As a result, McCloskey decided to get involved, even though doing so meant breaking his usual rules. He rarely took on a case where the defendant already had a legal team in place, as Brandley did. Brown had not abandoned him the way trial attorneys often do in death penalty cases, leaving their clients in the lurch. Nor had Brown's investigator, Reyna. They continued to give full cooperation to attorneys DeGeurin and Nugent, who had come forward to handle the appeal, working harder than ever (at great personal sacrifice) after Brandley was convicted. Indeed, they stuck with the case until the very end. Thus it could be argued that Brandley needed McCloskey's help less than many other prisoners who sought it.

On the other hand, Brandley was only a few weeks away from a date in the execution chamber. He needed all the help he could get, and he needed it quickly. McCloskey agreed to work with Reyna, rather than alone, and for several weeks the two men traveled the state, knocked on doors, and collected new evidence that would make the pieces of the puzzle fit together.

They began by talking with John Sessum, whose testimony at the evidentiary hearing suggested that he was the most likely one of the three janitors to break down. Defense investigators had already noticed, when they tried to interview Acreman, that he kept asking what Sessum had told them. Sessum, they figured, might know more than he was letting on. When McCloskey (wearing his clerical collar) and Reyna found Sessum, it quickly became clear that getting him to talk was not going to be easy. To the surprise of his two visitors, however, Sessum suddenly volunteered to re-enact what he knew of the crime. Yet when they met him at the high school a few days later, as scheduled, Sessum stood at the bottom of the stairs where he said he had seen Acreman talking to Fergeson and simply stopped in his tracks, silent. Apparently he had changed his mind; he would tell the investigators nothing.

Another week passed before they were again able to convince him that he should talk. This time they even persuaded him to let them videotape his remarks. With the tape running, he elaborated on his court room statement of a few months earlier. Not only had he seen Acreman with the victim—he had also seen James Robinson. He admitted he had turned away, in cowardly fashion ("I guess I've got a little rabbit in me"), and therefore had not seen which of the two had grabbed the girl. But he had heard the victim's cries of "No!" and "Don't!" coming from inside the rest room, for "a couple or three minutes." Then silence. "She meant it," Sessum said. "My mind and heart told me that."

McCloskey and Reyna next confronted Acreman with the news that a witness had changed his testimony. Acreman began to shake so hard that he had to sit on his hands to keep them still. With McCloskey urging him on, saying he would feel better for getting it all out, Acreman—like Sessum—agreed to make a statement on videotape. His account of what had happened was that Robinson alone had abducted the victim. Later Acreman tried to take back his testimony. Then, his mood wildly vacillating, he instead agreed to make another videotape to clarify his story. On the second video, he confirmed what he had said in the first and added that he had seen Robinson dispose of Fergeson's clothes in the dumpster.

Still later, according to the prosecution, Acreman recanted both tapes. But when word of the recantation came out, two entirely new witnesses surfaced. The *Dallas Times Herald* quoted attorney Mike DeGeurin as saying these witnesses, two women, were "reliable, upright citizens." They told the defense they had more than once heard Acreman say, "Clarence did not kill that girl. I know who did. Clarence did not do it, but I will never tell."

On March 20, Judge Coker granted a stay of execution, largely on the strength of the videotaped statements by Acreman and Sessum. The countdown to execution had reached six days.

Having thus gained time for further investigation, the defense promptly filed a request for yet another evidentiary hearing. Icky Peace, the janitor who had been the State's chief witness, was by then willing to repeat for the defense his recollection of the police officer saying to Brandley, "Since you're the nigger, you're elected." Other evidence of overt racism was turning up, too, quite apart from the brute fact that a black man charged with raping and killing a white girl had been tried by two all-white juries.

There was the way William Srack, the lone holdout for Brandley's acquittal in the first trial, had repeatedly been called a "nigger lover." The defense also learned that reference books used by the district attorney's office were racist, containing, for example, explicit recommendations that prospective black jurors be rejected, whether for cause or by peremptory challenge. There was also racial tension in the court room itself during the trial. A witness testified that she had heard an old woman chanting, "Kill that nigger. Kill that nigger." Although those remarks had been drawn to the attention of court officers, the woman had not been removed.

The defense established that the locks on the auditorium door were so faulty that no one really needed keys to get in—and that Brandley was in any case not the only person with keys to the room. Furthermore, the bruises on the victim's body were consistent with one person having held her down while another raped her. District Attorney Speers, however, was not convinced; he remained adamant about his judgment that Brandley, and Brandley alone, was the guilty party. He told the *New York Times,* "There is absolutely no way that anyone else on the face of the earth could have committed this crime." Nonetheless, by the end of March Speers had added his voice to those requesting an investigation by the state attorney general's office. He hoped the independent examination would deflect the defense team's criticisms and deflate the groundswell of support that Brandley was beginning to receive.

A long editorial in the *Dallas Times Herald* on March 29 urged the

U.S. Department of Justice to conduct an investigation into the possibility that Brandley's civil rights had been violated. Such a review was promised, and the FBI also decided to intervene. Five days later, the *Austin American Statesman* ran an editorial under the title "Brandley case points up problem of death penalty."

On June 30, 1987, the Texas Court of Criminal Appeals ordered that an evidentiary hearing be held to investigate the defense team's allegations. The hearing opened in Conroe in September, before Special State District Judge Perry Pickett. Pickett, 71, had been on the bench for thirty-three years. He had retired in 1981, but still heard cases when a visiting judge was needed. District Attorney Henry Wade of Dallas said of him, "He's one of the nicest fellows I've known, and I don't think he has a dishonest bone in him. He's about as fair a judge as you can find." A few days into the hearing, the scores of Brandley's supporters in the court room generally agreed with that assessment.

On the first day of the hearing, William Srack offered his testimony about having been called a "nigger lover." When he heard that, Judge Pickett promptly concluded that "there exists here a volatile and explosive situation not conducive to the administration of justice," and he moved the hearing from Conroe to Galveston. But there was more. Srack went on to recount what had happened when he later applied for a position as the county's purchasing agent. The county's district judges had conducted the interview; most of the questions, Srack stated, had concerned his vote on the Brandley case. He was told that his "Not guilty" vote was evidence he could not get along with people. He did not get the job.

Gary Acreman tried to recant his videotaped remarks while he was on the stand, but he stuck with his recent recollection that Robinson had indeed been at the high school when the murder occurred. Acreman also repeatedly said that Brandley had nothing to do with the murder—that he was "being railroaded." Then Icky Peace, too, admitted that he had perjured himself at trial. He had done so because he was afraid of Texas Ranger Wesley Styles and of being prosecuted for perjury if his testimony differed from his initial written statement. He claimed that Styles had come to his home one evening, thrown him against a wall, started to choke him, and threatened to "blow his brains out," all because he showed signs of wanting to back away from his trial statement.

Ranger Styles denied these allegations, but the spotlight continued to shine on his shoddy investigative work and his "blind focus" on Brandley. Styles said he had spent five hundred hours on the case, but when pressed he admitted that all but the first few of those hours came after Clarence Brandley was already in jail, charged with the murder. "The Ranger and other investigators were not trying to find the murderer; they were trying to convict Clarence Brandley," declared defense lawyer Paul Nugent. It was Styles who had met with Acreman, Martinez, and Sessum a week after the murders, re-creating for them the sequence of events on the day of the crime with the help of Gary Acreman (who had done most of the talking). And it was during that "walk through" with Styles, according to Sessum, that the janitors had been coached to produce a consistent story. Sessum also repeated for the judge his videotaped statement that he had initially lied on the witness stand and insisted that, in truth, he had seen Acreman grab Cheryl Fergeson.

Among the others who testified at the Galveston hearing were some individuals who had worked at the Conroe court house during the Brandley trials. Janet Dial, who had been Judge Martin's secretary at the time, testified that working on the case had been "like working on a project to convict Clarence Brandley." Court reporter Mary Johnson added several minor points that helped re-create the trial atmosphere. First, for example, she insisted that the missing evidence could never have been thrown out by mistake, as the prosecution had suggested. "I do not know how anybody could have thrown those exhibits away thinking they were trash," she said. In other words, she thought their disappearance must have been deliberately arranged. Second, Judge Martin had promised to decide whether to grant probation to a client of defense attorney Mike DeGeurin's brother, also an attorney, based on how DeGeurin treated him in the court room in the Brandley hearing. Third, Judge Martin had agreed to set January 16 as the execution date for Brandley at the request of his clerk; she wanted the execution to take place on her birthday. Judge Martin denied all these claims, but Judge Pickett concluded that his judicial colleague's testimony "was simply not credible."

The defense also used the hearing as an occasion to report on new research showing that in Texas, other factors being held constant, the race of the victim is a strong predictor of who is sentenced to death. The person most likely to receive the death penalty in Texas is a black man convicted of raping and murdering a white woman.

The hearing before Judge Pickett ended on October 9 with a dramatic victory for Brandley. The judge's ringing condemnation of the procedure was much quoted in the Texas newspapers: "For the past ten days, I have presided over the evidentiary hearing to try to determine if equal justice under the law has been self-evident from all of the evidence adduced under oath. The litany of events graphically described by the witnesses, some of it chilling and shocking, leads me to the conclusion [in this case that] the pervasive shadow of darkness has obscured the light of fundamental decency and human rights."

The judge found the State's investigative procedure to be "so impermissibly suggestive that false testimony was created, thereby denying . . . due process of law and a fundamentally fair trial." He went on to say that the State had "wholly ignored any evidence or leads to evidence that might prove inconsistent with their premature conclusion that Brandley had committed the murder. The conclusion is inescapable that the investigation was conducted not to solve the crime, but to convict Brandley." As if that were not condemnation enough, Judge Pickett added that "in the thirty years that this court has presided over matters in the judicial system, no case has presented a more shocking scenario of the effects of racial prejudice . . . and public officials who for whatever motives lost sight of what is right and just." Leaving no doubt at all about what he thought lay behind Brandley's conviction, Pickett wrote, "The court unequivocally concludes that the color of Clarence Brandley's skin was a substantial factor which pervaded all aspects of the State's capital prosecution against him."

Judge Pickett could not free Brandley; he could only make a recommendation. But to the applause of hundreds of Brandley's supporters, led by Brandley's parents, he announced a willingness to propose to the Texas Court of Criminal Appeals that Brandley receive a new trial—and that it be held outside Montgomery County. He went further, stating that "the testimony . . . unequivocally establishes that Gary Acreman and James Dexter Robinson are prime suspects and probably were responsible for the death of Cheryl Dee Fergeson."

The next move was up to the Court of Criminal Appeals. Brandley rejoined his 260 companions on Texas's death row for another long wait. It was a month before Judge Pickett's written recommendations were forwarded to the court in Austin, and the spring of 1988 had rolled around before written briefs were requested from Brandley's attorneys and from District Attorney Speers. In October, when there still had been no ruling, Judge Pickett spoke out on the failure of the appeals court to act on his recommendation. "To put it as delicately and diplomatically as possible," the *Dallas Times Herald* quoted him as saying, "I'm a little surprised it's taken a year. This is the anniversary of the hearing in Galveston and nothing has happened." At the end of November 1988, the court at last requested oral arguments on the case, which were held on January 18, 1989. In October 1989, Brandley passed the second anniversary of the Galveston hearings still waiting in his cell on death row.

Finally, on December 13, 1989, the long-awaited ruling came: Brandley would be given a new trial. The court split, however, and the disagreement among the judges was acrimonious. The *Dallas Times Herald* described the court's opinion in these words: "In unusually nasty asides, [Judge David A.] Berchelman accuses [a dissenting judge] of quoting testimony out of context, offering 'gratuitous personal observations' and making 'an impassioned attempt' to refute 'overwhelming evidence' that Brandley was hounded to Death Row by a racist team of police and prosecutors who refused to consider evidence that could have proven Brandley innocent."

The court's ruling was clear. "Our society wins not only when the guilty are convicted but when criminal trials are fair," said Judge Berchelman, writing for the majority; "our system of justice suffers when an accused is treated unfairly." He concluded that, in Brandley's case, "the State's investigative procedure produced a trial lacking the rudiments of fairness."

The presiding judge, in his dissent, mocked the defense's (and the majority opinion's) contention that racism was involved. "The majority . . . reasons that the presence of a racial slur in and of itself can exonerate [the] applicant," he wrote. He went on to give solace to District Attorney Speers by saying "there is no evidence which remotely tends to exculpate applicant or to show that he is not guilty." Berchelman in reply had strong words of his own: "The violent end to Cheryl Fergeson's young life is both senseless and tragic. . . . Our outrage over her murder, however, cannot justify the subversion of justice that took place during the investigation, which ultimately affected the trial of her accused perpetrator."

After the Court of Criminal Appeals handed down its ruling, Jim McCloskey emphasized to the press that Brandley's case was not unique. "Clarence Brandley is lucky. He's lucky because his case developed a lot of notoriety. A lot of good and competent people came to his aid—the public, lawyers and investigators. He's lucky because there are a lot of Clarence Brandleys and they are still buried in prison or on Death Row."

Brandley, in his cell in Huntsville, received the good news from reporters. "It will make my Christmas," he said. "It's something I didn't think would come this year." But Brandley was not to be home for Christmas; the Court of Criminal Appeals refused to free him while he awaited his new trial. And on December 14, District Attorney Speers said he would ask the court to rehear the case and to alter its retrial order.

On January 17, 1990, the rehearing was denied. Immediately Speers, who continued in his confident insistence that Brandley was guilty (he said the three dissents showed he was right), announced he would appeal to the United States Supreme Court. Meanwhile, bail was set at $75,000, and when bond was posted a week later, Brandley's nine-year confinement on death row came to an end. A photograph of Clarence Brandley walking out through the prison gates made its way into newspapers around the world.

On October 1, more than ten years after the murder of Cheryl Fergeson, the Supreme Court denied certiorari, thereby rejecting prosecutor Speers's request to overturn the decision of the Court of Criminal

Appeals. A few hours after the Supreme Court's ruling, Speers capitulated, asking for all charges against Brandley to be dismissed. With no evidence on which to base a retrial, there was little else he could do. Speers's appeal to the Supreme Court turned out to have been no more than a public relations bluff and a way to prolong Clarence Brandley's agony as long as possible.

In the months following his release on bail, Brandley was ordained a Baptist minister. He worked as an apprentice electrician in Houston, and a short time later he was married. None of the police, prosecutors, or judges who played a role in erroneously convicting Brandley was ever disciplined.

※

THE VULNERABILITY of a black defendant to an unjust conviction and a death sentence is nowhere more evident than in rape-murder cases like Brandley's. But a charge of rape, even without murder, when the offender is black and the victim white has often proved just as catastrophic. Two cases that occurred years before Brandley's illustrate the point.

Late in December 1931, some months after the Scottsboro Boys had been arrested in Alabama, 22-year-old Jess Hollins, black, was taken into custody near Tulsa, Oklahoma. A white woman, joined by her brother-in-law, had brought charges against Hollins for rape. Fearful of lynching and without legal counsel, he waived his right to a jury trial and pleaded guilty in the belief that doing so would spare him the electric chair. The plea was accepted by Judge Gaylord Wilcox, who promptly sentenced Hollins to death. From beginning to end, the proceedings took less than an hour.

As with the Scottsboro Boys, so with Hollins: The International Labor Defense Committee of the American Communist Party vied with the NAACP in pursuing appellate relief. Both organizations were convinced that Hollins was innocent of any crime—and that he had merely engaged in consensual sexual relations with his accuser, a 17-year-old girl. Local support for Hollins was led by editor Roscoe Dunjee of the Oklahoma *Black Dispatch*. Good news came in September 1932 when the state appeals court reversed the conviction, acknowledging that "this ignorant, defenseless Negro, with the terror of the mob in his mind, did not and could not voluntarily do anything"; his guilty plea was thus legally worthless.

Hopes for Hollins plummeted in February 1934 when, at a retrial before an all-white jury, he was again convicted and again sentenced to death. His accuser, Alta McCullom, told the jury that Hollins had encountered her along a country road and repeatedly raped her. The defense offered black witnesses who testified that she was an habitué of local black dance halls and that her reputation left much to be desired. But few white Oklahomans in 1936 were ready to believe a white woman would voluntarily have sexual relations with a black man—and even fewer were willing to believe something like that on a black man's word against a white woman's denial.

Hollins was scheduled to be electrocuted on May 13, 1935. When only thirty hours remained and Hollins's head had already been shaved for the electrodes, Charles H. Houston of the NAACP obtained a stay of execution pursuant to a hearing before the United States Supreme Court. On the day of Hollins's scheduled execution, the Supreme Court ordered his conviction reversed on the ground that blacks had been systematically excluded from the jury, in violation of the equal protection clause of the Fourteenth Amendment.

In February 1936, at his third trial—again before an all-white jury—McCullom presented much the same testimony against Hollins. Taking the stand in his own defense for the first time, Hollins admitted to having sexual intercourse with the defendant, claiming she had consented after they met at a dance. Again, defense witnesses testified to McCullom's frequenting black dance halls and that blacks viewed her as white trash. W. Shearer Brown, Hollins's counsel, charged that she had accused his client of rape only because her brother-in-law had come upon the pair in flagrante delicto. The jury reconvicted Hollins, but this time sentenced him to life in prison.

Exhausted from his four-year struggle to avoid death row, Hollins refused to appeal his conviction and gave up the fight to clear his name. He died in prison, largely forgotten, in 1950.

"THE SOUTH Kills Another Negro," wrote author William Bradford Huie after he had witnessed the trial of Roosevelt Collins in Alabama. The South did, indeed, and it did so under the aegis of the law, in one of the gravest miscarriages of justice recorded in this book.

In July 1937, while the Scottsboro Boys rape case was continuing its odyssey through the courts, Collins, 22, was charged in Anniston, Alabama, with rape of a white woman. Collins's young life was in the hands of two aging white attorneys who reluctantly accepted the court's assignment as his defense counsel. Arrayed against him were the Alabama attorney general as well as the local prosecutor and his subordinates.

Collins's accuser was (in Huie's words) a "husky, loose-jointed farm woman, perhaps thirty, with big, red hands, big feet, and a matted mass of blonde hair." Her husband sat grimly beside her. On the stand, she told the crowded court room and the all-white jury that she had been assaulted in a potato field by Collins, who—gun in hand—had forced her to submit. Other witnesses testified that he had then run off into the woods when some white farmers chased after him. No explanation was given for why the alleged victim, whom Huie described as weighing a good thirty pounds more than Collins, did not "knock him silly when he laid the gun down."

After the noon recess, Collins took the stand in his own defense. Huie covered the case in person, and wrote: "If you had struck a match while [Collins] was walking to the stand, the courtroom would have exploded. I have never felt such tension, such organized hate focused on one insignificant object." Collins, in telling his version (as Huie reported it), said he had asked her "de question an' she lukked aroun' an' said she wuz willin'. . . ."

That was the spark; the court room exploded. Amid shouts and threats, the woman's husband whipped out a .45 pistol, fired it at Collins, missed, and fired again. Before he could get off another shot he was wrestled to the floor and disarmed. With order eventually restored, Collins finished his testimony and then faced an hour's aggressive cross-examination. He stuck to his story and calmly insisted on his innocence. The jury recessed for four minutes and brought back a guilty verdict and a death sentence.

Huie heard all the testimony and thought Collins was telling the truth. So did the trial judge and several of the jurors, he discovered in later interviews. Yet as one of them told him, it didn't matter that Collins was innocent and the woman had lied under oath. "What the hell, he deserves the chair for messin' around with a white woman." In April 1937, the Alabama Supreme Court sustained the conviction. Without further ceremony, Collins was put to death that June.

PART THREE

CORRUPT

PRACTICES

7

A

SMEAR

OF BLOOD

AND PAINT

O N   A   S A T U R D A Y afternoon late in November 1955, 12-year-old Jimmy May and his dog, Cuddles, cut across the railroad freight yard near his house in Canton, Illinois. He knew the area well; the freight yard with its piles of abandoned railroad mine cars was his usual short cut to his grandmother's house.

This time was different, though. Jimmy and his older brother, Bill, were supposed to have been watching their little sister Janice, but she had disappeared from the house when they went out briefly. The two brothers had set out in opposite directions to look for her. As Jimmy told it later, "I got to the cars and heard a noise. I looked under one car and thought it was a dog that went under there to die. I ran home to tell my brother."

It wasn't a dog that Jimmy had found, as the boys quickly discovered when they went back to the freight yard together. Bill crawled between the empty mine cars, and there he found 8-year-old Janice on her knees, with her face in the dirt. She was moaning. The boys could see that she had been badly beaten and cut; all she had on was her shirt and her shoes, and there was a lot of blood around. Terrified, they ran for help.

In fact, Janice—a blond-haired, blue-eyed third grader with deep dimples—had suffered a brutal injury to her head, multiple skull fractures, and severe internal bruises. She had clearly been sexually assaulted. Barely alive when she was found, the child was dead two hours later.

For the year 1955, the FBI reported 6,850 cases of murder and nonnegligent manslaughter in the United States. Janice May was one of those victims.

On the day of Janice's death, Lloyd Eldon Miller, Jr., slept late. A Canton cab driver on the night shift, he needed his rest. By 5:00 P.M. on that Saturday, he was back behind the wheel of his yellow cab, ready for another long night's work. For the next eight hours he responded to calls in Canton and the surrounding area as usual. The murder was soon the talk of the town. In conversations with the local police and with others during the evening, Miller showed some interest in the crime, and even stopped by the police station a couple of times to find out what was going on. After working his cab until the early hours of Sunday morning, the day after the murder, Miller went back to the rooming house where he lived. He packed a suitcase and drove his cab out of Canton, headed toward Detroit.

By making a phone call, Miller learned that he could catch a 5:55 A.M. Illini-Swallow bus in Pekin, twenty miles east of Canton. He drove across the Illinois River and abandoned the cab on a side road. It was only a short walk to the bus stop, and he was soon on his way to Champaign. By mid-morning he was in Danville, on the Indiana border. There, too tired to continue traveling, Miller registered in a hotel. He slept until late the next morning.

Lloyd Miller was not a man of predictable behavior or regular habits. He was 29 years old, an army veteran of World War II. After discharge from the service, he had drifted from job to job and from marriage to marriage; in the space of seven years, he had married four different women. He was, as his attorney later described him, "a man of flaws." No big trouble with the law, mind you, except for a tendency to go A.W.O.L.—first from the United States Army, then from the Coast Guard—and then turn himself in. This time he was A.W.O.L. from the cab company. His family life was no steadier than his employment record. As his fourth wife once told him, he was "not too good a husband." Though his second wife bore him a son, fatherhood didn't suit him, either. On the day before Janice May was murdered, Miller had received a letter from his son's mother threatening to have him arrested for failure to provide court-ordered child support. That made leaving town seem like a good idea.

When Miller finally roused himself in Danville on Monday morning, he went down the street from his hotel looking for some breakfast. While he was eating, he was alarmed to hear on the radio that he was wanted in Canton for the murder of Janice May. Scared and uncertain what to do next, he decided to continue on his way to Detroit. He figured that by the time he arrived there, the police would have the true culprit under arrest, and his name would be cleared.

What Miller didn't know was that in the hours following his departure from Canton, every police officer in the city had been called in to search for the killer. The Canton police station was soon swarming with local and state police, deputy sheriffs, and police officers from several nearby communities. When it occurred to the attorney for the State that there might be a connection between the murder and the cab reported missing, its driver—Miller—became his prime suspect.

When Miller entered the Danville bus station asking for schedule information and a ticket, the alert ticket agent stalled. Thinking Miller fit the description of the suspect wanted for the murder of Janice May, the agent called the police. Within minutes, Miller was under arrest. One of the arresting officers was John Anderson, the former sheriff of Fulton County, acting as a special deputy. He had already tracked Miller as far as Danville. One reason Anderson had been sent out on Miller's trail was that he had known Miller for four years and so would easily recognize him on sight. That might also have been a factor in Miller's prompt admission, as he was being arrested, that he had taken and then abandoned the cab. But equally quickly, Miller said in later testimony, he stoutly maintained that if they wanted him for the killing of "the little girl over at Canton," they had the wrong man. "I didn't do it," he insisted.

Two days later, however, Miller signed a full confession. After one mistrial in June of 1956, he was convicted in September of murdering Janice May and sentenced to death in November. He thus became one of 147 prisoners on death rows in the nation's prisons that year. He was scheduled to be executed on January 18, 1957.

The events of the next few years took Lloyd Miller on an emotional roller-coaster ride. First, the scheduled execution was stayed for an appeal to Illinois's supreme court. That court affirmed the conviction and sentence, and in 1958 Miller was rescheduled for electrocution. Then the second death date, like the first, was canceled, when execution was again stayed. In fact, over a five-year period, Miller faced a total of seven death dates; once he came within seven and a half hours of being executed. Each time, however, he received a stay of execution. Thus in a way, despite everything, Lloyd Miller has to count as a lucky man—because in the end, the re-investigation of the evidence against him established that he was not guilty of the crime. Even so, it was not until 1967, after eleven years of incarceration, that Miller was freed. And it was 1971 before the indictment was dismissed, ending all proceedings.

Miller's innocence was established because of the industry of his postconviction attorneys, especially Willard J. Lassers. The Miller family had turned to the American Civil Liberties Union (ACLU) for help and Lassers was one of several volunteer attorneys who became involved at the request of the Illinois chapter. It was Lassers who obtained a reversal of the conviction that brought Miller to the brink of the electric chair. And it was Lassers who wrote up the story in his book, *Scapegoat Justice,* producing in the process one of the finest case studies on record of wrongful conviction involving a death sentence. The Miller case, Lassers said, was not merely an "isolated failure of the American legal system," but rather a "demonstration of the weakness of an institution." For Lassers, the story was more than a dramatic tale of one individual's terrifying ordeal, the life-and-death struggle of an innocent man. The Miller case showed clearly the "ineptness, crudity, and unfairness" of the American system of criminal justice.

Miller was repeatedly the victim of due-process errors: prejudicial pretrial publicity, inexperienced defense counsel, inadequate investigation of the crime, incorrect rulings by the trial judge, suppression of evidence by the prosecution, perjury by witnesses, and more. But these errors do not go to the heart of the matter; by themselves they might not have led to the erroneous conviction. That error rested primarily on three factors.

First, Miller was convicted because he confessed and because the police, the prosecutor, and the jury believed his confession. Second, Miller confessed because the circumstantial evidence with which the police confronted him made it look as though he was sure to be convicted, and he feared he might be sentenced to death unless he confessed. And third, once the authorities learned that Miller had left town shortly after the murder, their search for other possible suspects abruptly ended. They concentrated on finding ways to re-inforce their belief that Miller was guilty; they allowed themselves to be persuaded by the superficial and indirect appearance of his guilt.

A frightened suspect, a patchwork quilt of physical evidence, and complacent police work combined to rob Lloyd Miller of eleven years of his freedom. How did it happen? How could the American system of justice be capable of such "gross, shocking and scandalous abuses," as Lassers put it?

After being arrested in Danville that Monday afternoon in November 1955, Miller was taken to the offices of the Illinois Bureau of Criminal Identification and Investigation in Springfield, the state capital. There he agreed to take a lie detector test. First, though, the police fingerprinted him and took samples of his blood and his pubic hair. Then the serious questioning began. (Police records give a version of what happened and how long it all lasted that differs from Miller's account, though some of the details are undisputed.)

Miller explained that he had left Canton because "I had a—been threatened by a child abandonment warrant from my . . . wife." The police were unimpressed. They showed him a gray jacket found in a stream a few blocks from the freight yard, and suggested that he had been wearing it when the murder occurred. Miller denied it was his, only to be told by his interrogators that he was lying. Then he was shown a pair of white jockey shorts with what appeared to be dried blood on them. The shorts had been found in an empty apartment building across from the railroad yard; the police believed they belonged to the murderer. Miller denied that the shorts were his, insisting that he always wore boxer shorts. The police next showed him a piece of bloody concrete, presumed to be the murder weapon, found beside Janice May's body. They asked him to admit that he had gone to pick up clothes at the cleaner's on the fateful Saturday afternoon, showing him a ticket with the name "Miller" on it; they showed him photographs of the dead girl. Miller denied knowledge of all these things.

Then, according to Miller, one of the polygraph operators asked, "Why don't you admit this so we can get you to a mental institution for mental care?" To that he replied, "I am not admitting to no crime that I didn't do. I am not admitting to no crime that I did not commit." The interrogation went on for hours; finally, around 3:00 A.M., the exhausted Miller was ushered back to his cell.

After a twelve-hour respite, Miller was again taken from his cell for questioning. This time he was in for a further surprise. Seated across from him next to the police officer was Betty Baldwin, a Canton waitress he had been dating. More than that, she claimed that he had asked her to marry him. She had given the police a statement with her version of the events of the evening after the murder, and the officer read it to Miller.

According to Baldwin's story, she and Miller had driven around together in his cab on Saturday evening. The key passages in her statement were remarks she attributed to Miller, words that could be interpreted as veiled allusions to his having just done something awful. Other comments she claimed she'd heard him make suggested that he had gotten rid of some incriminating evidence by throwing it onto a passing freight train.

That part of her statement especially shocked Miller. "Do you want me to go to the chair for something I didn't do?" he asked her in disbelief. She "just grinned," he later testified, while the police led her out of the room. Miller's defense counsel did not see the text of Baldwin's statement until six years after Miller had been convicted, though it clearly was a crucial piece of the evidence piling up against him.

The police then said they had proof that Miller's pubic hair matched hairs found on the victim's body. Miller asked to look through the microscope to see for himself. Inexperienced though he was in such matters, he thought the mismatch was clear. "The hairs don't match!" he snorted in indignation. "Them hairs don't belong to me." The authorities apparently thought otherwise. The police did concede, however, that the results of their lie detector test were "inconclusive." At first Miller thought this would surely get him off the hook. "I know that lie detector test is telling the truth," he said. "I mean it too." Before long he began to worry, though. The police kept hinting that things would go worse for him if he did not confess. To Miller, as he said in later testimony, it seemed clear that he was in danger of "getting the chair" unless he confessed to the murder.

On the second day, after another five hours of questioning, Miller was presented with a written "confession," drawn up in the form of his answers to questions the police had asked. The text neatly summarized their view of what Miller had done immediately before, during, and after the murder. The authorities later testified that they had read the statement to Miller; he said they had not. In any case, he broke down and signed the document, thinking he had no other option. Much later, he explained himself: "I was so worn out and tired and I did not know what to do. . . . I finally signed the paper. I did not read it and it was not read to me. I signed the paper because, I tell you, I don't want to go to the electric chair for something I didn't do."

From the time of his arrest to the time he signed the confession. Miller was on his own. No lawyer, no telephone call to anyone, no contact with his parents. At one point he was even told his parents had said they wanted nothing to do with him. He did not believe it. "I says 'You are lying,' " he later testified. "I know my parents." (As it subsequently turned out, he was right.) Given the circumstances, it is not surprising that Lloyd Miller caved in under pressure. Although no one ever accused the Illinois authorities of using third-degree methods to get Miller to confess, there is no doubt they were extremely persistent and persuasive. And they seemed to have the deck stacked in their favor.

The "confession" had Miller stating that, at about 2:30 on Saturday afternoon, he met young Janice May and enticed her into taking a walk with him along the railroad tracks. There he sexually molested her, and then when "she started screaming and crying . . . I went hysterical, . . . struck her, . . . she fell and hit her head on a cement block." After shoving the girl under the railroad car, he went into an abandoned apartment building nearby where he removed his bloody jockey shorts and his gray jacket (which also had some blood on it) and put his trousers back on. From there he went to the cleaner's to pick up a clean shirt and pair of pants, which he had left to be laundered a few days earlier. He changed into the clean clothes back in his room, threw his bloodstained trousers into an open boxcar on a passing train, dropped his jacket over a bridge into a creek, picked up his girl friend (the waitress Betty Baldwin), and drove off with her in his cab.

This account of Miller's behavior was more or less consistent with that given in Baldwin's statement. From the time Miller got on the bus to the time of his arrest, the police knew his every move; their own observations and investigations supplied the details. But without the confession, there would have been no case against Miller at all—and the prosecution knew it.

Most of the confession later proved to be inconsistent with various facts of the murder. All of it having to do directly with the crime itself was worthless. Yet both the police and the prosecution believed it, perhaps in part because they so badly wanted to. When the confession was introduced at Miller's trial, it must have made the plea of "Not guilty" entered on his behalf look like a mere formality. When he himself took the stand and repudiated the statement, it must have seemed he was lying and simply going through the predictable motions of a doomed man.

Miller's confession came, however, only after the police had confronted him with numerous pieces of physical evidence. The chunk of bloody concrete, the dry cleaner's ticket, the discarded gray jacket, the pubic hairs under a microscope, and the crucial jockey shorts appeared to forge a chain of circumstantial evidence linking him to the murder of Janice May. The police had also talked about clothes supposedly found on a freight train and the clothes they said Miller had picked up from the cleaner's (using the claim ticket they had in hand). The cumulative effect of all this on Miller, in the immediate aftermath of his arrest, was overwhelming. He was frightened and confused.

In truth, though, the physical evidence—once it was properly understood—failed to incriminate Miller at all. Take the claim ticket, for example. In her original statement to the police, the clerk from the dry cleaner's declared that late on the afternoon of the murder a man who had "what looked like blood on the front of his clothes" handed her a ticket with a "dark smear" on it. He reclaimed a shirt and pair of trousers. When it was put in evidence, the ticket—showing a date five days prior to the murder—had the name "Miller" penciled on it.

But was the smear on the ticket blood? Was there really blood on the man's clothes? Was "Miller" a reference to *Lloyd* Miller? Was the name written on the ticket before or after the crime and arrest? And was Lloyd Miller the man who picked up a shirt and pair of trousers at the cleaner's on the afternoon of the murder?

The clerk testified that the man was Miller and that he picked up the clothes about an hour after the murder. She added that, as he left the store, she noticed his hands "had red smudges on them." The ticket was never put into evidence by the prosecution, however, and the precise time the clothes were collected was never established. And quite in contrast to what was stated in the confession prepared for Miller's signature, the clothes themselves apparently were never found—certainly not in Miller's possession. Miller consistently denied ever having gone to the cleaner's or having had a dry cleaner's claim ticket.

Significantly, the cleaner's clerk did not testify that the gray jacket the police had found in the freight yard was the jacket worn by the man who came to the store to pick up his cleaning. In addition, the State's chemist testified during the trial that the jacket had bloodstains on it but said they were so few and so slight that it was not possible to determine the blood type, or even whether it was human blood. The apparent discrepancy between these two pieces of testimony (so much blood on the jacket that the clerk could easily see it, and so little that chemical testing and analysis of it was impossible) was supposedly explained by the chemist's claim that the water in the creek where the jacket was found could have washed out bloodstains. But in any case, no evidence or testimony except for Miller's own confession ever linked him to the gray jacket.

The confession also included a statement that Miller had thrown a bundle of bloody clothes into an empty boxcar on a passing train. Presumably this included the shirt and trousers he had worn at the time of the killing. But no such bundle was ever discovered in any boxcar of any train that went through Canton on the afternoon or evening of the murder. Furthermore, years after the trial, careful examination of freight-train schedules showed that it was not possible for Miller or anyone else to have thrown anything into a boxcar immediately following the murder: There were no trains routed through Canton during the period between the murder and the time when the cab dispatcher's records began to document Miller's comings and goings.

Then there was the pubic hair. At the autopsy done on Janice May, a vaginal smear was taken; the specimen was then bottled and turned over to the police. It so happened that a stray hair got onto the specimen, probably without the knowledge of the forensic expert. Later, when Miller was in custody and the State's chemist examined the specimen and compared it with the sample hair taken from Miller, the comparison failed to implicate Miller. As the examiner wrote in his report, a "common origin of the two hair samples is not probable." (That was precisely what Miller himself had thought when he looked through the police microscope.) Exactly whose hair it was that contaminated the specimen was never determined, however. It could have been the assailant's; it was not Miller's.

The authorities must have realized that this piece of evidence did not confirm Miller's guilt; they never introduced it in court against him, even though the police interrogators had used it as part of their effort to convince Miller that they had damning physical evidence of his assault on Janice May. The defense did not learn about the lab report on the hair samples until seven years after Miller's conviction.

But it was the "bloodstained" jockey shorts that were the single most important piece of physical evidence against Miller. In the confession Miller had said they were his, despite his otherwise consistent denial that he ever wore jockey shorts. At trial, the State's chemist testified for the prosecution that the shorts were stained with type A blood, supposedly the same as the deceased's blood type. He also testified that Miller's blood type was O, not A, so the staining blood could not have come from Miller.

Years later, the defense learned that the clothes in Miller's suitcase, taken by the police when he was arrested, included two pairs of boxer shorts. There were no jockey shorts. And post-trial examination of the jockey shorts also established that they were too small to fit Miller. Still, the really crucial discovery, which was not made until 1963, had nothing to do with the size or style of Miller's underwear.

During the original trial, defense motions to submit the shorts to a laboratory examination were denied. But six years later, armed with a federal court order, Miller's attorney engaged a New York hematologist to examine the shorts. The hematologist's examination proved, incredibly enough, that the stains were not blood at all. Just to be sure, attorney Lassers took the shorts to another expert, who confirmed the finding. Further chemical tests revealed that the dark brown stains were simply dried paint! If there had been any blood on the shorts in 1956, the tests that were used in 1963 would still have detected it. Thus it became clear that, although Miller's confession stated that the shorts were his and that the stains had come from the victim's blood, the truth was that the shorts—which didn't even fit Miller—were nothing but an old paint rag. This raised serious questions about the validity of any aspect of the confession.

The defense was in for an even greater shock: The police had known all along that it was paint on the shorts. They had, however, kept this knowledge to themselves and concocted a far-fetched story to explain it. After the murder, they said, Miller had run into the abandoned building, taken off his shorts, and to cover up the blood had smeared paint on them from some empty paint cans nearby. He had then left the shorts on the floor and run off. Whether this story would have convinced a jury no one knows. The prosecution of course never had to explain in court how paint stains were found on the shorts, because the defense's request at trial for chemical analysis—which would have revealed that the stains were paint rather than blood—had been denied.

The truth was simply that investigations by the police had turned up a pair of paint-stained jockey shorts near the scene of the crime, but no evidence linked them either to the crime itself or to Lloyd Miller. The basis for the trial testimony by the State's chemist that the shorts had type A bloodstains on them was never satisfactorily explained. In any case, an adequate defense at trial should have been able to establish at least some portions of this truth. The prosecution's concealment of its knowledge that the stain was paint rather than blood later proved critical: It was the decisive consideration cited by the United States Supreme Court in 1967 in reversing Miller's conviction.

Another crucial piece of information that surfaced only very late was the extreme unreliability of Betty Baldwin's testimony. About four months after Miller's arrest and her original statement to the police, and still three months before his trial opened, she phoned Miller's attorney and insisted on giving him a long statement. This statement was at complete variance with her earlier one. On the witness stand at the trial, however, she reverted to a version of the facts consistent with the first statement she had made (and with the prosecution's theory of the crime), when she claimed Miller had made self-incriminating comments like "You know they will blame me for it" and "You know I done it." Six years after Miller's conviction, Baldwin again switched to the second version, repudiating her trial testimony that Miller had admitted killing Janice May.

So which version was correct? Was it the pretrial statement and its postconviction reaffirmation? Was Baldwin's statement to the prosecution and on the witness stand therefore perjury? Or was it just the reverse? At hearings in 1963 in federal court the discrepancies finally came to light, and Judge J. Sam Perry declared that Betty Baldwin was "a most unreliable and unbelievable witness and the jury did give consideration to her testimony. The jury did not have before it the type of unreliable person that she is." On this basis, the judge granted Lloyd Miller habeas corpus relief. It was the prosecution's appeal of this decision to the Supreme Court that, four years later, finally resulted in Miller's complete vindication.

Two last points. First, why did Miller leave Canton the night of the murder, abandoning his cab miles from town and taking a bus headed for Detroit, if he wasn't guilty of a crime? Second, if Miller didn't kill Janice May on that Saturday afternoon, what was his alibi? What was he doing at the time of the murder?

Miller's flight from the scene of the crime was apparently interpreted by the authorities as an indication of his "consciousness of guilt." This was a factor in criminal prosecution used against Tom Mooney in 1916 in California and made famous in the 1923 trial of Sacco and Vanzetti in Massachusetts. In those two cases the theme of flight-as-consciousness-of-guilt was explicitly presented to the jury. Although that did not happen in the Miller case, the authorities seemed to have had that in mind when they treated Miller as the culprit essentially from the start. According to Betty Baldwin, Miller had his bag packed because he had decided that he wanted to get married to her the very next day. She added, in one of her versions of that evening's events, that he had said to her "the way people felt about him in Canton and the way they treated him that they'd lay this on to him and that he wanted to just go ahead and go." At the trial, however, Miller's sister testified that, the day before the murder, he had told her he was "going to leave this weekend and . . . go to Detroit or thereabouts for a job," because he "wasn't making enough money." And Miller's employer, the owner of the cab company, testified that he had been half expecting Miller to quit and leave.

Miller himself testified at his trial that he left Canton when he did to avoid arrest on a "warrant out for me for child abandonment." Years later, he gave a different account of his hasty departure as a somewhat impulsive and ill-thought-out venture. "It's just one of those things. In fact in those days, that's the way I was living—more of a wild life and I made too many quick decisions. . . ." This account does, indeed, fit with Miller's somewhat erratic life-style at the time. Whatever the reasons for his actions that night, his precipitate departure from Canton was conveniently consistent with the prosecution's theory.

Miller's attempt at trial to exonerate himself by alibi labored under an obvious difficulty: It was at variance with his confession. Persuading a jury to believe his alibi would have been difficult in any case, however, partly because at trial the prosecution never established the precise time of the assault. The defense failed, too; the jury was never provided with an exact chronology of Miller's whereabouts over the relevant two hours or so. During the five years that intervened between the trial and the first appeal in federal court, the prosecution concluded that the murder had occurred about 4:00 P.M. Years after the trial, Miller's landlady informed the defense that on the day of the murder Miller had been asleep in his room until 4:00. He left the house a half hour later, she said, to run an errand for her at the pharmacy before he started work. He returned with her prescription at 5:30, between fares. The landlady's grandchildren, the ones who had actually gone to wake Miller at 4:00, as he had requested, confirmed this account. Their story also matched exactly Miller's testimony at the original trial.

No evidence was ever brought forward that contradicted this version of the events. And if this account is indeed correct, it is virtually impossible that Miller could have been at the dry cleaner's with bloody hands and clothes to pick up his dry cleaning "about an hour after the murder." More to the point, it is utterly inconsistent with his having killed Janice May at 4:00 P.M.

Why was Miller made the fall guy? He had no previous record. There is no evidence that the local police or the townspeople who testified against him at his trial had been just waiting for an excuse to saddle him with responsibility for a grisly crime. He does not seem to have been marked in people's minds as a suspicious or unsavory character. But no doubt the hasty way he left Canton in the "stolen" cab, his failure to produce a convincing alibi, the waitress Betty Baldwin's incriminating testimony, and the absence of leads to any other suspect all worked against him and helped persuade authorities that in arresting Miller they had the right man. His confession finished the job.

Though Lassers (now a circuit court judge in Cook County) used the title *Scapegoat Justice* for his book about the case, what he actually wrote suggests that he did not think Miller had been deliberately framed or that the authorities attempted to convict a man they knew was innocent. Rather, Lassers contended, the authorities needed a suspect and quickly convinced themselves of Miller's guilt. Then, almost from the start, they interpreted in that light every piece of evidence that came to their attention. The Miller case thus is a clear demonstration of the break-down—"the failure," as Lassers's subtitle rightly asserts—"of the American legal system." Again and again, discrepancies in the fit between the evidence and Miller's guilt were explained away. The most dramatic instance of this was the way the police and the prosecution dealt with the "bloodstained" jockey shorts, but it was true of the way they handled other evidence as well.

Still and all, without Miller's false confession, the prosecution would have had an uphill job to make its case. According to Miller, he "confessed" because he was afraid of being executed. Whether without the threat of the death penalty he would have insisted more stubbornly on his innocence, no one can say. What is clear is that "confessing" made him look guilty and did not spare him the harshest sentence. Despite the confession he thought would save him from the electric chair, the jury sentenced him to death. Perhaps if the confession had been followed by a plea of guilty Miller would have received a different sentence. Again, no one will ever know. But as Willard Lassers wrote: "For the exercise of his constitutional right to a determination of his innocence or guilt by a jury"—that is, for refusing to deny his innocence—"he had to stake his life." He almost lost it.

✳

LLOYD MILLER'S plight was not caused even in part by his race, as was Clarence Brandley's, or by a previous criminal record, as was James Foster's, or by community uproar in response to a symbolic attack on the entire social fabric, as were Mooney's and Billings's. Rather, his case is like scores of others in which shoddy police investigation, a pressured (if not exactly coerced) confession, evidence withheld from the defense, and overzealous prosecution all work against a defendant with no resources for self-protection. Those causes of error appear in most of the hundreds of cases discussed in this book; they are starkly evident in a case from California in the 1930s and another from Georgia in the 1970s.

In August 1936, two deputy sheriffs and a vacationing harbor captain were shot and killed in the Siskiyou Mountains of northern California. An armed posse of angry men was soon searching for two mixed-blood Native Americans from Oklahoma, Coke Brite, 35, and his brother, John, 31. (Two years earlier, irate residents of the area had lynched a man suspected of killing a law officer.) The Brites successfully eluded their would-be captors for a few weeks, but—perhaps convinced there was no way to escape eventual capture—they walked out of the woods one day and peacefully surrendered, frustrating the angry lynch mob that was hot on their heels.

Their trial in December lasted three weeks. The jury convicted the brothers of first-degree murder and made no recommendation of mercy; the judge accordingly sentenced them to death. They were transported south to Folsom Prison to await execution.

Few in the community were afflicted with any doubts about the Brites' guilt. The story generally accepted was that the crime took place in the woods when the two brothers were awakened after a hard day's work on their gold claim and a long night's drinking in town. While carousing, they roughed up some locals, and the sheriff put out warrants for their arrest on charges of assault and battery. In the early morning hours two sheriff's deputies and their companion found the brothers asleep in their tent, woke them up, and announced they were under arrest. The response from inside the tent was a fusillade of rifle fire that left all three visitors dead. The account, as one can read it today in the yellowed pages of newspapers from nearly sixty years ago, leaves no room for any speculation about their guilt. The California Supreme Court, in 1937, unanimously affirmed both convictions.

In some quarters, however, there were doubts about whether the trial had been fair. Pretrial publicity had been considerable during the period when the Brites were fugitives, and community sentiment was extremely hostile to the defendants. Their first execution date was postponed, principally owing to investigative work and publicity by reporters from the *Sacramento Bee*. During the next two and a half years, the brothers received six more stays of execution. Finally, on the ground that the Brites had not been tried and convicted in "a detached judicial atmosphere," Governor Culbert L. Olson commuted their sentences to life in prison.

There were also a few who thought the Brites were actually innocent and that the publicly disseminated version of events was completely false. The facts were not unraveled until the early 1950s, when Erle Stanley Gardner's Court of Last Resort took an interest in the case and established a totally different account of the killings.

It seems that the Brites were strongly disliked by their neighbor, Baker, a crotchety homesteader. The night before the shooting took place, he and his friend the harbor captain—aptly named Seaborn—went up to the brothers' tent, and (with what intention, no one ever established) rousted them out. The two unwelcome visitors were roughed up and sent on their way; the Brites were tough mountain men and well able to fend for themselves. The chastened visitors promptly swore out a warrant for the Brites' arrest.

Around midnight Baker and Seaborn, this time accompanied by two armed deputies, returned to the Brites' campsite. Standing outside the tent, the two officers yelled something like "There they are. Pour it to those sons of bitches." With that, they pounced on the awakening brothers, pummeling them with fists and clubs through the canvas and bedding. Gunfire broke out. When the smoke cleared, the two Brites were badly beaten and dazed. One of them was holding a broken rifle in his hands; three dead men lay at their feet. Baker, the fourth intruder, had fled into the night, and as the sole survivor it was he who created the story that initially prevailed.

The district attorney, James Davis, himself part-Indian, was inclined to think that Coke and John Brite had done no more than shoot in self-defense. No convincing evidence had been presented that the deputies had first shouted, "Come out with your hands up—this is the deputy sheriff and you're under arrest," or words to that effect. The fact that the Brite brothers had later turned themselves in without a fight cautioned him against premature suspicions of their guilt, despite overwhelming community sentiment to the contrary. In fact, he flat out refused to prosecute them. An assistant took over the case, and Davis's budding political career in Siskiyou County abruptly came to an end.

Gardner's Court was later able to establish that the prosecution's theory of the killings was completely inconsistent with the physical evidence. The bullet wounds in the dead men could not have come from the .30.30 rifle the Brites used to fight back. How the sleeping brothers, thoroughly beaten under their blankets while lying on the ground, could have gotten up and shot their three assailants (with only two bullets) is baffling. Baker's several versions of the night's events endlessly contra-dicted themselves. One had to conclude that his testimony, the prosecu-tion's chief evidence, was worthless. The Brites not only had not killed in self-defense—they hadn't killed at all.

It also turned out that a critical piece of evidence, known to the prosecution, had been withheld from the defense. A careful search of the ground under one of the deputies, dead with two bullet holes in his head, failed to turn up any spent bullets. This undercut the prosecution's whole theory of the killing, based on Baker's testimony, which had one of the Brite brothers bending over the deputy and firing twice with his rifle directly into the man's head. As Gardner observed, "If the defense had known of that point it is possible that the conviction of the Brite brothers might have been reversed. . . ."

Thanks to the investigation by the Court of Last Resort, the Brites were released from Folsom Prison in September 1951, after spending fifteen years behind bars. Some years later, John Brite was returned to prison for parole violation; he died in 1972, murdered by another inmate. His brother, Coke, ceased reporting to his parole officer and disappeared.

IN MAY 1971, two medical pathologists in Marietta, Georgia—Drs. Warren and Rosina Matthews—were found murdered in their home. Evidence indicated that a robbery attempt had turned violent. Police rounded up seven men as their suspects: James Creamer, George Emmett, Larry Hacker, Bill Jenkins, Hoyt Powell, Charles Roberts, and Wayne Ruff. Their convictions in Cobb County Superior Court were based largely on the word of Deborah Ann Kidd, who testified under immunity. She claimed she had accompanied the men to the Matthews home. Creamer—the supposed gunman—received a death sentence, the others life imprisonment.

In two separate decisions in 1974, the Georgia Supreme Court unani-mously upheld all seven convictions and sentences. But in April 1975, having learned (in part thanks to an investigation undertaken by the *Atlanta Constitution*) that the prosecution had intentionally withheld evidence from the defense, attorneys for Creamer and Emmett sought habeas corpus relief in federal court. In his opinion, Judge Charles A. Moye of the United States District Court declared that the prosecution had concealed from the defense transcripts of previous statements that Kidd had made to the police. These statements showed that she had produced a series of different versions of what had happened at the crime scene, of who really shot the victims, even of who was really there with her. At one point she went so far as to "confess" that she was the killer, rather than any of the men. None of this mass of inconsistent information by Kidd had been made available to the defense. (As if any more were needed, it was established that prior to the trial Kidd was regularly high on drugs and was sexually involved with one of the detectives assigned to the case.) The result, the judge observed, was a trial that "bordered on the Kafkaesque."

Judge Moye ordered the convictions reversed and charged the prosecution with willful destruction of the taped testimony Kidd had given during sessions with a hypnotist arranged by the police. The prosecution appealed the district court's rulings to the federal circuit court.

A few months later, while the State's appeal was pending, additional new evidence was put before the Georgia Supreme Court. Debbie Kidd made a formal admission that she had lied in her original trial testimony. But since a liar's admission that she has lied may be merely another lie, the court put greater weight on very different evidence from another quarter that implicated three other men. Billy Birt, at the time under death sentence in Georgia for another crime, confessed that he and two friends, Billy Davis (then in federal prison) and Willie Hester (a fugitive), were the actual murderers. As a result, reversals were secured for all seven defendants. Emmett, Jenkins, Powell, and Roberts were released on bail; the others remained in prison serving time for prior crimes.

Court-watchers said that the reversals handed down by the state court were a prelude to the prosecution's dropping the charges against Creamer and his six co-defendants. They were right. In September 1975, District Attorney George W. ("Buddy") Darden, expressing some residual misgivings about the complete innocence of all the defendants, nonetheless withdrew the indictment against them. Despite protests, he refused to prosecute Deborah Kidd for perjury. Bobby Lee Cook, counsel for the former defendants, complained, "It is utterly shocking and appalling to me that seven innocent men were convicted on fabricated testimony, . . . and for the district attorney to say he did not intend to prosecute [Kidd]."

When interviewed after his release, George Emmett told a newspaper reporter, "I never thought we would be exonerated. . . . We've claimed all along that we're innocent and people are now beginning to believe that we were telling the truth."

District Attorney Darden lost his job to a rival at the next election, though he was later elected to the state legislature. In 1983 he ran for Congress, and in response to criticism for his handling of the Matthews murder trial, he defended himself as well as he could. "A district attorney," he said, "is only as good as a case presented to him by law enforcement officers." Perhaps so. But suppression by the prosecution of evidence cannot be blamed on the police, and the court's criticism of the way the district attorney's office prosecuted the case stands unrebutted.

8 GULLIBLE POLICE AND A VULNERABLE SUSPECT

O N   H I S   W A Y   H O M E from work on the evening of December 30, 1959, Benjamin Yount dropped in at his favorite bar, The Speak Easy, in Boutte, Louisiana. A tiny hamlet of 155 residents just off the main highway, Boutte lay seventeen miles southwest of New Orleans. Yount, 48, was a drilling supervisor for Pan American Petroleum Company. He was married and had four children but was also good friends with the bar's owner, Hermine Fiedler. Sometimes he helped her with her account books. On this particular evening, he just wanted to say hello. After all, both a year and a decade were coming to an end.

The next morning, a few hours after The Speak Easy had closed, the custodian arrived to set the place in order. When he entered the back room, a combination kitchen and office, he found Yount awkwardly slumped over, partly on the table and partly on the floor. Alive but unconscious, Yount had obviously been shot in the back of the head, but the room showed no other signs of violence or of a struggle. Neither did robbery appear to be the motive. Yount's wallet lay on the table in front of him, with about $80 still in it, next to a pack of cigarettes and a lighter.

At a nearby hospital, Yount underwent emergency surgery. The doctors removed an odd, badly mangled bullet—a .22 slug—from Yount's brain, but to no avail. He never regained consciousness, and three days later he died.

The crushed bullet was partially covered with some kind of bright yellow metallic substance. Rumors began to spread that the murderer had used a gold-plated bullet. The State Police soon concluded that the color came from a copper alloy, however, not gold, so visions of an exotic murder weapon evaporated. Furthermore, although the copper alloy was relatively rare in .22 bullets, it was not rare enough to make tracing the bullet feasible. Thus, despite the unusual slug, the police had almost nothing to go on.

Hermine Fiedler, owner of The Speak Easy, was nowhere to be found. A 37-year-old German immigrant who had been in the United States some two years, Mrs. Fiedler was a war widow with two children; her husband had been killed on the Russian front. Some people naturally speculated that she might have been Yount's killer, but no obvious motive suggested itself. Most of the patrons at the bar on the night of the murder were regulars who knew both each other and Yount at least casually. Though some of them later remembered seeing Yount and Fiedler talk off and on during the course of the evening, no one recalled the two of them arguing.

The other obvious possible explanation for Fiedler's mysterious disappearance was that she, too, was dead. But no one had noticed any strangers in the bar or any unusual activity. The stragglers among the customers remembered Mrs. Fiedler getting ready to close around 1:30 in the morning; none of them, questioned later, remembered noticing whether Yount was still there at that hour.

About seventy-five miles west of Boutte, between Six-Mile-Lake and the Gulf of Mexico, lies Patterson, another small Louisiana town. There on January 4, less than twenty-four hours after Yount had died, a young couple out walking on a levee across marsh land discovered a woman's body in the reeds. They reported it to the police, who soon determined that it was the missing Hermine Fiedler. Like Yount, she had been shot from behind at close range. Another similarity in the two shootings was that the bullet that killed Fiedler also turned out to be a mangled .22 slug. That raised the possibility that the two bullets had been fired from the same gun. And if they were, it seemed likely that Yount's murderer and Fiedler's murderer were the same person.

The police soon concluded that robbery *was* a motive for the Fiedler murder. Mrs. Fiedler was known to have been carrying some $500 the night she vanished, money she had intended to use to renew the annual liquor license for her bar. But when she was found, her purse—lying a few feet away—contained only some cosmetics.

A closer look at the condition of Hermine Fiedler's body revealed several interesting facts. Despite rain the night of January 2 heavy enough to leave the ground quite wet, Mrs. Fiedler's body, clothes, and purse were dry; so was a book of matches picked up at the scene. There was also not much evidence of blood. All of this suggested that she had been killed elsewhere and that her body had simply been dumped in the marsh some time after the rainstorm.

On the other hand, Mrs. Fiedler's body was lying sprawled out in an awkward position, and her clothes were in considerable disarray, as if she had struggled with her assailant right there on the levee. When the autopsy report confirmed that she had not been sexually assaulted, however, a new theory emerged. She might have been mortally wounded but not yet dead when she was left in the marsh. Convulsive twitching or thrashing about in the throes of death could explain both the position of her body and the condition of her clothing. None of this was any help in figuring out who might have murdered her, however.

The medical examiner later established the time of death as "on or about January 2, 1960." That was hardly a precise finding, but it made sense if Mrs. Fiedler had been kidnapped and held captive for a couple of days before she was killed. No one had reported seeing her between the time she closed the bar, early on the morning of December 31, and January 4, when her body was found.

The police did find a couple of other possible clues, though they didn't know what to make of them. There were some white hairs on the dead woman's clothes, which certainly were not hers; they looked as if they might have come from a white Persian cat. Under the corpse the police also found a large piece of fingernail, colored with an unusual red polish, which looked as if it could have been broken off in a fight or struggle. The nail clearly was not Mrs. Fiedler's, but the police didn't know whose it was, either.

For fourteen months the murders remained unsolved. The police were stymied, and a $2,000 reward went unclaimed.

The Hampton family hailed from Sandy Hook, Kentucky, where Routes 7 and 32 cross in the hills between Daniel Boone National Forest and the West Virginia border. Mary Katherin Hampton, one of eight children, had an I.Q. of barely over 70. A ninth-grade dropout, she lived at home and helped with the younger children. Dark-haired and blue-eyed Mary Kay (as she was called) was attractive, despite being a little on the chubby side.

She was 16 in 1958 when Emmitt Monroe Spencer breezed into town with a fancy car and pocketful of cash. Both the automobile and the money later turned out to have been stolen, but Mary Kay didn't know that, and Spencer initially cut a pretty impressive figure in her eyes. He was slimmer and taller than she, and quite a bit older, and he had a quick, glib way of talking that made his attention to her all the more flattering. He was also a rambling but effective storyteller. Mary Kay

Hampton, bored with home and more than a little aroused by her admirer, left Sandy Hook in May 1959 with Emmitt Spencer. The road to adventure and excitement stretched before her.

What Mary Kay didn't know was that she was running off with an ex-convict. Spencer failed to tell her that he had just been released from the Kentucky state penitentiary after completing a twelve-year term for voluntary manslaughter. She soon began to get a clearer picture of the man she had run away with, and she didn't like what she saw. As they traveled together, she quickly learned that he was a holdup artist with a propensity toward violence, for one thing. Within a few months Mary Kay wanted to leave Spencer, but by then she was pregnant and scared to go home. Besides, every time she talked about leaving him, Emmitt threatened he would track her down and kill her, even if he had to go "all over the world" to get her. She believed he would (he could be very intimidating and persuasive), and so she stayed with him—a frightened, pregnant teenager. During the eleven months that Mary Kay remained with Emmitt, they went to Florida, drifted back and forth across the South, and then headed for the Pacific Northwest before returning to the South via California.

In Idaho, things turned really ugly. Not far from the town of Gooding, on the edge of the lava-strewn countryside around Craters of the Moon National Monument, Spencer forced another motorist off the road and attacked him for no apparent reason. (The facts here are somewhat uncertain. In another version of the story, Spencer stopped when he saw a man standing near a parked car at the side of the road and approached him, map in hand, on the pretext of asking directions.) With the help of a hitchhiker he had picked up somewhere along the line, Spencer attempted to rob the man. When the intended victim resisted, Spencer shot him dead. Hampton, sitting in the car watching this senseless murder, became hysterical. Slowly it was dawning on her that Spencer might be every bit the murderer he had bragged to her he was.

The dead man left by the side of the road was John Hunt, Jr., a botanist and forester scheduled to join the faculty of Yale University that autumn. The authorities searched in vain for his killer; Spencer and his two companions were by that time on their way to California. Though the hitchhiker soon went his own way, Hampton stayed with Spencer, thoroughly under his thumb. They hung around the San Diego area for a while before returning to Florida. Once there, en route from Jacksonville to Key West, Spencer killed two more people—again for no apparent reason. Leon Hammell and Virginia Tomlinson had been planning to marry and spend their lives together; in the end, they did not even die together. Hammell was shot to death at Big Coppitt Key, and Tomlinson was stabbed to death near Vero Beach.

By then Mary Kay was truly terrified, fearing for her own life. A couple of times she broke off with Emmitt, but—helpless alone—she always went back to him. One time she made it home to Sandy Hook briefly. While she was there, another brutal murder was committed in Key West, which also turned out to be Emmitt Spencer's handiwork. Indeed, he bragged about it to Mary Kay when she rejoined him in Florida.

Shortly afterwards, on April 14, 1960, Spencer and Hampton—with yet another hitchhiker, James Jobe—were driving near Clermont, in Central Florida, when they were stopped by a State Highway Patrol officer on a routine traffic violation. Spencer was behind the wheel; when asked to produce a driver's license, he did so. The alert officer noticed that the license looked as if it belonged to a considerably older and heavier person. He confronted Spencer, who appeared nervous; the trooper asked all three to get out of their vehicle. As they walked toward the squad car, Spencer bolted. Jobe, the hitchhiker, tried to stop him. Hampton started to scream. Spencer made a dash back to the automobile, grabbed a hidden pistol, shot and wounded the officer, jumped into the car, and sped off into the night. Hampton and Jobe rushed to the aid of the police officer, who radioed for a back-up.

After a chase at speeds of more than a hundred miles an hour, Spencer was apprehended near Leesburg, about thirty miles away. As he tried to run a police roadblock, some three dozen bullets from a machine gun stopped him. He emerged from the car hands over his head, with nothing but superficial scratches. Authorities traced the bullet-ridden vehicle and quickly discovered that both it and the driver's license Spencer was carrying had been stolen from John T. Keen, a naval base pipefitter who lived in Key West. When the police went to Keen's small cottage to tell him they had recovered his car, they found him lying in bed—dead. He had been robbed and literally hammered to death. In fact, he had been struck with a ball-peen hammer so many times that it was impossible to count the number of blows.

Both Spencer and Hampton were taken into custody. While Spencer kept trying to make a deal with the authorities, Mary Kay Hampton told the terrifying story of her months with Emmitt. She made a complete statement, which included details of the murder of John Hunt in Idaho. She told about the murders of Virginia Tomlinson and Leon Hammell; she provided information on an unsolved murder in Miami, the knife-slaying of Ethel Little. All Mary Kay's disclosures were verified. When she was released by the Florida police, she returned to Kentucky.

Mary Kay and Emmitt's child was born on the Fourth of July in 1960. She immediately put the baby boy up for adoption.

On August 24, 1960, Spencer was convicted of murdering John Keen and sentenced to die in Florida's electric chair. The key to his conviction and death sentence was Hampton's testimony against him. "Emmitt told me he put that man out of this world," she had said. From the death house in Raiford, Spencer vowed to get even. A guard reported he heard Spencer say, "I'll get that bitch if it's the last thing I do."

Emmitt Spencer began his campaign of retaliation by confessing to murder after murder, implicating Hampton in each one. He provided lurid details, and insisted that she was a vicious "torture killer" and "homicidal lesbian." During his first six months on death row, he confessed to thirty-six murders. (Once he got going, he couldn't seem to stop; by August 1966, the count had reached forty-eight.) Prominent on his list were the still-unsolved murders of Benjamin Yount and Hermine Fiedler in Louisiana. "Me and Mary Kay did it," he said, adding that in those crimes she had been the actual trigger person, his "gun moll."

Soon Spencer had police investigators in ten different states running off on one wild goose chase after another. None of the details given in any of his confessions could be verified, however, except for those previously reported in the press. His stories just did not make sense. One person he said he had killed, for example, later showed up alive and well at the local police headquarters. Spencer claimed to be a serial murderer, and probably he was. He certainly had become a serial confessor.

The only murder Emmitt Spencer flatly denied was the one for which he was sentenced to death. And the only one for which he did not try to shove at least some of the blame off onto Mary Kay Hampton was a murder he admitted committing when Mary Kay was only five years old.

There were numerous discrepancies between the catalogue of murders Emmitt confessed to and the list of those that Mary Kay accused him of committing. In her favor was the fact that each story she told turned out to be completely accurate, whereas his tales kept proving to be extravagantly false. Nevertheless, Louisiana law-enforcement officials traveled to the prison in Raiford to see what they could learn from Emmitt about the Yount and Fiedler murders. For three days he rattled on about the gold-plated bullet, the white Persian cat hairs—and Mary Kay Hampton, the alleged killer. Unlike authorities from several other states, who by this time had become skeptical of Spencer, those from Louisiana chose to believe him. He was a convincing storyteller and good-natured with his questioners. "If I get the chair in Louisiana on crimes committed there, then I'll walk in and try to help the gentlemen strap me in," he jested.

Soon afterward, on February 26, 1961, the Louisiana authorities had Mary Kay Hampton arrested in Kentucky. Spencer had made it easy for the law officers to find her; he had drawn a map showing the road to her family's farm in Sandy Hook. Hampton was as compliant as ever, and when the police told her she was needed "to identify some things" in Louisiana, she agreed to go with them. Once there, she was charged with the Yount and Fiedler murders, despite insisting she was innocent. One of the arresting officers later said, "She was just an ignorant farm girl, that's all. She was scared to death of Spencer." Always emotionally unstable, she was frightened and overwhelmed with guilt about her on-again, off-again relationship with a convicted murderer. She would not, however, confess to crimes she knew nothing about.

For six weeks Mary Kay was interrogated, and for six weeks she cried and denied any guilt. Then, forty-three days after she had been taken to Louisiana in custody, she finally cracked. On April 11, 1961, Mary Kay Hampton went before the judge in St. Charles Parish Court and pleaded "guilty without capital punishment" to one count of first-degree murder in the death of Benjamin Yount. On April 17 she was sentenced to life imprisonment. A day later, in the criminal court of St. Mary Parish, she again pleaded "guilty without capital punishment" to the murder of Hermine Fiedler. She was immediately given a second life sentence. In neither court appearance was there a trial. The State of Louisiana entered no evidence to establish her involvement in either crime. No proof was offered of her guilt "beyond a reasonable doubt." There was not even a formal confession from Mary Kay, nor did she or anyone else make any statement explaining her role in the murders. Her guilty pleas relieved the State from the burden of having to prove anything. For once Emmitt Spencer had spoken the truth; he had said that if Louisiana acted on his tip, all the State would have to do was "throw in the cards and rake in the pot."

Her court-appointed attorneys had been of little or no help to Mary Kay Hampton. For one of her two court appearances, she had first met her attorney only a few minutes before she was sentenced. At the other, the attorney had let her plead guilty without ever bothering to ask her whether she had actually had anything to do with the crimes. Neither did it occur to anyone, in either proceeding, to raise the issue of Hampton's marginal mental capacity and whether that might affect the legal status of her plea. A psychiatrist, Dr. Kenneth Ritter, had examined her and found her sane and able to assist her lawyers in her own defense. He in turn had asked psychologist Robert N. Dorsey to give her another professional evaluation. Before Dorsey had had a chance to complete his examination, however, Mary Kay had pleaded guilty. No one asked for Dorsey's report, and so no one at the time knew that he disagreed with Ritter about her mental state and competence to stand trial.

Hampton later insisted that she pleaded guilty both times out of fear. The authorities were threatening to "fry" her in the state's electric chair, she said. "They told me if I pleaded guilty, I'd only get maybe a couple of years. If I didn't, I'd go to the chair for sure."

Mary Katherin Hampton was moved to St. Gabriel, Louisiana, home of the Louisiana Correctional Institution for Women, in the bayou country northwest of New Orleans. The prison was built in the nineteenth century, an imposing place despite being only one story high, thanks to its gray stone and fortress style. There, along with roughly 150 other prisoners, she began to serve her time.

The first person to raise questions about Mary Kay's conviction was Warren D. Holmes, a homicide detective with the Miami Police Department. Holmes had a reputation as one of the best crime investigators in the South. He had met Emmitt Spencer several times in the course of murder investigations and had learned to view his "confessions" with great skepticism. Holmes had concluded that Spencer was a fantastic storyteller with a phenomenal memory, someone who could absorb details of crimes he had read about in detective magazines and then rattle off the facts as if they were based on his own firsthand knowledge.

Knowing as much as he did about how unreliable Spencer's stories were, Holmes was by no means persuaded that Hampton was guilty. His misgivings were further aroused when he learned that nothing implicated her in the murders except Spencer's vengeful accusations and her own ill-advised guilty pleas. He decided to interview Hampton himself. When he did so, in the prison at St. Gabriel in September 1962, Holmes became thoroughly convinced that she was totally innocent. "Her behavior," he observed, "is entirely consistent with her circumstances of fear, terror, emotional instability, low intelligence and true guilt overtones for having lived with Spencer." There was, however, little Holmes could do, given that he was not a Louisiana law officer. He made his findings available to the Louisiana authorities, who—perhaps not surprisingly—chose to ignore the information. Hampton continued to sit in prison, unable to help herself, but telling anyone who would listen that she was innocent.

Holmes was not ready to give up. Having resigned from the police department in order to set up shop as a private lie detector consultant, he had greater latitude in what he could undertake. In November 1963, about a year after meeting Hampton, Holmes mentioned her case to Gene Miller, a 29-year-old *Miami Herald* reporter. Miller had joined the *Herald* staff in 1957; most of the time he worked as a general assignment reporter, writing on a wide range of subjects. He had a long-standing commitment to human rights, however, which sparked his interest in the Hampton case after Holmes drew it to his attention, and which kept him working on it for the next three years. (Four years later, in 1967, his dedication and the results of his work earned him a Pulitzer Prize.)

Miller's investigations quickly convinced him that Holmes was right in believing Mary Kay was innocent. As time went by and his involvement in the case deepened, Miller—by his own admission—lost his objectivity as a reporter, but he did not pretend otherwise. In column after column in the *Herald,* he made his position clear. Fearing the media's efforts to be neutral were masking a terrible injustice to a helpless and innocent prisoner, he could not sit idly by. "I sometimes think that if the 20th Century press could report the crucifixion of Christ, the second paragraph would be an explanation from Pontius Pilate," he once wrote. In an effort to clarify why he had become so personally engaged in the Hampton case, he added, "Mary Hampton, in my opinion, no more committed the crimes for which she is incarcerated than did Grandma Moses or Mamie Eisenhower."

Despite being based in Miami, far from Louisiana, Holmes and Miller decided to do whatever was necessary to get Mary Kay released. On January 13, 1964, after Miller had been writing about the Hampton case for three months, he and Holmes traveled to St. Gabriel; there Holmes introduced him to Hampton. While in Louisiana, they also made a photocopy of the five-hundred-page transcript of the interviews that officials had conducted with Spencer at the prison in Raiford. Study of the transcript enabled Miller and Holmes to see just how many important details of the murders of Benjamin Yount and Hermine Fiedler were missing from Spencer's rambling tales—presumably because he did not know them. These included such basic facts as the dates, times, and locations of the crimes, as well as the weapons used.

For instance, Spencer said he had had six accomplices in the two Louisiana murders, and he gave leads to thirty people he said could verify that he and Hampton were in the vicinity of the crimes. None of these accomplices or witnesses could be found. Nor was there any trace of the five different cars that—in his various accounts—he claimed they had used. His instructions on where to find the murder weapons (he was inconsistent about them, as well, mentioning four different guns that ranged widely in caliber and type) led nowhere. In short, as Miller later wrote, "Spencer displayed total ignorance of the true facts of the crime." The amazing thing, given the inconsistencies and holes in his story, was that the Louisiana authorities had ever believed him. The only thing to be said for taking his wild tales at face value was that doing so enabled the authorities to clear up the Yount and Fiedler murders in the preferred way—with a conviction—once they had successfully browbeaten Hampton into pleading guilty.

The morning after Holmes and Miller got their copy of the transcript of the interviews with Spencer, they presented their findings at a previously scheduled meeting of Louisiana's board of pardons. The two men had grown increasingly confident of victory as they accumulated evidence of Hampton's innocence. They never dreamed how unreceptive the State authorities would be. "I have learned from bitter experience," Miller wrote later, "that innocence is not enough." In fact, officials wouldn't even listen to Miller and Holmes. Hampton's attorney, they said, should submit a written brief. But the attorney, retained for Hampton by a sympathetic prison priest, had no real interest in her plight. He was not going to sit down and write a detailed brief without assurance that he would be paid. Holmes and Miller concluded that they, despite being completely untrained in the law, would have to write the brief themselves. And so they did, producing a fifty-page document and assembling seven and a quarter pounds of exhibits as an appendix, in an effort to give the pardons board what it wanted. Pleased with what they had accomplished, they were certain this time that they would soon be able to hold a "Welcome Home" party for Mary Kay.

Authorities for the State remained unimpressed, however, and were unwilling to admit even the possibility that a mistake had occurred. It became apparent to Holmes and Miller that bringing in a hard-working, skillful lawyer for Mary Kay was their only chance of success. They boldly turned to Boston's F. Lee Bailey, considered one of the best criminal attorneys in the country, though he was only 33. Fresh from a widely publicized victory in Dr. Sam Sheppard's case in Ohio (Sheppard had been released on bond and would be acquitted two years later), Bailey agreed to take Hampton as a client. A New Orleans television reporter helped find a local attorney, Salvador Anzelmo, to join Bailey on the case. James M. Russ, a lawyer in Orlando, Florida, also enlisted in the legal task force that challenged the State of Louisiana on Mary Katherin Hampton's behalf. Like Holmes and Miller, none of these attorneys received a fee for his services.

Lee Bailey didn't think much would come of further appeals to the pardons board. Instead, on January 12, 1965, he went back to the Louisiana courts, filing a motion to withdraw Hampton's plea of guilty in the Yount case. This approach, too, led to a dead end. The motion was denied by the trial court, and on March 29, 1965, the denial was affirmed by the state supreme court. By that time, Mary Kay had been in prison four years.

The attorneys next sought a writ of habeas corpus in federal court. When Bailey said, "We can prove that the petitioner is innocent of the crimes for which she is incarcerated," Judge G. Gordon West listened closely. Wanting to be sure he had heard correctly, he interrupted to ask, "Is it my understanding that there never was a factual admission of guilt?" Bailey assured him that this was, indeed, true. Mary Kay Hampton had pleaded guilty, but she had never confessed to the murders of Yount and Fiedler. When it began to look as if the judge would require a full evidentiary hearing, the prosecutor became visibly nervous. The State did not want a federal court to be the forum for review of its case. An assistant attorney general told the judge that the State would be happy to grant a full hearing—in a parish (county) court room. And so on June 2, 1966, without ruling on the merits of the case, the district court denied Hampton's request for federal habeas relief, saying she would have to exhaust state remedies before the federal courts had jurisdiction. She would therefore first have to seek a writ of habeas corpus in Louisiana courts.

Hampton wrote to Gene Miller from St. Gabriel—her letters arrived stamped with the censor's "C"—saying, "I can't stay here much longer and remain a sane person. I can't face another disappointment. There isn't any justice for me." As it turned out, she did not have much longer to wait. On August 25, 1966, a hearing on the habeas writ opened in the state court in Plaquemine, Louisiana, not far from Baton Rouge. The State was still unhappy about having to re-examine Hampton's conviction. As Miller noted, "Under the eight old-fashioned ceiling-blade fans, the courtroom atmosphere reeked of hostility." Nevertheless, the defense was able to produce some genuine support for Mary Kay. For the first time, testimony in the case was given under oath from the witness stand. Major John R. Thomas, chief of detectives for the Louisiana State Police, testified that he did not think Hampton was guilty; the only evidence against her had been the word of Emmitt Spencer. Major Thomas's testimony was reinforced by that of three law enforcement officials from Florida who had paid their own way to Louisiana to testify on behalf of the convicted murderer. Each testified to Emmitt Spencer's complete unreliability and to the veracity of everything Mary Kay Hampton had told them when she was in custody in Florida.

The defense had yet more evidence to present. The most important pieces Warren Holmes had uncovered several years before: a Florida traffic ticket and a cash appearance bond. Up to this point, however, Holmes had never had a forum in which to present what he had found. Attorney Bailey was finally in a court room where he could use it.

During the period when Holmes had been trying to verify some of Spencer's confessions, he had learned about a traffic violation involving Spencer in Crestview, Florida—330 miles from New Orleans. A traffic ticket had been issued to him there on New Year's Eve 1959. At 10:30 P.M. that same night, the records in Crestview showed, Spencer was posting a $35 cash bond; he had been charged with driving without a license. The records further showed that Hampton was a passenger in the car with him at the time. That was less than twenty-four hours after Yount was murdered in Boutte, Louisiana, and about thirty-six hours before Fiedler's body was discovered near Patterson, Louisiana.

But that wasn't all. Earlier in the day on New Year's Eve, according to several witnesses prepared to testify under oath, Hampton and Spencer had been even farther from Boutte and Patterson. They had driven from Sneads, Florida, to Bainbridge, Georgia—a full 470 highway miles from the scene of the Yount shooting—and then to DeFuniak Springs, Florida, before they ever got to Crestview. Furthermore, three of these alibi witnesses had been interviewed by Louisiana authorities before Hampton had entered her guilty pleas. Their statements had, however, been suppressed, and as a result Hampton's court-appointed defense attorneys had known nothing about the existence of possible alibi testimony. It was Holmes and Miller who later obtained photostats of these statements. Taken together, the accumulated evidence strongly argued that Spencer and Hampton had been hundreds of miles away, in Florida, within a few hours of the Louisiana crimes. They simply could not have committed either, let alone both, of the murders. "No one," as Miller put it, "can be two places at the same time."

At the August 25th hearing, the defense hoped to have testimony from Dr. Robert N. Dorsey, the psychologist who had examined Hampton on April 8 and 9, 1961—shortly before her guilty pleas. As Miller summarized Dorsey's findings in one of his articles, Hampton "was highly disturbed, terrified of electrocution, extremely suggestible and . . . totally incapable of helping in her own legal defense." Because the defense team had no money to bring Dorsey (or its seventeen other witnesses) to the court room, Bailey tried to enter what is known as "proffered testimony" (testimony given on behalf of a person absent from court but otherwise willing to testify). The judge would have none of it. Nor would he allow Bailey to enter into evidence an elaborate, seven-page confession Spencer had made to a Miami murder—another false confession—that would have conclusively demonstrated his readiness to fabricate a pack of lies regarding his criminal past.

Even so, the Louisiana authorities had their backs against the wall, and they knew it. When a witness told how he had heard a prosecutor explain to Mary Kay that she could "fry" in the electric chair, Miller thought he saw the prosecutor begin to squirm in his chair. Indeed, almost immediately and very abruptly, he rose and strolled over to the railing of the court room well. "Will you take commutation?" he asked Hampton and her attorney. The prosecutor was offering everyone an easy way out. As Miller later wrote, he was certain—given the relationship of trust he had established with her—that Mary Kay would do whatever he suggested. Wanting the decision to be hers, he carefully explained that if she accepted commutation she would never be officially exonerated. She told him she figured there were two options: be in prison or be out. She wanted *out*, as fast as possible. She would take commutation.

On September 30, 1966, Louisiana's board of pardons—composed of the lieutenant governor, attorney general, and sentencing judge—unanimously voted to commute Hampton's sentence to ten and a half years, a term short enough that she would be eligible for parole virtually right away. A few weeks later Governor John J. McKeithen concurred. Guilt or innocence was not at issue; Hampton would still stand convicted of the murders. But at least she would be able to leave the prison almost immediately.

Almost, but not quite. Back in Florida, Emmitt Spencer was furious when he heard the news of Mary Kay's commutation. He went to authorities at Raiford prison once again and accused Mary Kay of still another murder. Then, in November, he testified in front of a Florida grand jury. Incredibly, he was once again believed, and Hampton was indicted for that crime. Fortunately for her, this indictment was quickly voided because of faulty wording, and the case was returned to the grand jury for re-examination. Lee Bailey was there for her once again. During three days of argument, he painstakingly demonstrated the many flaws in Spencer's testimony. Members of the grand jury deliberated only fifteen minutes before deciding not to return an indictment.

Ten days later, on November 30, 1966, Mary Kay Hampton was freed. Looking drawn and tired, and unable to control a facial tic that had developed while she was incarcerated, she walked out of prison wearing a cheap mail-order suit from Sears, Roebuck. She had spent five years and nine months behind bars. She was no longer the attractive 18-year-old who had been arrested; she was in her mid-twenties, she had lost weight, and she had acquired a tremble and a stutter. But Mary Kay could not wait to return home. From St. Gabriel she took a bus to New Orleans; a plane to Washington; a bus to Huntington, West Virginia; and a car for the last sixty-eight miles to Sandy Hook. Today, she still lives in Kentucky. She is married and has two children. In 1970 Emmitt Spencer's death sentence was vacated, and he was resentenced to natural life; in 1979 he was transferred from Florida to Iowa, where he continues to serve out his prison term.

The authorities still do not know who murdered Benjamin Yount and Hermine Fiedler; their investigation ended fourteen months after the crimes, as soon as Mary Katherin Hampton pleaded guilty. At the start, when the murders were first reported, some had speculated that the killer was Hermine Fiedler's sister, Gerda Sheridan, though she had a strong alibi for the days before her sister's body was discovered. Sheridan was quoted as saying, "I know I was the prime suspect before that girl pleaded guilty." Shortly after Mrs. Fiedler's funeral, investigators noticed that a part of one of Gerda Sheridan's fingernails was missing. Her finger was photographed, and at least two police investigators concluded that the broken nail fit the piece found under her sister's body. Even Gerda admitted that it was probably hers, but she said she had no idea how it got there. "Maybe the police planted it," she suggested vaguely. And Gene Miller said that though he couldn't prove it, he "always felt . . . Gerda Sheridan was the killer. Or, if not she, someone she knew."

The much-discussed white hairs were never precisely explained or identified. Mrs. Fiedler's children, Lothar and Carmine, both told Gene Miller that their neighborhood teemed with cats, so it is quite possible that the white hairs on Mrs. Fiedler's coat were a clue of no significance. But no one will ever know; no cat hairs were submitted to a laboratory for comparison.

Another suspect, Robert H. Allen, a tugboat captain from St. Louis, had been arrested a few weeks after the murders and held in jail for fifty-eight days. He was released after he proved that on the day of the murders he was on his ship with ten crewmates, five hundred miles from Boutte and Patterson. The police had suspected him because in his motel room near the murder scene they had found a gun. Ballistics tests eventually showed that the gun could not have been the murder weapon.

Without the traffic ticket, Mary Kay Hampton's alibi defense would never have come to light. Without the volunteer efforts of detective Holmes, reporter Miller, and attorneys Anzelmo, Russ, and especially Lee Bailey, she might even yet be in prison. Holmes said after it was all over, "The Mary Kay matter is no indictment of our system of justice, nor of our system of laws. It is a tragic example, though, of what can happen if facts are taken for granted instead of being pursued to the bottom. She . . . was frightened into pleading guilty to a crime she did not commit because someone told her she would 'fry in the electric chair' unless she did so. She didn't realize what she was doing until it was too late. It took four years of hard work . . . to undo that mistake."

❋

LIES FROM a prisoner on death row, exhausting police interrogation, and terrible fear of a threatened death sentence were the three critical factors that led to Mary Kay Hampton's false guilty plea. For a false accusation of an innocent person—peddled from death row—to be taken seriously enough to victimize that innocent individual is highly unusual. But false confessions under pressure from the police are by no means uncommon; one dramatic example comes to light in the story of a Maine case told next. And when the police questioning takes place against the background of death row and possible execution, an innocent defendant is even more likely to crumble in fear, as happened in the Ohio case recounted below.

Late in 1959, prison doors in Maine at last opened for Paul Dwyer, 40, who by the time of his release had served twenty-two years of a life sentence for a murder he did not commit. The case had begun in October

1937. Dwyer, then 17, was arrested in North Arlington, New Jersey, when curious police officers stopped to investigate a parked car with a pair of feet sticking out the window. The feet belonged to Paul Dwyer, asleep in the vehicle. The police also discovered two bodies in the trunk.

Contact with the authorities in South Paris, Maine, where Dwyer lived with his mother, revealed that the car belonged to the deceased, Dr. James C. Littlefield and his wife, Lydia, who had been reported missing from their home in South Paris under suspicious circumstances. Dwyer readily signed a confession to both murders. In fact, he gave three confessions, offering different versions of a wild tale of his having driven eight hundred miles across New England after bludgeoning Dr. Littlefield and then strangling Mrs. Littlefield when she discovered her husband had been murdered. His motive, Dwyer told the police, was robbery.

Returned the next day to South Paris under custody—he had waived extradition proceedings—Dwyer was placed in the hands of Deputy Sheriff Francis M. Carroll, 43, a war veteran and father of five (including two girls—Barbara, 15, and her younger sister, Betty). Dwyer promptly confessed once more—with another new version of the facts. Because his stories were so extraordinary and his behavior in other ways aberrant, he was briefly transferred to a state mental institution for observation. The court then appointed a local attorney, E. Walker Abbott, as Dwyer's counsel, and Dwyer was brought to trial in November 1937. No witnesses and no circumstantial evidence linked him to the crimes. Yet there was the unarguable fact that the bodies of the deceased had been found hundreds of miles from South Paris, in their own car, with Dwyer behind the wheel. And there were his several confessions. But faced with the need to state his plea before the court, Dwyer chose to plead not guilty.

Suddenly, on the third day of the trial, Dwyer announced he wanted to change his plea to guilty. This conveniently saved the prosecution from having to produce any evidence or even any theory of the crime to convince the jury. The trial judge accepted Dwyer's plea and promptly sentenced him to life imprisonment. (Fortunately, Maine had long been without the death penalty, having abolished it in 1887.)

Once in prison, Dwyer changed his story yet again. In a long, hand-written statement, he claimed that Deputy Carroll had murdered the two Littlefields and forced him to dispose of the bodies, threatening to kill Dwyer's mother, too, if he refused. (During the trial, Carroll had stood silently behind Mrs. Dwyer as she sat in the court room; young Dwyer said this had served as a vivid and ominous reminder to him of the threat that hung over his mother if he wavered in his new plea of guilty.) Dwyer also stated that as soon as he was arrested and returned to jail in South Paris, Carroll had renewed his threats, and that it was Carroll who had insisted he change his plea from not guilty to guilty. Fear of death—not for himself in the electric chair, but for his mother—was Dwyer's motive for his confessions and guilty plea. Or so he said.

It also emerged that Dwyer had earlier conveyed to his counsel this version of the facts and the reason he had abruptly changed his plea, but that the lawyer had kept the matter to himself and allowed the guilty plea to go on record. The district attorney, however, learning of Dwyer's accusations, decided to investigate the charges. So did Sheriff Fernando F. Francis. As a result, only six months after Dwyer went to prison, South Paris was stunned by another arrest. The sheriff abruptly took into custody his deputy, Carroll—on a charge of incest. Behind the Littlefield murders lay sexual molestation of Barbara Carroll by her own father. Meanwhile, the investigation into the murders continued, and in August 1938 Francis Carroll was tried for those crimes. Paul Dwyer was the chief witness against him. Only then did the complicated story finally unfold. Paul Dwyer, it turned out, had fallen in love with Barbara Carroll. Before long an adolescent crush became an intimate affair. Barbara revealed to Paul that she was not a virgin; she even put the story of her father's molestation in writing in letters to Paul. Shocked and angry, Dwyer threatened Carroll: If he continued to direct his illicit attentions to his daughter, Dwyer would give Mrs. Carroll the evidence of her husband's sordid behavior.

Carroll's response was to demand that the damning letters be turned over to him, but Dwyer refused—only to have Carroll tell him that Barbara was pregnant and that it was his fault. Carroll offered to "take care of" the pregnancy, but only if the letters were put into his hands. Dwyer would not be bluffed; he asked Dr. Littlefield to verify the pregnancy. Carroll confronted Littlefield and Dwyer, furious about the doctor's intervention. Littlefield (as Dwyer recounted it later from the witness stand) told Carroll that he knew the full story and said that, if what he had learned from Dwyer was true, "you belong in the state prison." Enraged, Carroll attacked and killed the doctor.

Carroll, when he learned that Dwyer had told Mrs. Littlefield who had killed her husband, murdered her as well. By that time, Dwyer not surprisingly feared for his life (as well as his mother's); it was then—in a desperate attempt to appease Carroll—that he began the wild odyssey that ended with his arrest three days later.

The State's case against Carroll rested not only on Dwyer's testimony, but on convincing physical and other circumstantial evidence as well. The jury found him guilty of murder and sentenced him to prison. After twelve years, in 1950, Carroll was released; he died a few years later.

But Dwyer fell through the cracks. Even though no part of the prosecution's theory of the murders or any of its evidence had involved a claim of conspiracy between Dwyer and Carroll, Dwyer remained behind bars—despite Carroll's having been convicted of the same crime. Dwyer's attempts to convince the authorities that his guilty plea had been anything but voluntary fell on deaf ears.

His plight did not go unnoticed among friends and supporters, but their efforts proved unavailing until seven years after Carroll—the real culprit, whose threats had induced Dwyer to make false confessions and enter a false guilty plea—had already been released from prison. In May 1957, Harold Bennett—an ACLU-affiliated attorney persuaded to take action in the case—filed with the superior court a five-part assignment of error, citing various due-process grounds for a new trial. The court rejected all his arguments. Dwyer's attorney appealed to the supreme court of Maine for certain exceptions.

That court ruled in his favor on an important point. The evidence of Dwyer's testimony in the Carroll trial (plus that of other witnesses), the court ruled, could indeed be used after all these years in a new trial for Dwyer. The court in essence declared that since Dwyer had not been tried with Carroll, the State in using him as its chief witness to convict Carroll had implicitly accepted his version of the facts. That included his insistence on his innocence, irrespective of his earlier confessions and guilty plea. He had explained those, in his testimony against Carroll, as arising from duress.

Before further legal issues surrounding a new trial could be settled, prison authorities acted on their own, deciding it was time to release Paul Dwyer on parole. The State of Maine, however, never officially admitted it had wrongly convicted Paul Dwyer on the basis of his own false guilty plea, or that its failure to terminate his prison sentence after Carroll's conviction had done him any injustice.

KIDNAPPING, RAPE, and murder were the charges flung at Jack Allen Carmen in August 1975 when he was arrested in Columbus, Ohio. Three days earlier, the violated body of a 14-year-old girl had been found in a field. An alert traffic officer spotted Carmen crossing the street and thought he resembled a composite drawing in the newspaper that had been based on descriptions of two alleged eyewitnesses to the crime. Carmen, 26, was a mentally retarded junior high school dropout who lived in town in a hotel managed by Volunteers of America. In no time at all, police said, he confessed.

Carmen's court-appointed attorney (described by the prosecution as "active" and "experienced") arranged for Carmen to plead guilty to the murder charge. Fear of the death penalty, according to later information, had played a role in his client's decision. (Ohio's new death penalty statute was only a year old.) The guilty plea meant the prosecution had no need to introduce Carmen's confession as evidence; as a result, the defense never was able to examine it. Despite considerable public protest at the idea of having Carmen plead—many in town knew he lacked normal mental abilities—the court allowed him to do so. Within a fortnight of the crime, Carmen had been convicted and sentenced to life in prison.

A few days later, local ACLU attorneys came to Carmen's defense, seeking a rehearing on the ground that he was incompetent to plead to any charge, much less to a crime that could have sent him to his death. It was well established that, eight years earlier, Carmen had been declared mentally incompetent and given a civil commitment to a state institution. His competence aside, three witnesses were also located who insisted they had seen Carmen at his hotel during the time of the crime.

A hearing was held before Judge Frederick Williams in January 1977 on the competency issue. The prosecution, having solved the crime to its satisfaction, vigorously protested the idea of nullifying Carmen's conviction by forcing withdrawal of his guilty plea. The prosecutor argued that painstaking efforts had been made to explain to Carmen the significance of his plea, and that he had surely understood what he was doing—this, despite evidence that Carmen's I.Q. ranged somewhere between 43 and 55. Psychiatric testimony established that Carmen had an extremely faulty memory, could not always recognize his attorneys, asserted and then denied the very same things, and so on. Judge Williams ruled for the defense, Carmen's plea was withdrawn, and his conviction was nullified.

While the state appellate court judges considered the ticklish question of whether Carmen could be ruled competent to be tried (even if he was incompetent to plead or to waive his rights prior to trial), Jack Carmen remained behind bars. Nearly two years had elapsed since his arrest.

The legal issues weighed by the appellate court were resolved in favor of Carmen's competence to be tried, and so he faced a jury in late December 1977. The trial, according to one reporter, was described by many spectators as "like something out of Perry Mason." Many in the court room thought Carmen was "a pathetic figure." Evidently he had "the sympathy of the spectators during most of the trial." His usual demeanor during the trial consisted of staring at the defense table, although he did give a sheepish smile to the sheriff's deputies when he entered or left the court room. He looked up from the defense table only once—when the judge mentioned the "electric chair." Meanwhile, alibi witnesses gave unchallenged testimony on Carmen's behalf: At the time of the murder Carmen had indeed been inside a Volunteers of America shelter, nowhere near the site of the crime.

A week before Christmas 1977, the jury of five women and seven men voted to acquit Carmen of all charges. As Judge Fred J. Shoemaker read out the jury's verdict, the crowd in the court room burst into applause.

Carmen's defense counsel, David Riebel and Thomas Tyack, wept at the good news for their client. When asked by reporters how he felt about his acquittal, Jack Carmen said, "I'm happy to be free again," adding, "I wish you guys a Merry Christmas."

9 ✳ WRONG PLACE, WRONG TIME

O N   A   L A T E autumn afternoon in 1974, Jerry Banks, a 23-year-old irregularly employed truck driver, stumbled on an awful scene in a wooded area of Henry County, Georgia. He made his discovery just off a country road near Stockbridge, twenty-five miles southeast of Atlanta. Banks was rabbit hunting at the time, and his attention was drawn by the frantic barking of his dog to bloodstains on the ground. Following the dog into some underbrush, he found a red bedspread—and then saw that it was partly covering two bodies.

The deceased, it turned out, were local musicians: 38-year-old high school band instructor Marvin W. King (the bedspread later proved to have belonged to him), and 19-year-old Melanie Ann Hartsfield, a former student of his and an assistant choir director at a nearby junior high school. They had obviously been murdered. Each had been hit by two shotgun blasts, one in the back and one in the head, apparently fired from close range. The autopsy reports led the police to conclude that the shootings had taken place at approximately 2:30 P.M. on November 7, 1974, a couple of hours before Banks discovered the bodies.

Banks occasionally did odd jobs for a neighbor, Grace Slaughter, and he had spent most of that day at her home. Toward the latter part of the afternoon, he decided to go hunting with his dog. He headed for the woods off an unpaved lane known as Old Rock Quarry Road, created when Rock Quarry Road was straightened and paved. The abandoned stretch had become a favorite place for teenagers to park and for hunters to leave their cars. Jerry had hunted there in the past, with his brother, so he knew the area well. When he unexpectedly uncovered the bodies of King and Hartsfield, he rushed directly to the main road and flagged down a passing motorist, who in turn alerted the authorities.

By the time the police arrived, the light had already faded so much that they could not really examine the scene. The next morning, however, the sheriffs found two red shotgun shell casings nearby. They also discovered bloodstains about 130 feet from where the victims had been lying. A hypothesis for the crime quickly emerged: The murderer, having shot Hartsfield and King, dragged their bodies to the spot where Banks found them and then attempted to cover them with the spread taken from King's car.

Unfortunately for Banks, the hunting weapon he had been carrying was a shotgun. He had made no effort to hide that fact from the authorities, who—when they found the shells—asked him for his gun. Then a routine background check established that four years earlier Banks had been convicted of manslaughter, which added to the suspicions against him. To make matters worse: He was black, the victims were white.

The murders remained unsolved for more than a month. During those weeks, the police had difficulty finding any clues connected with the crime. For instance, King's car was located between one mile and three miles (accounts vary) from the bodies, but the only hairs or fingerprints inside the vehicle were Hartsfield's and King's, so that was no help. Melanie Hartsfield's car turned up several miles away; it had been deliberately disabled (someone had pulled a coil wire). What significance that had for the murder investigation was unclear.

The police returned Banks's shotgun to him. They then asked him for it a second time so that they could test-fire it, but that did little to resolve their uncertainties; the results from the police laboratory's examination of the fired shells were suggestive, not conclusive. (Firing a shotgun leaves no bore markings on spent cartridges.) Thus it was impossible to say confidently that Banks's gun was the murder weapon, though the report from the crime lab did indicate with some certainty that the red shells found near the bodies came from Banks's shotgun. When he was questioned about this, Banks insisted that he had not fired the shotgun on the day of the murders and that he had not thrown out any used shells in the area. Hence, the presence of the shells at the scene was a mystery. At one point, Banks told the authorities that he had loaned his gun to a friend on the day of the murders. However, when the friend failed to confirm this, Banks admitted he had lied "to get the officers off my back."

Then, in early December, a month after the murders, a detective reported that he had found a third red shotgun shell near the murder site. It, too, had apparently been fired from Banks's gun. That was enough for the police. On December 10, Jerry Banks was arrested and charged with murder.

Banks was too poor to hire private investigators to do the kind of work that was desperately needed in his case. He did scrape together some money to hire a local attorney, Hudson John Myers. But either because he felt he was not being paid enough (he later said he was asked to work for Banks for little more than "a mess of collard greens") or because of general ineptitude and lack of imagination, Myers utterly failed to pursue some of the potentially useful leads he should have. At the trial he also failed to call to the stand a key witness who could have supported Banks's account of what had transpired.

Six and a half weeks after Banks's arrest, in early 1975, the jury—with the prosecutor's case based entirely on circumstantial evidence—convicted Banks and as quickly sentenced him to death. (Years later, the United States Supreme Court would review data showing that between 1973 and 1979 in Georgia, other things being equal, those convicted of killing a white were more than four times as likely to be sentenced to death as those convicted of killing a black.) No motive for the murders was ever proposed, much less established. The jury apparently believed Banks was a hopelessly stupid young man: stupid enough to kill two white people for no particular reason; stupider still, to flag down a passing car so he could report the crime to the police and then to remain at the scene until the police arrived; and, stupidest of all, to keep the murder weapon and then hand it over to the police.

Jerry's brother, Perry, had testified at the trial that he had used the shotgun in question when he hunted near the crime site a week before the murders; he could have ejected the shells there at that time. He had also been hunting in the area in early December, a few days before the third shell was found. Members of the jury must have concluded that Perry's story was the simple-minded product of misguided brotherly love, however, because they obviously didn't believe it any more than the police had believed Jerry's.

Jerry's neighbor, Grace Slaughter, had also testified, to the effect that Jerry had been working at her house at the very time (according to the autopsy reports) that King and Hartsfield were being murdered. According to Mrs. Slaughter, Banks had arrived for work around 9:30 A.M. and did not leave until well after 2:30 P.M., the estimated time of the murders. The jury discounted her testimony as well.

Attorney Myers's failure to locate the motorist Banks had flagged down after discovering the bodies was critical. In the absence of this witness, police testimony on the issue went uncontested. The police claimed they did not know the man's name, opening the way for the prosecution skillfully to suggest that Banks had made up the story about the passing motorist and that he had reported the murders himself. If that was true, there was no telling how much of the rest of the story Banks had made up. The implication was obvious: Nothing he said could be trusted. Soon after the trial, however—no thanks to Banks's lawyer—the "passing motorist" identified himself. Andrew Eberhardt, on his own initiative, got in touch with the trial judge and insisted he had given his name to the police when he reported the murders at Banks's request.

Even Hudson Myers couldn't ignore this surprising turn of events. He knew that if Eberhardt's story was true, the police should have given this information to the defense attorney, and that their failure to do so was grounds for overturning Banks's conviction. Myers filed a motion demanding a new trial. The trial judge promptly denied the motion, but Myers was not about to give up so easily; he appealed. Georgia's supreme court reversed the denial, saying that the trial court had erred in overruling the defendant's motion, given that the identity of an important witness had been discovered after the original trial. The unanimous decision ordering a retrial was handed down in September 1975.

Confronted with the challenge to reconvict Banks, the prosecution tried to cut its losses by offering him a deal: life imprisonment in exchange for pleading guilty to the murders. Banks steadfastly refused, however, insisting he would never lie about his innocence in court, "even if they let me walk away free. I didn't kill those people."

When this attempt at plea bargaining collapsed, the prosecution opened the second trial, one year after the murders. Once again Hudson Myers failed his client: He did not offer even the minimum defense he had presented at the first trial. He did not have Banks testify in his own defense, and neither did he solicit testimony from Banks's neighbor (his alibi witness) or his brother—both of whom *had* testified at the first trial. The only person attorney Myers called to the stand on his client's behalf was Eberhardt, the motorist. The trial was over in two days.

For the second time Banks had received a completely inadequate defense, and for the second time he was convicted on two counts of capital murder. To experienced court-watchers, this was not surprising. Stephen Harrison, one of the volunteer lawyers who later helped take over Banks's defense, subsequently told a reporter, "In the case of an indigent accused of a severe crime, everything in our system is geared toward his conviction. Cases such as Jerry Banks's are not all that unusual."

The only remaining issue for the trial court to decide was Banks's sentence. The murderer, it had been determined, had stood only five feet from the victims. Since Banks's weapon was a single-barrel shotgun, it had to be reloaded after each shot. Assuming that Banks was the murderer and his shotgun the murder weapon, this meant that whichever of the two victims was the second to be shot had a few moments of horrible anticipation before the gun could be fired again. The jury concluded (in the language of the Georgia statute) that at least this second murder "was outrageously and wantonly vile, horrible, and inhuman," because "it involved torture to the victim or depravity of the mind on the part of [Banks] in that the death was caused by two shotgun blasts." Accordingly, Banks was again sentenced to death on both counts of murder. Under Georgia law, Banks's conviction and death sentence were automatically appealed once more. In July 1976 the Georgia Supreme Court unanimously affirmed the murder convictions and the death sentence for Jerry Banks.

How much difference it would have made if Banks's attorney had done even rudimentary investigation of the murders, or had called more than two witnesses at the first trial and one at the second, is difficult to say. It is more difficult to believe it would have made no difference at all. Even worse than Myers's sloppiness in deciding which witnesses to call was another failure: He never filed the routine motion requesting the prosecutor to turn over information in his possession favorable to the defendant's case—a motion prosecutors are required to heed, a motion no competent defense attorney fails to file.

A special report on the quality of defense attorneys in capital cases, published in the *National Law Journal* in 1990, opened with the following observation:

> Southern justice in capital murder trials is more like a random flip of the coin than a delicate balancing of the scales. Who will live and who will die is decided not just by the nature of the crime committed but by the skills of the defense lawyer appointed by the court. And in the nation's Death Belt, that lawyer too often is ill-trained, unprepared and grossly underpaid.

The *Journal*'s investigation uncovered a capital case in Florida in which the trial judge was asked by the prosecutor to begin each day in court by smelling the defense counsel's breath for the odor of alcohol. In a capital case in Louisiana, the prosecutor admitted that he had been dating the defense attorney; after her client's conviction, it developed that the two attorneys had actually been cohabiting during the trial. In another Georgia case, a month after being convicted and sentenced to death, a defendant ran into his attorney in the prison yard; the lawyer had just been arrested for drug possession. Nine years later that attorney signed an affidavit admitting his drug use and other personal problems had left him ill equipped to defend his client, John Young, at trial. Four days later Young was nonetheless executed.

From the time of Banks's arrest through the denial by Georgia's supreme court of the appeal of his second conviction and sentence, no one was paying much attention to whether he had been given a fair trial. In late 1976, public defender Alex Crumbley was visiting his clients at the Henry County Jail when Banks spotted him and asked whether he could spare a minute. Crumbley paused and then went over to Banks's cell to see what he wanted. Banks's request was quite simple: He had not heard from Myers in some time, and he wondered whether Crumbley could help him find out whether his attorney was still working on the case.

Crumbley checked. Myers, he learned, was in the process of being disbarred because of his incompetent performance in other cases. Preoccupied with his own troubles, Myers had quietly and without notice abandoned Banks to his fate. Crumbley, somewhat to his surprise, suddenly found himself handling Banks's case. Crumbley's involvement turned out to be the lucky break Banks so desperately needed.

Crumbley's first step was to ask the United States Supreme Court to review the case. It was a long shot, and Crumbley knew it. In April 1977, as he expected, the Court refused. Then in March 1978 Alex Crumbley was appointed to the bench and thus could no longer represent Banks. He had already done enough investigation of the case, however, to convince himself that Banks was not the murderer. Before taking on his new judicial duties, he resolved to find another attorney for Banks. He found two: A. J. "Buddy" Welch, Jr., and Stephen P. Harrison. Crumbley's younger brother, Wade, joined the defense team as soon as he graduated from the University of Georgia Law School, and this trio, all from McDonough, Georgia, agreed to work on the case without fee. Every bit as convinced as Alex Crumbley that Banks was innocent, each made a commitment to spend one day a week working pro bono to vindicate their client.

In the summer of 1978, the attorneys went to Judge Sam Whitmire of the superior court, asking for a new trial based on ineffective assistance of counsel. The disbarment proceedings against Myers were still incomplete, but Banks's new attorneys thought the evidence supporting the ineffective-assistance argument was convincing even without a formal ruling against Myers. They were able to point to numerous places in the second trial where an objection should have been made or a motion filed, and they prepared a strong criticism of the trial strategy and tactics that Myers had employed. But Judge Whitmire remained unpersuaded; he disagreed that the problems uncovered by the new defense team amounted to ineffective assistance and therefore denied Banks a new trial.

The legal criteria that define "ineffective assistance of counsel" are complex and extremely conservative, and over the years appellate courts have judged only a handful of attorneys in capital cases to be "ineffective." In Georgia, it happens only about once every two years. Though Myers's performance was not formally found ineffective, that hardly constitutes an endorsement of his work. There were sufficient omissions, failures, and oversights in his conduct of the defense to give seasoned lawyers convincing reasons to think that a different defense attorney, with at least average skills and energy, would have done a more thorough investigation and could have convinced a jury to acquit.

Banks's attorneys appealed Judge Whitmire's decision, but to no avail. In November 1978 the Georgia Supreme Court affirmed the ruling: A new trial would not be granted. In the meantime, the same court had decided to severely restrict Myers's future career at the bar, ruling that he could no longer practice before either the Georgia Court of Appeals or the state supreme court. These sanctions resulted from Myers's failure to file appeals in two criminal cases—one a rape conviction, the other a conviction for marijuana possession. (Later, Myers did indeed suffer the ultimate professional sanction of disbarment.) Despite the findings against Myers and his glaring failure to conduct an adequate defense when his client's life was at stake, Georgia's supreme court refused to declare that the way he had handled the Banks case warranted a reversal and a new trial.

Undaunted by this defeat, Banks's defense team continued efforts to shore up its case. They learned, for example, that there were other witnesses, never called at either trial, who could shed light on the murders. One was Chief Paul Collier of the Stockbridge police. On the day Marvin King and Melanie Hartsfield were murdered, it turned out, Collier and his son (also a police officer) had been near the scene of the crime—near enough to hear the shots. Chief Collier confirmed that at about 2:30 in the afternoon he had heard four shots, one right after the other. That was during the period when Banks, according to one of the witnesses at the first trial, had been at work. In addition, Collier reported that he and the mayor of Stockbridge had later visited the site of the murders and found two green shotgun casings. These casings carried a heavy shotgun load and could not have come from Banks's twelve-gauge, single-barrel shotgun.

The attorneys also found a former police detective who had been involved in the murder investigation. He had interviewed four carpenters who, on the day of the murders, had been working on a house about eight hundred yards from the spot where the bodies of King and Hartsfield were found. The four workmen had also heard the shotgun blasts; they, like the Colliers, stated that the series of shots came in very rapid succession. In fact, they said, the entire sequence of four shots took no more than five seconds. Even the authorities had agreed that Banks's shotgun could fire only one blast at a time; it required at least five seconds to reload. In the process of test-firing the shotgun, they had discovered something else about it. As it was being reloaded the old weapon frequently failed to eject the spent shell casing and often fell apart. Clearly, if the victims had been murdered by shotgun blasts that rapidly followed each other, the deadly shots could not have come from Banks's gun. A memo summarizing this information—devastating to the prosecution's theory—had been circulated among the detectives working on the case, but it had subsequently disappeared from the file.

Banks's attorneys located yet another person who had heard the shots. Dean Floyd, a farmer, was the seventh witness to say that the shotgun blasts had followed each other so quickly that they could not have come from a single-shot weapon. On the day of the crime, Floyd had been constructing a calf pen not far from where the murders occurred. He had passed near the site shortly after hearing the shots—he was on his way to pick up his son at the end of the school day—and had seen a white man holding an automatic shotgun, leaning against a parked van. Floyd said he had reported all this to the sheriff, but that no one had bothered to get back in touch with him.

An unidentified woman called Banks's lawyers several times urging them to contact a person named Leon Scruggs. When they did, and interviewed him, Scruggs reported that he had seen a small station wagon (a car like King's) pulled over on Hudson Bridge Road shortly after noon on the day of the murders. A woman was sitting in the car, but two white men were outside, arguing loudly. This suggested an altogether new interpretation of what had happened on the roadside that November afternoon: A fight between King and another man, perhaps over Harts-field, had ended with the second man murdering both her and King. In fact, newspaper articles published just after the murders had reported that the police were looking for two white men, suspected of being the killers—another fact that had not come out at either of Banks's trials.

None of these important witnesses had been identified, interrogated, and subpoenaed by the defense in support of an acquittal for Jerry Banks. Either Hudson Myers had never probed enough to learn about them, or he had failed to see the potential value of their testimony for his client. Whatever the explanation, Jerry Banks had clearly not received the kind of assistance he needed from his attorney in the first two trials.

Other tips from anonymous sources (the defense team referred to them as "Deep Throats") began to come in. Someone left a spent shell from a different kind of shotgun on attorney Welch's porch, and then phoned to tell him to look for it. A former detective suddenly volunteered to turn over police files to Crumbley, Welch, and Harrison—files they had been pressing to get for weeks. Diligent efforts to undermine Banks's conviction were beginning to pay off, and success appeared to be taking shape on the distant horizon. Crumbley, Welch, and Harrison took their impressive array of newly discovered evidence back to Judge Hugh D. Sosebee, who had presided at both of the trials (and years earlier, at the trial in which Banks had been convicted of voluntary manslaughter). Judge Sosebee remained unimpressed, however, and in January 1980 he denied the request for a new trial. The defense promptly appealed yet again to the state supreme court, and this time—finally—they scored a victory. On June 9, 1980, with only one judge dissenting, the court ordered a third trial for Banks.

The prosecutor could have simply conceded error and disposed of all charges, but instead he insisted on pursuing the case against Banks. For six months, the State and the defense attorneys prepared to go to trial for the third time, while Jerry Banks waited in his death row cell.

In the process of getting ready for court, the defense attorneys made still another discovery. This one concerned Philip S. Howard, a former sheriff's detective and the lead investigator in the King and Hartsfield murders. By 1980, six years after the double murder was committed, it had been established that Howard had mishandled evidence in several criminal investigations. Banks's lawyers decided it might prove worthwhile to look into whether he had perhaps mishandled evidence in the Banks case as well.

According to Howard's testimony at Banks's first trial, the murders occurred on a Thursday, the shells from Banks's gun were found in the woods the next day and sent to the state crime laboratory on Saturday, and Banks was asked to turn in his gun on Sunday. This sequence conflicted, however, with the statement of a former county commissioner. That official said he had seen Howard test-fire Banks's gun behind the court house on Friday, one day after the murders and one day before Howard said he had had the gun. Suddenly the possibility loomed that Howard had taken the shells found in the woods and had—behind the court house—switched them with shells fired by Banks's shotgun. At the very least, one could no longer be confident about the provenance of any of the shotgun shells, and when or how they came to be where they were allegedly found. There was also a very real possibility that the shells found at the scene of the murder had indeed been left in the woods by Banks's brother Perry when he used the shotgun, just as he and Jerry had said.

Howard's dishonesty in other cases did not of course prove Banks was innocent (any more than Hudson Myers's ineffective defense did), but it certainly looked like an issue worth pursuing. Tracking Howard down was no easy task, however. Numerous leads had to be followed, which required both time and money. As defense attorney Wade Crumbley said later, "If you are very poor and have a complex case, your chances of getting a fair shake are greatly reduced. . . . Most indigents cannot afford able counsel; they cannot afford to have the expertise of a pathologist; they cannot afford to hire an investigator like Doug Moss. Fortunately, in the Jerry Banks case, we were able to raise some money."

In fact, raising money to pay for expenses over and above their own pro bono work had been one of the defense lawyers' first tasks. One important consequence of their success was that they *were* able to hire Doug Moss, an experienced criminal investigator, to look for Howard. Putting Howard on the stand was crucial to the defense's strategy. Unless Howard appeared as a witness, the prosecution would be able to argue that his testimony from the earlier trial was sufficient and could be used in his absence. The defense team wanted more—to expose Howard, a thoroughly discredited ex-detective who had resigned from one police department and been fired from another before being indicted and then convicted of forgery. He had perjured himself in other cases as well, and—most revealingly—in a case having nothing to do with Jerry Banks, he had been shown to have "tampered with and manipulated evidence involving [shotgun] shells. . . ."

Doug Moss's experience and skill proved critical. With dogged relentlessness, he took advantage of various anonymous tips and did not allow dead ends to discourage him. Eventually he succeeded in finding Philip Howard, by then working as a subcontractor for Georgia Power in Waynesboro, near the South Carolina border. The defense attorneys immediately drove to Waynesboro, where they engaged Howard in a grueling, middle-of-the-night interview.

On December 16, 1980, just after District Attorney E. Byron Smith said that he would again seek a death sentence for Banks, the defense attorneys decided to reveal all they knew about Howard. They let the prosecution know that they would call him to the stand, and they made it clear that they would be able to utterly destroy his credibility as a witness.

That, finally, was enough for the district attorney. Three days later, he announced he would not reprosecute the case. He was also willing to agree that the evidence from the shotgun shells "lacks sufficient legal credibility to be believed." Only former detective Howard could attest to precisely when and how those shells were discovered and the "chain of custody" through which they were held before the trial, said the district attorney, and Howard's "veracity has been entirely discredited through recent investigation by the district attorney's office." Never mind that it was the defense team that had conducted the investigation.

Three days before Christmas in 1980, Jerry Banks was freed. He noted that his religious faith had been a major factor in giving him first the stamina to withstand his five-year ordeal on death row and then the calmness of spirit that allowed him to harbor no anger toward those who had done him such an injustice. "I couldn't sit here and tell you that I believe in God and [at the same time] say that I'm angry at anybody. We're all human. We all make mistakes," he said, according to one newspaper account.

Banks was back with his wife and children on Christmas Eve, and a picture of the smiling family appeared in the papers, signaling the apparently happy ending to this awful story. The desire to be reunited with Virginia and their three children—Jerry, Jr.; Elbert; and Felicia— had been Banks's other sustaining force while he was incarcerated. In his prison Bible, he had written out his most heartfelt prayer: "Dear God, I ask you to watch over and bless and hold us together as a family. . . ."

Publicity about the way justice had miscarried was sufficient to inspire several people to offer Banks a job. He was able to choose one close to home—so he could be near the children, according to one news account. But despite initial appearances, Jerry Banks's transition from the cells of death row to the free world was painful and difficult. Shortly after his release, he learned that the paths he and his wife had been following for six years did not lead in the same direction. Virginia could not endure the strain and filed for divorce. Jerry was distraught, above all at the prospect of losing his children. For the next three months he begged his wife to reconsider; she did not respond to his pleas.

On March 29, 1981, three days before the divorce would have become official, Banks went to the family's home and sent the children next door to their aunt's house. After some discussion with Virginia, he pulled out a pistol. He shot and wounded her severely as she fled from the house, put the .38 caliber pistol to his own chest, and pulled the trigger. Death was instantaneous.

Jerry left a note. "Everything I have in this world has been taken away," it read. His struggle on death row had not, to be sure, ended with a walk into the execution chamber. The State had not killed him physically, but it had certainly broken his spirit. The walk away from prison was itself a struggle. Banks's friend and counselor, the Reverend Murphy Davis, said, "It was something set into motion—a very powerful death machine— that just couldn't be stopped. You take six years of a person's life, you tell them they are going to die. You tell his wife and kids that, you set a tragedy in motion. At the end of six years you don't go back and say it was all a mistake. I don't think anybody could understand the pain and tragedy that tore up Jerry's heart." Six weeks later, in mid-May, Virginia Banks was also dead, a victim of the wounds Jerry had inflicted.

In May 1981, attorneys Wade Crumbley, Buddy Welch, and Stephen

Harrison received an "Indigent Defense Award" from the Georgia Association of Criminal Defense Lawyers, a dramatic indication that their fellow members of the Georgia bar recognized the value of their work and appreciated it. For their efforts on behalf of Jerry Banks, the three defense lawyers never received a dime, however. Not having been officially court appointed, they were not entitled to even the minimal compensation that public defenders receive. (Some states, such as Mississippi, Louisiana, and Arkansas, pay attorneys in death penalty cases as little as $1,000, regardless of the amount of time and effort they invest.) Welch, in an article he published several years after receiving the award, was quoted in a remark that makes clear the importance of adequate compensation for defense counsel: "If lawyers [were] certified to be competent, if they [were] paid a reasonable fee to afford them the time and finances to do investigative work and consult with expert witnesses, our system of justice would be strengthened considerably."

The three Banks children—the oldest of whom was 11 when their parents died—went to live with their aunt, Opel Lee Davis. In June 1981, Jerry's mother, Nannie L. Dodson, acting as the administrator of his estate, filed a $12 million suit on behalf of the children. Defendants were Jimmy Glass, the former sheriff of Henry County, and five of his deputy sheriffs; the suit cited their mishandling of the case, which Dodson believed was "motivated by racial prejudice." After nearly two years of negotiations, in March 1983, Dodson settled out of court for $150,000. It was the county's insurance company, however, not the individual law-enforcement officers, that paid the awarded sum into a trust fund for the children.

The State thus acknowledged that justice had miscarried. The State also in effect said that the lives of Jerry and Virginia Banks were each worth only $75,000. Around the time the settlement was announced, Jerry, Jr., was quoted in a news account speaking hopefully about his future. In a comment rich with poignancy, he said that when he grew up he wanted to "go into a law field."

Not even the peculiarly tragic aftermath of the Jerry Banks case has been sufficient to prod the criminal justice system into reforming itself. In Georgia and other states, the quality of investigation and representation afforded to most defendants facing the death penalty remains unchanged and wholly inadequate. As recently as 1990, the Georgia Supreme Court threw out death sentences for two black men defended by an 85-year-old attorney who, unbeknownst to them, had at one point been an Imperial Wizard of the Ku Klux Klan. Retained for a few hundred dollars by the defendants' impoverished families, this attorney had consistently missed meetings during the trial and had once fallen asleep while sitting at the defense counsel's table.

The great tragedy of the Jerry Banks case is that it was like compound interest on the mishandling of the tragic murders of Marvin King and Melanie Hartsfield. That two people were murdered was bad enough. But then an innocent man was convicted and condemned to die. When his conviction was found flawed, the State retried and reconvicted him in another flawed proceeding. Next the innocent defendant's innocent family was destroyed, first emotionally and then through a brutal murder-suicide. Jerry Banks's children, adjusting to a life with no parents, were three more innocent victims.

The bungled murder investigation and incompetent defense accomplished all this, and more; it drew a veil over the trail of the true killer, so that he (or she) remains unknown and unpunished. For all anyone knows, by now the killer may have killed again. At the time the out-of-court award was made to Jerry Banks's children, the *Atlanta Constitution* in a bold editorial called the payment "blood money" and went on to say, "No amount of money could ever really make up for what the system—all of us included—did to Jerry Banks and his family. But $150,000 doesn't even begin to address the level of damages, the lasting pain. In fact, it come closer to being an insult."

✳

CORRUPT PRACTICES by police or prosecution that lead to convicting the innocent take a wide variety of forms. In the Banks case, the preparation of false physical evidence—although it was not the only problem—appears to have been one of the factors that contributed to the erroneous conviction. In other cases we discuss, testimony known to be perjured was used. Two cases from California further illustrate the abuses and errors that can trap the innocent as well as the guilty.

Christmas 1971 in Long Beach, California, was wet with fog and rain. Despite the holiday, police officers were called away from their homes to investigate the brutal murder of William Staga. He had apparently been bludgeoned to death in his own apartment. The resident manager had discovered the body at 7:00 A.M., when—hearing a commotion and seeing someone run out Staga's front door with a television set—he entered the apartment. There he found Staga, dead, in the blood-smeared living room.

The police promptly found a bloody hammer in an alley behind the building. They also noticed a blue Plymouth parked at the curb directly outside Staga's place; it was registered to Lawrence Reyes. Within half an hour of learning about the crime, the police had located Reyes two blocks away—or rather he located them; he flagged down a patrol car to report that his car had been stolen. With him at the time was his childhood friend, Juan Venegas, visiting from Colorado for the holidays. Two days later, after rather hasty investigations, the police sought murder complaints against them both.

The evidence against Reyes was certainly suggestive: One of his hands showed recent cuts (he must have been in a fight), three of the witnesses identified him from his photo, a search of his home uncovered the victim's wallet and a pair of bloody trousers, and his palm print was found in Staga's apartment. Besides, his "stolen" car had been found parked right outside the murder scene.

Against Venegas, however, there was nothing—except his having been caught in Reyes's company. The district attorney authorized a charge against Reyes but not against Venegas. Further detective work by the police, however, established that Venegas and Reyes had been seen together just before the time of the crime, and that the clothes Venegas was wearing when stopped by the traffic police were like those on the man a witness claimed to have seen running off with the television from Staga's apartment. Once they had these pieces of information, the police charged Venegas, too.

The two men went to trial in July 1972. Reyes confessed. He said he had visited Staga, a casual friend, early Christmas morning in search of something to drink. When, to his surprise, Staga made a homosexual advance, Reyes went berserk and killed him. While walking home, Reyes decided to report his car as stolen. He asked Venegas to accompany him—and then they met the police. Venegas claimed not to have been with Reyes at all in the early morning hours, until they went out together to report the "stolen" car. Reyes confirmed the alibi, as did members of his family.

Medical evidence at trial supported the State's claim that two persons were involved in the Staga murder. With Reyes's confession in hand, the prosecution believed Venegas had to be lying. That belief was supported by testimony from a local bartender who claimed the two defendants had been drinking together in his bar just minutes before the murder. Other witnesses during the four-day trial gave less direct support to the prosecution's theory. Both defendants were found guilty of first-degree murder and sentenced to life in prison.

Two years later, however, in September 1974, the California Supreme Court reversed Venegas's conviction. The court insisted that the evidence at trial simply failed to warrant his conviction. The decision was unusual in that it amounted to retrying the case on the evidence—which is exactly what appellate courts never do (or at least never admit doing). After two years and three months in jail and prison, Venegas was released.

Venegas then turned prosecutor himself, in a civil suit against the city of Long Beach and its police. He named three officers and included in his argument a deposition from the bartender to the effect that his testimony—crucial to the conviction—was the result of intimidation by the police investigating the crime. When the case went before the jury, in September 1980, Venegas triumphed: The city and the three officers were found in the wrong, and Venegas was awarded $1 million. Jurors told his attorney that they "voted unanimously because they wanted to show there was no doubt that Mr. Venegas wasn't involved in the murder." Judge Ronald Swearinger of the Superior Court of Los Angeles County, who presided over the trial, said, "I think the jury was horrified at what happened to this man."

But the city of Long Beach and its employees appealed, and the controversy dragged on in the California courts. More than two years later, back in court—this time the Circuit Court of Appeals—Venegas argued that his federal civil rights had been violated. He asked for $3 million in damages. Over the years his wounds from the wrongful conviction had deepened: His Colorado farm had been taken from him, and his "criminal record" had made it impossible for him to get or hold a job. Once more the jury agreed; Venegas was awarded $2 million plus punitive damages and costs.

Again the police officers appealed, and again they lost. The final settlement in the case was an award to Venegas of $2.08 million plus attorneys' fees—to our knowledge, the largest award ever made for a wrongful conviction of murder.

AT THE SAME TIME Venegas was struggling to get the California courts to vindicate him, Tony Cooks was plunging into his own serious difficulties. On a dark January night in 1980, John Gould, 42, prematurely crippled with arthritis, was walking with his wife just outside their apartment in Paramount, California, twenty-five miles or so south of downtown Los Angeles. Suddenly, three teenaged black youths assaulted him, beating him to the ground, stabbing and shooting him. Helpless and screaming in terror, his wife watched. The assailants then ran off, laughing (or so a witness later attested). Two weeks later, still comatose in the hospital, Gould died.

Helen Foster, a neighbor, became the prosecution's chief witness. Looking out her apartment window, she said, she had watched the mugging take place sixty yards away. Detective Vernon Clover, assigned to his first homicide case, visited Mrs. Foster and showed her some photos of black youths from the neighborhood. She recognized one of the boys as the same one she had reported three weeks earlier to the police for molesting two little girls.

Shortly after Clover had gone, Mrs. Foster also left her apartment. At a nearby crosswalk, she noticed three young blacks on foot across the street. She immediately contacted the police again and said that one of them—Tony Cooks, just turned 18—was Gould's killer. She recognized Cooks, having seen him many times before. (In fact, six years previously, he and one of her sons had been in a minor fracas; her son had come out on the short end.)

Cooks was arrested in March. Although he suffered from epilepsy, during interrogation police refused to let him take his medication. When asked where he was the night of the crime, he said he was with another family and was unaware that any street assault had occurred in the neighborhood. (All members of this family would later confirm his alibi, though none was called at his original trial.) Told by Clover that the police knew he was guilty, Cooks was advised to confess.

When Mrs. Gould was shown Cooks's photo she told the detective, "I can't be positive, but I think that's him." Later, at trial, she would positively identify Cooks as the one who held her at bay while the others pummeled her husband to the ground.

Only days after Cooks's arrest, the police arrested a 14-year-old boy on the strength of Foster's accusation. Interrogated about the murder by Detective Clover, the boy fully confessed his own involvement in the mugging and accused Cooks and another youth. Two down and one to go.

Cooks went to trial in 1981. Gus Poole, Cooks's black defense attorney, had pressed hard on the white witnesses, asking them whether they thought "all blacks look alike." He managed to infuriate the witnesses by implying they were racists. White jurors were also incensed. The first trial ended with a hung jury, divided on racial grounds ten to two, whites against blacks.

The second trial was abruptly ended when the judge learned that a juror had decided, without authorization, to examine the murder scene. The third trial, like the first, ended with a hung jury, nine whites for conviction, three Latinos for acquittal. Finally, in the fourth trial, the jury—nine whites and three blacks—was unanimous: Guilty of murder, but only in the second degree.

Judge Roosevelt Dorn, black and a former deputy sheriff, was extremely unhappy with the verdict and simply refused to accept it, saying, "I have to be able to sleep at night and I have to be able to look in the mirror." The prosecution appealed, and the higher court ordered the jury's guilty verdict re-instated. Thus forced back into court to impose sentence on Cooks, Judge Dorn really vented his anger.

"I am convinced this is the worst job of [police] investigation I have ever seen," he said. He denounced defense counsel as "totally incompetent." He explained that the police had conducted "one of the most suggestive photo lineups I have ever seen. . . ." (The only picture of a light-skinned black in the group of photos shown to Mrs. Gould was of

Cooks, and she had earlier stated to the police that one of the assailants was a light-skinned black.) Judge Dorn scoffed at the idea that the witness Foster could have identified anybody at night in the street from her apartment window 177 feet away.

Deputy prosecutor Thomas Gray was also highly critical of Detective Clover's handling of the investigation. For one thing, the language in the confession by the 14-year-old—who was semiliterate—was totally implausible. In a later interview, the boy (then serving a term in a state reformatory for his part in the murder) claimed he had cast blame on Cooks in order to shift police attention away from his half-brother, who was a suspect in the crime.

The unfair photo line-up and dubious confession apart, the real basis for believing Cooks was innocent turned on discoveries in 1983 by David Johnston of the *Los Angeles Times*. His investigations established that two other eyewitnesses to the crime, in the same apartment building as the prosecution's chief witness, had given a completely different account of John Gould's murder—an account inconsistent with Cooks having been involved.

Even more significant, within five minutes of the murder and only two blocks away, police had stopped three black youths who fit witnesses' descriptions far better than Cooks did—and then released them. No one had mentioned this at Cooks's four trials.

After he had uncovered so much that was shabby about the police work that helped convict Cooks, journalist David Johnston interviewed Mrs. Gould. She viewed the case, he wrote, "as a travesty of justice," in which she had been forced to relive the terrible night of the crime again and again from the witness stand. She still thought Cooks guilty, but she admitted that "if the man . . . is innocent, this has been a nightmare for him."

In November 1986 Tony Cooks was awarded yet another new trial. Prosecuting him once again was Tom Gray, but in Cooks's corner was a new defense attorney, John Yzurdiaga. The accumulated evidence uncovered since 1981 was at last put before the jury. After six days of testimony and several hours of deliberation, the jury voted for acquittal. The jury foreman was later quoted as saying, "We felt the wrong identification was made, and it should have been Doug Henderson."

Henderson was one of the three youths the police stopped right after the murder but then completely ignored; he had appeared on the stand only in Cooks's fifth trial. There he denied any involvement in the crime. It turned out that he was also a client of Cooks's original defense attorney, Gus Poole, and that Poole had let it be known more than once that he believed Henderson, not Cooks, was one of the three who murdered Gould.

After acquitting Cooks, many of the jurors wanted the prosecution to indict Henderson, but even Yzurdiaga, Cooks's new attorney, agreed the trail of evidence against Henderson was by then too cold. A successful prosecution was highly unlikely.

The protracted ordeal was hard on the Cooks family. They lost their home to pay legal fees and bail bonds. Tony Cooks, by then 24, observed soberly, "Mr. Gray [the prosecutor] should have known a long time ago that I didn't do this. . . . Now I just want to put this behind me and start my life."

PART FOUR

RUSH TO

JUDGMENT

10 ✳ GUILTY AT FIRST SIGHT

D R. ELMER SCHMIERER arrived at Arcadia General Hospital at ten minutes past noon. He was taken immediately to examine the seven children who had just been admitted. After pronouncing three of them dead—two, he had been told, were dead on arrival; the third had just died—he entered another room where three more were laid out on stretchers. All were shaking and struggling to breathe. Their lungs were filled with fluid, and saliva was beginning to foam from their mouths. Schmierer guessed right away that they had been poisoned. The children were moaning loudly, and the air smelled of feces. Despite massive doses of atropine, all three died within an hour. The seventh child died at 5:30 the next morning.

When a child dies, people react with shock and anger, all the more so if the circumstances of the death are suspicious. Medical examiners give high priority to establishing the cause of death; police and prosecutors double their efforts to bring the killer or killers to justice. This is especially true in small towns where practically everyone knows everyone else. When *seven* children in one family die of poisoning, the public is truly horrified. Uncertainty over whether there has been foul play hangs thick in the air, and solving the crime becomes urgent business.

News of the tragedy that struck the dusty Florida town of Arcadia in October 1967 spread quickly. Reporters flocked to the region. For a few days, the deaths of those seven children, assumed to be murders, was one of the top stories in the nation. Yet despite all the immediate attention, it took more than twenty years for anything like the complete story to emerge.

James and Annie Mae Richardson, the dead children's parents, were people of color. Both were illiterate, and James was hard of hearing; his I.Q. of around 75 classified him as a slow learner. He and his wife worked as fruit pickers, earning 25¢ for each box of oranges they filled. In a good week, they might bring in $100 to $115—hardly enough to sustain a large family. The Richardsons did their best, but measured by material standards, that wasn't very good. They were desperately poor.

They were, however, determined to play Santa Claus as well as they could for their youngsters: 8-year-old Betty Jean; Alice, 7; Susie, 6; Doreen, 5; Vanessa, 4; Diane, 3; and 2-year-old James, Jr. Though Christmas was still two months away, Mrs. Richardson was making plans to bake a pecan pie and cook a goose for the family's holiday meal, just as she had done the previous year. She also later said that she and her husband had already started putting presents on layaway. "That's what you have to do when you have a large family. It ain't like having one child or two."

If all went well, Santa would bring a talking doll for Betty Jean ("one of the big old dolls where you pull a string and it talks," her mother said). Susie, too, wanted a doll, as well as a tea set. Doreen, in fact, had said they all wanted the same thing. James, Jr., the only boy, was in line for a toy car, and maybe even a tricycle and "one of those wagons to be pulled in."

Christmas never came for the seven Richardson children. On October 25, 1967, someone laced their lunch with what turned out to be parathion, a highly toxic agricultural pesticide. The poison brought on pulmonary edema (fluid in the lungs). It was so bad, one doctor testified, that as soon as you walked in the room you could tell from the children's raspy breathing—without even bothering with a stethoscope—that there was excessive moisture in their lungs. In effect, the children drowned in their own bodily fluids.

Arcadia, the seat of DeSoto County, lies in the southwest part of Florida between Sarasota and Fort Myers, thirty-five miles inland from the Gulf of Mexico. Outside the Everglades, there are few spots more remote in the state. Home in the 1960s to between six thousand and seven thousand residents, a third of whom were black, Arcadia provided laborers for the nearby citrus groves and cattle ranches, and for the large state hospital that had opened in 1949. The whites worked mostly in the mental hospital; the blacks picked the fruit. In 1967, though thirteen years had passed since the United States Supreme Court's decision in *Brown v. Board of Education*, a black minister could with accuracy (and no apparent embarrassment) refer to "the Negro school." There were rumors that the only movie theater in town had closed when it began to look as if blacks might try to buy tickets. The café at the Trailways bus depot prominently displayed a sign announcing management's right to refuse service, and Arcadia's restaurants were to all intents and purposes completely segregated. The cemeteries, too, were still separate and unequal. Today, outside the beautifully landscaped main cemetery, seven simple stones mark the seven graves of the Richardson children in the sandy field reserved for blacks.

The Richardsons were a close-knit family, used to being together. At the end of a workday, Richardson would later recount, he typically spent "all the time" with his wife and children. "I never let my wife get out of my sight. My wife never let me get out of her sight. My children—we laughed and played on the beds. Sometimes we tear up the bed, and my wife would get at me about letting the children jump all over the bed. She said, 'Do you love the children, James,' a heap of times." Indeed, when Annie Mae was asked about the relationship between James and the children, she said, "He loved every last one of them and treated all of them equal right." James himself said, "I really loved my children, and I don't think nobody in the whole world can give his love to their children more than me." Others told how he liked to run outside with the children and play with them there, or sing "Christian songs" to them.

Early on Wednesday morning, October 25, Annie Mae and James Richardson left as usual for work in a citrus grove some fifteen miles outside of town. They had to walk five or six blocks from their home at 131 Watson Avenue to the spot where a truck picked up workers. Once at the grove, workers were supposed to wait for the trees to dry in the morning air before they started picking. But Richardson, when he arrived at the job site, was impatient to earn as much as he could. "They told us it was dangerous to climb up into the wet trees," he recounted when talking about his job, but added that sometimes he would do it anyway, he was so eager to get to work. On this particular day, he and Annie Mae had filled about fifteen boxes of oranges when they stopped to take a lunch break. She ate a sandwich made from the chicken she had fried that morning; he had a ham sandwich.

Suddenly Fred Steven, one of the foremen, came running across the field. He yelled that Richardson must return to town; one of his children was ill. "Hurry up," Steven said. "They have been calling and calling on my phone." James and his wife did not like being separated, so they decided they would both quit for the day. They climbed into Steven's truck—James in the rear, Annie Mae up front in the cab ("because the back of the truck was too high for her to get up there")—and Fred Steven drove them straight to Arcadia General Hospital.

Bessie Reese, the next-door neighbor who had been in charge of the children for the day, was standing outside the hospital. When James asked her what had happened, she indicated that she didn't know. "Go inside," she said, "and they will tell you." Since James, Jr., had recently been sick, both parents assumed that he had taken a turn for the worse. "Okay," Richardson said, "probably James got sick."

James was sick, all right, but that was only part of the problem. Myrtice Jackson, a first-grade teacher at Arcadia's all-black Smith-Brown school, had been the first to notice that something was amiss. One of her students was Alice Richardson. When Alice returned to school from home, where she had eaten lunch, she began to perspire heavily almost as soon as she sat down. She clutched her desk tightly. Her mouth gaped open, and she was retching and trembling. She couldn't talk. Jackson, fearing the child might be having an epileptic fit—she'd never seen one, but couldn't think what else might be happening—summoned help. With another teacher, Ruby Fiason, she carried Alice to the principal's office. A few minutes later two more of the Richardson children, Susie and Betty Jean, were also brought to the office. Susie's symptoms were similar to Alice's. Betty Jean wasn't in quite such bad shape; at least she could walk. The principal and the teachers didn't hesitate long, however. They rushed the three girls to the hospital.

Susie's teacher, Gustava Luther, learning that there were other Richardson children still at home, decided to check on them. Sure enough, she found four preschoolers with their baby-sitter, Bessie Reese. Two children were lying weakly on Reese's porch. Another child was standing up, crying. Reese was holding the fourth. Luther grabbed two of the children and headed for the hospital. Close behind were other teachers, who took the last two preschoolers with them.

When James and Annie Mae arrived at the hospital, they had no idea that a tragedy was unfolding inside. And at first no one would talk to them. People were busily rushing about, but they either ignored the bewildered parents or made vague allusions to some difficulty. First the minister. Then the sheriff. Then the minister again, saying, "All of us must get down on our knees and start praying." When Richardson asked what they should pray for, the minister simply stated, "It is time to pray."

Even so, when the sheriff returned and said, "Boy, all of your children are dead," Richardson would not, could not, believe it. "You are a liar," he said. Those were strong words for a poor black man to address to a white sheriff, but Richardson was shocked by the news. His wife fell to her knees and wept.

The first police officer to arrive at the hospital was Lt. Joseph Minoughan of the Arcadia Police Department. He stayed only briefly. Thinking there might be other children in danger, he rushed to the Richardson home. By then the house was empty, but he did not otherwise sense anything wrong and simply asked a neighbor to watch the place. He went back to the hospital for a few minutes and then returned to the house. By that time two other officers had arrived on the scene: Arcadia's chief of police, Richard Barnard, and DeSoto County Sheriff Frank Cline. Chief Barnard's primary responsibility was local misdemeanors. This case, because it was a felony investigation, came under Sheriff Cline's jurisdiction. Since the felony had been committed within the city limits, however, the police chief was supposed to assist the sheriff.

The two men together searched the Richardson house and a small shed in the back yard. They discovered nothing suspicious in either place, though they did notice a strange metallic smell in the air. Cline recognized the odor, which could be detected from several yards away; he knew it came from parathion. There was, however, no parathion to be found in either the house or the shed.

In the ensuing hours, several others joined the case. Sheriff Cline, the county's Judge Gordon Hayes, and local prosecutor Frank Schaub would end up being at the center of the investigation. These three not only handled the search for clues but also eagerly gave regular updates to the media on each new fragment of evidence. They called press conferences whenever one of them had a new hunch and readily commented on the inquiry as it unfolded.

Chief Barnard and Lt. Minoughan, however, refused to make statements to the press, pose for pictures, or appear on television. But although Barnard quietly disapproved of the way Sheriff Cline and the others were managing the public relations aspects of the case, he continued to offer his assistance. Cline, however, did not need Chief Barnard. He had investigators from two state agencies—the health and agriculture departments—and the state attorney general's office supplementing the work he, his prosecutor, and the judge had already undertaken.

The mystery deepened the next morning, after the last of the seven children died. Someone called the police to report that a sack of parathion had been found in the shed behind the Richardson house. Even Sheriff Cline thought that was odd, given that the shack had been searched at least five times on the previous day without anything being uncovered. He was sure the parathion hadn't been there and promptly told reporters so, bluntly and directly: "It wasn't there yesterday." Cline's account of how the authorities learned about the parathion did not, however, correspond with Minoughan's. Later, for example, it became clear that they couldn't even agree on whether a man or a woman had made the tip-off call.

Quite independent of that, rumors began to surface that on the eve of the tragedy James Richardson had purchased life insurance for his children. This hardly seemed like the type of thing an impoverished laborer trying to save money for Christmas presents would do, but the rumors—combined with the discovery of parathion in the shed—provided a reason to focus the investigation on Richardson.

On Sunday, October 29, more than a thousand mourners filled a local gymnasium for the children's funeral. Annie Mae and James Richardson were of course there; both collapsed in tears. The national media were on hand, too, and the pressure on Cline to make an arrest was strong.

Two days later, on Halloween, James Richardson was arrested and charged with seven counts of first-degree murder—even though Chief Barnard was still not convinced Richardson was the culprit. Neither were the prosecutor and his assistants, Frank Schaub and John "Red" Treadwell; their doubts may have been behind the abrupt change in the charges from murder to child neglect. And though no explanation was given, Annie Mae Richardson was then also arrested.

Richardson protested his innocence from the start. "I loved those children hard," he said. But Sheriff Cline still thought Richardson was the killer, and on Wednesday he and Judge Hayes called another news conference. They announced that some years earlier, in Jacksonville, five other Richardson children had died under mysterious circumstances. (Hayes and Cline did not bother to point out that this was simply an unverified rumor; no charges had been filed on that occasion and no foul play was ever proved.)

Meanwhile, after the funeral, both Richardson and his wife were made to take lie detector tests. Sheriff Cline concluded that the results indicated the Richardsons were "lying from the very beginning." The motive, he and Judge Hayes contended, was $14,000 in insurance money. Hayes, who also served as the county coroner, decided to call a coroner's jury; by law, he could hand-pick its members. The sheriff and judge reasoned that once the coroner's jury gave its report, the prosecutors—Schaub and Treadwell—would have no choice but to issue murder warrants.

On Thursday, November 2, the coroner's jury met. Representatives of the media were invited to attend. Judge Hayes presided. He had been on the bench for more than thirty years, and no one doubted that he was one of the most powerful men in the area. Before the session opened, the judge made clear his view that the defendant was guilty and would be charged with murder. "We will meet today," he announced, "to instruct Frank Cline to file murder charges against Richardson." The assistant prosecutor, Treadwell, conducted the examination for the State.

Sheriff Cline reported that he had "evidence" about the earlier mysterious deaths of other Richardson children. (Perhaps he did, though he produced none at the hearing.) Also testifying was Bessie Reese, the babysitter from next door. Her daughter, Dorothy Bracey, usually cared for the Richardson children, but she had had to go to Sarasota that morning and had asked her mother to fill in. Thus it was Bessie Reese who actually served the children the deadly lunch. That much she acknowledged. But no one asked her why she had served food with such a pervasive odor of poison in it. (Much later she would tell an investigator who did ask that she never suspected anything was wrong with the food. "I didn't smell nothing," she said.) Further, though Treadwell conceded that Mrs. Reese was on parole for some crime or other, he did not go into details. No one asked about that, either.

Mrs. Reese did, however, tell the coroner's jury about an encounter with Charlie Smith, another black neighbor, on the day after the deaths. Smith had come over and suggested that they search for the poison, according to Mrs. Reese. He had headed straight for the shed, she said, where they promptly found the parathion.

Smith also took the stand. In his version of the story, it was Reese who proposed they look in the shed. Nonetheless, Judge Hayes seemed inclined to believe Reese rather than Smith. In fact, he ordered Smith arrested and held as a material witness. Charlie Smith remained in jail for the next two months.

Gerald Purvis, an insurance salesman, testified. Yes, he confirmed, on the evening before the children died he had stopped at the Richardson house and tried to sell some life insurance. Though Richardson had shown polite interest, he had explained that he simply couldn't afford it. Purvis had then said he would return the following week to see whether Richardson's finances were in better shape. Thus, Purvis made it clear, he had not sold Richardson a policy. The assistant prosecutor, Treadwell, suggested Purvis had given Richardson the impression that a policy was in effect, even though the premium had not yet been paid. Purvis denied having tried to get Richardson to think that, but after further questioning he allowed there was a chance Richardson might have misunderstood. Then he asserted again that he doubted it.

Richardson himself always insisted he knew his family did not have any insurance. At least one news report, written less than three weeks after the crime, supported Purvis and Richardson. It explicitly stated that "there would have been no insurance payoff for the accused father even if he had not been arrested: he had not been able to pay the policy's initial premium of $3.20." Nevertheless, at the coroner's hearing and thereafter, the potential insurance money became the murder motive in the eyes of many.

After a half hour of deliberation, the coroner's jury returned. Given the way Judge Hayes had opened the hearing, it was no surprise that the jurors concluded there was sufficient evidence of an indictable offense to make a charge: "Death with premeditation at the hands of James Richardson and party or parties unknown." Oddly, this verdict by the coroner's jury was almost the first reference to Richardson during the entire inquest. Other than Purvis, most of the witnesses had not even mentioned Richardson's name, despite all the details in their testimony. No new facts had emerged from the hearing, and nothing presented at the inquest was new to Schaub and Treadwell.

At the same time, public opinion had solidified, and a kind of hysteria had arisen. The jury's conclusion convinced Schaub and Treadwell to get on the bandwagon. The prosecutors never again publicly expressed any misgivings about the case. They professed to be convinced, like most of the community, that Judge Hayes and Sheriff Cline were right: Richardson was their man. Frank Schaub also believed insurance was the motive and that Richardson did not love his children. (Years later, he continued to cling to that theory, explaining that—in his view—Richardson was trying "to avoid the responsibility of supporting the children. . . . He had no interest in his family or anyone else.")

Some years earlier, James Richardson had worked as a garbage collector in Daytona Beach, across the state from Arcadia. Coincidentally, it was in Daytona Beach that a 30-year-old civil rights advocate and family law attorney, John Spencer Robinson, took an interest in the case. Outraged at the daily televised rantings by the white sheriff and judge, Robinson (also white) wondered whether a fair trial would ever be possible. He called Jack Young, who ran the Daytona Beach garbage service and with whom he had negotiated contracts, to find out more about the accused man.

Young was unequivocal in his judgment. Although Richardson had worked only briefly for the city, Young was quick to say, "I know one thing—I can't believe he killed the kids. He loved those children. He was a good family man, a fine worker who never missed a day's work. I don't care what the papers say, I know I don't believe it." Robinson's initial concern had been simply that the man have a fair trial; Young's suggestion that Richardson might actually be innocent aroused Robinson's interest even further. He decided then that he would volunteer to help with the case and got in touch with Joel Atkins, head of the Florida NAACP and an old friend of his from years of involvement in civil rights issues.

Atkins, thus prompted by Robinson to take action, sent the head of the Arcadia NAACP to visit Richardson in jail. His task was to learn whether Richardson had an attorney and to suggest a few names if he didn't. Richardson knew none of the lawyers on the list of those who had offered assistance, but he chose Robinson. He felt good, he later said, about the similarity between the names "Robinson" and "Richardson." In this way, John Robinson soon found himself in the middle of his first murder case. It was to be the most difficult case of his career.

One meeting with Richardson was enough to convince Robinson that the grieving father was innocent. Though Robinson admitted that as a young lawyer he had made errors of judgment about a client's guilt or innocence, this time he was sure. And nothing that happened subsequently made him waver in his view. "I've never found that [Richardson] even exaggerated or strained the truth one iota," he would say later. Robinson had offered to provide advice until court-appointed counsel could take over, but he and his partner, Richard Whitson, ended up handling the whole case themselves at no charge.

In mid-November they took the first step, filing for a writ of habeas corpus. A habeas hearing would require the State of Florida to show cause for holding Richardson. If the State failed, the presiding judge, John D. Justice, would have to let Richardson go. Schaub and Treadwell had a weak case, and they knew it. They were eager to avoid the hearing. They tried to persuade Robinson to have his client plead guilty to some lesser charge, but Robinson—confident the State had no case—refused. Then at the last minute, though still unwilling to enter a guilty plea for Richardson, Robinson agreed to forego the hearing on the condition that the State set reasonable bail. To his surprise, the prosecution agreed—after some negotiation—to set the amount at $7,500. Bail so low was unheard of in a murder case, much less for a suspected mass-murderer. The prosecution's willingness to accept such a figure looked to Robinson like a clear acknowledgment that it knew it had no case.

Within a few days an anonymous source provided money for the bail, and James Richardson was released. So was Annie Mae, and the child-neglect charges against her were dropped. James remained free while he waited for the preliminary hearing on March 25, 1968. On that day, the defense attorneys and the defendant arrived at court confident that the murder charges would be dropped. The State, however, had a surprise—testimony from Ernell Washington and James Weaver, two men who had been locked up with Richardson in the Arcadia jail. Each claimed to have heard Richardson confess to the killings; their testimony was devastating. Bail was revoked, and Richardson was returned to jail. For the first time, it looked as if the State had some evidence that might convince a jury.

Trial was set for the last week of May. The judge granted a defense motion for a change of venue—not across the state to Miami, as requested, but to Fort Myers, in the next county to the south. Only an hour's drive from Arcadia, Fort Myers was not immune to the rumors and publicity that had been flooding the area for the previous seven months. It was, however, just far enough away that James Richardson's local reputation as a God-fearing, hard-working man was unlikely to do him any good.

On Monday morning, May 27, 1968, Judge John Justice gaveled the court to order. James Richardson was charged with the murder of his daughter Betty Jean, the oldest of the seven victims. If the jury failed to convict, prosecutors could try Richardson for the other six murders, one at a time, until they got a conviction. Although reporters had predicted that jury selection might take several days, by mid-afternoon of the first day eleven men and one woman had been chosen. All were white.

On the second day of the trial, James Weaver took the witness stand and repeated his allegation that Richardson, while confined at the Desoto County Jail, had confessed to the killings. Another former inmate, James Cunningham, also testified that he had heard Richardson confess. Ernell Washington did not appear. Not long after giving testimony at the preliminary hearing, he was released from prison; within a matter of weeks, he had been shot to death in a local bar.

Washington had been jailed on a charge of assault to commit murder. Having abused and terrorized several fellow prisoners, he was known as something of a "brute." He would hardly have made a stellar witness in front of a jury; his death thus actually worked to the State's advantage. Because no transcript of Washington's remarks at the preliminary hearing had been made, the State was permitted to present five witnesses who testified about their recollections of what he had said. These five included news reporters and Red Treadwell, the assistant prosecutor. All were far more respectable and credible than Washington could ever have been. Not surprisingly, the effect was to strengthen tremendously the impact on the trial jury of what Washington had earlier testified.

Early on the third day of the trial, Schaub abruptly announced that the State rested its case. Despite promises in his opening statement, he had failed to call three witnesses the defense considered critical: Bessie Reese, who had served the fatal meal; Charlie Smith, who with Reese had "discovered" the parathion; and Gerald Purvis, the insurance salesman whose visit to Richardson supplied the supposed motive for the murders. This was a terrible blow to the defense team, which had been counting on cross-examining these three witnesses. The lost opportunity was all the more important in the light of the evidence supplied by the jail-house informants—the only evidence that linked Richardson directly to the crime.

The defense opened by showing that Ernell Washington had received probation on his attempted-murder charge after Sheriff Cline had spoken in his behalf. Had Washington offered incriminating testimony against Richardson in exchange for getting a good deal? Shortly after the preliminary hearing, Washington had admitted to Robinson's partner, Whitson, that his incrimination of Richardson was a lie. Whitson tried to take the stand to testify on this point, but Schaub protested. "If it please the Court," the prosecutor said, "It is rather unusual. Mr. Whitson has been participating in the trial." Judge Justice threatened Whitson with disciplinary action if he proceeded. And so Whitson, who like Robinson was confident that their client would be acquitted, decided not to testify. Oddly enough, no one protested and no threat of disciplinary action was made when Treadwell testified about Washington, despite the fact that he, too, was "participating in the trial" as the assistant prosecutor.

Annie Mae Richardson took the stand and testified that James was a devoted husband and father, and that in any case she, not he, had prepared the children's lunch before the two of them left for work. A half dozen character witnesses followed her to the stand. Each testified that the Richardson family life was full of love; several explicitly mentioned the eager happiness with which the children greeted their father when he got home from work. Robinson also called Chief Richard Barnard. The attorney wanted to have Barnard tell the jury that from the start he had not believed there was a case against Richardson, but Judge Justice sustained the prosecution's objections to this line of inquiry. Robinson then tried to get the chief to give an opinion about Sheriff Cline's veracity, but this, too, was ruled inadmissible. Thus, the jury did not hear the testimony from Chief Barnard that would have immeasurably strengthened the case for the defense.

James Richardson, the man on trial for his life, took the stand to tell his story. Other witnesses, also former inmates of the DeSoto County Jail, said that they had never heard Richardson confess. Their testimony bolstered the argument that the prosecutors had made a deal with Ernell Washington. Then, after brief closing arguments, the trial was over.

Robinson and Whitson decided to take turns, in two-hour shifts, waiting for the verdict to come in. Whitson was on duty first; Robinson never got his chance. After just ninety minutes of deliberation, the jury returned, and it was all over. There wasn't even time to call Robinson at the nearby Holiday Inn, where he was attempting to rest.

It was all over for James Richardson, too, when the jury announced its verdict: Guilty of first-degree murder. When asked whether his client was ready for sentencing, Whitson requested time to confer with his partner. Robinson, reached by phone, at first thought Whitson was playing an unbelievably bad joke on him. Whitson was, unfortunately, in earnest. The two lawyers agreed there was no point in delaying the inevitable. Given that the jury had made no recommendation of mercy, the judge had no discretion in sentencing. Whitson returned to the court room alone to watch the judge impose the mandatory death sentence.

Judge Justice told Richardson to stand. "The Court adjudges you guilty of murder in the first degree," he intoned. "Do you have anything to say why I should not pronounce you guilty?" Richardson appeared dazed; he said he did not understand. The judge repeated the question; Richardson repeated, "Sir, I do not understand." It was a pathetic scene. A man had been put on trial for his life and found guilty; he was about to be sentenced to death, and he clearly did not comprehend what was going on.

Judge Justice lost patience and decided to wait no longer for the prisoner to understand; he proceeded with the sentencing (the first death sentence he had ever pronounced). Richardson, led away in handcuffs by a deputy, had little to say, though he apparently finally grasped that he had been sentenced to death. Whitson tried to sound reassuring, telling him he would be found innocent after a new trial. Richardson could only mumble a couple of times, "I trust you and Mr. Robinson."

Months later, a young lawyer from New York, Mark Lane, arrived in Arcadia to look into the murder of the seven children and the conviction of Richardson. Sheriff Cline proudly showed him the certificate he had been awarded by *Official Detective Magazine* for solving the crime so quickly. On hearing about that, Chief Barnard laughed—unimpressed; he had received the same award. "Can you believe that?" he said to Lane. "For my work on the Richardson case. . . . An award for me, and I don't even think there is a case." In fact, Barnard and Minoughan had steadfastly clung to their doubts about Richardson's guilt, convinced that the three jail-house informants who had helped convict him were liars.

Lane, a lawyer in the public eye a few years earlier because of his conspiracy theory about the assassination of President John F. Kennedy, helped keep doubts about Richardson's guilt alive. It was after reading a short item about the trial and conviction in *Newsweek* that he took an interest in the case. Eight months of work, 150 interviews, and thousands of miles of travel later, Lane was thoroughly convinced that Richardson was innocent. In 1970, two years after Richardson had been convicted, Lane published his account of the case in a book entitled *Arcadia*.

Among the people Lane interviewed in Arcadia was insurance salesman Gerald Purvis. Purvis said the newspapers had badly distorted the insurance motive. There was no insurance, he insisted, and he thought it unlikely that Richardson could have believed there was. Lane also interviewed baby-sitter Bessie Reese, who had fed the children their lunch but hadn't even been called to testify at trial. Lane was among those who had doubts about her. He learned that in 1955 she had been convicted of killing her second husband, and that she had served four years of a twenty-year term before being paroled. Her first husband had also died somewhat mysteriously. (The question had been raised but never resolved as to whether his death was a result of food poisoning.) Lane also found out that, shortly before the murders, the neighborly relationship between Richardson and Reese had soured. Her third husband, Johnny King, had gone to Jacksonville with Richardson and had fallen in love there with Richardson's cousin. King had decided not to return home, and Bessie

Reese blamed James Richardson for King's desertion. She had threatened to "get" Richardson.

Lane's suspicions about Bessie Reese were in no way lessened by her staunch denial that she had anything to do with the murders. Numerous inconsistencies emerged between what she told Lane and the accounts others had given. She brushed aside the oddity of Cline's having jailed her for only a few hours as a "material witness" (while Charlie Smith was held for two months) and precisely at the time John Robinson was in town trying to get in touch with her. Also, she persisted in saying that she had smelled nothing, though everyone else who visited 131 Watson Avenue had commented on the overpowering metallic smell of the poison.

Charlie Smith told Lane, as he had earlier told the court, that it was Bessie Reese who had found the bag of parathion on the day after the murders. In retrospect, he said, he believed Reese had put the bag in the shed and that she had cleverly arranged for him to "find" it in order to divert attention from herself. When Lane asked him directly whether Richardson had killed the children, Smith replied firmly, "I tell you this. That man didn't do it. That man did not kill his own. No sir. I know that."

Meanwhile, James Richardson's appeal to the state supreme court went forward, handled by John Robinson. Before the court announced its decision, Lane's book was published. Robinson hoped the judges might read it, that the entire case would at last be reviewed (not simply the selected parts of it that had been presented at trial), and that the judges might be persuaded to deliver a favorable ruling. Members of the defense team kept their fingers crossed.

But on April 21, 1971, Richardson's conviction and sentence were unanimously affirmed. Said the court, "A thorough review of the entire record reveals evidence more than adequate to establish defendant's guilt of murder in the first degree beyond and to the exclusion of a reasonable doubt." (The review was not sufficiently thorough to get Betty Jean's age correct; the court opinion said the 8-year-old was 11 when she died.) There was no evidence the judges had read Lane's book.

Richardson was not totally without luck, however. Florida hadn't executed anyone since the double execution of Sie Dawson and Emmett C. Blake on May 12, 1964. In fact, no person had been executed anywhere in the United States since Luis Jose Monge was gassed in Colorado on June 2, 1967. In Florida, all executions had been stayed pending review by the United States Supreme Court, and no death warrants were being signed. (Later news reports had Richardson on death watch, being shaved for execution, coming within a day or two of death, and watching his coffin being built. All these tales were false;

no death warrant for Richardson was ever signed, or even came close to being signed.)

On June 30, 1972, more than six hundred death sentences in the United States—including Richardson's—were voided by the Court's decision in *Furman v. Georgia*. As a result of that ruling, Richardson was resentenced by the Florida courts to life imprisonment. Lane's *Arcadia* had faded into obscurity (unlike his sensational book on the Kennedy assassination), and though it neither stimulated protests nor proved to be a quick ticket out of prison for Richardson, the author's investigative efforts provided useful insights and information for subsequent work on the case by him and by others. There was little for Richardson to look forward to except 1993, the year he would become eligible for parole.

As he sat in prison, however, Richardson had another stroke of good luck without even knowing it. It would in fact be years before he or anyone on his defense team learned about it. In 1979 a young white Arcadian named Remus Griffin had an opportunity to help, and—at great personal risk—he did so. Griffin, as it happened, was dating Red Treadwell's secretary. She told him Treadwell still had a thick file on the Richardson case, and that—when drunk—Treadwell would say he had helped frame Richardson. (Treadwell would later say that he had begun to have second thoughts about the case years earlier, but—when sober—he would admit nothing about a "framing.")

Griffin wanted the Richardson file. One night he borrowed his girl friend's keys, went to Treadwell's office, found the file, and took it. "That file is the property of the people of the State of Florida," he was later quoted as saying. "At worst, what I did is break into his office and get something that belonged to the State of Florida and give it back to them." When Griffin phoned Robinson to say he had the file, the lawyer didn't take it seriously; he had over the years gotten so many crank calls about the case that he was disinclined to believe any of them. With Robinson showing no interest, Griffin wasn't sure what to do. He eventually gave the file for safekeeping to a friend, a former dispatcher in the DeSoto County sheriff's office who disliked Sheriff Cline. For nine years the file sat and collected dust. So did James Richardson.

Then, in 1988, Mark Lane returned to Arcadia to see whether he could stir up interest in re-examining Richardson's conviction. By this time, Lane and Florida attorney Ellis Rubin were co-counsel for Richardson. John Robinson had withdrawn from the case, fearing that—if there were a new trial—Richardson would be found guilty again. It didn't seem worth the gamble, given that his client was soon to be eligible for work release and then parole.

Remus Griffin, after meeting Lane at a public rally, persuaded the friend who had been keeping the file to turn it over. Lane immediately recognized the file's value and undertook to put it to work. He could see that it contained what the courts would almost certainly regard as suppressed evidence. Prosecutors are required to give to the defense any evidence in their possession that suggests the defendant is innocent. In the Richardson case, the prosecution had failed to do this.

Other bits and pieces of information and potential evidence began to surface. Affidavits were obtained from two aides at the nursing home where the aging Bessie Reese was living. They said Reese had admitted to them that she was the one who killed the children. This could not be substantiated, however, because by the time the aides reported it to Lane, Reese was senile and suffering from Alzheimer's disease. The aides claimed that Reese had confessed before she became mentally incompetent; Frank Schaub suggested that whatever she said was just the raving of someone ridden with guilt for having unwittingly served food that was laced with poison. Others insisted her "confession" must have been subsequent to her mental incapacitation.

Chief Richard Barnard came forward and publicly stated what he had implied to Lane years earlier. In December 1988 he said in an affidavit, "I have concluded that James Richardson is innocent and that he was framed for the murder of Betty Bryant [Richardson's daughter Betty Jean] by Sheriff Frank Cline." Cline reportedly laughed when he heard that, saying, "I just wonder why after twenty years somebody comes up with this or remembers it." Barnard, it will be recalled, had never believed the State had a case, but had been prevented from saying so at the trial.

Attorney Ellis Rubin accused prosecutor Frank Schaub of obstructing justice and of virtually attempting to murder Richardson. Schaub, like Frank Cline, was undaunted. Still convinced that Richardson was guilty and that his office had done nothing improper, he promptly filed a $35 million defamation suit against Rubin—who responded in turn with an announcement that he welcomed the suit. It would, he said, allow him to take depositions from the participants in the trial, which could only speed Richardson's exoneration. The defense attorneys petitioned the governor for immediate release of Richardson. They also petitioned the state supreme court for a new trial.

That broke the dam for Virginia Dennis, 28, who then came forward and made a public statement. An 8-year-old girl at the time of the crime, she had been a friend of the Richardson children and had eaten breakfast with them on the day of their death. For years, her nightmares about the murders had kept her silent. Although parathion had been found in the remnants of both the breakfast and the lunch, young Virginia had never gotten sick. This revelation fit perfectly with another previously unexplained fact. On the day the seven children were murdered, Annie Mae Richardson had eaten a sandwich made of chicken cooked in the frying pan used at breakfast, and she had also never gotten sick. These incidents helped substantiate the theory that the poison was added to the leftovers after the breakfast had been eaten—and thus after James and Annie Mae Richardson had gone to work.

On February 1, 1989, Governor Bob Martinez of Florida appointed one of the state's top prosecutors, District Attorney Janet Reno from Dade County, to re-examine the case. A clemency hearing was scheduled for April. Frank Schaub, who had recently stepped down as district attorney, came out of retirement to argue anew that no miscarriage had occurred. "It's one of the strongest cases I've ever presented to a jury," he said.

Meanwhile, the Florida Supreme Court had appointed retired Circuit Judge Clifton Kelly to hear Richardson's request for a new trial. On April 11, 1989, Janet Reno filed her report. Because several witnesses had lied under oath, Reno concluded, the conviction should be vacated. The State, she went on to say, had not informed the defense about statements in its possession from two witnesses that would have helped bolster Richardson's claim that he had no insurance. Reno also noted that the first jail-house witnesses had made statements exonerating Richardson, which were similarly withheld by the prosecution; in their stead, only later statements incriminating Richardson were used. Furthermore, at least one of the prosecution's jail-house witnesses, James Weaver, admitted he had lied at the trial. The truth was, he said, that Richardson had never confessed in front of him. The report went on to accuse Sheriff Frank Cline of also perjuring himself when he told the jury that Richardson had purchased insurance and had gotten a receipt for it.

On April 25, Judge Kelly heard oral arguments in Arcadia. After thirty minutes of deliberation, he told a packed DeSoto County court room that he was convinced Richardson had not received a fair trial. He did not go so far as to say Richardson was innocent, but he did throw out the conviction and order Richardson released from the Tomoka Correctional Institution in Daytona Beach.

James Joseph Richardson was by then 53. His years of confinement for a crime he did not commit were finally at an end. But he was left with the stigma of having had people believe that he killed seven of his own children. Given that the only evidence against him was perjured jail-house testimony, the failure of the court to exonerate him fully has to count as a major disappointment.

Still, he was free at last after twenty-one years behind bars. He had made good use of his time in prison, teaching himself to read and write and earning a high school diploma. Immediately upon his release, Richardson was offered a $100,000-a-year job at the Diet and Health Resort in Panama City, Florida, run by civil rights activist Dick Gregory.

Though the job did not work out, the offer boosted Richardson's self-esteem and gave him a much-needed sense of security.

In August 1989 Richardson filed a $35 million suit against the State, DeSoto County, Sheriff Cline, and the prosecutor, Schaub. (Some sixteen months later, the Florida Bar Association opened an investigation of another murder case Schaub had handled, where there were "instances of misconduct too numerous to list." An official in the Bar's office in Tampa was quoted making the devastating comment that "the nature of the complaint [against Schaub] is interfering with justice.") Richardson, meanwhile, continues to wait and wonder whether he will ever receive any compensation for the years taken from him.

Having divorced Annie Mae (the strain of twenty-one years apart had taken its toll), James Richardson has now remarried. With his new wife, an eighth-grade schoolteacher, he waits for word that the movie version of the story of his life has been sold. Then, he thinks, perhaps he will finally have money enough to do as he wants.

But along with the waiting and wondering, he savors his freedom. In the summer of 1989, a few weeks after he was released, Richardson told a reporter, "Just being out here, looking at the world, seeing how precious it is, how marvelous life can be, people laughing, children playing, makes you feel like you want to survive again, it's like you're starting life all over again, like you just coming into the world."

✻

JAIL-HOUSE informants play an important role in many miscarriages of justice, for two reasons. Prison cell mates have the opportunity, hour after hour, day after day, to learn a great deal about each other. People will talk (or even brag) about the crimes they have committed, even to a perfect stranger, especially if the stranger is (or appears to be) in a similar plight—facing trial and severe punishment if convicted. So it is plausible for a jury to believe a prisoner's testimony that a cell mate has confessed.

Any prisoner in jail, moreover, has an incentive to embellish what a cell mate says—even to fabricate a cell mate's confession out of whole cloth—if there is reason to believe that reporting such a confession might reduce one's own risk of conviction, or perhaps result in better treatment or a reduced sentence. Similarly, prosecutors have an incentive to try to persuade prisoners to testify against each other, especially when they are concerned that without such testimony the rest of their evidence against the accused will not convince a jury.

And so a deal is often made between a prosecutor and a prisoner to help convict an accused suspect. The fact that this sometimes requires perjury, and that the perjury may result in the conviction of an innocent defendant (and possibly a death sentence), is outweighed by the selfish advantage gained. Perjured "evidence" of this sort was almost certainly responsible for Richardson being convicted, and it has proved crucial in many other cases as well.

In September 1932, a gas station attendant in Asheville, North Carolina, was murdered during a holdup. Witnesses reported seeing two men drive away from the crime scene; others stated that the day before, they had seen a car parked at the station with New Jersey license plates. Five days later, Gus Colin Langley and his friend Wilcey Johnson were arrested in Wilmington, North Carolina, and accused of the murder.

Although a native of Wilmington, Langley drove a car with Jersey plates because for the previous two years he had been working there as a housepainter. Those license plates were his undoing; the police could not locate any other car with New Jersey plates in the whole of North Carolina on the day of the murder.

One might have thought that Langley had an ironclad alibi. On the afternoon before the crime, headed home to Wilmington, he was near Fort Bragg, four hundred miles northeast of Asheville. There he gave a lift to some army officers. Thus his car couldn't have been seen in the Asheville gas station that day. Langley and Johnson spent that night in Elizabethtown, fretting over car trouble. The following morning, after making some repairs, Langley and Johnson continued their drive to Wilmington, where an argument at a toll booth over the Cape Fear River provided them with further alibi support. At the moment of the crime itself, Langley was at a party in his father's house in Wilmington with friends and neighbors.

The Asheville police were interested in Langley's explanation of his whereabouts prior to and during the murder, but they didn't follow up his story with any investigation. While in jail awaiting trial, Langley's own efforts to establish his alibi—he sent letter after letter to Fort Bragg officers and others who had seen him on his drive to Wilmington—received no response. (Later inquiries established that none of these letters reached its destination and that there was good reason to doubt whether any of them was ever mailed by the jailers.)

Langley went to trial in December 1932. No evidence was put before the court to establish that he was the holdup murderer, or even that he was in Asheville the day of the crime. Instead, the chief evidence against him was indirect. One witness testified that he had spoken with Langley near the gas station, but most of his testimony was utterly inconsistent with implicating Langley. All the witness really remembered was a car with New Jersey plates.

The other witness, the crucial one, was a man who had been in jail with Langley before trial. He testified that Langley had admitted the murder and then expressed his confidence that he would nonetheless get off because he would have a roomful of witnesses falsely confirming that he had been in Wilmington at the time of the murder. (After Langley's trial, pending charges against this witness were quietly dropped.)

When Langley took the stand in his own defense, he laid out the details of where he had been before and during the crime. Then, just as the jail-house informant testified he would, he produced several witnesses to his presence in Wilmington on the night of the murder. The prosecution openly sneered at this collusion of testimony: "A bunch of parrots could have been taken from a pet store and done as well." It took little more than two hours for the jury to convict Langley and sentence him to death. (The charges against Johnson, the co-defendant, were dismissed for lack of evidence.)

No higher court reviewed Langley's conviction; North Carolina law in 1932 provided no funds for the appeal of a capital conviction by a defendant who could not afford to pay his own way. In due course the date with the electric chair moved closer—so close, in fact, that as the chaplain arrived at his cell door, Langley was expecting to be escorted to the death chamber. Instead, he was informed that his execution had been stayed because of a technical error.

Langley's trial counsel had just discovered that at the time of sentencing, the trial judge had failed to include the words "first degree" in reporting the jury's verdict. The jury had, of course, convicted Langley of murder; but a death sentence had to be based on a conviction of "first-degree murder," not just "murder." So the judge's sentence was, strictly, unwarranted by the verdict as reported.

Close as this scare was, Langley had several others. Six more times he faced a death date only to be reprieved each time; the final one was like the first, coming with only minutes to spare.

The delays in execution, as well as Langley's ultimate exoneration, where the result of letters from angry witnesses in Wilmington, who *knew* that he was innocent. Several years of investigation slowly amassed the evidence supporting his original alibi, evidence not submitted at trial yet easily obtained. In August 1936, a few weeks short of four years after his arrest, Langley received word that the State had at last acknowledged its error; he was then granted a full pardon and released.

THE AVAILABILITY of a jail-house informant also discourages the police, in some cases, from following up other possibilities and seeking evidence against other suspects. That is clearly what happened to Neil Ferber in Pennsylvania.

On an evening in May 1981, mobster Chelsais Bouras was dining with eight friends (at least he had thought they were his friends) at the Meletis Restaurant in South Philadelphia. Suddenly two men burst in, searched out Bouras's table, and gunned him down along with his companion, Jeannette Curro.

Neil Ferber, 39, a resident of North Philadelphia, was arrested a month later on the basis of testimony by a husband and wife who told police they had seen a man dash out of the restaurant, yank a ski mask off his head, and flee down the street. When shown photographs of possible suspects, the woman picked out Ferber. Later, at a police line-up, she changed her mind; she was then certain Ferber was *not* the man with the ski mask. Her husband, however, disagreed; he still believed Ferber was the man they had seen. When arrested, Ferber protested his complete innocence.

At trial, additional testimony against Ferber came from Jerry Jordan. Jordan had the proverbial arm-long arrest record. Nevertheless, the prosecution put him on the stand, and the jury evidently believed him when he said that Ferber had confessed to the killings while the two men were in jail. Ferber was duly convicted and sentenced to death.

Four years later, in January 1986, Judge Robert Latrone, who had presided at Ferber's trial, reconsidered the case. The district attorney's office had informed the court that a polygraph test of Jordan, withheld from the defense at the trial, indicated that Jordan had lied to the police about Ferber's involvement. This statement to the court was the culmination of two years of growing doubts among some of Philadelphia's homicide detectives and prosecutors about the police work that had led to Ferber's indictment and conviction.

During that period, Jordan had also recanted his court-room testimony. He told the authorities that he had never really believed Ferber was involved—admitting, in effect, that he had perjured himself. Judge Latrone ordered Ferber's conviction reversed. Two months later, District Attorney Ronald Castile informed the court that his office would not retry Ferber. Sitting in the court room, Ferber heard the good news in person.

Dennis Cogan, whom Ferber had retained as counsel after the first trial and whose investigative work had uncovered the suppressed polygraph evidence, had meanwhile come up with another theory of the murder. At the dinner table when Bouras and Curro were slain, another mobster, Raymond "Long John" Martorano, was also present. Cogan believed that Martorano had arranged for Bouras's murder. Sometime after the two murders in the Meletis Restaurant, Martorano was convicted of hiring Willard Moran to kill Bouras, a mobster. Already convicted of murdering a local union president, Moran was convicted of the Bouras killing as well, though he maintained that—despite Martorano's having offered him a contract—someone else had beaten him to it.

In any case, regardless of whether Martorano and Moran were guilty of conspiracy to commit murder, Ferber was innocent. Fortunately, he was freed—though not until he had spent four and a half years in jail and prison.

11 ✳ THE LUCK OF THE DRAW

FLOYD "BUZZ" FAY was sound asleep in his mobile home in Perrysburg, Ohio, when the phone rang. It was four o'clock on a March morning in 1978. As he picked up the receiver, he instinctively thought it must be bad news. When the voice on the line told him his house was surrounded by police and that they had a warrant for his arrest, his concern turned to irritation. Someone's stupid idea of a joke. Fay hung up, intending to go back to sleep.

The phone rang again.

The second message was like the first, except for the caller adding that Fay should step outside and not try anything. By this time he was definitely awake, and baffled as well as annoyed. He couldn't imagine what was going on. But something about the tone of the voice on the phone made him think perhaps this wasn't a joke after all.

When Fay got out of bed and went outside to look, he faced four police officers with drawn guns pointed directly at him. In fact, there seemed to be police everywhere. They said they wanted to search his home. "You can do anything you want, just put those guns down," he told them. Floyd Fay was a husky two hundred pounds and 6'2"—a strong young man of 26—but he was not about to stand up to a group of armed law-enforcement officers.

The police entered the trailer and started searching. Whatever they were looking for, they didn't find it. They placed Fay under arrest anyway. He was, they told him, suspected of shooting the co-owner of a nearby convenience store a few hours earlier. Fay began to wonder all over again whether he was fully awake. The whole thing was obviously just a crazy mistake. It had to be. Besides, in a few hours he was supposed to be at work.

He was led away in police custody.

Fred Ery, 26, was working at Andy's Carry-Out on March 28, 1978. He was co-owner of the little Perrysburg store, on the southern flank of Toledo, and he often worked the evening shift. Around 9:30 on that particular evening, Ery was chatting with a customer, Debra Koehler, the only other person in the store. Her back was to the door, but Ery had a clear view of the man who burst through it (interrupting the conversation, as Koehler later told it). The intruder, wearing a blue ski jacket and a full ski mask, was a large man, and he was carrying what appeared to be a sawed-off shotgun.

For the next few minutes, everything moved on fast forward. Words were exchanged, a shot was fired, Ery fell to the floor, the intruder ran off. Ery had been hit in the shoulder and was bleeding profusely when John Bondelier, a Perrysburg police officer, arrived on the scene a few minutes later. While he was waiting for help, Bondelier asked Ery whether he knew who had shot him. "It looked like Buzz," Ery mumbled, "but it couldn't have been."

Police always hope for a positive identification of the assailant. Fred Ery's remark about the intruder having "looked like Buzz," though mumbled, seemed like just such an identification. A short time later, the police chanced upon another piece of information. Asking around town, members of the department learned that Floyd Fay, an occasional customer at Andy's Carry-Out, was called "Buzz." A solid tip. There aren't too many people with that nickname.

By the time the police were arresting Buzz Fay a few hours later, Fred Ery was dead. Between the shooting and the death, as Ery lay dying at the hospital, he kept muttering about "Buzz." But what with a considerable loss of blood and several large doses of Demerol, most of Ery's remarks either had become incoherent or had collapsed into terse bluntness. Before he died, five hours after he had been shot, his initial remark— "It looked like Buzz, but it couldn't have been"—had evolved into the briefer but more incriminating "Buzz did it." With that the police thought they had the crucial eyewitness identification they needed. And the eyewitness was none other than the victim himself.

There was only one problem. The police had no other evidence that Fay was the killer. Furthermore, the blond, blue-eyed, and solidly middle-class Fay did not fit the stereotype of a holdup murderer. A former University of Florida student, he was employed as a carpenter. His boss at Conrail, in Perrysburg, said he was the best on the crew. He had no criminal record. His only prior arrest was for DWI (driving while intoxicated), five years earlier.

At first, the police relied entirely on Ery's dying remark about "Buzz." Then someone told them Fay owned a gun—a shotgun, no less. That made him a plausible suspect after all. The police failed to find the murder weapon or a ski mask in Fay's trailer, but they were not really surprised. A shrewd person, after all, *would* have gotten rid of such incriminating physical evidence.

Debra Koehler, though unable to give much of a description of the intruder, said she did remember the jacket he was wearing. The police arranged a kind of "jacket line-up" for her; she picked out two of the ski jackets, saying they were like the one worn by the gunman. No one seemed to notice that the jacket taken from Fay's trailer was not one of the ones she identified, or that the two she pointed to weren't even very much like his. As for the killer's gun and ski mask, they never were recovered. Not in Fay's mobile home, and not anywhere else.

Meanwhile, Fay kept thinking the whole thing would quickly blow over and that he would soon be joking with his friends about the absurd mix-up. It simply did not make any sense for the police to charge him with aggravated murder. So, although he was naturally upset after his arrest, he didn't really panic. "They'll find the right person, they'll get this straightened out, they'll let me go tomorrow," he kept saying to himself and to anyone else who would listen.

The police had no evidence, and Fay knew it, just as he knew he hadn't killed Ery. "I wasn't even going to hire a lawyer," he recalled later. But the police didn't have any other suspects, and they wanted to solve the case. Furthermore, they had Ery's dying remarks about "Buzz." Ery's widow, Lynda, had also informed police that her husband and Buzz had never much liked each other. Then someone remembered that, a few weeks before the shooting, Fay had gotten angry when Ery refused to sell him beer on a Sunday.

That hardly seemed like a sufficient motive for holding up a man's store, let alone killing him. But with nothing better to go on, the prosecution came up with a theory to explain how the generally mild-mannered Fay could have turned into a brutal armed robber: He might have been suffering from a delayed reaction to some PCP (a psychedelic drug) he had allegedly smoked several days before. That could have been enough to make him go berserk and use his gun in anger directed at Ery. Or so they said.

Still, it didn't look as though they had much of a case against him. Hoping to strengthen it, the prosecutors decided to offer Fay a deal. First, he would have to submit to a polygraph, popularly known as a lie detector test. Buzz knew nothing about polygraph tests—"I had only seen lie detectors on TV shows," he said much later—but he assumed they worked. He thought taking the test would be a good way to show he was innocent. Assuming the test would be both objective and reliable, he was confident that it would corroborate his version of the story and show the authorities he was telling the truth. "I was thinking it finally was going to end, be all over," he said.

The prosecutors spelled out the deal to him. "The Ohio Bureau of Criminal Identification will administer the polygraph," they said. "If the results show you're telling the truth, we'll drop all charges. You'll be released." That sounded fine to Fay. "Furthermore," the prosecutors went on, "if the polygraph shows you're lying, we'll let you take another one, administered by a private operator. And if the results are different from the State's test, we won't use either one at the trial." Fay thought this, too, seemed fair. Besides, the results of the first test would show he was telling the truth, so that would be the end of it anyway. If both tests found Fay was lying, the prosecutors continued, he would still have a choice. If he agreed then to plead guilty to a charge of murder, they would ignore the polygraph tests. But if he refused to plead guilty to the lesser charge, he would be tried for *aggravated* murder (the equivalent in Ohio to what in most other states is called "first-degree murder")—and the polygraph results would be used against him.

At the time, aggravated murder in Ohio was punishable by death. Still, Fay figured he had nothing to worry about, because he was innocent; he accepted the prosecutor's offer. He understood the terms, and he was certain that he would be exonerated, that he would never have to take the second test, and that all charges against him would be dropped. End of episode. "I really thought I was going home the next day," he recalled two years later.

Buzz Fay had no idea how incompletely and inaccurately he understood the way lie detectors really work. He shared the popular misconception that polygraphs don't make mistakes, that they are truly objective. He had not thought about the role of the person who interprets the test results: Objectively achieved results gain what meaning they have only from subjective evaluation by the polygraph operator. Nor did he ever consider the possibility that apparently objective factors can be altered. "I believed the polygraph worked," he stated repeatedly in later years. "But it's ridiculous," he would add ruefully. "Any criminal who knows how to beat a polygraph can beat it."

That wisdom came later. Initially, Fay did not know that as little as fifteen to twenty minutes of coaching can enable many people to "beat" the tests; he did not know how easy it is for those with experience taking polygraph tests to fool the machine. Neither did it dawn on him that the conditions under which such tests are given can themselves affect the results. Fay had no idea, for example, that the antihistamine drug (Triaminic) he was taking for his cold might influence his performance. He also did not understand the tricky way what the experts call "probable lie" control questions are used. The questions tend to be of the "Have you stopped beating your wife?" variety. According to David Lykken, a professor of psychiatry at the University of Minnesota Medical School who has done extensive research on polygraph testing, such questions frequently trap precisely those who answer truthfully.

Unaware of all this, Buzz Fay took the first test. To his utter amazement, he failed it. "When I was told I had failed, I couldn't believe it." He submitted to the second, privately administered, test. A deal is a deal. Later he reported, "I felt intimidated, but still not really scared." The second polygraph examiner, like the first, found Buzz Fay was being "deceptive." Fay, told he had failed a second time, was absolutely stunned. He knew the deal he had made meant the prosecutors would not mention the polygraph results, if he would just plead guilty to a charge of murder. But he could not bring himself to do that, even though he realized that continuing to insist on his innocence meant the test results would be used against him at his trial. And so it came about that Buzz Fay, when he appeared before the trial court—knowing he was innocent—faced the more severe charge of aggravated murder because he refused to plead guilty. The results of both polygraphs were used against him.

Professor Lykken's research indicates that most jurors share the popular view that lie detector tests are reliable, just as Buzz Fay did. At the trial, the negative test results, Ery's dying comment, and Fay's failure to testify on his own behalf (he was counseled against doing so by his attorney) proved to be a bad combination. Even if the polygraph results were not the dominant factor in the jury's thinking (which is what some jurors later insisted), they were critical in another sense. If it hadn't been for the negative outcome of both tests, Fay would never have been put on trial at all, because the prosecution would have had no case—only a vague and implausible theory of the crime.

On August 11, 1978, after five hours of deliberation, the jury convicted Buzz Fay of aggravated murder. Fortunately for him, only a month earlier (in *Lockett v. Ohio*) the United States Supreme Court had declared Ohio's death penalty statute unconstitutional. If the case had gone to trial more promptly—three months after the crime instead of four—Buzz Fay could have been sentenced to death and executed. As it was, the jury had no sentencing discretion; their only choice was life imprisonment. Thus the stage was set for Fay's struggle to vindicate his claims of innocence.

When you are innocent, and you know it, and you take what seem like logical steps based on that knowledge—you expect things to work out. When you are nevertheless convicted of a crime you didn't commit, it's hard to know where to turn next. Buzz Fay stubbornly and persistently maintained his innocence, but that wouldn't have been enough if he hadn't also had some luck after his arrest and conviction. As he himself would later say, he benefited from "a lot of hard work by a lot of people." Chief among them was Adrian Cimerman, a public defender just out of law school in 1978.

From his prison cell, Buzz had sent the charts from the two polygraph tests to four of the country's top polygraph experts. He had read a magazine article about congressional hearings on polygraphs and had pulled the experts' names from that source. After examining the material that Fay sent them, the four were unanimous in their findings: None of the tests showed Fay was being "deceptive." Not surprisingly, the experts didn't agree on all the details. Some, in the interpretation most favorable to Fay, believed he was being truthful. Others judged that the test results at best gave inconclusive evidence of Fay's guilt—but that was as close as any of the experts came to confirming the prosecution's interpretation of his responses. Even those who thought the results showed Fay was telling the truth agreed that the tests had been administered incompetently. Because of that, all agreed, the jury should never have been told about either the tests or their results.

Fay's defense of his innocence at trial had used up all his savings, so he could not afford to hire an attorney for his appeal. It was up to the public defender's office to handle the case, but by that time Fay had learned to take a more active role in managing his own defense. He drafted his appeal himself, appended statements from the four polygraph experts, and sent the material off with a request that Adrian Cimerman be appointed counsel. The Fay case had first come to Cimerman's attention while he was working as a legal intern in the office of the Wood County public defender in Toledo. Cimerman had subsequently been hired to replace his mentor, and Fay's request was granted. Running the hurdles that prosecutors and appellate courts set up in the months ahead was made less difficult for Cimerman by his belief from the outset that his client was not guilty.

Fay first sought relief in the Ohio Court of Appeals. He challenged the State's explanation of the crime, especially the claim that his having allegedly smoked PCP several days before the crime had, in a delayed reaction, turned him into a vicious murderer. The appellate court agreed that at least this part of the State's argument didn't make much sense. On June 25, 1979, the court nonetheless affirmed Fay's conviction.

Cimerman promptly filed notice of appeal to Ohio's supreme court.

He took the line that the Court of Appeals was right in concluding that testimony on PCP and its possible effects should not have been admitted, but wrong in judging that its use at trial was only "harmless error." If it were so harmless, Cimerman argued, his client would not be facing life in prison. The argument fell on deaf ears. Exactly four months after the Court of Appeals had affirmed Fay's conviction, the Ohio Supreme Court announced its refusal to hear the case.

Neither Buzz Fay nor Adrian Cimerman was willing to give up. Cimerman knew that the opinions of the polygraph experts Fay had solicited could not be classified as "newly discovered evidence" that would warrant a new trial, but he believed that the incompetent way the tests had been administered should have impeached their results. An appellate court might rule that the experts' criticism did constitute "impeachment evidence." Cimerman decided it was worth seeking post-conviction relief on this narrow point, even though he was not optimistic; the trial judge had already made an independent ruling that the original polygraph examiners were competent and that, by implication, the results of the polygraph tests were reliable.

Indeed, Cimerman was beginning to sense that the trial court was hostile to his position and perhaps to Fay himself. When a prosecution motion to take a deposition from Fay was granted, over Cimerman's objection (on fifth amendment grounds), Cimerman appealed the decision. He was not worried about Fay incriminating himself, but as a matter of principle he thought it a poor precedent for the court to set. He was also stalling for time. Cimerman was still trying to gather evidence on the possible effects of the medicine Fay had been taking at the time the polygraph tests were administered.

While Cimerman was preparing this appeal, he got a phone call from Buzz's original trial attorney, Loren Zaner, who reported that he had been contacted by an attorney in Cleveland. The Cleveland attorney had in turn been approached by a man named James Sharpe, who claimed he had information about the Ery murder. The three attorneys—Cimerman, Zaner, and the lawyer from Cleveland—arranged to meet Sharpe on July 3, 1980, in a motel in Sandusky. At the meeting, Sharpe told the trio of lawyers that he had proof a former friend of his, Clifford Markland, had acted as a lookout during the robbery. Furthermore, Sharpe said, he knew that two other individuals had also been involved in the crime.

Who was Sharpe? Could he be trusted? Why was he volunteering this valuable—though incomplete—information? James Sharpe's interest in the case, it turned out, had nothing to do with a desire to help an innocent man. He simply wanted to get back at Markland, motivated by the fact that his estranged wife had recently decided to live with Markland. If it hadn't been for this bizarre twist of events—Sharpe's anger at Markland for moving in with his wife—Buzz Fay might still be in prison.

Once Sharpe had made his unexpected appearance, Cimerman and Zaner had something to work with. Sharpe played a secretly made tape recording for them, on which Markland's mother could be heard admitting that her son and two other men had been involved in Ery's murder. Fay had been insisting all along that he was innocent. For the first time there was independent evidence to support his claim—evidence that three completely different men were involved.

Cimerman undertook to learn all he could about Markland—not all that difficult, because Markland had a long police record. Among his prior arrests, Cimerman soon discovered, was one for a supermarket robbery in which the robbers had used ski masks. He also learned from one of Markland's former employers that Markland sometimes hung around with a friend—a big, husky, blond guy.

The next bit of information Cimerman uncovered was that the driver of the getaway car used in the supermarket robbery, Ted Goodman, had an extensive gun collection. If Markland was indeed involved in the Ery murder, Cimerman speculated that Goodman might have been one of the others—and the source of the murder weapon. Cimerman also learned that there might be one or more paternity suits on file against Clifford Markland. That meant there might be additional individuals with a sufficiently serious grudge against Markland to make them willing to tell what they knew about him.

Cimerman could find no record of active paternity suits against Markland, but he did eventually track down a woman who had at least initiated such proceedings. And she knew something about the Ery murder. She corroborated James Sharpe's account that Markland had served as the lookout in the robbery at Andy's Carry-Out. She also confirmed Cimerman's suspicion that Ted Goodman had been the driver of the getaway car.

Nor was that all. In the interview with Cimerman, the young woman named the actual murderer: William Quinn. It would later emerge, not so incidentally, that Quinn was the big, husky, blond fellow who sometimes hung around with Markland—and that he bore a striking resemblance to Buzz Fay. Suddenly Ery's gasped comment minutes after he was shot—"It looked like Buzz, but it couldn't have been"—took on a new meaning. The young woman went on to give Cimerman the name of another person who, she said, could back her up. Indeed, the second informant did just that. "He verified everything," Cimerman later reported.

Cimerman had accumulated all this evidence, thanks to a massive amount of investigative work, but he was uncertain what to do next.

Filing a motion for a new trial would result in making public the new information in his possession, and that could easily have two very undesirable results. For one, it would make it more difficult (perhaps impossible) to convict the guilty parties—something Cimerman wanted to do almost as much as he wanted to have Fay freed. There was also a risk of putting his informants in jeopardy. The young woman had already received a letter from Markland containing a thinly veiled threat against anyone who talked with authorities about his criminal past.

In addition, even though Cimerman thought a motion for a new trial would be granted, he expected continuing opposition from the prosecutor. The invitation he and Zaner had extended for someone from the prosecutor's office to attend the Sandusky meeting had been declined, on the ground that "our office does not feel that an injustice has been done to Mr. Fay and we are confident that he committed the crime for which he was convicted."

Cimerman decided the best move would be to try again to enlist the prosecution on his side. Thus it was that on October 24, 1980—just one day short of a year from the time the Ohio Supreme Court had refused to hear Fay's case—Cimerman presented all his findings to the Wood County prosecutor, John Cheetwood. Genuinely concerned that a miscarriage of justice might have occurred, Cheetwood pronounced himself prepared to cooperate. Indeed, he was ready to take an active lead in the re-investigation; the State would proceed swiftly, he said. He would not oppose Fay's release, if a confession from one of the three guilty men could be obtained.

Ted Goodman seemed the one most likely to be persuaded to confess in exchange for immunity. As the driver of the getaway car, he was the furthest removed from the murder. Besides that, he had a relatively good record. So that was the deal: If Goodman would come clean, he would be granted immunity, and Fay would go free. Though some additional obstacles did appear, this part of the saga had only a few more days to run.

By that time, however, Ted Goodman had joined the army and was stationed in Germany. Cheetwood, in an apparent attempt to avoid having to make a trip abroad, decided to confront William Quinn instead. No one wanted to grant immunity to him, if he really was the killer. He was, however, readily accessible—in custody in Indiana, serving jail time for a minor drug offense. Approaching him seemed like a reasonable step for the prosecution to take; a confession from Quinn would free Fay.

Easier said than done. When the prosecutor and his investigator interviewed Quinn, they were immediately struck by his strong resemblance to Fay, but otherwise they came away with very little. Confronted, Quinn was visibly shaken by the accusations; he even shed some tears.

But in the end he refused to talk. His detention in Indiana would be up in three days. His unwillingness to talk perhaps stemmed from a hope that he could continue to elude prosecution for the Ery murder and that he would never again see the inside of a prison.

Quinn's refusal to talk spared the prosecutors a decision on what kind of a deal to make to get his formal testimony. Considerable evidence had mounted that he was the actual murderer. As such, he was the most culpable of the three suspects, and there was a good chance of convicting him without granting immunity if one of the other two could be induced to come clean. Evidence from previous cases indicated that Clifford Markland would serve time rather than talk, however, so Goodman—despite being so far away—seemed the only real prospect. Prosecutor Cheetwood, an investigator, and a detective left for Europe after all, to interview Goodman there. While they were in Germany, Quinn completed his Indiana sentence and was released.

Five days after having turned his information over to the prosecution, Cimerman learned that his strategy had worked. Ted Goodman had indeed not only talked, but confessed, in exchange for immunity. When Cheetwood and his two colleagues returned from Europe, he stated unequivocally, "The evidence obtained in West Germany clearly indicates that Mr. Fay did not commit the crime for which he was convicted." The next day, October 30, 1980, William Quinn—forty-eight hours after getting out of an Indiana jail—was re-arrested. This time he was charged with murder.

As promised, John Cheetwood joined Adrian Cimerman in filing a motion asking for Fay's release. In their motion they stated, "It is submitted that the Prosecuting Attorney's office, acting on information given to it by the Attorney for the Defendant, performed an investigation leading to substantial proof that Floyd Fay . . . did not perform the crime for which he was tried and convicted. The investigation . . . has led to proof that other individuals committed the crime and not Floyd Fay."

Judge Gale E. Williamson, who had presided over the original trial, had the satisfaction of being the one to order the release of William Quinn's near look-alike, Buzz Fay. "All charges will be dropped," he said. "I'm happy the error was discovered." Fay's first words were "I made it!" By that time he was 28. He had spent two and a half years in prison for a murder he did not commit. Judge Williamson later commented, "The whole thing is totally unfortunate. . . . I couldn't be any sadder." He added that he was thankful Ohio no longer had the death penalty. "If we . . . had one, Buzz would be dead right now." Although that was something of an overstatement—even if Fay had been sentenced to death, he might not have been executed—the judge's point is clear.

Despite the State's explicit admission of error, Buzz Fay's repeated attempts to sue the State for his erroneous conviction and incarceration initially all failed. Finally, in 1988, he did win some compensation from the Ohio Court of Claims for the two years of freedom the State had taken from him. Under newly passed legislation, he was awarded $25,000 and back wages for the time he was in prison (though not for the nine months he spent in the Wood County jail prior to his trial). Most of that cash went for attorney's fees. (He still owed $10,000 to his original trial attorney, Loren Zaner.) Nonetheless, the symbolic value of the award was enormous.

On January 28, 1981, when the Judiciary Committee of the Ohio Senate was considering the enactment of a new death penalty statute, Buzz Fay was one of those who testified against it. He posed what he thought was a rhetorical question: "Could you live with yourselves if you vote for this bill and then an innocent person is electrocuted?" Not unlike the three participants in the Ery murder who were content to watch an innocent person be imprisoned for their crime, the state senators apparently concluded they could live with themselves. The death penalty bill passed by a large majority.

Ted Goodman was granted immunity as promised, after he confessed and identified and testified against his partners in crime. On January 30, 1981, William Quinn—who had previously refused to talk—pleaded guilty to the charge of murder in the Fred Ery case. He was sentenced to a minimum term of fifteen years and maximum of life, in the Ohio State Reformatory. Ten days later, on February 9, 1981, Clifford Markland pleaded guilty to the same charge and was given the same sentence.

Surprisingly, Buzz Fay is not—nor was he ever—a bitter man. "I'm not angry at the jury or the prosecutors," he said shortly after his release. "But that polygraph examiner hasn't seen the last of me." Fay has launched something of a crusade against lie detector tests. "I think the polygraph should be eliminated from all use everywhere," he says. "It's a farce." He has worked hard to bring to public attention the fact that the outcome of these tests can be affected by factors that bear no relation to the guilt or innocence of the person being tested. He wants to destroy the public's belief, which he once shared, that polygraph tests are either objective or infallible.

In addition to fighting against the use of polygraphs, Fay has begged legislators to learn the lessons his case and others like it can teach. Being erroneously convicted of murder has made Fay a dedicated opponent of capital punishment. He was convicted of a murder he did not commit, in part as a result of incredibly bad luck. But as he is well aware, he benefited at the same time from almost freakish good fortune. The Ery murder occurred when Ohio's laws provided the death penalty for that crime. Yet Fay's case did not come to trial immediately, and he was in fact tried and convicted during the brief period when Ohio had no death penalty. Had the Supreme Court decided *Lockett* a few months later, or had Fay been tried more promptly, a very different outcome might have resulted. A death sentence and the possible execution of an innocent person have rarely been avoided by such an arbitrary luck of the draw.

＊

THE UNRELIABILITY of polygraph evidence partially explains Buzz Fay's wrongful conviction. But its relative reliability has been used to support valid claims of innocence, too. Far more important in Fay's case was that peculiar remark of the dying victim ("It looked like Buzz, but it couldn't have been")—which seemed to implicate Fay even as it exonerated him. Fay is not alone in having been victimized by bad luck. The two very different cases below are among the many that show how a series of unlucky strikes can result in an innocent person being convicted. Offsetting good luck is often needed to get things set right.

Early on a July morning in 1943, two police officers—Robert Hatchell and W. M. Jolly—were in their car on regular patrol through the streets of Petersburg, Virginia, twenty miles south of Richmond. A car with out-of-state plates caught their attention. Ordered to pull over, the driver suddenly sped away and, after a high-speed chase, crashed in a dead-end street. The driver, a black man wearing a white cap, jumped out and ran off. While Hatchell chased the fleeing driver, Jolly arrested the two black passengers in the wrecked car, soldiers picked up while hitchhiking near Raleigh, North Carolina. (The wrecked car turned out to have been stolen in Raleigh.)

The driver of the car disappeared from view, and Hatchell ran off in search of the fugitive. Half an hour later, Jolly found his companion unconscious and bleeding from a bullet wound. The dying officer, his gun missing from its holster and nowhere in sight, had apparently been bested in a struggle with the hunted man for the weapon.

Two hours after that episode, Silas Rogers—wearing a sailor's white cap—was thumbing a ride out of town. A local newspaper once described him as "a shoeshine boy who was hoboing his way north." In fact he was hitchhiking from Miami to New York in order to report to his draft board. Rogers was black; Officer Hatchell was of course white (this was 1943). The police, having been alerted to look for a black man wearing a white cap, quickly spotted Rogers and took him into custody for questioning.

Under police interrogation, Rogers denied having anything to do with the stolen car or the shooting. A routine check confirmed at least part of his story; Rogers had no previous police record in New York, Florida, or Virginia. Still, the police were sure they had their man. Two different witnesses claimed they saw "a colored man" being chased by Hatchell. Rogers was the only "colored man" the police interrogated or arrested. And there was crucial incriminating testimony from the two soldiers, both of whom told the police that Rogers was the driver of the stolen car.

Rogers continued to claim he had no involvement in the crime. He said he had arrived in Petersburg on a freight train earlier in the morning on the day of the murder. In his walk from the rail yard to the bridge where he was arrested, he had never been near the scene of the shooting. A halfhearted check of his story by the police left many loose ends.

Within a week Rogers was indicted for the crime, and a month later the trial began. Supported by the testimony of the two soldiers, the prosecution's case was convincing. Rogers's defense attorney, a local lawyer appointed by the court, had no resources to investigate his client's alibi. Within two days the trial was over. The all-white jury convicted Rogers of first-degree murder and sentenced him to death. The execution was initially set for January 21, 1944, and was then postponed.

After the trial the case was reviewed on appeal to Virginia's supreme court. The conviction and sentence were unanimously affirmed, the court stating in part: "A careful analysis of the evidence leads to the conclusion that the guilt of the defendant has been proven beyond a reasonable doubt. . . ." Nevertheless, despite that ringing endorsement of the prosecution's case and the jury's verdict, in October 1945 the state's parole and pardon board agreed to commute Rogers's sentence to life in prison. The evidence, they thought, just wasn't convincing enough to put him to death.

It was when a reporter for the *Richmond News Leader* took an interest in Rogers's plight and published a sympathetic account of the case that his fate took a turn for the better. Rogers's brother read the newspaper story and sent a copy to Rogers, who mailed it to Erle Stanley Gardner. Other inmates had told him about the Court of Last Resort, and Rogers hoped his case might interest Gardner. In short order two investigators from the Court were hard at work, reconstructing Rogers's alibi. They discovered that none of the many fingerprints taken from the stolen car matched Rogers's. They verified stories of police brutality in the futile effort that had been made to get Rogers to confess. When he learned of these third-degree methods from Gardner's associates, Petersburg's new police chief, Willard Traylor, began to think that maybe Rogers really was innocent.

Further investigation spread over many months led to a major break. A railroad man was located who said he remembered kicking a young black hobo off a freight train in Petersburg the morning of the murder. When taken to see Rogers in prison, the trainman positively identified him as "the man I put off the train. . . ." With that, the State's case against Rogers crumbled. It also turned out, to everyone's surprise, that Rogers did not even know how to drive a car!

All this new evidence was put before Governor John Battle, and three days before Christmas 1952—nine and a half years from the time of the arrest—the governor granted Rogers his unconditional pardon and release. A free man, Rogers was quoted as saying, "I never gave up hope. I knew I'd get justice with the right kind of folks helping me." As for why the two hitchhikers had testified against Rogers, that remained a mystery. So did the identity of the real killer.

ON AN OCTOBER night in 1979, a dozen or so young people were gathered in an unlighted section of Marine Park, east of Coney Island on the edge of Brooklyn's Jamaica Bay. Known locally as "The Alley," the area was no safe haven for the casual stroller. Suddenly, three gunmen emerged from the shadows, ordered everyone down onto the ground, and started to empty wallets and purses. Not everyone complied. Robert Halstead, 19, jumped up to attack the robbers; he fell back dying, hit by a bullet in the stomach and another in the head. Panicked, the gunmen fled the scene, jumped in their van, and roared off.

One of the robbery victims, Robert Tobin, a boy of 15, sat in the police station that night, looking at the computerized rogue's gallery of photos of known local criminals. He spotted the picture of William Ferro, 20, who he said looked like one of the gunmen. Detective John D'Elia, assigned to handle the robbery-murder investigation, took a closer look at the photo. On the back was written a second man's name; according to the notation, Ferro and a Robert McLoughlin had been previously arrested together.

Excited by the possibility that he now had a lead on two of the three gunmen, Detective D'Elia went to the files; he got a photo and showed it to young Tobin. The youth said that he thought he recognized that face, too. Later, in a police line-up, Tobin picked out the man—though it was questionable whether Tobin remembered the face from the robbery or only from the photo. But the police were satisfied. Within two weeks of the crime, they had the man in the photo in their custody. Thus began the story of the wrongful conviction of Bobby McLaughlin, 19, and the six years he spent in jail and prison for a murder he did not commit.

The key error made by the police was in wrongly matching the name on the back of the photo ("Robert McLoughlin") with the photo in the files under the name "Robert McLaughlin." The names were similar, to be sure, but the persons were completely different—and Tobin was shown the photo of McLaughlin, not McLoughlin. The photo mix-up, the confusion of the two names, and the eventual unraveling of the case make as fascinating a story as any in the annals of wrongful convictions rectified. (Television producers apparently thought so. A dramatized version of the case—"Guilty Until Proven Innocent"—was presented on network television in September 1991.)

At the center of the story stands Bobby McLaughlin's foster father, Harold Hohne. Without his unflagging belief in his son's innocence, and his relentless efforts to free the young man, the error in the police station would never have been straightened out. No one would ever have learned how badly the police, the prosecution, and the jury had gone astray.

In 1980 McLaughlin went to trial. Young Tobin's testimony against him was critical; without it the prosecution had no case. None of the robbery victims except Tobin could identify McLaughlin. No circumstantial evidence linked him to the crime, to the gun, to the bullets, or even to Ferro—except for the photo with the name written on its back. Yet that photo, containing the crucial link that connected McLaughlin to the crime in the prosecution's eyes, was never submitted in evidence. As a result, the defense never had an opportunity to turn the photo over, see that the name was spelled differently, and raise the possibility of mistaken identity.

When he was interrogated by the police, McLaughlin claimed he was innocent, denied knowing any William Ferro, and insisted on an alibi. He was, he said, drinking in a parked car and smoking grass with several friends. At trial, McLaughlin was kept off the stand. His court-appointed counsel, Sarah Halbert, decided it was best if the jury did not learn that less then a year before the Marine Park murder, he had been arrested (but not indicted or tried) on an assault charge arising from a barroom quarrel. It was the arrest on that charge that had gotten his photo into the police files.

The trial was hardly a masterpiece of criminal defense. Among its several shortcomings was the failure to call as witnesses two of the robbery victims who saw the murder—and failed to pick McLaughlin out of the police line-up. Years later, McLaughlin's attorney claimed she never knew of these witnesses because the prosecution failed to turn over to the defense the minutes of the line-up proceedings.

When both prosecution and defense were finished, and the jury instructed, Judge Sybil Kooper confided to counsel at bar, "I think there might very likely be an acquittal here. It is an iffy case." But the jurors didn't think so. Their verdict was guilty of murder in the second degree (first-degree murder in New York was largely confined to killing a police officer); Bobby McLaughlin was given a sentence of fifteen years to life.

While Bobby's foster father, Harold Hohne, doggedly pursued leads, newsman Jack Newfield of New York City's *Village Voice* helped keep the case alive. He once observed, "It seems that everything that could go wrong did in this case." Detective Thomas Duffy, later one of Hohne's strongest supporters, agreed. "This case," he was quoted as saying, "was the worst thing I had ever seen. This kid got a very bad trial." The appellate court disagreed, however, and in October 1984 affirmed the conviction.

By this time, Harold Hohne had turned himself into a virtually full-time amateur detective. Interviews with witnesses, the complete trial transcript, documents, police reports, notes—the paper slowly piled up, stored in boxes in the Hohne residence. Bit by bit, the fundamental error in the photo identification was uncovered. At the trial the jury had been told that the killer's description, based on Tobin's eyewitness identification, had been fed into the police computer, and out popped McLaughlin's photo. But personal interviews with Detective D'Elia and others in the police station that night revealed a different story. Once the defense had the Ferro photo, saw the differently spelled name on the back, and learned of the other McLoughlin in police files, the gap in the prosecution's argument suddenly yawned for all to see. (Whether Ferro himself really had anything to do with the murder was never resolved, because he was in prison for another crime and died there before the McLaughlin case was straightened out. Neither was anyone ever able to connect the other McLoughlin with the murder.)

By May 1985 Harold Hohne was thoroughly frustrated; he simply could not get the authorities to re-open the case. In a last-ditch effort, he wrote a six-page letter, reviewing the case and the results of his investigations, and sent it to everyone he could think of who might be able to help. The letter met with a sympathetic response from three people—Richard Emery, a lawyer in New York's branch of the ACLU; newspaperman Jack Newfield; and the judge who had presided over the court that had turned down McLaughlin's appeal the previous October.

Thanks to months of persistent work by these three, as well as by Hohne and several loyal associates, in April 1986 the district attorney's office agreed to consider re-investigating the case. Politics now intervened. District Attorney Elizabeth Holtzman, who said on television, "We think Bobby McLaughlin should be set free," wanted Governor Mario Cuomo to dispose of the case by executive clemency. Many observers thought it was another instance of professional stubborness in the hothouse atmosphere of New York politics: An ambitious district attorney, rather than officially re-open a case—thereby admitting that her office had made a major mistake (under her predecessor)—wanted the governor to take the heat by using his clemency powers to rectify the injustice.

McLaughlin's attorney, Richard Emery, was able to get the prosecution's key witness, Tobin, to admit in an affidavit that the police had prompted him to pick out McLaughlin from the line-up after telling him they knew Ferro and his companion. Learning this, the district attorney's office realized its case had evaporated. Furthermore, additional evidence in the office files dating back to the time of the crime revealed that the description of the killer given by another youth who had struggled with the gunmen did not fit McLaughlin at all.

On the morning of July 3, 1986, in a Brooklyn court room, a rehearing in the case was at last held. Assistant District Attorney Peter Weinstein said that his office would not oppose a motion to free McLaughlin, admitting that the new affidavit from Tobin "fatally undermines the credibility of the identification testimony on which this conviction rests." Judge Anne Feldman immediately set aside the conviction and dismissed the original indictment.

McLaughlin, in court for the proceedings, broke into tears. His foster father, Harold Hohne, leaped over the court room seats, shoved the press aside, and embraced his son in a massive bear hug. "My family is whole again," he said, choked with emotion, "and I feel tremendous." The next day, during Independence Day celebrations, Bobby McLaughlin and Harold Hohne went to the World Trade Center in Manhattan to see the fireworks.

Three years later, the New York Court of Claims awarded McLaughlin $1.9 million for his "loss of liberty, mental stress, anguish, and reputation," as well as lost earnings and medical expenses. In commenting on his years in jail and prison, and how he had changed, Bobby McLaughlin observed, "When I went in I was a kid, 19, and now I guess you could call me a man. . . . I was also in favor of the death penalty before I went in but I'm totally against it now. If there was a death penalty in this state I would be ashes in an urn on my mother's mantle."

Possibly. If New York had had a broader death penalty statute in 1979, McLaughlin might indeed have been sentenced to death. His attorney, Richard Emery, agreed. The case, he said, was "the strongest argument against capital punishment that we have in this country. If Bobby McLaughlin had been convicted in Texas or Florida or Louisiana, he would have been executed long ago for a crime he didn't commit."

12

❋ | "IT'S A

SCAR THAT'S

BEEN PLACED

ON ME"

IN HIS BOOK *Sophie's Choice*, William Styron tells the gripping story of a mother who is forced to choose which of her children to save from the Nazi gas chambers. Her dilemma is agonizing, partly because it seems unnatural for parents to outlive their children, but primarily because most parents would rather die themselves than have to send any of their offspring to death. When children are innocent, watching them taken away to be killed is more than unnatural; it is cruel beyond comprehension. Even when a mother is not forced to play a decisive role in her child's death, as Sophie was, the agony is unspeakable.

Thus it was that on May 15, 1975, Flossie Mae Charles could not speak, but instead became hysterical, as she heard a jury recommend a sentence of death for her son. In a Savannah, Georgia, court room Earl Charles had just been convicted of a double murder.

As the judge pronounced the sentence and solemnly intoned, "May God have mercy on your soul," Charles jumped to his feet and shouted at the jury, "I'm innocent! I wasn't even in the state!" He turned in time to see police officers rushing through the spectators to reach his hysterical mother. As they unceremoniously grabbed her and began to drag her from the court room, she fainted. Charles's own sentencing upset him at the time far less, he later said—for one thing, he didn't really believe what had happened—than the spectacle of his mother being so roughly handled as she was removed from the court room. Newspaper accounts focused less on the way the woman was treated, however, than on her outburst of distress and her son's reaction to it. Reporters repeatedly described her as "the wailing woman."

The events leading up to this court room drama had begun seven and a half months earlier, late in the afternoon of October 3, 1974. Max Rosenstein, 76, and his wife Myra, 70, ran the Savannah Furniture Company on the low-rent end of Savannah's main street, a raw stretch of a vital urban nerve. Most of the Rosensteins' customers, if they had money at all, relied on their Social Security or welfare checks to pay for their purchases. The Rosensteins, who were white, were gradually preparing to turn over the reins of the family business to their son Fred, 42. On that particular mild, sunny Thursday afternoon, at 4:30, the three Rosensteins and their bookkeeper, Bessie Corcelius, were the only people in the store when two young black men walked in. Fred recognized them; they had been in the day before to look at stereos. He went to the front of the store to greet them, and when they expressed apparent interest in some equipment, he responded by showing them how it worked. Mrs. Corcelius, at her desk in a little office enclosure at the back of the store, continued counting the day's receipts. Max and Myra were in the office with her.

When Mrs. Rosenstein saw her son walking toward the office with the two shoppers right behind him, she assumed he had succeeded in making a sale and was coming to write it up. But before Fred had a chance to begin the paperwork, the taller of the two young men abruptly said, "This is it," and shoved a small pistol directly in Mrs. Corcelius's face. Mrs. Rosenstein thought he was just trying to frighten them into turning over the money. When he told them all to get down on the floor and instructed his companion to tie them up, she responded boldly, "You'll have to shoot me. You're not going to get the money." Instead of shooting her, the man picked up a heavy tape dispenser and smashed her in the face with it. She crumpled, bleeding profusely.

Max moved quickly toward Bessie's desk, apparently hoping he could sweep the stack of bills (a little more than $1,000 in cash) into the office safe. The gunman turned his attention away from the women, aimed his pistol at Max's head, and fired. Max fell onto the floor, next to his bleeding wife. When Fred rushed to his parents' aid, he too was shot. Bessie then threw herself to the floor and ducked under a desk, praying the robbers would ignore her. She heard the gunman say, "There's another one. Get her!" But the fellow with him was apparently interested only in the money. The two of them bolted out the back door of the furniture store, into the alley, and disappeared.

Bessie Corcelius waited until certain the way was clear, got up from under the desk, and ran outside yelling for help. A passerby called the police. They arrived to find that Max Rosenstein lay dead where he had fallen. Fred was rushed off to the hospital, but he died before arriving. Myra Rosenstein, also badly in need of medical care, was totally beside herself and unable to describe the two armed robbers. She was so distraught that the officers finally gave up trying to learn anything from her, either then or later. Bessie Corcelius, on the other hand, was able to help a little. But she, too, shortly after telling the police what she could, checked into a hospital. Her description, the .22 caliber bullets removed from the victims, and a few promising fingerprints were the only clues the police had to work with.

In the days that followed, the two surviving victims of the crime looked through police mug shots to see whether they could identify the killers. Included among the photos of various black men was a five-year-old photo of Earl Charles, but neither woman gave it a second look. Charles was also among those whose fingerprints the police compared to the prints taken from the scene of the murders, but the match was negative. Thus, when Detective Joseph Jordan, heading the investigation, heard that Charles and his next-door neighbor Michael Williams had left town just days after the crime was committed, he dismissed the information as uninteresting. Clearly, there was no reason to treat Charles as a suspect. Nonetheless, the police tried again, presenting a more recent photograph of Charles to the two women for examination. They still did not recognize him as one of the attackers.

Neither did they identify anyone else. Just how shaken and unsure Mrs. Corcelius was of what the two robber-murderers looked like became obvious one day shortly after the crime, when she raced to the police station saying she had seen them in downtown Savannah. The police tracked the two black men she had pointed out—and learned they were soldiers with an unshakable alibi. They had been on their army base, not walking around Savannah, on the afternoon of the murders.

A very different episode provoked Mrs. Corcelius to call Detective Jordan on another day; she wanted to report a disturbing encounter with one of the other police investigators. Detective F. W. Wade had come by her house to have her look at some additional mug shots. She was still unable to identify the gunmen. He assured her it didn't matter—he was going to get warrants issued anyway, because he was ready to make arrests. Bessie Corcelius would not be the last person to wonder about the degree of Detective Wade's professionalism in this case.

On November 14, 1974, a warrant was issued for the arrest of Earl Patrick Charles. The next day, he was apprehended in New Port Richey, Florida.

The police in Savannah knew Charles, 21, though he had hardly been one of their biggest headaches. His picture and fingerprints were in their files because he had been convicted of burglary and shoplifting; he had spent some fourteen months in youth homes and jails over the course of the previous five years. His mother had begun to worry about him when he started cutting classes at Beach High School, but she never gave up hoping that "in the back of his mind" he would remember what she had tried to teach him about the difference between right and wrong. And indeed, at least there were no felony convictions on Earl's record, and when he was released from jail once again in the summer of 1974, he decided it was time to try to put his life together. To him, this meant leaving Savannah. He had noticed, he said later, that "most people that leave always do better."

In early September, Charles bought a ten-year-old car and headed for Tampa, Florida, with his neighbor Michael Williams and Williams's girl friend, Jenny Owens. Tampa was more than three hundred miles from home, far enough away to make a fresh start possible. Once there, the two men found work as gasoline station attendants at a Kwik Pep service station. The station manager, Robert Zachery, was reluctant to trust his new employees; he asked a friend of his, Deputy Sheriff Lemon Harvey, to keep a careful eye on them and the station. Harvey obliged, making a regular habit of beginning his shift in the gas station's parking lot. He kept notes on whether Charles and Williams were on hand as they were supposed to be. Harvey's routine notes, made because of Zachery's misgivings about the new employees, would later prove to be critical.

Almost as soon as the trio from Savannah arrived in Tampa, Jenny had to be hospitalized. During her illness, Michael and Earl would generally spend their mornings at the hospital, visiting her until early in the afternoon when they would leave for work. The next setback came barely a fortnight after the two young men had begun their jobs at Kwik Pep: The station was robbed. Williams and Charles reported they had been forced into a storage closet and locked in while the holdup men got away with approximately $1,000. Zachery did not find their story altogether convincing—he thought Charles and Williams might have stolen the money themselves—and, to protect his own interests, he fired them both.

After the service station job ended, Charles started doing minor repairs and painting for a company that managed apartment buildings. Then on October 26, he and Williams and another friend—Raymond Ash—were arrested. The charge wasn't serious; they were taken in as "suspicious persons" after they were seen relieving themselves by the roadside. Before the three young men were released on $27.00 bond, however, a .22 caliber pistol was found strapped behind a toilet in the jail. The gun was never traced to Charles, Williams, or Ash, but the fact that it was discovered in the jail while Charles was behind bars there would later come back to haunt him.

Another three weeks passed. On November 15 Charles again was driving around with Williams and Ash. A fourth person—Ash's brother James Nixon, an ex-con—was also in the car. The four men drove north from Tampa and stopped for lunch at a restaurant in New Port Richey. Once inside, Nixon excused himself to get something out of the car. By the time the other three had finished eating, he still had not returned; they strolled out to the parking lot, expecting to find him waiting for them there. What they found instead was the owner of a neighboring store holding Nixon at gunpoint, accusing him of grabbing money out of her till. Nixon and his three companions were all taken to the police station for questioning.

When the names of Earl Charles and Michael Williams were entered into the police computer, the New Port Richey officers learned that there was a fugitive warrant out on them both: Earl Charles and Michael Williams were wanted in Georgia for murder, armed robbery, aggravated assault, and interstate flight to avoid prosecution. So much for the fresh start Earl Charles had hoped to make when he left Savannah.

Flossie Mae Charles first learned about her son's arrest when she watched the television news that night. By the time her husband, Patterson, arrived home from work a few minutes later, she was frantic. Patterson managed to calm Flossie Mae down; knowing that Earl had already left for Florida when the murders occurred, his parents had no reason to think he wouldn't quickly be released. Later that evening, Earl called from the jail in Florida. Curious about the crime he had been charged with, he asked his mother to fill him in on details. He assured his parents that there was no need for them to bother making the trip to Florida to see him. Getting to Dade City, where he was being held in the Pasco County jail, would have required them to take a bus ride of more than five hours. And Earl, like his parents, was confident he would soon be released.

An extradition hearing was held a month later, on December 19. Handcuffed to Williams and two other men, Charles was taken to the county court house. On the way into the court room, they passed two elderly women standing next to a man in the hallway. It later turned out that this trio consisted of Mrs. Rosenstein, Mrs. Corcelius, and Savannah police detective F. W. Wade. They were on hand to make the eyewitness identification that was crucial to extraditing the two suspects to Georgia.

In the Florida court room, faced with a makeshift police line-up, Mrs. Corcelius identified Charles as the gunman who had killed Max and Fred Rosenstein. Robert Young, the public defender, pressed her. How certain was she? She admitted to being "shook up" during the crime, but went on confidently to identify the man standing on Charles's left in the line-up as the one who had assaulted Mrs. Rosenstein with the tape dispenser.

Mrs. Corcelius later had second thoughts about him—as well she might have, since the man she identified so positively was known to have been in Florida's Raiford prison at the time of the murders!—but she remained certain that Charles was the gunman. She was insistent on the impossibility of forgetting the looks of a man who had stuck a gun in her face.

Then it was Mrs. Rosenstein's turn. When she looked at the line-up, she admitted that Charles "looked different" from the assailant, who had been wearing glasses and a hat. Even so, she was "ninety percent" certain that Charles was the gunman. Since neither eyewitness had fingered Michael Williams, he was released. But Charles, despite the less-than-completely-certain identification by the two women, was taken to Savannah two days before Christmas to stand trial. The State announced it would seek the death penalty.

Charles was held in custody for five months before his case came to trial in May 1975. The State's principal witnesses included not only Detective Wade and the two eyewitness survivors of the attack—Mrs. Rosenstein and Mrs. Corcelius (who at trial both confidently identified Charles)—but also the ex-con James Nixon. Nixon was the man who had been arrested for helping himself to cash from the till at a store in New Port Richey on that outing the previous November. He had transformed himself from a parolee and felony defendant into a jail-house informer. Insisting that no deals had been made to elicit his testimony, he claimed that while he and Charles were together in jail Charles had bragged about shooting two people—"a man and a little boy"—in a Savannah furniture store. Never mind that the "little boy," Fred Rosenstein, was 42, and that Nixon in his confusion several times reversed the defendant's name and gave it as "Charles Earl." Even with these errors, other inconsistencies, and the general incoherence of what Nixon had to say, his testimony was a devastating blow to the defense.

Charles's attorney called to the stand Robert Zachery, the manager of the Kwik Pep station where Charles and Williams had worked. Despite the fact that Zachery had fired the two young men, he had taken three days off work and driven to Savannah at his own expense to aid in their defense. He testified that on the day of the murders Charles was working at his gas station in Tampa. Zachery's supervisor had already taken the stand; he showed the court the time cards and payment vouchers that verified Charles's alibi. Jenny Owens, Williams's girl friend, testified that Charles had visited her in the hospital on the day in question. Jenny's sister added her testimony that she, too, had seen Charles at the hospital on that day, thus further solidifying Charles's alibi.

The defense had never been told that Mrs. Rosenstein and Mrs. Corcelius had failed to identify Charles when they were shown photos of him in the days immediately following the murders and therefore did not raise the point as a challenge to their eyewitness identifications. Nor was the defense adequately prepared for Nixon's surprise appearance as a witness for the prosecution. And they had no response at all to Detective Wade's testimony when he directly contradicted their main alibi witness. On the stand, Wade insisted that when he first went to Tampa to investigate the case, Zachery had told him that Charles was not at work on the day of the murders. This flat-out contradiction of Zachery's testimony confronted the jury of two blacks and ten whites with a simple question: Whom should they believe? An out-of-state gas station manager (black), or a member of the local police department (also black)? The jury chose to side with the local detective.

Then there was the matter of the gun that had been found in the Tampa jail while Charles was being held there. The claim by the prosecution that it was used in the Savannah murders was never substantiated. The gun had been turned over to District Attorney Andrew Ryan, however, and the implication that there was a connection between Charles and the .22 pistol found in the Tampa jail (and that the pistol was the murder weapon) was not discredited during the trial.

The jury found Charles guilty. The trial judge, George E. Oliver, later recalled that Charles's alibi had sounded plausible to him and that he was surprised the jury did not believe it. One journalist speculated that the jurors might have been skittish because they knew about the recent release in Savannah of another murder suspect on the basis of a similar alibi. In any event, regardless of the private doubts Judge Oliver later acknowledged having had, he did not question the jury's decision. Relying on the authority of Georgia's capital statute, which had been enacted only a few months before the Rosenstein murders, he sentenced Charles to death.

The law at that time required an inmate under sentence of death in Georgia to be held in jail in the county where the trial had taken place until the state supreme court ruled on the appeal. Accordingly, Charles was moved to the imposing but deteriorating Chatham County jail in Savannah. The building where he was held was later abandoned in favor of a new facility, but during his incarceration the ancient structure was still in use. The jail, in what may have looked to Charles like an unfortunate piece of symbolism, overlooked the city's Colonial Cemetery. The view inside wasn't very reassuring, either. The walls of the cell that was Earl Charles's home had recently been whitewashed, but the metal-grate door and the metal bunk beds added to the bleak atmosphere.

Earl lived for Tuesday, visiting day. From the top bunk he could just barely get a view of visitors turning in off the street; he would wait in his cell, watching. His mother came every week for the ten-minute visit through a steel grill that was all regulations allowed. Earl's father would also make the trek to see his son, when he could, but he was frequently sick during that period and could not visit often. Then, too, there were times when one or both of his parents would arrive at the jail only to discover that Earl Charles was on a "no visiting" list that day. Flossie Mae Charles was not, however, easily put off. "A lot of times she went through a lot of chains to try to see me," Earl said. "The first thing she'd do is call my attorney and get him down on the case and she'd go call the jailer and they would find out why. And she'd usually get it straightened out." Earl never quit praising his mother's efforts on his behalf: "She really showed me what parenthood is about during this ordeal. She really hung in there with me."

Anthony Schmitz, who wrote a 1982 article on the Charles case in the *Atlanta Weekly*, also paid tribute to Flossie Mae Charles's stubborn persistence. "Mrs. Charles never gave up her search for the shred of evidence that would set her son free," he wrote. She visited the furniture store, pleading with Mrs. Rosenstein and Mrs. Corcelius to concede that their eyewitness identification could have been erroneous. She put ads in the Tampa newspaper, searching for additional confirmation of her son's alibi—the alibi that had been ignored, despite seeming so airtight. She called Robert Zachery at the Kwik Pep station to see whether he could remember anything that might help.

Zachery had left Savannah to return to Tampa right after giving his testimony, "assuming Charles would be acquitted," according to a later account. When he learned from Mrs. Charles that Earl had been convicted and was facing a date with the electric chair, Zachery was dumbfounded. But having given his honest and accurate testimony, only to have it disbelieved, he could think of nothing further to do. Mrs. Charles called him regularly, however, desperately hoping he might yet come up with something else that would help.

After one such call from Mrs. Charles, Zachery finally mentioned again to his friend Lemon Harvey—the deputy sheriff he had asked to keep an eye on the station on the days when Charles and Williams were working there—his distress and annoyance at Mrs. Charles's repeated calls. Harvey knew about the double murder in Savannah, of course, and he knew that Zachery had gone to Savannah to testify on Charles's behalf. But he had assumed, or had thought he understood, that the crime had taken place some time *after* Charles and Williams had left their jobs at the Kwik Pep. Suddenly he realized that Zachery was telling him otherwise: The Rosensteins were murdered *while* Charles was working at the Kwik Pep.

Deputy Harvey always kept a diary of his daily rounds. With the relevant dates and the sequence of events at last clear in his mind, he checked his log. And there it was! His entry for October 3, 1974, unequivocally confirmed that Charles and Williams were in Tampa, pumping gas, at precisely the time someone was murdering Max and Fred Rosenstein more than three hundred miles to the north.

Zachery called Mrs. Charles; she in turn called Earl's attorney. Flossie Mae Charles's tireless efforts on her son's behalf were about to pay off. "Truth itself is gonna prevail," Earl later said his mother had told him the first time she saw him after his arrest. She had strongly believed in that, and it now looked as if she were going to be proved right. Officer Harvey was interviewed by both the defense and the prosecution. His story held firm.

Harvey's testimony undeniably cast a cloud over the original arrest of Charles, as well as his prosecution and conviction. According to a much later account in the *Poverty Law Report*, once Harvey came forward it began to look as if Detective Wade had obtained the warrant for Charles's arrest "by coaching eyewitnesses into identifying Charles as the murderer, or by simply falsifying records." It also appeared that he had committed perjury when he testified at the trial, and that he had struck a deal with parole violator James Nixon. In fact, when one of the attorneys on Charles's defense team talked with Nixon again, he recanted his trial testimony, admitting that Detective Wade had coached him. He had incriminated Charles—perjuring himself—he said, because he was told it would help his own case. Wade had promised him freedom—an unkept promise, Nixon pointed out bitterly from the Florida prison cell where he was being interviewed.

In February 1978, nearly three years after Charles was convicted, his attorneys filed a motion for a new trial. The district attorney, Ryan, ordered his chief investigator to examine the new evidence and again interview all the witnesses. More bits of information slowly emerged. One particularly significant item came from Zachery. When he first met with Detective Wade, he said, he had suggested that Wade should talk with Officer Harvey. Wade never bothered to do so.

The investigation undertaken by the district attorney's office turned up other new and troubling questions about Wade's testimony and what the defense regarded as additional improprieties that had occurred while Wade was working on the case. After the trip to Tampa during which he interviewed Zachery, for instance, Wade had written a seven-page report. That report included nothing about any claim by Zachery that Charles had not been at work on the day of the murders. The detective who accompanied Wade to Florida also said that he had not mentioned that Zachery had destroyed Charles's alibi—which, in light of Wade's testimony at the trial, was a stunning omission. Nor had Wade informed the district attorney that Charles's fingerprints failed to match the fingerprints found at the furniture store. Nor were the prosecutors told about Mrs. Corcelius's erroneous identification of the soldiers. And, of course, neither were Charles's defense attorneys given any of this exculpatory evidence.

The district attorney's investigation concluded with a major concession: "The evidence was consistent with [Charles's] alibi." Ryan announced that his office would not oppose the motion for a new trial—and, moreover, if the motion was granted, his office would not retry the case. In short, Earl Charles deserved an acquittal; no longer was there any question about his innocence. Judge Oliver promptly vacated the conviction.

After three years and seven months of being incarcerated for a crime he did not commit, Earl Charles was freed on July 5, 1978. He soon learned that the city of Savannah was not ready to take responsibility for the blunders and misconduct of its officials. One might have thought an internal police department investigation would look into at least some of Wade's shabby tactics. As the *Poverty Law Report* noted, however, "No such investigation was ever held, nor [were] any officers disciplined."

Charles's parents had spent their life savings and mortgaged their home to help pay the legal bills. Earl wanted some official acknowledgment of the error from the authorities, as well as compensation for himself and his parents. On June 20, 1979, with the help of attorneys from the Southern Poverty Law Center (SPLC) in Montgomery, Alabama, Charles filed suit against the city of Savannah and Detective Wade. The suit alleged false imprisonment and malicious arrest and prosecution—specifically, that Detective Wade had knowingly tainted the eyewitness identifications, persuaded James Nixon to commit perjury, withheld exculpatory evidence from the district attorney, and perjured himself at the trial. Charles sought $7.2 million: $3.6 million in compensatory damages and another $3.6 million in punitive damages.

As the suit was being prepared, SPLC attorneys discovered further evidence that James Nixon had lied—a letter he had written to Detective Wade clearly stating his expectation that he would be released from prison in exchange for offering the incriminating testimony Wade wanted. They also found a letter from Detective Wade and another Savannah detective written to the governor of Florida, requesting that Nixon be released from prison because of the testimony he had given against Charles. Wade was trapped.

For the civil suit, Charles and his attorneys wanted James Nixon to come forward and formally admit that his testimony at the original trial was false and had been solicited by promises of leniency from Detective Wade. Nixon was by then in the maximum security prison in Starke, Florida, however. The best they could hope for was a deposition from Nixon, sworn to from his prison cell. Judge Avant Edenfield, who presided over the civil trial in federal district court, refused to allow

Nixon to be deposed, and thus the judge and jury never heard his story. In April 1980 Edenfield also threw out the claim against the city, and a day later a jury found no personal liability against Wade.

The SPLC attorneys promptly appealed. In January 1982 a three-judge panel from the Fifth Circuit Court of Appeals reversed the judgment of the lower court, saying the district court "abused its discretion in denying plaintiff's motion to depose [Nixon, who was] confined in Florida prison." Though in part the lower court's opinion had been affirmed, the civil case was remanded for a new trial because of the reversal on this point.

At retrial, in October 1983, the defendants—Detective Wade and representatives of the city of Savannah—waived their right to a jury trial. District Judge Edenfield again presided, and the SPLC again argued the case for Charles. This time, although Judge Edenfield cleared the city of any responsibility, he assessed damages of $417,000 against Detective Wade. To that extent, it was a major victory for Earl Charles.

Both sides appealed the judgment—the SPLC lawyers on the ground that the city should not have been exonerated—but they soon entered into negotiations with each other. Few police officers are wealthy, and Detective Wade was no exception. He had virtually no assets; there was no way he could turn over $417,000 to Earl Charles. Finally, in 1984, the city of Savannah agreed to pay $75,000 to Charles on Wade's behalf; in return, all further litigation would be dropped. Charles's attorneys reluctantly urged him to accept, figuring it was the best deal he could get. Although the Southern Poverty Law Center had spent approximately $30,000 on the case, they waived all fees so that Charles could receive the entire award.

Compared to what happens in most cases where a defendant has been wrongly convicted, it *was* a good deal. Many victims of judicial error never receive any compensation at all. But no monetary award could really make up for the years Charles had spent behind bars. At the time the civil suit was filed, Dennis Balske—SPLC's chief attorney in Charles's case—had said, "The rest of us can't begin to imagine the trauma Earl has gone through. No amount of money could make him whole again." The years in prison take a toll, quite apart from the loss of freedom and the time itself. In 1981, testifying at a hearing before a state senate committee on a bill to abolish the death penalty in Georgia, Charles (according to a newspaper report) rejected "the argument that justice was accomplished in his case when he was released." He testified to the contrary with considerable emotion: "With the mental stress and financial strain me and my family went through all those years, I don't see no way in the sight of God that this can be justice."

From the time Charles was released, nothing went smoothly for him.

Even the return home with his parents was rich in irony: As one writer later pointed out in an article about the Charles case, the family lived in the section of Savannah known as "Liberty City." For Earl Charles, liberty was hard won. Not long after his release, he was asked whether he had had "any particular problem" since getting out. In what must have been an understatement, Charles said, "It was real difficult finding a job in Savannah." He worked first with his uncle, and then with a cousin, in the construction business. When he applied for a job with the city park department, he had to face questions about the Rosenstein murders. His minister described him as "resentful" and "withdrawn," when as a child he had been "jubilant and outgoing." His mother was saddened at the loss of her son's sense of humor.

Finally Charles decided—once again—that he needed to leave Savannah to get a fresh start; once again, he headed for Florida. This time he went to Jacksonville, where he had a sister, and there he found a job as a gardener. But the quiet work, even coupled with the internal peace he had struggled so hard to develop while he was in jail—the only way he could survive the madness there, he said—did not suffice to still the angry, whirring voices in his head. When a representative of Jacksonville Citizens Against the Death Penalty wrote to ask Charles's SPLC attorney, Dennis Balske, whether Charles might make a public appearance under their auspices, he encouraged the group to get in touch with him, but warned, "These are difficult times for him."

By 1981, Charles had moved to Alabama and was living in Montgomery, doing some work for SPLC. A fund-raising appeal—a letter telling his story—went out over his name, and he spent time visiting with relatives of death row prisoners. He told one reporter, "Every time I would talk to a mother who has a son on death row, . . . I would give them some type [of] hope. My major goal is to get off into counseling and help guys just coming out of prison. I want to work with them while they are in and then be somebody they can talk to when they get out. Most guys return to prison because when they first get out, they don't feel comfortable talking with anyone who hasn't been there."

Hardly surprisingly, he had become an ardent opponent of capital punishment. The desire to seek revenge for a killing, while understandable, Charles once said, needs to be curbed. "Through this experience I've realized now that that would be acting on emotion without any type of reason. And emotions running . . . wild? They're no more than a flame which burns to its own destruction. You have to really think about this thing. It's a real delicate thing. But the Truth itself stands bold. And capital punishment—there's no way in the world it can be right. And that's the truth of the matter. That's the truth of it."

Within the next year Charles had moved to Atlanta, where he found a job in a decorator's shop refinishing antique furniture. His attorney gave him an old typewriter, and he liked to sit in his basement apartment banging out essays and poems. He had begun writing poetry while he was in jail. He hoped to get his G.E.D. so he could go to college. But the burden of his wrongful conviction continued to weigh on him. When a newspaper interviewer asked him whether he felt some people doubted his innocence, he replied, "Yea. It's a scar that's been placed on me that I had nothing to do with, but still it's on me and I have to wear it. It's something that just constantly follows me." Several years later, the weight had not lifted. "I'm not bitter in any violent sense," he once told another newspaper writer, "but there is a certain amount of anguish there. . . . And I went through a lot of personal, emotional changes that nobody else understands."

The passage of time, as it turned out, would not erase the pain; after another decade, it simply became too much. According to a brief news item in the *Atlanta Constitution* in March 1991, Earl Patrick Charles "walked into the path of an oncoming car" in Cobb County, Georgia, and was killed instantly. His mother was quoted as saying, "He just never was quite right" after the ordeal of trial and the long months of wrongful incarceration. "He was locked up in a cell for three years and seven months," his mother reminded those who had forgotten. "That can play with your mind."

Indeed it can. Some years earlier, in a reflective moment that seems all the more poignant in the aftermath of his apparent suicide, Charles had told a reporter, "This has cost me time and time again. It just kind of consumes me." And then he went on to ask, rhetorically, "What can I tell a child of mine about this system of justice after what they've done to me?"

✸

WHEN POLICE have taken someone into custody and then learn the suspect has a record of previous criminal convictions—or even only of arrests—the discovery increases their suspicion. And when such a person goes to trial and presents an alibi, the jury is typically quick to find the alibi unconvincing. A guilty verdict is more likely to follow than not. Earl Charles's story illustrates these points, as do many others; the two cases below come from West Virginia and California.

In the spring of 1951 Robert Ballard Bailey, 35, sat in a West Virginia prison cell awaiting execution. The state legislature had recently decided to change the method of execution from hanging to the electric chair, and Bailey was scheduled to be the first to be put to death by the new method. Appeals in both state and federal courts had been to no avail (though the state court decisions against him had always been by a margin of only one vote). Death in the electric chair for Bailey was going to be the end of more than a decade of crime that included convictions for auto theft in 1933, armed robbery in 1938, and unarmed robbery in 1946. He had served two years for the unarmed robbery offense and was discharged in 1948.

Bailey, by trade a glassworker, was not an especially vicious criminal. His crimes (usually committed while he was drunk) were typically impulsive and often carried out quite ineptly. Nor did they involve personal violence to his victims. Yet here he was, three years after the end of his most recent prison term, about to be executed for first-degree murder. No attorney was at his side, pursuing last-ditch efforts on his behalf. With only a few days to go, his case looked hopeless.

But it turned out he did have a friend in the prison warden, Orel Skeen, who had become convinced of Bailey's innocence. Skeen had heard of Erle Stanley Gardner's Court of Last Resort, and he asked Gardner to take a look at the case. At the time, Gardner and his associates were in Michigan investigating the claims of another prisoner (Vance Hardy). They were sufficiently impressed with the story Skeen told them, however, to drop everything and drive to the state prison in Moundsvile, in the panhandle of West Virginia, southeast of Pittsburgh. They found Bailey "a nervous wreck."

Their first step was to put him through a polygraph test; Alex Gregory, one of Gardner's associates, pronounced the results supportive of Bailey's innocence. Armed with this encouraging evidence, they drove the next day to Charleston, seeking to get more information about the case from the trial judge who had privately written the governor urging commutation of Bailey's death sentence. The investigators' only hope was a reprieve from Governor Okey Patterson—who had already made known his view that Bailey was guilty. He was, however, open-minded enough to be impressed with Gardner's interest in the case; he agreed to meet with Gardner and his colleagues to hear what they had to say.

Three and a half hours later, Governor Patterson issued a reprieve for Bailey. After reviewing further information that Gardner provided him, Patterson commuted Bailey's death sentence to life imprisonment. He had concluded, as Gardner put it, that "in the present condition of the evidence he was far from satisfied with the verdict, [and] there was a reasonable doubt to say the least as to Bailey's guilt. . . ." (As a result, Harry Burdette, not Robert Bailey, became the first person to be put to death in West Virginia's new electric chair.)

What was the evidence that changed the governor's mind? First and foremost, there was Bailey's alibi. At the very moment that—according to some witnesses—Bailey was committing the murder, the Charleston police were trying vainly to arrest him, miles away, for drunk driving. So eager were they to stop him, they shot the rear of his car full of holes. Numerous witnesses who knew Bailey attested to his being very drunk at the time and to being the driver of the car that careened madly down the roads, hotly pursued by the police. None of the few witnesses who identified him as the murderer knew him. Another case of mistaken identity? Probably.

The murder occurred in the middle of an October afternoon in 1949. The victim was Rosina Fazio, 56, a member of a prominent local family. Apparently she had accepted a ride home from someone—perhaps an acquaintance, maybe a stranger. Newspaper accounts of the crime reported that before she died she "identified Bailey as her attacker." A witness who knew Mrs. Fazio specified the time exactly when she saw Fazio in a car being driven by a man the witness said was Bailey. Another witness, pinpointing the time as precisely as the first witness had, claimed to have seen a man he later identified as Bailey shoving the body of Mrs. Fazio out of his car. The car in question was not, however, the car the police shot up and that belonged to Bailey.

Successfully eluding the police, Bailey made his way home. In due course he recovered from his drunken stupor. When he examined his car and saw the bullet holes, he vaguely remembered that the police had been in hot pursuit of him the day before. Scared, Bailey made a stupid move: He ran. As an ex-con, he wanted no trouble with the police and foolishly thought promptly leaving town for parts unknown was his best gamble. He had no idea he was fleeing from a murder charge. He hadn't heard about the Fazio murder, though the police by then had identified him as the man wanted for the crime. They in turn had no reason to connect the unknown drunken driver who had eluded them with the suspected killer. The local papers and the police wires were soon hot with the news that Robert Bailey was wanted for murder in Charleston, West Virginia.

When finally located by the police, Bailey and his family were in hiding in Florida. Taken back to Charleston, he was tried in March 1950 and convicted. The jury accepted the damning testimony from the eyewitnesses and rejected the alibi. Bailey's status as a criminal in and out of prison was, by the time of the trial, well known. West Virginia law provided that first-degree murder could be punished either by death or by life in prison; Bailey's jury—after three hours of deliberation—decided on death.

Virtually snatched from the electric chair by the Court of Last Resort, Bailey remained in prison another nine years. Then, in 1960, Governor Cecil Underwood granted him a conditional pardon. Six years later the conditions were dropped.

ON A JANUARY evening in 1961, Morris Hassen, the owner of the Purity Market on West Eighth Street in Los Angeles, was dusting liquor bottles on the shelf. Suddenly, two men entered the store, and Morris's wife, Beulah, found herself looking at the muzzle of a gun. A moment later one of the gunmen fired, fatally wounding her husband.

Beulah Hassen didn't get a good look at the killer's face, but she did notice his hat and coat. Later, she identified the other robber from police file photographs. As it turned out, he had just been killed in a futile effort to escape after an abortive armed robbery of a gas station in Pomona, forty miles to the east. One of the others on that caper was Paul Kern Imbler. Not surprisingly, the police suspected he was involved in the Los Angeles holdup-murder ten days earlier.

At trial, the prosecution's chief witness was Alfred Costello. He told the jury that he had chased the gunman down the street and into an alley, recovered his coat and hat discarded during the chase, and found in the coat pocket the murder weapon (later confirmed by ballistics tests). Costello positively identified Imbler as the man he had chased. Other witnesses helped tighten the net around Imbler.

From the time of his arrest, Imbler had protested his innocence. He claimed he had spent the evening of the robbery in the company of several friends at various bars, drinking. But the only one of these companions who could be located by the defense was, alas, the third participant in the Pomona robbery that had led to Imbler's implication in the first place. In and out of jail and prison for fifteen years prior to the Hassen murder, Imbler was an aging recidivist familiar to the California police. Perhaps the chief thing to be said in his favor at the time was that, although he had managed to get away following the Pomona robbery attempt, he later turned himself in. He had no inkling that he was wanted in Los Angeles on a murder charge.

The jury convicted Imbler of felony-murder in the course of armed robbery, a capital offense, and sentenced him to die in the gas chamber. The California Supreme Court, in its automatic review of the conviction in 1962, reported that "the evidence . . . was more than sufficient to establish that [Imbler] did the shooting." Imbler's death date was set for mid-September, and he seemed reconciled to his fate. He even willed his corneas to an eye bank and the rest of his body to a medical school.

Meanwhile, however, evidence was being accumulated that cast doubt on Imbler's guilt. Leading the re-examination of the case were Russell Carroll, an investigator with the public defender's office in Los Angeles, and Dr. LeMoyne Snyder, an associate of Erle Stanley Gardner's with the Court of Last Resort. They learned that Costello, the one witness who had positively identified Imbler, was an ex-convict and former mental patient. Furthermore, on the stand Costello had lied about his background—and the prosectuion had known he was lying. Carroll and Snyder made two other discoveries about Costello: He was a runner in an illegal bookmaking operation that the Hassens carried on from their grocery store, and several bad-check charges were pending against him at the very time the Imbler trial was in progress.

Closer scrutiny of the physical evidence against Imbler established that it, too, was unreliable. The gun found in the killer's overcoat was never linked to Imbler. The one good fingerprint on the material in the overcoat pocket was not Imbler's. Neither the hat nor the coat fit Imbler. And the polygraph evidence used against him was unreliable. Snyder was the father of polygraph testing in police investigations, inaugurating its use in Michigan in 1931. When he finally located the polygraph test results used by the prosecution against Imbler, he concluded they proved nothing. (Later, a Los Angeles Police Department polygraph expert confirmed Snyder's judgment.)

With this evidence, Carroll was able to get Imbler a stay of execution with only a few days to spare. But in the following year, 1963, the California Supreme Court refused to grant a habeas corpus hearing on the basis of the new evidence, and another death date was set for March 1964. Imbler's attorneys then shifted their attack to the death sentence itself, ignoring the underlying conviction. They argued that prejudicial evidence had been introduced during the penalty phase of the trial. (California was one of the states to pioneer the bifurcated trial system that has become universal in capital cases since United States Supreme Court rulings in 1976.) They claimed that the judge's instructions to the jury about the law on parole eligibility were prejudicial to their client's hope for a life sentence. The petition was successful; the appellate court ordered a new trial on the issue of sentencing alone. At this trial, in 1964, the jury sentenced Imbler to life in prison.

Imbler's supporters next shifted their attention back to the task of overturning his conviction. Early in 1968 his attorneys filed a habeas corpus petition in federal court, and a year later, District Court Judge Warren Ferguson reversed Imbler's conviction. "There was no physical evidence whatsoever connecting [Imbler] with the crime. . . . Subsequent to the trial, investigation produced further corroboration by new witnesses of . . . petitioner's alibi. . . . There is no doubt that false testimony was given at petitioner's trial by Costello. . . ." As for the prosecution, Judge Ferguson charged it with "reckless use of highly suspicious false testimony. . . ." He went on in this vein for seventeen double-columned pages. The judge gave the State sixty days to retry Imbler or set him free.

The State was not inclined to give in, but two years of appeals in state and federal courts failed to overturn Judge Ferguson's order. By 1971 time had run out, and the retry-or-release order could no longer be evaded. The prosecution decided not to give Imbler a new trial before a new jury (ten years had elapsed since the crime was committed), but they also did not exactly set him free. Instead, they arranged to have him released on parole—which they could do because he still had hanging over him the sentence for the crime he had turned himself in for in 1961, the failed stickup of the Pomona gas station.

Out on the street again, Imbler decided to file a civil suit against the State, asking for $2.7 million for unlawful prosecution and other violations of his civil rights. The courts turned him down cold, despite having effectively admitted that they had made a gross error when they convicted him and sentenced him to death.

13 | EVEN

✳ | EXPERTS

MAKE

MISTAKES

B OB DOMER slowed his car to a stop just over the crest of the hill. He shifted into neutral, put on the parking brake, and left the motor running. Opening the door of his 1958 Buick sedan, he got out. This looked like the right place for what he had decided to do. The April night was cool and quiet, and he had this stretch of Ohio country road all to himself; it was dark except for the faint light cast by the stars. The nearest city, Massillon, was five or six miles away, and no houses were in sight. At 2:00 A.M. it was unlikely that any car would pass by.

Less than a hundred yards away, a straight shot down the steep hill, he could dimly see the double silvery lines of steel where the main line of the Pennsylvania Railroad between New York and Chicago crossed the road. In 1963 trains were running frequently, and Bob was sure that before long a freight would round the bend and head for the open-grade crossing. A train was essential to his plan. All he would need to do was release the brake, shift the car into gear, and push; the Buick would then roll, gathering momentum, down the road onto that crossing.

He opened the rear door of the car and wrestled the rigid body of Howard Riddle from the back seat into the front. Carefully he transferred his own driver's license from his wallet to the hip pocket of Riddle's trousers. Half an hour passed. Domer began to worry that a car might come along after all. What if the driver stopped to offer help, and he had to explain what he was doing! Suppose somebody recognized him! He wasn't all that far from home, and his clothes were a mess, especially for a middle-aged business executive. No car came down the lonely road, however—but neither did a train appear. Another half hour, perhaps an hour, went by. Where was that blasted train?

Suddenly it occurred to him that he could fake a better accident if he made sure there was a fire as well as a collision. He took out the spare gas can he always carried, unscrewed the cap, and doused Riddle's body and the interior of the car. In the process, some of the fuel spilled on his hand. He put the can back and then stood beside the car in the angle formed by the open door and the vehicle's side—waiting for the train.

Finally, in the distance, Domer heard the unmistakable sound he had been waiting for, steadily growing louder. He knew he had to act quickly; things had to be timed just right, or there wouldn't be any collision at the crossing. Nervously, he lit a cigarette and reached into the car, preparing the shift it into gear and release the brake as the train came into view. Abruptly, the interior of the car roared into flame. Domer leaped back, his hand and the right side of his face seared by the fire. Damn that cigarette and the gasoline he'd spilled on his hand!

Suddenly in a panic, with the car on fire and starting to roll, Domer checked the position of the approaching train. To his horror, behind the engine he saw a long row of dimly shining lights—a passenger train, not a freight! Oh God, he thought, this is awful; I can't let this burning car hit a passenger train. "I knew that I couldn't do that," he said later. "I had no option. I turned the wheel, pushed it into gear, and ran it down over the embankment, off the road and into a field."

Smoking and aflame, the Buick slid off the pavement, crashed through a fence, and came to rest a dozen yards from the tracks. The train roared by and disappeared into the darkness.

Domer stood in the road in the sudden stillness. What a fiasco! Left without a choice—exhausted, frightened, and confused—he decided to call it quits. Screwing up his courage for the ordeal that lay ahead, Bob Domer trudged down the lonely and now-silent tracks toward Massillon. Unwittingly, he was also walking straight toward Ohio's electric chair.

Robert K. Domer was about as unlikely a candidate for Ohio's death row as anyone could imagine. Son of a successful businessman, he grew up in northeastern Ohio in the city of Canton, went to college a few miles away in Alliance, entered the army just after Pearl Harbor, and married a local girl—Evelyn Miller. He served overseas and in 1946 was discharged with the rank of captain. Law school on the GI Bill beckoned, and Domer entered Western Reserve University in Cleveland, graduating in June 1948. Evelyn and the young attorney promptly returned to Canton.

Situated fifty miles south of Cleveland, just twenty miles from Akron on what is now Interstate 77, Canton in 1948 had a population of about 120,000. President William McKinley is buried there, but today far more visitors come each year to the Pro Football Hall of Fame than to visit the nearby presidential grave. The Timken Company, where Domer's father was a middle-level executive, was the city's largest employer. Bob and Evie Domer thought Canton, a stable midwestern town, was a good place to live, raise a family, and find steady employment.

Domer accepted a job as an investigator with a Canton law firm. But when he failed to pass the bar examination on his first attempt, he resigned. He soon found a position as an installment loan interviewer with a local bank. Later, after passing the bar, he was promoted and became a mortgage lending officer. Within a year he was elected assistant cashier, and in five years he was vice president. Two years later, he left that position to accept the presidency of the newly formed Mortgage Securities, Inc., in association with members of a major construction company. For a young man of 35, he was doing well.

For five years the company grew and prospered, until Domer's partners, preferring to concentrate on construction, arranged for the sale of their shares in the company without consulting him. The new owners then bought out Domer's interest. With the settlement, Domer formed Continental Mortgage Corporation. The mortgage market sagged, however, in one of its periodic downturns, and the struggling company was unable to find sufficient financial resources to continue. The troubles accelerated, and within two years the company was near collapse.

Domer had been trying for months to negotiate the sale of some mortgages the company had originated, or to find additional financing to carry the company through the bad times. Most of these efforts were unsuccessful, and the money shortage was squeezing the life out of the corporation. At the same time, one of Domer's employees was having financial troubles of his own—and coping with them by illegal means. Undertaking negotiations unilaterally, he had committed to several mortgages and managed to close on those loans without following regular escrow procedures. This necessitated immediate pay-outs, which the cash-starved company could ill afford. To make matters worse, the hapless employee pocketed some of the money for his personal use. The result was a crisis for Continental Mortgage.

When Domer learned about the fraud, he confronted the employee, who pleaded for time to repay the money. Pointing to his family of five children, he asked for help. Instead of turning him over to the police, Domer agreed to a short delay. Years later Domer observed ruefully, "I could see the handwriting on the wall. I should have called the police and just closed the company doors. That would have been the end of the business, but it would have been better than what did happen." The embattled employee took some company credit cards and fled the state, abandoning his wife and children to an uncertain future.

Domer still stubbornly clung to the faint hope that a miracle would save the business. The combination of the internal business crisis and the outside pressure from creditors, however, meant that his struggle to keep Continental's head above water was a losing battle. Evie knew something about the problems her husband was facing; she had been keeping Continental's books. Thus she was aware that the usual sources of funding were fast drying up and that banks were demanding liquidation of loans as well as refusing to extend further credit.

Bob was becoming desperate. With money borrowed from his father, he sought to staunch the outflow of cash. His complicated system of bookkeeping for mortgage payments required both a general operating account and a "clearing" account. By the end of March 1963, Continental's clearing account was thousands of dollars short. This included money owed to investors, which Domer had used in part to pay off the loans contracted by the absconded employee. That strategy backfired when one investor abruptly decided to send several auditors to examine Continental's books. They arrived on Friday, March 29.

Domer knew what they would find over the weekend; he knew that when they made their report on Monday, Continental Mortgage would be finished. He became convinced, too, that his whole world was collapsing around him. His manipulation of company funds clearly violated the law; the fact that it was his erstwhile employee rather than he who was primarily at fault, and that insurance would cover much of the loss, was immaterial. At the age of 43, he faced disgrace—as he saw it—in his home town and possible criminal charges. On Sunday, while the auditors were winding up their work, he concluded there was only one solution.

Some years earlier he had purchased a substantial insurance policy on his life with his wife as principal beneficiary. Although he was about to be ruined by the failure of his business, the insurance money would at least make it possible for his father to be repaid and his wife and children to be provided for—if they could gain access to it. Unfortunately, the only way to do that was to take his own life, making it look like an accident. (The insurance policy provided for double indemnity in the case of his accidental death.) Domer was by this time in a pathetic state, unable to think clearly and feeling driven to insane measures. A law-abiding citizen all his life—he had never even had a parking ticket—he was about to perpetrate a fraud in order to save himself terrible embarrassment, to cover up his unlawful handling of other people's money, and to get himself out of what looked to him like a totally hopeless situation.

On Monday morning, April 1, the Domers' two daughters left for school, with no inkling of what their father was planning. Evie Domer also left the house, headed for the office as usual and completely unaware of the bizarre scheme her husband had concocted over the weekend. Bob told Evie he'd be along a bit later. But instead, as soon as he was alone in the house, he left a rambling message on the family tape recorder, placed the machine on the kitchen counter where it would be easily found, and drove off in his car.

As he put distance between himself and Canton, Bob slowly realized that he didn't have a very exact plan in mind at all. Suicide, yes, and it had to look like an accident—but how, and where? Then he remembered a railroad underpass with a sharp right turn on a road near Ravenna, about a thirty-minute drive to the northeast. A large concrete abutment suddenly looms up, and dozens of accidents had occurred there over the years when cars, traveling too fast, couldn't make the turn. Domer decided that was the spot, thinking it would be easy to head into the underpass at high speed, swerve out of control too late, and crash into the abutment. As he approached the underpass, however, his courage failed him. "I got up there, and I raced my car toward that abutment, but at the last moment I turned the wheel. I just couldn't do it," he said later.

In Canton, when Bob did not show up at the office, Evie began to worry. She phoned home: No answer. Uneasy, she returned to the house and promptly found the tape recorder. Aghast when she heard the message Bob had left, with its vague reference to how she would read about this or hear about it from the police, she immediately called the police herself, hoping to head Bob off. Back at the office, the auditors finished their investigation, and Continental Mortgage Corporation was placed in receivership—just as Bob had anticipated.

During the rest of that Monday, indeed for the next two weeks, Domer drove around aimlessly, in a fog of confusion and uncertainty. He continued morosely and unsystematically to look for a plausible place to stage his "accident"—but to no avail. Either he couldn't find the right spot, or he would lose his nerve. At the same time, as his resolve slowly faded, he kept hoping he might think of some better way out of his dilemma. He had no inclination to flee the area for places unknown. "I was trying to screw up enough courage in my own mind to go home and face the music. At that point it would have been simply a failed company, and that would have been the end of it." Instead, he drove aimlessly here and there, crisscrossing the countryside for miles around Canton. Often he slept in his car rather than pay for a motel room. Even so, what little money he had with him was soon nearly exhausted. Relying on credit cards, he bought gas and food as he needed them. His unchanged clothes were rumpled, but he was clean shaven every day, thanks to an electric razor he could plug into the lighter on his dashboard. Old habits die hard, even for a man on the run.

On Friday evening, April 18, Domer found himself outside a bar in Akron. Although he had never been there before, he went in, sat down, and ordered a beer. At first he took no notice of the man on the next bar stool, but before long they struck up a casual conversation, as strangers will in such settings. The other man was Howard Franklin Riddle, in his late 50s or early 60s. He was shorter than Domer (as were most men—Domer was well over 6' and had played high school football). Domer soon figured Riddle to be a drifter and a boozer, not the sort of person he often met or in whose company he was likely to spend time. But under the circumstances it didn't much matter, and so they talked on, about nothing in particular. When Domer mentioned he was perhaps going to Cleveland, Riddle said he, too, was on his way to Cleveland and that he needed a ride. Domer backed off, not sure he wanted Riddle's company. Anyway, he wasn't going to Cleveland that night—maybe tomorrow. The two men talked a while longer and then left separately; Domer mentioned casually that he might be back later.

The next afternoon Bob did return to the bar—"I don't know why I chose to go back there," he said later—and there was Riddle. He still wanted to go to Cleveland with Domer, provided, of course, Domer was willing. Bob really didn't care whether he went to Cleveland or not, but decided he might as well go there as stay another day in Akron. So they got into his car and drove toward Cleveland, half an hour to the north.

The two men decided to take their time and first headed southwest to Wooster, where they stopped to eat. Thus, it was late Saturday night before they arrived in Cleveland and checked into a motel room. Riddle was not feeling well; he spent much of the evening coughing and vomiting.

The next morning Riddle felt better—and said that he really didn't want to stay in Cleveland. He suggested they go to Salem, southeast of Cleveland and less than twenty miles from the Pennsylvania border. Domer didn't much care. His behavior had continued to be as directionless as it had been in the first days of his flight, but at least he had someone to talk to, someone who would listen. That evening they stopped to eat at a Salem bowling alley. Riddle asked for frog legs, which struck Domer as a strange order for someone who had been so sick the previous night.

There in Salem, for no apparent reason, Bob suddenly decided it was time for him to go home to Evie and deal with the mess he had left behind, taking whatever consequences there might be. After three weeks on the road, he realized that he was not going to commit suicide—never mind making it look like an accident. That night, after eating—and with

Riddle still accompanying him—he drove to Canton and checked himself into a motel on the outskirts of town. He used an assumed name and, to get a cheaper rate, did not mention that he had a companion with him. About eleven o'clock, he left Riddle fast asleep in the room and got back into his car. He drove out past his home, toying with the idea of announcing his presence, unsure whether he was going to return to the motel. Up and down his street he drove; remarkably, no one saw him. Still unable to make a clean breast of it, however, he decided to continue driving around a bit, to spend one more night in the motel, and to go home in the morning.

It was about 1:00 A.M. when he let himself back into the motel room, fully expecting to find Riddle still asleep. Instead, he was greeted with an appalling scene: Riddle was propped up in bed, his face a gray mask, his hands clasped behind his head; vomit mixed with blood was splattered all over the bedding, the table, and the walls. An empty wine bottle lay on the floor.

Riddle was dead.

Domer could think of only one thing: He had to dispose of the body without anyone knowing. The Buick was parked right outside the door in a garage that could be entered directly from the room, a convenient arrangement for anyone who didn't want to be seen entering or leaving. Domer had backed the car in; it was not too difficult to drag the smaller man out the door and shove him onto the back seat. Domer covered the body and returned to the room to clean things up as well as he could, not thinking about how easy it would have been to leave without anyone knowing he had been there. Because he had not used his own name when he registered, no one had any idea that it was he who had arrived in Canton—or that anyone had been with him. He could simply have driven away, and no one would ever have connected him with Riddle's death.

Once he had cleaned up the worst of the mess, Bob exited quietly, making sure no one was watching, and drove off. By then dawn was approaching, and as he headed east toward Youngstown, all thoughts of returning home vanished. The need to dispose of Riddle's body absorbed all his mental energy. He drove around for hours; later he checked into another motel, making sure when he parked that the body wasn't visible through the car window (why he hadn't put it in the trunk was never clear). After dark, he drove toward the Pennsylvania border, where he was certain he could find an abandoned strip mine—just the kind of place to leave a body where it would not soon be discovered. He had spent much of the day driving here and there, trying to find a suitable location, where no one would see him coming or going. But a good spot to dump a body turned out to be just as difficult to come by as a good way to fake a suicide. Domer was thoroughly stymied. Years later he would say, "I didn't know what in the hell to do. Just that—plain and simple."

It was then that he thought of staging an accident that would appear to be the cause of his death. He wouldn't have to commit suicide after all. He would transfer his I.D. to Riddle's pocket, put the dead man in the front seat of the Buick, and crash the car at night into a speeding freight train on a remote country road. Brilliant!

Bob Domer reached Massillon as dawn broke. He found an unlocked shed and went inside; exhausted, he lay down and was soon asleep. Around noon that day he woke up and walked to the local YMCA, where he used a washroom to clean up. There for the first time he noticed the burns on his hand and wrist. At a nearby drugstore, he purchased some medication. Next he walked to the bus station and, using most of his remaining money, bought a ticket for the short ride to Canton. Still distraught, still desperately confused about what he was going to do with himself, he rode only as far as the county fairgrounds, where he found an empty barn, burrowed into a pile of straw, and again went to sleep. For five days he stayed there—eating nothing, drinking water from an outdoor tap, going out only at night—trying to make up his mind how to proceed. Finally, on April 28, four weeks less a day after he had disappeared, he walked the several miles to his home on the west side of Canton. It was a Sunday morning, his mother's birthday.

Still, he wasn't quite ready to bring his futile odyssey to an end. He assumed his family would soon be going to church (the Domers had always been staunch Lutherans), and so he hid in the garage, planning to wait until his wife and daughters had left before he went in to clean up and get ready to present himself upon their return. But even this small and seemingly rational part of his plan went awry.

Friends of the Domer family had come over to the house that morning to offer Evie and the girls their sympathy and support. While the adults were talking inside, the children went to the garage—only to find a strange man lurking in the shadows! Frightened by his appearance (they didn't recognize him), they ran back to the house to report what they had seen. Evie guessed immediately that it might be Bob. She sent the girls off with the visitors and within moments was helping her husband into the house. While he was in the bathroom getting ready to bathe, she called the sheriff's office to say that her missing husband was at last safe at home.

Two sheriff's deputies had arrived at the house before Bob was out of the bathtub; they waited at the bathroom door. In clean clothes but still unshaven, Domer agreed to accompany them to the county court house for "some questions." He did not know that the police had learned almost immediately about the bungled accident, because the engineer of the passenger train had called his dispatcher to inform the local police of the burning vehicle near the tracks. Identifying the Buick as Domer's was easy; he had made no attempt to destroy or switch the license plates. Almost as quickly, the police established that the dead man was not Domer. Riddle had false teeth. Evie's statement that her husband did not wear dentures was confirmed by his dental records.

With Domer back in town, the police were naturally eager to learn what he knew about the burned car and the unidentified body found inside it. At the very least, they figured he was probably guilty of illegal disposal of a human body (a misdemeanor). At most, well . . . they would have to see.

In the court house, otherwise empty on that Sunday afternoon, various local officials began to join the deputy sheriffs in talking with Domer. Increasingly worried, he asked to get in touch with an attorney; his repeated requests were ignored or denied. Soon the Stark County prosecutor, Norman Putman, joined the group, and Domer again asked for a lawyer. Eventually they agreed to phone George Davidson, who had served Continental Mortgage as legal counsel; he was the first lawyer whose name came to Bob's mind. But when Davidson came to the court house, Domer was not permitted to see or talk with him—was not even told Davidson was there. Perhaps it didn't matter; Davidson was not a criminal defense attorney anyway. The interrogation, getting nowhere because Domer refused to answer more questions without a lawyer on hand, finally stopped. The police took him to the local hospital for treatment of his burns and then to the county jail. There Domer got his first taste of what it was like to spend a night in a cell.

Early the next morning the police took Domer to the fairgrounds, and he identified the barn where he had spent five days in hiding. They next took him to visit the bar in Akron where he had met Riddle. Domer still had not been given the opportunity to talk with legal counsel. Nor had he been put under arrest. He was, however, kept in police custody. As the week went on, he talked with his wife from time to time and also, at last, with George Davidson. Evie and George then met with Davidson's partner, Harry Schmuck, a criminal defense attorney. They introduced him to Bob at the jail, but the authorities would not allow anything except perfunctory communication between the two.

On Friday, five days after his return home and detention, Robert K. Domer was indicted for the murder of Howard Riddle. In fact, he was indicted not on one but on two counts of murder—premeditated murder and felony murder (homicide committed during the course of kidnapping). With Domer formally under indictment for a capital crime, the authorities at last allowed him to meet with Harry Schmuck in private.

Joining Schmuck on the defense team later was another acquaintance of Domer's, Sherlock Evans, a well-known attorney from Massillon. Although Evans was not a criminal defense attorney—he was in general practice—he was a popular figure in the area, and Schmuck thought he could help the defense in various ways. (Both Schmuck and Evans were retained as counsel by Domer's father on his son's behalf.)

From the moment of the indictment, the local press began and maintained a drumbeat of stories about Domer, his family, the failed Continental Mortgage Corporation, Domer's wild and absurd flight, the near-collision with the train, and the mysterious death of Howard Riddle. Every time Domer was moved from the jail to the court house, it was a media circus. Schmuck and Evans managed to arrange for Domer to be taken to the State Mental Hospital at Lima, more than a hundred miles to the west, for a month's psychiatric evaluation. This was done less to lay the basis for an insanity plea than to afford Domer and his family some respite from the relentless attentions of the press and radio.

Right from the start there was considerable uncertainty among the officials about who had jurisdiction over the crime, and therefore over where Domer would be tried. Curiously enough, the county line ran right down the middle of the two-lane road where Domer had staged the accident. The burned car with Riddle's body in it had ended up in a field in Wayne County; it had been pushed from the side of the road in Stark County, however, and it was in Stark that Domer had been arrested and indicted. Norman Putman, the Stark County prosecutor, argued that it was his case to try. Despite the location of the victim and the car, the crime—he insisted—had occurred in his jurisdiction. With the publicity from this case behind him, he could count on an eventual appointment to the bench. (Or so Domer believed. In due course, events bore this out; for years, Norman Putman has been an appellate court judge in Canton, Ohio.)

As the summer of 1963 drew to a close, preparations got under way for the trial in the Court of Common Pleas. Impaneling the jury turned out to be a staggering problem. The first venire of seventy-five was quickly exhausted; everyone polled had not only heard about the case (what else could be expected?), but seemed to have views about Domer's guilt as well. As the second venire was being polled, prospective jurors were again disqualified right and left, for the same reasons. Both prosecution and defense began to wonder whether it would be possible to secure a jury in Canton and whether a change of venue might be in everyone's interest. Then another possibility emerged: waiver of a jury altogether in favor of trial before a panel of three Common Pleas judges. After discussions between counsel and Domer, and between counsel and the court, it was decided to follow that route.

Both Domer and Schmuck knew there were risks involved in taking such a course. The judges were all local; political differences divided most local politicians and the Domer family, so that there was no love lost between them. The defense could count on hostility from the bench at every turn. But Schmuck thought things looked grim for Domer no matter how or where the case was tried. He believed that the court would in all likelihood convict Domer, and that he would end up on death row regardless. The only real hope was to win on appeal and retrial. And, for those purposes, Schmuck did not want the first trial record to be replete with findings of fact from a jury, which would constrain an appellate court. By waiving the jury trial, the defense could also learn the prosecution's line of argument with minimum risk to its own case. That, Schmuck insisted, was the best way to prepare for the appeal.

The trial began in October and lasted for more than a month. (In late November, Domer was on the stand when proceedings were suddenly interrupted by the news flash from Dallas that President John F. Kennedy had just been assassinated. Immediately, trial was suspended for a week.) Particularly damaging to the defense was the tape-recorded message Domer had left for Evie. Listening to it in open court, Domer realized for the first time how ambiguous his "last words" were. Instead of clearly intimating nothing worse than an attempted suicide, his message could be construed to forecast an attempt to find and kill an innocent victim!

On November 29, the court announced its verdict. The three judges acquitted Domer of the first charge, felony murder, but not of the second—premeditated murder. The critical issue was whether Riddle had died of natural causes before Domer set the fire. If Riddle had burned to death, there would have been soot in his lungs and air passages as well as carbon monoxide in his blood. Neither was present. Even so, pathologists testified for the State that they had heard of one or two cases (which they were unable to cite) of death by fire where such findings were absent. With the help of that testimony, the prosecutor succeeded in downplaying the importance of the question, and Domer was convicted.

A month later, at the sentencing, the court asked him whether he wished to make a statement. Domer rose and stated simply: "I would like to say, I believe the evidence in this case and the decision of this Court does not prove me guilty. As God is my witness, I am innocent of this charge, now and always."

Attorney Schmuck added, "I offered . . . to submit the defendant for polygraph test or sodium pentothal test, if administered by an unbiased person, provided that it be introduced into evidence—and that was refused. As far as I am concerned this man is innocent. He is being sentenced for something he did not do." The judicial panel responded on December 30, 1963, by sentencing Robert Domer to death in the electric chair at the Ohio Penitentiary in downtown Columbus. His lawyer's motion for a new trial was dismissed out of hand the same day.

The death sentence was no surprise to Bob Domer. The three judges had shown their hostility from the start; Harry Schmuck just kept reminding Bob, "You know, we're gonna have to ride this one through." Domer clung to Schmuck's assertion that the case would be reversed on review by a higher court.

When Robert Domer arrived on Ohio's death row, seven other prisoners were already there ahead of him. Since 1897, the year Ohio's first electric chair was constructed, it had been kept in regular use. More than three hundred condemned prisoners had "ridden the white lightening" in that chair; it had most recently been used only two weeks prior to the day in March 1963 when the auditors descended on Domer's firm in Canton. Just three years earlier, the Ohio Legislative Service had issued a report stating that, on the average, only one of every four prisoners condemned to die in Ohio would beat the electric chair. Would Domer be one of the lucky few to survive?

As promised, Schmuck appealed the conviction. Having little choice, Domer settled into the routine of life on death row as he waited for the outcome of his appeal. "The thing about death row is the uncertainty, the not knowing. When you go there, it doesn't really sink in because the routine actually overwhelms you. We had no television, and only one radio station during the day and part of the evening. The officers dialed it, and each of us had a set of ear phones—it was listen to religious programs or whatever. We were permitted newspapers only if they came directly from the publisher. My dad subscribed to the hometown paper for me, but I really didn't care.

"The major discomfort is confinement for twenty-three hours and forty minutes each day, in a cell that is only four and a half feet wide and no more than eight feet long. I could take only three steps beside my bed. It was so narrow that I had to put my one leg up on the bed in order to sit on the john. The bed was riveted to the floor. We had no access to a window. And we were permitted to walk outside only when there wasn't a cloud in the sky, and then only three or four of us at a time—accompanied by not fewer than eight or ten guards. The routine denied outside air or walking as much as possible. There was no such thing as recreation. Officers were mostly cast-offs from regular prison guards. One captain of the guards on death row was later committed to a mental hospital. Once, when one of the guards became a father, I secured a card from a chaplain, and I got the guys to sign it. I was sent to the hole—solitary—for that.

"Evie visited with the children. They sat outside the screen with an officer on either side. One visit per month, 12:30 to 3:00. I don't think they ever missed a time. Whenever they came, I was absolutely crushed all over again. I hated for them not to come, but I also hated for them to come, because the procedures they had to go through were so bad." (Furthermore, the penitentiary in Columbus was two and a half hours by car from Canton.)

Nearly a year after Domer arrived on death row, the Court of Appeals announced its decision. Attorney Harry Schmuck's prediction, or at least part of it, was coming true: There would be a retrial. The appellate court opinion scolded the trial judges and the prosecutors for several errors, such as countering the defendant's insistence on his innocence with the false assertion that he had sought a plea bargain for second-degree murder. The court also criticized the prosecution's refusal to allow Domer counsel once he was in custody but prior to his indictment. In all, the defense was sustained on eight of the eleven errors alleged. All these violations of due process led to one conclusion: "The foregoing errone-ous and prejudicial conduct of the prosecutor [is] sufficient grounds to reverse the judgment as entered." But the chief ground for reversal, in the court's judgment, was simply that the evidence of Domer's guilt failed to support a murder conviction.

The prosecution protested, filing a motion for the appellate court to reconsider its reversal of the original judgment. That motion was denied in January 1965, and by May the Ohio Supreme Court had upheld the appellate court's decision. On May 28, 1965, after more than seventeen months on death row, Bob Domer was returned to Stark County to await his second trial.

Retrial began in August, in Canton—once again without a jury, but with an entirely new panel of judges. This time prosecutor Norman Putman spent a full fifty-six days presenting his case, mostly rehashing the questions of jurisdiction (Where, exactly, on County Line Road was Domer standing? Where did Howard Riddle actually die?), and inciden-tally trying to deal with the questions raised by the appellate court on the true cause of death. The essential issue to be resolved once more was whether Riddle had died of natural causes before the fire or as a result of it. Only in the latter instance could Domer be guilty of murder. Putman insisted that Domer had caused Riddle's death by setting the Buick's interior on fire. The defense maintained that Riddle was dead long before the fire; he had not been killed by Domer (or anyone else).

When Putman finally rested his case, the defense moved for an imme-diate verdict of acquittal. The court rejected the motion on a 2-1 vote. Then the defense called a single witness, Dr. Milton Helpern, the chief medical examiner for New York City. Testifying from the State's own autopsy report, he stated unequivocally that the victim *could not possibly* have been alive at any time during the fire in the car. It was, he stated, long accepted in United States law that there are exactly two infallible tests for determining whether death has resulted from fire: the presence of carbon monoxide in the blood, and the presence of soot particles in the victim's throat and lung passages. Helpern further stated that a body that exhibited evidence of neither of these conditions could be conclusively presumed no longer to have been alive when the fire began. Riddle's body, according to the autopsy report, showed no such traces of death by fire.

The prosecutor sought in vain to shake Helpern's categorical testimony. Helpern remained adamant. After the cross-examination, the defense again moved for immediate acquittal. This time the three-judge panel sustained the defense's motion, and the long trial abruptly ended. "I never thought for a moment that I was going to die," Domer said when reflecting on his case two decades later. "I knew that I had not committed *that* crime, and I knew that the good guys would win someday, somehow."

He was right, as it turned out, though it was far from being a foregone conclusion—however boldly optimistic and confident he and his attorneys had (or claimed later to have) been. Despite being a respectable member of the community from a respected family, Bob Domer came disturbingly close to being executed for a crime he did not commit—a crime that never occurred.

To be sure, Domer had knowingly broken the law as he tried to deal with an accumulation of business problems that loomed in his mind to catastrophic proportions. In desperation, confused and afraid, he had behaved in a wildly irrational manner. He had not, however, committed murder.

For the crimes he did commit—misappropriation of funds in the mortgage company (irregular handling of other people's money) and "uttering and publishing" (forging someone's name)—Bob Domer served time in federal prison in Terre Haute, Indiana. There he became involved in numerous activities, first teaching English and writing, then starting a group he called "Focus Forum" that brought speakers from Indiana State University to the prison. Later, he was active in the Gavel Club, organizing nearly five dozen inmates in a project to record books for the blind. When he left prison, the Gavel Club threw a surprise party for him. In attendance were not only other prisoners and the chaplains, but the warden and deputy warden as well.

In part because of these educational endeavors behind bars, when Domer was released he was able to find a job in the evening college division at the University of Akron. He thus moved directly from the penitentiary to being a student counselor. By the beginning of the following semester, he was teaching part-time. That in turn led to full-time teaching, eventually in the Department of Developmental Programs, where he taught children from the inner city.

Bob Domer paid his debt to society for the crimes he committed. As a teacher, as an active layman in the Lutheran Church, and as a committed advocate for the abolition of capital punishment, he has made exactly the kinds of contribution to society that one might expect someone of his background and abilities to make. Granted, Domer did some stupid things when he felt cornered, as many people do, but he harmed no one except himself and his family. And yet a court's erroneous judgment almost resulted in the State's executing him for an accidental death he did not cause.

✳

BOB DOMER'S CASE is unusual for two principal reasons. There was in fact no crime—at least no form of criminal homicide—and so there was no "real" culprit. Also, none of the usual factors that help cause and explain a wrongful conviction played any role in his case. The issue was not the defendant's race or the victim's race, the defendant's previous criminal record, a coerced confession, mistaken (or perjured) eyewitness testimony, or evidence withheld from the defense or fabricated by the police (though one might attribute a certain amount of unwarranted overzealousness to the prosecution). But Domer's case was not the first or only time that circumstances have supported the appearance of foul play and an attempt to cover it up, thereby leading to a wrongful conviction of murder. Two very different cases from California illustrate the same problem.

In October 1941, a passerby looked into the house where widower Courtney Rogers, 50, lived, and saw to his horror a room on fire and full of smoke. Investigators found lighted candles and fires that had been set in several rooms; when Rogers died of asphyxiation soon after being rescued from the burning house, the coroner's inquest ruled it a suicide. The police were, however, suspicious. Rumors of arson and murder were bruited about; attention focused on the deceased's 24-year-old son, Fred, a church organist. The young man's mother had died eight months earlier, in what had also been ruled suicide (by inhalation of chloroform). In retrospect, police began to wonder whether perhaps that, too, had been a well-disguised murder.

Four months after Courtney Rogers died, Fred was arrested on a charge of a fraudulent insurance claim, made in a feeble effort to cover some indebtedness. While they were checking out that crime, the police concluded the tandem suicides had really been double parricide, motivated in part by Fred's desperate need to pay off his heavy debts. (Fred

Rogers had received no insurance proceeds from his mother's death—although the house had been jointly held in his and her names and therefore belonged to him after she died—and only a couple of thousand dollars from insurance policies on his father's life. Thus the deaths of his parents did little to solve his money problems.)

Rogers later said to an interviewer, "I was extremely frightened when they arrested me. I didn't know anything about the law or the way the courts work. One of the officers told me that they had enough evidence against me to send me to the gas chamber. He told me that the only way I could escape the death penalty was to sign a confession. He said that would make them go easy on me."

The signed confession said in part: "I killed my mother because I had a bitter childhood. I wanted to get her property, but most of all I wanted to put her out of the physical pain she suffered. She had an unhappy marriage." As to his father's death, he said (again in part): "My father had come home intoxicated. We quarreled, as we had so many times before. He threatened to kill me and burn the house. . . . I turned on the gas, lighted five candles and walked out." What Fred did not say in his confessions was that he had been subjected to sixteen days of more-or-less continuous questioning before he produced these abject statements.

At trial in June 1942, Rogers retracted his confessions and pleaded not guilty. His defense to the murder charge was that both of his parents had indeed committed suicide. As a side issue, his counsel raised the question of insanity. Newspaper writers loved it. They reported that two forensic psychiatrists had examined Fred and pronounced him a "dangerous madman" who believed he was the reincarnation of a pharaoh, Cagliostro, Francis Bacon, and Cardinal Richelieu. The jury, however, refused to find Fred Rogers not guilty by reason of insanity—or for any other reason. He was convicted on two counts of murder and sentenced to death. So much for attempting to outflank the gas chamber by confessing.

When the California Supreme Court took a look at the trial proceedings in September 1943, it unanimously threw out the conviction. Evidence of several kinds that Mrs. Rogers's death had been by suicide was clear and convincing; evidence of her death by murder rested on nothing but her son's retracted confession. The same was true of Mr. Rogers's death. Neighbors testified that he was utterly despondent after his wife died, and that he had often spoken of taking his own life. They also spoke of his dread of being left alone after Fred, who was an only child, answered a draft call into the army; he was scheduled to report the day after the fatal fire.

The court in particular did not like the methods the police had used to persuade young Rogers to confess. Furthermore, as the court rightly noted, his confessions were of "unusual importance" because of the lack of other evidence against him. Judging the veracity of the confessions was, of course, a matter for the jury rather than the appellate court. But thanks to faulty jury instructions from the trial judge concerning this point—a relatively technical matter, one might argue—the convictions were overturned.

Fred Rogers had by then spent fourteen months on San Quentin's death row. At his retrial, in the face of no evidence whatsoever against him, the court dismissed the charges, and Rogers was released.

IN JANUARY 1965 Antonio Rivera and his wife, Merla, like many other Mexican Americans in the San Bernardino area, were on the ropes economically. Rivera, 28, was unable to support his family. He and his wife were less concerned about themselves than they were about their child, Judy, only 3. Convinced that they could not take adequate care of her—she was extremely ill—they decided in desperation to abandon her, hoping that some generous family would take her in, adopt her, and give her the medical care and other things they could not provide.

In order to reduce the risk of having the abandoned child traced to them, they drove north to San Francisco, where they left the little girl. The next day, the *San Francisco Chronicle* duly reported that a child had been found at a local gas station.

Back in San Bernardino, rumors surfaced when people noticed Judy was missing. The authorities could do nothing, however. There was no direct evidence of any crime, no witness, no confession.

In the years that followed, Rivera and his wife were divorced, and she remarried. The 1965 abandonment of their daughter suddenly came back to haunt the parents in 1973, when the skeletal remains of a dead girl were found in a crude grave some ten miles from where they had lived. It looked as though the child must have been beaten to death. That was all the district attorney needed: He charged the parents whose daughter had so mysteriously disappeared eight years earlier with criminal homicide.

Tried in March 1973 before Judge Thomas Haldorsen, Antonio Rivera and his ex-wife Merla Walpole told for the first time the pathetic tale of their motives for abandoning their daughter. The story failed to convince the jury, and the parents were found guilty of murder in the second degree. When court reconvened for sentencing a few weeks later, however, Judge Haldorsen took extremely unusual steps. Refusing to sentence them (they could have gone to prison for five years to life), he set the verdict aside, ordered a new trial, and directed the district attorney to investigate further. The murder charge still hung over their heads.

Timothy Martin, on the staff of the San Bernardino district attorney's office, proceeded to check the defendants' alibi. He attempted to locate their child in the Bay area, since that was where Rivera and Walpole claimed to have left her. There, in October 1975, Martin tracked down the girl who had been found in a gas station a decade earlier—she was called Judy "Gasse" because of where she had been discovered—living with the woman who had adopted her. But was she the girl Rivera and Walpole had abandoned ten years before? Was she really their child? Defense attorneys Larry Freeman and David Call thought she might be and set out to prove it.

First, they arranged for various tests to compare blood samples from the girl and the two alleged parents. Physical features of the three were also compared, including certain bone formations. All the results were consistent with the parental claims. The attorneys then set up a meeting for Judy, her adoptive mother, Walpole, and Rivera. According to Freeman, that meeting was conclusive. He was quoted as saying, "Not only are Rivera and Mrs. Walpole convinced that Judy Gasse is their daughter. So are the girl and her adoptive mother."

At Thanksgiving of 1975, Judge Haldorsen dismissed the charges against the two defendants. The *New York Times* reported that Judy, along with her adoptive mother, was planning a Christmas visit south to the homes of her natural parents.

✳ | # CONCLUSION

FOR ANY READER who has come this far, there is no need to belabor the point that in the United States not only do countless men and women get arrested for murders they did not commit—they get convicted and often sentenced to death as well. Occasionally they are even executed, and we document twenty-three such cases in this book.

With the important exception of those twenty-three, the rest of the stories—nearly four hundred—that we discuss in varying degrees of detail are those of the lucky defendants. They are the ones whose innocence was eventually established so convincingly that the State finally did, in one way or another, admit its errors and correct them. And 150 or so of those who were once wrongly under sentence of death did at least escape execution, their death sentences for a variety of reasons having been nullified before the ultimate tragedy occurred. Often, as we have seen, it was fickle good fortune rather than anything having to do with the rational workings of the criminal justice system that played the crucial role in sparing these innocent defendants. Yet luck was not sufficient to spare them time in prison (often many years), the agony of uncertainty over whether they would ever be vindicated and released, and blighted hopes for a decent life all too frequently destroyed by the ordeal and stigma of a murder conviction. Low though the odds of convicting the innocent are, the odds of innocent prisoners—once convicted—being able to marshal the resources essential to proving their innocence are lower still.

What lessons are to be learned from these chronicles of error? What do these cases—stretching back across the twentieth century and found in every region and almost every state—have to teach us? One naturally wonders whether the errors could have been avoided and whether comparable errors can be prevented in the century ahead. If not, what are the minimal accommodations with unavoidable error and the risk of terrible tragedy that a civilized society ought to make?

Before addressing these questions, we must first make clear that the scope of the problem of erroneous conviction in homicide cases is by no means entirely before us, even now. How many other cases there may be in which good fortune, hard work, or unflagging courage was absent and the erroneous conviction was never corrected or even adequately identified (except by the prisoner and a few supporters), we cannot say. We are confident, as a result of the years of work on which this book is based, that there are hundreds (perhaps even thousands) of other cases in which innocent people have been convicted of homicide or sentenced to death without having been able to prove their innocence to the authorities. We also have reason to believe that there are other cases, not yet known to us, in which states have officially acknowledged, one way or another, that an innocent person was convicted of homicide. Even today, after eight years of continuous and well-publicized research into this subject, we learn of new cases at the rate of one each month. Some of these cases date back twenty or thirty years; others crop up as current news reported in the daily papers.

Since the initial publication of our research in 1987, in which 350 cases were identified, we have examined more than 100 additional cases. After careful review, we have included 66 of them in our Inventory of Cases. There is no reason to believe that somehow, magically, on the eve of publishing this book, we have managed to produce a complete list of all the relevant cases. As James McCloskey of Centurion Ministries noted recently, "I believe that the innocent are convicted far more frequently than the public cares to believe, and far more frequently than those who operate the system dare to believe." Despite our efforts, it is quite possible that all we have done is trace the outlines of the proverbial tip of the iceberg.

What is true of cases yet to be discovered in which an innocent person was wrongfully convicted of murder is equally true regarding the execution of the innocent. We report in this book nearly two dozen cases where we believe an innocent person was executed.* We can be virtually

---

*The names of these defendants are: J. Adams, Anderson, Appelgate, Bambrick,

certain there are more cases that will probably never be documented in which innocent individuals were executed before they were able to prove their innocence. As Voltaire argued in the eighteenth century and Bentham in the nineteenth, we argue in the twentieth century that the risk of executing the innocent is and will remain one of the strongest objections to capital punishment.

Defenders of the death penalty have responded to this objection in two ways. Some want to challenge our research and the adequacy of the evidence we cite in support of the twenty-three cases where we believe an innocent person was executed. Reasonable and unbiased judges, they claim, would not be persuaded by the evidence that has persuaded us. These critics remind us that no court, chief executive, or other official body has ever acknowledged that an innocent person has been executed in this century—as if that constituted evidence that it has never happened. Other critics are willing to concede, at least for the sake of argument, that some two dozen erroneous executions may have occurred, but they insist that this is a small price to pay for the benefits they claim the death penalty provides. They further argue that reasonable people would no more abolish the death penalty because of the risk of fatal error than they would outlaw truck driving because of the risk of fatal accidents.

Both these objections deserve serious thought and a considered reply. In regard to the initial objection, we would grant that more research is desirable regarding the cases of wrongful execution that we cite; we would welcome the interest of other scholars, journalists, writers, and civil rights advocates in re-opening all these cases to public scrutiny. Unfortunately, much of the further research that needs to be done is likely to prove inconclusive or impossible to carry out. More often than not, the important witnesses and other participants in the case are dead, and the relevant physical evidence has long ago vanished or been destroyed. Future research efforts might very well leave us no better informed than we are now.

Our investigations lead us to believe that the small number of cases we have identified in which an innocent person was executed is an indication not of the fairness of the system but rather of its finality. Very few death penalty cases in this century have attracted the sustained interest of persons in a position to undertake the research necessary to challenge successfully a guilty verdict meted out to a defendant later executed; funds are rarely available to investigate execution of the allegedly innocent (there are not even adequate funds available to investigate thoroughly those in prison who claim to be innocent).

Becker, Cirofici, Collins, Dawson, Garner, Grzechowiak, Hauptmann, Hill, Lamble, Mays, McGee, Rybarczyk, Sacco, Sanders, Sherna, Shumway, Tucker, Vanzetti, and Wing. See the Inventory of Cases for details.

The 1974 Florida case of James Adams, discussed in the Introduction, is a perfect example. Once the defendant is dead, the best source of evidence is gone. So is the primary motive for re-investigating the case. Further, as we have also already indicated, the limited resources of the defense lawyers (the ones in the best position to direct additional investigations into their deceased client's guilt or innocence) are quickly absorbed by the legal battles to save the lives of others still on death row. The result is that, as time passes, the possibility of continuing an effective investigation slowly disappears.

Neither is there now (nor has there ever been) any organization whose purpose is to gather and sift the evidence of a defendant's possible innocence after that defendant has been executed. The best-known previous investigators of wrongful convictions—Yale law professor Edwin Borchard; federal judge Jerome Frank and his attorney-daughter, Barbara; journalists Edward Radin and Eugene Block—worked essentially alone and ignored the claims to innocence of those already executed. Erle Stanley Gardner's Court of Last Resort did a remarkable job of investigating a few capital cases, and our Inventory is indebted to its labors. But we know of no instance where the Court attempted to re-open any case of allegedly erroneous execution. Moreover, that organization was in business less than two decades, and it never confined its attention to defendants under a death sentence. Centurion Ministries, founded in 1981 by James McCloskey, has helped free many innocent prisoners—including one on death row. But it understandably devotes none of its slender resources to investigating a case after a prisoner has been executed.

As if these difficulties were not enough, no matter how much evidence we might gather concerning a given case, there is simply no tribunal before which it can be placed and from which an authoritative posthumous judgment can be rendered on the innocence of an executed convict. Bluntly put, there is no forum—as we pointed out in the Introduction—for hearing the case for innocence of someone already dead. We are necessarily confined to less formal methods and procedures, whose adequacy can always be challenged by the skeptic.

As for the fact that responsible officials have never publicly acknowledged that an innocent person has been lawfully executed, we do not think their silence ought to be taken as evidence that the system makes no fatal errors. Those involved in pressing a death penalty case from arrest to execution, whether private citizens or government officials, not surprisingly tend to close ranks and resist admission of error. More distressingly, they have been known to obstruct others even from exploring charges of erroneous execution—as every serious investigator of wrongful convictions has pointed out.

A silent witness or the real culprit is even less likely to step forward if their failure to do so earlier has already cost the life of an innocent person. Randy Schaffer, attorney on the appeal for Randall Dale Adams (discussed in Chapter 3), commenting on *The Thin Blue Line* and the failure of the film to persuade any of the jurors who convicted Adams and sentenced him to death that they had the wrong man, said: "I think a decision of the magnitude of sentencing another human being to death is one that is not arrived at lightly. But once you've arrived at it, I think it would take wild horses to convince you that you have convicted someone in error." What is true of most jurors is equally true of most prosecutors, witnesses, and judges. After sending a defendant to death— or even death row—few are willing to admit the possibility that they were in error.

Finally, if one concedes (as any fair-minded reader of this book must) that there have been hundreds of innocent persons wrongly convicted of murder, then it seems strange and implausible to insist that the evidence is wholly insufficient to show that even one innocent person has ever been executed in the United States during this century. Are we to believe that although hundreds of demonstrably innocent persons have been erroneously imprisoned, *not even one* has been wrongfully executed? Surely there is nothing about the penalty of death and the way it is administered to make us sanguine on this point, nothing to ensure that the innocent have never been and will never be executed. On the contrary, it seems to us a virtual certainty that some, perhaps many innocent persons—one can only speculate on the exact number—have been executed, just as hundreds have been imprisoned.

One cornerstone of this judgment is to be found in the more than two dozen cases we have identified where at the very last—days, hours, or minutes prior to execution—a reprieve or stay saved the life of a prisoner later exonerated. In Chapter 2 we reported the case of Isidore Zimmerman, saved within two hours of electrocution; Chapter 7 related the story of Lloyd Miller, spared from execution seven times—including once when he was just seven hours from death. These cases are not unique; we know of twenty-five more, all reported in our Inventory of Cases. Among them are the following:

In 1932 in North Carolina, Gus Langley had his head shaved ready for electrocution when a technical error in his death sentence was discovered that stayed the execution. Later, new evidence proved that his alibi was legitimate.

In 1942 in North Carolina, William Wellman was seated in the electric chair when the governor, having just learned that another man had confessed, issued a reprieve.

In 1957 in Ohio, Harry Bundy was only three days from execution when a witness to the crime chanced to read about the case, notified the authorities, and secured a stay of the execution. As the Columbus, Ohio, newspaper observed, "It was sheer luck that saved [Harry] Bundy from execution."

In 1983 Joseph Green Brown came within thirteen hours of electrocution in Florida before a federal district court judge granted a stay of execution. Three years later, his conviction was vacated by the Eleventh Circuit Court of Appeals when it was discovered that the prosecution had used perjured testimony to obtain the conviction. All charges against Brown were then dropped.

That same year, also in Florida, half-brothers William Jent and Earnest Miller came within sixteen hours of sitting in the electric chair. As in Brown's case, the convictions were later vacated in federal court. This time the reason was the discovery that the prosecution had suppressed exculpatory evidence.

Jent and Miller and the others mentioned here were not the only lucky ones.* But can anyone seriously believe that *all* innocent murder convicts sentenced to death have been equally lucky?

The second response death penalty advocates make to our claim that innocents have been executed concedes that terrible errors have occurred—and will occur again—but argues that this is a price worth paying. Our reply to this objection rests on two considerations. First, there is only the weakest possible analogy between a state-imposed system of capital punishment on the one hand and risky but lawful practices such as undersea exploration, skydiving, mining, and the ordinary operation of motor vehicles on the other. In all these activities, innocent people are occasionally killed. But although no one engaging in them behaves in an intentionally lethal manner toward anyone, the death penalty *is* deliberately—and inherently—lethal. None of the activities mentioned above coerces its participants; the death penalty most assuredly does coerce its victim. Interfering with skydiving or mining by prohibiting it under law would constitute an unreasonable interference with voluntary behavior (and on unacceptable paternalistic grounds). Abolishing the death penalty would interfere with no one's liberty.

Deciding to engage in practices that take "statistical lives" (the predictable death of innocents unidentifiable in advance in the course of risky but not intentionally lethal social practices) is justifiable only because there are otherwise unobtainable benefits to society (and given the presumed tacit consent we all give to life in a society in which such risks

---

*The other defendants who came within seventy-two hours of being executed are: Bailey, Bernstein, J. B. Brown, Cero, Draper, Hollins, Irvin, T. Jones, Labat, Larkman, Morris, Poret, Reno, Sherman, Charles Smith, Stielow, Vargas, Weaver, and Zajicek. See the Inventory of Cases for details.

are created). We believe the death penalty provides no social benefits not achievable by long-term imprisonment. In any event, the costs outweigh any possible benefit by so much that a fair and reasonable cost/benefit analysis of capital punishment in our society would surely favor its abolition.

Crime control or social defense, in the form of incapacitation (*preventing* the killer from killing again) and deterrence (*discouraging* others from imitating the killer), and tax economies are the chief benefits allegedly flowing from use of the death penalty. Some want to add as further benefits such things as giving the public what it wants, vindicating the authority of the law against murder, and enhancing respect for human life. We believe, on the contrary, that these "benefits" are illusory or worse. To be sure, this is a complex matter that cannot be discussed here in the detail it deserves. Nevertheless, we believe that the existing evidence (in sources readily available in libraries throughout the nation) clearly establishes several important points:

***There is no adequate evidence that the death penalty is a better deterrent than long-term imprisonment. Such meager evidence as there is (all of it developed since the mid-1970s, relying on highly technical statistical methods, and none of it produced by criminologists) is of little or no significance when measured against the counter-evidence of more numerous and more reliable investigations.

***Incapacitation can be achieved for all convicted murderers, as for persons convicted of other crimes, with existing forms of imprisonment. States such as Michigan, Wisconsin, and Minnesota—none of which has used the death penalty in this century—have amply demonstrated the feasibility of incarceration as an alternative to the death penalty.

***The public wants protection from victimization at the hands of criminals. However, survey research purporting to show overwhelming popular support for the death penalty in recent years is extremely misleading, in that it usually measures support for the death penalty against the implicit alternative of mild punishment—or no punishment whatever—for the offender. If given the choice, public opinion favors life imprisonment and compensation to the victim's family over the death penalty.

***The costs of a system of capital punishment are considerable and irreducible, unless we are prepared to sacrifice altogether the rights of due process and equal protection of the law that we all depend on—and that all who are accused and convicted deserve. A criminal justice system (like Michigan's or Canada's) that never raises the controversial question of the death penalty in a murder case is far less expensive to operate than a system (like California's or Texas's) that regularly raises the issue in every case of aggravated murder.

***Vindicating the law and showing due respect for the lives and welfare of all citizens does not require killing any prisoners already safely in custody. If anything, the nation's selective—that is, arbitrary and discriminatory—use of the death penalty constantly risks bringing the whole system of criminal justice into disrepute. "Justice" is not obtained by a punishment that is based as much on issues of race or social class or quality of attorney as it is on the heinousness of the crime.

Believing these propositions, as we do, we obviously cannot believe that the benefits of capital punishment outweigh its social and economic costs.

What, then, is to be done with a criminal justice system like ours that has been shown to be so prone to error? There seem to be only two alternatives. One is to remove the causes of error, or at least render them rare, and preserve the death penalty for very occasional use in only the gravest cases. The other is to accept the impossibility of doing much more than has already been done to reduce the risk of error, and then to eliminate the worst harm that can result from the inevitable errors by not executing (or holding under death sentence) anyone. We favor the latter alternative. Perhaps the most convincing argument for our conclusion is to be found by exploring the former alternative more fully.

Previous investigators of wrongful convictions in our system of criminal justice who brought to the subject extensive training and experience in the criminal law—notably, Edwin Borchard in 1932 and Jerome and Barbara Frank in 1957—were naturally led to propose various reforms that they believed would appreciably reduce the likelihood of miscarriages of justice. Of all such proposals, those by Borchard were the more extensive and will serve here to illustrate the futility of this approach to the problem.

Borchard advocated seven specific changes in criminal procedure: (1) prior convictions of the defendant, if any, should be introduced into evidence only in regard to sentencing, and thus only after conviction; (1a) if the preceding proposal is thought to be too restrictive, then prior convictions may be cited during trial insofar as they are for crimes like the one(s) for which the defendant is currently being tried; (2) no confession may be introduced as evidence unless it was given before a magistrate and in the presence of witnesses; (3) expert witnesses ought to be in the employ of the public and not retained solely by the defense or by the prosecution; (4) indigent defendants ought to have the services of a public defender; (5) in cases where a conviction may have been erroneous, an independent investigative body ought to be appointed to review the case; (6) appellate courts ought to be empowered to review not only the law under which the defendant was convicted but also the facts introduced into evidence against him or her; (7) no death sentence ought to issue against a defendant convicted solely on circumstantial evidence.

In the seventy years since these proposals were first introduced, no jurisdiction has seen fit to adopt them all. Except for one or another version of proposal (4)—public defenders for the poor—none has been adopted by all jurisdictions. In particular, no jurisdiction has adopted the most restrictive of Borchard's ideas, proposals (2)—limits on admissibility of confessions, and (7)—no death penalty on circumstantial evidence alone. We see no likelihood that in the future these proposals, or any like them, will find favor with the American bar and bench. And without widespread support, they will continue to be merely the utopian ideas of an all-but-forgotten Ivy League law professor.

But suppose, contrary to fact, that all Borchard's proposals had been commonly part of American criminal law throughout the twentieth century. Would they have eliminated all or at least a large fraction of the cases recorded in this book? They would not. To understand why, one must remember that the erroneous convictions described in this book rest on factors not touched by Borchard's proposed remedies and often immune to later review: mistaken eyewitness testimony, unreliable polygraph evidence, perjury by prosecution witnesses, suppression of exculpatory evidence, sloppy (not to mention corrupt) police investigation, and false confession by the accused. Most of these factors cannot be eliminated by changes in the rules of criminal procedure. Those that can (for example, not allowing the prosecution to use in court a defendant's confession) would require such drastic revision of the rules as to be impossible to enact. Hence, miscarriages of justice in capital (and noncapital) cases will continue. We deceive ourselves if we think otherwise.

Current capital punishment law already embodies several features that probably reduce the likelihood of executing the innocent. These include abolition of mandatory death penalties, bifurcation of the capital trial into two distinct phases (the first concerned solely with the guilt of the offender, and the second devoted to the issue of sentence), and the requirement of automatic appellate review of a capital conviction and sentence. All three developments have taken place within the past twenty years. Yet, as our Inventory of Cases shows, more than one hundred miscarriages of justice in homicide cases (including forty innocent defendants who were sent to death row) occurred during these same years—despite these protections. Like the procedural reforms urged by Borchard in the 1930s, the reforms actually adopted in the 1970s leave untouched the major causes of grave error. They also do not alter the fact that most of the errors caught in time are corrected not thanks to the system but in spite of the system—that is, in spite of the obstacles to re-investigating and re-opening a case, to persuading a higher court to reconsider, and to securing executive intervention to halt the march to the execution chamber.

Sixty years ago the German refugee scholar and lawyer Max Hirschberg, in his study of wrongful convictions, rightly observed, "Innocent men wrongfully convicted are countless. It is the duty of science to open our eyes to this terrible fact. It is the duty of ethics to rouse indolent and indifferent hearts." As for capital punishment, he added, "*Every* doubt, and not merely 'reasonable' doubt, should be over before a death sentence is imposed." But, as Hirschberg must have realized, it is impossible to operate a criminal justice system in which "every doubt" is resolved in favor of the accused. His demand, like Borchard's reforms, simply cannot be implemented in practice. Against the background of sixty years of studying the problem, from Borchard's day to our own, it is absurd to grope any further in the forlorn hope of eliminating the risk of executing the innocent by reforming criminal procedure.

If it is impossible, for diverse reasons, to introduce into the criminal justice system reforms that would appreciably reduce the likelihood of fatal error in capital cases, then we must live with a system essentially like the present one—and expect more errors in the decades ahead to be added to those documented in this book. Many Americans seem willing to accept such errors because they believe that the really brutal killers—a multiple murderer like Gary Gilmore or a serial murderer like Ted Bundy, for example—simply *must* be executed; they believe that justice for the victims requires no less. Isn't it worth it to be able to punish cunning and remorseless killers with a richly deserved death?

There are many replies to this rhetorical question, but the argument of the present book parries it with a counter-question: What reason is there to believe that our criminal justice system can effectively distinguish between the Gilmores and Bundys who are guilty and arguably "deserve" to die, and the Zimmermans, Domers, and Brandleys who unarguably do not? The evidence is starkly against the capacity of police, prosecutors, witnesses, jurors, judges—the people on whom the system depends—to make this distinction with unfailing and consistent perfection, as the unimpeachable record shows.

The history of capital punishment in western civilization might well be said to have begun with the execution of the innocent—Socrates in Athens in 399 B.C. and Jesus in Jerusalem in A.D. 30. In the centuries from those days to the present, countless others who were innocent have been put to death. Most were not famous; their names, if remembered at all, are known but to a few. Just a century ago, Illinois executed three of the Haymarket anarchists—August Spies, Adolph Fischer, and George Engel—only to have them all later exonerated by Governor Altgeld (one of the rare instances in any century that such an error has been officially admitted). What errors of the same sort in our time will historians record a century from now?

Voltaire's naive Candide, despite the endless folly and horror he encounters, stoutly maintains that his mentor, Doctor Pangloss, is right— we *do* live in "the best of all possible worlds." But Candide's beloved, the no-nonsense Cunigunde, disagrees. We side with her; we believe our world could be made significantly better by ending the death penalty for every crime, once and for all. We agree also with Voltaire's younger contemporary, the Marquis de Lafayette, who uttered these oft-quoted words: "Till the infallibility of human judgment shall have been proved to me, I shall demand the abolition of the death penalty."

The information on which we have relied concerning each case discussed in the preceding chapters and in the following pages will be found cited in the Sources (pp. 361–78), under the name(s) of the defendant(s). All quotations, whether attributed or not, will be found in the materials cited there as well.

The date following a defendant's name refers to the year of the conviction.

ADAMS, JAMES *(black). 1974. Florida.* See Introduction.

ADAMS, RANDALL DALE *(white). 1977. Texas.* See Chapter 3.

AMADO, CHRISTIAN *(black). 1980. Massachusetts.* Amado was convicted of first-degree murder and sentenced to life imprisonment. On appeal, the conviction was overturned, and the trial court was ordered to enter a judgment of acquittal. The only evidence linking Amado to the crime was an eyewitness who, as the court noted, first told police that Amado (in a photo) resembled the killer and then testified on the witness stand "that he was 'positive' that the defendant was not the killer." In 1982 Amado was released after having served two years.

ANDERSON, WILLIAM HENRY *(black). 1945. Florida.* Anderson was convicted of the rape of a white woman, sentenced to death, and executed in 1945 without an appeal having been made. The execution took place only five months after Anderson's arrest, perhaps in part because the sheriff wrote to the governor, "I would appreciate special attention in this case before some sympathizing organization gets hold of it." The victim had not resisted, screamed, or used an available pistol to escape Anderson's advances. Anderson's sister and one of his co-workers presented affidavits to the governor claiming that Anderson and the victim had been consensually intimate for several months before rape charges were filed. Anderson's attorney also wrote to the governor that "there exists well founded belief . . . that William Henry Anderson and the prosecutrix were intimate since August 1944. This belief is widespread among Negroes, but white people have been heard to express opinions likewise."

ANTONIEWICZ, JOSEPH, WILLIAM A. HALLOWELL, *and* EDWARD H. PARKS *(all white). 1952. Pennsylvania.* Antoniewicz, Hallowell, and Parks—all under 18—pleaded guilty. They were each convicted of felony-murder and sentenced to life imprisonment. The victim died nine days after being attacked and robbed by the youths. In 1968 the

Philadelphia medical examiner testified that the victim "died as a result of a coronary heart disease which was not caused, contributed to, or aggravated by the assault." The defendants were ordered released, though the State won the right to retry them. In acting on the petition to release the defendants, the judge ruled that "at most, a $15.00 robbery and assault had occurred."

APPELGATE, EVERETT *(white)*. *1936. New York.* Appelgate was convicted, with Frances Q. Creighton, of the murder of Appelgate's wife; both were sentenced to death in 1936. The conviction was affirmed on appeal. Creighton had been tried and acquitted on two separate occasions for similar murders a dozen years before she met Appelgate. In this case, she testified that she killed the victim (by arsenic poisoning) at Appelgate's instigation. During the investigation of the case, she also confessed to one of the previous murders. "Virtually no evidence against Appelgate existed beyond Mrs. Creighton's unsupported word." Appelgate had no previous criminal record, and Creighton's version of the crime changed somewhat during the investigation. Appelgate admitted having had sexual relations with Creighton's 15-year-old daughter; that fact did not earn him any sympathy from the jury. Governor Herbert Lehman, who had doubts about Appelgate's guilt, requested the prosecutor's support for clemency for Appelgate; it was not forthcoming, and clemency was denied. Appelgate was executed (as was Creighton) in 1936. A few weeks after the execution all investigation of Appelgate's innocence ended.

ARROYO, MIGUEL *(Hispanic)*. *1965. New York.* Arroyo was convicted of manslaughter for killing a boy during a street fight between Puerto Ricans and blacks outside his store. The trial judge immediately set aside the verdict when Arroyo's defense counsel produced a series of eyewitnesses to testify that they saw another man kill the boy. In 1966 the other man was arrested and indicted for murder; key witnesses who had testified against Arroyo recanted their testimony. The indictment against Arroyo was then dismissed.

ARROYO, ROGELIO, ISAURO SANCHEZ, IGNACIO VARELA, *and* JOAQUIN VARELA *(Hispanic)*. *1982. Illinois.* All four were convicted of a quadruple murder and sentenced to life imprisonment. The defendants (who did not speak English) and the victims were undocumented workers, as were some witnesses who could have established the defendants' innocence (but who feared deportation if they stepped forward). On appeal their convictions were upheld by the state appellate court. Further appeals to the state and U.S. Supreme Courts were denied. In 1990 their sentences were commuted to time served by Governor James Thompson. They were released after an investigation by the Illinois State Police confirmed what the defendants' attorney had learned: The actual killers, one of whom had admitted guilt, had fled to Mexico. Three witnesses who had not testified at trial but who could establish the defendants' innocence were also found. Even so, when Governor Jim Edgar pardoned them in 1991 he insisted it was "not because I'm saying they're innocent, [but] because of the hardship on their families." In exchange for full pardons the men agreed not to sue the state for false imprisonment.

BACHELOR, BRETT (*white*). *1979. Florida.* Bachelor was convicted of second-degree murder and sentenced to 15 years in prison. At the subsequent trial of an alleged co-defendant, evidence showed that a key witness had erroneously identified Bachelor. The co-defendant was acquitted. Eight months after Bachelor had been found guilty, the trial court ordered him released from prison.

BAILEY, ROBERT BALLARD (*white*). *1950. West Virginia.* See Chapter 12.

BAMBRICK, THOMAS (*white*). *1915. New York.* Bambrick was convicted of murder and sentenced to death. The conviction was affirmed on appeal. Evidence was later discovered that convinced Warden Thomas Mott Osborne and the prison chaplain that another man had committed the crime. Osborne knew who that man was. Although Bambrick also knew the man's identity, he refused to "squeal" on him. Osborne commented, "It is almost as certain that Bambrick is innocent as that the sun will rise tomorrow." Bambrick was executed in 1916.

BANKS, ALF, JR., ED COLEMAN, JOE FOX, ALBERT GILES, PAUL HALL, ED HICKS, FRANK HICKS, J. E. KNOX, JOHN MARTIN, FRANK MOORE, ED WARE, WILL WORDLOW, *and* 39 other defendants (*all black*). *1919. Arkansas.* See Chapter 5.

BANKS, JERRY (*black*). *1975. Georgia.* See Chapter 9.

BARBATO, JOSEPH (*white*). *1929. New York.* Barbato was convicted of first-degree murder and sentenced to death. The conviction was reversed after evidence showed that Barbato's four-word confession had been coerced. A physician's report verified that Barbato had been beaten while in custody. Following a recommendation by the prosecutor, the trial judge released Barbato; he had already spent 11 months in prison, more than half of them on death row.

BARBER, ARTHUR (*white*). *1967. New York.* Barber was convicted of first-degree murder and sentenced to life. On appeal, the conviction was affirmed. In 1975, on further appeal in federal court, the conviction was reversed because Barber had been arrested without probable cause, beaten by the police, and subjected to numerous other illegal police tactics. The court stated that Barber's confession had been obtained by the police through "a pattern of lawlessness which shocks the conscience." Charges were then dismissed.

BEALE, CLYDE (*white*). *1926. West Virginia.* Beale was convicted of first-degree murder and sentenced to death. After the first execution date passed (while the conviction was being appealed), the trial judge refused to set another date for execution and tried to commute the sentence to life imprisonment. "[The trial judge] has been convinced of the innocence of the defendant and has felt that the prisoner had not had a fair and impartial trial . . . and that the witnesses upon whose testimony Beale was convicted have admitted that their evidence was false, and have pleaded that the life of Beale be spared." Nonetheless, the state supreme court ordered the judge to reschedule the execution. In 1929 the judge followed these orders, but shortly thereafter the governor commuted the sentence to life. In 1933 Beale was granted a conditional pardon and released.

BEAMON, MELVIN TODD *(black). 1989. Alabama.* Beamon was convicted of a 1988 murder in Montgomery and sentenced to 25 years' imprisonment. After being arrested by police detectives, he was held for 17 hours without being given access to an attorney or to a phone. While Beamon was in custody, the officers allegedly beat him, and at one point threatened to shoot him if he did not confess. At trial they gave false testimony against Beamon, as did other witnesses they had threatened. Six weeks later, when an eyewitness to the crime exonerated Beamon, both the district attorney and Beamon's defense attorney asked the court to vacate the conviction. The request was granted, and all charges were later dismissed.

BECKER, CHARLES, *and* FRANK ("DAGO") CIROFICI *(both white). 1912. New York.* Becker and Cirofici were convicted of murder and sentenced to death; Cirofici was executed in 1914 and Becker in 1915. The victim, Rosenthal, was a gambling-house owner. Shortly before the homicide, Rosenthal had implicated Becker, a police lieutenant, in gambling activities. Becker had earlier made the gambling world angry because of his vigorous work in suppressing its members' activities. He was convicted largely on the testimony of gamblers and ex-convicts in the glare of extensive newspaper publicity about police corruption. These witnesses, allegedly middlemen hired by Becker, were given immunity for their testimony by an ambitious district attorney. The alleged motive was graft, although no evidence was produced to support the theory.

Less is known about Cirofici, one of four gunmen put to death for the crime. The then warden of Sing Sing Prison, James Clancy, allegedly believed that two of the executed gunmen were innocent. Another former Sing Sing warden, Thomas Mott Osborne, who knew the closest friends of the gunmen, stated that these friends all agreed Cirofici had nothing to do with the murder and was not even present when it occurred. Warden Osborne also believed that Becker was not guilty.

BEEMAN, GARY L. *(white). 1976. Ohio.* Beeman was convicted of aggravated murder and sentenced to death. The defense alleged that the main prosecution witness, an escaped prisoner named Claire Liuzzo, was the actual killer. In 1978 the district court of appeals ordered a retrial because Beeman's right to cross-examine Liuzzo had been unfairly restricted. At retrial in 1979, Beeman and Liuzzo continued to accuse each other of the crime. Five witnesses testified that they had heard Liuzzo confess to the murder, however, and Beeman was acquitted.

BELL, CRAIG H. *(white). 1987. Virginia.* Bell was convicted of second-degree murder for killing his girl friend and was sentenced to 20 years. Bell and the victim had quarreled a few days prior to her murder, and blood, clothes, and cigarettes found at the scene were consistent with his guilt. He was convicted despite the failure of the police to identify mysterious fingerprints, clothing, and hair samples found at the scene. These were eventually traced to another man who confessed to the crime two months later. Charges against Bell were dropped, and he was released. Said the district attorney, "Even with safeguards that we are so proud of, the system is still human-engineered and human-run. Innocent people can be convicted of crimes very easily." The circuit judge who ordered Bell's release commented, "We do as much as we can to ensure that innocent people are not convicted. This is one of those cases that didn't work."

BENNETT, LOUIS WILLIAM *(white). 1957. Oklahoma.* Bennett was convicted of manslaughter and sentenced to 35 years in prison. "He said he pleaded guilty, though he knew he was innocent, because he feared he would get a death sentence if convicted." The police demanded the guilty plea after finding Bennett's fingerprints on the victim's door. Bennett had been drinking and had no recollection of his activities. Later he remembered he had painted the door for the victim, who had been a friend. In 1960, after three years in prison, Bennett was given an unconditional pardon and released. A Texas prisoner, Leonard McClain, had confessed to the crime, and authorities had verified the confession.

BERNSTEIN, CHARLES *(white). 1933. District of Columbia.* Bernstein was convicted of first-degree murder and sentenced to death. At the trial, six witnesses testified that Bernstein was in New York at the time of the crime, and only one of the five eyewitnesses at the scene of the crime could identify him as the killer. In 1935, minutes before Bernstein's scheduled execution, President Franklin D. Roosevelt commuted the sentence to life. In 1940 Bernstein was released on a conditional pardon after eight years in prison. In 1945 he received an unconditional pardon from President Harry S. Truman. (Many years earlier, Bernstein had been erroneously convicted in Minnesota of a bank robbery; he was released and pardoned in that instance, too, after the prosecutor discovered that the eyewitnesses who had identified him were in error.)

BERTRAND, DELPHINE *(white). 1944. Connecticut.* Bertrand was convicted of manslaughter after a guilty plea and sentenced to 10–15 years. In 1946, after the actual killers (two men) confessed, the indictment against Bertrand was dismissed, and she was released. The two men were later convicted of the crime. They and a third man, along with Bertrand, had visited the victim the night of the murder. Bertrand and the third man were sexually intimate in another part of the house when the murder occurred. Apparently thinking it better to be branded a killer than to reveal her sex life during the trial, she had voluntarily confessed to the crime.

BIGELOW, JERRY D. *(white). 1980. California.* Bigelow was convicted of first-degree murder. He and Michael Ramadanovic escaped from a Canadian jail; the murder victim had picked them up hitchhiking in Sacramento. Tried separately from Bigelow, Ramadanovic pleaded guilty to the murder and was sentenced to life imprisonment. Bigelow was sentenced to death. In 1983 the California Supreme Court vacated Bigelow's conviction because he had acted as his own attorney at trial, which it was decided constituted ineffective assistance of counsel. At Bigelow's retrial in 1988, the defense argued that Ramadanovic had acted alone in the murder while Bigelow, intoxicated, slept in the back seat of the car. Several fellow prisoners testified that they had heard Ramadanovic boast about the killing and take sole responsibility for it. Bigelow's initial confession to the murder was countered by evidence showing he had a history of confessing to crimes he had not committed. He was acquitted. The trial judge promptly declared a mistrial, on grounds of inconsistencies in the jury's verdict of acquittal. The state court of appeals then unanimously ordered acceptance of the jury's verdict.

BILGER, GEORGE, *and* RUDOLPH SHEELER *(both white). 1939. Pennsylvania.* Although tried separately, both defendants were convicted of murdering a police officer. Bilger was tried and convicted of the murder with a recommendation of death, but the trial judge set aside the jury's verdict, accepted a plea of guilty, and sentenced him to life imprisonment. Nearly two years later Sheeler, who happened to be visiting Philadelphia, was arrested (without warrant) as a co-felon, held incommunicado, tortured, and forced by the police to confess. One week before Sheeler's arrest, the actual killer of the police officer was himself killed by the police in a gunfight. A police informant then gave perjured eyewitness testimony against Sheeler, who was sentenced to life. After Sheeler's arrest, Bilger was released and transferred to a mental hospital. In 1951 a new trial was granted for Sheeler, with a directed verdict of acquittal. It was said to be "one of the most shameful cases ever brought to the public notice."

BILLINGS, WARREN K., *and* THOMAS J. MOONEY *(both white). 1916. California.* See Chapter 4.

BLANTON, ROBERT H., III *(white)*. *1974*. *Louisiana*. Blanton was convicted of murder and sentenced to life imprisonment. The conviction was affirmed on appeal. On further appeal, the conviction was reversed. According to the State's theory, Blanton was one of three people hired to kill the victim. The court argued that the State failed to disclose to the jury the agreements it had made with prosecution witnesses, who had admitted their own role in the crime and testified against Blanton in exchange for lighter sentences. Blanton's alibi at the trial was supported by several witnesses. The court ruled that this alibi testimony would have been given more credence by the jurors had they known about the plea-bargaining agreements with the incriminating witnesses. On remand, all charges against Blanton were dropped.

BOGGIE, CLARENCE GILMORE *(white)*. *1935*. *Washington*. Boggie was convicted of murder and sentenced to life. Perjured testimony suborned by the prosecution was used to obtain the evidence. A prison chaplain was able to interest the Court of Last Resort in the case. In 1948 Boggie was conditionally pardoned by Governor Monrad Wallgren when considerable evidence pointed to the guilt of another person. (Boggie had previously been erroneously convicted of a bank robbery, but he was pardoned when the error was discovered.)

BOWLES, JOE *(white)*. *1919*. *North Carolina*. Bowles was convicted of murder and sentenced to death with his co-defendants Joe and Gardner Cain. The conviction was affirmed on appeal, but in 1920 Bowles's sentence was commuted to 20 years, and in January 1921 Governor Thomas Bickett commuted the sentence to expire in June 1921. On May 27, 1921, the newly elected governor, Cameron Morrison, issued Bowles a complete pardon on the "very earnest" recommendation of the prosecutor. Bowles had been present at the time of the murder, but he was feeble-minded and made intoxicated by his co-defendants; there was no evidence that he ever had a weapon. The Cain brothers were executed for the crime.

BOYD, PAYNE *(black)*. *1925*. *West Virginia*. Boyd was convicted of first-degree murder, but the trial court set the verdict aside on technical grounds and ordered a new trial. He was reconvicted and sentenced to life imprisonment despite testimony of 31 witnesses who said he was not Cleveland Boyd, known to be the real killer. The only issue in the trials was whether the prisoner before the court was Cleveland Boyd. An appellate court ordered a third trial. In this trial, also in 1925, fingerprint evidence was used to show that the prisoner was really Payne Boyd. He was acquitted and released after having served 18 months in prison.

BRANDLEY, CLARENCE LEE *(black)*. *1981*. *Texas*. See Chapter 6.

BRANSON, WILLIAM *(white)*. *1916*. *Oregon*. Branson was convicted of second-degree murder and sentenced to life imprisonment. The conviction was reversed on appeal because of improper jury instructions. In 1917 he was retried, reconvicted, and resentenced to life. The State Parole Board reported to the governor that "we . . . are satisfied after a full and complete investigation of this case that the accused was not guilty of the crime with which he was charged." The trial judge also wrote to the governor and requested the pardon. In 1920 Branson was granted an unconditional pardon by Governor Ben Olcott.

BRIGGS, JOSEPH ("JOCKO") (white). 1905. Illinois. Briggs was convicted of murder and sentenced to death. The state supreme court granted a new trial because of improper consideration of alibi witnesses. The court also held that the verdict had been granted against the weight of the evidence. In the new trial, Briggs was acquitted. "A captain of police has told me more than once, that he knew absolutely that Briggs was innocent."

BRITE, COKE (white). 1936. California. See Chapter 7.

BRITE, JOHN (white). 1936. California. See Chapter 7.

BROADY, THOMAS H., JR. (white). 1973. Ohio. Broady was convicted of first-degree murder and sentenced to 10–25 years in prison. On appeal, the conviction was reversed on the ground of newly discovered evidence—evidence available to police before the first trial, but suppressed. The victim had been killed during the robbery of his store. Another man had confessed to the robbery and implicated a third man as his partner and the real killer, but his testimony was not introduced at Broady's trial. Mistaken eyewitness identification led to the erroneous conviction. At retrial Broady was acquitted of the homicide, but he was subsequently convicted of a different robbery and sentenced to 10–25 years. Alibi witnesses were not permitted to testify. In both trials, Broady was mistaken for the real criminal, a look-alike. In 1978 the judge in the murder trial and a police detective who had originally investigated the murder, convinced of Broady's innocence in both crimes, testified in support of his release. Broady was paroled after having served five years in prison.

BROWN, ANTHONY SILAH (black). 1983. Florida. Brown was convicted of first-degree murder and sentenced to death, despite a jury recommendation of life imprisonment. The only evidence against Brown came from the testimony of a co-defendant, who was sentenced to life for his role in the crime. On appeal, the conviction was reversed and a new trial ordered because Brown had not been notified before the State took a crucial deposition in the case and had thereby been deprived of his right to confront and cross-examine an adverse witness. At retrial in 1986, the co-defendant admitted that his incrimination of Brown at the first trial had been perjured, and Brown was acquitted.

BROWN, BRADFORD (black). 1975. District of Columbia. Brown

was convicted of second-degree murder and sentenced to 18 years to life. Mistaken eyewitness identification led to the conviction, which was affirmed on appeal. In 1979 an informant came forward and told police that Brown had not been involved in the homicide. The informant implicated another man, who was arrested, pleaded guilty to manslaughter, and was convicted. The police detective who investigated the tip that freed Brown admitted to doubts about capital punishment: "I kept thinking about what could have happened if Bradford had been in a state with the death penalty." After the error was discovered, the judge who wrote the opinion of the appellate court that had unanimously affirmed the conviction, stated: "The system worked but unfortunately convicted a man who was legally and factually innocent."

BROWN, J. B. (black). 1901. Florida. Brown was convicted of murder and sentenced to death. The conviction was affirmed on appeal, despite the court's statement that there was very little testimony beyond a disputed confession to connect the defendant with the crime. Cell mates testified that they heard Brown confess while in custody; this testimony, later found to have been perjured, was sufficient to obtain the conviction. The hanging was averted at the gallows only because the execution warrant erroneously listed the jury foreman's name instead of Brown's. In 1902 the sentence was commuted to life. In 1913 another man gave a deathbed confession admitting guilt. Governor Park Trammell granted Brown a full pardon, and Brown was released after having served 12 years in prison. In 1929 he was indemnified by the State ($2,492).

BROWN, JOSEPH GREEN (black). 1974. Florida. Brown was convicted of first-degree murder and sentenced to death. The conviction rested on the testimony of Ronald Floyd, who claimed to have played a minor role in the crime and to have heard Brown confess to the murder. On the day before the murder, Brown and Floyd had committed a robbery together, and Floyd was angered when Brown turned himself in to the police, confessed to the robbery, and implicated Floyd as his partner. At the murder trial, Brown argued that Floyd's testimony against him was a product of anger for Brown's implication of him for the robbery, and, further, was given in exchange for lenient treatment on the robbery charge. Floyd denied any deals had been made, and the prosecutor stood silent, but two months after the conviction Floyd retracted his testimony (he later retracted the retraction when threatened with a perjury prosecution, but later again admitted the original testimony was a lie). A dozen years later, after the case had been affirmed by the state supreme court and Brown had come to within 13 hours of execution, a new trial was ordered by the Eleventh Circuit Court of Appeals. "The prosecution knowingly allowed material false testimony to be introduced at trial," wrote the court. A year later, in March 1987, the State decided not to retry the case, and Brown was released.

BROWN, ROBERT, *and* ELTON HOUSTON *(both black). 1984. Illinois.* Brown and Houston were convicted of the 1983 murder of a gas station attendant on Chicago's South Side, and sentenced to 35 years in prison. One eyewitness identified Brown as a participant; two other eyewitnesses identified Houston. These turned out to be good-faith but erroneous eyewitness identifications. In 1989 a police investigation of local gang activities netted three others who confessed to the killing and also assisted defense counsel for Brown and Houston in securing their clients' freedom.

BROWN, WILLIE A., *and* LARRY TROY *(both black). 1983. Florida.* Both were convicted of first-degree murder and sentenced to death for stabbing a fellow prisoner. No arrests were made until 17 months after the murder, when the authorities identified three inmates who claimed to have witnessed the crime. Two of these inmates had histories of mental problems, so the testimony of the third, Frank Wise (whose original statements exonerated the two accused), was crucial. Wise was in prison for murdering Troy's cousin, and said before the trial that he hated both men so much that he would like to see them executed even if they were not guilty. A few months after Brown was sent to death row, a prison visitor fell in love with him, and over the next few years she invested $70,000 in re-investigating the case. In 1987 the convictions were reversed by the state supreme court because the State had improperly conducted a pretrial deposition. Wise then approached Brown's girl friend, admitted he had lied at the trial, and offered to confess it publicly for $2,000. The girl friend (assisted by law enforcement officials) taped this offer, thereby destroying Wise's credibility, and all charges against Brown and Troy were dropped. Forty minutes after Brown's release, he and his girl friend were married. (For a year Wise was jailed awaiting trial for perjury; this charge was also eventually dropped.)

BUNDY, HARRY DALE *(white). 1957. Ohio.* Bundy was convicted of first-degree murder and sentenced to death. The conviction was affirmed on appeal. Bundy had helped police investigate four murders committed by a friend; when this "friend" turned himself in to the authorities, he implicated Bundy in two of the murders. Three days before Bundy's scheduled execution, a woman read a story about the crimes in a detective magazine and recognized the co-defendant's picture. She came forward and insisted the man had told her he had already murdered four people and was in the process of arranging to murder a fifth, only this one would be "legal." Bundy's execution was immediately stayed. In a hearing for a new trial, it was asserted that the co-defendant was the actual killer and had implicated Bundy as his accomplice in an effort to have him executed, as revenge for Bundy having helped police investigate the other murders. The conviction was reversed, and a new trial was ordered. Bundy was acquitted and released after spending one year in prison. "It was sheer luck that saved Bundy from execution. . . ."

BURT, LAVALE (black). 1985. Illinois. Burt was convicted of murder. The conviction was based on his confession, which he retracted two days after it was given. Burt claimed that he confessed because the police slapped him around, told him he would be sentenced to death (and not probation) if he did not confess, said they had two eyewitnesses who had incriminated him, and failed to advise him that he could have an attorney. While sentencing was pending, the grandmother of the victim contacted the judge and told him that she had discovered a gun, and that she believed her daughter—and not Burt—was the killer. Results of ballistics tests on the weapon showed she was correct. The judge then vacated the conviction and entered a judgment of acquittal.

BURTON, SAMUEL L., and SYLVANUS L. CONQUEST (both white). 1907. Virginia. Burton and Conquest were both convicted of voluntary manslaughter and sentenced to 10 years in prison. The convictions were reversed by the state supreme court because of the trial court's refusal to grant a change of venue. The defendants were later retried, reconvicted of voluntary manslaughter, and sentenced to one year. The convictions were again reversed because the court held that the evidence was "wholly insufficient . . . to sustain the verdict. . . . There is not a scintilla of evidence that either Burton or Conquest countenanced, encouraged, counselled, aided, abetted, advised, or consented" to the crime. In 1908 charges were dropped, and both defendants were released.

BUTLER, LOUISE, and GEORGE YELDER (both black). 1928. Alabama. Butler and Yelder were both convicted of murder and sentenced to life imprisonment. Two months later, both received pardons and were released when the supposed victim was discovered alive in another county. Butler at first confessed to the crime but repudiated her confession in court. The main witnesses for the prosecution were two children, Butler's daughter and niece, who perjured themselves.

CALLOWAY, WILLIE (black). 1945. Michigan. Calloway was convicted of first-degree murder and sentenced to life imprisonment. In 1953 two prison wardens learned that a key witness had admitted giving false testimony against Calloway, under duress. Convinced of Calloway's innocence, the two wardens urged Detroit Free Press reporter Ken McCormick to investigate. McCormick, a Pulitzer Prize winner, interviewed a co-defendant who had confessed and implicated Calloway. This co-defendant, like the other witness, retracted his incriminating statements. After reports of these initial findings were published, two alibi witnesses came forward, as did yet another witness who admitted he was present when a friend of his did the killing. The alibi witnesses signed affidavits saying that Calloway was at work at the time of the crime. A new trial was then ordered by the trial court. Acknowledging Calloway's innocence, the prosecution dropped the case. In late 1953, after nearly nine years in prison, Calloway was released.

CARDEN, RONALD Q. *(white)*. *1982. Arkansas.* Carden was convicted of first-degree murder and rape and was sentenced to life. Prompt investigation by *Arkansas Democrat* reporter Mike Masterson led to a reversal of the conviction by the trial court and an order for a new trial. A confession by another man (who subsequently confessed that he had also murdered his own wife), physical evidence that connected this suspect with the victim, and an FBI finding that discredited the physical evidence linking Carden to the victim all led the prosecutor to drop the charges against Carden. Seven months after his conviction, he was freed. "Masterson believed in Carden's innocence and he fought to prove it for nearly seven months."

CARMEN, JACK ALLEN *(white)*. *1975. Ohio.* See Chapter 8.

CARTER, NATHANIEL *(black)*. *1982. New York.* See Chapter 3.

CASHIN, HARRY F. *(white)*. *1931. New York.* Cashin was convicted of first-degree murder for killing a police detective during an attempted robbery and was sentenced to death. One of the robbers was killed by police; Cashin was implicated as the other robber because he had once worked for this man. None of the five eyewitnesses to the shoot-out initially identified Cashin as the escaped robber, but later (and again at trial) one of them did. No other incriminating evidence was entered against the defendant at trial. Furthermore, testimony from several other witnesses indicated another person must have been the real culprit, and three witnesses confirmed Cashin's alibi. Despite all this he was convicted. In 1932 the New York Court of Appeals ordered a new trial because "the verdict [went] against the weight of evidence." Cashin was released on $5,000 bail after spending seven months on death row. In 1933 charges were dropped when the eyewitness who had "identified" Cashin admitted her testimony was false.

CERO, GANGI *(a.k.a.* CERO GANGI) *(white)*. *1927. Massachusetts.* Cero was convicted of first-degree murder and sentenced to death. The conviction was affirmed on appeal. Because of persistent efforts by Cero's brother, an eyewitness to the shooting was located, who identified another man, Samuel Gallo, as the actual murderer. This evidence secured a reprieve for Cero only four hours before his scheduled execution. In 1929 Gallo was tried and convicted of the murder. Both defendants were granted new trials by the trial court. In 1930 Cero and Gallo were jointly retried, with each defendant trying to implicate the other. Gallo was reconvicted of first-degree murder, and Cero was acquitted. On appeal,

Gallo's conviction was affirmed. Later, after still another trial, Gallo was acquitted. As Borchard notes, "Cero Gangi was the victim of a chain of circumstances which brought him to the shadow of the electric chair and then by a miracle snatched him back. . . . The case presents a striking argument for the abolition of the death penalty in cases resting on circumstantial evidence."

CHAMBERS, ISIAH ("IZELL"), CHARLIE DAVIS, JACK WILLIAMSON, and WALTER WOODWARD (all black). 1933. Florida. All were convicted of first-degree murder and sentenced to death. In a case that became known as "Little Scottsboro," numerous black suspects were arrested in a police dragnet for the murder of a white man. The exact number of men caught by the police appears to be in some dispute. (The Florida Supreme Court estimated the number to be 12 to 14. Associate Justice Hugo Black, in his opinion for the U.S. Supreme Court, initially stated that 25 to 40 men were arrested, then later in his opinion referred to "thirty to forty negro suspects.")

After five days of continuous questioning, four defendants, dubbed the "Four Pompano Boys," confessed. Although these confessions were the only evidence against them, three of the four pleaded guilty. Their court-appointed attorneys offered only a perfunctory defense. The convictions were affirmed on appeal. After hearing allegations that the confessions and guilty pleas had been coerced, the state supreme court allowed the defendants to apply for a writ of error coram nobis. When the writ was later denied by the trial court judge, the state supreme court ruled the issue should be resolved by a jury. After a jury ruled against the defendants, the state supreme court again reversed, this time on the ground of erroneous jury instructions. After a change of venue, another jury ruled against the defendants. Counsel for the defendants failed to pursue an appeal to the state supreme court, even after receiving a 30-day extension. The court affirmed the convictions after reviewing the trial transcript forwarded by the prosecutor. In 1940 the U.S. Supreme Court unanimously ruled that the confessions were coerced and reversed the convictions on the ground of denial of due process. Shortly thereafter one of the defendants (Chambers) was transferred to a mental hospital; in 1942, at retrial, the other three received a directed verdict of acquittal.

CHAMBERS, LEON (black). 1969. Mississippi. Chambers was convicted of killing a white police officer and was sentenced to life imprisonment. One of dozens in a crowd who were fired upon by police during an unsuccessful attempt to make an arrest, Chambers was hit and left for dead. Apart from one witness, who claimed that he had seen Chambers shoot the victim, there was no evidence to connect Chambers to the crime. Furthermore, shortly after Chambers's arrest, another man confessed to the crime (both orally and in writing). Although the confession was retracted before Chambers's trial, two witnesses at the trial testified that they had seen this second man shoot the officer; three witnesses who had heard the confession repeated on separate occasions were not permitted to testify. On initial appeal the conviction was affirmed. On further appeal, the U.S. Supreme Court reversed the conviction. After the conviction was reversed, all charges against Chambers were dismissed.

CHARLES, EARL PATRICK *(black)*. *1975*. *Georgia*. See Chapter 12.

CIROFICI, FRANK ("DAGO") *(white)*. *1912*. *New York*. See BECKER, CHARLES.

CLARK, CHARLES LEE *(black)*. *1938*. *Michigan*. Clark was convicted of felony-murder and robbery, and was sentenced to life imprisonment. During the late 1950s, Clark refused to apply for parole or accept a commutation of his sentence on the ground that to do so would imply that he was guilty when in fact he was entirely innocent. In 1968 initiatives by the Detroit Legal Aid and Defender's Association led to a new trial for Clark. At the retrial, the victim's daughter—the only eyewitness from the original trial—admitted that she had never been able to identify Clark and that her testimony had been affected by a police detective telling her at the line-up, "That's the man who shot your father." On motion from the prosecutor the case was dismissed, and Clark was released. In 1972 Clark was awarded by the legislature an indemnity of $10,000 for his 30 years in prison.

CLARK, EPHRAIM R., LINDBERG HALL, *and* SCEOLA KUYKENDALL *(all white)*. *1961*. *Michigan*. All were convicted of first-degree murder and sentenced to life. The convictions were based on erroneous eyewitness identification and perjury by a woman who claimed to have driven the getaway car. The prosecutor, because he "felt . . . that these men were not guilty," spent 600 hours working on the case. Nearly a year later, one of the actual killers (in prison on another conviction) confessed, and the State's chief witness admitted perjury. The witness, a former drug addict, testified she had perjured herself because the police promised her lenient treatment for another crime if she would implicate these men. Prosecutors confirmed that such a deal had been made. The trial judge ordered a new trial and freed the three defendants, and murder charges against them were dismissed.

COBB, PERRY, *and* DARBY WILLIAMS *(a.k.a.* DARBY TILLIS) *(both black)*. *1979*. *Illinois*. After two mistrials because of hung juries, Cobb and Williams were convicted by an all-white jury (the prosecution used peremptory challenges on 36 of 38 black jurors) of first-degree robbery-murder of two white men in 1977 and were sentenced to death. The key witness for the prosecution, Phyllis Santini, claimed that she had heard Cobb and Williams talking about the robbery. In 1983 the convictions were reversed by the state supreme court. The retrial in 1986 resulted in yet another hung jury, despite testimony from Michael Falconer, a former co-worker and friend of Santini's—by then he was an assistant state attorney—that Santini had told him that her boy friend was the actual murderer. Falconer gave this testimony again in another retrial in 1987 before a judge without a jury. At this trial—the fifth time Cobb and Williams had been tried for the same crime—the two defendants were finally acquitted and released. They had spent nearly a decade in prison, including four years on death row.

COLEMAN, ED *(black). 1919 Arkansas.* See Chapter 5.

COLEMAN, ROBERT *(white). 1929. Georgia.* Coleman was convicted of murdering his wife and sentenced to life imprisonment. He had himself reported the crime to the police and was amazed to be arrested as the prime suspect. The evidence at his trial was wholly circumstantial. In 1932 the real killer (then in prison for another crime) confessed; in 1933 Coleman was granted an unconditional pardon. Eight years later, in 1941, he was indemnified by the legislature.

COLLINS, ROOSEVELT *(a.k.a.* ROOSEVELT WILSON) *(black). 1937. Alabama.* See Chapter 6.

CONNOR, MATTHEW *(black). 1980. Pennsylvania.* After a mistrial (the result of a hung jury), Connor was convicted of first-degree murder and rape, and was sentenced to life imprisonment. The conviction was based on the inability of a witness to confirm the defendant's alibi and the testimony of another witness who saw a man she later identified as Connor at the site where the victim's body was found. In 1986 a fellow prisoner of Connor's, believing in his innocence, wrote to private investigator James McCloskey, head of Centurion Ministries, calling the case to his attention. Numerous inconsistencies in the witnesses' statements were found, as was exculpatory evidence that the prosecutors had withheld from the defense. Much of this evidence suggested that the real culprit was the victim's stepbrother, who by then had died. The district attorney's office also re-investigated the case, and in 1990, at its urging, a new trial was ordered and Connor was released after having spent 12 years in jail and prison. One month later, all charges were dropped.

CONQUEST, SYLVANUS L. *(white). 1907. Virginia.* See BURTON, SAMUEL L.

COOKS, TONY *(black). 1981. California.* See Chapter 9.

COOPER, C. D. *(white). 1921. South Carolina.* After one mistrial, Cooper was convicted of a murder committed in Bennettsville in 1919 and sentenced to life in prison. The conviction was affirmed by South Carolina's supreme court. In 1925 Cooper escaped from prison, went to California, and established a new life there. He was recaptured in 1933 and returned to prison in South Carolina. In 1934, less than a year later, Governor Ibra Blackwood granted a full pardon, and Cooper was freed.

In his statement, the governor declared that he had granted clemency because "there was always some doubt as to [Cooper's] guilt," and "one of the principal witnesses at his trial practically admitted that bias and prejudice entered into her testimony." This was a reference to the testimony given by the former wife of Cooper's brother, who had admitted in an affidavit in 1923 that her trial testimony was "mainly hearsay" and that "as far as actual knowledge of the crime is concerned I know nothing." Among the 250 Californians who had petitioned for clemency for Cooper was film actress Mae West.

COOPER, RALPH, COLLIS ENGLISH, MCKINLAY FORREST, JOHN MCKENZIE, JAMES THORPE, and HORACE WILSON (all black). 1948. New Jersey. Known as the "Trenton Six," they were convicted by an all-white jury of robbery-murder and sentenced to death. Five of the six signed separate and inconsistent confessions, although the six had solid alibis. None was identified by eyewitnesses nor was there any physical evidence to connect the defendants with the crime. On appeal, the convictions were reversed; among the grounds cited was that the confessions were tainted by police coercion. In 1951 four of the defendants won acquittal in a second trial; the other two (Cooper and English) were reconvicted and sentenced to life imprisonment. These convictions were reversed on appeal. Before retrial, Cooper was released after he pleaded "no defense"; English had died in prison. In 1956 the physician who had testified at the first trial that the defendants appeared normal when they signed the (coerced) confessions, but who at the second trial reported that they appeared to be drugged, was convicted of perjury for his initial testimony. "There is little reason to doubt that in this case several innocent men were subjected to a cruel experience as a result of public hysteria which the press helped to whip up."

COX, ROBERT CRAIG (white). 1988. Florida. Cox was convicted of first-degree murder and sentenced to death. He was an early suspect in the 1978 murder because he and his family were staying at a motel near the scene of the crime and he sought surgical repair of his tongue—part of which had just had been bitten off, indicating a recent struggle—the day after the murder. He was not charged, however, until 1986, when he was tried and convicted for kidnapping and assault in California. No witness had ever seen him with the victim, and Cox contended his injured tongue was the result of a bar fight. In 1989 the Florida Supreme Court in a per curiam decision vacated the conviction and ordered the trial court to acquit Cox on all charges because "the evidence is insufficient to support [the] conviction." The court declared that the evidence created, at best, "only a suspicion" of the defendant's guilt.

CRAIG, ALVIN, and WALTER HESS (both white). 1929. Missouri. Craig and Hess were both convicted of second-degree murder and sentenced to 10 years in prison. Within a year, one of the actual killers voluntarily came forward and confessed. Hess and Craig were pardoned by Governor Henry Caulfield, and the real killers were convicted. "The Hess and Craig case exemplifies the danger of conviction for first-degree murder on circumstantial evidence; only the prosecutor's belief that he might not be able to sustain that charge induced his request for the alternative second-degree charge, which under the circumstances was equally erroneous."

CREAMER, JAMES, GEORGE EMMETT, LARRY HACKER, BILLY JENKINS, HOYT POWELL, CHARLES ROBERTS, *and* WAYNE RUFF *(all white)*. *1973. Georgia*. See Chapter 7.

CRUTCHER, WILLIE, JIM HUDSON, JOHN MURCHISON, *and* CLEO STATEN *(all black)*. *1920. Alabama*. All were convicted of first-degree murder and sentenced to life imprisonment. The convictions were based on perjured testimony. Several years after the crime, in 1926, the nephew of the victim (white) admitted that he had conspired with the victim's wife to murder her husband. Three months later, when affidavits containing these facts were presented to the Board of Pardons, Murchison and Staten were released on parole. Meanwhile, Crutcher and Hudson had died in prison. In 1927 Governor Bibb Graves gave Staten a full pardon, but Staten died a few days before it was formally issued. Murchison was denied a pardon because of his bad conduct in prison, but in 1931 he was awarded compensation ($750) by the state legislature.

DABNEY, CONDY *(white)*. *1926. Kentucky*. Dabney was convicted of murder and sentenced to life imprisonment. A year later, the supposed victim turned up alive, and Dabney was immediately pardoned. The conviction had been obtained on false testimony, and the witness who gave it was convicted of perjury.

DAVINO, FRANK *(white)*. *1940. New York*. Davino was convicted of first-degree murder and sentenced to death. The conviction was based entirely on eyewitness identification, but a new trial was ordered by the Court of Appeals because of insufficient evidence. At retrial in 1941, Davino was again convicted and sentenced to death. In addition to the original eyewitnesses, four prison inmates also testified against him; one of them said he saw Davino commit the murder, and two others claimed to have heard him confess. The fourth, who had spent the day of the murder with Davino, denied seeing him that day, thus destroying his alibi defense. The convictions rested on erroneous eyewitness identification and perjured testimony. Also, at both his trials, Davino had testified in his own defense, thereby bringing to the attention of the juries his prior criminal record. In 1942 the guilty verdict was again set aside by the Court of Appeals, because of insufficient evidence. Four months later the indictment was dismissed, and Davino was released. He had spent 17 months under death sentence.

DAVIS, CHARLIE *(black)*. *1933. Florida*. See CHAMBERS, ISIAH.

DAWSON, SIE *(black)*. *1960. Florida*. Dawson was convicted of first-degree murder and sentenced to death. The victim was the two-year-old son of a white woman for whom Dawson worked. (Although the boy's mother was also murdered, Dawson was not tried for that offense.) The conviction by an all-white male jury was based on a confession obtained from Dawson after he had spent more than a week in custody without the assistance of counsel and on an accusation by the victim's husband. Dawson had an I.Q. of 64. At trial he repudiated his confession, claiming it had been given only because "the white officers told him to say he killed Mrs. Clayton or they'd give him to 'the mob' outside." On appeal, the conviction was affirmed on a 4–3 vote. Dawson was executed in 1964. Years later, newspaper stories revived doubts that had surrounded the conviction from the beginning. Dawson had claimed that the victim's husband had committed the murders. There were no eyewitnesses, and the circumstantial evidence was slight and inconclusive.

DEAN, SARA RUTH *(white)*. *1934. Mississippi*. Dean, a doctor, was convicted of murder and sentenced to life imprisonment. The conviction, based on the victim's dying declaration that Dean attacked him after he had announced an end to their romantic relationship, was affirmed on appeal. Evidence showed, however, that it was Dean who initiated the breakup, after she had become engaged to another man. In 1935 Governor Martin Sennett Conner granted Dean a full pardon, which she had requested because "she was wholly innocent of the charge upon which she was tried and convicted."

DEDMOND, ROGER Z. *(white)*. *1967. South Carolina*. Dedmond was convicted of the murder of his wife and sentenced to 18 years in prison. At Dedmond's trial, a police officer testified that Dedmond had confessed to the murder. Dedmond, however, testified that he had no memory of where he was at the time of the crime. In 1968, three months after Dedmond began serving his sentence, he was released on bond when another man confessed to the homicide. This man, who also confessed to several other murders, was subsequently tried, convicted, and sentenced to life imprisonment for the murder of Dedmond's wife. After that sentencing, the trial court dismissed all charges against Dedmond.

DE LOS SANTOS, GEORGE ("CHIEFIE") *(Hispanic)*. *1975. New Jersey*. De los Santos was convicted of first-degree murder and sentenced to life in prison. In 1983 theological student James McCloskey devoted a year to studying the case. In the course of his investigations, he discovered proof that the prosecutors had suppressed evidence that undermined the credibility of their star witness. Other alleged eyewitness testimony against de los Santos had also been discredited. The conviction was voided by a federal district court because the original testimony of the star witness "reek[ed] of perjury." The perjured testimony was provided by a cell mate, who had claimed to hear de los Santos confess after he was arrested.

DeMore, Louis *(white). 1934. Missouri.* DeMore was convicted of murder and sentenced to life imprisonment. He had just moved to St. Louis when, on his first night in town, a police officer was slain by a fleeing robber. DeMore jokingly commented to three police officers that he fit the description of the killer and was promptly arrested. Thinking he was in danger of being sentenced to death, DeMore confessed after being assured that this would get him a life sentence instead. Ten days later the real culprit was arrested and, after five months in prison, DeMore was pardoned by Governor Guy Park.

Domer, Robert K. *(white). 1963. Ohio.* See Chapter 13.

Donnelly, James *(white). Circa 1910. Federal (Hoopa Valley Indian Reservation, California).* Donnelly was convicted of first-degree murder on circumstantial evidence and sentenced to life. A deathbed confession by another person was offered at trial, but it was excluded as inadmissible evidence under the hearsay rule (the man who had confessed died before Donnelly's trial and so could not testify in person). Donnelly's conviction was affirmed by a divided vote of the U.S. Supreme Court; he thus became a victim of a "technical rule originally laid down for his protection."

Dove, Frank, Fred Dove, *and* George Williams *(all black). 1922. North Carolina.* All three were convicted of first-degree murder and sentenced to death. A fourth defendant, on the morning of his execution in 1923, stated that these three men had nothing to do with the crime; his perjured testimony—apparently coerced—had been the basis for their convictions. Shortly thereafter, on petition from (among others) the trial judge, Governor Cameron Morrison commuted the sentences to life imprisonment. In 1928, on petition from the prosecutor, some of the arresting officers, and some of the original jurors, the three men received an absolute pardon from Governor Angus McLean and were released.

Dove, Fred *(black). 1922. North Carolina.* See Dove, Frank.

Drake, Henry *(white). 1977. Georgia.* Drake was convicted of murder and sentenced to death. The chief testimony against him came from his co-defendant, William "Pop" Campbell, who had been sentenced to death for the murder a year earlier. No physical evidence linked Drake to the murder, and witnesses confirmed his alibi. In 1984 the Circuit Court of Appeals vacated Drake's death sentence and in 1985 ordered a new trial. By then, Campbell had recanted his testimony; in 1983 he died of natural causes. At retrial, the jury split 10–2 for acquittal, requiring another retrial. In 1987, Drake was again convicted; this time he was sentenced to life. Five months later, the State Parole Board voted unanimously to release Drake, persuaded by evidence (confirmed by Campbell's attorney) that Campbell had exonerated him and by testimony from the medical examiner that bloodstains at the murder scene did not support the theory (as the prosecution alleged) that the victim had struggled with two assailants. Drake had spent eight years on death row.

DRAPER, AYLIFF *(white). 1935. Arkansas.* Draper was convicted of first-degree murder and sentenced to death. The chief evidence against him was the testimony of a co-defendant, Roy House, who was tried first. House admitted that he and Draper had robbed the victim, but he claimed that Draper alone had committed the murder. The jury convicted House and sentenced him to death. Draper was then tried and convicted on the strength of House's testimony. On appeal, the conviction was unanimously affirmed by the State Supreme Court. In 1936, a few hours before both defendants were scheduled to die in the electric chair, House admitted sole responsibility for the killing and directed the authorities to the murder weapon. House was duly executed, but Governor Junius Futrell commuted Draper's sentence to life imprisonment. Many of the original jurors, as well as all the local officials in the county where the trial had been held, joined in a plea for clemency. In 1938 Governor Carl Bailey granted Draper a full pardon, and he was released.

DULIN, WILLIAM *(white). 1933. California.* Dulin was convicted of first-degree murder and sentenced to life imprisonment. The victim was a former boxer; the State alleged that the homicide occurred in an argument over division of funds realized from the sale of a diamond ring. The State's main witness testified that a co-defendant had told her the details of the crime, but the defense contended that this witness was threatened with a prison sentence unless she gave testimony against the defendants. In court, the co-defendant admitted his sole responsibility for the crime. On appeal, Dulin's conviction was affirmed. In 1936 Governor Frank F. Merriam granted Dulin a full pardon because of his innocence. This action had been requested and supported by a number of officials, including two deputy sheriffs, two deputy district attorneys, and the judge who tried the case.

DWYER, PAUL N. *(white). 1937. Maine.* See Chapter 8.

ELLISON, ELLA MAE *(black). 1974. Massachusetts.* See Chapter 3.

EMMETT, GEORGE *(white). 1973. Georgia.* See Chapter 7.

ENGLISH, COLLIS *(black). 1948. New Jersey.* See COOPER, RALPH.

ESTES, CORNELL AVERY *(black)*. *1979. Maryland*. Estes was convicted (at age 16) of murder and sentenced to 20 years. After nearly a year in prison, he was released when the real killer confessed. In 1983 Governor Harry Hughes pardoned Estes, noting the defendant "has been conclusively shown to have been convicted in error of those criminal offenses." In 1984 the State Board of Public Works awarded Estes $16,500 in damages for the erroneous confinement.

FAVOR, JACK GRAVES *(white)*. *1967. Louisiana*. Favor, a world champion rodeo star, was convicted on two counts of murder and sentenced to life imprisonment. The case against Favor was based entirely on the word of career-criminal Floyd Cumbey, who admitted his own involvement in the 1964 murder. A second confessed participant in the crime, Donald Yates, agreed that a third person was involved but denied that it was Favor. The trial judge ruled that he could not give this testimony to the jury. During Favor's trial, Cumbey pleaded guilty to murder and was sentenced to life. After the trial he was allowed to change his plea to guilty of manslaughter; he received suspended sentences of 21 years on each count. Seven months after Favor's trial, Cumbey was released, and two days later he killed two women in Oklahoma. Meanwhile, a fellow prisoner and jail-house lawyer, Ron Wikberg, took an interest in Favor's case and filed an appeal on his behalf. In 1972 a federal district court granted Favor a new trial. At retrial in 1974, Yates testified that Favor was uninvolved, and the jury acquitted him. His suit for false imprisonment against the State was eventually settled for $55,000. Wrote Angola Prison Warden C. Murray Henderson, "Jack Favor . . . was obviously innocent, and information available to the judicial process from the very beginning of his ordeal could have cleared him before a miscarriage of justice cost him his health and seven years of his life. . . . The moving case of Jack Graves Favor serves to emphasize the dangers inherent in a criminal justice system out of control and willing to convict on even the most questionable evidence, a system which could make almost anyone its victim and run rampant over most defendants."

FAY, FLOYD ("BUZZ") *(white)*. *1978. Ohio*. See Chapter 11.

FEATHERSTONE, FRANCIS *(white)*. *1986. New York*. Featherstone was convicted of second-degree murder. Six months later, when he appeared in trial court for formal sentencing, his conviction was vacated because the prosecution by then had learned that the real killer was a man named Bokun. During the killing (which grew out of a gang's internal rivalry) Bokun had disguised himself to resemble Featherstone, who had been tried and acquitted on three previous murder charges. Bokun's guilt had been known by his attorney for nearly a year before Featherstone's trial. But in a bizarre twist, because he also represented Bokun, the attorney did not inform the court of Bokun's guilt, believing that to do so would violate attorney-client privilege. Said the prosecutor, the "bottom line, despite the defendant's past, is still that we are convinced that Francis Featherstone did not shoot (the victim), and that William Bokun did."

FERBER, NEIL *(white). 1982. Pennsylvania.* See Chapter 10.

FEWELL, STANFORD ELLIS *(white). 1952. Alabama.* Fewell was convicted of second-degree murder and sentenced to 30 years in prison. After 13 days of continuous questioning, Fewell, in his third conflicting statement, confessed to the 1949 sex murder of his 9-year-old cousin. He repudiated this confession almost immediately. "Except for the confession . . . there was no case." The conviction was affirmed on appeal, and his request to petition for a writ of error coram nobis was denied. Subsequent investigation by the former city editor of the *Birmingham News* and the Court of Last Resort led to four persons who confirmed Fewell's alibi. In 1959, after this new evidence was introduced, the Alabama Parole Board released Fewell.

FISHER, WILLIAM *(white). 1933. New York.* Fisher was convicted of first-degree manslaughter and sentenced to a prison term of 15 to 30 years. In 1944 he was paroled, having served 11 years. In 1958 the New York Court of Appeals reversed two lower courts' denials of Fisher's application for a writ of error coram nobis. The judgment of conviction against Fisher was vacated because the prosecuting attorney at the original trial had offered in evidence as the murder weapon a gun that he knew had not been fired by the defendant. The prosecutor had also suppressed evidence that clearly demonstrated Fisher's innocence. Six bills allowing Fisher to sue the State were passed by the New York Legislature but were vetoed by Governors Nelson Rockefeller, Hugh Carey, and Mario Cuomo. Finally, in 1984, the State waived its immunity in a bill signed by Governor Cuomo, and in 1986 the courts awarded Fisher $750,000 for his wrongful imprisonment.

FORREST, MCKINLAY *(black). 1948. New Jersey.* See COOPER, RALPH.

FOSTER, JAMES FULTON *(white). 1956. Georgia.* See Chapter 1.

FOSTER, LOCK, GEORGE FRICK, GEORGE URY, *and* two others *(all white). 1901. Ohio.* All five defendants were convicted of murder (in Wyandotte County) and sentenced to life imprisonment. Three of them died in prison. The only evidence against the men came from what turned out to be an erroneous identification by the victim's widow. According to the State Board of Pardons, the men were "victims of a plot to railroad them to prison to satisfy public feeling, which had been aroused by a series of crimes in the county for which no one had been punished." In 1911 the Board recommended Frick's release because "he has already served more than ten years for a crime which he did not commit." In

1913, despite repeated objections of the county prosecutor, Ury was pardoned by Governor James Cox, who agreed that Ury had a "complete alibi."

FOWLER, WALTER, *and* HEYWOOD PUGH *(both black). 1936. Illinois.* Fowler and Pugh were both convicted of murder and sentenced to life imprisonment. Fowler had a prior felony record; Pugh, 19, did not. "There was no corroborative evidence to link either of them to the murder." Nonetheless, Fowler confessed quickly, as did Pugh after sustaining beatings over a period of several days while in custody. At trial the police perjured themselves by denying the beatings. In 1955 Pugh finally convinced a volunteer attorney to re-examine the case. The reinvestigation established that the prosecution had suppressed evidence of two eyewitnesses who had identified the true killer as white. Pugh's conviction was reversed (Fowler had in the meantime died in prison in 1949), the prosecution dropped the charges, and the State later awarded Pugh a settlement of $51,000.

FOX, JOE *(black). 1919. Arkansas.* See Chapter 5.

FRANK, LEO M. *(white). 1913. Georgia.* Frank was convicted of murder and sentenced to death. The conviction was sustained on appeal. In 1915 Governor John Slaton commuted the death sentence to life imprisonment because of doubts about Frank's guilt. Two months later, Frank was lynched. The conviction had been obtained in an atmosphere of strong anti-Semitism on perjured testimony from Jim Conley, the person who probably was the real culprit. In 1982 a witness to the crime admitted having seen Conley carry the victim's body on the first floor of the factory where the murder took place. This contradicted Conley's testimony at trial that, on Frank's orders, he had carried the body on the elevator directly from the second floor to the basement. In 1983 the Anti-Defamation League of B'nai B'rith, the American Jewish Committee, and the Atlanta Jewish Federation presented a petition and 300 pages of evidence and supporting documents to the Georgia Board of Pardons and Paroles in an effort to obtain a posthumous pardon. In 1986 a pardon was granted because of blatant due-process violations.

FREDERICK, JOHNNY, *and* DAVID R. KEATON *(both black). 1971. Florida.* Frederick and Keaton were both convicted of the murder of an off-duty deputy sheriff during a robbery; Frederick was sentenced to life imprisonment and Keaton to death. Along with three other men who were indicted for this crime, they were called the "Quincy Five" by groups defending their innocence. (Of these three other defendants, one was found incompetent to stand trial, and the second was acquitted; charges against the third were dropped.) Their convictions were based mainly on mistaken testimony by five eyewitnesses, as well as on coerced confessions. A year later three other men were arrested for the crime based on extensive circumstantial evidence, including the presence of their fingerprints at the scene of the crime. Two confessed, and all three were convicted. The state supreme court ordered a new trial for Keaton because of the newly discovered evidence. In 1973 both Frederick and Keaton were released after the State decided not to reprosecute. "The case of the Quincy Five stands as a classic [example] of eyewitness misidentification, or racial skew," noted one psychologist.

FRICK, GEORGE *(white)*. *1901. Ohio.* See FOSTER, LOCK.

FRY, JOHN HENRY ("TENNESSEE") *(white)*. *1958. California.* Fry was convicted of manslaughter and sentenced to 1–10 years in prison. Charged with the murder of his common-law wife, Fry had been too drunk to remember the events and finally pleaded guilty to the reduced charge of manslaughter. In 1959 another man (Richard Cooper) was arrested in connection with an unrelated murder; he confessed to the killing for which Fry had been convicted. Cooper was convicted, sentenced to death, and executed in 1960 for both murders. In 1959, less than a month after Cooper's confession, Fry was released and pardoned by Governor Edmund G. Brown. The State Board of Control voted to award Fry $3,000 compensation.

FUDGE, E. J. *(white)*. *1916. Florida.* Fudge was convicted of first-degree murder for killing his two daughters and was sentenced to life in prison. On appeal the conviction was reversed, and a new trial was ordered. According to the court, a suicide note written by one of the children and the absence of a motive for murder by their father indicated that the two deaths were a murder-suicide caused by one of the girls. "While the testimony raises a vague and attenuated suspicion that by some rare chance the plaintiff in error might have murdered his children, there is no whit of it that points with any certainty in that direction...." In 1918 all charges against Fudge were dropped.

GAINES, FREDDIE LEE *(black)*. *1974. Alabama.* Gaines was convicted of second-degree murder and sentenced to 30 years in prison. In 1985 he was released on parole. In 1990 a man who closely resembled Gaines confessed to the murder, and in a 1991 hearing that lasted five minutes an Alabama circuit judge vacated Gaines's conviction. The district attorney said he was convinced Gaines was innocent. "I don't know of any system that's perfect . . . and I can't apologize for the state. It's certainly an injustice. It's regrettable and I hate that it happened." Gaines observed, "I really could have been somebody but they took that away—13 years of my life gone down the drain. A dead life."

GARCIA, FRANCISCO *(Hispanic)*. *1913. New Mexico.* Garcia was convicted of voluntary manslaughter and sentenced to a prison term of seven to eight years. The state supreme court reversed the conviction and noted that it was "physically impossible for Francisco Garcia to be guilty of any crime in this connection." Garcia had been shot by the victim and was unconscious when another man committed the homicide. "A man has been convicted . . . where there is, not only no evidence to support the verdict, but where the evidence conclusively established his innocence." A new trial was awarded, and the charges were dropped.

GARNER, VANCE, *and* WILL JOHNSON *(both black)*. *1905*. *Alabama*. With Jack Hunter, Garner and Johnson were convicted of murder and sentenced to death, despite their claims of innocence. No appeals were undertaken. In 1905 Garner and Hunter were hanged. From the gallows Garner maintained his complete innocence; Hunter admitted his own guilt and absolved both Garner and Johnson. In 1906 Johnson's sentence was commuted to life. A fourth man, Bunk Richardson, who was charged with perjuring himself in Garner's behalf, was lynched three nights after Johnson's death sentence was commuted.

GARRETT, SAMMIE *(black)*. *1970*. *Illinois*. Garrett was convicted of murder and sentenced to 20–40 years in prison. The female victim (white) and Garrett had been lovers, although each was married to someone else. After the affair was discovered, she became depressed and talked of committing suicide. A suicide note, uncontestably written in her hand, was found next to the body, but Garrett was with her when she died, and the State contended that the evidence proved it was impossible for the deceased to have shot herself. All the evidence against Garrett was circumstantial. Four years later Garrett's attorneys found a report, by the pathologist who did the autopsy, that was consistent with the theory of death by suicide. In 1975 the conviction was reversed by the Illinois Supreme Court, and Garrett was released after having served five years.

GARVEY, MIKE, HARVEY LESHER, *and* PHIL ROHAN *(all white)*. *1928*. *California*. All three were convicted of murder and sentenced to life. The persistent efforts of their defense attorney uncovered several holes in the State's case. In 1930 full pardons were granted by Governor Clement C. Young, and Rohan was indemnified ($1,692). Perjured testimony plus mistaken identification by a 10-year-old boy contributed to the convictions.

GIDDENS, CHARLES RAY *(black)*. *1978*. *Oklahoma*. After the all-white jury deliberated for 15 minutes, Giddens was convicted of first-degree murder for the death of a grocery store cashier and sentenced to death. The main evidence against the 18-year-old Giddens came from the testimony of Johnnie Gray (never indicted), who claimed to have accompanied him to the murder scene. In 1981 the Oklahoma Court of Criminal Appeals reversed the conviction on the ground of insufficient evidence, describing Gray's testimony as "replete with conflicts." In 1982 the same court held that Giddens could not be retried without violating the prohibition against double jeopardy, so the case was remanded with an order to dismiss it. After having spent 52 months on death row, Giddens was finally released.

GILES, ALBERT *(black)*. *1919*. *Arkansas*. See Chapter 5.

GILES, JAMES, JOHN GILES, *and* JOSEPH JOHNSON, JR. *(all black)*. *1961*. *Maryland*. All were convicted of the rape of a 16-year-old white girl and sentenced to death. (The Giles brothers were tried first; Johnson was not tried until 1962.) Several citizens believed the men were not guilty and, led by a local scientist, Harold Knapp, continued to investigate the case. New evidence was discovered, and five jurors wrote to the governor to say that—had they been aware of this information—they would not have found the defendants guilty. In 1963, after extensive further investigations, Governor J. Millard Tawes commuted the sentences to life. In 1967 the U.S. Supreme Court, noting several problems with the credibility of the victim, ordered additional hearings on the case. In 1967, at a postconviction hearing in the county circuit court, both the prosecuting attorney and the state attorney general conceded that the original convictions rested in part on erroneous testimony, and a new trial was awarded. After re-indictment, the prosecutor moved to drop all charges, and the brothers were released. Johnson, however, was not released until receiving a full pardon from Governor Spiro Agnew in 1968. The essence of the case, as it appeared to the Giles–Johnson Defense Committee, was that the victim had willingly consented to sexual intercourse with all three defendants and had accused them of rape only to protect herself from charges as a delinquent minor when the police found her and one of the defendants in flagrante delicto.

GILES, JOHN *(black)*. *1961*. *Maryland*. See GILES, JAMES.

GLADISH, THOMAS V., RICHARD WAYNE GREER, RONALD B. KEINE, *and* CLARENCE SMITH, JR. *(all white)*. *1974*. *New Mexico*. See Chapter 2.

GOODWIN, PAUL *(white)*. *1936*. *Oklahoma*. Goodwin was convicted of murder and sentenced to life imprisonment. He was paroled in 1961 but was returned to prison in 1962 for parole violation. In 1968 his petition for a writ of habeas corpus was denied in the state court. In 1969, however, after the material facts had been fully developed, a federal district court judge ordered Goodwin's immediate release, finding that Goodwin had been denied effective assistance of counsel, that the prosecution had suppressed exculpatory evidence (the statement of an eyewitness), and that prejudicial pretrial publicity had prevented a fair trial. This judgment was affirmed on appeal. The only evidence against Goodwin was a written statement made by a co-defendant who twice before had admitted sole responsibility for the killing. The co-defendant's trial attorney (later Speaker of the Oklahoma House of Representatives) also testified that his client alone was responsible. The district court was "convinced that petitioner did not shoot and kill the deceased."

GRACE, FRANK ("PARKY") (black). 1974. Massachusetts. Grace, with his brother, was convicted of murder by an all-white jury and sentenced to life in prison. Initial attempts to overturn the conviction failed. Finally, in 1983, an evidentiary hearing was ordered. Investigation by staff of the New England American Friends Service Committee showed that Grace, a former Black Panther and political activist, had been targeted by the New Bedford police as an extremely dangerous trouble-maker. Arrested more than a dozen times, he was never found guilty of any crime prior to the murder conviction. "He was arrested [for the murder] by a police officer who had a long standing antipathy toward him, . . . he was sentenced although there was no evidence to convict him, and he remains in jail although proof of his innocence abounds." In 1984 hearings on Grace's request for a new trial, a key prosecution witness admitted he had lied at the original trial, and Grace's brother also acknowledged sole responsibility for the killing. Finally, in 1985, Frank Grace was granted a new trial and freed.

GRAY, RUSSELL LEON (black). 1987. Virginia. Gray was convicted of first-degree murder and sentenced to 52 years in prison. He had a previous criminal record and was known in his neighborhood as a "real bad actor," which no doubt played a role in his becoming a prime suspect. The defense attorney, Cary Bowen, persisted with his investiga-tion of the case and eventually demonstrated that the conviction had been based on erroneous eyewitness identification by the State's chief witness. The eyewitness then identified another man, Michael Harvey; other witnesses, who had not testified at Gray's trial, agreed that Harvey was the gunman. Harvey finally confessed. In 1990 a police investigation verified Harvey's confession, and he was convicted. The district attorney then joined Gray's defense attorney in requesting a gubernatorial pardon. Two days after Harvey's conviction, Governor Douglas Wilder granted a complete pardon, and Gray was released after 3 years in prison.

GREASON, SAMUEL (black). 1901. Pennsylvania. Greason was con-victed of first-degree murder on the testimony of the victim's wife and was sentenced to death. On appeal, his conviction was affirmed. Greason had been under a death warrant ten different times in four years before the victim's wife recanted her testimony against Greason in 1905, leading the Pennsylvania Supreme Court to remand the case to the trial court on the ground of newly discovered evidence. After retrial later that year, the victim's wife confessed to the murder herself and completely exoner-ated Greason. Following a request by the district attorney, the judge directed a verdict of acquittal.

GREEN, NELSON, and CHARLES STIELOW (both white). 1915.

New York. Stielow was convicted of murder and sentenced to death. Green pleaded guilty to second-degree murder to avoid the electric chair and was given a 20-year-to-life term. The prosecution alleged Stielow had confessed; Stielow maintained the confession had been obtained by intimidation. His conviction was affirmed on appeal. Prison officials and a private attorney, convinced the confession had not been voluntary, took up the case. Stielow faced five dates with the electric chair, once receiving a stay after he had already been led to the execution chamber. In 1916 his death sentence was commuted to life by Governor Charles Whitman. In 1918 the real culprit confessed to friends. After a detailed investigation by a lawyer had uncovered ballistics evidence proving Green's and Stielow's innocence, both men were pardoned and released.

GREEN, WILLIAM S. *(black). 1947. Pennsylvania.* Green was convicted of first-degree murder and sentenced to life imprisonment. The judgment was affirmed on appeal. In 1957 one of the two "excellent eyewitnesses" against Green convinced the district attorney that he had been paid by the other witness to give perjured testimony in an effort by that witness to get "revenge" against Green. The State then joined in Green's petition for a new trial. Governor George Leader pardoned Green after he had served 10 years. Green had earlier turned down an opportunity for parole because he wanted first to have his name cleared.

GREENLEE, CHARLES, WALTER LEE IRVIN, *and* SAMUEL SHEPHERD *(all black). 1949. Florida.* See Chapter 5.

GREER, RICHARD *(white). 1974. New Mexico.* See Chapter 2.

GROSS, LOUIS *(white). 1932. Michigan.* Gross was convicted of first-degree murder and sentenced to life imprisonment. He had three previous convictions for larceny and attempted larceny. In 1945 a rabbi, convinced of Gross's innocence, persuaded the Court of Last Resort to re-investigate the case. Meanwhile, all official records of the case had mysteriously disappeared. Evidence was discovered of a "frame-up" by the police and of perjured testimony by the State's chief witness. In 1948 the prosecutor obtained a new trial for Gross and announced his intention to dismiss the indictment. The judge stated, "It appears to me that this man, Louis Gross, has been framed." Gross was freed after having served 16 years. "There was no necessity for any pardon. In the eyes of the law he had never been convicted of this crime."

GROWDEN, GERALD *(white). 1931. Michigan.* Growden was convicted of murder and sentenced to life imprisonment. In 1932 two other men confessed to the murder, all charges against Growden were dismissed, and he was released after having served nine months. His conviction had been based on erroneous eyewitness identification and the testimony of fellow inmates who claimed that Growden had confessed to the crime.

GRZECHOWIAK, STEPHEN, *and* MAX RYBARCZYK *(both white).* *1929. New York.* Grzechowiak and Rybarczyk were both convicted of felony-murder and sentenced to death. Co-defendant Alexander Bogdanoff insisted that neither Grzechowiak nor Rybarczyk had been involved in the crime, and that each had been mistakenly identified by the eyewitnesses. He refused, however, to reveal the names of his true accomplices. Grzechowiak and Rybarczyk were executed in 1930, after their convictions were affirmed on appeal. In their final words, they maintained their innocence, and Bogdanoff again declared that the two were innocent.

GUNTER, THOMAS *(white). 1929. Mississippi.* Gunter was convicted of murdering his son-in-law, mainly on the basis of the perjured testimony of his daughter (the deceased's wife) and his 7-year-old granddaughter. He was sentenced to five years in prison. Several months later, his daughter admitted killing her husband; she pleaded guilty and received a suspended sentence. Meanwhile, Gunter had been temporarily released from prison. After his daughter received the suspended sentence, Gunter was ordered to return to prison. Governor Theodore Bilbo declared that "somebody ought to be in the penitentiary all the time for the murder of a sleeping man." Gunter, however, had already fled the state.

HACKER, LARRY *(white). 1973. Georgia.* See Chapter 7.

HAINES, ERNEST *(white). 1916. Pennsylvania.* Haines, with Henry Ward Mottorn, was convicted of first-degree murder and sentenced to death. Haines had a subnormal intellect. Both defendants were juveniles, and the impending execution of the two youths led to an effort to abolish Pennsylvania's death penalty statute. The only evidence against Haines was the testimony of his co-defendant, who admitted the killing but claimed that Haines was involved in the plot. Haines denied this, and Mottorn's testimony was deemed reversible error by the state supreme court because he had discussed an earlier unrelated burglary that he and Haines had allegedly perpetrated. At retrial Haines was acquitted; the next year Mottorn's sentence was commuted to life.

HALL, GORDON ROBERT CASTILLO *(Hispanic). 1978. California.* See Chapter 1.

HALL, JAMES *(black). 1974. Iowa.* James Hall was convicted of second-degree murder and sentenced to 50 years in prison. On appeal, the conviction was affirmed. Hall and his attorneys continued to insist that he was innocent, however, and in 1983 they found that the prosecution had suppressed exculpatory evidence. Shortly thereafter, the conviction was overturned, a new trial was ordered by a state district judge, and Hall was released on bail. In 1984 the original indictment was dismissed. The decision cited "racial slurs" made by the prosecutor in front of the grand jury and stated that the prosecutor had failed to present evidence that pointed to other suspects in the case. It was also found that a state investigator had lied to the grand jury about comments Hall had allegedly made during an interview.

HALL, LINDBERG *(white). 1961. Michigan.* See CLARK, EPHRAIM R.

HALL, PAUL *(black). 1919. Arkansas.* See Chapter 5.

HALL, PHYLLIS ELAINE *(white). 1985. Florida.* Hall was convicted of first-degree murder and given a sentence of 25 years to life in prison. In 1986 the Florida District Court of Appeal ruled unanimously that the evidence was insufficient to support her conviction. The court also ordered the charges dismissed and Hall released. The evidence showed that Hall's lover, Albert Freer, was involved in the murder. Hall was seen with Freer before and after the murder, and she lied to the police in an attempt to give Freer an alibi. However, there was no evidence to connect her with the crime, and hence the State's theory that she aided and abetted in the murder was completely unsupported. Said the appellate court, "The entire position of the State is based on stacking inference upon inference."

HALLOWELL, WILLIAM A. *(white). 1952. Pennsylvania.* See ANTONIEWICZ, JOSEPH.

HAMBY, LOREN *(white). 1940. Colorado.* Hamby was convicted of first-degree murder for a filling station robbery-murder in 1937 and sentenced to life imprisonment, even though the chief prosecution witness—who initially claimed he had driven Hamby to the scene of the murder—asserted on the witness stand at Hamby's trial that the incrimination was false. The conviction was affirmed on appeal, with two justices dissenting, despite the acknowledgment that Hamby's "alibi was well supported. . . ." The court also recognized that the trial record "seethes with palpable perjury" but refused to rule on which testimony was false. In 1946 Governor John Vivian appointed a commission to reinvestigate the case. The alibi was confirmed, and the governor issued a full pardon, stating that the conviction had been obtained because perjured testimony had been used to discredit the alibi. Hamby was released after having served six years in prison.

HAMPTON, MARY KATHERIN *(white). 1961. Louisiana.* See Chapter 8.

HANKINS, LEONARD *(white). 1933. Minnesota.* Hankins was convicted of first-degree murder and sentenced to life. The erroneous conviction was based on mistaken eyewitness identification and misleading circumstantial evidence. A co-defendant, who had pleaded guilty, said that he had never seen Hankins until after the crime. Other members of the "gang" that was responsible for the robbery during which the murders took place also said the Hankins was not involved. Nevertheless, the conviction was affirmed on appeal. In 1936 an Associated Press reporter, notified by a prison warden who was certain Hankins was innocent, re-investigated the case. All but one of the eyewitnesses, after seeing a picture of one of the confessed killers, admitted that their identification could have been erroneous. As the years went by a succession of Minnesota governors and attorneys general became interested in the case, only to abandon it. The county attorney who prosecuted Hankins apparently opposed any re-opening of the case, fearing exposure of a prosecutorial mistake. In 1953 Hankins was given a "final unconditional release" and indemnified, and his sister was reimbursed by the state legislature for her expenses in exonerating him.

HARDY, VANCE *(white)*. *1924. Michigan.* Hardy was convicted of first-degree murder and sentenced to life. Perjured eyewitness testimony, given under coercion, was the basis of the conviction. Hardy's sister provided an unsuccessful alibi, but—convinced of his innocence—she secured the help of Erle Stanley Gardner. As a result, a new trial was granted, a quarter century late. When the identifying witness at the earlier trial repudiated his testimony, admitting that it was perjured and the result of unscrupulous police pressure, all charges against Hardy were dropped. Some years earlier this witness had attempted to correct his testimony in order to assist Hardy, but he was deterred from doing so by what he regarded as a threat of prosecution for perjury. After having served 26 years, including 10 in solitary confinement, Hardy was released.

HARRIS, FRANK *(white)*. *1926. Pennsylvania.* Harris was convicted of first-degree murder and sentenced to life imprisonment. The victim was Harris's companion when the two of them attempted to resist arrest. (Harris had served two short sentences after convictions on minor charges.) The prosecution argued that Harris fired the fatal bullet. Harris protested his innocence to anyone who would listen, but to no avail. In 1946 a volunteer lawyer, convinced of Harris's innocence, re-investigated the case. In 1947 Governor James Duff commuted the sentence after it had been demonstrated that the bullet that killed the victim could not have come from Harris's gun. Harris was then released. In 1951 he was detained as a parole violator, and he applied for a writ of habeas corpus. The court denied Harris's application but, noting that the ballistics test indicated that Harris had not fired the fatal shot, recommended that he should apply for a pardon or a new trial.

HARRIS, L. D. *(black)*. *1947. South Carolina.* Harris was convicted of murder and sentenced to death. After hours of interrogation (by white police officers), physical abuse, and threats, he confessed to the crime. The trial judge told the jury that without the confession there was no evidence to support a guilty verdict. Harris's conviction was appealed solely on the involuntariness of the confession; by a vote of 3–2 the South Carolina Supreme Court refused to order a new trial. On further appeal to the U.S. Supreme Court, the conviction was reversed. No retrial was held. In 1957 a man originally suspected of the murder was arrested for similar murders; he confessed to the murder for which Harris had been convicted and convinced authorities that his confession was authentic.

HAUPTMANN, BRUNO RICHARD *(white)*. *1935*. *New Jersey*. See Chapter 4.

HEFNER, CECIL *(white)*. *1920*. *North Carolina*. Hefner was convicted of second-degree murder and sentenced to 15 years' imprisonment. Five months later, following a recommendation by the prosecutor and the trial judge, Hefner was pardoned by Governor Cameron Morrison. The prosecutor reported that his post-trial investigation "proves conclusively" that Hefner was not present when the victim was killed.

HENNIS, TIMOTHY B. *(white)*. *1986*. *North Carolina*. Hennis was convicted of three counts of murder and sentenced to death. A staff sergeant in the army, Hennis was at first identified by a witness who claimed to have seen him leaving the murder scene. The witness later said he was mistaken, only then to say—under pressure from the prosecutor—that he was certain his identification was correct. A surprise prosecution witness was also called, who remembered seeing someone who looked like Hennis use the bank card of one of the victims shortly after the murders. (This witness had at first told investigators that she remembered nothing, but 10 months after the murders she came forward with her newly found memory). In 1988 the state supreme court granted a new trial because the jury had been shown inflammatory photos of the victims. The court's opinion also described the first witness's identification as "tenuous" and the second's as "extremely tentative." At retrial in 1989 the defense produced a neighbor of the victims—a man who closely resembled Hennis and who liked to stroll in the neighborhood—and argued that he was the man seen by the eyewitness. Furthermore, the testimony of the witness at the bank was discredited when it was demonstrated, on the strength of her A.T.M. bank receipts, that she had arrived at the bank after the person who used the victim's card had departed. Hennis was acquitted.

HESS, WALTER *(white)*. *1929*. *Missouri*. See CRAIG, ALVIN.

HICKS, ED *(black)*. *1919*. *Arkansas*. See Chapter 5.

HICKS, FRANK *(black)*. *1919*. *Arkansas*. See Chapter 5.

HICKS, LARRY *(black)*. *1978*. *Indiana*. Hicks was convicted on two counts of murder and sentenced to death. Two weeks before the scheduled execution, a volunteer attorney became interested in the case. After Hicks passed lie detector tests, the Playboy Foundation provided funds for a thorough re-investigation. In 1980 the original judge ordered a new trial because Hicks (who had a "low normal" I.Q.) had not understood the proceedings well enough to assist in his own defense. Later that year, at the new trial, evidence established Hicks's alibi and that eyewitness testimony against him in his original trial was perjured. He was acquitted and released: "The case of a young man with no family, friends or funds who avoided the electric chair mainly by a stroke of extraordinary good luck."

HILL, CHRISTINA *(black)*. *1990. Massachusetts*. Hill was convicted of second-degree murder after a closed trial before a judge and was committed to the Department of Youth Services. The evidence against Hill, 16, came from the testimony of a friend, who claimed she had heard Hill confess. Another friend of both Hill and that witness subsequently testified that the witness's testimony was given because of strong pressure by a *Boston Herald* newspaper reporter who was investigating the case. The reporter told the witness and her friend that the two of them would be in trouble with the law if they did not help convict Hill. Other witnesses also said that the witness had privately repudiated her testimony, but did not want to recant under oath for fear of being prosecuted for perjury. Under the trial de novo system in Massachusetts, Hill then requested a jury trial. In 1991 she was retried and acquitted.

HILL, JOE *(originally known as* JOSEPH HILLSTROM*)* *(white)*. *1915. Utah*. Hill was convicted and sentenced to death for the murder of two storekeepers. The prosecution was based on sketchy circumstantial evidence and was in part the result of collusion between the prosecution and the trial judge in an atmosphere of anti-union hostility. Despite several appeals from President Woodrow Wilson to the Utah authorities for a reprieve, Hill was denied a new trial. He was also denied executive clemency. His appeal to the Utah Supreme Court was unsuccessful and he was executed in 1915. Hill appears to have been an innocent victim of "politics, finance and organized religion, . . . a powerful trinity"; his conviction and death are "one of the worst travesties of justice in American labor history."

HOFFMAN, HARRY L. *(white)*. *1924. New York*. Hoffman was convicted of second-degree murder and sentenced to 20 years to life. Upon learning that he was a suspect, Hoffman tried to manufacture an alibi that would help him avoid both lynching and the death penalty. He was inspired to this folly by his fear that he would otherwise be another Leo Frank (q.v.). The false alibi was exposed at trial, and the jury viewed it as evidence of guilt. The conviction was reversed on a technicality (faulty wording in the original indictment). At retrial, a mistrial was declared when Hoffman's defense counsel collapsed from a heart attack. The third trial resulted in a hung jury. In 1929, at the fourth trial, it was shown that the original eyewitness testimony was perjured and that the fatal shots could not have come from Hoffman's gun. Hoffman was acquitted in the end because "the jury had realized how treacherous circumstantial evidence could be."

HOFFNER, LOUIS *(white). 1941. New York.* Hoffner was convicted of first-degree murder and sentenced to life. He had a previous criminal record and had served a prison sentence for larceny. The conviction was affirmed on appeal. In 1947 a New York newspaper reporter re-investigated the crime and confirmed Hoffner's alibi. In 1952 the prosecutor moved to re-open the case and set aside the conviction, on the grounds that the district attorney's office had withheld information on an eyewitness's misidentification (made under police pressure). Hoffner was released, and in 1955 the State indemnified him for false imprisonment ($112,290).

HOLBROOK, ERNEST, JR., *and* HERMAN RAY RUCKER *(both white). 1982. Ohio.* Both Holbrook and Rucker were convicted of the rape and murder of a child and sentenced to life imprisonment, although no physical evidence linked either defendant to the crime. The convictions rested entirely on the shaky testimony of two witnesses and the jury's refusal to believe the defendants' alibis. After a key witness recanted his testimony, Rucker was awarded a new trial, and in 1983 he was acquitted. The witness was then convicted of perjury. In 1984 Holbrook was released after the prosecutor dismissed all charges against him. (By that time, another man had been convicted and sentenced to death for crimes similar to the offenses for which Holbrook and Rucker had been convicted.)

HOLLAND, KENNETH R. *(white). 1948. Virginia.* Holland was convicted of first-degree murder and sentenced to 20 years in prison. He was a former police officer, and the victim was the husband of a friend. The conviction was reversed on appeal because of insufficient evidence. In 1950 Holland was acquitted at retrial.

HOLLINS, JESS *(black). 1931. Oklahoma.* See Chapter 6.

HORN, GEITHER *(white). 1935. Washington.* Horn was convicted of first-degree murder and sentenced to life imprisonment. When three police officers took him to an open grave and told him they were going to bury him alive unless he confessed to murdering a farm hand, Horn confessed. The confession was used at the trial despite Horn's subsequent claim of innocence. His original application for a writ of habeas corpus was denied. In 1959, after having served 24 years, he was freed by a federal judge. In 1963 the legislature awarded Horn $6,000 for his false imprisonment, and an insurance company settled Horn's civil suit against the three officers out of court.

HOUSTON, ELTON *(black). 1984. Illinois.* See BROWN, ROBERT.

HUDSON, JIM *(black). 1920. Alabama.* See CRUTCHER, WILLIE.

IMBLER, PAUL KERN *(white). 1961. California.* See Chapter 12.

IRVIN, WALTER LEE (black). 1949. Florida. See Chapter 5.

JACKSON, EDMOND D. (black). 1971. New York. Jackson was convicted of murder and felony murder and sentenced to two concurrent terms of 20 years to life in prison. On initial appeal, the convictions were affirmed. In 1978, on a petition for habeas corpus in federal court, the conviction was reversed on grounds of unreliable eyewitness testimony (by four people) and the fact that "not a scintilla of [other] evidence was offered at the trial to connect petitioner with the crime." In ordering Jackson freed after he had spent eight years in prison, the judge said, "I shudder to think what the situation would have been in this case if there had been a mandatory death penalty." In addition, the judge criticized the district attorney for proceeding with the trial "on such highly dubious evidence and in light of the incomplete and negligent investigation conducted by the detectives." The police had ignored evidence that pointed to another suspect after they had decided that Jackson was guilty.

JACKSON, JOHN WILLIAM (white). 1984. Florida. Jackson was convicted of first-degree murder and sentenced to life imprisonment. The victim, a woman, had also been raped. The chief evidence against Jackson was given by a forensic odontologist, who concluded that "the bite mark on the victim's wrist was consistent with Jackson's teeth impressions." However, this expert also testified that the bite mark evidence was not strong enough to justify arresting Jackson. In addition, Negroid pubic hair was found on the victim, and Jackson was white. Furthermore, in a statement given before she died, the victim indicated that her assailant had been driving a car with Michigan license plates; Jackson's car had Florida plates. In 1987 the conviction was vacated by the Florida District Court of Appeal because the evidence was insufficient to support a verdict of guilt.

JACKSON, SERGEANT (white). 1974. California. Jackson, arrested without a warrant, was convicted of first-degree murder and first-degree robbery; he was sentenced to life imprisonment. Shortly after his conviction, another man came forward and implicated himself in the crimes. He was subsequently tried and convicted. After having spent seven months in prison, Jackson was set free and the judgment against him was vacated. A wallet in his possession had been erroneously identified as belonging to the victim. A jury awarded him $280,000 for false imprisonment, but this judgment was reversed on the ground that he could sue only for his detention under warrantless arrest. The California Court of Appeal described Jackson as "an innocent man, convicted and imprisoned for crimes he did not commit." The city of San Diego later paid Jackson $17,000.

JAMES, TYRONE, and WINFRED J. ("WILBUR") PETERSON (both black). 1982. South Carolina. Both James and Peterson were convicted of murder and sentenced to life imprisonment, primarily on the testimony of a police officer who stated that he overheard them making incriminating statements while in custody after their arrest. Two months later, prompted by testimony from a previously silent witness that implicated four other men, the court ordered a new trial. Subsequently a grand jury dropped the charges against both James and Peterson (and two others who had not yet been tried for the crime). Each of the four men implicated by the new witness was arrested, and at least one of these men pleaded guilty and was sentenced to life imprisonment.

JARAMILLO, ANIBAL *(Hispanic). 1981. Florida.* Jaramillo was convicted on two counts of first-degree murder and sentenced to death, even though the trial jury had unanimously recommended a sentence of life imprisonment. At trial, one prosecution witness admitted under cross-examination that he had seen another "anxious-looking" man, a roommate of the victims, less than one mile from the scene shortly after the time of the crime; another prosecution witness admitted that shortly thereafter she and her husband drove this same frightened man back to the house where the killing occurred. The failure of this man to mention having seen any signs of a fight or of the dead victims suggests he may have been implicated in the crime (although he was never indicted). On appeal, Jaramillo's convictions were reversed, and he was released on the ground that the circumstantial evidence against him was "not legally sufficient to establish a prima facie case. . . ."

JENKINS, BILLY *(white). 1973. Georgia.* See Chapter 7.

JENKINS, LONNIE *(white). 1931. Michigan.* Jenkins was convicted of first-degree murder and sentenced to life imprisonment for killing his wife. Initially, a coroner's jury found that Mrs. Jenkins had committed suicide by shooting herself. Jenkins was later arrested, charged with murder, and convicted largely because a teenaged girl testified that she had forged the wife's suicide note at Jenkins's instigation. Subsequent investigation by Jenkins's dedicated daughter revealed that the handwriting was indeed her mother's, however, and that the testimony against her father had been perjured. Jenkins's attorney had conducted a prior investigation also showing Jenkins's innocence. In a macabre twist of fate, the attorney shot himself in the head while presenting a simulation of Mrs. Jenkins's suicide. In 1940 a motion for a new trial was granted. The prosecutor informed the court that a mistake had been made, and Jenkins was released after nine years in prison.

JENNINGS, JASPER *(white). 1906. Oregon.* Jennings, convicted of first-degree murder for killing his father, was sentenced to death. The state supreme court reversed the conviction because of improper testimony by a prosecution witness. On motion at retrial, the charges were dismissed because Jennings's sister had told others that she had committed the crime.

JENT, WILLIAM RILEY, *and* EARNEST *(a.k.a.* ERNEST) LEE MILLER *(both white). 1980. Florida.* Jent and Miller, half-brothers, were convicted of rape and first-degree murder and were sentenced to death (despite a jury recommendation of a life term in prison for Miller). The convictions, based largely on testimony from three alleged eyewitnesses, were affirmed by the Florida Supreme Court on appeals in 1981–82. In 1983 the brothers came within 16 hours of execution before they received a stay from a federal judge. In 1986 the identity of the victim was finally established, and suspicion was cast on her boy friend (by then suspected of murdering another girl friend in Georgia in a similar manner). Also, re-examination of the autopsy report uncovered errors: The crime as described by the three eyewitnesses had never taken place. Furthermore, when the actual time of the murder was established, it turned out that Jent and Miller had an airtight alibi. In 1987 a federal district court ordered a new trial because of prosecutorial suppression of exculpatory evidence, and in 1988 the brothers were freed immediately after they agreed to plead guilty to second-degree murder. They repudiated their pleas as soon as they left the court room. In 1991, victims of incompetent police investigation and corruption of witnesses, they were awarded $65,000 in compensation by the Pasco County (Florida) Sheriff's Department.

JOHNSON, COOPER, *and* BENNIE YOUNG *(both black). 1922. Texas.* Johnson and Young were convicted on three counts of murder; Johnson was sentenced to death and Young to life imprisonment. Circumstantial evidence against them was weak and inconclusive, but both defendants originally confessed out of fear of lynching. At trial each recanted his confession, but to no avail. In 1923 another man confessed to the murders, as well as to others. He was convicted of several of them and was hanged. By then Johnson, still waiting for a death warrant, had died of natural causes. In 1934 Governor Miriam Ferguson granted a pardon to Young after being informed by the trial judge and prosecuting attorney that they did "not believe he was guilty."

JOHNSON, EMMA JO *(white). 1951. Nevada.* Johnson was convicted of second-degree murder and sentenced to 10–12 years. After Johnson quarreled with her landlady, the latter died from a blood clot. In 1954 a physician who had examined the victim the day before her death testified that the quarrel had nothing to do with the death; the victim had been suffering from the blood clot for some time. "There had been no crime." Johnson was imprisoned for 33 months before being pardoned and released.

JOHNSON, JOHN *(white). 1911. Wisconsin.* Johnson was convicted of murder and sentenced to life imprisonment. A former mental patient, Johnson feared being lynched, and he confessed when he was told that a mob was about to break into his cell. A former judge was convinced of Johnson's innocence, however, and continued to pursue the case. Governor John Blaine commuted Johnson's sentence, and in 1922 Johnson was released after the victim's father was shown to have committed the crime. "There was no reason at all to connect Johnson with the crime; but the need for a scapegoat seemed to furnish the necessary motive for pinning the crime upon the poor fellow."

JOHNSON, JOSEPH, JR. (black). 1961. Maryland. See GILES, JAMES.

JOHNSON, LAWYER (black). 1971. Massachusetts. Johnson was convicted of first-degree murder and sentenced to death. In 1974 the conviction was reversed on appeal to the state supreme court because of improper limits placed on Johnson's opportunity to cross-examine witnesses. Retried, he was reconvicted of second-degree murder and sentenced to life imprisonment. On initial appeal the reconviction was affirmed. Both juries that convicted Johnson were all-white; the murder victim was also white. In 1982 Johnson was awarded another new trial when a previously silent eyewitness came forward and identified the real killer as the man who had testified against Johnson in the first two trials. Johnson was released after the district attorney decided not to retry the case. In 1983 a bill was filed in the state legislature to obtain compensation for Johnson; it initially passed in both houses, but proponents of the bill failed to secure its final enactment before the end of the year.

JOHNSON, WILL (black). 1905. Alabama. See GARNER, VANCE.

JONES, HARLLEL B. (black). 1972. Ohio. Jones was convicted of second-degree murder and sentenced to life imprisonment. A leader of a black nationalist organization, Jones was charged with ordering random shootings in retaliation for the shooting of a member of his organization by a security guard. The chief witness against Jones, a co-defendant (the admitted triggerman) who had turned FBI informant, had first-degree murder charges against him dismissed in exchange for testifying against Jones. But two others who were present said Jones had nothing to do with the crime, and another co-defendant's written version of the homicide failed to mention any involvement by Jones. This written statement and the prosecutor's agreement to drop charges against the chief witness were withheld from the defense. In 1977, after Jones had spent five years in prison, his petition for habeas corpus relief was granted on the basis of the State's suppression of exculpatory evidence, and he was released on bail to await a new trial. Efforts by the State to return Jones to prison prior to retrial were unsuccessful. In 1978 all charges against him were dropped. In 1979 Jones filed a $4.2 million damage suit against 11 defendants, but it was dismissed because the statute of limitations had expired.

JONES, TOM *(white)*. *1936*. *Kentucky*. Jones was convicted of murder for killing his wife and was sentenced to death. The conviction was affirmed, but after further appeal to the federal district court, a stay was granted—only five hours before the scheduled execution. Petitions for executive clemency had been signed by more than two thousand citizens, including the original jurors. The conviction was reversed on further appeal after investigation by the Kentucky attorney general led him to state that he was "strongly inclined to the view that Tom Jones was convicted on perjured testimony." The defense contended that the gun was discharged in a scuffle for its possession when the wife threatened suicide. The indictment against Jones was then dismissed.

JORDAN, THEODORE V. *(black)*. *1932*. *Oregon*. Jordan was convicted of first-degree murder and sentenced to death. The state supreme court affirmed the conviction on appeal. From the start Jordan contended that his confession (the only evidence against him) was coerced. After public outcry arose, a special gubernatorial commission was appointed to re-investigate the case. In 1934 Governor Julius Meier commuted the sentence to life, on the recommendation of the commission, and in 1954 Jordan was paroled. In 1963 he was picked up as a parole violator after leaving the State without the consent of the parole board, and this led to further investigation of the homicide. In 1964 the murder conviction was set aside, and the prosecution dropped the indictment.

JORDAN, WILLIAM *(white)*. *1934*. *Alabama*. Jordan was convicted of second-degree murder and sentenced to 25 years in prison. After the conviction, the police continued their investigation, and another suspect confessed to the killing. Shortly thereafter, the state supreme court reversed Jordan's conviction because his guilt was only "a remote possibility," there was no motive, and all the evidence against him was circumstantial. A month later all charges against Jordan were dropped.

KAMACHO, DANIEL *(Hispanic)*. *1946*. *California*. Kamacho was convicted of first-degree murder and sentenced to life imprisonment. Having been arrested and identified in a police line-up by an eyewitness, Kamacho confessed after admitting that he had been "high" at the time of the murder. Prior to trial, however, he retracted his confession, claiming to remember that he had been in Mexico when the crime was committed. This statement was corroborated by his sister's testimony at the trial, but the jury was not convinced. A public defender volunteered to challenge the conviction, and in 1947, when the alibi was verified by the Mexican authorities, the conviction was set aside and Kamacho was released.

KANIESKI, EDWARD F. *(white)*. *1952*. *Wisconsin*. Kanieski was convicted of first-degree murder and sentenced to life imprisonment. He consistently maintained his innocence, but his petitions for writ of error and for habeas corpus were denied. In 1972, on further appeal, the conviction was reversed, and the state supreme court ordered Kanieski released after he had served nearly 20 years. The court found that the evidence was not sufficient to sustain the conviction and directed that Kanieski was "thus entitled to release from custody and his freedom, without the possibility of a new trial." After Kanieski's claim for compensation was denied, his case became instrumental in changing Wisconsin's criteria for compensating innocent convicts; the requirement for proof of innocence "beyond a reasonable doubt" was dropped in favor of "clear and convincing" evidence of innocence.

KAPATOS, THOMAS *(white)*. *1938. New York.* Kapatos was convicted of second-degree murder and sentenced to 20 years to life imprisonment. He was paroled in 1960 but returned to prison in 1961 when he pleaded guilty to a charge of receiving stolen goods. In 1962 a federal judge overturned the murder conviction on the ground that the prosecutor had prejudiced the case by concealing from the trial court and the defense the exculpatory testimony of an eyewitness. This eyewitness had seen two men, neither of whom was the defendant, running from the scene of the crime. Such testimony, the court wrote, "would have supported a conclusion that someone else had committed the crime."

KASSIM, AHMAD *(white)*. *1958. New York.* Kassim was convicted of first-degree manslaughter and sentenced to 5–10 years in prison. In 1965 the conviction was vacated on the ground that Kassim's confession was involuntary. The defendant was unfamiliar with the English language, and his "supposed admissions . . . actually were the words of the District Attorney." In addition, another person had confessed to the crime. In 1966 a new trial was ordered, the indictment was dismissed, and Kassim was released after having spent seven years in prison. In 1984, for the third time, the New York Legislature passed a bill enabling Kassim to sue the State; this time it was signed by the governor. In 1986 a New York court awarded Kassim $501,653 for loss of civil rights, humiliation, mental anguish, and lost earnings.

KEATON, DAVID R. *(black)*. *1971. Florida.* See FREDERICK, JOHNNY.

KEINE, RONALD B. *(white)*. *1974. New Mexico.* See Chapter 2.

KENDALL, HAMP, *and* JOHN VICKERS *(both white)*. *1906. North Carolina.* Kendall and Vickers were convicted of second-degree murder and sentenced to 30 and 26 years' imprisonment respectively. Their convictions were affirmed on appeal, with the court noting, "There is abundant evidence from which the prisoners might have been convicted of murder in the first degree." In 1917, however, an investigation by

Governor Thomas Bickett concluded that the men had been framed by the actual killers (who had at one point been arrested and acquitted). Kendall and Vickers were both granted unconditional pardons. One of the actual killers had testified against them; in 1922 he had a coffin built for himself, confessed, and then committed suicide.

KIDD, ROBERT LEE *(white). 1960. California.* Kidd was convicted of first-degree murder and sentenced to death. In 1961 the state supreme court reversed the conviction. The murder weapon was allegedly a sword belonging to the victim, but the prosecution had prevented the defense from informing the jury that shortly after the murder the coroner had told reporters that the suspected sword could not have been the murder weapon. In addition, the jury falsely perceived that a three-page document produced by a police witness at trial and described as the defendant's "rap sheet" implied that Kidd had a long series of previous arrests. At retrial, Kidd was acquitted as evidence emerged that the prosecutor had suppressed information that showed the victim was alive several hours after Kidd was alleged to have murdered him. Subsequent investigation revealed that the police had photographic evidence in their files indicating that the murder weapon was a revolver used to beat the victim to death; no evidence connected this weapon to the defendant. In 1974 Kidd filed a $200,000 damage suit against the prosecutor, but the complaint was dismissed.

KIRKES, LEONARD M. *(white). 1951. California.* Kirkes was convicted of second-degree murder and sentenced to five years to life in prison. The state court of appeals reversed the judgment and the order denying a motion for a new trial; the superseding decision of the California Supreme Court also reversed the judgment and order on the grounds of prosecutorial misconduct and faulty instructions by the judge. In 1953, at retrial, evidence revealed that the key eyewitness against Kirkes had a history of hospitalization for mental illness. The judge advised the jury to acquit Kirkes, which it did.

KNOX, J. E. *(black). 1919. Arkansas.* See Chapter 5.

KRAUSE, JULIUS *(white). 1931. Ohio.* Krause was convicted of first-degree murder and sentenced to life imprisonment. In a 1935 deathbed statement, Krause's co-defendant implicated another man as his actual partner. In 1940 Krause escaped from prison and found this man, who was later tried and convicted. Krause voluntarily returned to prison, thinking he would be promptly released. Instead, he was kept in prison until 1951, when he was paroled. Although he was never officially cleared of the crime, "no one doubts his complete innocence."

KUYKENDALL, SCEOLA *(white). 1961. Michigan.* See CLARK, EPHRAIM R.

LABAT, EDGAR, *and* CLIFTON ALTON PORET *(both black). 1953.*

Louisiana. Labat and Poret were convicted of aggravated rape and robbery of the rape victim's companion (both victims were white) and were sentenced to death. The convictions and sentences were affirmed on appeal. In 1957, after many stays of execution, the men were abandoned by their attorneys. In a desperate effort, they smuggled out of death row an appeal for help that was published as an advertisement in the *Los Angeles Times.* A sympathetic reader saw their ad and hired new attorneys, and in 1960 another stay of execution (the ninth) was granted—this one with only three hours to spare. Eventually one of the three original witnesses recanted his testimony, and a second admitted that his testimony, given under police pressure, had been perjured. The testimony by the victim was found to be full of inaccuracies and discrepancies. Alibi witnesses also came forward, and it became evident that one of the defendants had been beaten by the police into confessing. In 1966 the convictions were reversed, and a new trial was ordered. The State's appeal to vacate this order was denied. In 1969 the Louisiana courts, reluctant to admit their errors, sentenced the men to time served—16 years on death row—and released them. "If it were not for the long delays of executions brought about by the oft-damned 'legal loopholes,' these two men would have been executed sixteen years before they were finally released, and their cases closed with nobody giving a hang that they had been unjustly convicted."

LAMBERT, HENRY J. *(white). 1901. Maine.* Lambert was convicted of first-degree murder and sentenced to life imprisonment. The conviction, based on circumstantial evidence in an atmosphere of great public alarm, was affirmed on appeal. The defendant, a French Canadian, could not speak English. The trial judge believed in Lambert's innocence, and after the conviction several citizens continued to demand a re-investigation. In 1923, after Governor Percival Baxter and the Executive Council became convinced that Lambert was innocent, the defendant received a full pardon. He had spent 22 years in prison. After his release, he was driven directly from the prison to be welcomed to freedom by the governor. As Borchard wrote: "[The evidence] demonstrates how the impossible may be transformed into reality when one is blinded by prejudice or a revengeful spirit, as the prosecution and the jury must have been. . . . Reviewing the case impartially, it seems almost incredible that a jury acting on the evidence introduced could have found a verdict of guilty against Lambert."

LAMBLE, HAROLD *(alias* GEORGE BRANDON*) (white). 1920. New Jersey.* Lamble was convicted of murder and sentenced to death. Testimony of an alleged accomplice and Lamble's admission on the witness stand of his previous convictions led to his conviction, which was affirmed on appeal. Lamble consistently asserted his innocence, but he was executed in 1921. After the execution, Governor Edward Edwards refused requests to appoint a special counsel to investigate the case, despite what the *New York Times* called a "rather widespread fear that perhaps" Lamble was innocent. Lamble's attorney was disbarred for mishandling the defense.

LAMSON, DAVID *(white)*. *1933*. *California.* Lamson was convicted of first-degree murder for killing his wife and was sentenced to death. On appeal, the conviction was reversed and a new trial ordered. In his book, *We Who Are About to Die,* Lamson (a graduate of Stanford University and an employee of Stanford University Press) explains that when he went to trial he and his attorneys were confident his innocence would be established. "It never occurred to any of us that anything but an acquittal might result." The conviction was based entirely on circumstantial evidence; no murder weapon, evidence of motive, or confession was introduced at trial. The California Supreme Court concluded in part: "Every statement of the defendant, capable of verification, tends to support his claims. It is true that he may be guilty, but the evidence thereof is no stronger than mere suspicion. It is better that a guilty man escape than to condemn to death one who may be innocent." Lamson spent 13 months on death row in San Quentin. The jury in a second trial was unable to agree on a verdict, as was the jury in a third trial. Shortly thereafter, the judge dismissed all charges on the recommendation of the prosecutor, who claimed that it was impossible to obtain a jury to convict the defendant. Thirty years later a journalist described Lamson as "one of the 20th century's most distinguished victims of a capital error."

LANDANO, V. JAMES *(white)*. *1976*. *New Jersey.* Landano was convicted of felony-murder in the death of a Newark police officer and was sentenced to life in prison. He was implicated by a childhood friend (who participated in the crime) and convicted despite having an alibi and bearing no resemblance to the killer as originally described to the police. The conviction was based on perjury, erroneous eyewitness identification (suborned by pressure from the prosecutor), and suppression of exculpatory evidence. In 1981 the prosecutor informally admitted that he thought Landano's childhood friend was the actual murderer and that witnesses in the case had been coerced. In 1985, other records discovered in the prosecutor's files—which had never been seen by the defense—supported the theory that the childhood friend was the real culprit. In 1987 the federal district court refused to reconsider the case, despite acknowledging there was a "risk" that Landano was innocent. Higher federal courts refused to reverse this decision. In 1989 a federal judge ruled that the prosecution had withheld information, and he ordered Landano released. He spent 13 years in prison. The error was uncovered thanks to the efforts of volunteer investigator James McCloskey and his organization, Centurion Ministries.

LANGLEY, GUS COLIN (white). 1932. North Carolina. See Chapter 10.

LANZILLO, LUIGI (white). 1918. Connecticut. Lanzillo was convicted of second-degree murder and sentenced to life imprisonment. He was implicated when the gun found near the murder scene was identified as his. He declared that his brother, Carmello, had taken it without his knowledge. The brother and two others were also convicted of the crime, and the three of them were sentenced to death and executed in 1918. A confession from the condemned men, written just days before their execution, absolved Lanzillo of any participation in the crime. Not until 10 years later, however, after sustained pleas from concerned citizens (including attorneys for two of the three men executed for the crime), was Lanzillo pardoned and released. (In some news reports, Lanzillo appears under the surname "Longello," but the State Board of Pardons reports no record of a pardon for anyone of that name, and execution records list a Carmello Lanzillo).

LARKMAN, EDWARD (white). 1925. New York. Larkman was convicted of murder and sentenced to death. The conviction, based on erroneous eyewitness identification, was affirmed on appeal. In 1927, only ten hours before the scheduled execution—with Larkman's head already shaved for the electric chair—Governor Alfred Smith commuted the sentence to life imprisonment. In 1929 another convict confessed to the crime, yet it was four more years before Smith's successor, Governor Herbert H. Lehman, unconditionally pardoned Larkman.

LEASTER, BOBBY JOE (black). 1971. Massachusetts. Leaster was convicted of first-degree murder and sentenced to life imprisonment. In 1977 two attorneys, convinced of Leaster's innocence, volunteered to work on the case (a commitment that ultimately resulted in approximately $400,000 worth of volunteered time). In 1986 a Boston constable read about the case and came forward to report that he had seen two men, neither of whom was Leaster, fleeing from the crime scene. The conviction had been based on erroneous eyewitness identification. It was also discovered that the murder weapon had been used in a robbery two weeks after Leaster's arrest. A new trial was ordered, Leaster was released, and the State dismissed charges. He had spent 15 years in prison.

LEE, CHOL SOO (Asian). 1974. California. Lee was convicted of first-degree murder and sentenced to life imprisonment. The case became a cause célèbre for the San Francisco Asian-American community. In 1977, while in prison, Lee was convicted of murdering a fellow inmate and was sentenced to death. In the course of a review of his conviction for the prison murder, it was discovered that his previous conviction was a miscarriage of justice. That conviction was overturned on appeal because of erroneous eyewitness identification and the prosecution's suppression of exculpatory evidence. In 1982, at retrial, Lee was acquitted. In 1983 Lee's conviction for the prison killing was also overturned because of improper jury instructions, and he was released from prison. Later that year he pleaded guilty to the prison homicide in exchange for a sentence of time already served.

LEE, WILBERT, *and* FREDDIE PITTS *(both black). 1963. Florida.* Lee and Pitts were convicted of murder in connection with the deaths of two white men and sentenced to death. No physical evidence linked the defendants to the crime; the convictions were the result of their guilty pleas, testimony of an alleged eyewitness, and incompetent defense counsel. Pitts claimed that his confession had been beaten out of him; both defendants, when interviewed by the FBI, maintained they were innocent. Nonetheless, on appeal the convictions were affirmed. In 1966 another man (already in prison for a crime similar to the one for which Pitts and Lee had been convicted) confessed to being the real killer. In 1968 the eyewitness recanted her accusations, but the prosecution withheld this fact from the defense for four years. At a rehearing in 1969, the court vacated the convictions and ordered a retrial. In 1970, however, the state court of appeals reinstated the convictions and death sentences. In 1971 the Florida attorney general conceded that the State had unlawfully suppressed evidence; the state supreme court ordered a new trial. Lee and Pitts were again convicted and sentenced to death, again before an all-white jury who knew nothing about the other man's confession. On appeal, the reconviction was affirmed. Finally, in 1975, however, Governor Reubin Askew granted Pitts and Lee a full pardon, saying "I am sufficiently convinced that they are innocent." In 1972 their appellate attorney had said that the defendants, "although totally innocent, were convicted because they were black." Their eventual vindication was the result largely of the unrelenting efforts of Gene Miller, a *Miami Herald* reporter.

LEFEVRE, FRANK *(white). 1942. Wisconsin.* LeFevre was convicted of first-degree murder and sentenced to life imprisonment. Alibi testimony and results of lie detector tests (not admitted at trial) supported his claim of innocence. On appeal, the conviction was reversed on the ground that the evidence was insufficient to sustain the conviction, and LeFevre's release was ordered. However, he failed to receive compensation from the State under a standard that required him to establish his innocence "beyond a reasonable doubt." (In 1980 the legislature eased the standard for proving claims against the State to the level of "clear and convincing" evidence; see also the case of Edward Kanieski.)

LESHER, HARVEY *(white). 1928. California.* See GARVEY, MIKE.

LETTRICH, GEORGE *(white). 1950. Illinois.* Lettrich was convicted of killing a 10-year-old girl and sentenced to death. He confessed to the crime after being held incommunicado for 60 hours, but after the trial he repudiated his confession, claiming it had been extorted from him by third-degree methods. In 1952 the state supreme court said, "there [was] not a scintilla of evidence to connect [Lettrich] with that crime except his repudiated confession. . . . That confession does not coincide with many of the known facts and cannot be entirely true." The defense had also been denied the opportunity to inform the jury that another person had confessed to the murder. A new trial was ordered. In 1953 the State's attorney asked the trial court to drop all charges, saying "there is a very grave doubt in my mind about the guilt of the defendant."

LEYRA, CAMILO *(white). 1950. New York.* Leyra was convicted on two counts of first-degree murder (for killing his parents) and sentenced to death. On appeal, the convictions were reversed on the grounds that his confession was coerced and in any case did not really amount to an admission of guilt. Leyra was retried, reconvicted, and resentenced to death. On appeal to the U.S. Supreme Court, the convictions were again reversed, once more because of the questionable confession. A second time Leyra was retried, reconvicted, and resentenced to death. In 1956, finally, the New York Court of Appeals reversed the conviction, stating that other than the dubious confession, "the prosecution has produced not a single trustworthy bit of affirmative, independent evidence connecting defendant with the crime. . . . It may well be that the law enforcement officials, relying too heavily on the 'confessions' . . . , failed to do the essential careful and intensive investigatory work that should be done before a defendant is charged with crime, certainly with one as serious as murder." The court ordered the indictment dismissed and Leyra released. By the time of his release in 1956, Leyra had spent nearly five years on death row. He stated he planned to spend the rest of his life looking for the person who killed his parents.

LINDLEY, WILLIAM MARVIN ("RED") *(white). 1943. California.* See Chapter 1.

LINDSEY, LLOYD *(black). 1975. Illinois.* Lindsey was convicted at age 17 of four counts of murder and sentenced to 40–80 years in prison. The victims, aged 7 to 17, died in a fire. The evidence against Lindsey came principally from two witnesses. One was the victims' 13-year-old brother, who went to officials 35 days after the deaths (which until then had been considered accidental) and said that he had seen Lindsey and two other men rape and kill the victims. The second witness, a boarder at the home, also claimed to have been an eyewitness; his testimony was "pivotal," but his mental retardation was not revealed to the jury. When

Lindsey heard that these witnesses had implicated him to the police, he confessed. In simultaneous trials, the jury for the alleged accomplices acquitted them, while Lindsey's jury (the only one to hear his confession) voted for conviction. In 1979 the Illinois Appellate Court unanimously reversed the conviction and ordered that Lindsey be freed. The court found the confession clearly inconsistent with the physical facts. "The inconsistencies in the testimony [of the two witnesses] were not only contradictory but diluted this evidence to the level of palpable improbability and incredulity. . . ."

LINSCOTT, STEVEN PAUL *(white)*. *1982. Illinois.* Linscott was convicted of murder and sentenced to 40 years' imprisonment. A student at a local Bible college, Linscott had a dream about a neighbor's murder that, he realized, closely paralleled the story of a real murder in the vicinity. Thinking his dream might provide some clues to help the police solve the real crime, he reported it to them. Despite no evidence connecting Linscott to the crime, the police theorized he must have been the murderer, and he was charged. In 1985 the conviction was reversed by the Illinois Appellate Court because of the insufficiency of evidence. That decision, however, was reversed by the Illinois Supreme Court, and the case was remanded to the Appellate Court for further proceedings. In 1987, again ruling in the case, that court reversed the conviction because of "outright fabrications" by the prosecution, which had "simply made up" evidence that connected Linscott to the crime.

LOBAUGH, RALPH W. *(white)*. *1947. Indiana.* Lobaugh was convicted on three counts of rape and murder and sentenced to death. He had voluntarily confessed to the crimes and pleaded guilty, and an eyewitness implicated him at the trial. By 1950 another man had been convicted of one of the crimes, and a third man, Franklin Click, had confessed to the other two crimes and been executed for them. In 1951, following a State investigation, Lobaugh's sentence was commuted to life by Governor Henry Schricker, who stated that Lobaugh was "a degenerate and a homosexual, not a fit person to be free on the streets of any city, but not guilty of killing any of these three women." Lobaugh was immediately transferred to a mental hospital. In 1975 Governor Otis Bowen ordered an investigation that resulted in Lobaugh's release on parole in 1977. He had been confined for 30 years, 28 of them after the State's investigation had proven him innocent. After two months of freedom, Lobaugh voluntarily returned to prison, telling officials that he could not relax on the outside.

LONG, ELI J. *(white)*. *1918. Wisconsin.* Long was convicted of murder and sentenced to life imprisonment. In 1920 he was released by court action on the basis of newly discovered evidence. Efforts to obtain compensation from the State failed. In 1927 the Wisconsin Legislature passed a bill awarding Long $2,750 "for his wrongful imprisonment . . . for a crime of which he was innocent," but the bill was vetoed by Governor Fred Zimmerman because Long "was required not only to have been convicted of an offense of which he was not guilty, but he must have served his term" before being entitled to compensation.

LUCAS, JESSE, and MARGARET LUCAS *(both white). 1909. Illinois.* Both defendants (son and mother) were convicted of first-degree murder and sentenced to life imprisonment (after the jury failed by one vote to impose a death sentence on Jesse). The trial court granted Margaret's motion for a new trial; charges against her were then dropped. Jesse's conviction was affirmed on appeal. He continued to maintain his innocence, rejecting advice that he would be paroled if he admitted guilt. In 1931 the actual killer made a deathbed confession, and after further investigation a key witness at the original trial admitted that her testimony had been perjured because her life had been threatened. The only other witness against Lucas had been a prison inmate, who had perjured himself as a means of reducing his sentence for an unrelated crime. Lucas was released after having served 23 years.

LUCAS, MARGARET *(white). 1909. Illinois.* See LUCAS, JESSE.

LUDKOWITZ, MAX. *1934. New York. (white).* Ludkowitz was convicted of murder and sentenced to death. The only evidence against him was the uncorroborated dying declaration of the victim. In 1935 the conviction was reversed by the New York Court of Appeals. "There was no testimony on the part of any eyewitness directly or indirectly connecting appellant with the crime or which indicated that he was in the vicinity of the [murder scene] on the evening in question. . . . Under such circumstances to permit a conviction to stand would shock one's sense of justice." At retrial, Ludkowitz was acquitted.

LYONS, ERNEST *(black). 1909. Virginia.* Lyons was convicted of second-degree murder and sentenced to 18 years' imprisonment. The conviction was based on circumstantial evidence. Lyons was released in 1912 after a friend, convinced of Lyons's innocence, located the supposed victim—alive and well in North Carolina. Governor William Hodges Mann promptly granted Lyons a pardon.

MACFARLAND, ALLISON M. *(white). 1912. New Jersey.* MacFarland was convicted of first-degree murder for killing his wife and sentenced to death. Four months later the conviction was reversed because the State, in an attempt to establish a motive, had improperly used correspondence between MacFarland and another woman. At retrial the other woman admitted writing the letters, but sustained MacFarland's contention that he had merely wished to divorce his wife. In addition, it was shown that the poison taken by Mrs. MacFarland had been kept in a medicine cabinet next to her sleeping pills, and that she easily could have taken the poison by mistake. MacFarland was acquitted.

MACGREGOR, ROBERT *(white)*. *1912. Michigan.* MacGregor, a physician, was convicted of murder and sentenced to life imprisonment. The conviction, based entirely on circumstantial evidence, was affirmed on appeal. In 1916, after a thorough review of the case by Governor Woodbridge Ferris, MacGregor was granted a full pardon. Governor Ferris stated: "I am firmly convinced that Dr. MacGregor is absolutely innocent of the crime for which he was convicted. I am satisfied that in sending him to prison, the State of Michigan has made a terrible mistake."

MAJCZEK, JOSEPH, *and* THEODORE MARCINKIEWICZ *(a.k.a.* TED MARCIN) *(both white). 1933. Illinois.* Majczek and Marcinkiewicz were both convicted of first-degree murder and sentenced to life imprisonment. The convictions were affirmed on appeal. In 1944 Majczek's mother convinced the *Chicago Times* to re-investigate the case. They found that testimony perjured with the collusion of the police had secured the conviction. In 1945 Majczek received an unconditional gubernatorial pardon, and was released after having served nearly 12 years. The next year he was awarded $24,000 by the state legislature. In 1949 Marcinkiewicz refused an effort by the governor to commute his sentence to 75 years, which would have made him eligible for parole in 1958 (this was the first time an Illinois prisoner had ever refused a gubernatorial commutation). He was freed on a writ of habeas corpus by a Cook County judge in 1950, five years after Majczek's pardon. In 1965 Marcinkiewicz was awarded $35,000 by the state legislature for his wrongful conviction. (In 1948 the story was made into the movie *Call Northside 777,* starring James Stewart.)

MALLOY, EVERETT BAILY *(white). 1984. Texas.* Malloy was convicted of murder and sentenced to 15 years' imprisonment. He was released two months later when an anonymous tip led police to a woman who had witnessed the murder. Her information led to the filing of charges against the real killer and freedom for Malloy. The conviction had been based on erroneous eyewitness identification by four people.

MANSELL, ALVIN *(black). 1925. North Carolina.* Mansell was convicted of the rape of a white woman and was sentenced to death. Before trial, Mansell was saved from a lynch mob (15 members of this mob were later convicted for their actions). Although defense counsel was not appointed until the day before Mansell's trial, a request for postponement to allow time to study the case was denied. The conviction was affirmed on appeal, but Mansell's attorneys continued to investigate the case. They discovered that the victim's initial descriptions of her assailant were contradictory and did not match the defendant, that two physicians who had examined the victim on the day of the attack "believed it impossible that Mansel [*sic*] had assaulted her," and that Mansell could not have been at the scene of the crime. A petition signed by four thousand citizens supported clemency. In 1926 Governor Angus McLean commuted the sentence to life imprisonment, and in 1930 Governor O. Max Gardner ordered Mansell freed, declaring that he was "absolutely convinced" that the mentally retarded defendant was innocent.

MARCINKIEWICZ, THEODORE *(white). 1933. Illinois.* See MAJCZEK, JOSEPH.

MARINO, TONY *(white). 1925. Illinois.* Marino was convicted of murder and sentenced to life imprisonment. He could not speak or read English, was unrepresented by counsel at trial, and steadfastly maintained his innocence. Nevertheless, the trial record falsely showed that he had signed a guilty plea. One of the two interpreters appointed to assist him at the trial was the arresting police officer. In 1947, after Marino had been imprisoned for 22 years (during which time he learned English), he wrote a letter to the U.S. Supreme Court, and certiorari was granted. The Court ordered his release because of the deprivation of due process. The Illinois attorney general confessed to having made an error and consented to a reversal of the judgment.

MARSH, GUY GORDON *(white). 1973. Maryland.* Marsh was convicted of first-degree murder and sentenced to life imprisonment. The conviction rested on the testimony of a jail-house informant and a witness who claimed she saw Marsh fleeing from the scene of the crime. In 1985 a woman who had fallen in love with Marsh hired an attorney to re-investigate the case. Two years later, with the support of the prosecutor, Marsh was released from prison when the witness admitted that she had perjured herself; a newspaper investigation revealed that she had been in jail on a shoplifting charge when the robbery-murder occurred, and that she had testified against Marsh only because a police detective beat her and suborned her perjury (the witness was subsequently convicted of perjury). The jail-house informant also recanted his testimony, saying that it was the result of coercion by the police detective. After Marsh's release, charges were not immediately dropped because yet another inmate claimed to have heard Marsh confess to the murders. This inmate was released (apparently because of a clerical error) and allegedly murdered three people. All charges against Marsh were then dropped.

MARTIN, JOHN *(black). 1919. Arkansas.* See Chapter 5.

MATERA, PIETRO *(white). 1931. New York.* Matera was convicted of first-degree murder and sentenced to death. On appeal, the conviction was affirmed. In 1932 Matera's sentence was commuted to life by Governor Franklin D. Roosevelt. The real culprit's wife confessed on her deathbed in 1960 that she had "fingered Matera to save her husband." After having served 30 years in prison, Matera was released.

MAYNARD, WILLIAM A. ("TONY") *(black). 1971. New York.* After a hung jury and a mistrial, Maynard, who had a history of black militancy, was convicted of first-degree manslaughter for a 1967 killing and was sentenced to a term of 10–20 years. In 1972 the appellate division upheld the conviction, but in 1974 the state supreme court—on the request of the district attorney—dismissed all charges against Maynard and ordered his release because the prosecution had suppressed evidence of the unreliability of its chief witness. This witness had both a long history of psychiatric hospitalizations and a criminal record, facts the prosecutors had failed to reveal. Maynard had spent six and a half years in prison by the time he was released. His attorney described it as a "great wrong done to an innocent man."

MAYS, MAURICE F. *(black). 1919. Tennessee.* Mays was convicted of murder in the killing of a white woman and was sentenced to death. A white lynch mob terrorized the entire black community in Knoxville; several blacks were killed by white rioters; the National Guard had to be called out. Mays's conviction rested on the testimony of a police officer who had disliked him for years and on the testimony of an eyewitness who never got a clear look at the killer. On appeal, the conviction was reversed because the judge, rather than the jury, had fixed the penalty at death. Mays was retried, reconvicted, and resentenced to death, and this conviction and sentence were affirmed on appeal. In 1922 Mays was executed, still maintaining his innocence. In 1926 the real killer confessed in a written statement that revealed she was a white woman who had dressed up as a black man to kill the woman with whom her husband was having an affair. The authorities, however, never accepted this confession, no doubt because they had already executed Mays for the crime. Accepting the confession would have meant admitting an erroneous execution. Mays had been previously convicted in 1903 for killing a black man, but was pardoned for that crime.

MCDONALD, WILBUR *(white). 1971. Illinois.* McDonald was convicted of murder and sentenced to a prison term of 100–150 years. The conviction was based on misleading circumstantial evidence. In 1973 he was released from prison when another man confessed to the killing after having been arrested for a similar murder. In 1974 McDonald was granted a full pardon.

MCGEE, WILLIE *(black). 1945. Mississippi.* McGee was convicted of the rape of a white woman and was sentenced to death by a white jury that deliberated for only two and a half minutes. The conviction was reversed on appeal because a request to change venue had not been granted. After a change of venue McGee was retried, reconvicted, and resentenced to death by another all-white jury (this time deliberation lasted 11 minutes). The second conviction was reversed because of the exclusion of blacks from juries in the indicting county. In 1948 McGee was re-indicted, retried, reconvicted, and again resentenced to death; three blacks were on the jury, but there was no change of venue. On appeal the conviction was affirmed, and the U.S. Supreme Court declined to intervene. The chief evidence against McGee was a coerced confession that he had given while being held incommunicado for 32 days after his arrest. Furthermore, the victim's husband and her two children, asleep in the next room, never heard any commotion from the alleged attack. Investigation by journalist Carl Rowan revealed that the victim had been consorting with McGee for four years and was angry at his efforts to terminate their relationship. Local blacks were too intimidated to give this evidence in court, and local whites felt the woman's consent was impossible or irrelevant. An attempt to win a retrial on the basis of newly discovered evidence failed, and McGee was executed in 1951.

MCINTOSH, WALTER *(black). 1980. Georgia.* McIntosh was convicted of a double murder and sentenced to confinement for life in a mental hospital. At first he denied any knowledge of the crimes; then he confessed and pleaded guilty but insane. The county sheriff was convinced of McIntosh's innocence. The defendant's niece had been a suspect in the case and in 1982 was indicted for the crimes, but the State did not proceed because of insufficient evidence. In 1984 the niece and a friend both confessed their guilt and were convicted of manslaughter. McIntosh, however, had already died in confinement.

MCKENZIE, JOHN *(black). 1948. New Jersey.* See COOPER, RALPH.

MCKINNEY, CLARENCE LEROY *(white). 1922. Ohio.* McKinney was convicted of first-degree murder and sentenced to life imprisonment. McKinney had a previous criminal record; his conviction was obtained by circumstantial evidence and mistaken eyewitness identification. While an appeal was pending, two other men confessed to the murder, and they were indicted and convicted. In 1923 McKinney was awarded a new trial by an appellate court judge. The indictment was dismissed, and he was released after having served five months in prison.

MCLAUGHLIN, ROBERT *(white). 1981. New York.* See Chapter 11.

MCMULLEN, EDWARD A. *(white). 1956. Ohio.* McMullen was convicted of first-degree murder in the course of a robbery and sentenced to life imprisonment. In 1963 McMullen's attorney learned that the police had suppressed evidence showing that the gun used in the killing had been used in a prior burglary committed by three other men. The ballistic evidence available to the prosecution showed that the defendant's gun was not the murder weapon. In 1965 McMullen's conviction was overturned, and at retrial he was acquitted.

MERRITT, GEORGE *(black). 1968. New Jersey.* Merritt was convicted of first-degree murder and sentenced to life imprisonment for killing a white police office during a "race riot." Merritt was one of a dozen persons charged for this crime. The case against Merritt rested solely on the testimony of one witness. The prosecutor had failed to disclose a report of a pretrial police interview with this witness that was completely at variance with the testimony given at trial. The appellate division reversed, and the state supreme court affirmed the reversal. At retrial in 1974, Merritt was again convicted and sentenced to life imprisonment. On appeal in 1976, this conviction was also reversed. In 1977 he was again retried and reconvicted. In 1980, on habeas corpus petition to the federal courts, the third conviction was reversed. After 10 years in prison, Merritt was freed. When he was released, his attorney asked, "What would the proponents of the death penalty have to say if Merritt had been executed before the discovery of the concealed document?"

MILLER, EARNEST LEE *(white). 1980. Florida.* See JENT, WILLIAM RILEY.

MILLER, LLOYD ELDON, JR. *(white). 1956. Illinois.* See Chapter 7.

MONTGOMERY, OLEN, CLARENCE NORRIS, HAYWOOD PATTERSON, OZIE POWELL, WILLIE ROBERSON, CHARLIE WEEMS, EUGENE WILLIAMS, ANDREW WRIGHT, *and* LEROY ("ROY") WRIGHT *(the "Scottsboro Boys") (all black). 1931. Alabama.* See Chapter 5.

MOONEY, THOMAS J. *(white). 1916. California.* See Chapter 4.

MOORE, FRANK *(black). 1919. Arkansas.* See Chapter 5.

MORALES, SANTIAGO VENTURA *(Hispanic). 1986. Oregon.* Morales was convicted of murdering a fellow migrant worker; he was sentenced to life in prison. Immediately after sentencing, two of the trial jurors—convinced they had made a terrible error—started work to reopen the case. The conviction of Morales, 17, was based largely on eyewitness testimony, later recanted and explained as caused by the witness's fear of what would happen to him if he did not testify as the prosecutor wanted. Investigation also uncovered evidence that another migrant worker, after returning to Mexico, had confessed to a shaman (medicine man) that he, not Morales, had killed the victim. This confession was confirmed by the man's aunt. In 1991 a circuit judge ordered Morales freed, citing grave defects in the conduct of the defense. When Governor Neil Goldschmidt offered to issue a conditional pardon to block the district attorney from appealing the release order, the state attorney general agreed not to contest the judge's ruling. Four months later, on recommendation on the district attorney, the trial judge dismissed all charges.

MORELLO, RAFFAELO E. *(white). 1918. New Jersey.* Morello was convicted of the murder of his wife and was sentenced to life in prison. A native Italian, he had admitted through an interpreter at the coroner's inquest that he was "responsible" for her death. No appeal was undertaken. In 1926 he was pardoned after he had learned enough English to explain that his wife had committed suicide after he told her he had been drafted into the army. Investigation by welfare workers cleared his name; he was freed after having served eight years. "A fatally wrong meaning was given to his testimony through misunderstandings of the interpreter."

MORRIS, GORDON *(white). 1953. Texas.* Morris was convicted of murder and sentenced to death. All in one day, the jury was selected, the trial conducted, the jury verdict announced, and the sentence imposed. Subsequent investigation by the victim's brother demonstrated that Morris was physically incapable of committing the crime, and that the conviction had been obtained by mistaken eyewitness testimony. In 1955, three days before the scheduled execution, Morris's sentence was commuted to life. The foreman of the jury, sought out by news reporter Don Reid, re-investigated the case and located all other members of the jury; together they urged a pardon. In 1976 the Board of Pardons and Paroles responded by granting Morris parole.

MURCHISON, JOHN *(black). 1920. Alabama.* See CRUTCHER, WILLIE.

NORRIS, CLARENCE *(black). 1931. Alabama.* See Chapter 5.

NORWOOD, ALBERT E. *(black). 1983. Missouri.* Norwood was convicted of second-degree felony-murder in the killing of a police officer and was sentenced to probation. Prior to sentencing the prosecutor sought to have the conviction reversed and the murder charge dropped on the ground of newly discovered evidence. The indictment had alleged that, because Norwood had possessed marijuana, he was criminally liable for the death of a policeman killed in a shoot-out while he was delivering a search warrant. Norwood argued that he was uninvolved in the shooting, had no knowledge of the drugs discovered in the house, and therefore was not liable for the officer's death. The prosecutor agreed and dropped the murder charge after the jury's guilty verdict (but before sentencing). The judge refused to accept the prosecutor's motion, however, and stated his intention to sentence Norwood for the murder. Without addressing the substantive issues in the case, the state supreme court refused to intervene, arguing that the judge's refusal was within the trial court's discretion.

OLSON, HENRY *(white)*. *1927*. *Illinois*. Olson was convicted of murder and sentenced to life imprisonment after a previous trial had ended in a hung jury. Released on bond pending decision on a motion for a third trial, Olson vanished, but his attorney continued to work on the case. Later, two youths confessed to the crime and were tried and convicted. Olson was eventually located, returned, and acquitted in his third trial; mistaken eyewitness testimony had been the basis for the conviction. All three trials occurred within a six-month period.

OWENS, AARON LEE *(black)*. *1973*. *California*. Owens was convicted on two counts of first-degree murder and sentenced to life imprisonment. In 1980, following a denial of parole for Owens, the original prosecutor (by then in private practice) talked with him and decided to re-investigate the case. His investigation determined that another man, who resembled Owens, was guilty of the crime. In 1981 Owens was released when the State admitted its case was based on erroneous eyewitness identification. Owens had served nine years in prison.

PADGETT, EUGENE *(white)*. *1940*. *Texas*. Padgett was convicted of murder after a guilty plea and sentenced to 99 years' imprisonment. He confessed to the crime while in prison serving a 20-year burglary sentence. He appealed the murder conviction, saying he had confessed to the crime because he thought his trial for murder would necessitate his being held in a small town jail, from which escape would be easy. The appeal was not heard until the burglary sentence was completely served, however, and it was 1955 before the state court of appeals finally freed Padgett.

PADGETT, WILLIAM H. *(white)*. *1936*. *Michigan*. Padgett was convicted of first-degree murder in the death of a policeman and was sentenced to life in prison. Six years later, the conviction was overturned. Padgett was retried, reconvicted, and resentenced to life. In 1949, after 14 years in prison, Padgett was given a "truth serum" injection; on the basis in part of the results from this test and in part on other evidence, the parole board released him with a full pardon. The conviction, it turned out, had been based on mistaken eyewitness testimony by two people.

PARKS, EDWARD H. *(white)*. *1952*. *Pennsylvania*. See ANTONIE-WICZ, JOSEPH.

PARKER, GEORGE *(white)*. *1980*. *New Jersey*. Parker was convicted of aggravated manslaughter and sentenced to 20 years in prison. The chief evidence against him came from two eyewitnesses, one of whom was later indicted and convicted of the murder, and both of whom were subsequently convicted of perjuring themselves at Parker's trial. Parker at first confessed to the crime, but later claimed that he had done so because he was in love with the woman who had actually committed it. On appeal the appellate court affirmed the conviction, and the New Jersey Supreme

Court denied review. In 1986, after the convictions of the two women, Parker was awarded a new trial. The appellate court found that "the State essentially conceded that Parker's confession . . . was false," and that the newly discovered evidence "is the State's camouflaged concession that defendant was convicted on the basis of perjured and false testimony." It concluded that "in light of the subsequent convictions [of the two women], the prosecution's case against Parker has been wholly discredited."

PARROTT, LEMUEL, *and* SAM THOMPSON *(both white). 1947. North Carolina.* Parrott was convicted of first-degree murder and sentenced to death; Thompson was convicted of second-degree murder and sentenced to 30 years' imprisonment. Parrott's appeal was denied. The convictions were based on Thompson's confession and his implication of Parrott. Thompson later retracted this testimony and claimed that both he and Parrott had been several hundred miles from the scene of the crime. This claim was corroborated by an investigation conducted by the state bureau of investigation. A retrial for Parrott was ordered, and he was acquitted. Despite the new evidence, however, Thompson's conviction was permitted to stand. A charge of perjury against Thompson for his false testimony was filed but later dropped, because he had spent so much time in prison. In 1959 he was finally paroled.

PATTERSON, HAYWOOD *(black). 1931. Alabama.* See Chapter 5.

PECHO, WALTER A. *(white). 1954. Michigan.* Pecho was convicted of second-degree murder in the killing of his wife and was sentenced to 15–20 years in prison. When Pecho's attorney learned that the prosecution had concealed fingerprint evidence showing that the death was actually a suicide, he filed a motion for a new trial, but it was denied. Further investigation led to another motion for a new trial on the ground of newly discovered evidence; again the motion was denied. In 1960, after the parole board had conducted its own inquiry, Governor G. Mennen Williams granted an unconditional pardon, saying, "This is a case of miscarriage of justice. . . . An innocent man was convicted."

PEEK, ANTHONY RAY *(black). 1978. Florida.* Peek was convicted of first-degree murder and sentenced to death. The only evidence directly linking Peek with the crime was his fingerprints, found on the victim's car. The conviction came despite Peek's claim that he had discovered the abandoned car the day after the crime and had opened its door to look inside, and despite witnesses who supported his alibi testimony that at the time of the murder he was asleep at a nearby halfway house where he lived. On appeal, the conviction was affirmed by the state supreme court. In 1983 the trial judge granted a new trial because an expert's testimony concerning hair identification evidence was shown to have been false. At retrial (during which the judge referred to Peek's family as "niggers") in

1984, Peek was again convicted and sentenced to death. On appeal, the state supreme court again ordered a new trial, this time because evidence that Peek had been convicted of an unrelated rape was inappropriately introduced at his second trial. In 1987, at his third trial, Peek was acquitted.

PENDER, JOHN *(white). 1914. Oregon.* After one hung jury, Pender was convicted on two counts of first-degree murder and sentenced to death. Nine months later, after an outcry of public sympathy, the sentence was commuted to life by Governor Oswald West. In 1920, after a mental patient confessed to the crime and both trial judges appealed for clemency, Pender was pardoned by Governor Ben Olcott.

PERSICO, CHARLES F. *(white). 1981. California.* With charges of murder and the possibility of a life sentence pending, Persico (who had a criminal record and a history of drug abuse) entered a plea of guilty to manslaughter, saying that he did not want to take the chance of being convicted of murder. In 1984 he was paroled. In 1987 a Los Angeles police officer, William E. Leisure, was charged with murder for the same crime; in 1991 he was convicted for it, after pleading "no contest" to second-degree murder. The assistant chief of police and the district attorney admitted that their investigation proved that Persico was completely innocent. In 1987 Persico filed a $62 million suit in federal court against (among others) the city of Los Angeles and several police officials for his erroneous conviction.

PETERSON, WINFRED J. *(black). 1982. South Carolina.* See JAMES, TYRONE.

PETREE, JOHN WILSON *(white). 1981. Utah.* Petree was convicted of second-degree murder and sentenced to five years to life. At the time of the crime, both Petree and the victim were 15 years old. On appeal, the conviction was reversed for insufficiency of evidence, and the defendant was ordered released from custody. The court found that there was "no other evidence of admissions [by Petree], no physical evidence, and no motive for the homicide." Petree spent a year and a half in prison before being freed.

PFEFFER, PAUL *(white). 1954. New York.* Pfeffer was convicted of second-degree murder and sentenced to 20 years to life. At his trial Pfeffer claimed that his confession had been obtained by coercion. On the day of his conviction another man, John Roche, was arrested in connection with other killings and confessed to the murder for which Pfeffer had been tried. On the basis of this confession, and after passing a series of lie detector tests, Pfeffer was granted a new trial. One newspaper observed at the time, "The Pfeffer-Roche case dramatically illustrated to New York the built-in danger of its capital punishment law: the ever-present possibility of executing an innocent man." (Roche was never tried for this crime. For the other killings, he was tried, convicted, and executed in 1956.) Pfeffer was re-indicted for first-degree manslaughter. In 1955, while trial on that charge was pending, he was indicted and tried in a completely different case, convicted of second-degree murder, and sentenced to 20 years to life. A month later, the manslaughter charge in the first case was dropped.

PHILLIPS, RICHARD *(black)*. *1900*. *Virginia*. Phillips was convicted of first-degree murder and sentenced to death. The only witness against Phillips was Grant Watts, who was acquitted on the same charge a week after Phillips's conviction. Phillips's attorney had been appointed only two hours before the trial. In 1901 a special jury found Phillips insane; he was transferred to a mental hospital, and the execution was postponed pending his recovery. His attorney then learned that Watts was indeed the murderer. He also learned that the fatal shot could not have been fired from Phillips's weapon, something he had been unable to demonstrate in court because he had lacked the time to investigate the case before trial. Thinking Phillips was hopelessly insane, the attorney made no effort to correct the record. In 1930 Phillips's sister got in touch with the attorney (by this time a state attorney), and he informed the governor of these facts. He added: "I am morally certain this man was convicted of a crime he did not commit, and if anyone was ever entitled to clemency, or rather justice, he is." A month later Governor John Pollard granted a pardon, and Phillips was released.

PITTS, FREDDIE *(black)*. *1963*. *Florida*. See LEE, WILBERT.

PORET, CLIFTON ALTON *(black)*. *1953*. *Louisiana*. See LABAT, EDGAR.

POWELL, HOYT *(white)*. *1973*. *Georgia*. See Chapter 7.

POWELL, OZIE *(black)*. *1931*. *Alabama*. See Chapter 5.

PREVOST, LLOYD *(white)*. *1919*. *Michigan*. Prevost was convicted of first-degree murder and sentenced to life. The conviction was affirmed on appeal. In 1930, because of Prevost's exceptional prison record, the State Pardon Board re-opened the case and concluded he was innocent and the conviction had been obtained by unscrupulous prosecution methods, perjury, and mistaken expert ballistics testimony. The board recommended a pardon, and that year it was granted. "Prevost's refusal to talk before trial . . . certainly did not help him. . . . On the whole, the case may be deemed to show that the supposed privilege against self-incrimination is of but little if any help to an innocent man."

PUGH, HEYWOOD *(black)*. *1936*. *Illinois*. See FOWLER, WALTER.

PYLE, HARRY *(white)*. *1935*. *Kansas*. Pyle was convicted of first-degree murder and robbery and was sentenced to life. The conviction was affirmed on appeal. Pyle claimed the conviction was based on perjured testimony coerced from witnesses by the State and on the State's suppression of exculpatory evidence. In 1941 a letter to Pyle from the prosecuting attorney, submitted in Pyle's application for habeas corpus, stated, "Your conviction was a grave mistake." A letter from a witness admitting perjury was also enclosed. The appeal was nevertheless denied. After the trial of another man for complicity in the same crimes, in which evidence was produced that contradicted the evidence used in Pyle's trial, the U.S. Supreme Court ruled that the new evidence "clearly exonerates petitioner," and Pyle was released.

RAMOS, JUAN F. *(Hispanic). 1983. Florida.* Ramos was convicted of first-degree murder and sentenced to death, although the jury had recommended a sentence of life imprisonment. The victim, who lived near where Ramos worked, had been raped and died of multiple stab wounds. Ramos was convicted largely because the police had no other suspect, a neighbor contradicted Ramos's alibi, and his clothing was picked out in a line-up by dog scent discrimination. No physical evidence linked Ramos to the victim or to the scene of the crime. In 1987 the Florida Supreme Court vacated the conviction and ordered a new trial because of improperly used evidence. At retrial in 1987, Ramos was acquitted.

REICHHOFF, KENNY RAY *(white). 1975. Wisconsin.* Reichhoff was convicted on two counts of first-degree murder and sentenced to life imprisonment. In 1977 an investigation by *Wisconsin State Journal* reporter Richard Jeager raised many doubts and revealed major discrepancies in the prosecutor's case. On appeal, the conviction was overturned on the technical ground that the judge erred in allowing the jury to infer that the defendant's silence at the time of his arrest was a tacit admission of guilt. Later in 1977 Reichhoff was acquitted at retrial; after nearly three years in prison he was released. The fight to prove his innocence cost Reichhoff tens of thousands of dollars. In 1980 attempts to pass a special bill in the state legislature to compensate him for these costs and lost income failed.

REILLY, PETER A. *(white). 1973. Connecticut.* Reilly was convicted of first-degree manslaughter and sentenced to 6–16 years in prison. He was released on bond after attracting the interest of playwright Arthur Miller and author William Styron, and following a special investigation by the *New York Times* that uncovered evidence exonerating Reilly and showing that police had coerced him into making a false confession. In 1976 Reilly won a new trial. According to the court, new evidence established that "a grave injustice had been done." Before the new trial began, all charges were dropped when it was found the prosecution had suppressed evidence confirming Reilly's alibi. Reilly's efforts to sue the Connecticut State Police were unsuccessful.

REISSFELDER, GEORGE A. *(white). 1966. Massachusetts.* Reissfelder was convicted of armed robbery and first-degree murder and was sentenced to life. In 1972 his co-defendant, in a deathbed confession to a former prison chaplain, said that Reissfelder had been incorrectly identified by eyewitnesses. At a special hearing in 1982, five policemen, an FBI agent, a probation officer, and the prison chaplain to whom the co-defendant had confessed gave evidence supporting the contention that the co-defendant had not known Reissfelder before the latter's trial. A new trial was ordered. The prosecutor decided to dismiss the charges, and Reissfelder was released. In 1985 a bill to compensate Reissfelder ($900,000) was defeated in the state legislature.

RENO, RALPH *(white). 1925. Illinois.* Reno was convicted of murder and sentenced to death. In an earlier trial, after his conviction and a jury recommendation of death, the trial judge refused to impose the sentence and ordered a new trial on the ground that the evidence was totally insufficient. Reno was charged with two counts of murder and one count of attempted murder; he was tried for only one of the murders. The sole evidence linking him to the crime was the testimony of a neighbor of the murder victims, who claimed that Reno had also tried to kill her (her story changed somewhat between the two trials). Reno's wife, with whom he had been asleep at home, was prevented from giving alibi testimony at the trial. In 1926, just seven hours before the scheduled execution, Reno received a stay in order to pursue an appeal. His appeal was aided by the volunteer efforts of the judge from the first trial, who was convinced of Reno's innocence. A new (third) trial was ordered. In that trial the witness again changed her testimony, and Reno was promptly acquitted. An indictment for the second murder was quashed, and Reno was acquitted on the attempted-murder charge. In 1928, after three years in prison, he was released. He later wrote that when he came out, his "health had been ruined . . . and I had a complete breakdown. . . . Everything that I had built in my first thirty-six years of life was gone— money, job, home, wife and baby, and my good health!"

REYNOLDS, MELVIN LEE *(white). 1979. Missouri.* See Introduction.

RICHARDSON, JAMES *(black). 1968. Florida.* See Chapter 10.

RIPAN, ALEXANDER *(white). 1919. Michigan.* Ripan was convicted of first-degree murder and sentenced to life. In 1929 he escaped, but he was recaptured in 1935. Ripan's prosecutor helped him obtain a new trial. At the retrial, the charges were dismissed. A ballistics expert, using newly developed techniques, proved that the fatal bullet could not have come from Ripan's gun. Ripan had spent 14 years in prison.

RIVERA, ANTONIO, *and* MERLA WALPOLE *(both Hispanic). 1974. California.* See Chapter 13.

ROBERSON, WILLIE *(black). 1931. Alabama.* See Chapter 5.

ROBERTS, CHARLES *(white). 1973. Georgia.* See Chapter 7.

ROBERTSON, DAVID WAYNE *(white)*. *1980. Maryland.* Robertson was convicted on two counts of first-degree murder and sentenced to two life terms. Robertson was present when a friend murdered two victims; as a co-defendant, the "friend" testified falsely against him. The perjured testimony represented the prosecution's price for an agreement with the co-defendant not to proceed against him at trial under the State's death penalty statute. In 1983 the conviction was reversed because of improper jury instructions. In 1984 Robertson was acquitted at the retrial. The co-defendant is serving a life term in prison.

ROBINSON, DERRICK *(black)*. *1989. Florida.* Robinson was convicted of second-degree murder and sentenced to seven years in prison. With a record of prior arrests but no convictions, Robinson pleaded no contest to the charges to avoid the threat of the death penalty after an eyewitness implicated him. "If I had gone to trial, I would have been railroaded. I had no choice. I knew I was innocent, but the jury would have judged me on how I looked." His court-appointed attorney, never satisfied that Robinson was guilty, pursued the investigation with his own funds. The eyewitness eventually recanted. In 1991 three eyewitnesses came forward and implicated another suspect (then in custody on a charge of attempted murder), and the district attorney agreed to dismiss the charges. After two and a half years in prison, Robinson was freed. The judge said, "I've never seen anything like this before. This was an injustice."

ROBINSON, VAN BERING *(black)*. *1981. New Mexico.* Robinson was convicted of armed robbery and felony-murder of a police officer and was sentenced to life. On appeal the convictions were overturned on the ground that the prosecutors had subjected an eyewitness to prejudicial questioning in the attempt to impeach him. The witness had testified that Robinson was not the perpetrator. In 1983, at retrial, Robinson was acquitted.

RODRIGUEZ, SANTOS *(Hispanic)*. *1954. Massachusetts.* Rodriguez was convicted of second-degree murder and sentenced to life. The conviction was based on a coerced confession and Rodriguez's lack of comprehension of English (he was semiliterate and had recently emigrated from Puerto Rico). His appeal was dismissed for late filing, but in 1957, after having served 39 months, he was released with a full pardon when another man pleaded guilty to the killing. The legislature subsequently approved a $12,500 indemnity for Rodriguez.

ROGERS, COURTNEY ("FRED") *(white)*. *1942. California.* See Chapter 13.

ROGERS, SILAS *(black)*. *1943. Virginia.* See Chapter 11.

ROHAN, PHIL *(white)*. *1928. California.* See GARVEY, MIKE.

ROSS, JOHNNY *(black)*. *1975. Louisiana.* Ross, 16, was convicted of the rape of a white woman and sentenced to death; he confessed after being beaten by the police. His trial lasted only a few hours. No alibi witnesses were called to testify, and the eyewitness testimony—including that of the victim—was of dubious value. The conviction was affirmed on appeal, but because the death penalty had been imposed under a mandatory sentencing statute that was later invalidated, the case was remanded with directions to impose a sentence of 20 years. Beginning in 1975, the Southern Poverty Law Center sought to obtain a new trial for Ross. In 1980 the blood type of the sperm found in the victim was compared with Ross's, and it was established that the two were not the same. Presented with this evidence, as well as a federal habeas corpus order, the New Orleans district attorney's office agreed to Ross's release in 1981.

RUCKER, HERMAN RAY *(white). 1982. Ohio.* See HOLBROOK, ERNEST, JR.

RUFF, WAYNE *(white). 1973. Georgia.* See Chapter 7.

RYBARCZYK, MAX *(white). 1929. New York.* See GRZECHOWIAK, STEPHEN.

SACCO, NICOLA, *and* BARTOLOMEO VANZETTI *(both white). 1921. Massachusetts.* See Chapter 4.

SANCHEZ, ISAURO *(Hispanic). 1982. Illinois.* See ARROYO, RO-GELIO.

SANDERS, ALBERT *(black). 1917. Alabama.* Sanders was convicted, with Fisher Brooks, of murder, and sentenced to death. The conviction was affirmed on appeal. Though he had nothing to gain by helping Sanders, Brooks testified at Sanders's trial that Sanders was innocent. Another fellow prisoner testified that he had heard Sanders confess, however, and both Brooks and Sanders were executed in 1918. In a statement from the scaffold, Brooks again insisted on Sanders's innocence, as did Sanders himself before he was hanged.

SANTANA, RENE *(Hispanic). 1976. New Jersey.* Santana was convicted of murder and sentenced to life imprisonment. The defendant, a political refugee from the Dominican Republic, had entered the U.S. in the 1960s and worked as an undercover informant with the Bureau of Alcohol, Tobacco and Firearms in New York. Having participated in an undercover operation against illegal gunrunning, he was charged with murder and armed robbery, despite an alibi. In 1986 a new trial was ordered because the State had not told the defense about the criminal record of two of its chief witnesses and that pending criminal charges against one of them had been dropped in exchange for testimony implicating the defendant. The head of Centurion Ministries, James McCloskey, who had re-investigated the case, said he "had absolutely no doubts whatsoever" that Santana was innocent. Santana was released after he pleaded guilty to a lesser charge (supplying the weapons that were used in the murder), which he denied as soon as he was freed. Once released, he was deported to the Dominican Republic.

SBERNA, CHARLES *(white)*. *1938. New York.* Sberna was convicted of first-degree murder of a police officer and sentenced to death. His conviction was affirmed on appeal. Sberna's co-defendant, Salvatore Gati, testified at the trial that Sberna was innocent, and in prison both Gati and Sberna convinced Isidore Zimmerman (see Chapter 2) that Sberna was innocent. Gati also said the head of the New York Homicide Bureau, Jacob Rosenblum, admitted he knew Sberna was innocent and that he would clear him if Gati would reveal the name of his real accomplices. Gati refused to do this. Later it turned out that Rosenblum had also been involved in wrongfully convicting Zimmerman. Sberna and Gati were both executed in 1938. The prison chaplain said of Sberna, "This is the first time I've ever been positive that an innocent man was going to the chair, and there is nothing I can do about it. If only people would make sure they know what they are talking about before they swear a man's life away."

SCHUYLER, JOHN EDWARD *(white)*. *1907. New Jersey.* Schuyler was convicted of first-degree murder and sentenced to death. The conviction was based wholly on circumstantial evidence, but it was affirmed on appeal. In 1914 Schuyler was pardoned and released after the real murderer confessed. "Had it not been for the persistent efforts of ex-Governor [Edward] Stokes and of the New York banker, Mr. C. Ledyard Blair, . . . the death chamber would have had him as its victim."

SCOTT, BRADLEY P. *(white)*. *1988. Florida.* Scott was convicted of first-degree murder and sentenced to death. He had been an early suspect in the case, but the state attorney had declined to seek an indictment against him because he had produced a convincing alibi. Ten years later, after evidence corroborating this alibi had been lost, Scott was indicted and convicted on the basis of testimony from witnesses who identified him as the man they had seen talking with the victim shortly before her death. In 1991 the Florida Supreme Court vacated the conviction and ordered Scott released because the circumstantial evidence was insufficient to support the conviction. Each of the identifications had been plagued with inconsistencies and shortcomings. "We find that the circumstantial evidence presented by the prosecution could only create a suspicion that Scott committed this murder. Suspicions cannot be a basis for a criminal conviction. Our law requires proof beyond a reasonable doubt and a fair trial for a defendant."

SCOTT, SCOTTY *(white)*. *1983. Arkansas.* Scott was convicted of first-degree murder and sentenced to 25 years in prison. After his first trial (in 1982) ended with a deadlocked jury, the conviction at retrial was based on the identification of three witnesses who thought they had seen Scott near the crime scene. In 1984 a serial killer on death row in Texas, Henry Lee Lucas, confessed to the killing. The Arkansas Court of Appeals granted a motion ordering the lower court to review a videotape of the confession pursuant to deciding whether to order a new trial for Scott. At that hearing the judge ordered a new trial. In 1985 Lucas retracted his confession; nevertheless, in 1986 the order for a new trial was upheld by the Arkansas Supreme Court. In 1989, after a long delay of the retrial because he was in poor health, Scott was retried and promptly acquitted in proceedings that lasted only 80 minutes. "No one feels uneasy about the verdict," said the jury foreman.

SEATON, TERRY (black). 1973. New Mexico. Seaton was convicted of first-degree murder and sentenced to life imprisonment. His conviction was affirmed on appeal. In 1979 a state district judge ruled the conviction was based on perjured testimony given by another person in exchange for a lighter sentence on other charges. Evidence also indicated that the State had suppressed the confession of a third person. A new trial was ordered, the prosecution dropped the charges, and Seaton was released after having served six and a half years in prison. In 1983 a federal court jury awarded Seaton $118,000 in damages from the county, the sheriff, and a deputy. The State also paid attorneys' fees of $217,500.

SHAFFER, HOWARD, CHARLES STEVENS, and WILLIAM TROOP (all white). 1927. Florida. Shaffer, Stevens, and Troop were all convicted of first-degree murder and sentenced to death. On the ground of new evidence, the trial judge granted a motion for retrial, but the defendants were convicted and sentenced to death a second time. On appeal the convictions were reversed, and a third trial was ordered. The only evidence against the defendants was the testimony of an alleged eyewitness, the victim's husband. An alcoholic and drug addict, this man had previously threatened to kill his wife with an axe (which was the murder weapon), and he had beaten her on several occasions. In granting the new trial, the court cited the complete lack of any motive for the slaying by the defendants and the numerous discrepancies between the testimony from the victim's husband (as well as his own prior testimony) and that of "credible disinterested witnesses." "Law enforcement officers familiar with the case frequently expressed doubts as to the guilt of the trio." At the new trial in 1930, the judge ordered that the charges be dropped and the defendants be immediately released.

SHEA, JOSEPH FRANCIS (white). 1959. Florida. Shea was convicted of murder and sentenced to life. His conviction was based entirely on his false confession, which he later said he gave because he had suicidal urges and wanted to die in the electric chair. In 1966, after an investigation led by Miami Herald reporter Gene Miller, Shea was retried and acquitted.

A key to his acquittal was the admission by a police detective that he had denied Shea access to counsel and lied to him about having evidence against him in order to elicit the false confession. In the U.S. Air Force at the time of the crime, Shea was dishonorably discharged and then spent six years in prison before being released. A Miami police officer commented, "Shea was a neurotic, of low intelligence, who wanted to be punished. . . . All the evidence was against his being the killer, but the authorities just didn't want to know." In 1967 Shea received an indemnification of $45,000 from the state legislature.

SHEELER, RUDOLPH *(white). 1939. Pennsylvania.* See BILGER, GEORGE.

SHEPHERD, SAMUEL *(black). 1949. Florida.* See Chapter 5.

SHEPPARD, SAMUEL H. *(white). 1954. Ohio.* Sheppard, a physician, was convicted of second-degree murder for killing his wife and sentenced to life imprisonment. On initial appeal, the conviction was affirmed. At the beginning of the Ohio Supreme Court decision, Justice Bell commented, "Murder and mystery, society, sex and suspense were combined in such a manner as to intrigue and captivate the public fancy to a degree perhaps unparalled in recent annals." In 1966, after considerable litigation, Sheppard's conviction was overturned and a new trial ordered, on the ground that massive, pervasive, and prejudicial publicity had attended his prosecution. At retrial it was established through bloodstain patterns that Sheppard was not his wife's killer and that, unlike the killer, he was right handed. Sheppard was acquitted.

SHERMAN, DAVID *(black). 1907. Tennessee.* Sherman was convicted (with two co-defendants) of murder and sentenced to death. No appeal was taken. In 1907, a few days before the scheduled executions, one co-defendant (Beulah McGhee) absolved Sherman of guilt. McGhee was hanged, but Governor Malcolm Patterson granted a reprieve for Sherman and the other co-defendant. In 1908 their sentences were commuted to life. The conviction had been obtained by "the uncorroborated statements of one of the parties who was a witness." Then in 1911 Governor Patterson pardoned Sherman after the Board of Pardons concluded, "This appears to us quite a remarkable case of a miscarriage of justice." The attorney general, who prosecuted the case, wrote that "the prisoner had nothing to do with the murder."

SHUMWAY, R. MEAD *(white). 1907. Nebraska.* Shumway was convicted of the first-degree murder of his employer's wife on circumstantial evidence and sentenced to death. One juror, the only one to hold out against the death penalty, told his friends he "had not slept well any night since the trial." He later left a note in which he expressed "great worry at the trial," and he then killed himself. Shumway was executed in 1909. His last words were: "I am an innocent victim. May God forgive everyone who has said anything against me." In 1910 the victim's husband confessed on his deathbed that he had murdered his wife.

SMITH, CHARLES ("RED") *(black). 1983. Indiana.* Smith was convicted of first-degree murder for killing a woman during a robbery and sentenced to death. He was implicated by a man who claimed to have driven the getaway car; charges against this self-confessed accomplice were dropped in exchange for his testimony against Smith. The defense suspected that a relative of the witness was the actual culprit, but because the State had lost or destroyed physical evidence from the crime, it was impossible for the defense to support this argument. At one point Smith came within three days of execution. In 1989 the Indiana Supreme Court awarded Smith a new trial because of ineffective assistance of counsel. At retrial in 1991, Smith was acquitted after presenting an alibi defense and evidence that the witnesses against him had lied under oath.

SMITH, CLARENCE *(white). 1974. New Mexico.* See Chapter 2.

SMITH, FRANK A. *(white). 1922. Texas.* Smith was convicted of murder and sentenced to 15 years. The actual murderer, a serial killer named Euzebe Vidrine (hanged for other murders in Louisiana in 1924), confessed in an autobiography written shortly before his death to the murder of which Smith had been convicted.

SMITH, GRACE M. *(white). 1945. Virginia.* Smith was convicted of first-degree murder for killing her husband and sentenced to 20 years in prison. On appeal, the conviction was reversed because the evidence indicated the deceased might have taken his own life. "The result of the evidence is that only by speculation or guess can it be said that this defendant aided or abetted in the commission of the crime and the verdict against her must be set aside." Upon remand, the case against Smith was dismissed.

SMITH, LARRY THOMAS *(white). 1976. Ohio.* Smith was convicted of aggravated murder and sentenced to life imprisonment. Despite the testimony of alibi witnesses, Smith was convicted by a 2–1 vote of a three-judge panel. The main evidence against him came from the victim's girl friend, who, according to the defense, had a history of drug abuse. In 1978 the sheriff's department re-opened the investigation, found evidence implicating another suspect in the slaying, and fought on Smith's behalf for a new trial. In 1980 the three-judge panel ordered a new trial. Later that year, at retrial, the evidence pointing to the other suspect was introduced, as was alibi testimony, and Smith was acquitted. As the Akron *Beacon-Journal* commented, "His story makes another strong argument against reinstituting the death penalty in Ohio."

STAPLES, F. N. *(white). 1905. California.* Staples, a physician, was convicted of first-degree murder and sentenced to death. His wife had been suffering from typhoid fever and then died. When Staples moved to

San Francisco a mere month later and was joined there by a neighbor's wife, their conduct "doubtless awoke the indignation of the residents . . . and generated a suspicion as to the cause of his wife's death." The body was exhumed, an autopsy was performed, ·and traces of arsenic were found. On appeal, the evidence was held insufficient to establish the existence of a crime. (The appellate court found it was "quite apparent" that the arsenic was introduced into the body through embalming and that the death of Mrs. Staples was consistent with the type of death experienced by victims of typhoid fever.)

STATEN, CLEO *(black)*. *1920. Alabama.* See CRUTCHER, WILLIE.

STEVENS, CHARLES *(white)*. *1927. Florida.* See SHAFFER, HOWARD.

STIELOW, CHARLES *(white) 1915. New York.* See GREEN, NELSON.

STORICK, MAUDE CUSHING *(white). 1923. Michigan.* Storick was convicted of first-degree murder and sentenced to life imprisonment. The victim was Storick's husband; it was her remarriage only a month after his death that led to speculation that he had been murdered. (She was convicted of poisoning him with bichloride of mercury.) In 1949, after 26 years in prison, Storick received a gubernatorial pardon. Investigation by a volunteer attorney had established that the deceased was in the habit of using the poison as a throat gargle, and that the prosecutor in the case (by then deceased) had also believed Storick was innocent.

SWEENEY, JAMES *(white). 1926. New Jersey.* Sweeney was convicted of first-degree murder and sentenced to life. In 1928 the Board of Pardons exonerated and freed him when the true culprits confessed. The conviction had been obtained by mistaken eyewitness identification, perjury, and circumstantial evidence (despite several alibi witnesses).

SYNON, MICHAEL J. *(white). 1900. Illinois.* Synon was convicted of the murder of his wife and sentenced to death. On appeal, the conviction was reversed because of prejudicial remarks by the judge, and a retrial was ordered. At the retrial, after several reputable witnesses testified that Synon was four miles from the scene of the crime when it was committed, he was acquitted. Governor Edward Dunne, who had presided over the second trial as judge before being elected governor, stated, "Only those words which the court had committed an error in uttering stood between him and the cruel tragedy of which my state would have been guilty."

THOMPSON, SAM *(white). 1947. North Carolina.* See PARROTT, LEMUEL.

THORPE, JAMES *(black). 1948. New Jersey.* See COOPER, RALPH.

THROWER, ALLAN E. *(black). 1973. Ohio.* Thrower was convicted of first-degree murder in the ambush death of a police officer and sentenced to life imprisonment. He was convicted despite his lack of motive, claims of innocence, and testimony from three alibi witnesses that placed him in Detroit at the time of the crime. The only evidence against him was eyewitness identification by another police officer, the victim's partner. On appeal the conviction was affirmed. In 1978 an internal police investigation revealed that the eyewitness had perjured himself when testifying against Thrower. The officer, who admitted making the false statements, was suspended, and a police detective who had falsely testified that he heard two of the alibi witnesses plotting to perjure themselves resigned. In 1978 the trial court ordered a new trial (at the request of the prosecutor), and Thrower was released after having spent five years in prison. In 1979 the prosecutor formally dropped the charges.

TIBBS, DELBERT (black). 1974. Florida. See Chapter 2.

TORRES, PEDRO (Hispanic). 1985. Texas. Torres was convicted of murder and sentenced to 75 years in prison. Three witnesses identified him as the killer. Three months later, the trial judge ordered the defense attorney to file a motion for a new trial so that he could inspect Torres's work records, which had not been presented at trial. These records revealed that Torres was at work, 250 miles away, at the time of the murder. The judge reversed the conviction and ordered Torres's immediate release. An illegal alien, Torres had been confused with a different Pedro Torres, who had actually committed the crime.

TREADAWAY, JONATHAN CHARLES, JR. (white). 1975. Arizona. Treadaway was convicted of sodomy and first-degree murder (of a 6-year-old boy) and was sentenced to death. On appeal the conviction was reversed because evidence of a prior criminal act by the defendant had been improperly introduced at trial. At retrial Treadaway was acquitted by the jury after five pathologists testified the victim probably died of pneumonia and that there was no evidence he had been sodomized. Members of the jury reported having voted to acquit because the prosecutors failed to present enough evidence to establish that Treadaway was even inside the victim's home.

TROOP, WILLIAM (white). 1927. Florida. See SHAFFER, HOWARD.

TROY, LARRY (black). 1983. Florida. See BROWN, WILLIE A.

TUCKER, CHARLES LOUIS (white). 1905. Massachusetts. Tucker was convicted of first-degree murder and sentenced to death. The conviction, based on circumstantial evidence, was affirmed on appeal. More than 100,000 Massachusetts residents signed petitions on behalf of clemency. Among those convinced of his innocence were the county medical examiner (who lost his job because of his stand) and a clergyman who said a witness had told him she had perjured herself at the original trial. Tucker was nonetheless executed in 1906.

URY, GEORGE *(white)*. *1901. Ohio*. See FOSTER, LOCK.

VALLETUTTI, JOHN *(white)*. *1947. New York*. Valletutti was convicted of first-degree murder and sentenced to death, despite the jury's recommendation of life imprisonment. Valletutti had been beaten by police officers into signing a confession, which was the chief evidence against him. The admitted killer, convicted six months prior to Valletutti's trial, testified in Valletutti's defense that he had initially inculpated Valletutti as his accomplice only to avoid further police beatings. Valletutti's conviction was reversed on appeal because of the coerced confession, and he was released after two years in prison when the district attorney requested that the indictments be dismissed.

VANZETTI, BARTOLOMEO *(white)*. *1921. Massachusetts*. See Chapter 4.

VARELA, IGNACIO *(Hispanic)*. *1982. Illinois*. See ARROYO, ROGELIO.

VARELA, JOAQUIN *(Hispanic)*. *1982. Illinois*. See ARROYO, ROGELIO.

VARGAS, ANASTACIO *(Hispanic)*. *1926. Texas*. Vargas was convicted of murder and sentenced to life imprisonment. On appeal the conviction was reversed, and a new trial was ordered. At retrial Vargas was again convicted and sentenced to death. On appeal, the conviction was affirmed. Vargas's head had already been shaved for execution, and he had been served his last meal, when a look-alike confessed to the crime. The judge investigated the case and commuted the sentence to life. In 1929 Vargas was granted a full pardon and released after four years in confinement. In 1965 he belatedly sued the State for damages and was awarded $20,000; the State appealed, but the award was affirmed.

VASQUEZ, DAVID *(white)*. *1985. Virginia*. Vasquez, whose I.Q. was below 70, was convicted of second-degree murder (in connection with rape) and sentenced to 35 years in prison after he pleaded guilty out of fear of being sentenced to death. In 1987, when a nearly identical murder occurred, detectives began to question the verdict. Tests of the semen found on the first victim's body conclusively linked the slaying to another man. The prosecutor, on learning of this evidence, petitioned the governor to pardon Vasquez. In 1989 Governor Gerald L. Baliles granted the petition, and Vasquez was released unconditionally. In 1990 a bill was filed in the legislature to award Vasquez $500,000 as an indemnity for his four years of wrongful imprisonment.

VEGA, DAMASO *(black)*. *1982. New Jersey*. Vega was convicted of murder and sentenced to life imprisonment. The conviction was based largely on the testimony of three witnesses, one of whom alleged that Vega had confessed to him and another of whom identified Vega as the man he had seen at the scene of the murder. In 1989 a new trial was ordered after re-investigation by James McCloskey, head of Centurion Ministries. All the witnesses recanted their testimony, claiming that they had been manipulated under pressure by the police detective who investigated the case. Unbeknownst to the defense, pending criminal charges against one of these witnesses were dropped after his testimony. The police detective was sharply criticized by the judge for "alter[ing]" or "dressing up" files and failing to turn them over to the prosecution. Said the judge, "There are many aspects of this case which truthful[ly] terrify me to think that these things can still occur within our justice system." A month after the new trial was ordered, all charges against Vega were dismissed.

VENEGAS, JUAN *(Hispanic). 1972. California.* See Chapter 9.

VICKERS, JOHN *(white). 1906. North Carolina.* See KENDALL, HAMP.

VINDIOLA, BERNARD *(Hispanic). 1977. California.* Vindiola was convicted of second-degree murder and given a sentence of five years to life imprisonment. On appeal the conviction was reversed because of the admission of hearsay evidence that identified Bernard, rather than his brother Eddie, as the culprit, and because evidence tending to impeach Eddie's testimony had been excluded. The court also questioned the quality of the eyewitness identification. "Much evidence pointed to Eddie as the killer. . . . There was persuasive evidence that it was Eddie, not appellant, who entered the back seat of the car where . . . the killer sat." A prosecution informant also came forward and admitted she had told law-enforcement officials that Bernard had not committed the crime. The prosecution as a result dropped all charges.

WALKER, LEE DELL *(black). 1954. Michigan.* Walker was convicted of first-degree murder and sentenced to life imprisonment. A gun used in the killing was found in Walker's car, and Walker, under duress, confessed to the crime. In 1965 the Michigan Supreme Court remanded the case back to the trial court to determine whether the confession was voluntary. The trial court concluded that it was, and on appeal the supreme court of the state affirmed. Further appeals also failed. In 1972 the case was re-investigated by the *Detroit Free Press.* Alibi witnesses were located, Walker's claim that his confession had been coerced was confirmed, and a new trial was then granted. The prosecutor moved to drop all charges, and Walker was released after having served 18 years. In 1974 an indemnity bill ($25,000) unanimously passed the state senate, but failed in the lower house after the prosecutor claimed that Walker was indeed guilty. Walker's efforts to sue the prosecutor for defamation failed.

WALLACE, EARNEST *(black). 1916. Illinois.* Wallace was convicted of murder and sentenced to death. An eyewitness identified Wallace as the culprit, but three other witnesses stated the gunman was masked, thus making identification impossible. Three alibi witnesses also testified for Wallace. A volunteer attorney and five private citizens fought on his behalf, and, in the words of a state senator, "were able to convince the public finally that Wallace was absolutely innocent." On appeal, the conviction was reversed because the evidence was insufficient.

WALPOLE, MERLA *(Hispanic). 1979. California.* See Chapter 13.

WAN, ZIAN SUNG *(Asian). 1919. District of Columbia.* Wan was convicted of murder and sentenced to death. The conviction was reversed on appeal because his coerced confession was improperly admitted at trial. Juries in two later trials refused to reconvict, and the indictment was dropped. Wan, a native of China, was released after seven years in prison. "The review exercised by the [U.S.] Supreme Court in this case is seldom assumed by that Court. But for this unusual intervention Wan would have been executed. . . ."

WARD, WILLIAM *(black). 1975. Alabama.* Ward was convicted of first-degree manslaughter and sentenced to 10 years in prison. Two years later, the original investigating police detective (Tuscaloosa Detective Shirley Fields), who had never been comfortable with the conviction, discovered that the fatal bullet could not have come from Ward's gun. Ward had fired his weapon into the air, and witnesses had erroneously believed that this harmless shot was the cause of the victim's death. The trial court ordered a new trial, the indictment was dismissed, and Ward was released.

WARE, ED *(black). 1919. Arkansas.* See Chapter 5.

WEAVER, JOSEPH *(black). 1927. Ohio.* Weaver was convicted of first-degree murder and sentenced to death. His conviction was affirmed on appeal. Despite Weaver's alibi witnesses, a co-defendant who had confessed to the crime testified against him. In 1929, a few days before Weaver's scheduled execution, the co-defendant (serving a life term after being convicted of manslaughter) retracted his implication of Weaver. Three days later, on further appeal, the Ohio Supreme Court granted a retrial on the technical ground that certain hearsay evidence was inadmissible. Later that year, after 22 months under death sentence, Weaver was retried. When his attorney demanded a directed verdict of acquittal and the prosecutor did not object, the court ordered his release. In 1933 the legislature awarded Weaver $15,000 "for the damages he suffered by reason of the erroneous conviction."

WEEMS, CHARLIE *(black). 1931. Alabama.* See Chapter 5.

WELLMAN, WILLIAM MASON *(black). 1942. North Carolina.* Wellman was convicted of rape of a white woman and was sentenced to death. On appeal, the conviction was affirmed. On the morning of the scheduled execution, Governor J. Melville Broughton received word that another man had confessed to the crime. Wellman had already been seated in the electric chair when the reprieve came. An investigation by the State Parole Commission, ordered after a routine request for executive clemency, showed that on the day of the crime Wellman was "unquestionably" at work some 350 miles away. Six months later he received a full pardon and was released. The pardon report described the victim as "an honorable woman of the highest integrity," though it was on the basis of her testimony that Wellman had been convicted.

WENTZEL, GERALD C. *(white). 1947. Pennsylvania.* Wentzel was convicted of second-degree murder and sentenced to 10–20 years. The conviction was affirmed on appeal. The conviction was based wholly on circumstantial evidence; the jury refused to believe Wentzel's alibi that he was out of town at the time of the crime. Chief Justice George W. Maxey, in a strong dissent joined by two other justices, stated: "The Commonwealth produced no evidence which justified a verdict of guilty of murder against this appellant and the trial judge should have given binding instructions for acquittal." Through the efforts of the victim's mother and sister, the Court of Last Resort intervened. In 1950, after another man's confession convinced the Board of Pardons that the wrong man had been convicted, Wentzel was released. His sentence was commuted by Governor John Fine to time served after the Board unanimously recommended a pardon. As Gardner notes, "This [result was] a compromise, something of a sop to all parties concerned, but it . . . automatically prevented [Wentzel] from claiming damages from the State for false imprisonment."

WILKINSON, ROBERT *(white). 1976. Pennsylvania.* Wilkinson was convicted on five counts of murder in the firebombing of a home, but he was not formally sentenced because an appeal was immediately filed. An investigation by the *Philadelphia Inquirer* indicated that Wilkinson's confession had been coerced, and that at least seven other people had been beaten, threatened, or otherwise coerced by the police into making false statements. One witness admitted he had lied at the trial, and another man confessed and pleaded guilty to the firebombing (for which two others were indicted) before the mildly retarded Wilkinson was freed; he had spent 15 months in prison. The convictions of several Philadelphia police officers for civil rights violations arising from their "brutal and unlawful" mistreatment of Wilkinson were sustained on appeal. Wilkinson was later awarded damages of $325,000.

WILLIAMS, DARBY *(a.k.a.* DARBY TILLIS*) (black). 1979. Illinois.* See COBB, PERRY.

WILLIAMS, EUGENE *(black). 1931. Alabama.* See Chapter 5.

WILLIAMS, GEORGE *(black). 1922. North Carolina.* See DOVE, FRANK.

WILLIAMS, JOSEPH S. *(white)*. *1920*. *Virginia*. Williams was convicted of voluntary manslaughter in the death of his wife and was sentenced to five years in prison. The cause of death was a brain hemorrhage, which the State argued resulted from a fight between the spouses two days prior to the wife's death. On appeal, the conviction was reversed because "there was no bruise or outward physical evidence of any blow on the head," and "there is no evidence in the case to support the verdict in the finding that the corpus delicti was proven." Prior to retrial, all charges were dropped.

WILLIAMS, ROBERT *(white)*. *1956*. *California*. Williams was convicted of first-degree murder and sentenced to life at the age of 18. He had falsely confessed to the murder to kindle interest from his girl friend, who he believed was about to marry someone else. He was paroled in 1975 and three years later established that he was completely innocent; police records showed that he had been in custody at the time of the murder. In 1978, after testimony on Williams's behalf from the former prosecuting attorney (who nonetheless was not totally convinced of Williams's innocence), a superior court judge ordered his release from parole.

WILLIAMS, ROBERT *(white)*. *1958*. *California*. Williams was convicted of murder and sentenced to life imprisonment. While in prison on a previous conviction (see preceding paragraph), he falsely confessed to a murder in order to convince the prison authorities that an innocent person could indeed be convicted on a false confession. For the second time, he was proved right. In 1975 he was paroled, and in 1978 he was released from parole.

WILLIAMS, SAMUEL TITO *(black)*. *1948*. *New York*. Williams was convicted of first-degree murder for the killing of a teenaged girl and was sentenced to death, despite a jury recommendation of life. The conviction was affirmed on appeal. In 1949 his sentence was commuted to life by Governor Thomas Dewey. In 1963 the conviction was reversed by federal court on the ground that Williams's confession had been coerced. The confession had been the only evidence against him. Williams was freed after 22 months on death row and almost 16 years in prison. He later won $40,000 in compensatory damages from the city of New York for "malicious prosecution."

WILLIAMSON, JACK *(black)*. *1933*. *Florida*. See CHAMBERS, ISIAH.

WILSON, BILL *(white)*. *1914*. *Alabama*. Wilson was convicted of first-degree murder and sentenced to life, despite testimony of five eyewitnesses that the victim was alive after the date of the alleged homicide. The conviction was based on perjured testimony and was affirmed on appeal. In 1916 the trial judge was among those who petitioned the governor for a commutation. In 1918 Wilson was fully pardoned after his persistent attorney found the "victim" alive and well in Indiana. In 1919 Wilson was indemnified by the legislature ($3,500), but most of this money was stolen by a probate judge who had been named a trustee of the account.

WILSON, DAVID RONALD *(black). 1967. Florida.* Wilson was convicted of second-degree murder and sentenced to 20 years. In 1968 the conviction was affirmed on appeal. In 1971 the prosecution concluded that its chief witness had lied at the trial; independent polygraph examinations of another eyewitness (who had never testified) and of the defendant confirmed that Wilson was innocent. At the request of the state attorneys, the conviction was set aside by the trial court, and Wilson was released. At the time he was released, authorities were attempting to locate another suspect who meanwhile had become a fugitive on armed robbery charges.

WILSON, HORACE *(black). 1948. New Jersey.* See COOPER, RALPH.

WILSON, SHELIA *(white). 1979. Kentucky.* Wilson was convicted of first-degree murder and sentenced to 20 years in prison. Her conviction was affirmed on appeal. In 1983 a federal court found that the evidence of her " 'intent' to murder her husband was insufficient to support a jury conviction of first-degree murder." Wilson had driven off in a car with her husband (the victim) and a friend (at the time a fugitive from justice, having murdered his wife). The two men quarreled; Wilson stopped the car by the road, and the men got out. Shots were fired, and Wilson and the friend left in the car. The federal court noted that she was guilty of hindering prosecution (which was not charged), but not of murder. As one attorney noted, "The triggerman gave a sworn deposition stating [Wilson] was 'in no fashion or form' involved in her husband's murder. This could have been a capital case but was not prosecuted as such."

WING, GEORGE CHEW *(Asian). 1937. New York.* Wing was convicted of first-degree murder (after a 30-minute trial) and sentenced to death. His conviction was affirmed on appeal. A participant in the killing testified against Wing and was sentenced to 20 years. While he was in prison awaiting execution, Wing convinced several observers that he had been falsely identified by eyewitnesses and that perjured testimony had been used against him. Warden Lewis Lawes also questioned his guilt, but Wing was nonetheless executed in 1937.

WOODMANSEE, ERNEST *(white). 1947. California.* Woodmansee was convicted of first-degree murder in the killing of a special police officer during a robbery and was sentenced to life. The chief evidence at the trial was the testimony of a self-confessed participant in the murder (who had been granted immunity) that connected Woodmansee with another co-defendant, Trujillo. Trujillo was executed for his role in the crime. Although one state supreme court justice argued in dissent that the evidence connecting Woodmansee with the crime was insufficient, in 1948 his conviction was affirmed on appeal. After intervention by the Court of Last Resort, the testimony that had been used against Woodmansee was impeached, and the murder weapon was found in the possession of the witness's sister. In 1956 Woodmansee was released on parole.

WOODWARD, WALTER *(black)*. *1933*. *Florida*. See CHAMBERS, ISIAH.

WOON, LEM *(Asian)*. *1908*. *Oregon*. Woon was convicted of first-degree murder and sentenced to death. The conviction was affirmed on appeal. Woon presented an alibi defense and always maintained his innocence. Two state supreme court justices, dissenting from the denial of rehearing, argued that the evidence was insufficient for conviction. In 1913 Governor Oswald West commuted the sentence to life, and in 1914 he granted Woon a pardon, conditional on his return to China. Woon did not leave the country, however, and therefore in 1927 Governor I. L. Patterson revoked the pardon. In 1935 Governor Charles Martin granted Woon another pardon, again conditional on his deportation.

WORDLOW, WILL *(black)*. *1919*. *Arkansas*. See Chapter 5.

WRIGHT, ANDREW *(black)*. *1931*. *Alabama*. See Chapter 5.

WRIGHT, LEROY ("ROY") *(black)*. *1928*. *Alabama*. See Chapter 5.

YELDER, GEORGE *(black)*. *1928*. *Alabama*. See BUTLER, LOUISE.

YOUNG, BENNIE *(black)*. *1922*. *Texas*. See JOHNSON, COOPER.

ZAJICEK, HERMAN *(a.k.a. HERMAN BILLIK) (white)*. *1907*. *Illinois*. Zajicek was convicted of murder and sentenced to death. He received a stay three days before the scheduled execution, and in 1908 the sentence was commuted to life by Governor Charles Deneen. In 1916, when the prosecution's key witness admitted having given "false and perjured testimony," Zajicek was granted a full pardon by Governor Edward Dunne. An investigation by the State Pardon Board had concluded that the prisoner "is at present an inmate of the prison hospital, in poor health, and, as we believe, an innocent man."

ZIMMERMAN, ISIDORE *(white)*. *1937*. *New York*. See Chapter 2.

alibi   Lat. for "in another place." The plea of a defendant that, having been elsewhere at the time of the crime, he or she cannot be guilty.

amicus curiae   Lat. for "friend of the court." A person—other than the parties to a case—entitled to file a brief or argue in the case (provided both parties give their permission).

bifurcated trial   A two-stage jury trial, especially in capital cases, where the jury first hears evidence on the issue of the defendant's guilt and then—if the verdict is one of guilty—the defense and prosecution may introduce further evidence bearing on the jury's choice of sentence (e.g., between life imprisonment and death).

certiorari, writ of   Lat. for "to be informed." Filed by a convicted defendant with an appellate court, seeking re-examination of a lower court's decision. Granting or denying such a writ is discretionary.

challenge, peremptory   A power of the prosecution and the defense during the *voir dire* (q.v.) to dismiss a prospective juror without giving a reason. Used by each side to remove from the trial jury someone deemed likely to be sympathetic to the other side. The number of such challenges may be limited by court regulations. Contrasted with *challenge for cause*, where a prospective juror is challenged by the defense and dismissed by the judge for a particular reason (e.g., the person is a relative of the victim and cannot be presumed to be unbiased).

coram nobis, writ of   Lat. for "before us." An order providing for review by a court of a proceeding in a prior action by that same court.

deposition   Written statement of a witness under oath given outside of court for use in court, hence a way of obtaining testimony from a person who is unable to appear at trial.

en banc   Fr. for "on [the] bench," a proceeding before a full court of judges, rather than before one judge presiding alone.

ex parte   Lat. for "by [or for] one party only." In the name of a case, the phrase means that the party named immediately following "ex parte" was the one who made the application to the court.

ex rel.   Short for *ex relatione*, Lat. for "out of relation [i.e., information]," hence a term used in the name of a decided case to indicate that the government—as the active party—although acting officially on behalf of the State, is doing so also to protect the interest of a private individual (the "relator").

habeas corpus, writ of   Lat. for "may you have the body." An ancient writ by which a court orders that a defendant being held in custody be brought before it so that the defendant's claims of wrongful detention may be reviewed. Federal habeas corpus has become an important route for state prisoners to obtain review in federal court of constitutional issues in their cases.

in flagrante delicto   Lat. for "[caught] in the very act of committing the crime."

jurisdiction   The legal entity (local, state, or federal) that has the authority to hear a case.

jury, coroner's   A body convened and sworn to hear evidence concerning cause of death where the death is violent, sudden, or suspicious.

jury, grand   A body convened and sworn to consider whether an indictment for a crime ought to be issued against a person (known or unknown), based on argument and evidence from the prosecutor.

nolle prosequi   Lat. for "[I do] not wish to further prosecute," hence the filing by a prosecutor before a court to drop further proceedings against a defendant.

non vult   Lat. for "[he/she] does not wish [to contest the charge]," hence a defendant's statement to a trial court that amounts to pleading guilty. In some jurisdictions, such a plea is accepted in the form *nolo contendere* (Lat. for "I do not wish to contest the charge"). Once such a plea is entered and accepted, the defendant is ready for sentencing.

per curiam   Lat. for "by the [whole] court," hence a phrase used to introduce an appellate court's opinion in a case where there are no concurring or dissenting opinions and where no one judge is singled out as author of the opinion.

prima facie   Lat. for "at first appearance," hence a way of describing evidence that presents a strong case, on its face, for one and only one outcome.

pro bono   Short for *pro bono publico*, Lat. for "for the public good," hence legal services provided free of charge to indigent defendants so that their interests will be properly represented in court.

pro se   Lat. for "for him/herself," hence used to describe a defendant who appears as his or her own attorney in court.

recuse   To withdraw from a case as judge, on the ground of a conflict of interest or other reason of conscience.

remand   Order by a high court to a lower court, sending a case back to that court for further proceedings.

severance   Decision by co-defendants to be tried separately rather than as a group.

venire   Lat. for "to come," hence the group of persons summoned to appear before a trial court for possible jury duty and from among whom a trial jury will be selected. Anyone so summoned is called a *venireman* or *venireperson*.

venue   Fr. for "place," hence the location—within a jurisdiction—where a trial is to be held. A *change of venue* is often sought in a criminal trial by the defense in order to avoid prejudicial pretrial publicity, which can make jury selection difficult or impossible.

voir dire   Fr. for "to see, to speak," used to refer to the oral examination each prospective juror undergoes before being sworn onto the jury or dismissed, and hence by extension a way of referring to the transcript of such an examination.

ALABAMA (25) M. Beamon, Butler and Yelder, Collins, Crutcher and three others, Fewell, Gaines, Garner and Johnson, W. Jordan, Montgomery and eight others (the "Scottsboro Boys"), Sanders, Ward, B. Wilson
ALASKA (0)
ARIZONA (1) Treadaway
ARKANSAS (54) A. Banks and 50 others, Carden, Draper, S. Scott
CALIFORNIA (31) Bigelow, Billings and Mooney, Brite and Brite, Cooks, Dulin, Fry, Garvey and two others, G. Hall, Imbler, S. Jackson, Kamacho, Kidd, Kirkes, Lamson, C. Lee, Lindley, Owens, Persico, Rivera and Walpole, C. Rogers, Staples, Venegas, Vindiola, R. Williams (twice), Woodmansee
COLORADO (1) Hamby
CONNECTICUT (3) Bertrand, Lanzillo, Reilly
DELAWARE (0)
DISTRICT OF COLUMBIA (3) Bernstein, B. Brown, Wan
FLORIDA (38) Adams, Anderson, Bachelor, A. Brown, J. G. Brown, J. B. Brown, Brown and Troy, I. Chambers and three others, Cox, Dawson, Frederick and Keaton, Fudge, Greenlee and two others, P. Hall, J. Jackson, Jaramillo, Jent and Miller, Lee and Pitts, Peek, Ramos, Richardson, D. Robinson, B. Scott, Shaffer and two others, Shea, Tibbs, D. Wilson
GEORGIA (14) J. Banks, Charles, Coleman, Creamer and six others, Drake, Foster, Frank, McIntosh
HAWAII (0)
IDAHO (0)
ILLINOIS (28) R. Arroyo and three others, Briggs, Brown and Houston, Burt, Cobb and Williams, Fowler and Pugh, Garrett, Lettrich, Lindsey, Linscott, Lucas and Lucas, Majczek and Marcinkiewicz, Marino, McDonald, Miller, Olson, Reno, Synon, Wallace, Zajicek
INDIANA (3) Hicks, Lobaugh, C. Smith

IOWA (1) J. Hall
KANSAS (1) Pyle
KENTUCKY (3) Dabney, T. Jones, S. Wilson
LOUISIANA (6) Blanton, Favor, Hampton, Labat and Poret, Ross
MAINE (2) Dwyer, Lambert
MARYLAND (6) Estes, Giles and two others, Marsh, Robertson
MASSACHUSETTS (12) Amado, Cero, Ellison, Grace, C. Hill, L. Johnson, Leaster, Reissfelder, Rodriguez, Sacco and Vanzetti, Tucker
MICHIGAN (16) Calloway, C. Clark, E. Clark and two others, Gross, Growden, Hardy, Jenkins, MacGregor, W. Padgett, Pecho, Prevost, Ripan, Storick, Walker
MINNESOTA (1) Hankins
MISSISSIPPI (4) L. Chambers, Dean, Gunter, McGee
MISSOURI (5) Craig and Hess, DeMore, Norwood, Reynolds
MONTANA (0)
NEBRASKA (1) Shumway
NEVADA (1) E. Johnson
NEW HAMPSHIRE (0)
NEW JERSEY (18) Cooper and five others (the "Trenton Six"), de los Santos, Hauptmann, Lamble, Landano, MacFarland, Merritt, Morello, Parker, Santana, Schuyler, Sweeney, Vega
NEW MEXICO (7) Garcia, Gladish and three others, Robinson, Seaton
NEW YORK (33) Appelgate, Arroyo, Bambrick, Barbato, Barber, Becker and Cirofici, Carter, Cashin, Davino, Featherstone, Fisher, N. Green and Stielow, Grzechowiak and Rybarczyk, Hoffman, Hoffner, E. Jackson, Kapatos, Kassim, Larkman, Leyra, Ludkowitz, Matera, Maynard, McLaughlin, Pfeffer, Sberna, Valletutti, S. Williams, Wing, Zimmerman
NORTH CAROLINA (13) Bowles, Dove and two others, Hefner, Hennis, Kendall and Vickers, Langley, Mansell, Parrott and Thompson, Wellman

NORTH DAKOTA (0)
OHIO (21)   Beeman, Broady, Bundy, Carmen, Domer, Fay, L. Foster and four others, Holbrook and Rucker, H. Jones, Krause, McKinney, McMullen, Sheppard, L. Smith, Thrower, Weaver
OKLAHOMA (4)   Bennett, Giddens, Goodwin, Hollins
OREGON (6)   Branson, Jennings, T. Jordan, Morales, Pender, Woon
PENNSYLVANIA (13)   Antoniewicz and two others, Bilger and Sheeler, Connor, Ferber, Greason, W. Green, Haines, Harris, Wentzel, Wilkinson
RHODE ISLAND (0)
SOUTH CAROLINA (5)   C. D. Cooper, Dedmond, L. D. Harris, James and Peterson

SOUTH DAKOTA (0)
TENNESSEE (2)   Mays, Sherman
TEXAS (10)   R. Adams, Brandley, C. Johnson and Young, Malloy, Morris, E. Padgett, F. Smith, Torres, Vargas
UTAH (2)   Hill, Petree
VERMONT (0)
VIRGINIA (11)   Bell, Burton and Conquest, Gray, Holland, Lyons, Phillips, S. Rogers, G. Smith, Vasquez, J. Williams
WASHINGTON (2)   Boggie, Horn
WEST VIRGINIA (3)   Bailey, Beale, Boyd
WISCONSIN (5)   J. Johnson, Kanieski, LeFevre, Long, Reichhoff
WYOMING (0)
FEDERAL GOVERNMENT (1)   Donnelly

TOTAL CASES: 416

✳ SOURCES

Introduction

Adams, James. Application for Executive Clemency in re James Adams (May 1, 1984).
Bennett, Willie. *Boston Herald*, Oct. 26, 1989, p. 1; *Boston Globe*, Oct. 4, 1990, p. 1; Sept. 12, 1990, p. 1; Sept. 1, 1990, p. 21; Jan. 29, 1990, p. 1; Jan. 28, 1990, p. 1; Jan. 5, 1990, p. 1; Oct. 26, 1989, p. 1; Oct. 25, 1989, p. 1; *N.Y. Times*, Mar. 29, 1990, p. 16; Jan. 15, 1990, p. 1; Jan. 5, 1990, p. 1.
Reynolds, Melvin Lee. State v. Reynolds, 619 S.W.2d 741 (1981); *Kansas City Star*, Oct. 16, 1983, p. 1; *Kansas City Times*, Oct. 14, 1983, p. 1; *L.A. Times*, Mar. 17, 1985, p. 1; *N.Y. Times*, Oct. 15, 1983, p. 7; *St. Louis Post-Dispatch*, Oct. 17, 1983, p. 5; Oct. 16, 1983, p. 1; Oct. 14, 1983, p. 1; Ganey 1989.

Chapter 1

Foster, James. Foster v. State, 100 S.E.2d 426 (1957); letter from G. L. Wacaster to HAB, Sept. 18, 1989; *Birmingham Post Herald*, July 5, 1958, p. 1; Martin 1960; Wood 1960. Our account depends almost entirely on the last two sources; where they disagree, we relied on Wood's version.
Hall, Gordon. In re Hall, 637 P.2d 690 (1981); *L.A. Times*, Feb. 19, 1982, p. II-2.
Lindley, William Marvin ("Red"). People v. Lindley, 161 P.2d 227 (1945); *S.F. Examiner*, Apr. 18, 1947; Gardner 1952:3–14.

Chapter 2

Gladish, Thomas V., Richard Wayne Greer, Ronald B. Keine, and Clarence Smith, Jr. *Detroit News Magazine*, Jan. 11, 1976, p. 14; *Detroit News*, Dec. 16, 1975, p. 1.
Tibbs, Delbert. Tibbs v. State, 337 So.2d 788 (1976); Tibbs v. Florida, 397 So.2d 1120 (1981); Tibbs v. Florida, 457 U.S. 31 (1982); McClory, "Justice for Mr. Tibbs," *The Reader* (Chicago), Feb. 11, 1983, p. 1; *Chicago Sun-Times*, Aug. 29, 1985; *Ft. Myers News-Press*, Nov. 7, 1982, p. 1; *Miami Herald*, July 29, 1976; June 8, 1982, p. 1; *Miami Times*, Sept. 16, 1982, p. 3; Cannon 1976; Gettinger 1979:183–84.
Zimmerman, Isidore. People v. Guariglia et al., 18 N.E.2d 324 (1938); People v. Zimmerman, 179 N.E.2d 849 (1962); Zimmerman v. City of N.Y., 40 Misc.2d 179 (1963); 44 Misc.2d 66 (1964); 52 Misc.2d 797 (1966); Zimmerman v. State, 116 Misc.2d 521 (1982); *Boston Phoenix*, Oct. 26, 1982, p. 18; *Florida Times Union* (Jacksonville), Nov. 17, 1982, p. 3; *Newsweek*, June 13, 1983, p. 82; *N.Y. Times*, Oct. 14, 1983, p. 25; June 8, 1983, p. 22; June 1, 1983, p. 1; Feb. 3, 1962, p. 19; Apr. 23, 1938; Apr. 15, 1938, p. 11; Apr. 12, 1938; July 26, 1937, p. 12; Apr. 23, 1937, p. 2; Apr. 16, 1937, p. 48; Apr. 11, 1937, p. 21; Zimmerman 1964. We relied mainly on Zimmerman's book and the introduction to it by Drew Pearson.

Chapter 3

Adams, Randall Dale. Adams v. State, 577 S.W.2d 717 (1979); Adams v. Texas, 448 U.S. 38 (1980); 624 S.W.2d 568 (1981); Ex parte Adams, 768 S.W.2d 281 (1989); Harris v. Texas, Texas Court of Criminal Appeals No. 69,634 (Sept. 13, 1989); "The Thin Blue Line" (unpublished synopsis of film by Errol Morris [1988]); *Austin American-Statesman*, Dec. 3, 1988, p. B2; Dec. 2, 1988; *Boston Globe*, Jan. 11, 1989, p. 65; *Dallas Morning News*, Dec. 3, 1989, p. 37A; Oct. 7, 1989, p. 33A; Oct. 6, 1989, p. 27A; Apr. 5, 1989, p. 19A; Mar. 14, 1989, p. 19A; Feb. 1, 1989, p. 19A; Dec. 20, 1988; Dec. 3, 1988, p. 1A; Dec. 2, 1988, p. 29A; Dec.

1, 1988, p. 33A; Nov. 28, 1988, p. 15A; Oct. 1, 1988, p. 15A; Sept. 27, 1988; *Dallas Times-Herald*, Mar. 1, 1989, p. 1; Feb. 26, 1989, p. 1; Jan. 31, 1989, p. 1; Dec. 9, 1988, p. B1; *Gainesville Sun*, Mar. 22, 1989, p. 5A; *L.A. Times*, Mar. 2, 1989, p. 1; *N.Y. Times*, Dec. 7, 1988, p. C19; Oct. 31, 1988; *People Magazine*, Apr. 10, 1989, pp. 155–56; *Washington Post*, Mar. 2, 1989, p. D1; Cartwright 1987; Fricker 1989; Rosenbaum 1990. We relied most heavily on articles by P. Applebome, M. Brower et al., R. Fricker, D. Pasztor, and R. Rosenbaum, and the movie *The Thin Blue Line*. The book by Adams et al. (1991) appeared too late for our use.

Carter, Nathaniel. *N.Y. Times*, Mar. 26, 1984, p. B2; Mar. 16, 1984, p. B1; Mar. 15, 1984, p. B1; Jan. 26, 1984, p. B5; Jan. 19, 1984, p. B9. Our account relied especially on the articles by P. Shenon.

Ellison, Ella Mae. Commonwealth v. Ellison, 379 N.E.2d 560 (1978); letter from Max Stern (defendant's attorney) to MLR, May 9, 1985.

Chapter 4

Billings, Warren K., and Thomas J. Mooney. People v. Billings, 168 P. 396 (1917); People v. Mooney, 171 P. 690 (1918); Frost 1968; Gentry 1967; Lofton 1966:88–91; Weihofen 1939. We relied especially on the books by R. T. Frost and C. Gentry.

Hauptmann, Bruno Richard. Bryan 1990–91; Fisher 1987; Kennedy 1985; Scaduto 1976; Seidman 1977; Waller 1961; Whipple 1989.

Sacco, Nicola, and Bartolomeo Vanzetti. Commonwealth v. Sacco, 151 N.E. 839 (1926); Proclamation of the Governor of Massachusetts (July 19, 1977), reprinted in Executive Department of Massachusetts, Report to the Governor in the Matter of Sacco and Vanzetti (1977); *N.Y. Times Book Review*, May 25, 1986, p. 10; Avrich 1991; Ehrmann 1969; Frankfurter 1927; Joughlin and Morgan 1948; Russell 1962; Russell 1986; Young and Kaiser 1985.

Chapter 5

Banks, Alf, Jr., Ed Coleman, Joe Fox, Albert Giles, Paul Hall, Ed Hicks, Frank Hicks, J. E. Knox, John Martin, Frank Moore, Ed Ware, Will Wordlow, and thirty-nine other defendants. Banks et al. v. State, 219 S.W. 1015 (1920); Ware et al. v. State, 225 S.W. 626 (1920); 252 S.W. 934 (1923); Hicks et al. v. State, 220 S.W. 308 (1923); Moore et al. v. Dempsey, 261 U.S. 86 (1923); Martin v. State, 257 S.W. 752 (1924); *N.Y. Times*, Nov. 6, 1919, p. 17; Cortner 1988; Kluger 1976:112–14; McCool 1970; Rogers 1960; Waterman and Overton 1951–52; White 1919; White 1948:47–51. Our account of this case relied largely on the book by R. C. Cortner.

Greenlee, Charles, Walter Irvin, and Samuel Shepherd. Shepherd et al. v. State, 46 So.2d 880 (1950); Shepherd et al. v. Florida, 341 U.S. 50 (1951); Irvin v. State, 66 So.2d 288 (1953); *The Crisis*, Oct. 1949, pp. 266–68; *Florida Times Union* (Jacksonville), Mar. 14, 1956, p. 21; Nov. 9, 1951, p. 16; *Orlando Morning Sentinel*, July 19, 1949, p. 1; July 18, 1949, p. 1; July 17, 1949, p. 1; *St. Petersburg Times*, Mar. 7, 1969, p. B1; Jan. 14, 1955, p. 6; Nov. 13, 1951, p. 8; Nov. 11, 1951, p. 1; Nov. 9, 1951, p. 1; Nov. 8, 1951, p. 1; Apr. 7,8,9, 1950; *Tampa Tribune*, Feb. 17, 1956, p. 1; Dec. 16, 1955, p. 1; Clendenin 1972; Horne 1988:192–93; Kennedy 1951; Kluger 1976:561; Lawson et al. 1986; Moore 1982; Trippett 1972; Wagy 1985:64–8. Among these sources, we relied most heavily on the articles by N. Bunin; also useful were the articles by D. Clendenin and T. Wagy, S. Lawson et al., O. Powers, and F. Trippett.

Montgomery, Olen, Clarence Norris, Haywood Patterson, Ozie Powell, Willie Roberson, Charlie Weems, Eugene Williams, Andrew Wright, and Roy Wright (the "Scottsboro Boys"). Powell v. Alabama, 287 U.S. 45 (1932); Norris v. Alabama, 294 U.S. 587 (1935); Patterson v. Alabama, 294 U.S. 600 (1935); Carter 1979;

Norris and Washington 1979; Patterson and Conrad 1950; White 1948:125–33. We relied heavily on the book by D. T. Carter.

Chapter 6

Brandley, Clarence. Brandley v. State, 691 S.W.2d 699 (1985); Ex parte Brandley, 781 S.W.2d 886 (1990); *Dallas Morning News*, Dec. 14, 1989, p. 19A; Mar. 19, 1987; *Dallas-Times Herald*, Dec. 14, 1989, p. A1; Apr. 5, 1987, p. A1; Mar. 29, 1987, p. L2; Mar. 19, 1987, p. B5; Mar. 17, 1987, p. A1; *Houston Chronicle*, Dec. 14, 1989, p. A1; Oct. 10, 1987, p. A1; Sept. 22, 1987, p. 1; *N.Y. Times*, Mar. 29, 1987; Mar. 22, 1987; Mar. 21, 1987, p. 1; Curtis 1987; Rohrlich 1990. We relied heavily on articles by P. Applebome; K. Fair; C. Gordon; J. McCormack; P. McKay and C. Robison; and L. Montgomery; the articles by T. Curtis and T. Rohrlich were indispensable. Details from these sources were confirmed in Davies 1991, which became available only after this chapter had been written.

Collins, Roosevelt. Collins v. State, 174 So. 296 (1937); Huie 1964. Our account relies entirely on the article by W. B. Huie (who refers to Collins as "Roosevelt Wilson").

Hollins, Jess. Ex parte Hollins, 14 P.2d 243 (1932); Hollins v. State, 38 P.2d 36 (1934); Hollins v. Oklahoma, 295 U.S. 394 (1935); Kluger 1976:161; Martin 1980; Styles 1937:46–47. We relied heavily on the article by C. H. Martin.

Chapter 7

Brite, Coke, and John Brite. People v. Brite et al., 72 P.2d 122 (1937); *S.F. Examiner-Chronicle*, "This World," June 3, 1990, p. 16; Gardner 1952:123–53. Bedau and Radelet (1987:100) erred in reporting the Brites' race. Our account relies especially on the discussion by E. S. Gardner.

Creamer, James, George Emmett, Larry Hacker, Billy Jenkins, Hoyt Powell, Charles Roberts, and Wayne Ruff. Creamer v. State, 205 S.E.2d 240 (1974); Emmett v. State, 205 S.E.2d 231 (1974); Emmett v. Ricketts, 397 F.Supp. 1025 (1975); letter from Bobby Lee Cook (defendant's attorney) to MLR, May 11, 1991; *Atlanta Constitution*, Oct. 29, 1983, p. 1B; Sept. 3, 1975, p. 1A; Aug. 28, 1975, p. 1A; Aug. 27, 1975, p. 1A; Apr. 4, 1975, p. 1A.

Miller, Lloyd Eldon, Jr. People v. Miller, 148 N.E.2d 455 (1958); Miller v. Pate, 386 U.S. 1 (1967); Lassers 1973. In preparing this chapter, we relied heavily on the book by Lassers (who refers to the prosecution witness Betty Baldwin as "June Lang").

Chapter 8

Carmen, Jack. *Columbus Citizen-Journal*, Dec. 20, 1977, p. 1; June 8, 1977, p. 8; June 7, 1977, p. 13; Jan. 31, 1976, p. 1; Jan. 16, 1976, p. 1; Sept. 12, 1975, p. 22. Our account relies especially on the article by H. Franken.

Dwyer, Paul N. Dwyer v. State, 145 A.2d 100 (1958); *ACLU Weekly Bulletin* No. 2021, Dec. 7, 1959, pp. 2–3; *Boston Herald*, Aug. 11, 1938, p. 1; Aug. 5, 1938, p. 1; Aug. 3, 1938, p. 1; *Boston Traveler*, Aug. 8, 1938, p. 1.

Hampton, Mary Katherin. Hampton v. Allgood, 254 F. Supp. 884 (1966); Spencer v. State, 133 So.2d 729 (1961); Lowall, "How Lee Bailey Freed the 'Hillbilly' Lolita," *Argosy*, Mar. 1967, pp. 58–61, 123; Lowall, "The Riddle of Mary K: Double Murderess or Innocent Dupe?" *Argosy*, Feb. 1965, pp. 14, 18, 123–24; letter from Gene Miller to MLR, July 9, 1985; letter from Florida Dept. of Corrections to MLR, Jan. 1, 1992; *Miami Herald*, Dec. 1, 1966, p. 1; Aug. 24, 1966, p. 16; Aug. 23, 1966, p. 7D; Aug. 22, 1966, p. 5B; Aug. 21, 1966, p. 6B; May 8, 1966, p. 1F; Aug. 17, 1964, p. 16; Hohenberg 1980:46–47. The series of articles by G. Miller was indispensable; articles by G. Lowall were also helpful.

Chapter 9

Banks, Jerry. Banks v. State, 182 S.E.2d 106 (1971); 218 S.E.2d 851 (1975); 227 S.E.2d 380 (1976); Banks v. Glass, 250 S.E.2d 431 (1978); 268 S.E.2d 630 (1980); Bailey v. State, 228 S.E.2d 357 (1976); Patrick v. State, 233 S.E.2d 757 (1977); *Atlanta Constitution*, Apr. 1, 1983, p. 10A; Mar. 22, 1983, p. 14A; Mar. 18, 1983, p. E1; Jan. 6, 1981, p. 1; Dec. 23, 1980, p. 1; *National Law Journal*, Nov. 19, 1990, p. 1; *N.Y. Times*, Dec. 26, 1980, p. 31; Oct. 17, 1980, p. 31; Gleason 1982. The most valuable source was the article by D. Gleason; we also relied on articles by L. Field and T. Cooper, N. McCall and T. Thompson, B. Mooney and T. Wicker, as well as an editorial in the *Atlanta Constitution*.

Cooks, Tony. *L.A. Times*, Nov. 11, 1986, p. I-3; Dec. 12, 1983, p. II-1; Nov. 27, 1983, p. VI-1. We have relied on the articles by D. Johnston.

Venegas, Juan. People v. Reyes and Venegas, 526 P.2d 225 (1974); Venegas v. Wagner, 704 F.2d 1144 (1983); Venegas v. City of Long Beach et al., No. 66285 (California Court of Appeals, Aug. 22, 1983); Venegas v. Wagner et al., 831 F.2d 1514 (1987); Venegas v. Mitchell, 867 F.2d 527 (1989); 110 S.Ct. 1679 (1990); *Jury Verdicts Weekly*, Aug. 8, 1986, vol. 3, no. 32, p. 26; *Long Beach Press-Telegram*, Mar. 18, 1990, p. D1; Nov. 15, 1987, p. B1; Feb. 28, 1986, p. E1; *National Law Journal*, Sept. 22, 1980, p. 5.

Chapter 10

Ferber, Neil. *Philadelphia Daily News*, Mar. 7, 1986, p. 9; *Philadelphia Inquirer*, Mar. 8, 1986, p. 1B; Jan. 4, 1986, p. 1B.

Langley, Gus Colin. Radin 1964:75–81. Our account relies entirely on E. Radin.

Richardson, James. Richardson v. State, 216 So.2d 2 (1968); 247 So.2d 296 (1971); 546 So.2d 1037 (1989); *Ft. Meyers News-Press*, May 1, 1989; *Gainesville Sun*, May 6, 1989, p. 3B; Apr. 29, 1989; Apr. 26, 1989, p. 1; Feb. 5, 1989; Jan. 24, 1989, p. 2B; Jan. 22, 1989, p. 3B; Jan. 5, 1989, p. 3B; Dec. 26, 1988, p. 3B; Dec. 23, 1988, p. 3B; Dec. 8, 1988; Aug. 12, 1988; Feb. 26, 1988, p. 3B; *Newsweek*, Apr. 24, 1989, p. 68; Nov. 13, 1967, p. 36; *N.Y. Times*, Apr. 27, 1989, p. 16; Apr. 23, 1989; *Orlando Sentinel*, Apr. 12, 1989; *Sarasota Herald Tribune*, Mar. 11, 1989, p. 1; *Tampa Tribune*, Dec. 14, 1990, p. 3B; May 7, 1989, p. 1B; Achenbach 1989; Lane 1970. We relied heavily on M. Lane's book; especially useful articles were those by J. Achenbach, R. Buck, J. Gibeault, L. W. Hicks, and M. Worth.

Chapter 11

Fay, Floyd ("Buzz"). State v. Fay, No. 78-CR-24 (Wood Cty., Ohio, Court of Common Pleas, Aug. 11, 1978); WD-78-32 (Ohio Court of Appeals, June 22, 1979); State v. Quinn, No. 80-CR-158 (Wood Cty., Ohio, Court of Common Pleas, Jan. 30, 1981); State v. Markland, No. 81-CR-9 (Wood Cty., Ohio, Court of Common Pleas, Feb. 9, 1981); *Denver Post*, Jan. 4, 1981, p. 17; *Fremont* (Ohio) *News-Messenger*, Oct. 31, 1980; *L.A. Times*, Dec. 22, 1980, p. 1; *N.Y. Times*, Nov. 3, 1980, p. C20; *Toledo Blade*, Oct. 31, 1989, p. 1; Cimerman 1981; Lykken 1981. We relied heavily on an article by A. Cimerman, and also on articles by D. Lykken and B. Siegel. Floyd Fay provided details unavailable elsewhere.

McLaughlin, Robert. State v. McLaughlin, 480 N.Y.S.2d 151 (1984); *N.Y. Law Journal*, July 9, 1986, p. 1; June 2, 1986, p. 1; *N.Y. Times*, July 20, 1986, p. 24; July 4, 1986, p. B10; *Village Voice*, July 15, 1986, p. 13; June 10, 1986, p. 14; Aug. 5, 1985, p. 14. We relied especially on the articles by J. Newfield.

Rogers, Silas. Rogers v. Commonwealth, 31 S.E.2d 576 (1944); record of pardon (Dec. 22, 1952) Exec. Jrnl., office of Secretary of the Commonwealth; *Petersburg* (Va.) *Progress-Index*, Dec. 23, 1952, p. 1; Block 1963:144–56; Ehrmann 1962:18.

Chapter 12

Bailey, Robert Ballard. Bailey v. West Virginia, 340 U.S. 905 (1950); State ex rel. Bailey v. Skeen, 340 U.S. 949 (1951); telephone interview with W.Va. parole board office, Aug. 2, 1983; *Charleston* (W.Va.) *Gazette*, Dec. 28, 1960, p. 1; July 9, 1950, p. 40; Bedau 1982:238; Gardner 1952:232–45; Gardner 1970:539. Our account relies heavily on E. S. Gardner.

Charles, Earl. State v. Charles, No. 23,392 (Georgia Superior Court, July 5, 1978); Charles v. Wade, 665 F.2d 661 (1982); *Southern Poverty Law Center Report*, Apr. 1984, p. 1; Jan./Feb., 1982, p. 7; July /Aug., 1979, p. 1; *The Trumpet* (Clearinghouse on Georgia Prisons and Jails, May/June, 1982), p. 1; *Atlanta Constitution*, Mar. 7, 1991; Mar. 22, 1983, p. 9A; Nov. 19, 1981, p. 29A; Jan. 6, 1981, pp. 1, 8 (two articles); *Florida Times Union* (Jacksonville), June 28, 1979; Schmitz 1982. We relied heavily on the article by A. Schmitz; also useful were the *SPLC Report* and the articles by K. Brewer and B. Mooney.

Imbler, Paul Kern. People v. Imbler, 371 P.2d 304 (1962); 379 U.S. 908 (1964); In re Imbler, 393 P.2d 687 (1964); Imbler v. Craven, 298 F. Supp. 795 (1969); Imbler v. California, 424 F.2d 631 (1970); 400 U.S. 865 (1970); Imbler v. Pachtman, 424 U.S. 409 (1976); *S.F. Examiner and Chronicle*, May 4, 1969, p. 8A; Wolfe 1973:335–41. We have relied mainly on B. Wolfe's account of this case.

Chapter 13

Domer, Robert K. State v. Domer, 204 N.E.2d 69 (1965); interview with Domer by authors, Feb. 2, 1991. Domer himself reviewed and contributed to several drafts of this chapter.

Rivera, Antonio, and Merla Walpole. Letter from David W. Call (defendants' attorney) to MLR, Sept. 4, 1985; *L.A. Times*, Nov. 23, 1975, p. 2; *N.Y. Times*, Nov. 23, 1975, p. 42; *S.F. Examiner*, Nov. 24, 1975; June 4, 1974.

Rogers, Courtney ("Fred"). People v. Rogers, 141 P.2d 722 (1943); Moskowitz, "You Can't Apologize to the Dead," *Inside Detective*, Dec. 1962, pp. 46–47, 70–71.

Conclusion

Columbus Dispatch, June 20, 1958, p. 16A; *Dallas Morning News*, Oct. 1, 1988, p. 15; Avrich 1984:417–23; Borchard 1932:xvi–xxi; Hirschberg 1940:20, 46; McCloskey 1989:1.

Inventory of Cases

Adams, James. See Sources for Introduction.

Adams, Randall Dale. See Sources for Chapter 3.

Amado, Christian. Commonwealth v. Amado, 439 N.E.2d 257 (1982); letter from Frank C. Kelleher to HAB, Apr. 22, 1985; *Boston Globe*, Aug. 21, 1982, p. 13.

Anderson, William Henry. Letter from Walter Clark (Broward Cty. sheriff) to John Wigginton (executive secretary to the governor), Apr. 9, 1945; letter from L. E. Thomas to Gov. Millard F. Caldwell, July 20, 1945. Materials on the Anderson case are located in the collection of governors' clemency files, Florida State Archives, Raymond Gray Library, Tallahassee.

Antoniewicz, Joseph, William A. Hallowell, and Edward H. Parks. Commonwealth v. Antoniewicz, 244 A.2d 687 (1968); *N.Y. Times*, Feb. 15, 1968, p. 49; MacNamara 1969:60.

Appelgate, Everett. People v. Creighton, 2 N.E.2d 650 (1936); Brown 1958:90–116; Kilgallen 1967:190–230; Lawes 1940:333–35.

Arroyo, Miguel. *N.Y. Times*, July 26, 1966, p. 41; July 22, 1966, p. 32.

Arroyo, Rogelio, Isauro Sanchez, Ignacio Varela, and Joaquin Varela. *Chicago Tribune*, Sept. 5, 1991, p. II-2.

Bachelor, Brett. *Gainesville Sun*, July 25, 1980, p. 7A.

Bailey, Robert Ballard. See Sources for Chapter 12.

Bambrick, Thomas. People v. Bambrick, 113 N.E. 1063 (1916); *N.Y. Times*, Oct. 7, 1916, p. 1; Bye 1919:82–83.

Banks, Alf, Jr., Ed Coleman, Joe Fox, Albert Giles, Paul Hall, Ed Hicks, Frank Hicks, J. E. Knox, John Martin, Frank Moore, Ed Ware, Will Wordlow, and thirty-nine other defendants. See Sources for Chapter 5.

Banks, Jerry. See Sources for Chapter 9.

Barbato, Joseph. People v. Barbato, 172 N.E. 458 (1930); *N.Y. Times*, Nov. 27, 1930, p. 25.

Barber, Arthur. People v. Barber, 306 N.Y.S.2d 878 (1969); 282 N.E.2d 329 (1972); 286 N.E.2d 464 (1972); letter from the Bronx Cty. Supreme Court to MLR, Oct. 18, 1985; *N.Y. Times*, Sept. 11, 1975, p. 47.

Beale, Clyde. State ex rel. Chafin v. Bailey, 144 S.E. 574 (1928); letter from K. D. Knapp (assistant commissioner, W.Va. Department of Corrections) to MLR, Sept. 3, 1985.

Beamon, Melvin Todd. Complaint in Beamon v. Hornsby et al. (filed by attorney David Schoen on Oct. 26, 1990, in U.S. District Court, Montgomery, Ala.); *Alabama Journal* (Montgomery), Oct. 31, 1990; *Montgomery Advertiser*, Dec. 13, 1990; Oct. 31, 1990.

Becker, Charles, and Frank ("Dago") Cirofici. Bye 1919:77–78; Klein 1927; Kunstler 1960:59–73; Logan 1970; Sullivan 1961:21–40.

Beeman, Gary L. *Ashtabula* (Ohio) *Star Beacon*, Oct. 5, 1979, p. 1; Sept. 29, 1979, p. 14; Sept. 25, 1979, p. 11; Sept. 5, 1979, p. 1; Apr. 11, 1978, p. 10; July 28, 1976, p. 9; June 5, 1976, p. 1; Greenberg 1982:920 n. 69.

Bell, Craig H. Ryder, "An Innocent Man Cleared—A Sex Slayer Nabbed!" *Inside Detective*, Mar. 1989, pp. 18–20, 49–50; *Virginia Pilot* (Norfolk), Oct. 29, 1987, p. D1; Oct. 16, 1987, p. A1.

Bennett, Louis William. *Oklahoma City Times*, Dec. 22, 1960, p. 3; Dec. 21, 1960, p. 26; Radin 1964:154–55; Reid and Gurwell 1973:136.

Bernstein, Charles. Bennett 1970:159–61; Bernstein 1965; Greenwald 1963; Radin 1964:107–10.

Bertrand, Delphine. Radin 1964:146–48.

Bigelow, Jerry D. People v. Bigelow, 37 Cal.3rd 731 (1983); *L.A. Times*, July 16, 1989, p. VI-1; July 6, 1989, p. 3; June 23, 1989, p. 3; Mar. 21, 1989, p. 3; *The Recorder* (San Francisco), Mar. 21, 1989, p. 1; Smith 1988; Bryan 1990–91.

Bilger, George, and Rudolph Sheeler. Sheeler v. Burke, 79 A.2d 654 (1951); Barnes and Teeters 1959:222, 267; Frank and Frank 1957:167–80; Radin 1964:27–34.

Billings, Warren K., and Thomas J. Mooney. See Sources for Chapter 4.

Blanton, Robert H., III. State v. Blanton, 312 So.2d 329 (1975); State v. Blackburn, 494 F. Supp. 895 (1980); letter from Lewis O. Unglesby (defendant's attorney) to MLR, Apr. 19, 1985.

Boggie, Clarence Gilmore. Block 1963:157–69; Gardner 1952:27–85.

Bowles, Joe. State v. Cain, 100 S.E. 884 (1919); N.C. Board of Paroles, Book of Pardons, Vol. 3, 1917–1932, p. 302 (May 27, 1921); letter from the N.C. Department of Cultural Resources, Division of Archives and History, to MLR, Nov. 20, 1984.

Boyd, Payne. Borchard 1932:22–27.

Brandley, Clarence Lee. See Sources for Chapter 6.

Branson, William. State v. Branson, 161 P. 689 (1916); *The Oregonian*, Sept. 12, 1920, p. 1.

Briggs, Joseph ("Jocko"). Briggs v. People, 76 N.E. 499 (1905); *Chicago Tribune*, Dec. 21, 1905, p. 2; Barbour 1919:506.

Brite, Coke, and John Brite. See Sources for Chapter 7.

Broady, Thomas H., Jr. State v. Broady, 321 N.E.2d 890 (1974); letter from the Ohio

Department of Rehabilitation and Correction to MLR, Aug. 26, 1985; *Columbus Citizen-Journal*, Oct. 3, 1978, p. 14; *Columbus Dispatch*, Sept. 14, 1978, p. B1.

Brown, Anthony Silah. Brown v. State, 471 So.2d 6 (1985); *Pensacola News*, Mar. 2, 1986, p. 1; Feb. 20, 1986, p. 1B; Feb. 15, 1986, p. 1; Feb. 13, 1986, p. 1B; Feb. 9, 1986, p. 1B; July 27, 1983, p. 1.

Brown, Bradford. State v. Brown, 372 A.2d 557 (1977); *S.F. Chronicle*, "This World," Mar. 12, 1989, p. 11; *N.Y. Times*, Dec. 31, 1979, p. 10; *Washington Post*, Aug. 23, 1979, p. C2.

Brown, J. B. Brown v. State, 32 So. 107 (1902); Borchard 1932:32–38.

Brown, Joseph Green. Brown v. State, 381 So.2d 690 (1980); 439 So.2d 872 (1983); Brown v. Wainwright, 785 F.2d 1457 (1986); *L.A. Times*, May 10, 1987, p. 1.

Brown, Robert, and Elton Houston. Warden 1990:36–37.

Brown, Willie A., and Larry Troy. Brown v. State, 515 So.2d 211 (1987); *Gainesville Sun*, Sept. 18, 1988, p. B1; Mar. 25, 1988, p. 1; *St. Petersburg Times*, Mar. 25, 1988, p. 1.

Bundy, Harry Dale. *Columbus Dispatch*, June 20, 1958, p. 16A; Radin 1964:130–36, 249–50.

Burt, LaVale. Warden 1990:43–46.

Burton, Samuel, and Sylvanus L. Conquest. Burton v. Commonwealth, 60 S.E. 55 (1908); 62 S.E. 376 (1908); letter from the Circuit Court, city of Norfolk, to MLR, Oct. 19, 1984.

Butler, Louise, and George Yelder. Borchard 1932:39–44.

Calloway, Willie. McCormick 1964.

Carden, Ronald Q. *Arkansas Democrat*, Dec. 28, 1982, p. 1; Dec. 21, 1982, p. 1; Dec. 19, 1982, p. 1F; Guzda 1983.

Carmen, Jack Allen. See Sources for Chapter 8.

Carter, Nathaniel. See Sources for Chapter 3.

Cashin, Harry F. People v. Cashin, 182 N.E. 74 (1932); Murray, "I Snatched My Client From the Death House," *Crime Confessions*, Mar. 1942, pp. 28–31, 50; *N.Y. Times*, Apr. 28, 1962, p. 25; Mar. 31, 1933, p. 9; Dec. 16, 1932, p. 8; July 29, 1932, p. 16; July 20, 1932, p. 18; Apr. 30, 1932, p. 2; Apr. 8, 1931, p. 6; Feb. 20, 1931, p. 1.

Cero, Gangi (a.k.a. Cero Gangi). Commonwealth v. Cero, 162 N.E. 349 (1928); Commonwealth v. Gallo, 175 N.E. 718 (1931); Borchard, memorandum on Cero Gangi case (unpublished manuscript, Yale University Library, Dec. 21, 1931); Ehrmann 1962:19.

Chambers, Isiah ("Izell"), Charlie Davis, Jack Williamson, and Walter Woodward. Chambers v. State, 151 So. 499 (1933); 152 So. 437 (1934); 158 So. 153 (1934); 167 So. 697 (1936); 187 So. 156 (1939); Chambers v. Florida, 309 U.S. 227 (1940); *Ft. Lauderdale News*, Mar. 10, 1942, p. 1; Feb. 12, 1940, p. 1; *Palm Beach Post*, Mar. 11, 1942, p. 5; Mar. 10, 1942, p. 1; Styles 1937:31, 161–64.

Chambers, Leon. Chambers v. State, 252 So.2d 217 (1971); Chambers v. Mississippi, 410 U.S. 284 (1973); telephone interview with George West (defendant's attorney), Oct. 10, 1985; Miller 1975:304.

Charles, Earl Patrick. See Sources for Chapter 12.

Clark, Charles Lee. People v. Anderson, 205 N.W.2d 461 (1973), at 472 and 484; act approved Jan. 28, 1972, No. 1, 1972 Mich. Pub. Acts 1; *Boston Globe*, Jan. 29, 1972, p. 2; *Detroit Free Press*, Dec. 17, 1971, p. 6B; *Washington Post*, June 12, 1981, p. 16A.

Clark, Ephraim R., Lindberg Hall, and Sceola Kuykendall. *Detroit Free Press*, Nov. 25, 1961, p. 3; Nov. 19, 1961, p. 3; Nov. 15, 1961, p. 2; Radin 1964:18–23.

Cobb, Perry, and Darby Williams. People v. Cobb et al., 455 N.E.2d 31 (1983);

Chicago Lawyer, Oct. 1986, pp. 6–7; Nov. 1983, p. 5; *Chicago Tribune*, Sept. 4, 1988, p. V-1; Jan. 21, 1987, p. II-3.

Coleman, Robert. Borchard 1941:202–3; Frank and Frank 1957:190.

Collins, Roosevelt. See Sources for Chapter 6.

Connor, Matthew. *Philadelphia Inquirer*, Oct. 5, 1990, p. 1B; Mar. 30, 1990, p. 1B; Mar. 3, 1990, p. 1B; Feb. 22, 1990, p. 1A.

Cooks, Tony. See Sources for Chapter 9.

Cooper, C. D. State v. Cooper, 110 S.E. 152 (1921); *True Detective Mysteries*, Oct. 1935, p. 13; *The State* (Columbia, S.C.), Aug. 15, 1934, p. 1.

Cooper, Ralph, Collis English, McKinlay Forrest, John McKenzie, James Thorpe, and Horace Wilson. State v. Cooper, 67 A.2d 298 (1949); 92 A.2d 786 (1952); *N.Y. Times*, Feb. 10, 1956, p. 46; Nov. 28, 1951, p. 34; Bedau 1964a:37; Bliven 1949; Horne 1988:131–54; Lofton 1966:191–92.

Cox, Robert Craig. Cox v. State, 555 So.2d 352 (1989); *N.Y. Times*, Dec. 22, 1989.

Craig, Alvin, and Walter Hess. Borchard 1932:93–98.

Creamer, James, George Emmett, Larry Hacker, Billy Jenkins, Hoyt Powell, Charles Roberts, and Wayne Ruff. See Sources for Chapter 7.

Crutcher, Willie, Jim Hudson, John Murchison, and Cleo Staten. Borchard 1932:160–65.

Dabney, Condy. Borchard 1932:50–57.

Davino, Frank. People v. Davino, 31 N.E.2d 913 (1940); 43 N.E.2d 472 (1942); Fischbein, "My Greatest Criminal Case," *Crime Detective*, Dec. 1945, pp. 46–51; *N.Y. Times*, Nov. 10, 1942, p. 29; Dec. 10, 1941, p. 52; Dec. 5, 1941, p. 11.

Dawson, Sie. Dawson v. State, 139 So.2d 408 (1962); *St. Petersburg Times*, Sept. 20, 1977, p. 1; *Tallahassee Democrat*, May 20, 1979, p. 1; Bedau 1982:236–37. Additional materials are located in the governors' clemency files, Florida State Archives, Raymond Gray Library, Tallahassee.

Dean, Sara Ruth. Dean v. State, 160 So. 584 (1935); letter from Sara Ruth Dean to Gov. Sennett Conner, May 28, 1935 (on file in the Mississippi Department of Archives and History).

Dedmond, Roger Z. Letter from Frank B. Sanders (Director, Division of Public Safety Programs, State of S.C.) to MLR, Feb. 1, 1984; *Atlanta Constitution*, Sept. 17, 1968, p. 2; *Charlotte Observer*, Mar. 1, 1968, p. 1; MacNamara 1969:60.

de los Santos, George ("Chiefie"). De los Santos v. O'Lone, No. 82-1717, slip opinion (U.S. District Court of N.J., July 6, 1983); *Newark Star-Ledger*, Jan. 13, 1984, p. 35; *N.Y. Times*, July 28, 1983, p. B6; *Philadelphia Inquirer*, Aug. 9, 1983, p. B1; July 28, 1983, p. 8B.

DeMore, Louis. Radin 1964:151–54, 251–52.

Domer, Robert K. See Sources for Chapter 13.

Donnelly, James. Donnelly v. United States, 228 U.S. 243 (1913); Bye 1919:83–84.

Dove, Frank, Fred Dove, and George Williams. N.C. Board of Charities and Public Welfare, *Special Bulletin No. 10: Capital Punishment in North Carolina*, pp. 45–49 (1929).

Drake, Henry. Campbell v. State, 240 S.E.2d 828 (1977); Drake v. State, 247 S.E.2d 57 (1978); Zant v. Campbell, 265 S.E.2d 22 (1980); Drake v. Francis, 727 F.2d 990 (1984); Drake v. Kemp, 762 F.2d 1449 (1985); *Atlanta Constitution*, Dec. 24, 1987, p. 1; *L.A. Times*, Dec. 23, 1988, p. 1; Dec. 22, 1988, p. 1.

Draper, Ayliff. Draper v. State, 192 Ark. 675 (1936); proclamation of Gov. Carl E. Bailey, Aug. 19, 1938, on file with the Arkansas History Commission, Little Rock; Roy Emery, "Hillbilly Horror: Mountain Justice Uses High Voltage Third Degree," *Crime Detective*, Dec. 1939, pp. 68–71, 106–8.

Dulin, William. People v. Hayes, 25 P.2d 995 (1933); 30 P.2d 21 (1934); *L.A. Times*, Aug. 15, 1936, p. 1; May 2, 1933, p. 8; Apr. 18, 1933, p. II-8; Apr. 15, 1933,

p. II-2; Apr. 14, 1933, p. II-8; Apr. 13, 1933, p. II-8; Apr. 12, 1933, p. II-8; Apr. 11, 1933, p. II-8; *S.F. News and Examiner*, Aug. 20, 1936; Aug. 15, 1936; Aug. 14, 1936.

Dwyer, Paul. See Sources for Chapter 8.

Ellison, Ella Mae. See Sources for Chapter 3.

Estes, Cornell Avery. Letter from Mary Humphries (assistant attorney general) to Carl Beritela (management analyst, Maryland Division of Management Analysis and Audits), Jan. 4, 1984; *Baltimore Sun*, Mar. 22, 1984, p. C16.

Favor, Jack Graves. Favor v. Henderson, 348 F. Supp. 423 (1972); 472 F.2d 1382 (1973); Butler and Henderson 1990:5, 72–98.

Fay, Floyd ("Buzz"). See Sources for Chapter 11.

Featherstone, Francis. *N.Y. Times*, Sept. 6, 1986, p. 29; Rosenbaum 1990–91.

Ferber, Neil. See Sources for Chapter 10.

Fewell, Stanford Ellis. Fewell v. State, 66 So.2d 771 (1953); Ex parte Fewell, 73 So.2d 558 (1954); *Argosy*, July 1959, p. 41; July 1958, p. 12; May 1958, p. 56; Apr. 1958, p. 16; Feb. 1958, p. 8; Raab 1967:236–37.

Fisher, William. People v. Fisher, 151 N.E.2d 617 (1958); Memorandum in Support of S. 8082, 207th Leg. (N.Y. 1984) (Mar. 5, 1984), passed as Act of Dec. 21, 1984, ch. 1007, 1984 N.Y. Laws 2836; *Newsday*, Feb. 18, 1986, p. II-3; *N.Y. Times*, July 3, 1983, p. 18A.

Foster, James Fulton. See Sources for Chapter 1.

Foster, Lock, George Frick, George Ury, and two others. Miller v. State, 76 N.E. 823 (1906); *N.Y. Times*, June 7, 1913, p. 1; Dec. 8, 1911, p. 1.

Fowler, Walter, and Heywood Pugh. Raab 1967:234–36.

Frank, Leo M. Frank v. State, 80 S.E. 1016 (1914); Frank v. Magnum, 237 U.S. 309 (1915); *Atlanta Constitution*, Apr. 26, 1983, p. 1B; *N.Y. Times*, Mar. 12, 1986, p. 10; Dec. 23, 1983, p. 10; Dec. 13, 1983, p. 22; Mar. 8, 1982, p. 12; Busch 1952:15–74; Dinnerstein 1968; Frey and Thompson-Frey 1988.

Frederick, Johnny, and David R. Keaton. Keaton v. State, 273 So.2d 385 (1973); *Tallahassee Democrat*, Mar. 27, 1983, p. G1; Lickson 1974; Miller 1975:253.

Fry, John Henry ("Tennessee"). People v. Cooper, 349 P.2d 964 (1960); *S.F. Examiner*, Mar. 9, 1962; June 17, 1959, p. 10; June 5, 1959; Block 1962:64–65. Bedau and Radelet (1987:116) erred in reporting Fry's race.

Fudge, E. J. Fudge v. State, 78 So. 510 (1918); court journal entry of nolle prosequi, State v. Fudge, No. 1916-24117-CA-01, Minute Book X, p. 281 (Escambia Cty. Circuit Court, filed Apr. 10, 1918).

Gaines, Freddie Lee. *Birmingham News*, Feb. 12, 1991; Feb. 11, 1991; *San Francisco Banner Daily Journal*, Feb. 13, 1991, p. 6.

Garcia, Francisco. State v. Garcia, 143 P. 1012 (1914).

Garner, Vance, and Will Johnson. *Birmingham News*, Feb. 12, 1906, p. 9; Dec. 29, 1905, p. 8; *Tallahassee Weekly True Democrat*, July 21, 1905, p. 4.

Garrett, Sammie. People v. Garrett, 339 N.E.2d 753 (1975); Warden 1990:51–52.

Garvey, Mike, Harvey Lesher, and Phil Rohan. *S.F. Examiner*, June 21, 1930, p. 1; Feb. 21, 1928, p. 1; Borchard 1932:137–43.

Giddens, Charles Ray. Giddens v. State, No. F-78-164 (Court of Criminal Appeals, Nov. 17, 1981); Giddens v. Benson, No. 0-82-128 (Court of Criminal Appeals, June 30, 1982); Stowers, "The View from Death Row," *D Magazine*, Apr. 1986.

Giles, James, John Giles, and Joseph Johnson, Jr. Giles v. Maryland, 386 U.S. 66 (1967); *Washington Post*, Oct. 31, 1967, p. A1; Abramowitz and Paget 1964:161; Strauss 1970.

Gladish, Thomas V., Richard Wayne Greer, Ronald B. Keine, and Clarence Smith, Jr. See Sources for Chapter 2.

Goodwin, Paul. Goodwin v. Page, 444 P.2d 833 (1968); 296 F. Supp. 1205 (1969); 418 F.2d 867 (1969); *L.A. Times*, Mar. 9, 1969, p. 6.

Grace, Frank ("Parky"). Commonwealth v. Grace, 352 N.E.2d 175 (1976); 412 N.E.2d 354 (1980); *Outlook on Justice* (newsletter of the New England American Friends Service Committee), Mar.–Apr., 1985, p. 1; Dec. 1983–Jan. 1984, p. 1; *Boston Globe*, Jan. 29, 1985, p. 17; Jan. 16, 1985, p. 19; Sept. 14, 1984, p. 17; *Boston Phoenix*, Mar. 19, 1985, p. 1.

Gray, Russell Leon. *Richmond Times-Dispatch*, Apr. 13, 1990, p. A9; Apr. 12, 1990, p. A1.

Greason, Samuel. Commonwealth v. Greason, 53 Atl. 539 (1902); 57 Atl. 349 (1904); In re Greason, 55 Atl. 788 (1903); *N.Y. Times*, June 17, 1905; *Reading* (Pa.) *Eagle*, June 16, 1905, p. 1.

Green, Nelson, and Charles Stielow. People v. Stielow, 112 N.E. 1069 (1916); Block 1963:203–20; Borchard 1932:241–52; Brandon 1949.

Green, William S. Commonwealth v. Green, 56 A.2d 95 (1948); 128 A.2d 577 (1957); *Philadelphia Daily News*, Apr. 19, 1957, p. 3; Feb. 22, 1957, p. 5; Barnes and Teeters 1959:267; Radin 1964:139–40.

Greenlee, Charles, Walter Lee Irvin, and Samuel Shepherd. See Sources for Chapter 5.

Gross, Louis. Block 1963:237–52; Gardner 1952:163–80.

Growden, Gerald. *Washington Post*, June 19, 1932, p. 11; Frank and Frank 1957:190.

Grzechowiak, Stephen, and Max Rybarczyk. People v. Bogdanoff, 171 N.E. 890 (1930); *Buffalo News*, Mar. 26, 1989, p. 1; *N.Y. Times*, July 18, 1930, p. 21; July 17, 1930, p. 14; Elliott 1940:244–45; Lawes 1940:314–15.

Gunter, Thomas. Borchard 1932:335–37.

Haines, Ernest. Commonwealth v. Haines, 101 A. 641 (1917); Bye 1919:87.

Hall, Gordon Robert Castillo. See Sources for Chapter 1.

Hall, James. State v. Hall, 235 N.W.2d 702 (1975); 249 N.W.2d 843 (1977); 434 U.S. 822 (1977); State v. Hall (Johnson Cty., Iowa, District Court, May 17, 1984); *N.Y. Times*, Sept. 2, 1984, p. 29.

Hall, Phyllis Elaine. Hall v. State, 500 So.2d 661 (1986); *Gainesville Sun*, Jan. 17, 1987, p. 2B.

Hamby, Loren. Hamby v. People, 128 P.2d 993 (1942); executive order of Gov. J. C. Vivian, Apr. 3, 1946, in files of the clemency coordinator, Office of the Colorado Governor.

Hampton, Mary Katherin. See Sources for Chapter 8.

Hankins, Leonard. State v. Hankins, 258 N.W. 578 (1935); Houts 1958:161–62; Radin 1964:81–82.

Hardy, Vance. Gardner 1952:183–214.

Harris, Frank. Commonwealth ex rel. Harris v. Burke, 96 A.2d 909 (1953); *N.Y. Times*, July 13, 1947, p. 32.

Harris, L. D. State v. Harris, 46 S.E.2d 682 (1948); Harris v. State of South Carolina, 338 U.S. 68 (1949); *Augusta* (Ga.) *Chronicle*, July 18, 1979, pp. 1W–3W.

Hauptmann, Bruno Richard. See Sources for Chapter 4.

Hefner, Cecil. Pardon report for Cecil Hefner (Apr. 4, 1921), available at the N.C. Department of Archives and History.

Hennis, Timothy B. State v. Hennis, 372 S.E.2d 523 (1988); *News and Observer* (Raleigh, N.C.) May 9, 1989, p. 1; May 8, 1989, p. 1; May 7, 1989, p. 1.

Hicks, Larry. *Playboy*, May 1981, p. 66; Aug. 1980, p. 62.

Hill, Christina. Telephone conversation with John Cunha (defendant's attorney), Apr. 4, 1991; *Boston Globe*, Jan. 29, 1991, p. 15.

Hill, Joe (orig. Joseph Hillstrom). State v. Hillstrom, 150 P. 935 (1915); *L.A. Times*, Aug. 19, 1990, p. 20; Foner 1965; Smith 1969; Stegner 1948.

Hoffman, Harry L. People v. Hoffman, 220 N.Y.S. 249 (1927); 157 N.E. 869 (1927); Gilman 1929:90; Reynolds 1950:35–62.

Hoffner, Louis. People v. Hoffner, 42 N.E.2d 15 (1942); Hoffner v. State, 142 N.Y.S.2d 630 (1955); see also act approved Apr. 29, 1955, ch. 841, 1955 N.Y. Laws 1992; Special Commission Established For the Purpose of Investigating and Studying the Abolition of the Death Penalty in Capital Cases, *Report No. 2575 to the Massachusetts House of Representatives of 1958* (Dec. 30, 1958); *N.Y. Herald Tribune*, June 17, 1955, p. 1; Block 1962:63; Hohenberg 1959:128–31; Radin 1964:110–12.

Holbrook, Ernest, Jr., and Herman Ray Rucker. *Atlanta Constitution*, May 5, 1984, p. 8A; *N.Y. Times*, Apr. 16, 1984, p. 19.

Holland, Kenneth R. Holland v. Commonwealth, 55 S.E.2d 437 (1949); *Norfolk Virginian-Pilot*, Apr. 15, 1950, p. 13.

Hollins, Jess. See Sources for Chapter 6.

Horn, Geither. Horn v. State, 328 P.2d 159 (1958); 358 U.S. 900 (1958); Horn v. Rhay, No. 59-1385 (Eastern District, Washington, June 27, 1959); Horn v. Bailie, 309 F.2d 167 (1962); Radin 1964:26.

Imbler, Paul Kern. See Sources for Chapter 12.

Jackson, Edmond D. People v. Jackson, 322 N.E.2d 272 (1974); Jackson v. Fogg, 465 F. Supp. 177 (1978); 589 F.2d 108 (1978); *N.Y. Times*, Dec. 23, 1978, p. 1.

Jackson, John William. Jackson v. State, 511 So.2d 1047 (1987).

Jackson, Sergeant. Jackson v. San Diego, 175 Cal. Rptr. 395 (1981); letter from the San Diego City Attorney's Office to MLR, May 14, 1985; *L.A. Times*, Oct. 27, 1974, p. III-20; Oct. 20, 1974, p. 3.

James, Tyrone, and Winfred J. ("Wilbur") Peterson. Letter from David I. Bruck to MLR, Aug. 19, 1985; *The State* (Columbia, S.C.), Sept. 29, 1982, p. 3C; Sept. 26, 1982, p. 7C; Sept. 24, 1982, p. 1C; Sept. 15, 1982, p. 1C; Sept. 9, 1982, p. 3C; Aug. 27, 1982, p. 1C.

Jaramillo, Anibal. Jaramillo v. State, 417 So.2d 257 (1982); *Miami Herald*, July 9, 1982, p. D1.

Jenkins, Lonnie. *Detroit Free Press*, Dec. 24, 1940, p. 1; Radin 1964:159–65.

Jennings, Jasper. State v. Jennings, 87 P. 524 (1906); Bedau 1965:24.

Jent, William Riley, and Earnest Lee Miller. Jent v. State, 408 So.2d 1024 (1982); 435 So.2d 809 (1983); Miller v. State, 415 So.2d 1262 (1982); 435 So.2d 813 (1983); Miller and Jent v. Wainwright, 798 F.2d 426 (1986); Miller and Jent v. Dugger, 820 F.2d 1135 (1987); *Miami Herald*, Jan. 16, 1988, p. 1; Dec. 14, 1987, p. 1; Nov. 4, 1987, p. 1; Nov. 2, 1987, p. 1; Nov. 1, 1987, p. 1; *St. Petersburg Times*, Feb. 21, 1988, p. 1; *Washington Post*, Aug. 25, 1985, p. B1.

Johnson, Cooper, and Bennie Young. E. M. Farmer, "Saga of the Phantom Slayer," *Master Detective*, July 1947; pardon proclamation, Mar. 7, 1934 (Texas State Library, Austin).

Johnson, Emma Jo. Radin 1964:115–16.

Johnson, John. Borchard 1932:110–19.

Johnson, Lawyer. Commonwealth v. Johnson, 313 N.E.2d 571 (1974); 361 N.E.2d 212 (1977); 429 N.E.2d 726 (1982); *Newsletter of the Massachusetts Citizens Against the Death Penalty* (Boston), Winter 1984, p. 3; *Boston Globe*, Oct. 20, 1982, p. 25; July 1, 1982, p. 15.

Jones, Harllel B. Jones v. Jago, 428 F. Supp. 405 (1977); Jago v. United States District Court, 570 F.2d 618 (1978); Jones v. Jago, 575 F.2d 1164 (1978); 439 U.S. 883 (1978); Jones v. Shanklin, 800 F.2d 77 (1986); *Newsletter of Cleveland ACLU*, Aug. 1985, p. 1; *Cleveland Plain Dealer*, Oct. 19, 1978, p. 1.

Jones, Tom. Jones v. Commonwealth, 102 S.W.2d 345 (1936); 97 F.2d 335 (1938); Anderson v. Buchanan, 168 S.W.2d 48 (1943); Miller 1938; Warder 1941:963.

Jordan, Theodore V. State v. Jordan, 26 P.2d 558 (1933); *Oregon Journal*, Nov. 6, 1964, p. 21; Bedau 1965:23.

Jordan, William. Jordan v. State, 157 So. 485 (1934); *Geneva County Minute Book*, vol. 8, p. 593 (1934); *Geneva County Reaper*, Nov. 23, 1934, p. 1; Sept. 14, 1934, p. 1; Sept. 7, 1934, p. 5.

Kamacho, Daniel. Radin 1964:149–51.

Kanieski, Edward F. State v. Kanieski, 141 N.W.2d 196 (1966); Kanieski v. Gagnon, 427 F.2d 401 (1970); 194 N.W.2d 808 (1972); *Wisconsin State Journal* (Madison), May 4, 1980, p. V-1; Mar. 7, 1980, p. III-1; Feb. 4, 1979, p. 4; Jan. 1, 1978, p. 1; Mar. 8, 1972, p. IV-1; Mar. 3, 1972, p. 1.

Kapatos, Thomas. In re Kapatos, 208 F. Supp. 883 (1962); *N.Y. Times*, July 10, 1962, p. 35.

Kassim, Ahmad. *N.Y. Times*, Nov. 9, 1986, p. 25; Jan. 6, 1985, p. 22E.

Kendall, Hamp, and John Vickers. State v. Kendall, 57 S.E. 340 (1907); Radin 1964:144–45, 251.

Kidd, Robert Lee. People v. Kidd, 366 P.2d 49 (1961); *S.F. Examiner*, Sept. 19, 1974, p. 26; July 11, 1962, p. 1.

Kirkes, Leonard M. People v. Kirkes, 243 P.2d 816 (1952); People v. Kirkes, 249 P.2d 1 (1952); *L.A. Times*, May 6, 1953, p. II-7; May 5, 1953, p. II-6; *Santa Barbara News-Press*, May 5, 1953, p. 1; Apr. 30, 1953, p. 1; Apr. 29, 1953, p. 1; Apr. 28, 1953, p. 1; Apr. 24, 1953, p. 1; Apr. 16, 1953, p. 4.

Krause, Julius. Letter from Linda Sneed (chief of the Bureau of Records Management, Ohio Department of Rehabilitation and Correction) to MLR, Sept. 25, 1986; Radin 1964:16.

Labat, Edgar, and Clifton Alton Poret. State v. Labat, 75 So.2d 333 (1954); Labat v. Sigler, 162 F. Supp. 574 (1958); 267 F.2d 307 (1959); U.S. ex rel. Poret and Labat, 234 F. Supp. 171 (1964); Labat v. Bennett, 365 F.2d 698 (1966); Bennett v. Labat, 386 U.S. 991 (1967); Maas 1960; Wolfe 1973:296–98.

Lambert, Henry J. State v. Lambert, 53 A. 879 (1902); Borchard, memorandum on the Lambert case, pp. 10, 14 (unpublished manuscript, Yale University Library); files of the Maine State Archives; *Bangor Daily News*, July 25, 1923, p. 1; *Daily Kennebec Journal*, July 25, 1923, p. 17; *N.Y. Times*, July 25, 1923, p. 6.

Lamble, Harold. Lamble v. State, 114 A. 346 (1921); In re McDermit, 114 A. 144 (1921); Public Hearing on Assembly Bills Nos. 33 & 34 (Abolition of Capital Punishment) Before the N.J. Assembly, Judiciary Committee, p. 26A–34A (typescript, June 19, 1958) (second day, testimony of J. C. Deardorff, Jr.); *New Orleans Times-Picayune*, Apr. 30, 1929, p. 1; *N.Y. Times*, Aug. 30, 1921, p. 14; Aug. 29, 1921, p. 4; Aug. 26, 1921, p. 4; Aug. 25, 1921, p. 12; Aug. 24, 1921, p. 6; Aug. 23, 1921, p. 10; July 16, 1920, p. 7.

Lamson, David. People v. Lamson, 36 P.2d 361 (1934); Moskowitz, "You Can't Apologize to the Dead," *Inside Detective*, Dec. 1962, pp. 46–47, 70–71; *N.Y. Times*, Apr. 4, 1936, p. 4; Mar. 25, 1936, p. 46; May 15, 1935, p. 44; Lamson 1936.

Landano, V. James. State v. Landano, 425 A.2d 264 (1980); 483 A.2d 153 (1984); Landano v. Rafferty, 670 F. Supp. 570 (1987); 856 F.2d 569 (1988); 126 F.R.D. 627 (1989); *N.Y. Times*, Aug. 3, 1989, p. B1; *The Press* (Atlantic City), July 30, 1989, p. 6.

Langley, Gus Colin. See Sources for Chapter 10.

Lanzillo, Luigi. Letter from the Connecticut Board of Pardons to MLR, Nov. 11, 1985; *Hartford Courant*, May 8, 1928, p. 1; *New Haven Journal-Courier*, May 8, 1928, p. 1.

Larkman, Edward. People v. Larkman, 155 N.E. 873 (1926); *N.Y. Times*, Jan. 14, 1927, p. 12; Frank and Frank 1957:188–89; Williams 1962:237–38.

Leaster, Bobby Joe. *Boston Globe*, Dec. 29, 1989, p. 23; Dec. 27, 1986, p. 1; Nov. 21, 1986, p. 8; Nov. 16, 1986, p. 1; Nov. 5, 1986, p. 33; Nov. 4, 1986, p. 1; Oct. 9, 1986, p. 106; Sept. 16, 1986, p. 17; Apr. 1, 1986, p. 17; Kenney 1986; Kenney 1988.

Lee, Chol Soo. In re Chol Soo Lee, 163 Cal. Rptr. 204 (1980); *L.A. Times*, Aug. 11, 1983, p. 16; Sept. 26, 1982, p. IV-1; *S.F. Chronicle*, Sept. 4, 1982, p. 2; *S.F. Examiner*, Aug. 25, 1983; Mar. 29, 1983, p. B1; Jan. 16, 1983, p. B2.

Lee, Wilbert, and Freddie Pitts. Lee v. State, 166 So.2d 131 (1964); 380 U.S. 917 (1965); State v. Pitts, 227 So.2d 880 (1969); 234 So.2d 123 (1969); Pitts v. State, 247 So.2d 53 (1971); 307 So.2d 473 (1975); 423 U.S. 918 (1975); *St. Petersburg Times*, Sept. 20, 1985, p. 2B; *N.Y. Times*, Sept. 20, 1975, p. 1; Greenberg 1982:919; Miller, unpublished epilogue (1975); Miller 1975.

LeFevre, Frank. LeFevre v. State, 8 N.W.2d 288 (1943); LeFevre v. Goodland, 19 N.W.2d 884 (1945); *Wisconsin State Journal* (Madison), Mar. 7, 1980, p. III-1; Jan. 1, 1978, p. 1.

Lettrich, George. People v. Lettrich, 108 N.E.2d 488 (1952); *Official Detective Stories*, Sept. 1953, p. 50.

Leyra, Camilo. People v. Leyra, 98 N.E.2d 553 (1951); Leyra v. Denno, 347 U.S. 556 (1954); People v. Leyra, 134 N.E.2d 475 (1956); *N.Y. Times*, May 3, 1956, p. 25; Apr. 28, 1956, p. 36; Kunstler 1960:194–203.

Lindley, William Marvin ("Red"). See Sources for Chapter 1.

Lindsey, Lloyd. People ex rel. Carey v. Strayhorn, 329 N.E.2d 194 (1975); People v. Lindsey, 392 N.E.2d 278 (1979); *Chicago Tribune*, June 27, 1979, p. 1.

Linscott, Steven Paul. People v. Linscott, 482 N.E.2d 403 (1985); 500 N.E.2d 420 (1986); 511 N.E.2d 1303 (1987); Warden 1990:46–47.

Lobaugh, Ralph W. *Atlanta Constitution*, Oct. 29, 1977, p. 2; *Boston Globe*, Aug. 25, 1977, p. 12; *Fort Wayne News-Sentinel*, Dec. 30, 1950, p. 1; Dec. 6, 1949; Radin 1964:190–98.

Long, Eli J. Long v. State, 187 N.W. 167 (1922); Wisconsin Assembly Bill No. 147, 58th Leg. (1927); Wisconsin Senate Bill No. 294, 58th Leg. (1927); Veto Message of Gov. Zimmerman to the Wisconsin Assembly Rejecting Bill 147, Act to Provide Indemnification for Eli Long, in *Journal of the Proceedings of the 58th Session of the Wisconsin Legislature*, p. 1648 (1927); Borchard 1932:xxix.

Lucas, Jesse, and Margaret Lucas. People v. Lucas, 91 N.E. 659 (1910); *N.Y. Times*, Sept. 28, 1931, p. 20; Squire 1937:266–72.

Ludkowitz, Max. People v. Ludkowitz, 194 N.E. 688 (1935); *N.Y. Times*, Dec. 17, 1941, p. 28; May 2, 1940, p. 2.

Lyons, Ernest. Borchard 1932:144–48.

MacFarland, Allison M. State v. MacFarland, 83 A. 993 (1912); *N.Y. Times*, Oct. 4, 1913, p. 10; Bedau 1964a:37.

MacGregor, Robert. People v. MacGregor, 144 N.W. 869 (1914); Borchard 1932:149–53; Holbrook 1941:113–25, 236–39.

Majczek, Joseph, and Theodore Marcinkiewicz. People v. Majczek, 195 N.E. 653 (1935); *Chicago Tribune*, Aug. 11, 1965, p. II-128; *L.A. Times*, June 2, 1983, p. 28; Frank and Frank 1957:28–30.

Malloy, Everett Baily. *Tallahassee Democrat*, Apr. 15, 1984, p. 5A.

Mansell, Alvin. State v. Mansell, 133 S.E. 190 (1926); *Norfolk Journal*, Nov. 15, 1930, p. 1; Corbitt 1931:749–59.

Marino, Tony. Marino v. Ragen, 332 U.S. 561 (1947); Gershenson 1963:137–44.

Marsh, Guy Gordon. *Baltimore Sun*, May 9, 1987, p. 7A; May 7, 1987, p. 2E; *The Capital* (Annapolis, Md.), Jan. 25, 1991, p. A10; Jan. 10, 1991, p. 10; May 23, 1987, p. 1; May 8, 1987, p. A1; *Chicago Tribune*, May 10, 1987.

Matera, Pietro. People v. Matera, 180 N.E. 333 (1932); *N.Y. Journal American*, July 24, 1961, p. 9.

Maynard, William A. ("Tony"). People v. Maynard, 337 N.Y.S.2d 644 (1972); 363 N.Y.S.2d 384 (1974); *N.Y. Times*, Aug. 24, 1974, p. 16; Feb. 6, 1973, p. 44.

Mays, Maurice F. Mays v. State, 226 S.W. 233 (1920), 238 S.W. 1096 (1921); Egerton 1983.

McDonald, Wilbur. McDonald v. Illinois, 557 F.2d 596 (1977); 434 U.S. 966 (1977); *Chicago Tribune*, Aug. 16, 1973, p. 1; *N.Y. Times*, Sept. 30, 1973, p. 47.

McGee, Willie. McGee v. State, 26 So.2d 680 (1946); 33 So.2d 843 (1948); 40 So.2d 160 (1949); 338 U.S. 805 (1949); 47 So.2d 155 (1950); 340 U.S. 921 (1951); Brownmiller 1975:263–71; Horne 1988; Martin 1987:45–49; Patterson 1971:157–58; Rowan 1952:174–92.

McIntosh, Walter. *Atlanta Constitution*, Aug. 28, 1984, p. 9; MLR telephone interview with Floyd Keeble (defendant's attorney), June 30, 1987.

McKinney, Clarence LeRoy. Borchard 1932:154–60.

McLaughlin, Robert. See Sources for Chapter 11.

McMullen, Edward A. McMullen v. Maxwell, 209 N.E.2d 449 (1965); Journal entry, Indictment for Murder in the First Degree, State v. McMullen, No. 7624 (Miami Cty., Ohio, Court of Common Pleas, filed Oct. 7, 1965); Lassers 1973:220.

Merritt, George. State v. Madden, 294 A.2d 609 (1972); U.S. ex rel. Merritt v. Hicks, 492 F. Supp. 99 (1980); *N.Y. Times*, Dec. 21, 1983, p. A26 (letter to the editor).

Miller, Lloyd Eldon, Jr. See Sources for Chapter 7.

Montgomery, Olen, Clarence Norris, Haywood Patterson, Ozie Powell, Willie Roberson, Charlie Weems, Eugene Williams, Andrew Wright, and Leroy ("Roy") Wright (the "Scottsboro Boys"). See Sources for Chapter 5.

Morales, Santiago Ventura. *N.Y. Times*, Jan. 24, 1991, p. D22; July 25, 1988, p. A14; *The Oregonian*, Apr. 12, 1991, p. A1; Jan. 10, 1991, p. A1; Jan. 7, 1991, p. B1; Jan. 6, 1991, p. 1; *Statesman Journal* (Salem, Oreg.), Jan. 6, 1991, p. A1; Jan. 5, 1991, p. A1.

Morello, Raffaelo E. *N.Y. Times*, June 5, 1926, p. 15; May 23, 1926, p. 4; May 21, 1926, p. 15; May 20, 1926, p. 27; Frankfurter 1927:109–10.

Morris, Gordon. Letter from Cecil Simpson (director, Institutional Services, Texas Board of Pardons and Paroles) to MLR, Oct. 29, 1985; Reid 1966; Reid and Gurwell 1973:101–5 (authors refer to Morris as "Horgan").

Norwood, Albert E. State ex rel. Norwood v. Drumm, 691 S.W.2d 238 (1985); letters from Mary Dames (defendant's attorney) to MLR, Apr. 17, 1984, and Aug. 30, 1984.

Olson, Henry. Borchard 1932:172–76.

Owens, Aaron Lee. *L.A. Daily Journal*, Mar. 6, 1981, p. I-2; *S.F. Chronicle*, Mar. 5, 1981, p. 2; *S.F. Examiner*, Feb. 23, 1982.

Padgett, Eugene. Ex parte Padgett, 230 S.W.2d 813 (1950); 278 S.W.2d 865 (1955); Radin 1964:155.

Padgett, William H. Michigan v. Padgett, No. 919 (Washtenaw Cty. Circuit Court, July 14, 1949); California Senate Committee on the Judiciary, *Hearing Report and Testimony on Senate Bill No. 1, 1960*, Second Extraordinary Session, pp. 60–61.

Parker, George. State v. Parker, 460 A.2d 665 (1983); State v. Parker, No. A-453-83T4 (N.J. Superior Court Appellate Division, Feb. 4, 1986); *N.Y. Times*, Feb. 9, 1986, p. 46.

Parrott, Lemuel, and Sam Thompson. State v. Parrott, 46 S.E.2d 851 (1948); State v. Parrott, 47 S.E.2d 21 (1948); *Kinston* (N.C.) *Daily Free Press*, July 10, 1959, p. 12; *Raleigh News and Observer*, July 10, 1959, p. 1; *Raleigh Times*, July 11, 1959, p. 4; *Washington* (N.C.) *Daily News*, July 15, 1959, p. 4.

Pecho, Walter A. *Lansing State Journal,* July 15, 1960, p. 13; Radin 1964:40–44, 293.

Peek, Anthony Ray. Peek v. State, 395 So.2d 492 (1980); 488 So.2d 52 (1986); *Tampa Tribune,* Jan. 18, 1987, p. 2B.

Pender, John. *The Oregonian,* Dec. 1, 1964, p. 26; Nov. 30, 1964, p. 34; Sept. 12, 1920, p. 1; Bedau 1965:33.

Persico, Charles F. *L.A. Times,* Nov. 2, 1991, p. A1; Dec. 18, 1987, p. II-8; *S.F. Examiner,* Dec. 28, 1987, p. B5; Humes 1991.

Petree, John Wilson. State v. Petree, 659 P.2d 443 (1983); *Salt Lake City Tribune,* Feb. 8, 1983, p. 7A.

Pfeffer, Paul. *N.Y. Herald Tribune,* Aug. 25, 1955, p. 17; Aug. 3, 1954, p. 17; July 20, 1954, p. 1; *N.Y. Times,* Jan. 10, 1956, p. 63; Dec. 10, 1955, p. 42; Nov. 23, 1955, p. 50; Oct. 25, 1955, p. 34; Cook 1956.

Phillips, Richard. Letter from Mr. B. Lewis to Gov. John Pollard, Oct. 17, 1930, quoted in Borchard, memorandum on the Phillips case, p. 2 (unpublished manuscript, Yale University Library); Executive Papers of the Secretary of the Commonwealth, Oct. 9–31, 1930 (available in Virginia State Library Archives).

Prevost, Lloyd. People v. Prevost, 189 N.W. 92 (1922); Borchard 1932:197–205.

Pyle, Harry. State v. Pyle, 57 P.2d 93 (1936); Pyle v. Amrine, 112 P.2d 354 (1941); Pyle v. Kansas, 317 U.S. 213 (1942); Gershenson 1963:207–11.

Ramos, Juan F. Ramos v. State, 496 So.2d 121 (1986); *Florida Today* (Cocoa Beach), Apr. 25, 1987, pp. A1, B1; Apr. 24, 1987, p. B1; Apr. 23, 1987, p. B1; Apr. 22, 1987, p. B1; Apr. 21, 1987, p. B1; *Orlando Sentinel,* Apr. 25, 1987, p. D1.

Reichhoff, Kenny Ray. Reichhoff v. State, 251 N.W.2d 470 (1977); *Wisconsin State Journal,* Dec. 30, 1982, p. 10; Oct. 17, 1977, p. 1; Feb. 5, 1976, p. 10; Jan. 1, 1976, p. III-1.

Reilly, Peter A. Reilly v. State, 355 A.2d 324 (1976); Reilly v. Leonard, 459 F. Supp. 291 (1978); *N.Y. Times,* Sept. 26, 1979, p. B2; Oct. 13, 1977, p. A1; Nov. 25, 1976, p. 1; Mar. 26, 1976, p. 18; Dec. 15, 1975, p. 1; Barthel 1976; Connery 1977.

Reissfelder, George A. *Boston Globe,* Dec. 15, 1985, p. 46; May 13, 1984, p. 1; Aug. 31, 1982, p. 40; Aug. 26, 1982, p. 28; July 23, 1982, p. 18; June 22, 1982, p. 21; *N.Y. Times,* Aug. 31, 1982, p. 10.

Reno, Ralph. People v. Reno, 155 N.E. 329 (1927); *N.Y. Daily News,* Feb. 20–28, 1932 (series of articles); *N.Y. Sunday News,* Nov. 15, 1931, p. 62; Reno 1931.

Reynolds, Melvin Lee. See Sources for Introduction.

Richardson, James. See Sources for Chapter 10.

Ripan, Alexander. Frank and Frank 1957:187–88.

Rivera, Antonio, and Merla Walpole. See Sources for Chapter 13.

Robertson, David Wayne. Robertson v. State, 457 A.2d 826 (1983); *Baltimore Sun,* Apr. 27, 1984, p. D1; Apr. 26, 1984, p. D14.

Robinson, Derrick. *Miami Herald,* Jan. 31, 1991, p. 1B; Jan. 30, 1991, p. 1A.

Robinson, Van Bering. State v. Robinson, 662 P.2d 1341 (1983); *Albuquerque Journal,* Oct. 20, 1983, p. A1; Oct. 13, 1983, p. A9; Mar. 22, 1983, p. A1.

Rodriguez, Santos. Commonwealth v. Rodriguez, 131 N.E.2d 774 (1956); *Boston American,* Jan. 16, 1958, p. 1; *Boston Daily Record,* Apr. 6, 1957, p. 3; *Boston Globe,* Apr. 10, 1957, p. 1; Apr. 5, 1957, p. 1; Apr. 4, 1957, p. 1.

Rogers, Courtney ("Fred"). See Sources for Chapter 13.

Rogers, Silas. See Sources for Chapter 11.

Ross, Johnny. State v. Ross, 343 So.2d 722 (1977); N.Y. State Defender's Association, *Capital Losses: The Price of the Death Penalty in New York State* (1982), p. 14; *Poverty Law Report,* Jan. 1982, p. 1 (newsletter of the Southern Poverty Law

Center, Montgomery, Ala.); letter from John L. Carroll (defendant's attorney) to MLR, Sept. 21, 1983.

Sacco, Nicola, and Bartolomeo Vanzetti. See Sources for Chapter 4.

Sanders, Albert. Sanders v. State, 79 So. 375 (1918); *Mobile Register*, July 20, 1918, p. 3; Aug. 4, 1917, p. 6; July 21, 1917, p. 1; July 20, 1917, p. 1; July 1, 1917, p. 10.

Santana, Rene. *Star-Ledger* (Newark), Feb. 25, 1986, p. 28; Feb. 19, 1986, p. 13; Aug. 6, 1985.

Sberna, Charles. People v. Gati, 18 N.E.2d 35 (1938); *N.Y. Times*, Aug. 4, 1939, p. 3; June 30, 1938, p. 16; Lawes 1940:337–39 (refers to Sberna as "Russell"); Reynolds 1950:347–57; Sauter and Abend 1979:77–79.

Schuyler, John Edward. State v. Schuyler, 68 A. 56 (1907); *N.J. Law Journal* 38:1–2 (1915); *N.Y. Times*, Dec. 24, 1914, p. 16.

Scott, Bradley P. Scott v. State, 581 So.2d 887 (1991); *Ft. Meyers News-Press*, June 1, 1991, p. 1; May 31, 1991, p. 1.

Scott, Scotty. *Arkansas Democrat*, May 12, 1989, p. 1; Sept. 7, 1988; Jan. 17, 1987, p. 1E; June 10, 1986; Sept. 1, 1984, p. 1; July 31, 1984, p. 1; July 1, 1982, p. 1.

Seaton, Terry. State v. Seaton, 525 P.2d 858 (1974); Seaton v. Eddy Cty., No. 81-0286 (N.Mex. District Court, Jan. 18, 1983); Curley, "Terry Seaton: Did Justice Misfire?", *Albuquerque Journal Magazine*, Aug. 28, 1979, pp. 6–11; *Albuquerque Journal*, Jan. 14, 1983, p. 1; Dec. 26, 1982, p. 16.

Shaffer, Howard, Charles Stevens, and William Troop. Troop v. State, 123 So. 811 (1929); *Florida Times Union* (Jacksonville), May 1, 1930, p. 15; Aug. 3, 1929, p. 1; *Jacksonville Journal*, Aug. 7, 1929, p. 1; Aug. 3, 1929, p. 2.

Shea, Joseph Francis. Act of July 12, 1967, ch. 910, 1967 Florida Laws, p. 620; *Miami Herald*, Mar. 20, 1966, p. 1; *N.Y. Daily News*, Nov. 6, 1965, p. 4; Miller 1975:76; Raab 1967:237–40.

Sheppard, Samuel H. State v. Sheppard, 128 N.E.2d 471 (1955); 135 N.E.2d 340 (1956); 135 N.E.2d 340, 342 (1956); Sheppard v. Maxwell, 384 U.S. 333 (1966); Bailey 1971:55–92; Holmes 1961; Israel 1979:247–66; Kilgallen 1967:231–304; Kunstler 1960:204–19; Pollack 1972; Sheppard 1966.

Sherman, David. *Galveston News*, Nov. 27, 1907, p. 2; *Nashville Banner*, Jan. 13, 1911, p. 13; Nov. 26, 1907, p. 3; *Nashville Tennessean*, Jan. 14, 1911, p. 5; Nov. 27, 1907, p. 6.

Shumway, R. Mead. Shumway v. State, 117 N.W. 407 (1908); *Lincoln* (Nebr.) *Star*, Mar. 5, 1909, p. 1; Jan. 16, 1908, p. 5; Barbour 1919:508.

Smith, Charles ("Red"). *Fort Wayne Journal-Gazette*, May 10, 1991; May 9, 1991; May 8, 1991; May 5, 1991; May 3, 1991; May 2, 1991; Apr. 30, 1991.

Smith, Frank A. *Birmingham Age Herald*, Aug. 9, 1924; *Weekly Gazette* (Evangeline Parish, La.), Aug. 9, 1924, p. 1; Briggs 1940:69–73.

Smith, Grace M. Smith v. Commonwealth, 40 S.E.2d 273 (1946); letter from Allen L. Lucy (clerk of the Virginia Supreme Court) to MLR, June 28, 1984; *Harrisonburg* (Va.) *Daily News Record*, Nov. 26, 1946, p. 1.

Smith, Larry Thomas. *Akron Beacon-Journal*, Nov. 26, 1980, p. 4; Nov. 22, 1980, p. E1; Nov. 20, 1980, p. C1; Nov. 17, 1980, p. D3; Nov. 12, 1980, p. B11; Nov. 10, 1980, p. D1; June 6, 1980, p. D1; Greenberg 1982:920 n.69.

Staples, F. N. People v. Staples, 86 P. 886 (1906).

Storick, Maude Cushing. Radin 1964:70–75.

Sweeney, James. Block 1962:61–62.

Synon, Michael J. Synon v. People, 59 N.E. 508 (1901); Barbour 1919:506; Bye 1919:84; Davis 1922:527.

Thrower, Allan E. State v. Thrower, No. 73AP-292, slip op. 3032 (Ohio Court of Appeals, Franklin Cty., Nov. 27, 1983); *Columbus Dispatch*, Jan. 5, 1979, p. 3;

Aug. 29, 1978, p. 1; Aug. 9, 1978, p. 1; July 21, 1978, p. B7; Nov. 27, 1973, p. 7; July 13, 1973, p. B1.

Tibbs, Delbert. See Sources for Chapter 2.

Torres, Pedro. *Corpus Christi Caller-Times*, Apr. 27, 1985, p. 2B; *N.Y. Times*, Apr. 28, 1985, p. 15.

Treadaway, Jonathan Charles, Jr. State v. Treadaway, 568 P.2d 1061 (1977); State ex rel. La Sota v. Corcoran, 583 P.2d 229 (1978); *Arizona Republic*, Oct. 10, 1978, p. 1; Sept. 22, 1978, p. B2; Sept. 15, 1978, p. B1; Sept. 14, 1978, p. B1; Sept. 7, 1978, p. B1; Sept. 1, 1978, p. B2; Greenberg 1982:920 n. 69.

Tucker, Charles Louis. Commonwealth v. Tucker, 76 N.E. 127 (1905); Gross 1963:157–79; Hewett 1983.

Valletutti, John. People v. Valletutti, 78 N.E.2d 485 (1948); *N.Y. Times*, Sept. 29, 1948, p. 19; Mar. 12, 1948, p. 33; June 18, 1947, p. 10; June 8, 1947, p. 41; Radin 1964:24–26.

Vargas, Anastacio. Vargas v. State, 284 S.W. 564 (1926); 298 S.W. 591 (1927); State v. Vargas, 419 S.W.2d 926 (1967); 424 S.W.2d 416 (1968); *Houston Post*, Mar. 7, 1968; Feb. 8, 1968; Apr. 15, 1965; Nov. 21, 1958; Ehrmann 1962:18.

Vasquez, David. *Richmond News Leader*, Jan. 6, 1989, pp. 5, 10; Jan. 5, 1989, p. 1; *Richmond Times Dispatch*, Dec. 12, 1989, p. B2; Jan. 6, 1989, p. C1; Jan. 5, 1989, p. 1; *Washington Post*, Jan. 5, 1989, p. 1; Nov. 5, 1988, p. B1; Oct. 13, 1988, p. D1; Oct. 12, 1988, p. 1.

Vega, Damaso. State v. Vega, transcript of decision (Nov. 15, 1989) (Superior Court of N.J., Middlesex Cty.); *Asbury Park Press*, June 23, 1989; *Star-Ledger* (Newark, N.J.), Dec. 15, 1989; June 23, 1989.

Venegas, Juan. See Sources for Chapter 9.

Vindiola, Bernard. People v. Vindiola, 158 Cal. Rptr. 6 (1979); letter from Curtis B. Sisk (defendant's attorney) to MLR, July 18, 1986.

Walker, Lee Dell. People v. Walker, 124 N.W.2d 761 (1963); 132 N.W.2d 87 (1965); 149 N.W.2d 912 (1967); 393 U.S. 1028 (1969); Walker v. Cahalan, 296 N.W.2d 18 (1980); *Detroit Free Press*, Dec. 24, 1972, p. B1; Feb. 27, 1972, p. B1; *Lansing State Journal*, July 16, 1974, p. B3.

Wallace, Earnest. People v. Wallace, 116 N.E. 700 (1917); *Chicago Tribune*, June 22, 1917, p. 1; Barbour 1919:508–9.

Wan, Zian Sung. Wan v. United States, 266 U.S. 1 (1924); *N.Y. Times*, June 17, 1926, p. 3; Frankfurter 1927:108–9.

Ward, William. Bass, "And the Truth Shall Set You Free," *Inside Detective*, June 1977, p. 20.

Weaver, Joseph. Weaver v. State, 166 N.E. 594 (1928); 165 N.E. 569 (1929); H.B. 55, 90th Gen. Assembly, Reg. Sess., 1933 Ohio Laws 56; Borchard, memorandum on Weaver case (Sept. 14, 1931) (unpublished manuscript, Yale University Library); *Cleveland Plain Dealer*, Apr. 6, 1929, p. 9; Apr. 5, 1929, p. 10; Apr. 4, 1929, p. 6.

Wellman, William Mason. State v. Wellman, 222 N.C. 215 (1942); *Raleigh News and Observer*, Apr. 16, 1943, p. 1 (quoting the pardon report); Hart, "Gas Chamber Executioner," *Amazing Detective Magazine*, Nov. 1945, p. 42 (in which the crime is erroneously reported as "murder"); *Raleigh News and Observer*, Apr. 16, 1943, p. 1.

Wentzel, Gerald C. Commonwealth v. Wentzel, 61 A.2d 309 (1948); Block 1963:254–65; Frank and Frank 1957:119–29; Gardner 1952:154–62; Lofton 1966:202–4.

Wilkinson, Robert. United States v. Ellis, 595 F.2d 154 (1979); Wilkinson v. Ellis, 484 F. Supp. 1072 (1980); *N.Y. Times*, Dec. 21, 1976, p. 20; *Philadelphia Inquirer*, Dec. 21, 1976, p. 1.

Williams, Joseph S. Williams v. Commonwealth, 107 S.E. 655 (1921); *Richmond Times-Dispatch*, Oct. 5, 1921, p. 14.

Williams, Robert. *N.Y. Times*, Dec. 24, 1978, p. 22.

Williams, Samuel Tito. People v. Williams, 83 N.E.2d 698 (1949); 84 N.E.2d 446 (1949); Williams v. New York, 337 U.S. 241 (1949); United States ex rel. Williams v. Fay 323 F.2d 65 (1963); Williams v. City of New York, 508 F.2d 356 (1974); *N.Y. Times*, Sept. 11, 1964, p. 16.

Wilson, Bill. Wilson v. State, 67 So. 1010 (1915); Borchard 1932:303–10.

Wilson, David Ronald. Wilson v. State, 208 So.2d 479 (1968); *Miami Herald*, July 1, 1971, p. 1C.

Wilson, Shelia. Wilson v. Commonwealth, 601 S.W.2d 280 (1980); Wilson v. Kassulke, Nos. 81-5633, 81-5680 (Sixth Circuit Court of Appeals, Jan. 4, 1983); letter from Kevin McNally (Kentucky Department of Public Advocacy) to MLR, Mar. 26, 1984.

Wing, George Chew. People v. Wing, 8 N.E.2d 611 (1937); *N.Y. Times*, Jan. 5, 1937, p. 2; Lawes 1940:323–26.

Woodmansee, Ernest. People v. Trujillo, 194 P.2d 681 (1948); *Argosy*, Feb. 1956, p. 57; Jan. 1956, p. 28; May 1955, p. 92; Jan. 1953, p. 4; Cook 1956:196–97.

Woon, Lem. State v. Lem Woon, 107 P. 974 (1910); Lem Woon v. Oregon, 229 U.S. 586 (1913); pardon reports of Dec. 17, 1914, and Apr. 18, 1935 (Secretary of State's Records of Pardons, Permissions, and Commutations of Sentences, 1904–1954, Oregon State Archives); *The Oregonian*, Apr. 19, 1935, p. 20; Bedau 1965:33.

Zajicek, Herman. Report of the Illinois Board of Pardons (Oct. 1916) (in the Executive Clemency files, Illinois State Archives); *Chicago Tribune*, Apr. 21, 1908, p. 3; Barbour 1919:506.

Zimmerman, Isidore. See Sources for Chapter 2.

Abramowitz, Elkan, and David Paget. 1964. "Executive Clemency in Capital Cases." *New York University Law Review* 39 (January):136–92.

Achenbach, Joel. 1989. "Free At Last? Soon To Be A Major Motion Picture." *Tropic (Miami Herald)*, August 20:8–15.

Adams, Randall Dale, William Hoffer, and Marilyn Mona Hoffer. 1991. *Adams v. Texas*. New York: St. Martin's Press.

Avrich, Paul. 1984. *The Haymarket Tragedy*. Princeton: Princeton University Press.

Avrich, Paul. 1991. *Sacco and Vanzetti: The Anarchist Background*. Princeton: Princeton University Press.

Bailey, F. Lee. 1971. *The Defense Never Rests*. New York: Stein & Day.

Barbour, James J. 1919. "Efforts to Abolish the Death Penalty in Illinois." *Journal of the American Institute of Criminal Law and Criminology* 9 (February):500–513.

Barnes, Harry E., and Negley Teeters. 1959. *New Horizons in Criminology*, 3d ed. Englewood Cliffs, N.J.: Prentice-Hall.

Barthel, Joan. 1976. *A Death in Canaan*. New York: E. P. Dutton.

Bedau, Hugo Adam. 1964a. "Death Sentences in New Jersey, 1907–1960." *Rutgers Law Review* 19 (Fall):1–64.

Bedau, Hugo Adam. 1964b. "Murder, Errors of Justice, and Capital Punishment." Pp. 434–52 in Hugo Adam Bedau, ed., *The Death Penalty in America: An Anthology*. Garden City, N.Y.: Anchor Books/Doubleday.

Bedau, Hugo Adam. 1965. "Capital Punishment in Oregon, 1903–64." *Oregon Law Review* 45 (December):1–39.

Bedau, Hugo Adam. 1982. "Miscarriages of Justice and the Death Penalty." Pp. 234–41 in Hugo Adam Bedau, ed., *The Death Penalty in America*, 3d ed. New York: Oxford University Press.

Bedau, Hugo Adam, and Michael L. Radelet. 1987. "Miscarriages of Justice in Potentially Capital Cases." *Stanford Law Review* 40 (November):21–179.

Bedau, Hugo Adam, and Michael L. Radelet. 1988. "The Myth of Infallibility: A Reply to Markman and Cassell." *Stanford Law Review* 41 (November):161–70.

Bennett, James V. 1970. *I Chose Prison*. New York: Alfred A. Knopf.

Bernstein, Charles. 1965. Review of E. Radin, *The Innocents*. *Federal Probation* 29 (March):69–70.

Bliven, Bruce. 1949. "The Trenton Murder Case." *New Republic* (May 16):12–14.

Block, Eugene B. 1962. *And May God Have Mercy: The Case Against Capital Punishment*. San Francisco: Fearon Publishers.

Block, Eugene B. 1963. *The Vindicators*. Garden City, N.Y.: Doubleday.

Borchard, Edwin. 1932. *Convicting the Innocent: Sixty-Five Actual Errors of Criminal Justice*. New Haven: Yale University Press [the page numbers differ in various printings of the book].

Borchard, Edwin. 1941. "State Indemnity for Errors of Criminal Justice." *Boston University Law Review* 21 (April):201–11.

Brandon, Stuart K. 1949. "To the Rescue of Charlie Stielow." *Reader's Digest* (April):73–78.

Briggs, L. Vernon. 1940. *Capital Punishment Is Not a Deterrent*. Boston: Wright and Potter.

Brown, Wenzell. 1958. *They Died in the Chair*. New York: Popular Library.

Brownmiller, Susan. 1975. *Against Our Will: Men, Women, and Rape*. New York: Simon & Schuster.

Bryan, Robert R. 1990–91. "The Execution of the Innocent: The Tragedy of the Hauptmann-Lindbergh and Bigelow Cases." *New York University Review of Law & Social Change* 18:831–71.

Busch, Francis X. 1952. *Guilty or Not Guilty?* Indianapolis: Bobbs-Merrill Co.

Butler, Anne, and C. Murray Henderson. 1990. *Angola: Louisiana State Penitentiary—A Half-Century of Rage and Reform.* Lafayette, La.: Center for Louisiana Studies, University of Southwestern Louisiana.

Bye, Raymond T. 1919. *Capital Punishment in the United States.* Philadelphia: The Committee of Philanthropic Labor of Philadelphia Yearly Meeting of Friends.

Cannon, Terry. 1976. "The Delbert Tibbs Case." *The Nation* 223 (December 18):652–55.

Carter, Dan T. 1979. *Scottsboro: A Tragedy of the American South,* rev. ed. Baton Rouge: Louisiana State University Press.

Cartwright, Gary. 1987. "The Longest Ride of His Life." *Texas Monthly* (May):124–27, 187–94.

Cimerman, Adrian. 1981. "They'll Let Me Go Tomorrow: The Fay Case." *Criminal Defense* 8 (May–June):7–10.

Clendenin, Dudley. 1972. "The Legend of Iceman McCall Chills the Air in Lake County." *The Floridian (St. Petersburg Times Sunday Magazine),* November 5:19–22.

Connery, Donald S. 1977. *Guilty Until Proven Innocent.* New York: G. P. Putnam's Sons.

Cook, Fred J. 1956. "Capital Punishment: Does it Prevent Crime?" *The Nation* 182 (March 10):194–98.

Corbitt, David Leroy. 1931. *Public Papers and Letters of Angus Wilton McLean.* Raleigh, N.C.: Council of the State, State of North Carolina.

Cortner, Richard C. 1988. *A Mob Intent on Death: The NAACP and the Arkansas Riot Cases.* Middletown, Conn.: Wesleyan University Press.

Curtis, Tom. 1987. "Guilty Until Proven Innocent." *Texas Monthly* (September):94–97, 157–63, 170–71.

Davies, Nick. 1991. *White Lies: Rape, Murder, and Justice Texas Style.* New York: Pantheon Books.

Davis, Harry L. 1922. "Death by Law." *Outlook* 131 (July 26):525.

Dinnerstein, Leonard. 1968. *The Leo Frank Case.* New York: Columbia University Press.

Egerton, John. 1983. "A Case of Prejudice: Maurice Mays and the Knoxville Race Riot of 1919." *Southern Exposure* (July):56–65.

Ehrmann, Herbert. 1969. *The Case That Will Not Die: Commonwealth vs. Sacco and Vanzetti.* Boston: Little, Brown.

Ehrmann, Sara. 1962. "For Whom the Chair Waits." *Federal Probation* 26 (March):14–25.

Elliott, Robert G. 1940. *Agent of Death.* New York: E. P. Dutton.

Fisher, Jim. 1987. *The Lindbergh Case.* New Brunswick, N.J.: Rutgers University Press.

Foner, Philip S. 1965. *The Case of Joe Hill.* New York: International Publishers.

Frank, Jerome, and Barbara Frank. 1957. *Not Guilty.* Garden City, N.Y.: Doubleday.

Frankfurter, Felix. 1927. *The Case of Sacco and Vanzetti: A Critical Analysis for Lawyers and Laymen.* New York: Grosset & Dunlap.

Frey, Robert Seitz, and Nancy Thompson-Frey. 1988. *The Silent and the Damned: The Murder of Mary Phagan and the Lynching of Leo Frank.* Lanham, Md.: Madison Books.

Fricker, Richard L. 1989. "Crime and Punishment in Dallas." *ABA Journal* 75 (July):52–56.

Frost, Richard H. 1968. *The Mooney Case*. Stanford: Stanford University Press.

Ganey, Terry. 1989. *St. Joseph's Children*. New York: Carol Publishing Group.

Gardner, Erle Stanley. 1952. *The Court of Last Resort*. New York: William Sloane Associates.

Gardner, Erle Stanley. 1970. "Helping the Innocent." *UCLA Law Review* 17 (February):535–41.

Gentry, Curt. 1967. *Frame-up: The Incredible Case of Tom Mooney and Warren Billings*. New York: W. W. Norton.

Gershenson, Alvin H. 1963. *The Bench is Warped: Equal Justice Under Law?* New York: Vantage Press.

Gettinger, Stephen H. 1979. *Sentenced to Die: The People, the Crimes, and the Controversy*. New York: Macmillan.

Gilman, Mildred. 1929. "Without Apology: The State Releases Harry Hoffman." *New Republic* 59 (June 12):90–91.

Gleason, Dan. 1982. "Undue Process: The Jerry Banks Case." *Atlanta Magazine* 21 (March):50–53, 88–90.

Greenberg, Jack. 1982. "Capital Punishment as a System." *Yale Law Journal* 91 (April):908–36.

Greenwald, Howard M. 1963. "Ordeal of an Innocent Man." *Saturday Evening Post* 236 (October 5):82–86.

Gross, Gerald. 1963. *Masterpieces of Murder*. Boston: Little, Brown.

Guzda, M. K. 1983. "Reporter Helps Free Wrongly Convicted Man." *Editor And Publisher* 116 (December 24):16.

Hewett, David. 1983. "Shreds of Evidence." *Boston Magazine* 75 (November):133–38.

Hirschberg, Max. 1940. "Convicting the Innocent." *Rocky Mountain Law Review* 13 (December):20–46.

Hohenberg, John. 1959. *The Pulitzer Prize Story*. New York: Columbia University Press.

Hohenberg, John. 1980. *The Pulitzer Prize Story II*. New York: Columbia University Press.

Holbrook, Stewart H. 1941. *Murder Out Yonder*. New York: Macmillan.

Holmes, Paul. 1961. *The Sheppard Murder Case*. New York: David McKay Co.

Horne, Gerald. 1988. *Communist Front? The Civil Rights Congress, 1946–1956*. Rutherford, N.J.: Fairleigh Dickinson University Press.

Houts, Marshall. 1958. *From Arrest to Release*. Springfield, Ill.: Charles C. Thomas, Publisher.

Huie, William Bradford. 1964. "The South Kills Another Negro." Pp. 85–91 in Edward C. McGehee and William H. Hildebrand, eds., *The Death Penalty: A Literary and Historical Approach*. Boston: D. C. Heath (reprinted from *The American Mercury* [1943]).

Humes, Edward. 1991. "Is Bill Leisure the Most Corrupt Cop in L.A.?" *Los Angeles Times Magazine* (October 27):22–27, 39–43.

Israel, Lee. 1979. *Kilgallen*. New York: Dell.

Joughlin, G. Louis, and Edmund M. Morgan. 1948. *The Legacy of Sacco and Vanzetti*. New York: Harcourt, Brace.

Kenney, Charles. 1986. "The Trials of Bobby Joe Leaster." *Boston Globe Magazine* (July 27):18–27.

Kenney, Charles. 1988. "Justice for Bobby Joe." *Boston Globe Magazine* (February 28):14–15, 46–50, 53–57.

Kennedy, Ludovic. 1985. *The Airman and the Carpenter: The Lindbergh Kidnapping and the Framing of Richard Hauptmann*. New York: Viking Press.

Kennedy, Stetson. 1951. "Florida: Murder Without Indictment." *The Nation* 173 (November 24):444–46.

Kilgallen, Dorothy. 1967. *Murder One.* New York: Random House.

Klein, Henry H. 1927. *Sacrificed: The Story of Police Lieutenant Charles Becker.* New York: Isaac Goldmann Co.

Kluger, Richard. 1976. *Simple Justice: The History of Brown v. Board of Education and Black America's Struggle for Equality.* New York: Alfred A. Knopf.

Kunstler, William M. 1960. *First Degree.* New York: Oceana Publications.

Lamson, David. 1936. *We Who Are About to Die: Prison As Seen By a Condemned Man.* New York: Charles Scribner's Sons.

Lane, Mark. 1970. *Arcadia.* New York: Holt, Rinehart & Winston.

Lassers, Willard J. 1973. *Scapegoat Justice: Lloyd Miller and the Failure of the American Legal System.* Bloomington: Indiana University Press.

Lawes, Lewis E. 1940. *Meet the Murderer!* New York: Harper & Bros.

Lawson, Steven F., David R. Colburn, and Darryl Paulson. 1986. "Groveland: Florida's Little Scottsboro." *Florida Historical Quarterly* 65 (July):1–26.

Lickson, Jeffrey. 1974. *David Charles: The Story of the Quincy Five.* Tallahassee: Mockingbird Press.

Lofton, John. 1966. *Justice and the Press.* Boston: Beacon Press.

Logan, Andy. 1970. *Against the Evidence: The Becker-Rosenthal Affair.* New York: McCall Publishing Co.

Lykken, David T. 1981. "The Lie Detector and the Law." *Criminal Defense* 8 (May–June):19–27.

Maas, Peter. 1960. "The Man Who May Break Chessman's Death-Cell Record." *Look* (July 19):19–23.

MacNamara, Donal E. J. 1969. "Convicting the Innocent." *Crime & Delinquency* 15 (January):57–61.

Markman, Stephen J., and Paul G. Cassell. 1988. "Protecting the Innocent: A Response to the Bedau-Radelet Study." *Stanford Law Review* 41 (November):121–60.

Martin, Charles H. 1980. "Oklahoma's 'Scottsboro' Affair: The Jess Hollins Rape Case, 1931–1936." *South Atlantic Quarterly* 79 (Spring):175–88.

Martin, Charles H. 1987. "The Civil Rights Congress and Southern Black Defendants." *Georgia Historical Quarterly* 71 (Spring):25–52.

Martin, John Bartlow. 1960. "The Question of Identity." *Saturday Evening Post* (August 13):34–35, 66, 68–71.

McCloskey, James. 1989. "Convicting the Innocent." *Criminal Justice Ethics* 8 (Winter/Spring):1–9.

McCool, B. Boren. 1970. *Union, Reaction, and Riot: A Biography of a Rural Race Riot.* Memphis: Bureau of Social Research, Memphis State University.

McCormick, Ken. 1964. *Sprung: The Release of Willie Calloway.* New York: St. Martin's Press.

Miller, Gene. 1975. *Invitation to a Lynching.* Garden City, N.Y.: Doubleday.

Miller, Perry B. 1938. "State and Federal Administration of Criminal Justice: Tom Jones v. The Commonwealth of Kentucky." *Kentucky State Bar Journal* 4 (September):12–15.

Moore, Gary. 1982. "Rosewood Massacre." *The Floridian (St. Petersburg Times Sunday Magazine)*, July 25:6–18.

Norris, Clarence, and Sybil Washington. 1979. *The Last of the Scottsboro Boys.* New York: G. P. Putnam's Sons.

Patterson, Haywood, and Earl Conrad. 1950. *Scottsboro Boy.* New York: Collier Books.

Patterson, William L. 1971. *The Man Who Cried Genocide: An Autobiography.* New York: International Publishers.

Pollack, Jack Harrison. 1962. *Dr. Sam: An American Tragedy.* Chicago: Henry Regnery Co.

Raab, Selwyn. 1967. *Justice in the Back Room.* Cleveland: World Publishing Co.

Radin, Edward D. 1964. *The Innocents.* New York: William Morrow.

Reid, Don. 1966. "My 23 Years in the Death House." Pp. 122–36 in Phil Hirsch, ed., *Death House.* New York: Pyramid Books.

Reid, Don, with John Gurwell. 1973. *Eyewitness.* Houston: Cordovan Press.

Reno, Ralph. 1931. *In the Shadow of the Gallows.* Published privately by the author.

Reynolds, Quentin. 1950. *Courtroom: The Story of Samuel S. Leibowitz.* New York: Farrar, Straus & Giroux.

Rogers, O. A. 1960. "The Elaine Race Riots of 1919." *Arkansas Historical Quarterly* 19 (Spring):142–50.

Rohrlich, Ted. 1990. "Minister of Justice." *Los Angeles Times Magazine* (December 23–30):10–13, 16–17, 34–35.

Rosenbaum, Martin I. 1990–91. "Inevitable Error: Wrongful New York State Homicide Convictions, 1965–1988." *New York University Review of Law & Social Change* 18:807–30.

Rosenbaum, Ron. 1990. "Travels with Dr. Death." *Vanity Fair* (May):140–47, 166–74.

Rowan, Carl. 1952. *South of Freedom.* New York: Alfred A. Knopf.

Russell, Francis. 1962. *Tragedy in Dedham: The Story of the Sacco-Vanzetti Case.* New York: McGraw-Hill.

Russell, Francis. 1986. *Sacco and Vanzetti: The Case Resolved.* New York: Harper & Row.

Sauter, Joseph M., and Sheldon Abend. 1979. *The Guardians.* New York: Zebra Books.

Scaduto, Anthony. 1976. *Scapegoat: The Lonesome Death of Bruno Richard Hauptmann.* New York: G. P. Putnam's Sons.

Schmitz, Anthony. 1982. "In The Shadow of Death: Beyond Reasonable Doubt." *Atlanta Weekly (Atlanta Constitution),* May 30:6–8, 14–17.

Seidman, Louis M. 1977. "The Trial and Execution of Bruno Richard Hauptmann: Still Another Case That 'Will Not Die.'" *Georgetown Law Journal* 66 (October):1–48.

Sheppard, Samuel H. 1966. *Endure and Conquer.* Cleveland: World Publishing Co.

Smith, Gibbs M. 1969. *Joe Hill.* Salt Lake City: University of Utah Press.

Smith, Joan. 1988. "Not Guilty." *Image Magazine (S.F. Examiner),* October 30:20–25.

Squire, Amos O. 1937. *Sing Sing Doctor.* Garden City, N.Y.: Garden City Publishing Co.

Stegner, Wallace. 1948. "Joe Hill: The Wobblies' Troubadour." *New Republic* 116 (January 5):20–38.

Strauss, Frances. 1970. *"Where Did the Justice Go?" The Story of the Giles-Johnson Case.* Boston: Gambit.

Styles, Fitzhugh Lee. 1937. *Negroes and the Law.* Boston: Christopher Publishing House.

Sullivan, Harold W. 1961. *Trial By Newspaper.* Hyannis, Mass.: Patriot Press.

Trippett, Frank. 1972. "High and Mighty Sheriff." *Life* 73 (November 17):83–84.

Wagy, Tom. 1985. *Governor LeRoy Collins of Florida: Spokesman of the New South.* University, Ala.: University of Alabama Press.

Waller, George. 1961. *Kidnap: The Story of the Lindbergh Case.* New York: Dial Press.

Warden, Rob. 1990. "Guilty Until Proven Innocent." *Chicago Times Magazine* (January–February):34–59.

Warder, Smith. 1941. "Remedies Available to Convicted Defendant When New Facts Are Found." *Michigan Law Review* 39 (April):963–76.

Waterman, J. S., and E. E. Overton. 1951–52. "The Aftermath of Moore v. Dempsey." *Arkansas Law Review* 6 (Winter):1–7.

Weihofen, Henry. 1939. "The Effect of a Pardon." *University of Pennsylvania Law Review* 88 (December):177–93.

Whipple, Charles L. 1987. "A Reporter Illuminates Shady Evidence in Sacco-Vanzetti Testimony." *Nieman Reports* 41 (Winter):13–17.

Whipple, Sidney B., ed. 1989 [reprint of 1937 original]. *The Trial of Bruno Richard Hauptmann.* Birmingham, Ala.: Notable Trials Library.

White, Walter F. 1919. " 'Massacring Whites' in Arkansas." *The Nation* 109 (December 6):715–16.

White, Walter F. 1948. *A Man Called White.* New York: Viking Press.

Williams, Edward Bennett. 1962. *One Man's Freedom.* New York: Atheneum.

Wolfe, Burton H. 1973. *Pileup on Death Row.* Garden City, N.Y.: Doubleday.

Wood, James Horace, as told to John M. Ross. 1960. *Nothing But the Truth.* Garden City, N.Y.: Doubleday.

Yant, Martin. 1991. *Presumed Guilty: When Innocent People are Wrongly Convicted.* Buffalo, N.Y.: Prometheus Books.

Young, William, and David E. Kaiser. 1986. *Postmortem: New Evidence in the Case of Sacco and Vanzetti.* Amherst: University of Massachusetts Press.

Zimmerman, Isidore, with Francis Bond. 1964. *Punishment Without Crime.* New York: Clarkson N. Potter.

For a complete alphabetical list of the names of all persons wrongly convicted, see Inventory of Cases, pp. 282–356. For the jurisdiction in which a defendant cited in the Inventory was tried, see Jurisdiction of Cases, pp. 359–60.

conspiracy, alleged, 83, 84, 87–88
  see also "insurrection," alleged
conviction, causes of erroneous, 18–19,
    279
  see also alibi; counsel; evidence; per-
    jury; police; prosecution; record,
    defendant's; testimony
convictions, wrong-person, defined, 17
Cook, Bobby Lee, quoted, 156
Cooks, Tony, 190–93
  quoted, 193
Cooper, C. D., 296–97
Cooper, Ralph, 297
coram nobis, defined, 357
counsel, ineffective assistance of defense,
    42, 151, 163, 172, 173–74, 178,
    180, 181, 181–82, 184, 187, 232,
    287, 294, 307, 323–24, 326, 334–
    35, 339, 347, 349
Court of Last Resort, 39, 129, 154–55,
    230, 248, 249, 250, 274, 288, 303,
    309, 353, 356
Cox, Gov. James, 304
Cox, Robert Craig, 297
Craig, Alvin, 297–98
Creamer, James, 155–56
crime, conviction for nonexistent, *see*
    homicide, conviction for nonexist-
    ent crime of; rape, innocent per-
    son(s) sentenced to death for
Crumbley, Alex, 181
Crumbley, Wade, 181, 183, 184, 186
  quoted, 185
Crutcher, Willie, 298
Cunha, Edwin, quoted, 90–91
Cuomo, Gov. Mario, 233, 303

Dabney, Condy, 298
Daily Times (Gainesville, Ga.), quoted,
    32
Dallas, Tex., 60
Dallas Morning News, quoted, 70, 71
Dallas Times Herald, quoted, 131, 131–
    32, 134–35
Darden, George, quoted, 156
Davino, Frank, 298–99
Davis, Charlie, 294
Davis, Henry, quoted, 23
Davis, James, 154
Davis, Rev. Murphy, quoted, 186
Dawson, Sie, 209, 299
de los Santos, George ("Chiefie"), 299–
    300

Dean, Dr. Sara Ruth, 299
death penalty
  abolition of, 171
  alternative to, 277
  arguments for and against, 273–80
  cost of, 277
  as a deterrent, 277
  as incapacitation, 277
  popular support for, 277
  proposed law reforms in administer-
    ing, 278–80
death row, conditions of life on, 51,
    241, 264–65
death sentence
  commutation of, *see* commutation of
    death sentence
  defendant's fear of, 74, 136, 152,
    163, 168, 170, 173, 268, 286,
    309, 314, 342, 350
  mandatory, 97, 316, 342–43
Dedmond, Roger Z., 299
defendant(s)
  female, 73–74, 157–70, 269–70,
    286–87, 292, 299, 311, 314,
    318, 329, 347, 348, 355
  juvenile, 41–42, 104–9, 112, 117,
    118, 159–70, 171–73, 190–93,
    302, 310, 314, 327–28, 334,
    338, 342–43
  mentally impaired, 13, 40, 159, 163,
    168, 173, 174, 288, 299, 310,
    313–14, 318–19, 328, 330–31,
    333, 339, 345–46, 350, 353
DeGeurin, Mike, 129, 131
Delaware, *see Jurisdiction of Cases*
DeMore, Louis, 300
Deneen, Gov. Charles, 356
deposition, defined, 357
Detroit Free Press, 292, 351
Detroit Legal Aid and Defender's Asso-
    ciation, 295
Detroit News, reporters from, 56–57
Dewey, Gov. Thomas, 354
discrimination, racial, *see* racism
District of Columbia, *see Jurisdiction of
    Cases*
Domer, Robert K., 19, 253–67
  quoted, 263, 264–65
Donnelly, James, 300
Dorn, Judge Roosevelt, quoted, 191
Dorsey, Dr. Robert N., 163, 168
Dove, Frank, 300
Dove, Fred, 300

Drake, Camie, 30, 31
  quoted, 23–24, 26, 29, 38
Drake, Charles, 23–24
Drake, Henry, 300–301
Draper, Ayliff, 301
"Dr. Death," *see* Grigson, Dr. James
Duarte, Calif., 41
due process of law, violation(s) of, 9,
    16–17, 49–50, 53, 74, 97–98, 133–
    34, 144–46, 265, 269, 289, 294,
    304, 331
Duff, Gov. James, 312
Duffy, Thomas, 232–33
  quoted, 233
Dukakis, Gov. Michael, 4, 97
Dulin, William, 301
Duncan, Judge M. P., quoted, 71–72
Dunjee, Roscoe, 136
Dunne, Gov. Edward, 356
  quoted, 348
Dwyer, Paul N., 170–73

Edelbaum, Maurice, 52–53
  quoted, 53
Edgar, Gov. Jim, quoted, 284
Edwards, Gov. Edward, 324
Ehrmann, Herbert, 99
Elaine, Ark., 114
electrocution, 5, 51
Ellison, Ella Mae, 73–74
Emery, Richard, 233
  quoted, 234
Emmett, George, 155–56
  quoted, 156
en banc, defined, 357
Engel, George, 280
English, Collis, 297
erroneous conviction, causes of, *see* con-
    viction, causes of erroneous
erroneous execution, risk of, 271–72,
    273
  see also execution, erroneous
Ery, Fred, 219
Estes, Cornell Avery, 302
evidence
  disappearance of, after trial, 125–26,
    133, 309
  faked by police, 98–99, 108, 111–12,
    184–85, 303, 309, 322; *see also*
    police, mishandling or suppres-
    sion of evidence by
  misleading circumstantial, 61–62,
    122, 144, 145, 149, 171, 172,
    189, 219, 220, 261, 263, 267–

68, 269, 293–94, 296, 297, 297–
    98, 299, 306, 311, 314, 317,
    318, 320, 323, 324, 325, 329–
    30, 330, 332, 333, 344, 346,
    347–48, 348, 349, 352, 353, 355
  withheld from defense, 64–65, 69–70,
    89–90, 101, 145, 149, 155, 156,
    212, 216, 232, 296, 304, 310,
    315, 318, 319, 321, 324, 326,
    334, 337, 338; *see also* prosecu-
    tion, mishandling of evidence by
  see also polygraph, unreliability of
ex parte, defined, 357
ex rel., defined, 357
Examiner (San Francisco), 82
execution
  averted at the last moment, 40, 51–52,
    129–31, 137, 143, 215, 248,
    275–76, 286, 290, 291, 293,
    309, 318, 320, 323, 325, 335,
    341, 346, 347, 350, 352, 356
  erroneous, 5–10, 97–99, 99–101,
    137–38, 283, 284, 285, 299,
    306, 310, 314, 323–24, 332,
    332–33, 343, 344, 346–47, 349,
    355; difficulty of proving, 273–
    76
  see also death row, conditions of life
    on
executive clemency, award of, *see* com-
    mutation of death sentence
eyewitness testimony, *see* testimony; per-
    jury

Favor, Jack Graves, 302
Fay, Floyd ("Buzz"), 19, 218–29
  quoted, 220, 221, 222, 228
Featherstone, Francis, 302–3
federal government, *see Jurisdiction of
    Cases*
Federal Mediation Commission, 93–94
felony-murder-burglary, 100
female defendant(s), *see* defendant(s), fe-
    male
Ferber, Neil, 215–17
Fergeson, Cheryl, 119–20
Ferguson, Gov. Miriam, 318
Ferguson, Judge Warren, quoted, 251
Ferris, Gov. Woodbridge, quoted, 330
Fewell, Stanford Ellis, 303
Fickert, Charles, 83, 93, 95
  quoted, 84, 87
Fiedler, Hermine, 157–59, 169

Morris, Errol, 68, 69, 71–72
    quoted, 70
Morris, George, 123, 129
Morris, Gordon, 335
Morrison, Gov. Cameron, 288, 300, 313
Mosk, Judge Stanley, quoted, 42
Moss, Doug, 185
Mulder, Douglas, 64, 67, 69, 70
    quoted, 65
Münsterberg, Hugo, 39
Murchison, John, 298
Murphy, George W., 115
Myers, Hudson John, 178, 179, 181,
    182, 183, 184

NAACP Legal Defense and Educational
    Fund (LDF), 104, 107, 111, 137
Nadeau, Cynthia, 57–58
Nation, Lee, 12
National Association for the Advance-
    ment of Colored People (NAACP),
    104, 110, 114, 115, 118, 136, 137,
    204
National Law Journal, quoted, 180
Neal, Lonnie, quoted, 33
Nebraska, see Jurisdiction of Cases
Nelson, James, 75
Nevada, see Jurisdiction of Cases
New Bedford, Mass., 308
New Hampshire, see Jurisdiction of
    Cases
New Jersey, 97, 99
    see also Jurisdiction of Cases
New Mexico, 55
    see also Jurisdiction of Cases
New York, 18, 43, 74
    see also Jurisdiction of Cases
New York Legal Aid Society, 75, 76
New York Times, ix, 76, 88, 131, 270,
    340
    quoted, 324
Newfield, Jack, 233
    quoted, 232
Newsweek, 208
Nickerson, Vivian, 8
nolle prosequi, defined, 357
non vult, defined, 358
Norris, Clarence, 116–18
Norris v. Alabama, 118
North Carolina, 214, 275
    see also Jurisdiction of Cases
North Dakota, see Jurisdiction of Cases
Norwood, Albert E., 335

Nugent, Paul, 129
    quoted, 132

Official Detective Magazine, 208
Ohio, 19, 173, 218, 253, 275
    see also Jurisdiction of Cases
Oklahoma, 136
    see also Jurisdiction of Cases
Olcott, Gov. Ben, 289, 338
Olson, Gov. Culbert L., 154
    quoted, 96
Olson, Henry, 336
Oregon, see Jurisdiction of Cases
Osborne, Thomas Mott, 285
    quoted, 284
Owens, Aaron Lee, 336
Oxman, Frank, 88–90, 91–92, 95
    quoted, 89

Padgett, Eugene, 336
Padgett, Norma, 106, 107
Padgett, William H., 336
Paramount, Calif., 190
pardon, executive, 96, 97, 118, 215,
    231, 249, 284, 285, 286, 288, 289,
    290, 292, 296, 296–97, 298, 299,
    300, 301, 302, 303–4, 304, 305,
    306, 307, 308, 309, 311, 312, 313,
    318, 321–22, 323, 325, 326, 329,
    330, 332, 334, 335, 336, 337, 338,
    339, 342, 344, 346, 348, 350, 352–
    53, 353, 354–55, 356
    see also commutation of death sen-
    tence
Park, Gov. Guy, 300
Parker, George, 336–37
Parker, Marie, 75
Parks, Edward H., 282–83
Parrott, Lemuel, 337
Patterson, Haywood, 116–18
Patterson, Gov. I. L., 356
Patterson, Gov. Malcolm, 346
Patterson, Gov. Okey, 248
Patterson, La., 158
Pecho, Walter A., 337
Peek, Anthony Ray, 337–38
Pender, John, 338
Pennsylvania, 215
    see also Jurisdiction of Cases
per curiam, defined, 358
perjury, 95, 132, 133, 150, 152, 162,
    212, 229–30, 285, 292, 297, 298,
    304, 306, 308, 309, 310–11, 311,

prosecution (*cont.*)
    by, 226, 227, 295, 296, 307, 309,
    313, 315, 335, 336, 339–40
Pugh, Heywood, 304
Punishment Without Crime (Zimmerman), 50
Pyle, Harry, 339–40

Queens, N.Y., 74
"Quincy Five," 304
Quinn, William, 225, 226–27, 228

racism, 5, 6, 18, 187, 191, 282, 294,
    297, 304, 305, 310, 330, 333; *see
    also esp. Chs. 5 and 6*
Radin, Edward, 274
Ramos, Juan F., 340
rape, innocent person(s) sentenced to
    death for, 16, 58, 103, 109, 116–
    18, 136–37, 137–38, 282, 307,
    322–23, 330–31, 332–33, 342–43,
    352–53
record, defendant's
    prior arrest, 232, 342
    prior conviction, 26, 30, 39, 87, 96,
        97, 177, 237–38, 248, 250, 286,
        298, 304, 308, 315, 333, 337–
        38, 338, 349
"Red Scare," 97
Reese, Bessie, 199–200, 202–3, 208–9,
    211
Reichhoff, Kenny Ray, 340
Reid, Don, 355
Reilly, Peter A., 340
Reissfelder, George A., 340–41
remand, defined, 358
Reno, Janet, 212
Reno, Ralph, 341
restitution for wrongful conviction, *see*
    indemnity, award of
Reyes, Alfred, 41–42
Reyna, Richard, 127, 129, 130
Reynolds, Melvin Lee, 11–15
    quoted, 11, 12, 13
Rhode Island, *see Jurisdiction of Cases*
Richardson, Annie Mae, 198, 200, 202,
    205, 207, 211–12, 213
    quoted, 199
Richardson, Gov. Friend W., 95
Richardson, H. L., 41
Richardson, James, 19, 197–213
    quoted, 199, 208, 209, 213
    seven murdered children of, 197

Richmond News Leader, 230
Riddle, Howard, 253, 258–59
Riebel, David, 175
Ripan, Alexander, 341
risk of erroneous execution, *see* erroneous execution, risk of
Ritter, Dr. Kenneth, 163
Rivera, Antonio, 269–70
Roberson, Willie, 116–18
Roberts, Charles, 155–56
Robertson, David Wayne, 342
Robinson, Derrick, 342
Robinson, John Spencer, 204–5, 206–7,
    208, 209, 210
    quoted, 205
Robinson, Van Bering, 342
Rockefeller, Gov. Nelson, 54, 303
Rodriguez, Santos, 342
Roe v. Wade, 63
Rogers, Courtney ("Fred"), 267–69
    deceased parents of, 267
Rogers, Silas, 229–31
    quoted, 231
Rohan, Phil, 306
Rolph, Gov. James, Jr., 95
Roosevelt, Franklin D., 99, 286; as Gov.,
    331
Rose, Gus, quoted, 70
Rosenberg, Ethel and Julius, 96, 101
Rosenblum, Jacob J., 48, 50, 52, 344
Rosenstein, Fred, 236
Rosenstein, Max, 236
"Rosewood Massacre," 102
Ross, Johnny, 342–43
Rothschild, Charles Paul ("Rocky"), 33–
    38
    quoted, 37
Rowan, Carl, 333
Rubin, Ellis, 210, 211
Rucker, Herman Ray, 315
Ruff, Wayne, 155–56
Russ, James M., 166, 170
Rybarczyk, Max, 310

Sacco, Nicola, 97–99, 101, 151
Sacramento Bee, 153–54
St. Joseph, Mo., 10
St. Joseph's Children (Ganey), 12
St. Louis, Mo., 300
St. Louis Post-Dispatch, quoted, 15
St. Petersburg Times, 112
San Bernardino, Calif., 269
San Francisco, Calif., 79, 325, 348

Sanchez, Isauro, 283–84
Sanchez, Oscar, 41–42
Sanders, Albert, 343
Santana, Rene, 343–44
Savannah, Ga., 235
Sberna, Charles, 344
Scapegoat Justice (Lassers), 144, 152
Schaffer, Randy, 68–71
  quoted, 71, 275
Schaub, Frank, 201, 202, 205, 211, 213
  quoted, 204, 206, 212
Schmitz, Anthony, quoted, 242
Schmuck, Harry, 261–62, 264, 265
  quoted, 263
Schricker, Gov. Henry, quoted, 328
Schroeder, John, 73
Schuyler, John Edward, 344
Scott, Bradley P., 344
Scott, Scotty, 344–45
Scottsboro, Ala., 116
Scottsboro Boy (Patterson), 118
"Scottsboro Boys," 117, 136, 137
Seaton, Terry, 345
Self, Buck, 38
  quoted, 34
severance, defined, 358
Shaffer, Howard, 345
Sharpe, James, 224–25
Shea, Joseph Francis, 345–46
Sheeler, Rudolph, 287
Shenon, Philip, quoted, 76
Shepherd, Samuel, 18, 102–13
Sheppard, Dr. Samuel H., 166, 346
Sheridan, Gerda, quoted, 169, 170
Sherman, David, 346
Shumway, R. Mead, 346–47
Skeen, Orel, 248
Slaton, Gov. John, 304
Smith, Gov. Alfred, 325
Smith, Arthur, 55–57
Smith, Charles ("Red"), 347
Smith, Charlie, 203, 206
  quoted, 209
Smith, Clarence, 55–57
Smith, Frank A., 347
Smith, Grace M., 347
Smith, Larry Thomas, 347
Snyder, Dr. LeMoyne, 250–51
Sobell, Morton, 96
Socrates, 280
South Braintree, Mass., 97
South Carolina, *see Jurisdiction of Cases*
South Dakota, *see Jurisdiction of Cases*

South Paris, Me., 171
Southern Poverty Law Center (SPLC),
  244, 245, 246, 343
Speers, Peter, III, 127, 135–36
  quoted, 131
Spencer, Emmitt Monroe, 159–63, 165,
  167–68, 169
  quoted, 162
Spies, August, 280
Spry, Gov. William, 81
Staga, William, 188
Stanford Law Review, ix
Staples, Dr. F. N., 347–48
Staten, Cleo, 298
"statistical lives," 276
Steele, Michelle, 13
Stephens, Gov. William, 93–94, 95
Stevens, Charles, 345
Stielow, Charles, 308–9
Stockbridge, Ga., 176
Stokes, Gov. Edward, 344
Storey, Moorefield, 115
Storick, Maude Cushing, 348
Stuart, Carole, 3
Stuart, Charles, 3–5
  quoted, 3
Styles, Wesley, 132–33
  quoted, 121
Styron, William, 235, 340
suicide misjudged as murder, 267–69,
  305, 317, 335, 337, 347
Sunday Sentinel-Star (Orlando), quoted,
  103
  see also Morning Sentinel
Supreme Court, *see* United States Su-
  preme Court
Sweeney, James, 348
Synon, Michael J., 348

Tawes, Gov. J. Millard, 307
Taylor, Daniel, 97
Tennessee, *see Jurisdiction of Cases*
testimony
  by expert, misleading or erroneous,
    98–99, 100–101, 149, 189, 263,
    265–66, 268, 297, 316, 337,
    339; *see also* polygraph, unrelia-
    bility of
  by eyewitness, good faith but mis-
    taken, 7–9, 23–24, 26, 38, 39,
    40, 41, 57, 173, 190–91, 192,
    216, 219, 229–30, 231, 232,
    233, 239–40, 248–49, 282, 284,

White, Dennis, 67, 69
  quoted, 70
White, Walter F., 114
Whitman, Gov. Charles, 309
Whitson, Richard, 205, 206, 207, 208
Wickersham Commission, 94
Wikberg, Ron, 302
Wilder, Gov. Douglas, 308
Wilkinson, Robert, 353
Williams, Darby, 295–96
Williams, Eugene, 116–18
Williams, Franklin, 104, 107
Williams, Gov. G. Mennen, 337
Williams, George, 300
Williams, Joseph S., 354
Williams, Robert, 354
Williams, Samuel Tito, 354
Williamson, Judge Gale, quoted, 227
Williamson, Jack, 294
Wilson, Bill, 354–55
Wilson, David Ronald, 355
Wilson, Horace, 297
Wilson, Shelia, 355
Wilson, Woodrow, 93, 314
Wing, George Chew, 355
Wisconsin, 277
  see also Jurisdiction of Cases
Wisconsin State Journal, 340

Wood, James Horace, 24, 26–33, 34–37, 38
  quoted, 31, 32, 35
Wood, Robert, 61–62
Woodmansee, Ernest, 355–56
Woodward, Walter, 294
Woon, Lem, 356
Wordlow, Will, 114–16
Wright, Andrew, 116–18
Wright, Leroy ("Roy"), 116–18
wrong-person conviction(s), defined, 17
Wyoming, see Jurisdiction of Cases

Yelder, George, 292
Young, Bennie, 318
Young, Gov. Clement C., 95, 306
Young, Jack, quoted, 204
Young, John, 180
Young, William, quoted, 98
Yount, Benjamin, 157–58, 169
Yuba City, Calif., 39
Yzurdiaga, John, 192, 193

Zachery, Robert, 238, 240, 241, 242–43
Zajicek, Herman, 356
Zaner, Loren, 224, 225, 226, 228
Zimmerman, Gov. Fred, quoted, 329
Zimmerman, Isidore, 18, 43–55, 275, 344
  quoted, 52, 53